Contents

Acknowledgements

I want to thank each of the authors involved in this project for agreeing to be part of it, and for writing with passion and clarity about policy issues and processes. You are helping to educate the next generation of policy analysts and policy advocates.

My warmest appreciation to Brian Henderson, Carroll Klein, and Rob Kohlmeier at Wilfrid Laurier University Press for their support and encouragement. Carroll, I hope you are enjoying retirement, and more opportunity to do only the things you love. I want to thank Lisa LaFramboise for her careful attention to detail and Angela Hammond for her much-appreciated help with the index. My appreciation is also extended to the people with technical skills who made this project possible: Matt Regehr, who designed the graphics; Heather Blain-Yanke, who was responsible for production; Leslie Macredie, who developed the marketing plan; and Pam Woodland, who designed the interior and formatted the type.

Finally, warm thanks to my partner, Ken Westhues, my students, and my colleagues, who were patient when I was preoccupied with the book.

Preface to the Fourth Edition

It has been gratifying that the third edition of *Canadian Social Policy* has been so well received. Colleagues from across Canada and the United States have adopted the book for use in sociology, political science, family studies, theology, and Canadian studies courses, as well as social work courses. Students and faculty alike have expressed appreciation for the critical perspective and associated analysis that authors have brought to their subject, the broad range of current social policy issues covered, and the different standpoints from which the policy-making process is explained. Many have expressed thanks in particular for the emphasis on agency that is threaded throughout the book. While the majority of authors remain social workers, and this book is envisaged as primarily meeting the needs of social work educators and future practitioners, it is likely to be of value to people of all disciplinary backgrounds who are engaged—or want to become engaged—in effecting change through social policy at the individual, organizational, provincial, federal, or international levels.

One of the challenges in teaching social policy is remaining current across a broad range of issues. Policy can change with much public attention through consultations, lobbying, and media coverage preceding and following the change. An example of this would be the Civil Marriage Act passed by the federal government in July 2005 that grants same-sex couples the same right to marriage as opposite-sex couples. It can also change quietly, with less public scrutiny but just as much impact. The Supreme Court ruling of January 2003 on corporal punishment of children would be an example. While advocates did not receive the total ban on corporal punishment of children that they wanted, it is now clear that the Supreme Court understands it to be completely unacceptable with children under the age of two or teenagers. Further, the ruling restricts the circumstances under which teachers may apply force and directs that it only be used for "educative or corrective purposes" by parents or parent figures.

These social policies define a new dominant structure with respect to marriage and corporal punishment of children—a new set of rules that guide behaviour. Responsibility for the interpretation of the legislation and the Supreme Court ruling falls to policy analysts who write regulations and directives, and front-line service deliverers who implement them. These regulations and directives define both the responsibilities of service deliverers and the rights and responsibilities of people using the services.

To help teachers, students, and everyday citizens meet the challenge of remaining current on social policy trends, we have decided to release a fourth edition of *Canadian Social Policy* only three year after the third edition. All substantive chapters have been revised, with updated statistics cited and changes in policy since 2002 discussed. The theoretical literature drawn on in making a critical analysis of substantive issues also reflects sources that have been published since the third edition. Specifically, more attention has been given to the impact of the policy-making processes and substantive policy on the most vulnerable and marginalized groups in society. Following the recommendation of one of our anonymous reviewers, I have foregrounded the policy-making process by moving the chapters addressing this aspect of social policy forward in the book. In addition, I have added three new chapters to the fourth edition: one that examines the role of the courts in policy-making, one that explores mental health policy in Canada, and a third that critically assesses the current trend in Western child welfare of utilizing risk assessment measures to identify whether a child is sufficiently in need of protection to be taken into care.

We hope this continues to be a useful resource for those becoming acquainted with social policy issues and the ways in which policy is made, as well as for those wanting a quick update on current policy debates.

Preface to the Third Edition

One of our chief complaints when I was a social policy student at Wilfrid Laurier University in the mid-1970s was that few of the class materials spoke to us as Canadians. We used primarily American and British texts and articles, which taught us legislation that would not affect our practice; they taught us the history of a welfare state that was not ours, and they described policy-making processes that were generally applicable only in Canada. We found ourselves scouring the library, looking mostly in primary sources in the government documents section, for anything to do with Canadian social policy. While this may have given us a competence as researchers that is uncommon in students today, and breadth in our understanding of how other countries had addressed a range of policy issues, it left us feeling disconnected from—and somewhat confused about—Canadian social policy, with no sense of understanding about how, as social workers, we could change the social policies that would shape our practice.

Shankar Yelaja recognized this gap in knowledge, and produced the first edition of *Canadian Social Policy* in 1978 as part of the remedy of this situation. The considerable success of the book, and the subsequent second edition in 1987, is testimony that other students and teachers of social policy were also hungry for Canadian content. The first edition prompted one reviewer to say, "With its wealth of theoretical and factual material, assembled in a single volume, *Canadian Social Policy* will prove a valuable resource to teachers charged with the responsibility of introducing students to this subject area. It will also, one would hope, reach a much wider circle of readers, including policy makers themselves, and thereby contribute to a clearer understanding of major social problems facing the country."

In the years since the first edition of this book, social policy scholarship has flourished in Canada among social workers as well as political scientists, historians, and sociologists. Today, we can find journal articles on most policy issues as well as edited or authored books on a number of specific issues. The Internet gives us access to the most immediate information about legislation that has been introduced, and allows us to be well informed about the reactions of various stakeholders to proposed policy or legislation. There are now a handful of excellent books by Canadian social workers that teach us about the history of the welfare state in Canada and the policy-making process here.

There are still few books that address the full range of the objectives of the first edition: to help students of Canadian social policy begin to understand social welfare concepts, ideology, the process of social policy formulation, and the substantive issues from a Canadian perspective; and to stimulate discussion and debate on major social policy issues confronting Canadian society today. While the language we use has changed somewhat, these two primary objectives in introductory social policy courses remain. It therefore seemed that a revised and updated third edition of *Canadian Social Policy* would continue to be a valuable resource for both students and teachers.

The organization of the book remains essentially the same. It opens with a chapter defining social policy. Contributors then introduce readers to issues at the forefront of the policy agenda and the range of theoretical perspectives used to define policy issues. The third section focuses on the policy-making process, and the book closes with a fourth section identifying the challenges ahead.

A number of things have changed, though. First is the consciousness, reflected in all chapters, that policy is now made in a context that is global, not national. This is most explicit in the addition of the international level to the definition of policy-making levels. Second is the greater emphasis on advocacy or activism—efforts to change policy—which is discussed from the perspectives of working both within the system and outside of the system. Third is the conceptualization of issues. In the first edition, issues were framed broadly—for instance, housing, child welfare, income security, or policy for the elderly. In this edition, housing has transformed to homelessness, child welfare to child poverty, income security to workfare, and "the elderly" to caring and aging. We see new issues on the policy agenda, like heterosexism and ableism. Fourth, new theoretical perspectives inform the substantive analyses. Today, we see a feminist perspective incorporated into the analysis of issues like aging and caring, workfare, immigration and refugee policy, Aboriginal issues, and policy toward single mothers, while in the earliest edition this perspective was restricted to the chapter on social policy concerning women. We also see the use of new perspectives, like constructivism, postmodernism, anti-colonialism, and anti-oppression.

Perhaps most striking is the change in the disciplinary background and gender of the contributors, which I see as evidence of the maturation of the social work education system in Canada. In the 1978 edition, only three of the sixteen contributors were female, and five of the sixteen were social workers. In this new edition, ten of the twenty contributors are female, and fifteen of the twenty are social workers. This dramatic change is not just a reflection of different kinds of choices being made by the editor but indicative of the changes in the pool of social policy scholars now teaching and writing in Canada. In 1978, there were still only two schools in Canada that offered prospective social policy students an opportunity to study social work at the doctoral level, and the majority of graduates were male. Now there are eight programs spread across the country. As predicted, this greater accessibility has made it easier for women to engage in doctoral studies and the majority of graduates are now female, almost in proportion to the number of females graduating from master's programs. Policy analysis, once regarded as a male interest within the discipline, has been embraced by this new generation of female scholars.

Several of the contributors to the first book have passed on now, among them my two teachers at Laurier, Shankar Yelaja and Maurice Kelly. Both toiled through the 1970s and 1980s to create policy analysis and evaluation capacity within the profession. One of their dreams was to build the doctoral program at Laurier; five of the scholars who have contributed to this edition of *Canadian Social Policy* have graduated, or soon will graduate, from this program. This book is a tribute to the foundational work they did in paving the way for a new generation. I hope they would be proud of what they have inspired.

I   Introduction

Introduction to Part I

This section introduces you to the debate about what is meant by the term "social policy," and offers a definition that is inclusive of a broad range of human services and that recognizes the inextricable link between economic policy and social policy. A brief review is made of models of policy development, followed by a discussion of the dimensions of policy, or the levels, from the international to the organizational, at which it is made. The argument is set out that social workers have a responsibility to engage in advocacy in an effort to shape social policy to reflect the values that they support—values that are often inconsistent with the neo-liberal thinking of most governments in power in Canada today.

Anne Westhues

Social policy shapes our daily lives as social work practitioners and as citizens. It identifies what a majority of Canadians accept as legitimate public issues at a given moment in history—which is to say, the issues for which we see the state having a responsibility. It also gives direction to how that majority, represented by the government of the day, believes these issues should be dealt with. Social workers, along with others who deliver front-line-services—nurses, teachers, and police officers, for instance—are hired to implement these policies. We also have a responsibility, as reflected in the Canadian Association of Social Workers *Code of Ethics* (2005), to advocate for social policies that "uphold the right of people to have access to resources to meet basic human needs; that ensure fair and equitable access to public services and benefits; for equal treatment and protection under the law; to challenge injustices, especially those affecting the vulnerable and disadvantaged; and to promote social development and environmental management in the interests of all people" (Canadian Association of Social Workers [CASW] *Code of Ethics*, 2005, p. 5).

Following World War II, we saw a broadening of areas where Canadians were willing to make collective statements through social policy about the kind of society we wanted to create. Where once we saw violence against women and children as private matters to be dealt with by the family, for instance, we now have taken a position, reflected in the Criminal Code of Canada and in child welfare legislation in every province, that there are specified limits to allowable behaviour. Where once we accepted structural inequalities for women and racialized groups, now we have a Charter of Rights and Freedoms and human rights legislation in every province that commit to equal treatment of marginalized groups. This process of defining and redefining our vision of what we want to be as a society is continuous. There are supporters and there are critics for every policy decision taken, reflecting the variety of different interests within any society. New issues emerge as demographic, economic, and political realities change, and as individuals and peoples come to understand their realities differently than in the past, and to dream of a more just future.

Our purpose in this book is to introduce you to the discussion about what is meant by social policy, public policy, policy analysis, and social policy development; to familiarize you with the policy development process at the international, federal, provincial, and organizational levels; and to provide an overview of the major social policy issues currently being debated in Canada. We offer some ideas about how to evaluate the effectiveness of social policy and suggestions about how social workers can engage in advocacy to influence policy outcomes.

Defining Social Policy and Policy Analysis

There has been a long-standing debate within the literature as to what is meant by the term "social policy." The central issue that frames this discussion is how inclusive the domain of social policy is. Does it encompass only those areas that have been described as "personal social services," like income security, child welfare, and counselling (Kahn, 1979)? Does it include related human services like education and health care, or an even broader range of what some consider economic policies like labour legislation, decisions about budget deficit reduction, or free-trade agreements with the United States and Mexico? Does it include only decisions made with respect to the allocation of rights and resources by governmental bodies, or does it also include decisions made by transfer payment organizations or by non-governmental collectivities like unions? Is the role of policy analysts that of detached, dispassionate observers, or do they have a responsibility to advocate for a value-based position? While the debate may sometimes seem esoteric, the position taken on it defines the range of policy issues about which one believes social workers have a responsibility to be informed, and on which the profession has an ethical obligation to try to effect change.

Canadian authors have tended to emphasize a broader rather than a narrower definition of social policy. Yelaja (1987, p. 2), for instance, offers this definition: "Social policy is concerned with the public administration of welfare services, that is, the formulation, development and management of specific services of government at all levels, such as health, education, income maintenance and welfare services." In the same vein, Brooks (1993, p. 184) says, "Many of the most expensive activities carried out by the state in advanced capitalist societies are associated with the area of social policy. These functions include public education, health care, publicly subsidized housing, and the provision of various forms of income support to such segments of the population as the unemployed, the aged, and the disabled." At the opposite end of the spectrum, McGilly (1990, p. 12) suggests, "The least misleading simplification of social policy is to define it as society's struggle to keep up with the consequences of advancing industrialization." This broader definition, which recognizes an unequivocal linkage between social policy and economic policy, is reflected in the writing of Canadian social workers like Armitage (1988); Collier (1995); Graham, Swift, and Delaney (2003); Lightman

(1991, 2003); Moscovitch (1991); Moscovitch and Drover (1981); Riches and Ternowetsky (1990); Tester (1991, 1992); Wharf and McKenzie (2004). As we have inexorably shifted into a global economy over the past twenty years, it has become clear that social policy can no longer be discussed in a meaningful way without understanding the economic context of policy decisions.

Defining Social Policy and Policy Analysis

Parallel to the shift in thinking more globally has been an increased emphasis on understanding how policy relates to practitioners locally. Pierce (1984), writing from a social work perspective, suggests that there are eight levels at which social policy shapes our work as practitioners. These include the three levels of federal, provincial, and local government that political scientists like Pal (2006) and Brooks (1993) include in the domain of public policy. Pierce also suggests that what Flynn (1992) calls "small scale policy systems" like social service organizations and professional associations be included. This reflects his understanding that an integral part of practice is the development of operational policies that define how a service user will experience a policy that is generally set at a larger-system level: for instance, "minimum intervention" into the lives of families with children, "normalization" for people who have disabilities, or a commitment to equity for marginalized groups.

Pierce (1984) includes the family and the individual practitioner as system levels relevant to understanding social policy as well. He argues that decisions made by the individual practitioner when implementing policy define how service users experience social services, and the social policies that shape those services. Every worker has some discretion in how he or she interprets policy. For instance, a social assistance worker may choose to accept fewer contacts with employers as acceptable job search activity because a person receiving benefits has been ill, or not. Or a worker determining the eligibility for a child care care subsidy may choose to advise an applicant who is ineligible because of savings to reduce those savings. How the worker chooses to act in these two instances gives a very different message to service users about the social policies affecting them. Similarly, decisions taken by a family with respect to the amount of care they are willing to provide to an older family member or a child with a disability will have an influence on how the person needing care feels about the care they receive.

Flynn (1992) reinforces the importance of this broader perspective for the social work practitioner. Citing Kahn, he says that policy shapes and delineates what the practitioner does, how he or she relates to the service user, and the manner in which discretion is allowed or exercised. Further, he argues that understanding how policies at the agency, or even individual level, affect what the practitioner may or must do, and how they can be changed, is a way to empower practitioners.

Another important issue discussed in the current literature is the role of the policy analyst. Mirroring the debate in the social sciences about whether positivist, constructivist, or critical theory approaches are most appropriate for social science research today (Cresswell, 2002; Kirby & McKenna, 1989; Lincoln & Guba, 1985; Maguire, 1987; Neuman, 1994; Strauss & Corbin, 1998),

academic approach

applied approach

the question explored is whether the role of the policy analyst is to provide balanced information to decision-makers that will help them make more informed decisions (Friedmann, 1987), or whether the analyst has a responsibility to engage in some form of advocacy with his or her analyses (Moscovitch, 1991). As we saw above, the latter position is consistent with the Canadian Association of Social Workers *Code of Ethics*.

So how do I propose to use the term "social policy"? I build upon Pal's (2006, p. 2) definition of public policy: "a course of action or inaction chosen by public authorities to address a given problem or interrelated set of problems." Then I both broaden and narrow his definition. I broaden it by including in the definition of "public authorities" front-line service deliverers at the various levels of government and in social service organizations who make decisions that define the way service users experience policy. Unlike Pal, I do not see these front-line people as merely "policy takers" (2006, p. 2) or implementers of the directions defined by others, but as people who have some scope of discretion in the way that they work within broader policy guidelines. I believe it is through this exercise of agency that policy and practice are connected (Wharf & McKenzie, 2004) and that organizational and social structures are changed (Giddens, 1979; 1984). These displays of agency, like all policy decisions, reflect a particular set of values, or ideology. Then, borrowing from Flynn (1992), I narrow the definition to include only a subset of the issues than are addressed in public policy, the issues that "deal with human health, safety or well-being."

When all of these considerations are incoporated into my definition of social policy, it reads as follows: *Social policy is a course of action or inaction chosen by public authorites to address an issue that deals with human health, safety or well-being. These public authorities include those who work directly with service users, bureaucrats working in international organizations and at all levels of government, and elected officials. Policy decisions at the international and governmental levels reflect the values acceptable to the dominant stakeholders at the time that the policy decision is taken. Decisions taken by front-line workers may reinforce the intent of these policy decisions, or may resist it when they are understood to be inconsistent with the values of the front-line professionals.*

Definition

If social policy is action taken to address a given problem, policy analysis is "the disciplined application of intellect to public problems" (Pal, 2006, p. 14). In his earlier work, Pal differentiates between academic policy analysis and applied policy analysis, the domain of social work practitioners. He suggests that the academic is primarily concerned with theory, explanation, understanding how policy came into being, and attempts to retain some impartiality in making the analysis. The practitioner, he suggests, is more interested in specific policies or problems than in theory, in evaluation rather than explanation, in changing policies, and in advocating for the interests of consumers of service (Pal, 1992, p. 24). In his more recent work, he appears to have accepted this more applied domain as legitimate academic activity (Pal, 2006).

Moroney (1981) explains this difference in orientation between the traditional academic approach to policy analysis and the practice-based approach as being about making value-based choices. In support of this position, Kelley (1975, quoted in Flynn, 1992) suggests that all policy analysis must make explicit the values or criteria that are being used to choose among policy alternatives. He identifies three criteria that he believes must be considered in all policy analyses. These include adequacy (the extent to which a specified need or goal is met if program objectives are carried out), effectiveness (the extent to which the outcomes obtained are a result of policy intent and program activity), and efficiency (the measure of goal attainment in terms of the expenditure of the least number of resources). Other values that might be considered when analyzing social policy issues include impact on client identity and impact on self-determination. Values that might guide the policy development process include informed decision-making, public accountability, procedural fairness, and openness and accessibility to the process (Ogilvie, Ogilvie, and Company, 1990). When these values coalesce to define an identifiable world view, we call them ideology. Most typically, we associate ideology with political parties, but it is also identified with social movements such as the women's movement (feminist), the human rights movement (anti-oppression), or the anti-globalization movement.

Models
of Policy
Development

Models of Policy Development

Another aspect of social policy and policy analysis that academics and practitioners have tried to understand is the complexity of the policy-making process (Jansson, 1994; Kahn, 1969; Kingdon, 1995; Mayer, 1985; Meyerson & Banfield, 1955; Pancer & Westhues, 1989; Perlman & Gurin, 1972; Pierce, 1984; Westhues, 1980; Wharf & McKenzie, 2004; York, 1982). Earlier models that tried to elucidate how policy is made were less detailed than are more recent ones. Meyerson and Banfield (1955), for instance, defined only three stages in policy development: (1) the decision-maker considers all options open to him or her; (2) the consequences of adopting each alternative are identified and evaluated; and (3) the alternative that seems to have the best fit with the valued ends is selected.

As the social sciences moved into a period in which positivism and rationality were highly valued, models became more detailed, and emphasized the technical skills of the policy analyst as researcher (Kahn, 1969; Mayer, 1985; York, 1982). When our competencies in these areas developed more fully, concern was raised that insufficient attention was being given to the political, or value-based, aspects of policy development, and models were proposed that attempted to rectify this imbalance (Gil, 1981; Jansson, 1994; Perlman & Gurin, 1972; Wharf & McKenzie, 2004).

The model that I find most useful when thinking through a policy problem is neither the least nor the most complex of models that have been proposed. It has six stages, which are not linear as they appear when set out below, but recursive, with movement back and forth among the first four stages until agreement is reached on what policy will be at the end of a given discussion. This process of discussion never really stops, but slows for a time when new legislation or some other policy outcome is reached. The stages in this model are: (1) defining the problem to be addressed; (2) agreeing on goals (values, criteria, principles); (3) identifying policy alternatives; (4) choosing an alternative; (5) implementing the policy; and (6) evaluation of the new policy.

Policy Dimensions

The major difficulty in developing a model that captures the complexity of the policy-making process is precisely its complexity, as is so ably described by Kenny-Scherber in chapter 5. Social policy can be made at the international, federal, provincial, and local levels of government in Canada, as well as within the agency or organizational context. It is helpful to deconstruct policy by conceptualizing policy subsystems that affect practice and the experience of service users. A framework that I have found useful identifies a second dimension of policy, defining its purposes as strategic, legislative, program, and operational (Ogilvie, Ogilvie, and Company, 1990). These dimensions, all of which might be shaping front-line practice simultaneously, are explored in more depth below.

Before our shift to a more global economy and a more global perspective in the early eighties, we thought of social policy in a national context. The generosity of the safety net that a country put into place was understood to be related to its level of industrialization, its level of affluence, and the extent to which its cultural values supported the assumption of a public responsibility for the well-being of all citizens (Moscovitch & Drover, 1981). With the shift to global capitalism (Cameron & Stein, 2000; Collier, 1995; Teeple, 1995), however, international policies have begun to have more important influences on our social and economic well-being. Following the introduction of the Free Trade Agreement between Canada and the United States in 1989 and the North American Free Trade Agreement between Canada, the United States, and Mexico in 1992, it has become evident that there are economic and political pressures to "harmonize" social policy in all three countries. While ideally that may have meant that American and Mexican social policy would come to look like Canadian social policy, in fact the safety net that was so carefully woven over a period of fifty years or more in Canada is gradually being weakened, coming to look more like its less sturdy Amercian cousin.

United Nations agreements like the UN Convention on the Rights of the Child (1989) also shape social policy initiatives in Canada. Article 8 of the convention, for instance, says, "State Parties undertake to respect the right of the child to preserve his or her identity, including nationality, name and family relations as recognized by law without unlawful interference." This entitlement, which Canada agreed to by becoming a signatory to the convention, has implications for international adoption, for instance. If a child has a right to maintain his or her identity, Canada must now attempt to ensure that information is gathered on the child's background and that there is a mechanism for passing this information to the child at some specified age, in both non-identifying and identifying forms.

Policy at the international level may have each of the four purposes identified above. The **strategic** framework includes development of a vision and mission statement, and is associated with what we have come to call strategic planning. The **legislative** framework includes legislation and the regulations, directives, and guidelines that are intended to facilitate the implementation of legislation. The **program** framework involves program design, the service delivery structure, and the implementation plan. This area of policy is sometimes called program planning. Lastly, the **operational** framework includes decisions that we have trationally called administrative: human resources policies, budgeting, and decisions with respect to the operating structure of an organization, like how fundraising will be carried out and hours of operation (Ogilvie, Ogilvie, and Company, 1990). This policy may be set through bilateral or multilateral **agreements** like free-trade legislation, or through administrative agreements between Canada and individual countries for issues like international adoption. International policy may also be made by international organizations like the United Nations or the more recently formed World Trade Organization (WTO). We are coming to understand the enormity of the influence that the establishment of the WTO has had, and will continue to have, on all aspects of public policy through a variety of multilateral agreements. Developed out of the Uruguay Round of the General Agreement on Tariffs and Trade (GATT) talks, this body defines public policy in areas such as the environment, genetically modified food, and labour rights as part of its mandate to regulate international trade (Shrybman, 1999; Cameron & Stein, 2000).

Social policy in Canada is shaped by what is called the "divided sovereignty" (Van Loon & Whittington, 1976) of the British North America Act of 1867, and now the Constitution Act, 1982. This means that jurisdiction has been given to the federal government for some areas of policy development and to the provinces for others. Provinces are responsible for "the establishment, maintenance and management of public and reformatory prisons in and for the provinces," and "the establishment, maintenance and management of hospitals, asylums, charities, and eleemosynary institutions" (Splane, 1965). While it is generally agreed that the intention of the legislation was to limit the role of the provinces and to create a strong federal government, judicial interpretations of the legislation over time have limited the role of the federal government in the direct provision of human services.

Depending on the policy area of concern, then, the federal government may play a greater or lesser role. Legislation pertaining to young people in trouble with the law—the Youth Criminal Justice Act currently—falls within the federal jurisdiction. Each province has enabling legislation to serve as an

Policy
Dimensions

implementation guide, however. In all cases, this is a section of provincial child welfare legislation. By contrast, the federal government has no jurisdiction within the area of child welfare. This means that it cannot pass legislation that will directly shape the provision of child welfare services.

The one way in which the federal government has influenced child welfare policy and programs is through the provision of federal funding for approved child welfare services, or the exercise of its "spending power." The Canada Assistance Plan was the mechanism for this provision from 1966 to 1996. It allowed the federal government to match provincial spending on approved social services, including child welfare, an agreement known as cost-sharing. This federal-provincial agreement was replaced in 1996 with the Canada Health and Social Transfer, legislation that still allows the transfer of federal funds to the provinces, but now in the form of a block grant. This meant that the provinces would have more control over how federal funds were allocated within the areas of health, education, and social services than they had under the Canada Assistance Plan or the Established Programs Financing Act, the legislation that facilitated the flow of money to the provinces in the areas of health and education. In addition to legislative policy at both the federal and provincial levels, policy at these levels of government may also have strategic, program development, and operational purposes.

Local governments (municipal and regional) have a limited policy jurisdiction with respect to social services in all provinces in Canada (Graham, Phillips & Maslove, 1998; Tindal & Tindal, 1984). Their primary areas of responsibility include land use, water, roads, and recreation. In most provinces they do not deliver any social services, and so have no legislative jurisdiction or any reason to set policy within the strategic, program, or operational areas. Ontario and Nova Scotia municipalities have some jurisdiction in the area of social services, a jurisdiction that has increased in the past few years in Ontario. Local governments in Ontario must now cost share 50% of the spending on social assistance, long-term care, and child-care subsidies, and carry the full cost (100%) of social housing and community health (Melchers, 1999). Since provincial spending must match local spending, this means that local governments play a key role in determining the annual budget of the Province of Ontario in the areas of social assistance, child-care subsidy and long-term care. Policy initiatives at the local level are primarily in the strategic, program, and operational areas, with the province setting legislation.

Service delivery in all provinces occurs through some mix of government employees and transfer payment agency employees (that is, organizations that enter into purchase of service agreements with the provincial and local governments). These dimensions of social policy are summarized in Figure 1.1.

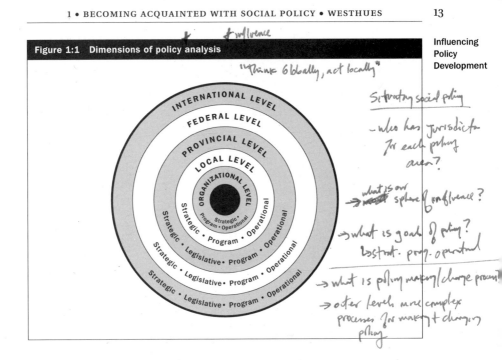

Figure 1:1   Dimensions of policy analysis

[handwritten annotations in figure:]
↑ influence
"Think globally, act locally"
Situating social policy
— who has jurisdiction for each policy area?
→ what is our sphere of influence?
→ what is goal of policy? [strat. prog. operationl]
→ what is policy making/change process?
→ other levels more complex processes for making + changing policy

[right margin:] Influencing Policy Development

Influencing Policy Development

Social workers, as noted above, have a responsibility within their *Code of Ethics* to advocate for social change that will improve the well-being of the people we work with. A key way in which this can be done is by attempting to influence the policies that shape people's experience of the services delivered. To do this effectively, it is first necessary to identify the appropriate system to be addressed for the policy issue of concern. If you are interested in increasing the number of beds in shelters for abused women, for instance, the provincial government should be lobbied rather than the federal or local governments.

Once the appropriate system has been identified, it is necessary to understand the policy-making process within that system. Figure 1.2 outlines this process in detail at the provincial level. Figure 1.3 provides further detail on this process, specifying the approvals required for each type of policy change, whether a change to legislation, regulations, or operational policy, procedures, or guidelines. What is striking about these two figures is how many approvals are required before any change can be effected.

At the federal level, the process of effecting change is even more complex, with the additional approval of each of the provinces required on social policy issues. The failed agreement on the Meech Lake and Charlottetown Accords is testimony to this complexity, although the Social Union Framework Agreement demonstrates that it is possible and identifies clear guidelines for future federal-provincial decisions (Mendelson, 1999). At the local level, it is much simpler, generally requiring only the approval of the social service

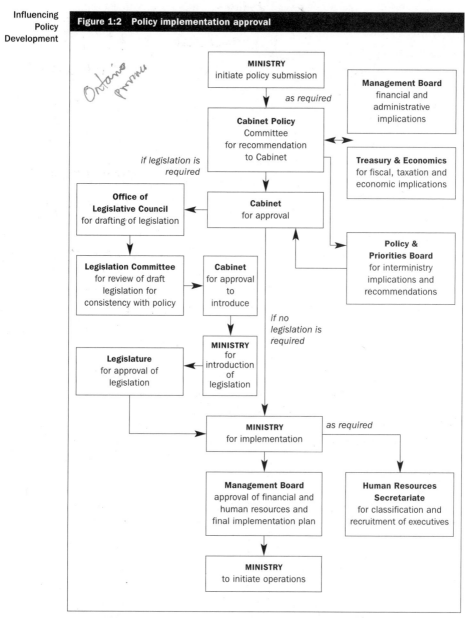

Figure 1:2   Policy implementation approval

Source: The Ontario government: Structure and functions, by G.G. Bell and A.D. Pascoe, 1988 (Toronto: Wall and Thompson), p. 28.

department, the commissioner of social services, the social services committee, and regional or municipal council. At the organizational level, the process is most similar to local government, with approvals required by the program unit, executive director, and the board of directors. Depending on the model

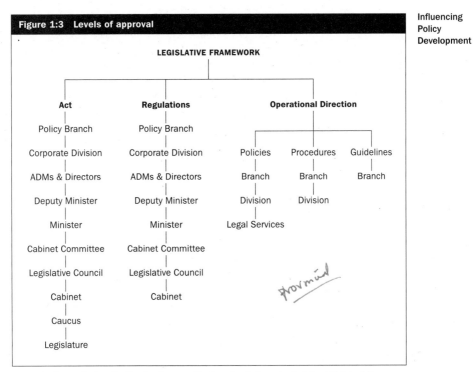

Figure 1:3   Levels of approval

Influencing
Policy
Development

Source: *Policy analysis and policy development: Tools and techniques,* by Ogilvie, Ogilvie and Company, 1990 course handbook (Toronto), p. 4.

of board governance, approval may be required by a standing committee of the board and the executive committee before the matter is presented to the board of directors itself (Carver, 1990).

What these models fail to convey is the politically charged environment in which many policy decisions are made. While Bell and Pascoe (1988) identify the first step in the policy-making process as the ministry initiating a policy submission, in fact there is often considerable political activity, sometimes over a prolonged period, before a ministry believes that an issue has a high enough priority to be addressed. Kenny-Scherber describes the variety of institutions, interests groups, and ideologies that interact with one another, vying for influence in shaping a policy outcome in chapter 5. These lobbying efforts are sometimes conceptualized as advocacy, or community organizing (Ross, 1967; Taylor & Roberts, 1985; Tropman, Erlich, & Rothman, 1995), and planning and policy analysis are described as more rational processes that attempt to bring a policy issue to the attention of policy-makers. It is important to understand that both internal and external politics are influential in this process: not only the various stakeholders external to government, but the bureaucrats making decisions themselves will promote different interests (Chappell, 2002; Kelly, 1999; Tindal & Tindal, 1984).

Influencing
Policy
Development

The effort to educate the general public about abuse of women is a good case example of this political process, one that is lucidly described by Gillian Walker (1990). Through the women's centres set up to raise consciousness about women's rights in the early 1970s, it soon became evident that a major concern of women experiencing relationship difficulties was assault by their partners. In response to this concern, women's shelters began to spring up across the country as places for women to take refuge when they were under attack. To obtain funding for these shelters, it was necessary to convince the United Way and local and provincial governments that wife assault was sufficiently widespread that funding was warranted for shelters. Walker makes an insightful analysis of how the problem of wife assault came to be defined and of the conflicting politics of feminists and professionals in this process. For feminists, it was an instance of women's oppression, grounded in the patriarchy that influences family relationships and social institutions like the law. The only possible remedy, for them, was fundamental social change, with the objective a system that supports social, political, and economic equality for women. By contrast, for professionals the problem was defined as that of outdated sex roles, traditional attitudes, and inadequate institutional procedures. Their remedy was to develop programs that educate men and women about gender equality and that institute therapeutic interventions to deal with the trauma of assault.

Skills Required

Whether policy analysis is a primary job responsibility or a secondary one, two sets of skills are required: what have been called process (Rothman & Zald, 1985), interpersonal (Tropman, 1995), or interactional skills (Perlman & Gurin, 1972); and task (Rothman & Zald, 1985), intellectual (Tropman, 1995), or analytic skills (Perlman & Gurin, 1972). Table 1.1 outlines both the analytic and interactional skills required at each stage in the policy development process. The analytic skills identified draw heavily from an earlier article by Pancer and Westhues (1989).

In addition to the general skill of thinking analytically, at the initial stage of the policy development process, when the problem is defined, analytic skills are needed in two areas: values analysis and needs assessment. To complete a values analysis, the analyst must know how to conduct opinion polls or to cull useful information from opinion polls conducted by others; carry out key informant interviews; use group techniques like the nominal group technique, the Delphi technique, focus groups, and community forums; and do preference scaling. To complete a needs assessment, the analyst has to know how to identify and interpret social indicators; carry out surveys; and use the group approaches identified above. Interactional skills required at this critical first stage of the process include leadership in setting up a process that will allow the exchange of ideas on the issue; ability to create a safe environment so people feel they can express their feelings about the issue; facilitation skills,

Table 1.1 Skills required at each stage of policy development		
STAGE IN POLICY DEVELOPMENT	**ANALYTIC SKILLS**	**INTERACTIONAL SKILL**
Defining the Problem	**Values Analysis** • opinion polls • key informant interviews • group approaches (nominal group technique, Delphi, community forum) • preference scaling **Needs Assessment** • social indicators approaches • surveys • group approaches	**Leadership** • creating a safe environment • ensuring participation • active listening • public speaking • clear, concise writing
Agreeing on Goals	**Goals Analysis** • *Goal formulation*: surveys, community forums, rating of goal characteristics • *Priority Setting*: estimate— discuss—estimate procedure, Q-sort, paired comparisons, multiattribute utility measurement, decision-theoretic analysis	**Engaging People in Process** • clarifying intent • brokering • mediating • persuading
Identifying Alternatives	**Policy Logic Analysis** • review of theories of causation • review of outcome evaluations in policy area • concept development	**Sharing Knowledge** • facilitating
Choosing an Alternative	**Feasibility Study** • investigation of funding sources • cost-benefit analysis • cost-effectiveness analysis • price analysis • administrative feasibility assessment	**Sharing Knowledge** • facilitating • guiding
Implementing the Policy	**Implementation Assessment** • Gantt charts • milestone charts • PERT–CPM networks	**Information Gathering** • manufacturing commitment
Evaluating the Policy	**Process** • collection of data from information systems • peer review ratings • client satisfaction surveys **Outcomes** • experimental approaches • quasi-experimental approaches • single case design • client satisfaction surveys • social impact assessments	**Sharing of Expertise** • safe environment • ensuring participation in developing design • communication of results

to ensure that all stakeholders have an opportunity to participate in the process of constructing the problem; active listening skills, to ensure that the nuances of different stakeholder perspectives are not missed; competence in working with people who differ on culture, "race," class, gender, sexual orientation, and ability; public speaking skills, if one is going to advocate for a particular policy position; and clear, concise writing skills, whether one is playing the role of neutral internal policy analyst at some level of government or that of community-based advocate.

At the next stage, agreeing on goals, analytic skills are again needed in two areas: goal formulation and priority setting. To formulate goals, skills are needed to carry out surveys, conduct community forums, and rate goal characteristics. Procedures like the estimate-discuss-estimate procedure, the Q-sort, paired comparisons, multiattribute utility measurement, and decision theoretic analysis can be used to set priorities. To support the analytic tasks, interactional skills that permit the analyst to engage stakeholders in the process of reaching agreement on goals are needed, as well as skills in clarifying, brokering, and mediating. If the analyst is acting as an advocate, she or he will also need to be skilled in persuasion. Again, competence in working across differences is needed to ensure not only that marginalized groups are included in these processes but also that their preferences, if not the same as those of the majority, are taken into account.

Policy logic analysis, a variant of program logic analysis (Rush & Ogburne, 1991), can be used to facilitate the identification of policy alternatives that, in light of a specified theory of causation of the identified problem, could be expected to achieve the policy goals agreed upon. A review of any outcome evaluations of these policy alternatives would identify empirical evidence, which could either support the implementation of a particular alternative or suggest that it would not, in fact, achieve the anticipated outcomes. Theory often precedes practice, so another skill required by the analyst is the ability to discern the implications for practice of a particular theoretical perspective for policy development. The interactional skills required at this stage include being able to summarize and share knowledge in a way that is both interesting and concise, and the ability to facilitate discussion to generate alternative ideas.

Feasibility studies provide information that assists in choosing among policy alternatives. Assessing feasibility includes determining whether funds would be available for the various alternatives; completing cost-benefit or cost-effectiveness analyses on each alternative; completing a political feasibility assessment using a technique like PRINCE (Probe, Interact, Calculate, Execute); and assessing the administrative feasibility of the alternatives. Good skills in presenting information in an interesting and concise way are required at this stage as well. In addition, the analyst must be able to guide the process in selecting an alternative.

An implementation assessment permits the analyst to identify how much time would be required to implement the alternative selected, which jurisdictions would need to be involved, and which approvals required. Pressman and Wildavsky (1973) alerted us to the importance of this stage thirty years ago, when they discovered that many policies never have their intended effects because they fail to make it through the long string of decisions necessary for the policy to be implemented. Analyzing these approval processes before-hand and identifying potential blocks will provide greater assurance that the policy will, in fact, be implemented. The primary interactional skills required at this stage are the ability to gather information on complex systems and to generate commitment on the part of service providers to the new policy alter-native, so that it will, in fact, be implemented as intended.

Limitations of Policy Analysis

Finally, any policy must be systematically evaluated to assess what has happened in light of its intended effects. Process evaluation includes a review of who has been served, for what reasons, and what service they have received. Peer reviews are made of cases to determine whether defined standards of care have been met. Client satisfaction surveys assess whether consumers received the expected service, whether they were served in a timely fashion, and whether they found it helpful. Outcome evaluations may focus on individual goals or program goals, and are intended to assess the extent to which the changes that are intended to occur for the client have, in fact, occurred. The interactional skills required of the policy analyst as evaluator include sharing his or her knowledge about how evaluations may be designed, creating a feel-ing of safety with respect to the evaluation, ensuring that all those affected by the evaluation participate in its design, engaging service deliverers in the data collection process, and communicating the results of the research to all those involved.

Limitations of Policy Analysis

With all of its promise for improving the well-being of Canadian citizens, what are the limitations of policy analysis as an area of practice? First, the process may be exceedingly slow. Even within an agency setting, to make a change in policy may take a year or longer from the point that a concern is identified until a new policy has been implemented. If the local, provincial, or federal governments are the focus of change, it is likely to take even longer. This means that a commitment to effect change must be a long-term one.

Second, efforts to make changes in policy can be very resource intensive. It takes time, energy, and money to raise awareness about an issue. The more complex and controversial the issue, the more resources will be required. It is essential to learn to build coalitions, to create organizations where none exist to advocate for an issue, and to identify and link with existing ones that might share your concern. It may also be necessary to raise funding to sup-port your policy change initiatives. This means that a commitment to effect change is an opportunity to develop a set of social work skills that are quite different from those within the clinical domain.

Third, even with the investment of considerable resources, it may not be possible to effect changes that are consistent with social work values at a particular time. An example would be the mandatory work requirement introduced for social assistance recipients in a number of provinces in the mid-nineties. While most social workers support the development of job-training opportunities for people on assistance, requiring people to work in return for benefits is in conflict with our belief that receipt of social assistance is a right, albeit one coupled with a responsibility to provide for oneself when possible. Abundant data show that the great majority of people work when given the opportunity. Job readiness programs offered by the various levels of government in Canada have typically been oversubscribed (Snyder, 2000). In spite of this empirical evidence, the belief persists that people on assistance are lazy and need to be coerced to accept work. As long as a government in power holds this belief, and refuses to alter it in light of evidence to the contrary, efforts to change workfare policies are unlikely to be fruitful. This means that a commitment to effect change may not always be successful in the short term, and can be the source of considerable discouragement if a longer-term perspective is not maintained.

Fourth, for the policy analyst working within an organization or at some level of government, it is essential that there is a clear understanding between the policy analyst and the employer about which kinds of political activity are acceptable. Traditionally, the role of government employee was defined as that of a rational, apolitical analyst. Partisan political activity was not only discouraged but could be the grounds for dismissal. While that has now changed, there may still be limits on what is allowed. An employee at the local government level may be free to engage in efforts to change provincial legislation with respect to regulation of social workers, for instance, but not to lobby his or her member of Parliament to withdraw the mandatory aspect of the workfare program. This means that a commitment to effect change requires a careful assessment of one's work environment and clear communication about the boundaries on political activity.

Finally, policy analysis skills and tools are not yet sufficiently developed to ensure that issues of "difference" are systematically and fully considered when social policy is made. It is only in 1995 that the Government of Canada committed to review all public policy initiatives from a gender perspective (Status of Women Canada, 1998). Evidence of the utilization of a gender-based analysis can be found on various government websites now, among them a detailed gender analysis of the 2001 Immigration and Refugee Protection Act (Citizenship and Immigration Canada, 2002). The framework first developed to guide this analysis was revised in 1998, and it could serve as the inspiration to develop parallel frameworks to assess the impact of policy on other marginalized groups, but this does not appear to have been done yet.

Conclusions

Social workers have come to accept the development of social policy as an essential component of our work as professionals. While the prospect of trying to change legislation, the vision of an organization, or agency policy with respect to service delivery may seem daunting, our successes in these efforts not only provide us with an opportunity to develop a complementary set of skills to those we use as clinicians but also teach us that it can be done. Whether we choose to focus on issues at the international, federal, provincial, local, or organizational level, our efforts improve the well-being of individual clients, build a sense of community, and empower us as individuals and as a profession. Ultimately, the values we promote, infused throughout social policy, will shape and give definition to a more just and inclusive Canada.

References

Armitage, A. (1988). *Social welfare in Canada: Ideals, realities and future paths.* Toronto: McClelland and Stewart.

Bell, G.G., & Pascoe, A.D. (1988). *The Ontario government: Structure and functions.* Toronto: Wall and Thompson.

Brooks, S. (1993). *Public policy in Canada: An introduction* (2nd ed.). Toronto: McClelland and Stewart.

Canadian Association of Social Workers. (2005). *Code of ethics.* Online at <www.cassw-acts.ca>.

Cameron, D., & Stein, J.G. (2000). Globalization, culture and society: The state as place amidst shifting spaces. *Canadian Public Policy 26*(suppl. 2), S15–S34.

Carver, J. (1990). *Boards that make a difference: A new design for leadership in non-profit and public organizations.* San Francisco: Jossey-Bass.

Chappell, L.A. (2002). *Gendering government: Feminist engagement with the state in Australia and Canada.* Toronto: University of British Columbia Press.

Citizenship and Immigration Canada. (2002). *Bill C-11: Immigration and Refugee Protection Act; Gender-based analysis chart.* Online at <www.cic.gc.ca/english/irpa/c11-gender.html>.

Collier, K. (1995). Social policy versus regional trading blocs in the global system: NAFTA, the EEC and "Asia." *Canadian Review of Social Policy, 35*(1), 50–59.

Cresswell, J.W. (2002). *Research design: Qualitative, quantitative and mixed methods approaches.* Thousand Oaks, CA: Sage.

Flynn, J.P. (1992). *Social agency policy: Analysis and presentation for community practice.* Chicago: Nelson-Hall.

Friedmann, J. (1987). *Planning in the public domain: From action to knowledge.* Princeton, NJ: Princeton University Press.

Giddens, A. (1979). *Central problems in social theory: Action, structure and contradiction in social analysis.* Berkeley: University of California Press.

Giddens, A. (1984). *The constitution of society.* Berkeley: University of California Press.

Gil, D.G. (1981). *Unravelling social policy* (3rd ed.). Cambridge, MA: Schenkman.

Graham, J., Swift, K., & Delaney, R. (2003). *Canadian social policy: An introduction.* Toronto: Prentice Hall.

References   Graham, K., Phillips, S.D., & Maslove, A.M. (1998). *Urban governance in Canada: Representation, resources and restructuring.* Toronto: Harcourt Canada.

Jansson, B. (1994). *Social policy: From theory to policy practice* (2nd ed.). Pacific Grove: Brooks/Cole.

Kahn, A.J. (1969). *Theory and practice of social planning.* New York: Russell Sage.

Kahn, A.J. (1979). *Social policy and social services* (2nd ed.). New York: Random House.

Kelly, J.B. (1999). Bureaucratic activism and the Charter of Rights and Freedoms: The Department of Justice and its entry into the centre of government. *Canadian Public Administration, 42*(4), 476–511.

Kingdon, J.W. (1995). *Agendas, alternatives and public policies.* New York: Longman-Addison.

Kirby, S., & McKenna, K. (1989). *Experience, research, social change: Methods from the margins.* Toronto: Garamond.

Lightman, E. (1991). Support for social welfare in Canada and the United States. *Canadian Review of Social Policy, 28*(2), 9–27.

Lightman, E. (2003). *Social policy in Canada.* Don Mills: Oxford University Press.

Lincoln, Y.S., & Guba, E.G. (1985). *Naturalistic inquiry.* London: Sage.

Maguire, P. (1987). *Doing participatory research: A feminist approach.* Amherst, MA: University of Massachusetts, Center for International Education.

Mayer, R.R. (1985). *Policy and program planning: A developmental perspective.* Englewood Cliffs, NJ: Prentice-Hall.

McGilly, F. (1990). *Canada's public social services: Understanding income and health programs.* Toronto: McClelland and Stewart.

Melchers, R. (1999). Local governance of social welfare: Local reform in Ontario in the nineties. *Canadian Review of Social Policy, 43*(2), 29–57.

Mendelson, M. (1999). The new Social Union. *Canadian Review of Social Policy, 43* (2), 1–11.

Meyerson, M., & Banfield, E.C. (1955). *Politics, planning and the public interest.* New York: Free Press.

Moroney, R.M. (1981). Policy analysis within a value theoretical framework. In R. Haskins & J.J. Gallager (Eds.), *Models for analysis of social policy: An introduction* (pp. 78–102). Norwood, NJ: Ablex Press.

Moscovitch, A. (1991, Winter). Citizenship, social rights and Canadian social welfare. *Canadian Review of Social Policy, 28*, 28–34.

Moscovitch, A., & Drover, G. (1981). *Inequality: Essays on the political economy of social welfare.* Toronto: University of Toronto Press.

Neuman, W.L. (1994). *Social research methods: Qualitative and quantitative approaches* (2nd ed.). Toronto: Allyn and Bacon.

Ogilvie, Ogilvie, and Company. (1990). *Policy analysis and policy development: Tools and techniques.* Course handbook. Toronto: Author.

Pal, L. (1992). *Public policy analysis: An introduction.* Toronto: Nelson Canada.

Pal, L. (2006). *Beyond policy analysis: Public issue management in turbulent times.* (2nd Canadian ed.). Toronto: Thomson Nelson.

Pancer, S.M., & Westhues, A. (1989). A developmental stage approach to planning. *Evaluation Review, 13*(1), 56–77.

Perlman, R., & Gurin, A. (1972). *Community organizing and social planning.* New York: John Wiley and Sons.

Pierce, D. (1984). *Policy for the social work practitioner.* New York: Longman.   References

Pressman, J.L., & Wildavsky, A.B. (1973). *Implementation.* Berkeley: University of California Press.

Riches, G., & Ternowetsky, G. (1990). *Unemployment and welfare: Social policy and the work of social work.* Toronto: Garamond Press.

Ross, M.C. (1967). *Community organization: Theory, principles and practice.* New York: Harper and Row.

Rothman, J., & Zald, M.N. (1985). Planning theory in social work community practice. In S.H. Taylor & R.W. Roberts (Eds.), *Theory and practice of community social work* (pp. 125–153). New York: Columbia University Press.

Rush, B., & Ogborne, A. (1991). Program logic models: Expanding their role and structure for program planning and evaluation. *Canadian Journal of Program Evaluation, 6*(2), 95–106.

Shrybman, S. (1999). *A citizen's guide to the World Trade Organization.* Ottawa: Canadian Centre for Policy Alternatives and James Lorimer.

Snyder, L. (2000). Success of single mothers on social assistance through a voluntary employment program. *Canadian Social Work Review, 17*(1), 49–68.

Splane, R.B. (1965). *Social welfare in Ontario 1791–1893: A study of public welfare administration.* Toronto: University of Toronto Press.

Status of Women Canada. (1998). *Gender-based analysis: A guide for policy-making.* Online at <www.swc-cfc.gc.ca/pubs/gbaguide/gbaguide_e.html>.

Strauss, A., & Corbin, J. (1998). *Basics of qualitative research: Techniques and procedures for developing grounded theory.* Thousand Oaks: Sage.

Taylor, S.H., & Roberts, R.W. (1985). *Theory and practice of community social work.* New York: Columbia University Press.

Teeple, G. (1995). *Globalization and the decline of social reform.* Toronto: Garamond Press.

Tester, F.J. (1991). The globalized economy: What does it mean for Canadian social and environmental policy? *Canadian Review of Social Policy, 27*(1), 3–12.

Tester, F.J. (1992). The disenchanted democracy: Canada in the global economy of the 1990s. *Canadian Review of Social Policy, 29/30*(2), 132–157.

Tindal, C.R., & Tindal, S.N. (1984). *Local government in Canada* (2nd ed.). Toronto: McGraw-Hill Ryerson.

Tropman, J.E. (1995). Policy management in the social agency. In J.E. Tropman, J.L. Erlich, & J. Rothman (Eds.), *Tactics and techniques of community intervention* (3rd ed., pp. 288–291). Itasca, IL: F.E. Peacock.

Tropman, J.E., Erlich, J.L. & Rothman, J. (Eds.). (1995). *Tactics and techniques of community intervention* (3rd ed.). Itasca, IL: F.E. Peacock.

Van Loon, R.J., & Whittington, M.S. (1976). *The Canadian political system: Environment, structure and process* (2nd ed.). Toronto: McGraw-Hill Ryerson.

Walker, G.A. (1990). *Family violence and the women's movement.* Toronto: University of Toronto Press.

Westhues, A. (1980, September). Stages in social planning. *Social Service Review, 54,* 331–343.

Westhues, A. (2002). Social policy practice. In F.J. Turner (Ed.), *Social work practice: A Canadian perspective* (pp. 315–329). Toronto: Prentice Hall.

Wharf, B., & McKenzie, B. (2004). *Connecting policy to practice in the human services.* Toronto: Oxford University Press.

References Yelaja, S.A. (1987). *Canadian social policy* (Rev. ed.). Waterloo, ON: Wilfrid Laurier
University Press.

York, R.O. (1982). *Human service planning: Concepts, tools and methods.* Chapel
Hill: University of North Carolina Press.

Additional Resources

The Canadian Policy Research Network promotes a more just, prosperous, and caring society through research, networking, and dissemination, and by providing a valued neutral space within which an open dialogue among all interested parties can take place. Their reports are available online at <www.cprn.com>.

Decision-making processes and central agencies in Canada: Federal, provincial and territorial practices, a detailed review of the policy-making process within the federal government and within each of the provinces and territories except Nunavut. Online at <www.pcobcp.gc.ca/default.asp?Page=Publications& Language=E&doc=Decision/decision_e.htm>.

Policy.ca is a non-partisan resource for the public analysis of Canadian policy issues. Online at <www.policy.ca>.

Social policy in Ontario: An online guide is a collaborative project of Laurentian University, the Ontario Social Development Council, and the Social Planning Network of Ontario. Online at <www.spo.laurentian.ca>.

United Nations. Online at <www.un.org/>.

The Voluntary Sector Initiative (vsi) is a unique undertaking between the Government of Canada and the voluntary sector to enhance their relationship and strengthen the sector's capacity. Over the five-year initiative, they are working together to address issues such as funding practices, policy dialogue, technology, volunteerism, and research about the sector. Online at <www.vsi-isbc.ca/eng/index.cfm>.

World Trade Organization. Online at <www.wto.org>.

II   Policy-Making Processes

Introduction to Part II

Part II of the book contains seven articles on the policy-making process at the international, federal, provincial, and program levels.

In chapter 2, Tim Wichert gives us a fascinating look at the complexities of attempts to influence international policy from the standpoint of a staff member in a non-governmental organization (NGO). Using refugee policy as an example, he first describes the policy-making process within the United Nations. We learn that it is perhaps even more replete with diverse perspectives than policy-making within a national or provincial context because of the enormous variation in the cultural and economic backgrounds of the countries involved in decision-making. He describes for us the partnership that has evolved between the NGO sector and the United Nations High Commissioner for Refugees in shaping refugee policy over the years and relates the satisfaction of shaping policy at a level that will have a worldwide impact.

John English and Bill Young then provide us with an intriguing insight into the policy-making process at the federal level in chapter 3, based upon their experience as, respectively, elected official and parliamentary policy analyst. Using a historical perspective, they set out in careful detail the struggles of the 1990s with debt and deficit, which led to the introduction of the Canada Health and Social Transfer, the National Child Benefit, and the Social Union Framework Agreement. They conclude that the period can best be characterized by the continued struggle to clarify the responsibilities of federal and provincial governments with respect to the funding of social programs and to define the conditions under which new programs can be introduced by the federal government.

Ailsa Watkinson adds a new chapter to the fourth edition that elucidates the influence of the courts in shaping social policy. Most often, these court cases involve a Charter challenge. She begins by explaining the links between human rights and the social work profession, and between human rights and the Charter of Rights and Freedoms. By recounting her own experience with a 2004 challenge to the Criminal Code provision that "reasonable use of force" is acceptable with children, Ailsa provides us with insight into how a social policy advocate can engage in a Charter challenge to effect change.

Carol Kenny-Scherber leads off chapter 5 with a challenge to social workers to draw on their knowledge of service user needs and how the human service system works to actively participate in the public decision-making process that determines the provincial government's response to social issues. She provides an insider's perspective on how policy is made at the political, pre-legislative, and legislative phases. The chapter concludes with a wealth of suggestions on how social workers can participate in the policy-making process through involvement with political parties, as advocates, and as professional social workers.

Mac Saulis makes an insightful analysis of the policy and program development processes within the mainstream, and from a holistic, Aboriginal perspective in chapter 6. He explains the meaning of The Circle, and how this world view could be applied to policy development. It differs most dramatically from the mainstream perspective in its emphasis on four aspects of humans—not only the emotional and the mental, or what the mainstream might call cognitive, but on the physical and the spiritual as well. He also explains the importance of inclusiveness for Aboriginal peoples in the policy-making process, and how this could be accomplished if we were to work from this cultural perspective. He notes the parallels between postmodern approaches to planning and the traditional Aboriginal perspective.

Chapter 7, by Joan Wharf Higgins, John Cossom, and Brian Wharf, reinforces the previous two chapters when it argues that there is insufficient citizen input into the policy-making process. Wharf Higgins, Cossom, and Wharf use Dahl's concept of "affected interests" to argue that everybody impacted by a policy decision should have a right to participate in making that decision and to offer some guidance on how one would define the players and the relative influence of each. They offer practical suggestions for fostering a more inclusive process, whether one is dealing with "ordinary issues" like promoting healthier communities or "grand issues" like the influence of the World Trade Organization in shaping the economy of nation-states.

The final chapter in this section, chapter 8, discusses an essential but sometimes overlooked aspect of the policy-making process—evaluation of social policy and programs. Anne Westhues argues that the shift from a positivist (modern) to a more humanist (postmodern) way of thinking over the past twenty-five years has had an impact on the role of the evaluator, the kinds of questions asked in evaluation, and the way we design research, collect data, and report our results. Most significant in this shift is the valuing of the subjective experiences of people affected by policies and programs. While we now see political leaders promoting a return to an emphasis on traditional measurable outcomes, Westhues suggests that by consciously committing to work from a critical perspective, social workers engaged in evaluation can ensure that we do not lose focus on these subjective experiences.

Tim Wichert

The international stage has become an important place to engage in social policy debate. Various agencies of the United Nations (UN) were created in the twentieth century to deal with social issues, including the World Health Organization, the United Nations High Commissioner for Refugees, the UN Children's Fund (UNICEF), and the UN Commission on Human Rights. The UN Charter, which created the United Nations at its founding conference in San Francisco on June 26, 1945, sought to "reaffirm faith in fundamental human rights, in the dignity and worth of the human person, in the equal rights of men and women," and to "promote social progress and better standards of life" (United Nations, 1945).

A positive approach to social policy development at the international level requires an understanding of the process and choosing how best to be involved. The international policy process involves a complex set of interactions involving individual states, regional groups of states, international agencies within the UN system, and private actors like non-governmental organizations (NGOs). Implementation of international standards ultimately requires governments to incorporate them into national legislation. However, political and cultural differences between states and regions result in different levels of understanding and commitment. Even if there is general agreement that certain social policy issues may be universal, how they are implemented at a national or local level varies considerably.

Non-governmental organizations have played an important role in developing international social policy because of their understanding of these local dynamics. NGOs that are most effectively engaged in international social policy tend to be those with programs in various parts of the world focused on human health, safety, and well-being. NGOs therefore play an important role in both representing civil society at the international level and interpreting international social policy for everyday use.

My perspectives on international social policy-making result from having ten years of experience in the NGO sector with the Mennonite Central Committee (MCC), which included a three-year secondment to the Quaker United Nations Office in Geneva, Switzerland. While MCC is an agency of Mennonite

Churches in North America, its mandate is to work among people suffering from poverty, conflict, oppression, and natural disaster, and to work for peace, justice, and the dignity of all people (Mennonite Central Committee, 2000). Much of my work has focused on refugees and policies related to the human rights of refugees. This chapter will examine developing international policy related to these issues.

Understanding International Policy Process

Policies for human rights related to refugees and asylum seekers have been developed through a vast array of instruments at the international, regional, and national level.

At the international level, these policies have developed throughout the United Nations system. The Universal Declaration of Human Rights gives everyone the right to seek and enjoy asylum (Article 14). As long as people cannot have their basic human rights protected in their own country, asylum remains their most effective means of protection. In the aftermath of World War II, governments were concerned about the refugee crisis in Europe and wanted to create a policy framework for dealing with the crisis.

The UN High Commissioner for Refugees (UNHCR) was created in 1951 by a resolution of the UN General Assembly.[1] A statute set out general provisions and functions of the high commissioner. The UNHCR was to provide protection to refugees falling within the scope of the UN statute. It was also authorized to seek permanent solutions for the "problem of refugees."[2] In July 1951, a conference in Geneva completed the drafting and signing of the Convention Relating to the Status of Refugees. Together with the UNHCR statute, this refugee convention provided the legislative framework for the vision outlined in the original resolution of the UN General Assembly.

The refugee convention remains the most comprehensive codification of the rights of refugees at the international level, though it was augmented by a protocol in 1967 to include those who became refugees after January 1951. The convention sets out the popular definition of a refugee that is still used today, namely a person who has a well-founded fear of being persecuted for reasons of race, religion, nationality, membership of a particular social group, or political opinion, and who is outside his or her country of nationality or habitual residence.[3] It also sets out specific provisions regarding housing, public education, social security, and travel documents for refugees. For example, governments that have signed the convention "shall accord to refugees the same treatment as is accorded to nationals with respect to elementary education."[4] However, Article 42 of the convention allows states to make reservations to some of these provisions when signing, thereby limiting their obligations.

At the original conference, twenty-six governments were represented by delegates and two others by observers. Only eight were from outside Europe and North America: Brazil, Colombia, Cuba, Egypt, Iran, Iraq, Israel, and

Turkey. Today, 146 countries have ratified the refugee convention or protocol. The refugee convention has evolved over time through both policy and practice. For example, the Organization of African Unity (OAU), comprising countries within Africa, has articulated a definition of refugees that includes those fleeing more generalized violence and civil war; and countries like Canada and the United States have specifically included violence and persecution aimed at women as a ground for refugee status in national policy.

International policy is continually developed by the Executive Committee of the UNHCR, known as Excom. Excom is made up of states that have a "demonstrated interest in and devotion to the solution of the refugee problem."[5] These have tended to be important asylum countries or major donors to UNHCR programs. Currently, sixty-eight states are members of Excom. They meet annually in Geneva to agree upon decisions and conclusions for ultimate adoption by the UN General Assembly.

In addition to the refugee convention and the Universal Declaration of Human Rights, a number of other key international treaties provide important rights for refugees and asylum seekers (Gorlick, 2000). These include the International Covenant on Civil and Political Rights, and the International Covenant on Economic, Social and Cultural Rights (both adopted in 1966), the International Convention on the Elimination of all Forms of Racial Discrimination (1965), the Convention on the Elimination of all Forms of Discrimination against Women (1979), the Convention Against Torture and Other Cruel, Inhuman or Degrading Treatment or Punishment (1984), and the Convention on the Rights of the Child (1989). Each of these treaties have established supervisory mechanisms, usually committees of international experts. They provide authoritative interpretation of treaty provisions and assess compliance of the standards by state parties that must report to the committees. Four of these treaties provide a mechanism for bringing individual complaints against a government (Civil and Political Rights, Torture, Racial Discrimination, and Discrimination against Women).

This array of human rights is available to all people within the territory or under the jurisdiction of a state that is subject to the treaty. Refugees who have been forced to flee their country of nationality because of persecution have had these international human rights violated. After they flee to another country, they are still entitled to these rights, not because they are refugees but because these rights should be applicable to everyone.

Implementation of human rights obligations will vary from country to country. Individual states will often choose to comply with their international obligations on the basis of national policy priorities. They must choose whether to formalize international obligations by enacting national legislation, whether to establish national mechanisms for dealing with human rights complaints, and whether to interpret constitutional rights in a narrow or restrictive manner. Goodwin-Gill (1996) suggests that while implementation may vary, obligations should at the very least be implemented in good faith.

Governments can be pressured into complying with international obligations through these human rights mechanisms or through political pressure from other states. The UN Commission on Human Rights, which meets each spring in Geneva, is an intergovernmental body made up of fifty-three government members elected on a regional basis. Most other states send observers to participate. The political nature of the process offers mixed results for policy-making. It allows pressure to be brought to bear on offending states for their human rights violations, especially through the use of rapporteurs who report on specific country or thematic issues. It has arguably been an important factor in achieving progress in recent decades in places like Chile, Argentina, and South Africa. However, it also allows states to avoid censure through political manipulation and negotiation; at the 2005 World Summit, the UN General Assembly agreed to replace the Commission with a smaller, revamped Human Rights Council.

Non-governmental organizations play an important role in raising awareness of the obligations and issues at a national level. Canadian NGOs were instrumental in raising refugee-related concerns at the Canadian government's first appearance before the UN Committee on the Rights of the Child (CRC) in 1995. The Inter-Church Committee for Refugees of Toronto prepared a detailed brief outlining a number of concerns, including the issue of family reunification for refugee children. The CRC, in its report, recommended that the Canadian authorities take all feasible measures to facilitate and speed up family reunification, and that solutions should be sought to avoid deportations causing separation of families (Gorlick, 2000). The latter is an issue when children have been born in Canada during the asylum process. Since they are Canadian citizens, the CRC suggested that their "best interests" should be considered in determining whether their parent or parents should ultimately be deported from Canada if their refugee claim is rejected.

Canadian policy was further clarified on this issue by the Supreme Court of Canada in the 1999 case of Mavis Baker, following legal interventions by NGOs, which raised the CRC decision and Canada's international legal obligations. As a result, the new Immigration and Refugee Protection Act of 2002 specifically included the "best interests of the child" terminology in a number of places. Further, it codified provisions of the UN Convention against Torture, prohibiting the return to torture. It included a specific requirement in section 3 that the Act is to be "construed and applied in a manner that complies with international human rights instruments to which Canada is signatory." NGOs in Canada were instrumental in getting these provisions included in the new law, and will continue to be instrumental in ensuring further development.

UN Treaty bodies, like the Committee on the Rights of the Child, acknowledge that Canada basically sets a good example in terms of its policies and programs. For example, on the international spectrum, children in Canada are better off than they are in almost all other countries in the world. Nonetheless, the committee's conclusions and concerns are one of the few ways in which international pressure can be brought to encourage better protection of children's rights in Canada. While offering its encouragement and expressing its concerns, the committee is very dependent on other actors within Canada to take these concerns forward.

It is also important to note the array of regional human rights mechanisms that have been established in Europe, Africa, and the Americas (Buergental, 1995). Canadian NGOs have used the mechanisms of the Organization of American States to promote social policy. In 2000, the Inter-American Commission on Human Rights issued a detailed report on the state of human rights of asylum seekers within the Canadian refugee determination system following a visit to Canada by a six-person commission delegation (Inter-American Commission on Human Rights, 2000). The commission held discussions with numerous high-level political, administrative, legislative, and judicial authorities, as well as representatives of NGOs and other sectors of civil society. NGOs subsequently used the commission's report when advocating for changes to the Canadian legislation on citizenship and immigration and refugees adopted in 2002.

International policy development is not simply about encouraging states to implement their obligations, however. On occasion, the Canadian government and other states have played a significant role in the policy process at the international level. The Canadian government in recent years has focused its foreign policy on issues related to human security (Canada, 2000). Part of this strategy was to play a leading role in the completion of the UN Convention on Land Mines in Ottawa in December 1997. More recently it has been instrumental in developing and promoting the "Responsibility to Protect," a concept of international intervention to protect civilians in the midst of human rights abuses and war. R2P, as it is known, was adopted in principle by the UN General Assembly at the 2005 World Summit. Further, the Canadian government continues to promote international recognition of the right to seek refugee asylum on the basis of gender-based persecution.

International policy-making therefore involves a complex set of processes. Effectively working within this system requires an understanding of where to focus attention.

Developing a Thematic Focus

International refugee policy is enhanced by having an institutional base within the office of the UN High Commissioner for Refugees [UNHCR]. The UNHCR provides a programmatic framework for designing and delivering programs for refugees. It has over 5,000 staff in 120 countries, with an annual budget of US$1 billion (UNHCR, 2000). The Executive Committee of the UNHCR approves and supervises the material assistance program of UNHCR, for which various governments provide financing. It also advises the high commissioner on the exercise of his or her functions. In practice, the work of Excom is largely influenced and guided by the UNHCR itself, especially through its policy papers and speeches given by the high commissioner. Policies are continually developed through guidelines and policy papers generated within UNHCR.

Excom is helped and hindered equally by its guiding principle to build consensus. Public debate is dominated by government responses to the issues raised by UNHCR, and by burning issues arising from specific refugee contexts. The final "conclusions" are the product of closed meetings between UNHCR and governments. Achieving consensus on decisions and conclusions is a difficult task, and important matters are often in danger of being excluded in the interest of agreement. However, once agreed upon, they arguably take on added significance.

Apart from programming, UNHCR is also instrumental in urging states to support and implement the policy standards they have set. The refugee convention does not have a monitoring mechanism like the expert committees of other human rights conventions.

The dilemma for UNHCR, which is perhaps typical in international policy-making, is that while it is striving to uphold the rights and interests of refugees, and must criticize states when necessary, it is also almost entirely dependent on those states for its funding and ongoing mandate. As a result, the role of the NGO sector, which is much more independent from governments, has become fundamental to policy development.

There is an increasing awareness and understanding among NGOs of the opportunities for effective participation in the UNHCR process. This increasing participation has involved a number of things, including recognizing the importance of coalitions and alliances with policy advisers within the Canadian government, with NGOs from Canada and other countries, with officials within the UN system, and also with policy advisers from other national governments. International policy development is not simply about creating utopian policies and highlighting the violations of acceptable behaviour. It also involves working together with those governments and international agencies that are seriously attempting to implement and demonstrate acceptable behaviour and urging others to do the same. Through such alliances, important strides have been made in the past decade on international refugee policy for women and children.

Women share the same protection needs as other refugees. They need protection against forced return to their countries of origin, security against armed attacks, legal status that grants adequate social and legal rights, and access to basic necessities like food, shelter, and medical care. In addition, refugee women and girls have special protection needs. They are vulnerable to sexual and physical abuse, exploitation, and discrimination in the delivery of goods and services (UNHCR, 1999). In particular, they may endure physical and sexual attacks during conflict in their home countries, during flight to asylum, and even during asylum (Human Rights Watch, 1995; UNHCR, 1995b). National policies in countries of asylum may not provide legal recognition or proper documentation.

Although gender is not specifically articulated in the refugee definition of the refugee convention, there have been important steps in recent years to include it in practice. In 1985, the European Parliament called on states to grant refugee status "to women who suffer cruel and inhuman treatment because they have violated the moral or ethical rules of their society" (UNHCR, 1997, p. 196). That same year, Excom conclusion no. 39 recognized that states were free to adopt the interpretation that women asylum seekers could, in certain situations, be considered a "particular social group" within the convention definition. In 1995, Excom took this further with a conclusion calling on states to develop guidelines on persecution aimed at women, suggesting that these guidelines should recognize as refugees those women whose persecution consists of sexual violence or is otherwise gender-related. Canada continues to promote this issue, having pioneered such guidelines in 1993 when the chairperson of the Immigration and Refugee Board issued gender guidelines for use in refugee determination hearings.[6]

In 1996, UNHCR hosted a symposium on gender-based persecution. Later that year, an Excom conclusion called on states to adopt an approach that is "sensitive to gender-related concerns," and which "ensures" that persecution through sexual violence or which is otherwise gender-related is indeed persecution under the refugee convention.

International protection for vulnerable groups goes beyond legal principles, however. Protection of refugee women requires practical programs and priorities that ensure their safety and well-being. In 1991 UNHCR produced *Guidelines for Protection and Care of Refugee Women*, and in 1995 they produced *Sexual Violence against Refugees: Guidelines on the Prevention and Response*.

These guidelines have been prepared to help the staff of UNHCR and its implementing partners to identify the specific protection issues, problems, and risks facing refugee women. The guidelines cover traditional protection concerns such as the determination of refugee status and the provision of physical security; but they also provide suggestions on actions that can be taken, particularly within traditional assistance sectors, to prevent or deter protection problems from arising. These encourage practical interventions such as the early assessment of protection issues (e.g., ensuring that services and facilities are easily accessible with good lighting), involving women in decision-making structures (e.g., the design of health programs), monitoring the nutritional status of women and children to identify problems in food distribution, and using female staff when trying to elicit information from female refugees (UNHCR, 1999).

In 1994, UNHCR also developed a training module called *People-Oriented Planning* (POP). Although it was developed by the senior coordinator on refugee women within UNHCR, it provided a broader focus to include women, men, and children. The premise for the tool was that for staff to do the best job possible in providing protection and assistance to refugees in any particular situation, they must know specific things about who the refugees are in that

particular setting. The POP programming tool helps UNHCR staff and partners identify the important facts about any group of refugees, and then organize that information to make programming decisions and to implement effective programs (Anderson, 1994).

NGOs were instrumental in initiating and encouraging discussions on the
importance of addressing the needs of refugee women. They encouraged the
development of the guidelines and the creation of a focal point within UNHCR
to address these needs. The Canadian government funded the first senior
coordinator for refugee women within UNHCR in 1994.

While much progress has been made, NGOs and others continue to express
concern about the implementation of the UNHCR guidelines relating to refugee
women. There was also concerted action by NGOs in 1997 when UNHCR suggested ending the mandate of the senior coordinator for refugee women
because of the belief that the issues had been adequately "mainstreamed"
within the overall work of UNHCR. NGOs and various states didn't agree, and
because of the pressure placed on UNHCR from both NGOs and states (which
were prepared to continue funding the position), the position was retained.
It is clear that even within the institutional framework of UNHCR, there are
issues related to the adequate implementation of social policies that have
been developed.

There has also been progress on policy related to refugee children. In 1987
Excom requested a set of guidelines for refugee children,[7] which UNHCR published the following year. Following an evaluation in 1991, UNHCR prepared a
policy on refugee children in 1993, which was adopted by UNHCR Excom in
October 1993, and a revised version of the guidelines in 1994 (UNHCR, 1994). At
the same time, UNHCR established the position of senior coordinator for
refugee children, with financial assistance from the government of Sweden,
to encourage the implementation of the guidelines and policy.

The policy arose because of the recognition that refugee children have
special dependence, vulnerability, and developmental needs. When resources
are scarce, they are often the first to die. Refugee girls are even more vulnerable than boys to neglect, abuse, and exploitation. Girls' participation in education programs is often prematurely curtailed (UNHCR, 1994).

The policy also originated around the same time that the UN was completing the Convention on the Rights of the Child in 1989. This widely ratified
convention set the normative international standards in which UNHCR could
develop a framework of practical implementation. This in turn led to the
directives of UNHCR Excom, which ultimately adopted a policy specific to
refugee children.

The Canadian government has also taken steps to ensure some of these
issues are incorporated into national policy. In particular, the chair of the
Immigration and Refugee Board issued guidelines on child refugee claimants
in September 1996. Among other things, these guidelines focus on appropriate procedures for assessing the refugee claims of children who are not accompanied by their parents. The guidelines stress the need to consider the best

interests of the child, and they make specific references to both the Convention on the Rights of the Child and the UNHCR guidelines on refugee children. As such, they are another example of how policies developed at the international level make their way into national legislation where they have an ongoing practical application.

Effecting Change

The role of non-governmental organizations in effecting the policies discussed cannot be underestimated. There were twenty-nine NGOs represented at the conference that created the refugee convention in 1951, including the World Council of Churches, Friends World Committee for Consultation (Quakers), World Jewish Congress, and YWCA. NGOs were allowed to submit written or oral statements to the conference.

Now over 150 NGOs are registered for the annual meetings of the UNHCR Executive Committee. Through a program called Partnership in Action, NGOs and UNHCR have increased their dialogue and cooperation through the use of NGO focal points from other regions of the world. Issues raised by NGOs include refugee children, urban refugees, detention of asylum seekers in the West, internally displaced people, women, and peacemaking. While many NGOs that go to Geneva for Excom emphasize their contacts with UNHCR and other NGOs, there is increasing attention to government delegates.

NGOs generally, and in particular those engaged in policy development at the international level, tend to have a commitment to social change. Many of them focus on and advocate for those who are vulnerable and voiceless. The most effective NGO advocates are those whose advocacy is rooted in actual programs, where expertise has been developed and best practices identified, along with gaps in social policy that need to be changed. There is also an increasing awareness and understanding among NGOs of the opportunities for effective participation in social change at the international level. I would like to highlight a number of specific interventions I was involved with in Geneva.

The UNHCR policy process, as outlined above, revolves around the Executive Committee of the UNHCR. Although UNHCR officials may prepare policy papers and guidelines, these must ultimately be approved by the Executive Committee of the UNHCR. Although UNHCR officials may prepare policy papers and guidelines, these must ultimately be approved by the Executive Committee of government representatives. In 1995, Excom adopted new working methods that delegated authority for much of its decision-making to a new standing committee that met quarterly throughout the year. It was given greater decision-making authority than the two subcommittees it replaced.

This had a number of implications. Firstly, the standing committee became the essential forum for directing international refugee policy. Secondly, participation in the standing committee became an important issue, in particular for NGOs and government observers that wanted to participate in this policy-making process. At the time, governments that were not Excom members were still allowed to participate in the standing committee, but

NGOs were not. A number of Geneva-based NGOs informally created a working group to lobby for a role for NGOs in the new structure. The outgoing chair of the Executive Committee had signalled his interest in having NGOs participate. The incoming chair for 1996, when the decision was to be taken by the new standing committee on working methods, was supportive as well. We prepared a discussion paper that articulated why NGOs should be involved (Quaker United Nations Office, 1996a). For example, we argued that NGOs are primary agents of protection and assistance for refugees, often as UNHCR implementing partners. They have important expertise and first-hand knowledge, are a source of current information, offer important analysis and ideas, and can engage in constructive and critical dialogue.

The NGOs that worked together on this initiative did not always agree on the nature of the participation requested. Some wanted full participation for any interested NGOs, with the ability to make oral or written presentations, while others were content to gain admission to the meetings even without the right to speak. Some suggested that since NGOs are allowed only one oral intervention at the annual meeting of the Executive Committee, we could not expect greater involvement at the standing committee. Other issues raised included the de-restriction of documents, so that NGOs could access UNHCR policy papers before they were presented to the standing committee for decisions. Gaining access to these papers would allow NGOs to provide useful inputs and commentary beforehand.

As a result of these efforts, the Executive Committee decided to "initiate consultations" among Excom members on this issue of NGO participation. After further consultations, which included the NGO working group, the standing committee decided in June 1997 to allow NGO participation in future meetings.[8] NGOs were given access to standing committee meetings upon written request, documents would be made available through established networks, NGOs would be permitted to make written contributions, and one oral NGO statement would be allowed on each standing committee agenda item (with NGOs making the selection based on expertise or direct knowledge of the issue).

Securing NGO access to this critical decision-making process ensured that NGOs would be able to participate more effectively in the policy process. It was successful for a number of reasons. There was a clear issue to work on, namely whether NGOs should be allowed to participate in the new committee process. The duration of the process was also quite clear, and NGOs knew that a decision was to be made within a year. Although NGOs did not always agree on the specific details of the request for greater NGO involvement, they nonetheless agreed that NGOs should have greater involvement. Speaking with one voice made a significant impact. Important political connections were fostered with government representatives that were based in Geneva and supportive of the NGO position. Others that were critical to the decision-making process, but were still uncertain about NGO participation, were also targeted through processes like informal lunch meetings. The senior bureaucrat within UNHCR was also involved in the critical discussions to ensure that the process was transparent and that NGOs were aware of the correct administrative details.

Many of the informal meetings through this process took place at the Quaker United Nations Office (QUNO). Quakers have had an official presence in Geneva since 1926, when they set up a liaison office for the League of Nations and other international agencies. Over the years, they became known for their independence and impartiality, and informal luncheons became a trademark for off-the-record dialogue on important policy issues (Bailey, 1993; Yarrow, 1978). Because of this history, NGOs, UN staff, and government delegates in Geneva were usually interested in participating in these discussions when invited. Staff at QUNO played the role of both advocate and broker. On issues like NGO participation in the Executive Committee process, we obviously had a position we wanted to convey. At other times, the purpose was to provide an opportunity for dialogue that might not otherwise happen.

For example, just prior to the Executive Committee meeting in October 1997, we organized an informal meeting for about twenty diplomats and NGO representatives. The purpose of the meeting was to provide an opportunity for dialogue on a variety of issues on the upcoming Excom agenda. There are numerous opportunities for informal meetings throughout the Excom process, between government delegates and UNHCR staff, and also between NGOs and UNHCR staff; but informal meetings between NGOs and a group of government representatives rarely occur. We also wanted to provide a forum for informal cross-regional dialogue, and we ensured that governments were represented from all regions of the world. At another level, we wanted an opportunity to raise specific issues and demonstrate that we had an articulated interest. We had prepared a draft NGO statement, which we presented for discussion.

The meeting was successful in many respects. Participants expressed appreciation for the opportunity to get together in an informal way, and some diplomats said they heard positions from their colleagues that hadn't arisen in other informal discussions. The good turnout implied that diplomats were interested in this kind of forum and this kind of discussion, both with NGOs and with each other. Some expressed disappointment that we had not discussed the draft conclusions for the upcoming session of Excom, and were surprised to learn that NGOs were not allowed prior access to these. They were willing to encourage NGO inputs and feedback. Other issues raised included the relative importance of Excom conclusions, why some members of the Executive Committee have refused to sign the Refugee Convention, and whether there needs to be a stronger reporting mechanism under the refugee convention. The meeting highlighted the importance of informal channels for discussion. We can try to create new channels for formal dialogue, but the more interesting and useful discussions will continue to take place informally.

Another feature of our policy-making in Geneva was to draw on our particular expertise and knowledge of given situations. We would facilitate informal meetings for people working in countries like Uganda and Burundi to offer current perspectives to UN staff and diplomats in Geneva concerned with the human rights and humanitarian agenda. We would also highlight particular concerns related to peacemaking efforts and reconciliation work in situations of conflict.

At the Executive Committee in 1996, we decided to highlight the important role of refugees in national reconciliation. In particular, we wanted to urge the UNHCR and member states of the UNHCR Executive Committee to put the necessary resources into a program for peace education and training in conflict management and conflict resolution. QUNO prepared a written brief that highlighted the reasons why reconciliation and peace-building were important to achieving durable solutions, and why refugees were important participants in this process.

In 1995, the Executive Committee had recognized the role that refugee community education can play in national reconciliation. It specifically encouraged UNHCR to strengthen its support for education, and in particular to introduce elements of education for peace and human rights.[9] UNHCR also includes peace education in its *Refugee Children: Guidelines on Protection and Care*. Specifically, they indicate that "peace education, including teaching different methods of conflict resolution, may be relevant to children who are victims of conflict" (UNHCR, 1994, p. 113). The QUNO statement also highlighted documents that UNICEF had prepared for teaching and training children about conflict resolution and peace. Finally, it urged UNHCR to facilitate the efforts of NGOs and other UN agencies with experience and expertise in working at peace education, reconciliation, and conflict management; to develop a training process that specifically incorporates elements of conflict management into the planning process for refugee programs, especially within education and social services programming; and to allocate the necessary resources, both human and financial, to such a program and seek out donors to provide funding for initiatives in this area (Quaker United Nations Office, 1996b).

We discussed our proposals beforehand with UNHCR senior staff in the education and social services departments. They had been trying to implement programming related to peace education and training, but were glad for NGO support for putting the appropriate policy framework in place and soliciting political will and resources to implement it. We also shared the briefing paper with a number of key government representatives. One of them was particularly interested. He pursued the issue during the closed negotiations for the final conclusions (which involve only government representatives and UNHCR staff) and was successful in including language on the importance of reconciliation and education for peace and human rights.

This initiative was successful for a number of reasons. Although we had not obtained widespread NGO support, we had clearly articulated reasons for promoting reconciliation, which arose out of our own experience and that

of other agencies. We also focused on key contacts within UNHCR and government. These were contacts that had been fostered before this particular issue
arose, so they were already familiar with the work of the Quaker office.

Other issues for which NGOs have been instrumental in effecting policy
change through the UNHCR Executive Committee include refugee women
and children, mentioned earlier, as well as detention of asylum seekers, family reunification, and the importance of resettlement in third countries like
Canada.

It is also worth highlighting some of the specific work that has been done
by NGOs at the UN Commission on Human Rights, which meets in Geneva.
The commission provides an opportunity for formally linking human rights
with refugees and internally displaced people (IDPs). It focuses on the abuse
of human rights as a cause of forced displacement, and on the human rights
of refugees and IDPs themselves.

Internally displaced people are those who are forcibly displaced for reasons similar to those that displace refugees, namely armed conflict and violations of human rights. There are an estimated 25 million IDPs throughout
the world (Global IDP Project and Norwegian Refugee Council, 2005). Unlike
refugees, they do not cross international borders, and so must rely primarily
on their own governments to uphold their rights and provide assistance, even
though those governments may be implicated in causing displacement. They
cannot rely on the international protection of the refugee convention.

However, at the urging of NGOs in Geneva, in particular the Quaker UN
Office, the World Council of Churches, and Caritas Internationalis, the commissioner on Human Rights requested the UN's secretary-general to appoint
a representative for IDPs in 1992. Through NGO networking and careful advocacy with key government representatives prior to the commission, they were
able to draft a resolution that garnered sufficient support among members of
the commission, articulate the relevant human rights concerns related to
IDPS, and create a mechanism for examining the issue.

As a result of the work done by the representative, Dr. Francis Deng (who
was replaced by Professor Walter Kälin of Switzerland in 2004), international
awareness of the existence of IDPs has increased substantially. He visited
more than twelve countries with acute IDP problems, including Sri Lanka,
Burundi, and Colombia, to look at internal displacement. He also issued
reports for the commission and follow-up recommendations.[10]

In 1996, Deng prepared a significant compilation and analysis of international legal norms relating to IDPs. Then, in 1998, the commission endorsed
a set of guiding principles for IDPs, based on the earlier compilation. These
thirty guiding principles were published in a compact and useable handbook by the UN Office for the Coordination of Humanitarian Affairs (1998).
They set out key rights and obligations for IDPs as articulated in international
humanitarian and human rights law. While they restate existing law, they
make its application more specific to the needs of IDPs. For example, while

existing law says that all people must have recognition before the law, the guiding principles specify that IDPS should be given documents that they need.

NGOS have continued to raise the problems related to IDPS, and increasingly both NGOS and UN agencies have been addressing the needs of IDPS. For example, the International Committee for the Red Cross, the UNHCR, and the World Food Program now provide substantial assistance for IDPS. Indeed, over 25% of the people assisted by UNHCR are actually IDPS, even though UNHCR was set up to provide protection and seek solutions for refugees under the refugee convention. UNHCR has creatively justified this involvement by stressing that these IDPS are in "refugee-like" situations (UNHRC, 2005).

The process of getting internally displaced people officially on the international agenda is one of the most significant contributions that NGOS have made. Current efforts are now under way to have refugee rights more clearly articulated as well through the Commission on Human Rights. The commission's resolution on mass exoduses, first introduced by Canada in 1980, has consistently called upon all states to promote human rights and fundamental freedoms, and to refrain from denying these for reasons such as race and ethnicity. As a result of informal NGO interventions in 1996, gender was also included in this list.

For the past few years, Canadian NGOS have encouraged the Canadian government to refocus this resolution on the rights of refugees. In 2001, the Canadian Council of Churches (CCC) prepared a statement for the Commission on Human Rights that specifically requested such a resolution. While the link between refugees and human rights is increasingly being made within UN bodies, there needs to be a clearer articulation of the human rights of refugees in the context of asylum. Placing refugees more clearly on the agenda of the Commissioner on Human Rights through a specific resolution would ensure that refugees and human rights are clearly linked. There is increasing support among NGOS for such a resolution, and a number of government representatives are tentatively prepared to consider it, but this is an issue that will likely require sustained advocacy for the next few years, thus underlining the long-term nature of international policy development.

Closing Comments

Important social policy development has taken place at the international level. While international bodies like the United Nations may seem ponderous at times, numerous benchmarks have been set in the area of social policy. They offer us all in the global community something to strive for.

While the process may seem complex from afar, there is a way of working through the system to achieve desired results. Understanding the complexities and determining where to focus attention is the first step. Experience shows that alliances can be built with numerous stakeholders, including nongovernmental organizations, United Nations staff, and government officials, including those from the Canadian government.

Perhaps the most satisfying aspect of social policy development at the international level is the possibility of setting high standards with universal applicability. Human rights have no borders. Public authorities can pursue an ideal vision of a society free from racial discrimination, where civil, political, and other rights prevail. Pursuing this vision at the international level can arguably be done without requiring the same level of public support that is needed at the national level. The general public is much less aware of international social policy than they are of the policies at a local or national level, which have a more recognizable or understandable impact.

Yet without this widespread public support, governments are less inclined to feel the need to implement international obligations. In this context, the role of non-governmental organizations takes on added significance. Because of their expertise and experience, they provide valuable inputs into the international policy-making process. They have the unique ability to serve as both advocates and brokers within the complexities of this system; and they serve an important function by raising awareness of international standards at the national level. Creative ways must continually be found to ensure that we help those we are obliged to help, while also expanding our concepts of those in need. Ultimately, how we help those in need reflects our commitment to social policy.

Notes

1   GA Resolution 428(v) of December 14, 1950.
2   Statute of the Office of the United Nations High Commissioner for Refugees, chap. 1.
3   Convention Relating to the Status of Refugees, Article 1.
4   Convention Relating to the Status of Refugees, Article 22.
5   Statute of the Office of the UNHCR, chap. 1.
6   Pursuant to Section 65(3) of the Immigration Act.
7   Conclusion no. 47.
8   UN Doc. ec/47/sc/crp.39, dated May 30, 1997.
9   UN Doc. a/ac.96/860, General Conclusion on International Protection, s. 19(n).
10 See, for example, his main report for the 2001 Commission: E/CN.4/2001/5.

References

Anderson, M. (1994). *People-oriented planning at work: Using POP to improve UNHCR programming*. Geneva: UNHCR.

Bailey, S. (1993). *Peace is a process*. London: Quaker Home Service.

Buergental, T. (1995). *International human rights* (2nd ed.). St. Paul: West Publishing.

Canada. (2000). *Freedom from fear: Canada's foreign policy for human security*. Ottawa: Department of Foreign Affairs and International Trade.

Global IDP Survey and Norwegian Refugee Council. (1998). *Internally displaced people: Global survey*. London: Earthscan.

Global IDP Project and Norwegian Refugee Council. (2005). *Internal displacement: Global overview of trends and developments in 2004*. Geneva: Global IDP Project.

Goodwin-Gill, G. (1996). *The refugee in international law* (2nd ed.). Oxford: Clarendon Press.

References Gorlick, B. (2000, October). Human rights and refugees: Enhancing protection through international human rights law. *Nordic Journal of International Law, 69*(4). Online at <www.unhcr.org>.

Human Rights Watch. (1995, August). *The Human Rights Watch global report on women's human rights.* New York: Human Rights Watch Women's Project.

Human Rights Watch. (2001). *World report.* New York: Author.

Inter-American Commission on Human Rights. (2000, February 28). *Report on the situation of human rights of asylum seekers within the Canadian refugee determination system* (oea/Ser.1/v/ii.106). Washington, DC: Author.

Mennonite Central Committee. (2000). *Mission statement.* Winnipeg: Author.

Office for the Coordination of Humanitarian Affairs. (1998). *Guiding principles on internal displacement.* New York: Author.

Quaker United Nations Office. (1996a, July). *NGO participation in the UNHCR executive committee: NGO working group discussion paper.* Geneva: Author.

Quaker United Nations Office. (1996b, October). *Refugees and reconciliation: A role for UNHCR.* Briefing Paper for the 47th Session of the Executive Committee of the United Nations High Commissioner for Refugees Programme. Geneva: Author.

United Nations. (1945). *Charter of the United Nations.* New York: Author.

UN High Commissioner for Refugees. (1991). *Guidelines for protection and care of refugee women.* Geneva: Author.

UN High Commissioner for Refugees. (1994). *Refugee children: Guidelines on protection and care.* Geneva: Author.

UN High Commissioner for Refugees. (1995a). *Sexual violence against refugees: Guidelines on prevention and response.* Geneva: Author.

UN High Commissioner for Refugees. (1995b, June 8). *Women victims of violence project in Kenya: An evaluation summary.* EC/1995/SC.2/CRP.22. Geneva: Author.

UN High Commissioner for Refugees. (1997). *The state of the world's refugees: A humanitarian agenda.* Oxford: Oxford University Press.

UN High Commissioner for Refugees. (1999). *Protecting refugees: A field guide for NGOs.* Geneva: Author.

UN High Commissioner for Refugees. (2000). *Refugees by numbers.* Geneva: Author.

UN High Commissioner for Refugees. (2005). *2004 global refugee trends.* Geneva: UNHCR.

Yarrow, C.H. (1978). *Quaker experiences in international conciliation.* New Haven: Yale University Press.

Additional Resources

Alston, P., & Crawford, J. (2000). *The future of human rights treaty monitoring.* Cambridge: Cambridge University Press.

Canadian Council for Refugees. Online at <www.web.net/~ccr>.

Charlesworth, H., & Chinkin, C. (2000). *The boundaries of international law: A feminist analysis.* Manchester: Manchester University Press.

Freeman, M., & Van Ert, G. (2004) *International human rights law.* Toronto: Irwin Law.

Hathaway, J.C. (2005). *The rights of refugees under international law.* Cambridge: Cambridge University Press.

Ife, J. (2001). *Human rights and social work: Toward a rights-based practice.* Cambridge: Cambridge University Press.

Inter-Church Committee for Refugees. Online at < www.web.net/~iccr >. The work References
    of ICCR was subsumed by KAIROS: Canadian Ecumenical Justice Initiatives, in
    2001. Online at < www.kairoscanada.org >.
Mennonite Central Committee. Online at < www.mcc.org >.
Quaker United Nations Office, Geneva. Online at < www.quno.org >.
UN High Commissioner for Human Rights, includes Commission on Human Rights.
    Online at < www.ohchr.org >.
UN High Commissioner for Refugees (UNHCR). Refworld 2004, CD-ROM.
UN High Commissioner for Refugees (UNHCR). Online at < www.unhcr.org >.
UN Office for the Coordination of Humanitarian Affairs. Online at < www.relief
    web.int >.

The Federal Government and Social Policy at the Turn of the Twenty-first Century: Reflections on Change and Continuity

3

John English and *William R. Young*

The 1990s began with the cold war's end, the collapse of the Soviet Union, extraordinary hopes, and new or reinvigorated structures in global politics. Despite the optimism and excitement on the international scene, Canadians watched the beginning of the decade with much nervousness when it came to the future of their own country. The well-known poll published in the New Year's issue of *Maclean's* in 1990 described an "uncertain Canada" despite a period of economic growth. It is true that Canadians in 1989 were more optimistic than in 1985 about their personal economic prospects; yet Canadians also told the Decima pollsters in late 1989 that they were deeply divided, especially on the issues of national unity and the relationship between Quebec and Canada. There had been "a souring" of attitudes toward government since 1985 and a growing respect for "business." In 1984, when asked whether government, business, or unions "best look after your economic interests," the response was 49% government, 32% business, and 10% unions. In 1989 responses to the same question were 25% government, 50% business, and 15% unions (*Maclean's*, 1990, p. 24).[1] These two issues—the constitution and the efficacy of government—were to dominate Canadian politics and deeply influence Canadian social policy in the 1990s and into the twenty-first century.[2]

One critical element of this shift in reliance upon government and increasing questions surrounding the role of government—particularly the federal government—related to Canadians' concern about national unity and about federal–provincial relationships generally. By 1990, the Meech Lake Accord, which promised a fundamental reordering of responsibilities between federal and provincial governments and which had the support of all major parties and provincial premiers, was facing growing opposition. Serious implications for social policy in the accord came from limitations on the federal "spending power" and from the new constitutional provision that any province might opt out of new shared-cost programs without a fiscal penalty.[3]

The concept of "spending power" bedeviled federal-provincial relations in constitutional and non-constitutional discussions throughout the 1990s. This concept refers to the federal government's provision of program funds, either unilaterally or in cooperation with the provinces, for a variety of programs in the areas of health, education, welfare, and social development. Use of the spending power allowed the federal government to shape issues and programs that fall essentially within provincial jurisdiction. Historically, the provinces oppose this federal use of tax dollars and argue that because they run these programs that alter their spending and taxing priorities, the federal government should get their consent first. They also complain that citizens of provinces that opt out of the programs have paid taxes without receiving any benefit. On its side of the argument, the federal government believes that the spending power remains vital in maintaining equal opportunity for individual Canadians, in ensuring comparable provincial services, and in putting in place programs of national importance.

At the intergovernmental level, doubts about the Meech Lake Accord appeared first in New Brunswick, where Liberal Premier Frank McKenna asked for revisions in the historic agreement. The election of another Liberal, Clyde Wells, in Newfoundland made things even more difficult. Wells, *Maclean's* reported, was "less fearful of losing Quebec." Many Canadians, notably the supporters of Pierre Trudeau and some provincial Liberals, had serious doubts about or opposed the Accord outright. In terms of its implications for the federal role in social welfare, various groups as well as smaller provinces voiced concerns that Meech Lake might threaten national shared-cost programs. Citizens told provincial committees studying the Accord that it could threaten any future programs such as child care, weaken the federal government's ability to provide national health and welfare programs, and increase regional disparities in social services.[4] These concerns had an impact on the reaction to Meech Lake in both Manitoba and Newfoundland.

In terms of national unity, when asked about the effect of the failure of Meech Lake in late 1989, 60% of Quebeckers thought that the failure to ratify Meech Lake would make Quebec more likely to choose separation. The rest of Canada disagreed. The majority in every province, except British Columbia (which was evenly split at 49/49), thought the collapse of Meech would make no difference. The Prairies, where a new Reform Party was attracting attention, were most decisive in their opinion (38% yes, 58% no). In the Prairies and British Columbia, almost one quarter of the population (23%) thought Quebec should separate from Canada, only 10% less than in Quebec itself (*Maclean's*, 1990).

These views were put to the test after June 1990 when Meech Lake died as Elijah Harper, an Aboriginal member of the New Democratic Party and the Manitoba Legislature, used procedural tactics to deny approval by his province. That same month, the Liberal Party chose Jean Chrétien as its national leader after a bitter contest with runner-up Paul Martin. Martin had supported Meech; Chrétien had been ambiguous. Later that year in the province of Ontario, Premier David Peterson, who had vigorously supported Meech, unexpectedly lost the premiership to Bob Rae of the New Democratic Party (NDP). Federally, the New Democrats moved ahead of the Liberals in national polls, and the Liberal Party's future seemed difficult as it faced a strong challenge from the left. In Quebec, the provincial Liberals under Robert Bourassa were openly disdainful of their federal counterparts, and the NDP took office in Saskatchewan and British Columbia in 1991. With democratic socialists successfully reinventing their approach in Western Europe, Canadian socialists seemed poised to replace a Liberal Party seeking to define a future role for government.

The 1990s did not unfold as the decade's beginning promised. Canadians were wrong to be optimistic about their economic prospects at New Year 1990; their personal incomes in real terms fell throughout the decade. Moreover, their dollar lost one third of its value when buying American goods or taking Florida vacations. Some of the European postwar immigrants looked to the lands whence they had come and noticed that Canada's per capita GDP in 2000 (US$19,170) was lower than that of the Netherlands (US$24,780) Germany (US$26,570) and even the United Kingdom (US$21,410) (*Economist*, 2001).[5] Apart from Canadians who travelled outside of Canada, the groups that were affected the worst in the 1990s were government employees—teachers, provincial and federal public servants, and military personnel—whose salaries were, in many cases, frozen for years and who faced strong pressure to accept early retirement offers. Others, such as the employees of Canadian National Railway, became a part of the private sector.

While Canadians were wrong about their economic prospects in 1990, their other responses forecast the principal themes of social and economic policy in the decade that followed. The shift to the left with the election of New Democrats in Ontario, Saskatchewan, and British Columbia weakened the national party, as the provincial governments became increasingly unpopular when they wrestled with their traditional union and activist supporters over difficult policy choices. The memoir by Bob Rae describes the uneasiness of the coalition among unions, feminists, social activists, and career politicians that ultimately caused the New Democrats to self-destruct in both Ontario and British Columbia (Rae, 1997).

Things went better for other political parties and groups. The Liberals, who chose the apparently left-leaning Jean Chrétien over the business favourite Paul Martin, took advantage of the three years between their leadership convention and the federal election to reshape their party as a "middle of the road" grouping that would focus on the possibilities of the "new economy." Chrétien shrewdly used Martin's reputation with the business community to place him in charge of developing a party platform. The central event was a policy conference at Aylmer, Quebec, in November 1991 where the keynote speakers were carefully chosen to stress that the Liberals had moved away from their economic nationalism of the 1988 free-trade election and were embracing market-oriented programs, government reform, and fiscal responsibility. Nevertheless, Chrétien and his party promised to adhere to "Liberal tradition," which since the 1960s had meant medicare, pension plans, and social programs.

The Liberals, however, were cautious about constitutional reform, a central consideration in the shaping of Canadian social programs, and the Mulroney government made one final attempt to redress the collapse of Meech in 1990. The Charlottetown Accord was a momentous agreement. In terms of its potential impact on social programs, Charlottetown contained the same opting-out provisions as Meech Lake, but also committed the federal and provincial governments to establishing a framework for federal expenditures in areas of provincial jurisdiction that would contribute to the pursuit of national objectives, reduce overlap and duplication, respect and not distort provincial priorities, and ensure equality of treatment of the provinces while respecting their differing needs and circumstances.

Once again, the major parties agreed on a package for major constitutional change, but this time it was not a single member of the Manitoba Legislature who cast a deciding vote but rather the Canadian public. On August 28, 1992, Canadians voted against the ratification of the accord in a remarkable repudiation of the political elites of the country. This rejection reflected the growing distrust of government and politicians that was apparent in the 1990 poll and also (for some) a suspicion of handing too much control over social programs to the provinces. Opposition to the accord came from the new Reform Party, organized by Albertan Preston Manning, a party that quickly eroded the Progressive Conservative Party's support in Western Canada and parts of Ontario. The most significant opponent, however, was former prime minister Pierre Trudeau.

The Liberal Party Red Book, its election platform, which bore Martin's ideas about innovation, government reform, and deficit reduction, became a shield to protect the Liberals against their own past and the party's own internal differences. It was remarkably effective, not least because of its careful balance between the economic fears of the time and the remembrance of such previous Liberal policies as the Canada Health Act. Its title, *Creating Opportunity* (Liberal Party of Canada, 1993), stressed employment and the economy, and it began with the statement that "A strong economy is the essence of a strong society." It promised "a balanced approach" that would deal with "the five major, interrelated problems facing the Canadian economy today: lack of growth, high unemployment, high long-term real interest rates, too high levels of foreign indebtedness, and excessive government debt and deficits."

What is striking about the Red Book is the place given to social programs. Part 2 of the Red Book, on "The Fabric of Canadian Life," promised no new programs, except in certain "niches," to use a term very popular at the time. There would be, for example, a Canada Prenatal Nutrition Program and an Aboriginal Head Start Program, but the financial promises were relatively small. There is a commitment to the preservation of universal medicare and a promise of a national forum on health. Still, the details are few, actual commitments rare, and the number of pages dealing with Canadian social policy significantly less than those devoted to the economy. Nevertheless, social policy did better than constitutional reform, the topic that had preoccupied Canadians for over a decade. It received no mention.

Although the Red Book reflected its principal authors (Martin and Chaviva Hosek, a former minister in the Ontario Liberal government) and, in its constitutional approach, Liberal Leader Jean Chrétien, it was also the product of profound intellectual shifts in North America and Western Europe. There was, as we have seen in the 1990 poll, dissatisfaction with the efficiency of the state, its employees, and its programs. For liberals in Canada and elsewhere, this dissatisfaction led to a program for "reinventing" government, and the successful American campaign of Clinton and Gore used the slogan. The Canadian political scientist Donald Savoie, who had extensive government experience, summarized the legacy of the 1980s in his 1994 study, *Thatcher, Reagan, Mulroney: In Search of a New Bureaucracy*. Savoie (1994, p. 319) pointed out that the three conservative Anglo-American leaders wanted government managers to emulate the private sector and that all three "shared the conviction that most of the perceived inefficiencies in government operations were simply a function of poor management." In redressing the problem, privatization, deregulation, and reduction of the activities of government were fundamental. Savoie thought that Canada under Mulroney had been less imaginative, less effective, and more willing to retain the bureaucratic tradition than Reagan, and especially Thatcher, had been. Savoie had edited an earlier book, *Taking Power: Managing Government Transitions*. In it, he noted the importance of the tendency to "blame the bureaucracy," not only in the Mulroney ministers, but also in the media and large parts of the public (Savoie, 1993, p. 217).

Attempts to "reinvent" and reduce government during the early 1990s as government deficits soared were generally perceived to be failures. At the same time, these efforts served as models for more successful measures that came later in the decade. Some commentators blamed the failure on the subtle shift of the policy function in government to ministers' offices. During the Mulroney years, the politicians' distrust of the bureaucracy showed up in the increasing size and strength of ministerial staff who took an active role, not just in providing overall direction, but in initiating and managing the policy functions of government. For whatever reason, Erik Neilson's task force, which reviewed and recommended cuts across the whole scope of federal spending, was deemed ineffective. Mulroney had also failed in his plan to reduce transfers to individuals. When he tried to limit increases in Old Age Security payments to individuals, he ran smack dab into a protest by seniors on Parliament Hill. It made for great television. When his government backed down on this issue, he damaged beyond recovery his credibility as a cost-cutter. Government spending soared in areas such as the Canada Pension Plan (disability) as eligibility criteria were loosened and premium increases did not keep pace. The Mulroney government also suffered, in business eyes at least, for putting in place "boutique spending programs," such as the National Strategy on the Integration of Disabled Persons, which were portrayed as succumbing to the wishes of so-called special interest groups. Thus, the federal budget of February 1992 announced its intention of eliminating, merging, or privatizing forty-six government boards or commissions; but critics on the right continued their complaints, and the federal deficit for 1992–1993 stood at $36.7 billion, up from $33.5 billion in 1991–1992.

Another effort at dealing with the growing cost of universal social programs and entitlements came in 1989. That was the year when federal income tax forms contained a formula to calculate a clawback of part or all of the federal government's Old Age Pensions or Family Allowances for everyone with a net income over $50,000. Apart from criticizing its inequity, social activists argued that the clawback unilaterally eliminated what they saw as a social contract between the federal government and families or seniors. It eliminated universality and effectively made pensions and family allowances income-tested. They believed that it changed the rules without the consent of seniors and reduced or eliminated income that they had counted on in planning for their old age (Battle, 1990).

Using the tax system as the instrument of choice for dealing with a social issue was hardly new. Over the years, it had become not just a means of managing the economy but also a way of treating social benefits. By its very nature, the tax system is a blunt instrument for delivering or cutting social programs, particularly because of the time lag between earning income, filing a tax return, and receiving benefits. For the federal government, the major advantage of the tax system lay in its bypassing the provinces and providing federal benefits directly to Canadians. This was the case of refundable benefits, like those provided through the Goods and Services Tax (GST), where a cheque could go directly to Canadians. Federal tax credits (refundable and non-refundable) can contribute to putting in place national standards for income support and, given the relationship between the federal and provincial tax systems, can trigger provincial benefits to individuals. From the perspective of the provinces, because the benefits go to individuals and not to governments, the tax system could deal with the demand side, but could not address the supply side (the number of services available). In addition, the provinces can always nullify any federal tax reductions by cutting their benefits or services to individuals.

In its 1992 budget, the Conservative government continued an ongoing trend of using the tax system to address social issues—in this case reducing benefits to Canadians. The 1992 measure introduced the Child Tax Benefit (CTB). The Conservatives justified this as a rationalization and simplification since the CTB replaced Family Allowances (introduced first in 1944) and other refundable and non-refundable tax credits for children, and eliminated the clawback on Family Allowances. Many commentators saw it as a means of dealing with a benefits system for children that had become irrational, unfair, complex, and inadequate (Battle, 1993). The CTB, however, was designed to contain costs since it was income-tested and varied according to the number of children in a family.[6] It was complemented by a supplement for children under seven and a working income supplement for working-poor families. The CTB was, however, to be only partly indexed to inflation so that its actual value would decline from year to year. Since 1985, the federal government had used de-indexation of the tax system as a tool for hiding increased taxes.

Another effort at cost-cutting led the Tory government right to the courts. While the federal government wanted to maintain its right to use spending power, it also wanted to be able to control the amount that it transferred to the provinces. In his 1990 budget, Finance Minister Michael Wilson announced measures to restrict federal transfers to the provinces by announcing an expenditure control plan that limited federal block grants to the provinces in the areas of education and health.[7] For three of the richest provinces (Alberta, British Columbia, and Ontario), he capped payments for social welfare made under the Canada Assistance Plan. These federal payments had increased at an average annual rate of 6.6% in part because the largest number of poor Canadians lived in these three provinces (plus Quebec). This cap on CAP aimed to control this rate of increase and to introduce an element of stability and predictability into federal transfers to the provinces. Until the cap on CAP, the federal costs had climbed because spending was determined beyond the control of the programs themselves and certainly beyond the control of the federal government. Only the provinces had the ability to contain costs— or not. As a result of increasing unemployment, the provinces' social assistance caseloads had inexorably mounted. "Needs are increasing which by law must be covered," explained the Nielsen task force (Melchers, 1990).[8] British Columbia challenged the constitutionality of the changes, but the Supreme Court of Canada accepted the federal government's argument that Ottawa must retain the right to control the federal purse strings. The Supreme Court's decision paved the way for further efforts by the federal government to contain costs and to eliminate the unpredictability and upward spiral of its fiscal transfers to the provinces. Critics, however, warned that the consequences of an expansion of the federal cost-containment exercise would jeopardize all health and social programs and potentially eliminate the opportunity to maintain national standards.

After Mulroney left office, his successor, Kim Campbell, linked the streamlining of government with a similar approach to income security in a speech on August 22, 1993. In that speech, she criticized existing skills-training programs, the existence of welfare that stops single mothers from taking work and, when plants close, the preference for "handouts" rather than training programs. "What we must do," she continued, "is reward, not penalize, effort and initiative. Any serious attempt to reform our new income security system must be a national endeavour" (Campbell, 1993). After she took power on June 25, 1993, Campbell moved dramatically and reduced the number of government departments and ministers significantly. In doing so, she combined all or part of five various departments concerned with human security issues to create a new Department of Human Resources.[9] Assessing this change, the Standing Committee on Human Resources Development pointed out in

2000 that the "positive synergies" anticipated in Campbell's initiative had failed to materialize. The amalgamation meant that the policies and debates among five departments and ministers no longer existed; the level of political scrutiny of departmental activities had been reduced. Matters that had formerly been discussed and decided at the political level were now treated as internal bureaucratic matters. Assistant deputy ministers took on a large part of what had previously been ministerial responsibilities. The committee's MPS believed that the change had also diluted the department's accountability to Parliament. They also found that the department lacked a unity of purpose and that employment-related policies and programs subsumed and controlled the social policy elements in the department's corporate culture. Social programs were treated as unwanted and subsidiary duties that got in the way of the jobs agenda (Standing Committee on Human Resources Development & the Status of Persons with Disabilities, 2000).

Campbell did not see the results of her handiwork from within government. Mulroney was unpopular, his party fragmenting, and Campbell, his successor, took over too late. Campbell gave up her office to Jean Chrétien after her election loss on October 25, 1993. Canada's founding political party won two seats as Quebec separatists and Western Reformers carved up the carcass of the Progressive Conservative Party. The New Democrats lost supporters among trade unionists and westerners to the Reform Party, and others who feared the shift to the right in North American politics voted Liberal despite ideological doubts. The New Democrats, who had led national polls in 1990, won only nine seats, and this weakness was most significant because that opposition from the left was to be muted in the new Parliament. The Conservative's disastrous electoral defeat also brought the Bloc Québécois to the Official Opposition benches and made the conservative Reform Party the third party in the House of Commons. The Bloc's focus upon Quebec and the constitution made it ineffective in the national debate on social policy except on the issue of constitutional authority, where it frequently expressed its view that the activities of the federal government in most social policy areas were infringements on provincial rights. Employment programs and labour market training were particular targets.

No one has done a better job of summing up the impact of the Conservative government on social policy and programs than the Caledon Institute of Social Policy. In a keynote address to the Seventh Social Welfare Policy Conference in Vancouver, the institute's Sherri Torjman (1995) pointed out that from the election in 1984 until its election loss, the Conservative government's actions undermined the policy rationale and operation of Canada's social welfare system, from the proposed limits on the federal spending power in the Meech and Charlottetown agreements, to the cap on CAP, the clawbacks, the partial indexation of social programs, changes in transfers to the provinces, and the use of the income tax system and its non-refundable tax credits. She pointed out that "Ken Battle [of the Caledon Institute] coined the term 'social policy by stealth' to describe these arcane technical measures.

And while many of the hidden cuts in transfers to individuals and provinces are neither recognized nor acknowledged, their devastating impact is still being felt [sic]. New cuts are over and above a declining base." (Torjman, 1995, p. 1). Torjman concluded that when the Liberals took power in 1993, social policy "reform" was already well under way.

From the Red Book, the Liberals brought the promise to reduce the federal deficit to 3% of GDP, a few commitments to new social programs (especially for children's and Aboriginal health), and a promise to continue the late Conservative moves to "streamline" or reinvent government. Campbell's Department of Human Resources was retained, and Lloyd Axworthy, widely regarded as Chrétien's most leftist minister, became minister of Human Resources Development. He inherited a department with enormous responsibilities and the largest amount of federal government spending.[10] Since 1988–1989, spending in some key areas had soared, as in the case of Old Age Security and Unemployment Insurance, which had risen, respectively, from $15.2 and $10.9 billion in 1988–1989 to $19.5 and $18.9 billion in 1992–1993 (Statistics Canada, 1994). Education had remained stable (postsecondary spending by the federal government had actually decreased from $2.71 to $2.64 billion), and health had fallen from $7.69 to $7.60 billion. Despite the measures taken by the previous government, federal expenditures on social welfare had risen from $5.30 to $6.87 billion, again in this same period (Statistics Canada, 1994). Throughout the 1990s, conservative think tanks like the Fraser Institute continued to point out the growth in spending on social programs and to argue strongly in favour of "big-time cuts in subsidy spending and a shift to old-fashioned investment-grade spending" of 15–25% (Riggs & Velk, 1995).

An activist by inclination, an intellectual by training, and an experienced politician with a strong tradition of using government to achieve social and economic ends, Axworthy grasped his opportunity quickly. In a speech in the House of Commons on January 31, 1994, he announced a national consultation that would culminate in a thorough revision of Canada's existing social policy.[11] His options, when presented, were breathtaking in scope, in that he promised to alter the fundamentals of Canadian federal social policy. Several aspects were obvious. Axworthy wanted to emphasize the federal role in social policy by making direct grants to individuals and thereby circumvent questions of provincial responsibility and an outcry from the provinces over unwarranted use of federal spending power. He also wanted to assure that funds went to those who needed them most, and in this respect he hoped to satisfy the fiscal regimen thought essential by his Cabinet colleagues, notably the minister of Finance and the prime minister.

The discussion paper that the HRD department prepared for Axworthy's Social Security Review proceeded from the assumption that "the status quo is not an option." Foreshadowing what was to come, it linked spending on social programs to the mounting debt and deficit, and noted that "if the next generation of Canadians is to obtain reasonable government services for the tax dollar, we must change our approach" (Human Resources Development Canada, 1994, p. 8). It portrayed social programs for the future as government strategies driven equally by a desire to create economic growth and by a wish to share the wealth and protect the disadvantaged. Finally, it mirrored the employment focus of the amalgamated HRDC and discussed social programs in the context of the primary objective of job creation. While the Social Security Review was touted as comprehensive, it was not because tax expenditures, increasingly a tool used by the federal government to deal with social issues, were excluded. Following the release of the discussion paper, a series of supplementary papers provided more information on the possible reforms, but again these echoed the overarching themes. These were all carefully vetted by officials from the Department of Finance.

The elements of Axworthy's review were a complicated affair: there would be a task force of "experts" supported by the bureaucrats in HRDC, as well as a national consultation by the House of Commons Standing Committee on Human Resources Development.[12] The committee received over 1,200 submissions and heard 637 witnesses before it approved its report on January 31, 1995. Over 200 members of Parliament consulted relevant groups in their constituencies: social workers, universities and their professors and students, activist groups, and health professionals. Over 25,000 Canadians completed and sent in a workbook, *Have Your Say*, to the Department of Human Resources Development. During the two years following the election of the Liberal government, social policy issues assumed a prominence that was unprecedented since the Green Book proposals of the Mackenzie King government in 1945. Given the complexity and the attention the Social Security Review was receiving, it was no small wonder that it quickly fell behind schedule.

The Liberal members of Parliament were deeply involved in the review. Most held so-called town hall meetings where the many groups interested in the substance of the review expressed their opinions. Those same groups appeared in constituency offices and, occasionally, picketed outside them. In university areas, student associations were generally opposed to the income-contingent approach, fearing that it would mean higher tuition even though many on the left supported it as a fairer way to approach the question of tuition. Business groups were puzzled by the review, and such associations as the local chambers of commerce did not present coherent critiques of it. On the one hand, they supported an overhaul of Unemployment Insurance; on the other hand, they were suspicious of Liberal designs, particularly when the artist was Lloyd Axworthy. Nevertheless, the reinventing and reduction of government were popular elements that Liberal MPs concentrated on in their speeches to business audiences.

What MPs soon realized during the course of the review was how many business interests employed social programs for their own needs. School bus lines relied on unemployment insurance to retain employees over the summer months. Various private educational firms used student loans to finance their work, and the scrutiny brought to the subject by the review was embarrassing to them: by far the highest rates of default came from students at these private schools. Sometimes labour and management came together to argue for retention of the current system around which they had constructed their employment practices, and the construction trades were especially active in this respect. The construction trade unions, unlike the industrial unions, were not affiliated with the New Democratic Party, and many had close ties with the Liberal Party or individual Liberal MPS. Social housing was also an area that united social activists with construction and architectural firms that had benefited greatly from past federal programs. The decision to transfer responsibilities to the province aroused much anger among MPS, especially in the province of Ontario after its voters elected the Progressive Conservatives in 1995.

In the case of grants through Human Resources Development (HRDC), members of Parliament signed an approval form, a practice that even most Reform Party members came to sign without dissent. Later, when such grants became controversial, those signatures became politically useful to the embattled Liberals as they defended the grants in the House of Commons. These grants were the sole example of MP involvement in the delivery of programs, at least in the province of Ontario. As a result, the contacts between the MP and the HRDC bureaucracy were many. When HRDC turned down an applicant, that applicant went to the MP's office, and when an MP needed information about a group, he or she contacted HRDC. This relationship, therefore, was affected when HRDC reduced significantly the number of employees, centralized administration, and sought to replace workers with technology.

In fact, one of the major tenets of the "reinventing government" movement was the importance of reducing "red tape" through technology, and HRDC, the largest deliverer of government services, was the department most affected. HRDC services were delivered primarily by clerical employees who were among the lowest-paid government workers and mostly female. With the freeze in government salaries in the 1990s, the technological challenge, and the uncertainty of employment, these employees had low morale. MPS often heard their complaints; they also heard complaints from clients of HRDC about poor service. Technology did help as kiosks with interactive screens listing jobs appeared in malls and elsewhere, but the department in the 1990s was drowning in its details.[13]

What happened in the constituencies reflected vividly the changing dynamics in Ottawa. This situation is described in detail in *Double Vision: The Inside Story of the Liberals in Power*, by journalists Edward Greenspon and Anthony Wilson-Smith. The book describes how Axworthy's ambitions crumbled as fiscal restraint and the politics of national unity gained pre-eminence:

> At the start of the government, Axworthy had been seen as the standardbearer for the social Liberals in cabinet. But their vision—indeed the Trudeau vision—had trouble getting airborne in this Liberal government.

> A competing vision, more fiscally grounded and provincially oriented, appeared to be gaining ascendancy, a vision most forcefully propounded by the intergovernmental affairs minister, Marcel Massé, and supported by his partner, the most powerful minister in the Chrétien government, Finance Minister Paul Martin. (Greenspon & Wilson-Smith, 1996, p. 152)

This interpretation is accurate in many respects, and there is little doubt that HRDC's plan for income-contingent student loans, a more imaginative approach to training through the Unemployment Insurance system, and a more focused approach to need had collapsed in the aftermath of the Quebec referendum of November 1995. Much less of the Axworthy plan remained (by the time he moved to Foreign Affairs in January 1996) than the review's driving forces had hoped. Unemployment Insurance had become Employment Insurance, but the impact of the referendum in Quebec brought federal assurance that labour training would be carried out by the provinces, with few federally imposed conditions. Moreover, the income-contingent loan scheme, despite its support from elements of the political left and right, did not survive strident opposition from student groups, opposition that included noisy protest in front of the private home of Denise and Lloyd Axworthy. In the end, the complex web of federal social policy created in the postwar era became a more simplified and considerably less restrictive Canada Health and Social Transfer, which some thought clarified federal and provincial roles, while others maintained that it permitted the federal government to gain credit for those funds it spent on social programs. In fact, the funds were less, and the province of Quebec, the major concern, did not thank the federal government for the less restrictive transfer program. Nevertheless, the 1995 budget, with its major cuts in federal government spending, the consolidation of federal transfers for health, welfare, and education in the Canada Health and Social Transfer, and the end of the ambitious Axworthy plan, marked a watershed in Canadian social policy whose impact remains in the twenty-first century.

Why? The reasons illuminate the dark area where process and substance intersect. To begin with, there were the questions of who was doing what, to whom, and when. To a large extent, the Liberals inherited a set of senior public servants who subscribed to the view of the primacy of the three "Ds"—dollar, deficit, and debt.[14] On the advice of his unpaid adviser, Mitchell Sharp, Prime Minister Jean Chrétien made it perfectly clear to his ministers that these public servants were their primary advisers. The Prime Minister's Office would deal with troublesome issues and provide direction. As a result, the ability of many departments to anticipate problems and consider options "atrophied" (Savoie, 1999). At the same time, the centre was, and is, limited in its resources and can be slow to make decisions. Ottawa observers noted that, instead of managing issues, policy resources were diverted into crisis management. This was certainly the case in Human Resources Development during the Social Security Review, particularly when Finance dropped the bomb in its proposal for the CHST. Gone were the large budgets and senior

ministerial staffs of the Conservatives with their policy expertise and control. Instead, the Liberal ministers, including Axworthy, were restricted in the
number of staff in their offices with the result that these mostly junior, inex-
perienced people were easily overwhelmed by their departments. To some
extent, at least in the economic areas, government relations firms—lobby-
ists—thought of themselves as the successors to the Conservatives' ministerial advisers and the counterweight to the bureaucrats. There was, however,
one key difference: their advice was self-interested, paid for by clients to
advance their cause. Axworthy realized this and brought in senior advisers
from outside, notably journalist Giles Gherson and former activist Patrick
Johnston; but this was too late in the game.

The cutbacks in the public service, moreover, meant that corporate mem-
ory was diminished and policy expertise downplayed or lost. When a government's major concern is downsizing and cutting costs, imaginative policy
solutions are deemed to be a distracting nuisance at best. As a result, much
of the policy thinking regarding social security reform took place outside government in think tanks and universities. Axworthy used the outside think
tanks, notably the Caledon Institute, but their input was always vetted through
the public servants. The question then—one that still remains—is about the
capacity within government to deal with the advice tendered from outside in
assimilating the information and converting it into public policy in a timely
fashion (*Inside Ottawa*, 1999).[15]

Finally, Axworthy's review achieved much less than anticipated because
it ran into the united front of the minister of Finance, his bureaucrats, and
their cost-cutting agenda. In effect, the Department of Finance took over the
review in midstream with the announcement of the Canada Health and Social
Transfer. With this, Finance also determined social policy. Axworthy's review
had always been constrained by the fiscal framework, no more clearly than in
the 1994 budget, which had kept on with the fiscal agenda: additional cuts to
federal transfers for social services, health, and education, and huge cuts to
unemployment insurance. As Axworthy's review fell behind schedule and
the ink was barely dry on the HRDC Standing Committee's report, the 1995
budget completed Finance's takeover of social policy. It announced the CHST
and raised questions that continue to be debated about the nature both of the
federal role in social programs (Is there one?) and any national standards in
their operation. Axworthy's successor in the HRDC portfolio, Douglas Young,
was not shy about disavowing a federal role in both of these. For the time
being, however, the 1995 budget stated that the job of the minister of Human
Resources Development was to negotiate with the provinces any principles or
objectives that would be attached to the transfer (Battle & Torjman, 1995).
The minister of Finance would determine the amount to be handed over.

The elements of the CHST are relatively straightforward. It combined the
money from the Established Programs Financing Act (EPF) for health and
education and the Canada Assistance Plan into a single block transfer with few
conditions. In effect, it eliminated the legislative basis that had underpinned

federal spending in the social area. It cut federal cash transfers to the provinces by $2.5 billion for 1996–1997 and by an additional $2 billion for 1997–1998. It eliminated the rules that had governed cost-shared programs under CAP and gave the provinces more or less full scope to spend federal transfer dollars as they wished (including on programs unrelated to assisting people in need). It did, however, retain the principles set out in the Canada Health Act and continued the prohibition on provincial residency requirements for applicants for social assistance.

Implications for the federal role were immense, particularly as the cash transfer to the provinces dropped annually as a proportion of the transfer as a whole.[16] If who pays the piper gets to call the tune, the federal government was getting increasingly hoarse. Even before the CHST, there were predictions that the EPF transfer would become cashless by the end of the 1990s and that the federal government would have then virtually no say over how this money was spent. Analysts did not need a crystal ball to see that removing the protection that CAP gave to the provincial services would mean that the impact of the cuts would be felt by people across the country as provincial governments trimmed in turn (Yalnizyan, 1995). In addition, the loose conditions attached to the transfer meant that the federal government and Canadian taxpayers had no way to measure how or where the money was being spent—in effect, the provinces were not accountable for the federal money they received. Commentators believed that the money would go to the provincial sectors with the squeakiest wheels and not necessarily to those who needed it most. They also questioned how the government would be able to achieve its other priorities such as eliminating child poverty (Clark & Carter, 1995). These predictions were proved correct as the share of provincial revenues spent on health care have crept higher in the interim, prompting the separation of the health transfer funds (Canada Health Transfer) from the education and social services transfer funds (Canada Social Transfer) in 2004 (Finance Canada, 2005).

The 1995 budget also signalled forthcoming changes to Canada's Unemployment Insurance program and set out the parameters that Axworthy would use to bring in the legislation, scheduled to take effect no later than July 1996. The aim of the changes was to help control the deficit and move money from areas that the budget saw as "creating dependence" to "investments in people to make them employable." As predicted, the newly renamed Employment Insurance (EI) tightened up the qualifying period, reduced the duration and level of benefits, and restricted expenditures for employment training to those who qualified for EI. Despite the doubts of some members of the federal Cabinet, devolution of labour market training to the provinces was pushed by ministers who wanted to show good faith to Quebec and to satisfy other provincial leaders who wanted more power. Theoretically, the argument in favour of moving responsibility to the provinces was to eliminate some duplication of programming between levels of government and allow training and other employment services to be integrated with provincial education programs.[17]

Although immigration remained an area of major federal involvement in the constituencies (although not in Quebec), the sense that the federal government was retreating from direct links with Canadians troubled many. The need to reduce the enormous deficit was almost universally accepted within the Liberal Party, and program review had almost no opponents. Yet the Red Book's promise of concentrating on where need was greatest led socially active MPs to create a social policy caucus. That caucus focused particularly on children's and disability issues. In the case of the former, there was much evidence that modern society's major victims were its children (Ross, Scott, & Smith, 2000; Torjman, 1995). With family dissolution increasingly common, single mothers and their children often slid into poverty and disadvantage.[18] The percentage of poor children in single-parent families reached 64.3% in 1993. Here, it seemed, was an area where the federal government could focus its more limited funds effectively. Think tanks such as the Caledon Institute had developed a series of proposals that were actively considered by the federal government and were readily available for committee meetings and private consultations. For the right-wing members of the Liberal government, however, there was little enthusiasm for new programs. Although poverty, particularly child poverty, is universally acknowledged as a serious problem, the effort to define poverty, poverty lines, poverty-level incomes, or minimum standards of living fuels debates among policy-makers inside and outside governments in Canada. In addition, both the deficit and the opposition of the provinces restricted the federal government's freedom of action. The result was the use of the tax system to deal with social policy, notably in the area of disability and children.

In the latter part of the 1990s, the federal government undertook several measures to deal with poverty—child poverty in particular. Estimates of the number of children living in poverty reached 1.4 million. The National Children's Agenda, developed between 1997 and 1999, has a common vision for children that acted as a catalyst for national discussions on policy issues between various levels of government and the community. One of its important components is its recognition that income support and integrated child and family services must be pursued simultaneously. It attempts to address the fact that many low-income parents on social assistance would lose benefits for their children if they found work. In this situation, known as the "welfare wall," some parents find themselves financially worse off in low-paid jobs than they are when on welfare because, without eligibility for welfare, they lose drug, dental, and additional health coverage for their children. Although the federal/provincial Canada Child Tax Benefit had improved the income levels of families living and working in difficult circumstances, the government decided to reinforce its child poverty initiatives by introducing the National Child Benefit and providing $850 million for it starting in July 1998. Subsequently, the federal government added significant other resources. The 2000 budget also used the tax system to promote this and other social objectives by restoring full indexation of tax benefits to inflation.[19] In essence, the Canada Child Tax Benefit (CCTB) goes to working poor families, while families receiving social assistance may have this reduced by the provinces and territories by an amount equal to the CCTB increase. The provinces committed themselves to reinvesting the money saved on social assistance into improving benefits and services for low-income families. The provinces agreed provided the federal investment was significant, incremental, and permanent, and they had the freedom to determine where to invest their savings from social assistance.

This program—the first new national program in two decades—would, therefore, help prevent and reduce child poverty and support parents in their transition to employment. The NCB was aimed at restructuring the system of income support for low-income families by replacing child benefits delivered through the welfare system with a national platform of income-tested child benefits delivered outside social assistance. Supposedly, by providing child benefits to all low-income families with children, regardless of their source of income, the NCB is levelling the playing field for families on social assistance and for the working poor.

The decade of the 1990s ended, as it began, with a federal/provincial agreement to deal cooperatively with social programs. Unlike Meech Lake, there was no attempt to use the constitution to achieve this goal in the Framework Agreement to Improve the Social Union for Canadians (SUFA), which was signed on February 4, 1999 (Canada, 1999). The current jargon uses the term "social union" to describe discussions and agreements among the federal, provincial, and territorial governments regarding social programs and social policy issues. The provinces began the social union discussions (without the federal government present) in 1995 to find ways of dealing with the CHST and the cuts to federal transfers. Initially, these talks were to encompass health, social services, and education, with children, people with disabilities, and youth as particular groups targeted. In 1996, when the federal government was invited into the tent, the discussions revolved around whether the outcome should be a broad federal–provincial–territorial framework agreement to guide social policy renewal, a limited framework agreement on the use of the federal spending power, or a step-by-step approach to conclude "sectoral" agreements in targeted areas with no overarching agreement.

However important it may be, the Social Union exercise has attracted little public interest; it is also a "yawner" for those who know about it and is very difficult to understand. So many of the discussions dealt with process and occurred behind closed doors. The nub of the discussions, however, continued to be the tug-of-war over social programs that began the decade of the 1990s—questions about the role of government and, from the perspective of Ottawa, the federal government. Should there be restrictions on the use of the federal spending power or not? Should there be enforceable national standards or not? Officials, ministers, and first ministers held an interminable series of meetings to find a middle way for almost three years. In negotiating positions reminiscent of the Meech Lake period, the provinces have intensified their efforts at controlling federal spending power since the 1998 budget, when the federal government had its first of eight consecutive years of surplus. Their bottom line remained the demand for restoration of cuts to federal transfers (approximately $6 billion). They have emphasized their health care needs—a cynic might think they were capitalizing on strong public support to maintain Canada's health system. For its part, the federal government wanted a flexible agreement that would preserve its discretion to spend as it wished and would recognize national principles, standards, and objectives. These aims, however, were recast in the language of "access," "mobility," "portability," and "common outcomes." Both sides agreed on the need for better accountability, including measuring outcomes of spending and publicly reporting on results.

The discussion of accountability regimes and outcomes, dull as it may appear, has the potential to affect social programs offered by all levels of government and the voluntary sector. For members of Parliament and other officials, the SUFA highlighted the ongoing challenge to ensure accountability and transparency of spending on programs, particularly social programs that affect groups whose interests cross over governmental and departmental boundaries. As a result, there is a stronger emphasis on the need to gather and make available information about the various programs in order to set national objectives or benchmarks. Outcome data provide an important foundation for discussions between the government and the community about what needs to be done—which goals have been met and which may need to be adjusted. In the area of social programs, positive outcomes need to be understood "horizontally." For example, employment for people with disabilities entails dealing with programs such as housing, transportation, supports and services, education and training, and programs that provide access to goods and services. In the current jargon, outcome measures provide feedback into the policy process and help to focus the government on its vision.

Given the linkage throughout the decade between cash and federal–provincial cooperation (or lack thereof), it is not surprising that the Social Union negotiations concluded just before the federal budget in 1999. The SUFA set the parameters for changing existing social programs and putting new ones in place. All the provinces except Quebec signed the agreement to recognize the need to ensure adequate, predictable, and sustainable funding for social programs; to modernize these programs to meet current needs; to restore the public's confidence by putting in place measures of citizen involvement, transparency, and accountability; and, finally, to better manage interdependence and encourage collaboration.

Who won? Overall, the federal government managed to retain a high level of flexibility, particularly in its unfettered ability to make transfers to individuals and organizations, to create the conditions required for access to national programs and mobility for Canadians, and to set up an accountability/reporting system. For their part, the provinces managed to get some limits on federal spending power, since new initiatives would require consultation and the approval of most provinces. In addition, the provinces retained the right to decide on program design, to secure agreement that the total federal transfer for a program does not necessarily have to be devoted to a given objective, and to require advance federal notice of changes to funding.

While the SUFA represents a considerable step forward in achieving the consensus that was denied at the beginning of the decade, it remains incomplete. What is required is to put meat on the bones in terms of real program and policy initiatives. Will it be respected? Will reports from the provinces be complete? What is a dispute resolution mechanism? Unfortunately, it is likely that ongoing attempts to clarify some of the language in the agreement will lead to ongoing preoccupation with processes, which means that actual program needs and design will take a back seat. The decade ended much as it began—with a struggle to understand the role of the federal government and to find an agreement that would be acceptable to the various levels of government and to the Canadian people. "'When I use a word,' Humpty Dumpty said, in a rather scornful tone, 'It means just what I choose it to mean—neither more nor less.' 'The question is,' said Alice, 'Whether you can make words mean so many different things.' 'The question is,' said Humpty Dumpty, 'Which is to be Master, that's all'" (Carroll, 1991, chap. 6).

Notes

1 The poll on business and government is found on p. 26. The following years brought a sharp recession to Canada. Some forecasters in the *Maclean's* issue warned of the possibility of recession.

2 This debate over the place of government and the nature of social security was taking place in most western countries. See Niels Ploug, "The Welfare State in Liquidation?" (1995).

3 Section 106a of the Meech Lake Accord stated that "The Government of Canada shall provide reasonable compensation to the government of a province that chooses not to participate in a national shared-cost program that is established by the Government of Canada after the coming into force of this section in an area of exclusive provincial jurisdiction, if the province carries on a program or initiative that is compatible with the national objectives.

4 For a summary of some of the presentations and arguments, see "Meech Lake" (1988).

5 In per capita GDP Canada had fallen from its postwar second place to twenty-second, but in terms of purchasing power it stood fourteenth, ahead of the United Kingdom but considerably behind some European countries, notably Norway, Denmark, and Belgium.

6 The maximum basic benefit was payable to all families with annual incomes less than $25,961 and was reduced at a rate of 5% of family net income above this amount.

7 The Established Programs Financing Act (EPF) was put in place in 1977 and replaced 50/50 conditional grants for hospital insurance and medicare with a combination of a single block grant (equal to 50%) of federal cash contributions indexed to GNP and provincial population. It also transferred to the provinces 13.5% personal income tax, 1% corporate tax points, and supplementary elements to compensate provinces to cover extended health care services. For the purposes of EPF, the provinces were not

obliged to spend to get federal money, although the federal government kept its ability to withhold its contribution if a province failed to meet the criteria set out in hospital insurance and medicare legislation (later the Canada Health Act of 1984). The EPF mechanism was criticized because it was alleged that a number of provinces took advantage of federal money and diverted it from health and education.

8   The Canada Assistance Plan put in place in 1966 had the objectives of alleviating poverty and preventing and removing the causes of poverty and dependence on public assistance. The CAP Act required provinces to enter into agreements with the federal government under which they agreed to comply with some general conditions on the administration and delivery of provincial social assistance and social services. In return, the federal government agreed to contribute 50% of eligible expenditures. CAP consisted of two elements: cost sharing of social assistance to people in need, which took two thirds of the funding, as well as social services for those in need or likely to become in need, which took the remaining one third. In 1990, the Canada Assistance Plan was the largest single source of funding for social services in Canada, accounting for an average of 38.5% of provincial spending in this area.

9   The new department consisted of the employment part of the former Department of Employment and Immigration, the welfare elements of the former Department of National Health and Welfare, the former Department of Labour, as well as parts of the former Department of Secretary of State and Multiculturalism and Citizenship. It was later renamed the Department of Human Resources Development, then Human Resources and Skills Development Canada, and more recently programs from five ministries delivered directly to individuals (such as employment insurance, the Canada Child Tax Benenfit, and immigration) have been amalgamated under Service Canada. See the Service Canada website at < www.servicecanada.gc.ca/en/about/about.html >.

10   This is still the case. By the end of the decade, in fiscal year 2000–2001 HRDC had responsibility for approximately $60 billion or approximately 45% of federal spending. Compared to other departments, HRDC spent five and a half times more than National Defence, twenty-six times more than Agriculture and Agri-Food, and thirty times more than Health Canada.

11   Chrétien announced a four-part review of federal government finances and programs on September 18, 1994, which resulted in *Agenda: Jobs and Growth*. Axworthy's review was one part of this as was Paul Martin's framework for economic growth, *A New Framework for Economic Policy*, released on October 17, 1994. This was followed by *Creating a Healthy Fiscal Climate*, which provided an update on the state of the economy and federal finances. The minister of Intergovernmental Affairs and minister responsible for Public Service Renewal (Marcel Massé) studied ways of streamlining programs and government operations to reduce expenditures. In late November 1994, the minister of Industry released *Building a More Innovative Economy*, which set out focused actions and strategies to foster economic growth.

12   The standing committee ultimately tabled a report in the House of Commons, *Security, Opportunities and Fairness: Canadians Renewing their Social Programs* (1995).

13   Many of these problems surfaced during the investigation of the administration of HRDC's grants and contributions programs that was carried out by Parliament. See Standing Committee on Human Resources Development and the Status of Persons with Disabilities, *Seeking a Balance: Final Report on Human Resources Development Canada Grants and Contributions* (2000).

14   See the commentaries prepared by the Caledon Institute throughout this period.

15   For another view, see Eva Kmiecic, "Canada's Policy Research Capacity: Observations from the Public Policy Forum" (2000).

16   Federal transfers dropped to $26.9 billion in 1996–1997 and then to $25.1 billion; the amount continued to be made up both of cash and tax points, but the cash component continued to drop as a percentage of the transfer.

References 17 For an evaluation of the changes to the income tax system, see Standing Committee on Human Resources Development and the Status of Persons with Disabilities, *Beyond Bill C-2: A Review of other Proposals to Reform Employment Insurance* (2001).

18 The child poverty rate rose from 15.4% in 1980 to 20.6% as a result of the recession, then declined during the economic recovery to 14.8%, and then increased again to 21.3% in 1993.

19 Following the initial $850 million, the federal government added $425 million in July 1999 and an additional $425 million in July 2000. Taking into account the restoration of indexation and the additional commitment in the 2005 budget, federal spending for the NCB will be increased by $965 million per year by 2007, bringing total CCTB benefits to over $10 billion annually. For details on how the NCB would work, see the *National Child Benefit Progress Report* (2001), online at < www.nationalchildbenefit.ca/ncb/ncb-2002/toceng.html >.

References

Battle, K. (1990). Clawing back. *Perception, 14*(3), 34.

Battle, K. (1993). *Missing a chance for a solid punch at poverty.* Caledon commentary. Ottawa: Caledon Institute of Social Policy.

Battle, K., & Torjman, S. (1995). *How finance re-formed social policy.* Ottawa: Caledon Institute of Social Policy.

Campbell, K. (1993). *Notes for an address.* Progressive Conservative Brunch, Montreal, August 22, 1993. Online at < collections.ic.gc.ca/discourspm/anglais/kc/2208993e.html >.

Canada. (1999). *A framework to improve the Social Union for Canadians: An agreement between the Government of Canada and the governments of the provinces and territories.* Online at < www.socialunion.ca/news/020499_e.html >.

Carroll, L. (1991). *Through the looking glass.* Millennium Fulcom Edition. Online at < www.cs.indiana.edu/metastuff/looking/looking.txt.gz >.

Clark, C., & Carter, S. (1995, Spring). Budget realities: Unravelling the social safety net. *Perception, 18*, 27–28.

Economist. (2001). *World in figures, 2001.* London: Profile Books.

Finance Canada. (2005). *Budget 2005: Delivering on commitments.* Online at < www.fin.gc.ca/budtoce/2005/budliste.htm >.

Greenspon, E., & Wilson-Smith, A. (1996). *Double vision: The inside story of the Liberals in power.* Toronto: Doubleday.

Human Resources Development Canada. (1994). *Improving social security in Canada: A discussion paper.* Ottawa: Author.

Inside Ottawa. (1999, October 4). 7(9).

Kmiecic, E. (2000). Canada's policy research capacity: Observations from the public policy forum. *Canadian Journal of Regional Science, 20*, 287–291.

Liberal Party of Canada. (1993). *Creating opportunity: The Liberal plan for Canada.* Author.

Maclean's. (1990, January 1), 14–18.

Meech Lake. (1988). *Perception, 12*(1), 16.

Melchers, R. (1990). The cap on CAP. *Perception, 14*(4), 19.

National Child Benefit progress report. (2001). Online at < www.nationalchildbenefit.ca/home_e.html >.

Ploug, N. (1995). The welfare state in liquidation? *International Social Security Review, 48*(2), 61.

Rae, B. (1997). *From protest to power.* Toronto: Penguin.

Riggs, A., & Velk, T. (1995). Social programs: Where they come from, where they are going. *Fraser Forum, 18.* Online at <www.oldfraser.lexi.net/publications/ forum/>.

Ross, D.P., Scott, K., & Smith, P.J. (2000). *Canadian fact book on poverty.* Ottawa: Canadian Council on Social Development.

Savoie, D. (Ed.). (1993). *Taking power: Managing government transitions.* Toronto: Institute of Public Administration.

Savoie, D. (1994). *Thatcher, Reagan, Mulroney: In search of a new bureaucracy.* Toronto: University of Toronto Press.

Savoie, D. (1999). *Governing from the centre.* Toronto: University of Toronto Press.

Standing Committee on Human Resources Development. (1995). *Security, opportunities and fairness: Canadians renewing their social programs.* Ottawa: House of Commons.

Standing Committee on Human Resources Development and the Status of Persons with Disabilities. (2000). *Seeking a balance: Final report on Human Resources and Development Canada grants and contributions.* Ottawa: House of Commons.

Standing Committee on Human Resources Development and the Status of Persons with Disabilities. (2001). *Beyond Bill C-2: A review of other proposals to reform employment insurance.* Ottawa: House of Commons.

Statistics Canada. (1994). *Canada Yearbook, 1994.* Ottawa: Author.

Summary of Provincial/Territorial/First Nations initiatives under the National Child Benefit 1999–2000. Online at <www.nationalchildbenefit.ca/ncb/ncb progress2000/summary.html>.

Torjman, S. (1995). *Milestone or millstone?* Ottawa: Caledon Institute of Social Policy.

Yalnizyan, A. (1995). Budget 1995: Open intentions, hidden costs. *Social Infopac, 13*(4), p. 1.

Human Rights Legislation, Court Rulings, and Social Policy

Ailsa M. Watkinson

Introduction

The International Federation of Social Workers (IFSW) and the International Association of Schools of Social Work (IASSW) define the social work profession as follows:

> The social work profession promotes social change, problem solving in human relationships and the empowerment and liberation of people to enhance well-being. Utilising theories of human behaviour and social systems, social work intervenes at the points where people interact with their environments. Principles of human rights and social justice are fundamental to social work. (2004)

The preamble of the Canadian Association of Social Workers' *Code of Ethics* (2005) confirms that the social work profession has "a particular interest in the needs and empowerment of people who are vulnerable, oppressed, and/or living in poverty. Social workers are committed to human rights as enshrined in Canadian law, as well as in international conventions on human rights created or supported by the United Nations." The CASW Code of Ethics identifies core social work values and the principles that underline those values. The core values are respect for the inherent dignity and worth of persons, the pursuit of social justice, service to humanity, integrity, confidentiality, and competence in professional practice.

Social work nationally and internationally is a practice grounded in social justice and human rights. The obvious emphasis on human rights means that familiarity with human rights principles and laws is extremely relevant to the practice of social work. Jim Ife (2001) promotes a practice of social work that more clearly identifies a social worker with an understanding of human rights. He states "that a human rights perspective can strengthen social work and [provide] a strong basis for an assertive practice that seeks to realize the social justice goals of social workers, in whatever setting" (p. 1). As I have noted elsewhere, the work associated with promoting and developing human rights is social work since the overall objectives of human rights laws are to promote equity, social justice, dignity, and well-being (Watkinson, 2001). Similarly, Reichert states that

> The study of human rights complements and broadens the perspective of social workers when carrying out policies and practices. By recognizing the importance of human rights, social workers can only enhance the profession. A foundation in human rights can provide a much clearer framework and structure with which to connect the social work profession to economic, political, and social aims. (2003, p. 13)

The purpose of this chapter is to discuss human rights principles and their relevance to social work practice and social policy. In particular this chapter will review human rights laws with a special focus on the Canadian Charter of Rights and Freedoms, its provisions, how it works, and the court's interpretation of it, and will explore recent changes brought about by the Charter's interpretation through court challenges that shape social policy in significant ways. I will use as an example my own involvement with the Charter in challenging the use of corporal punishment on children. I am using this example to illustrate how the Charter can be used by all citizens to influence changes to social policy, tradition, and oppression.

Human Rights Laws

Article 1 of the 1948 Universal Declaration of Human Rights begins with the statement that "All human beings are born free and equal in dignity and rights. They are endowed with reason and conscience and should act towards one another in a spirit of brotherhood." Respect for the inherent dignity of the human person is a common theme in all international, national, and provincial human rights documents arising from the Universal Declaration of Human Rights. Every province and territory in Canada has its own human rights legislation and a human rights commission or agency responsible for the administration of their laws. The first human rights legislation to be passed in Canada was Ontario's 1944 Racial Discrimination Act, which prohibited the publication or display of signs, symbols, or other representations expressing racial or religious discrimination. This was followed by Saskatchewan's Bill of Rights Act in 1947. The Saskatchewan legislation was more expansive than Ontario's, since it included protection of the fundamental freedoms of speech, press, assembly, religion, accommodation, employment, and business enterprises.

Today, most provincial, territorial, and federal human rights legislation prohibits discrimination in housing, employment, public services, education, contracts, and publications on the basis of stereotypical assumptions. The ability of individuals to acquire housing, employment, an education, health services, and other public services is essential to their sense of dignity and well-being. History has taught us that some of these basic needs are denied individuals only because of stereotypical assumptions based, for example, on their religion, age, or disability. The most common categories protected by provincial, territorial, and federal human rights laws are practices of discrimination based on sex, age, disability, colour, religion, creed, marital status, sexual orientation, family status, ancestry, nationality, place of origin, race, or perceived race.[1]   The Canadian Charter of Rights and Freedoms

Human rights agencies across the country, once they have received a complaint of discrimination that is within their mandate, will investigate it further. Their governing legislation allows them to review all documentation relevant to the complaint. An important benefit to filing a complaint with a human rights commission is that it does not cost the complainant any money. However, it can be a lengthy process that requires patience. A thorough discussion of human rights acts across the country is beyond the scope of this chapter, but the reader is encouraged to become familiar with local human rights acts and agencies.

The most significant change in the area of human rights protection in this country has been the inclusion of the Canadian Charter of Rights and Freedoms in Canada's constitution (a copy of the Charter is found in an appendix beginning on page 85). The Charter's purpose is to ensure that Canadian society is free and democratic and that the values and principles of a free and democratic society include "respect for the inherent dignity of the human person, commitment to social justice and equality, accommodation of a wide variety of beliefs, respect for cultural and group identity, and faith in social and political institutions which enhance the participation of individuals and groups in society" (*R. v. Oakes*, 1986, p. 136). Human rights legislation is about promoting and protecting equality, social justice, and human dignity; human rights legislation is synonymous with social work practice.

The Canadian Charter of Rights and Freedoms

In 1982, Canada patriated its constitution from the British Parliament and at the same time included a Charter of Rights and Freedoms. This was the culmination of years of work on the part of former prime minister Pierre Trudeau. There is little doubt that including, for the first time, fundamental freedoms and equality rights in Canada's constitution has had a profound impact on all Canadians.

The Canadian Charter of Rights and Freedoms is Canada's supreme social policy. Its status as a constitutional document means that the principles it enshrines are to be upheld in all government activity, including laws, policies, actions, and inactions. The extent of the Charter's reach is found in s. 32, which stipulates that the Charter applies to all federal, provincial, and territorial matters. This includes a wide range of social policy concerns, such as child protection, public health, prisoner welfare, social benefits, public education, and other items generally considered within the authority of governments. The Charter guarantees also apply to the actions and inactions of private organizations to which the government has delegated its public authority (*Eldridge v. British Columbia*, 1997; Watkinson, 2004).

Westhues, in chapter one of this book, defines social policy as "a course of action or inaction chosen by public authorities to address an issue that deals with human health, safety, or well-being" (p. 8). This definition illustrates nicely the Charter's connection to issues of social policy. The Charter is a template, a social policy assessor of sorts, against which all actions of public authorities are to be measured. Former Chief Justice Dickson of the Supreme Court of Canada stated, "the *Charter* represents an anchor in the storm of social evolution; it ensures that those values, unique to Canada as a nation and fundamental to Canada's orderly, democratic society, are immutable and shielded from encroachment by majority will. The goals sought to be achieved include: democracy, social justice, freedom, equality and human dignity" (2005, pp. 18–19).

It is important to understand the significance of the Charter's status. As has already been noted, it is part of our constitutional law and part of the "supreme law" of Canada (s. 52). The Charter can be amended only by reso-lution of the Senate and the House of Commons and by resolutions of the legislative assemblies of at least two thirds of the provinces comprising at least 50% of the population (s. 38). This means that changes in political ide-ologies cannot as easily interfere or alter what is constitutionally entrenched.

The Charter "provides a mechanism for progressive change in the legal relations of the individual with government by subjecting legislation and gov-ernment action [to] the scrutiny in the courts on the basis of fundamental rights and freedoms" (Dickson, 2005, p. 17). Any citizen can instigate a Char-ter challenge to policies and even to the lack of policies. If the challenge is suc-cessful, the law or policy may be declared invalid or altered (Watkinson, 1999, chap. 1). An understanding of human rights laws and their scope will assist advocates to turn what may have been deemed "an inevitable problem," into a right with legal recourse (Jochnick, 1999, p. 60).

A Charter challenge usually requires the services of a lawyer. This can be expensive. As I will discuss below, the Court Challenges Program provides funding for equality rights challenges if the issue is of significant national importance. In addition, some lawyers will provide pro bono (no charge) services. However, not all challenges will end up in the courts. Familiarity with human rights law is of benefit regardless of where a challenge may take you. If, for example, you are lobbying a politician or writing a submission on a new policy directive, framing the issue as a human rights matter will bring clarity to the policy under review. As noted above, it can turn "an inevitable problem," into a rights issue that cannot easily be ignored.

Charter of Rights and Freedoms

The Canadian Charter of Rights and Freedoms guarantees that all people are entitled to fundamental freedoms and equality rights. However, the rights and freedoms entrenched in the Charter may at times be limited. Section 1 of the Charter allows governments to limit rights and freedoms if they can show the limitation meets a sufficiently important objective and if the method chosen to limit the right or freedom is reasonable and demonstrably justified *The Canadian* (*R. v. Oakes*, 1986). The important fact to note is that once it has been shown *Charter of* that a government action violates the rights of an individual or group, the *Freedoms* onus switches to the government to justify why it has chosen to limit a Charter right. In addition, section 33 (referred to as the "notwithstanding clause"), can be invoked by governments to override legal and equality rights. It is a real threat available to governments, but one rarely exercised.

The rights and freedoms contained in the Charter include the right to freedom of conscience and religion and the right to freedom of expression (s. 2). These rights are considered the cornerstone of a democratic society. The Charter also guarantees the right of every citizen to vote in elections (s. 3) and the right to move in and out of Canada (s. 6). The Charter guarantees what are termed "legal rights." These rights are found in sections 7–12 and include the right to "life, liberty and security of the person" (s. 7), the right not to be subjected to unreasonable searches or seizures (s. 8), and the right not to be arbitrarily detained or imprisoned (s. 9). An individual arrested or detained is to be informed of his or her rights (s. 9), allowed access to a lawyer (s. 10), and have the case be heard within a reasonable time (s. 11). Other legal rights include the right to be free from "cruel and unusual treatment or punishment" (s. 12) and protection for witnesses in legal proceedings, including the right to an interpreter should it be required (ss. 13–14).

The most litigated section of the Charter is section 15, the equality rights section. It provides that all government policies, laws, directives, actions, and inactions must ensure that no person is affected in a negative way on the basis of age, sex, marital status and so forth. Greschner points out that section 15 is unique among the Charter provisions in that it is "aimed at ending discrimination against members of groups, those who suffer the harms of exclusion…. No other provision [in the Charter] has this broad goal" (2002, p. 305). The purpose of the equality section is to protect against the harm of exclusion. Greschner, in her examination of the purpose of section 15, comments that "one's human dignity, if it is a mark of anything is a mark of one's equality on some fundamental level with other human beings" (2002, p. 302). Former Chief Justice Dickson referred to section 15 as representing "one of the most important and dynamic forces of change on the road to social justice" (2005, p. 17).

Subsection 2 of the equality rights section recognizes the legitimacy of policies and programs designed to assist those who have suffered either directly or historically from discrimination. An example would be employment programs that encourage qualified or qualifiable women, members of racialized groups, or persons with disabilities to apply. The goal of such affirmative policies is to promote full membership of all persons in society. Greschner points out that distinctions are not necessarily harmful if, for example, they are called upon to allocate resources amongst members. Distinctions violate equality rights when they are used to exclude some members of the community because of their membership in what Greschner refers to as "identity groups"—groups that are "bound by common religious beliefs, language, sex, culture, ethnicity or history in ways that shape the experiences and characters of individuals" (2002, p. 302).

"A living tree"

The Charter has been described as a "living tree capable of growth and expansion" (L'Heureux-Dube, 2000). Recently the Supreme Court referred again to this metaphor, the origins of which came from the famous "Persons Case"[2] of 1929, saying, "our Constitution is a living tree which, by way of progressive interpretation, accommodates and addresses the realities of modern life" (*Reference Re: Same Sex*, 2004, para. 22). The metaphor is used to illustrate the need to interpret the Charter in a way that allows growth and changing societal standards. It acknowledges our uncertainty about what may be identified as a form of discrimination in years to come.

Since 1982, we have seen a great deal of growth. For example, the list of prohibited grounds of discrimination contained in section 15, the equality rights section, has been expanded to include "citizenship" (*Andrews v. Law Society of British Columbia*, 1989), "marital status" (*Miron v. Trudel*, 1995), "sexual orientation" (*Egan v. Canada*, 1995; *Vriend v. Alberta*, 1998), and those who face discrimination on the basis of "living on or off reserve" (*Corbiere v. Canada*, 1999). The prohibited grounds of discrimination listed in section 15 are referred to as the "enumerated" grounds of discrimination. Those added to the list through court decisions are referred to as "analogous" grounds of discrimination.

Whenever a court is asked to decide on a Charter matter, the court's decision provides new insight into how the Charter will be interpreted in the future. The most important decisions are those issued by the Supreme Court of Canada, the court of last resort, simply because its decisions are the final decisions (this does not imply there is nothing more to be done about an unfair policy—it means that energies will be placed elsewhere to attempt to change what is not right). A number of important understandings have come out of the Supreme Court concerning the Charter's interpretation. First, as discussed previously, the Charter is to be given a broad interpretation, in the same way as provincial and territorial human rights laws are to be interpreted broadly and liberally; and second, its application will be interpreted in the context of the situation under review. This latter point allows a substantive review rather than a formalistic and rigid interpretation of the law. A substantive review takes into account the impact of laws and policies on individuals and groups in the context of their lives by requiring an examination of "the impact of laws and polices on people to determine whether they are accorded full membership in the larger community" (Greschner, 2002, p. 294).

The prohibition against discrimination is perhaps one of the most valuable aspects of the Charter for social workers. There are countless incidents of discrimination facing those who are marginalized, but one area that is not included in the Charter is discrimination on the basis of "socio-economic status." There have been attempts by equality-seeking groups to have it included as a prohibited ground of discrimination in the Charter but so far to no avail (*Gosselin v. Quebec*, 2002). However, if a group is negatively impacted by a policy or government directive on the basis of poverty, it is worth considering whether it can be shown that those affected are disproportionately represented by another protected class such as gender, family status, marital status, being a member of a racialized group, or a person with a disability. If, for example, it can be shown that the policy impacts on a poor group of single parents, a complaint of discrimination could be built around marital status and/or family status.

Economic status was taken into account by the Nova Scotia Supreme Court in a 1993 Charter decision regarding the rights of a public housing tenant (*Dartmouth/Halifax County Regional Housing Authority v. Sparks*, 1993). The tenant, a single, black mother of two children, had lived in public housing for over ten years. Ms. Sparks had been given one month's notice to move out of her residence. According to the Residential Tenancies Act (1989), tenants in private housing who had lived in their residences for five years could not be evicted from their homes unless a judge was satisfied that the tenants were in default of obligations under their leases. The law protecting private housing tenants, however, did not extend to public housing tenants. The court ruled in favour of Ms. Sparks, noting that the law adversely affected protected groups under the Charter, namely single parents, females, and blacks. The court said "poverty is, in addition, a condition more frequently experienced by members of the three groups identified" (*Dartmouth/Halifax*, 1993, p. 233).

Similar arguments are being heard in an Ontario Charter challenge under way regarding the clawback of the National Child Benefit Supplement (NCBS) (*Chokomolin, Lance & Prine v. Her Majesty*, 2005). The case is supported by a provincial non-profit group, the Income Security Advocacy Centre.[3] As Hunter describes in chapter 9 of this book, the NCBS is part of a program introduced by the federal government in 1998 to reduce the depth of child poverty. The program, referred to as the Canada Child Tax Benefit (CCTB), includes a basic benefit plus the National Child Benefit Supplement. All provinces, except for Manitoba and New Brunswick, claw back the NCBS from families who are on social assistance. Only the working poor receive the benefits of the NCBS; the children of families on social assistance do not receive an increase in their income. The provincial governments' rationale is that this money will be reinvested into programs targeted at improving work incentives as well as benefits and services for low-income family employment incentives. The Charter challenge argues that the clawback violates their right to "life, liberty and security of the person" under section 7 of the Charter. They also argue that it disproportionately impacts on members of disadvantaged groups, namely women, single mothers, person with disabilities, Aboriginal persons, and racialized persons, and is therefore a violation of section 15 of the Charter.

Charter Challenges and Social Policy

There have been many court rulings of import that have influenced social policy over the past twenty years. The significance of these cases has been felt by every Canadian. In 1988, for example, the Supreme Court ruled that procedural requirements, as written in the Criminal Code of Canada governing a woman's access to abortion, interfered with a woman's right to liberty and security of her person as protected under section 7 of the Charter (*R. v. Morgentaler*, 1988). The Court ruled that the Criminal Code sections were no longer of any force or effect. This meant that the procedural requirements were technically wiped out, and thus women in Canada now have the right to determine, on their own, if they will terminate a pregnancy.

The Supreme Court was asked to consider whether a parent has a right to state-funded legal counsel when involved in a hearing regarding the placement of his or her child in government care (*New Brunswick v. G. (J.)*, 1999). In this case, the Minister of Health and Community Services in New Brunswick was seeking an extension of the custody of the mother's three children. The mother, who was poor and on social assistance, sought legal assistance from the provincial legal aid but was denied services because, at the time, legal aid did not provide services for those involved in child protection cases. The mother argued that the restriction on access to legal aid violated her rights to security of the person under section 7 of the Charter. The Supreme Court agreed and found that state "removal of a child from parental custody pursuant to the state's *parens patriae* jurisdiction constitutes a serious interference with the psychological integrity of the parent" (1999, para. 61). State removal of a child causes distress for the parent, interferes with the parent–child relationship, stigmatizes the parent as "unfit" and "is a gross intrusion into a private and intimate sphere" (para. 61). In light of the consequences to the parent, the Court said the government "was under a constitutional obligation to provide the appellant [mother] with state-funded counsel in the particular circumstances of this case" (para. 2). The Court noted that, since a large number of these cases involved single mothers, the issue was one of gender inequality and the right to equal benefit of the law. The results of this case can be used to support not only poor parents in child protection disputes, but other indigent people, such as prisoners, who find themselves fighting a government directive that limits their Charter rights.

In another case dealing with child protection and the security rights of parents, the Supreme Court ruled that the provisions in the Manitoba Child and Family Services Act, which allows the apprehension of children without a warrant, does not violate a parent's security rights (*Winnipeg*, 2000). The issue for the Court was whether the principles of fundamental justice in the child protection context require prior judicial authorization of apprehensions, that is a warrant, in non-emergency situations. Justice L'Heureux-Dube, speaking for the majority, said,

I am very conscious of the difficulties confronting social workers and others in obtaining hard evidence, which will stand up when challenged in court, of the maltreatment meted out to children behind closed doors. Cruelty and physical abuse are notoriously difficult to prove. The task of social workers is usually anxious and often thankless. They are criticized for not having taken action in response to warning signs which are obvious enough when seen in the clear light of hindsight. Or they are criticised for making applications based on serious allegations which, in the event, are not established in court. Sometimes, whatever they do, they cannot do right. (Winnipeg, 2000, para. 100)

The Supreme Court also determined that a child's right to health care overrides parental religious beliefs (*B.(R.) v. Children's Aid Society of Metropolitan Toronto*, 1995). The issue brought the rights of a child into conflict with her parent's religious beliefs. The child of Jehovah's Witnesses required medical attention. Her parents asked that no blood transfusions be administered as they objected to them for religious reasons. The medical team agreed, but when the situation became more serious, the Children's Aid Society requested temporary wardship of the child. This was granted, and she received a blood transfusion. The parents challenged the section of the Ontario Child and Family Services Act that allows for the wardship of children "in need of protection." They argued that this law infringed their freedom of religion under section 2(a) of the Charter. The Court did not uphold the Charter challenge and found that the provision in the Act was of sufficient importance in ensuring the life of the child—a right she had under section 7 of the Charter.

Charter challenges also forced the federal government to draft new legislation governing marriage after a number of decisions from across the country found that the common law definition of marriage, which identified marriage as between a man and a woman, violated the Charter equality rights of gays and lesbians (*Halpern v. Canada*, 2003). Once the government drafted its new law, it asked that Supreme Court to consider whether the proposed change was consistent with the Canadian Charter of Rights and Freedoms (*Reference re: Same Sex Marriage*, 2004). The proposed law was under intense criticism from various factions who argued that such a law would, among other things, discriminate against people on the basis of their religious beliefs as there are some religions that do not recognize the rights of same-sex couples to marry (para. 45). The Court found the proposed law to be consistent with the Charter, saying that it fosters the very principles that section 15(1) of the Charter was intended to. This case is another clear example of governments being forced, by Charter challenges, to alter policy. The new law has subsequently been passed by the Government of Canada.

A further example related to an amendment to the Criminal Code in 1995 to take into account alternative sentencing options available to courts when imposing a sentence on a prisoner. The change called upon the courts to take into consideration "all available sanctions other than imprisonment that are

reasonable in the circumstances ... for all offenders, with particular attention to the circumstances of aboriginal offenders."[4] It was argued that this
section amounted to "reverse discrimination" so as to favour Aboriginal people over others and thus was a violation of the equality right provision of the
Charter. The Supreme Court considered this argument and disagreed, noting
that it was an appropriate response to the problem of over-incarceration in
Canada. The Court said "our country is ... distinguished as being a world
leader in putting people in prison.... Canada's rate of approximately 130
inmates per 100,000 population places it second or third highest.... This
record of incarceration rates obviously cannot instill a sense of pride" (*R. v.
Gladue*, 1999, para. 52).While the over-reliance on incarceration is a problem, it is more so for Aboriginal Canadians. In Saskatchewan, for example,
60% of provincial admissions into jails are Aboriginal people, while they make
up approximately 13% of the total population. The Court said, "there is widespread bias against aboriginal people within Canada and 'there is evidence
that this widespread racism has translated into systemic discrimination in
the criminal justice system'" (*R. v. Gladue*, 1999, para. 61). The Court's decision
affirmed policy initiatives aimed at ameliorating the effects of discrimination caused in part by bias against Aboriginal people in Canada, which has
manifested itself in the justice system.

The cases highlighted so far are examples of what I would describe as
progressive decisions. They have worked to promote equality and dignity for
the marginalized—women, children, single parents, and sexual and racialized
minorities. However, not every case brought forward under the Charter turns
out the way one might hope. One case, instigated by the author, was a challenge to the use of physical punishment on children. The case was heard by
the Supreme Court, and it issued its decision in 2004 (*Canadian Foundation
for Children Youth and the Law v. Canada*, 2004). While the result was not
what I had hoped for, it still reaped some benefits.

Canadian Foundation for Children Youth and the Law

In 1995, an Ontario Provincial Court ruled that the physical punishment meted
out by an American tourist upon his five-year-old daughter in a restaurant
parking lot was "reasonable under the circumstances," and thus her father was
acquitted of assaulting her (*R. v. Peterson*, 1995). The father used a legal defence
to justify what would otherwise be an assault. The defence is found in section
43 of the Criminal Code of Canada, and it states, "Every school teacher, parent or person standing in the place of the parent is justified in using force by
way of correction toward the pupil or child, as the case may be, who is under
his care, if the force does not exceed what is reasonable under the circumstances." This defence has been in Canada's Criminal Code since 1892. At
that time, the Code also allowed the use of force on sailors, apprentices, and
prisoners. Over the years, the provision has been amended, leaving only children to be the recipient of this form of punishment.

Shortly after the case of *R. v. Peterson* made the news, I applied for funding through the Court Challenges Program to conduct research into the constitutionality of section 43. The Court Challenges Program is a federally funded program that funds challenges to Canadian law that may violate equality rights. In order to succeed in obtaining funding, the applicant must show that the violation is an equality rights matter, that it is of national significance, and that the law or action being challenged falls within federal jurisdiction.[5] Once I had completed my research (Watkinson, 1998), I applied for further funding from the Court Challenges Program to take the case forward as a Charter challenge. My application was successful. According to the mandate of the Court Challenges Program, an individual cannot take a case forward on her own, and so I was required to find an organization to carry the case forward for me. I selected the Canadian Foundation for Children Youth and the Law, an Ontario-based organization, since there was no other organization that I knew of that had a history of working with children and youth as well as experience with equality rights cases.

Our arguments were that section 43 of the Criminal Code violated the Charter rights of children under three sections. First, we claimed that section 43 infringed section 7 of the Charter, which protects all citizens from invasions of their security, and that the infringement could not be justified within the principles of fundamental justice. We also argued that section 43 violated a child's rights under section 12, which prohibits cruel and unusual treatment. Finally, we argued that section 43 is contrary to the equality rights protected under section 15 that protect all citizens from inequality in law and in the protection afforded by law.

Not surprisingly, the case caused a great deal of interest. This meant that a number of groups and organizations came forward seeking intervener status—an opportunity to comment on the case. Interveners are common in Charter cases. It is rare for a case to be heard before the Supreme Court that does not include a list of organizations representing strong views on the topic under review.

The Intervener supporting the challenge to section 43 was the Ontario Association for Children's Aid Societies. Other groups applied to intervene but were denied status. They included the Canadian Association of Social Workers and the National Youth in Care Network, among others. Once the case reached the Supreme Court level, two other interveners were accepted on our side: the Child Welfare League of Canada and the Commission des Droits de la Personne et des Droits de la Jeunesse. Those supporting the Government of Canada's position (represented by the Attorney General) were the Canadian Teacher's Federation and the Coalition for Family Autonomy. The Coalition for Family Autonomy is made up of REAL Women, Focus on the Family (Canada), the Canadian Family Action Coalition, and the Home School Legal Defence Association of Canada.

On January 30, 2004, the majority of the Supreme Court judges, in a 6–3 decision, sided with the Government of Canada, the Canadian Teacher's Fed-

(margin note) Charter Challenges and Social Policy

eration, and the Coalition for Family Autonomy and found that while the defence available to parents and teachers under section 43 violates a child's "security of the person" rights under section 7, it is not done in contravention of the principles of fundamental justice. They found that section 12, which guarantees freedom from cruel and unusual treatment, was not offended by section 43, since section 12 applies not to parents but to the actions of governments and their agents. While teachers are considered agents of the state, the Court ruled that section 12 did not apply, as the only force teachers could use on students was not "cruel and unusual."

Finally, the majority of the Court found that section 43 did not constitute discrimination against children. They acknowledged that section 43 "permits conduct toward children that would be criminal in the case of adult victims" (para. 50), but the distinction on the basis of age is, they said, designed to protect children by not criminalizing their parents and teachers. Chief Justice McLachlin, writing for the majority, said, "The decision not to criminalize such conduct is not grounded in devaluation of the child, but in a concern that to do so risks ruining lives and breaking up families—a burden that in large part would be borne by children and outweigh any benefit derived from applying the criminal process" (2004, para. 62). It was the majority's opinion that the benefit to be gained by the existence of section 43 outweighed the deleterious effects of the use of physical force on children.[6] However, even though the Supreme Court did not affirm the rights of the child in this regard, it did limit the scope of by whom and under what circumstances section 43 can be used as a defence.

The majority of the Court expanded on the limitations to section 43, specifically listing actions that would not be considered "reasonable." These actions enter what the Court called a "zone of risk," meaning that the section 43 defence will not be available in certain circumstances. First, "section 43 exempts from criminal sanction only minor corrective force of a transitory and trifling nature" (para. 40). Second, it is never justified when used by teachers: "Substantial societal consensus, supported by expert evidence and Canada's treaty obligations, indicate that corporal punishment by teachers is unreasonable" (para. 38). Section 43 will protect teachers from charges of assault only when "a teacher uses reasonable, corrective force to restrain or remove a child in appropriate circumstances" (para. 38). The Court said that it is never reasonable to use corporal punishment on children under two years of age because they do not have the capacity to understand "why they are hit" (para. 25, 40) Similarly, a child with a "disability or some other contextual factor" will not understand the reasons for the use of force (para 25). The Court said, "in these cases, force will not be 'corrective' and will not fall within the sphere of immunity provided by s. 43" (para. 25), since children must be capable of learning and have the capacity to successfully correct their behaviour. Corporal punishment is not to be used on teenagers as it can induce aggressive or antisocial behaviour in them (para. 37, 40). Corporal punishment cannot be justified under section 43 when an object or weapon Conclusion is used such as a ruler or belt, nor in cases involving slaps or blows to the head or when the force is "degrading, inhuman or harmful conduct" (para. 40). Section 43 cannot be used as a defence to charges of assault when corporal punishment is applied in anger stemming from "frustration, loss of temper or abusive personality" (para. 40).

In summary, those who use corporal punishment on children risk criminal sanctions, since they will not be able to use section 43 as a defence when

- it exceeds minor corrective force of a transitory and trifling nature;
- it is used by teachers;
- it is used on children under the age of two;
- it is used on children with disabilities;
- it is used on teenagers;
- an object is used;
- a child is hit on the head;
- the force is degrading or inhuman; or
- it is applied in anger.

The most distressing part of this case for me was the Court's unwillingness to extend to children the same rights and protections many of us take for granted. The reasoning used in this case is framed first and foremost around the rights of parents and teachers—not the rights of the child. The majority rejected the notion of children's rights and their entitlement to dignity, bodily integrity, and equality. Even so, the case changed policy by limiting the use of section 43 as a defence for parents, teachers, and others who use physical punishment on children. It was also successful in raising the issue of the harms associated with physical punishment of children in a very public way (Durant, Ensom, & Coalition on Physical Punishment of Children and Youth, 2004). The public's awareness of this issue has been heightened by the case and the use of force on children has, I hope, diminished.

Conclusion

The symbiotic relationship between social work and human rights works to the benefit of both. Familiarity with human rights principles and laws provides a basis for an assertive social work practice (Ife, 2001) and a structure within which to frame the lived experiences of the marginalized (Reichert, 2003). Human rights laws across the country, including the Charter of Rights and Freedoms, are essential tools available to social workers to analyze, articulate, and, if necessary, legally challenge inequities brought about by government action and inaction. As has been illustrated above, the Charter has brought significant changes to the lives of many marginalized people, demonstrating its potential as an invaluable tool in promoting social change and the well-being of all persons.

Notes

References

Notes

1 This list of protected grounds will vary slightly among provinces and territories. Please refer to your own local human rights act for further information. See the Saskatchewan Human Rights Commission website at www.gov.sk.ca/shrc/links.htm.

2 The case of *Edwards v. Attorney-General for Canada* (1930), the "Persons" case, determined that women were persons and as such could be appointed to the Senate of Canada. Up until this time women were not considered "qualified persons" for such an appointment. The case was brought forward by the Famous Five, which included Henrietta Muir Edwards, Nellie McClung, Emily Murphy, Louise McKinney, and Irene Parlby.

3 See the website of the Income Security Advocacy Centre, online at <www.incomesecurity.org>. This case is an important one to keep track of as it makes its way through the justice system.

4 The section under review was section 718.2 of the Criminal Code of Canada.

5 For more information on the Court Challenges Program, see the website at <www.ccppcj.ca>.

6 I have written more detailed critiques of the Court's reasoning: see Ailsa M. Watkinson "Corporal punishment and education: Oh Canada! Spare us!" and "Supreme Court of Canada stands behind corporal punishment—sort of" (both forthcoming).

References

Andrews v. Law Society of British Columbia, 1 S.C.R. 143 (1989).

B.(R.) v. Children's Aid Society of Metropolitan Toronto, 1 S.C.R. 315 (1995).

Bill of Rights Act. (1947). S.S. 1947, c. 35.

Canadian Association of Social Workers. (2005). *Social work code of ethics.* Ottawa: CASW.

Canadian Foundation for Children, Youth and the Law v. Canada (Attorney General), 1 S.C.R. 76 (2004). Online at <www.lexum.umontreal.ca/csc-scc/en/index.html>.

Charter of Rights and Freedoms. (1982). Online at <www.laws.justice.gc.ca/en/charter/>.

Chokomolin, Lance & Prine v. Her Majesty. Application for trial March 10, 2005.

Corbiere v. Canada (Minister of Indian and Northern Affairs), 2 S.C.R. 203 (1999).

Criminal Code. R.S.C. 1985, c. C-46.

Darmouth/Halifax County Regional Housing Authority v. Sparks, 101 D.L.R. (4th) 224 (N.S.C.A.) (1993).

Dickson, B. (2005). The Canadian Charter of Rights and Freedoms: Context and evolution. In G.A. Beaudoin & E. Mendes, *Canadian Charter of Rights and Freedoms* (4th ed., pp. 5–23). Markham, ON: Butterworths.

Durrant, J.E., Ensom, R., & Coalition on Physical Punishment of Children and Youth. (2004). Joint statement on physical punishment of children and youth. Online at <www.cheo.on.ca./english/1120.html>.

Edwards v. Attorney-General for Canada, A.C. 124 (P.C.) (1930).

Egan v. Canada, 2 S.C.R. 513 (1995).

Eldridge v. British Columbia (Attorney General), 3 S.C.R. 624 (1997).

Gosselin v. Quebec (Attorney General), 4 S.C.R. 429 (2002).

Greschner, D. (2002). The purpose of Canadian equality rights. *Review of Constitutional Studies, 6,* 291–323.

Halpern v. Canada (Attorney General), 65 O.R. (3d) 161 (2003).

Ife, J. (2001). *Human rights and social work: Towards rights-based practice.* New York: Cambridge University Press.

International Federation of Social Workers & International Association of Schools **References**
of Social Work. (2004). Ethics in social work, statement of principles. Online at
<www.ifsw.org/en/p38000324.html>.

Jochnick, C. (1999). Confronting the impunity of non-state actors: New fields for the
promotion of human rights. *Human Rights Quarterly, 21*(1), 56–79.

L'Heureux-Dube, C. (2000). The legacy of the "Persons Case": Cultivating the living
tree's equality leaves. *Saskatchewan Law Review, 63*, 389.

Miron v. Trudel, 2 S.C.R. 418 (1995).

New Brunswick (Minister of Health and Community Services) v. G.(J.), 3 S.C.R. 46
(1999).

Ontario. Child and Family Services Act. (2004). Online at <www.e-laws.gov.on
.ca/DBLaws/Statutes/English/90c11_e.htm>.

R. v. Gladue, 1 S.C.R. 688 (1999).

R. v. Morgentaler, 1 S.C.R. 30 (1988).

R. v. Oakes, 1 S.C.R. 103 (1986).

R. v. Peterson, 98 C.C.C. (3d) 253 (Ont. C.J. Prov. Div.) (1995).

Racial Discrimination Act. (1944). S.O. 1944, c. 35.

Reference re Same Sex Marriage, 3 S.C.R. 698 (2004).

Reichert, E. (2003). *Social work and human rights: A foundation for policy and
practice.* New York: Columbia University Press.

Saskatchewan Human Rights Commission. (n.d.). Human rights links. Online at
<www.gov.sk.ca/shrc/htm>.

United Nations. (1989). Convention on the rights of the child (UN Doc. A/RES/
44/25(1989)/).

United Nations. (1948). *Universal declaration of human rights* (U.N.G.A. Res. 217A
[III], 3[1], UN GAOR Res. 71, UN Doc. A/810 [1948]).

Vriend v. Alberta, 1 S.C.R. 493 (1998).

Watkinson, A.M. (1998) Prohibiting corporal punishment: In the name of the Charter, the child and societal values. In S. Natale (Ed.), *The management of values:
Organizational and educational issues* (pp. 301–332). Boston: University Press
of America.

Watkinson, A.M. (1999). *Education student rights and the Charter.* Saskatoon: Purich
Publishing.

Watkinson, A.M. (2001). Human rights laws: Advocacy tools for a global civil society. *Canadian Social Work Review, 18*, 267–286.

Watkinson, A.M. (2004). Equality rights and re-privatized public services: Religious
fundamentalism meets the Charter. In C. Schick, J. Jaffe, & A.M. Watkinson
(Eds.), *Contesting fundamentalisms* (pp. 137–151). Halifax: Fernwood.

Watkinson, A.M. (forthcoming). Corporal punishment and education: Oh Canada!
Spare us! In M.M. Casimir (Ed.), *The courts, the Charter, and the schools: The
impact of the Charter of Rights and Freedoms on educational policy and practice.* Toronto: University of Toronto Press.

Watkinson, A.M. (2006). Supreme Court of Canada stands behind corporal punishment … sort of. *International Social Work Journal, 49*(4), (in press).

Westhues, A. (2006). *Canadian social policy: Issues and perspectives* (4th ed.). Waterloo, ON: Wilfrid Laurier University Press.

Winnipeg Child and Family Services v. K.L.W. 2 S.C.R. 519, (2000).

References   **Additional Resources**

Canadian Association of Schools of Social Work. Online at <www.cassw-acess.ca>.

Canadian Supreme Court decisions. Online at <www.lexum.umontreal.ca/csc-scc/en/ index.html>.

Charter of Rights and Freedoms. Online at <laws.justice.gc.ca/en/charter/>.

International Association of Schools of Social Work. Online at <www.iassw.soton .ac.uk/>.

International Human Rights Laws. Online at <www.unhchr.ch/html/intlinst.htm>.

Saskatchewan Human Rights Code. Online at <www.gov.sk.ca/shrc/>.

APPENDIX
CANADIAN CHARTER OF RIGHTS AND FREEDOMS
Schedule B
Constitution Act, 1982

Enacted as Schedule B to the *Canada Act 1982* (UK) 1982, c. 11,
which came into force on April 17, 1982.

PART I
Canadian charter of rights and freedoms

Whereas Canada is founded upon principles that recognize
the supremacy of God and the rule of law:

Appendix.
Canadian
Charter of
Rights and
Freedoms,
Schedule B

1–6(4)

Rights and freedoms in Canada	1 The *Canadian Charter of Rights and Freedoms* guarantees the rights and freedoms set out in it subject only to such reasonable limits prescribed by law as can be demonstrably justified in a free and democratic society.
Fundamental freedoms	2 Everyone has the following fundamental freedoms: a) freedom of conscience and religion; b) freedom of thought, belief, opinion and expression, including freedom of the press and other media of communication; c) freedom of peaceful assembly; and d) freedom of association.
Democratic rights of citizens	3 Every citizen of Canada has the right to vote in an election of members of the House of Commons or of a legislative assembly and to be qualified for membership therein.
Maximum duration of legislative bodies Continuation in special circumstances	4 (1) No House of Commons and no legislative assembly shall continue for longer than five years from the date fixed for the return of the writs of a general election of its members. (2) In time of real or apprehended war, invasion or insurrection, a House of Commons may be continued by Parliament and a legislative assembly may be continued by the legislature beyond five years if such continuation is not opposed by the votes of more than one-third of the members of the House of Commons or the legislative assembly, as the case may be.
Annual sitting of legislative bodies	5 There shall be a sitting of Parliament and of each legislature at least once every twelve months
Mobility of citizens Rights to move and gain livelihood Limitation Affirmative action programs	6 (1) Every citizen of Canada has the right to enter, remain in and leave Canada. (2) Every citizen of Canada and every person who has the status of a permanent resident of Canada has the right a) to move to and take up residence in any province; and b) to pursue the gaining of a livelihood in any province. (3) The rights specified in subsection (2) are subject to a) any laws or practices of general application in force in a province other than those that discriminate among persons primarily on the basis of province of present or previous residence; and b) any laws providing for reasonable residency requirements as a qualification for the receipt of publicly provided social services. (4) Subsections (2) and (3) do not preclude any law, program or activity that has as its object the amelioration in a province of conditions of individuals in that province who are socially or economically disadvantaged if the rate of employment in that province is below the rate of employment in Canada.

Appendix.
Canadian
Charter of
Rights and
Freedoms,
Schedule B

7–15(1)

Life, liberty and security of person	7	Everyone has the right to life, liberty and security of the person and the right not to be deprived thereof except in accordance with the principles of fundamental justice.
Search or seizure	8	Everyone has the right to be secure against unreasonable search or seizure.
Detention or imprisonment	9	Everyone has the right not to be arbitrarily detained or imprisoned.
Arrest or detention	10	Everyone has the right on arrest or detention a) to be informed promptly of the reasons therefor; b) to retain and instruct counsel without delay and to be informed of that right; and c) to have the validity of the detention determined by way of *habeas corpus* and to be released if the detention is not lawful.
Proceedings in criminal and penal matters	11	Any person charged with an offence has the right a) to be informed without unreasonable delay of the specific offence; b) to be tried within a reasonable time; c) not to be compelled to be a witness in proceedings against that person in respect of the offence; d) to be presumed innocent until proven guilty according to law in a fair and public hearing by an independent and impartial tribunal; e) not to be denied reasonable bail without just cause; f) except in the case of an offence under military law tried before a military tribunal, to the benefit of trial by jury where the maximum punishment for the offence is imprisonment for five years or a more severe punishment; g) not to be found guilty on account of any act or omission unless, at the time of the act or omission, it constituted an offence under Canadian or international law or was criminal according to the general principles of law recognized by the community of nations; h) if finally acquitted of the offence, not to be tried for it again and, if finally found guilty and punished for the offence, not to be tried or punished for it again; and i) if found guilty of the offence and if the punishment for the offence has been varied between the time of commission and the time of sentencing, to the benefit of the lesser punishment.
Treatment or punishment	12	Everyone has the right not to be subjected to any cruel and unusual treatment or punishment.
Self-crimination	13	A witness who testifies in any proceedings has the right not to have any incriminating evidence so given used to incriminate that witness in any other proceedings, except in a prosecution for perjury or for the giving of contradictory evidence.
Interpreter	14	A party or witness in any proceedings who does not understand or speak the language in which the proceedings are conducted or who is deaf has the right to the assistance of an interpreter.
Equality before and under law and equal protection and benefit of law	15	(1) Every individual is equal before and under the law and has the right to the equal protection and equal benefit of the law without discrimination and, in particular, without discrimination based on race, national or ethnic origin, colour, religion, sex, age or mental or physical disability.

Appendix.
Canadian
Charter of
Rights and
Freedoms,
Schedule B

15(2)–20(2)

Affirmative action programs	**15** (2) Subsection (1) does not preclude any law, program or activity that has as its object the amelioration of conditions of disadvantaged individuals or groups including those that are disadvantaged because of race, national or ethnic origin, colour, religion, sex, age or mental or physical disability.
Official languages of Canada	**16** (1) English and French are the official languages of Canada and have equality of status and equal rights and privileges as to their use in all institutions of the Parliament and government of Canada.
Official languages of New Brunswick	(2) English and French are the official languages of New Brunswick and have equality of status and equal rights and privileges as to their use in all institutions of the legislature and government of New Brunswick.
Advancement of status and use	(3) Nothing in this Charter limits the authority of Parliament or a legislature to advance the equality of status or use of English and French.
English and French linguistic communities in New Brunswick	**16.1** (1) The English linguistic community and the French linguistic community in New Brunswick have equality of status and equal rights and privileges, including the right to distinct educational institutions and such distinct cultural institutions as are necessary for the preservation and promotion of those communities.
Role of the legislature and government of New Brunswick	(2) The role of the legislature and government of New Brunswick to preserve and promote the status, rights and privileges referred to in subsection (1) is affirmed.
Proceedings of Parliament	**17** (1) Everyone has the right to use English or French in any debates and other proceedings of Parliament.
Proceedings of New Brunswick legislature	(2) Everyone has the right to use English or French in any debates and other proceedings of the legislature of New Brunswick.
Parliamentary statutes and records	**18** (1) The statutes, records and journals of Parliament shall be printed and published in English and French and both language versions are equally authoritative.
New Brunswick statutes and records	(2) The statutes, records and journals of the legislature of New Brunswick shall be printed and published in English and French and both language versions are equally authoritative.
Proceedings in courts established by Parliament	**19** (1) Either English or French may be used by any person in, or in any pleading in or process issuing from, any court established by Parliament.
Proceedings in New Brunswick courts	(2) Either English or French may be used by any person in, or in any pleading in or process issuing from, any court of New Brunswick.
Communications by public with federal institutions	**20** (1) Any member of the public in Canada has the right to communicate with, and to receive available services from, any head or central office of an institution of the Parliament or government of Canada in English or French, and has the same right with respect to any other office of any such institution where a) there is a significant demand for communications with and services from that office in such language; or b) due to the nature of the office, it is reasonable that communications with and services from that office be available in both English and French.
Communications by public with New Brunswick institutions	(2) Any member of the public in New Brunswick has the right to communicate with, and to receive available services from, any office of an institution of the legislature or government of New Brunswick in English or French.

Appendix.
Canadian
Charter of
Rights and
Freedoms,
Schedule B

21–25

Continuation of existing constitutional provisions	21 Nothing in sections 16 to 20 abrogates or derogates from any right, privilege or obligation with respect to the English and French languages, or either of them, that exists or is continued by virtue of any other provision of the Constitution of Canada.
Rights and privileges preserved	22 Nothing in sections 16 to 20 abrogates or derogates from any legal or customary right or privilege acquired or enjoyed either before or after the coming into force of this Charter with respect to any language that is not English or French.

Language of instruction	23 (1) Citizens of Canada
	   a) whose first language learned and still understood is that of the English or French linguistic minority population of the province in which they reside, or
	   b) who have received their primary school instruction in Canada in English or French and reside in a province where the language in which they received that instruction is the language of the English or French linguistic minority population of the province,
	have the right to have their children receive primary and secondary school instruction in that language in that province.

Continuity of language instruction	(2) Citizens of Canada of whom any child has received or is receiving primary or secondary school instruction in English or French in Canada, have the right to have all their children receive primary and secondary school instruction in the same language.

Application where numbers warrant	(3) The right of citizens of Canada under subsections (1) and (2) to have their children receive primary and secondary school instruction in the language of the English or French linguistic minority population of a province
	   a) applies wherever in the province the number of children of citizens who have such a right is sufficient to warrant the provision to them out of public funds of minority language instruction; and
	   b) includes, where the number of those children so warrants, the right to have them receive that instruction in minority language educational facilities provided out of public funds.

Enforcement of guaranteed rights and freedoms	24 (1) Anyone whose rights or freedoms, as guaranteed by this Charter, have been infringed or denied may apply to a court of competent jurisdiction to obtain such remedy as the court considers appropriate and just in the circumstances.
Exclusion of evidence bringing administration of justice into disrepute	(2) Where, in proceedings under subsection (1), a court concludes that evidence was obtained in a manner that infringed or denied any rights or freedoms guaranteed by this Charter, the evidence shall be excluded if it is established that, having regard to all the circumstances, the admission of it in the proceedings would bring the administration of justice into disrepute.

Aboriginal rights and freedoms not affected by Charter	25 The guarantee in this Charter of certain rights and freedoms shall not be construed so as to abrogate or derogate from any aboriginal, treaty or other rights or freedoms that pertain to the aboriginal peoples of Canada including
	   a) any rights or freedoms that have been recognized by the Royal Proclamation of October 7, 1763; and
	   b) any rights or freedoms that now exist by way of land claims agreements or may be so acquired.

Other rights and freedoms not affected by Charter	26 The guarantee in this Charter of certain rights and freedoms shall not be construed as denying the existence of any other rights or freedoms that exist in Canada.
Multicultural heritage	27 This Charter shall be interpreted in a manner consistent with the preservation and enhancement of the multicultural heritage of Canadians.
Rights guaranteed equally to both sexes	28 Notwithstanding anything in this Charter, the rights and freedoms referred to in it are guaranteed equally to male and female persons.
Rights respecting certain schools preserved	29 Nothing in this Charter abrogates or derogates from any rights or privileges guaranteed by or under the Constitution of Canada in respect of denominational, separate or dissentient schools.(93)
Application to territories and territorial authorities	30 A reference in this Charter to a Province or to the legislative assembly or legislature of a province shall be deemed to include a reference to the Yukon Territory and the Northwest Territories, or to the appropriate legislative authority thereof, as the case may be.
Legislative powers not extended	31 Nothing in this Charter extends the legislative powers of any body or authority.
Application of Charter	32 (1) This Charter applies a) to the Parliament and government of Canada in respect of all matters within the authority of Parliament including all matters relating to the Yukon Territory and Northwest Territories; and b) to the legislature and government of each province in respect of all matters within the authority of the legislature of each province. (2) Notwithstanding subsection (1), section 15 shall not have effect until three years after this section comes into force.
Exception where express declaration	33 (1) Parliament or the legislature of a province may expressly declare in an Act of Parliament or of the legislature, as the case may be, that the Act or a provision thereof shall operate notwithstanding a provision included in section 2 or sections 7 to 15 of this Charter.
Operation of exception	(2) An Act or a provision of an Act in respect of which a declaration made under this section is in effect shall have such operation as it would have but for the provision of this Charter referred to in the declaration.
Five year limitation	(3) A declaration made under subsection (1) shall cease to have effect five years after it comes into force or on such earlier date as may be specified in the declaration.
Re-enactment	(4) Parliament or the legislature of a province may re-enact a declaration made under subsection (1).
Five year limitation	(5) Subsection (3) applies in respect of a re-enactment made under subsection (4).
Citation	34 This Part may be cited as the *Canadian Charter of Rights and Freedoms*.

Appendix.
Canadian
Charter of
Rights and
Freedoms,
Schedule B

26–34

Active Citizenship, Social Workers, and Social Policy

Carol Kenny-Scherber

The renewed interest among political theorists in citizenship—particularly concepts of active citizenship—offers a framework for social workers to engage in the social policy arena. Active citizenship is founded on the concepts that: political activity is a particular and meaningful manner of living together (Arendt, 1998), inclusion within the civil and political collectives is foundational (Baralet, 1988), and making claims for self and others breaks the culture of silence (Drover & Kerans, 1993). To think as an active citizen is "to switch from a generally passive outlook [to one] generated by the adoption of a political identity as a significant part of one's mode of life" (Clarke, 1996, p. 5). Citizenship affords the opportunity to combine, in rather unusual ways, the "public" and "social" with the "individual" aspects of political life (Held, 1991). In an era of social and economic restructuring, the well-being of many individuals depends on social workers' actively promoting the public good and holding political authorities accountable. As Habermas (1992, p. 7) notes, "the institutions of constitutional freedom are only worth as much as a population makes of them." This classical view of citizenship seeks a vision of society as a community where deliberations on the public good transcend private interests and market individualism (Ignatieff, 1991).

I challenge social workers, regardless of their practice field, to actively participate in the public decision-making that determines the government's response to social issues. I arrived at this view through being employed by the Ontario provincial government as a senior policy adviser for fifteen years and, for twelve years before that, as a social worker assisting people experiencing chronic unemployment. A social work perspective informs the best advice that I bring to labour force development policy, regardless of the ideology of the governing party. The view that it is necessary to involve the public in political decision-making is hardly disputed in the literature (Rosener, 1978). However, there is controversy over the public's role and authority in the decision-making process (Barber, 1984). The postmodern view of policy analysis holds out the prospect that social workers' involvement in the political implications of identity construction can contribute to public policies (Schram, 1993). In writing this chapter, my objective is not to critique the policy process

but to highlight opportunities that are present in the system. For social workers to be active citizens, we require an understanding of the provincial government's policy process, knowledge of participation opportunities, and
intervention skills that can be put to use. Social workers bring something
unique to the policy process: an understanding of clients' life circumstances
and the social world, knowledge of how means and ends can work together,
and a commitment for social change based on inclusion.

The View from Inside the Policy System

A multitude of definitions have been put forward since the 1920s when Charles
Merriam initially identified the policy sciences as a "cross fertilization of politics with science,… or more strictly with modern methods of inquiry and
investigation" (1921, p. 181). Since Harold Lasswell (1951) identified the basic
characteristics, others have described public policy as the binding course of
action (Pal, 1987) that results from government making the most important
choices (Lasswell, 1951) about what to do or not to do (Dye, 1972) in setting public goals and selecting the means to achieve the identified outcomes (Jenkins,
1978). In day-to-day practice, policy development is affected by the new public management models (Charih & Rouillard, 1997); the degree to which the
necessary decisions are imbedded (Jenkins, 1978); and the numbers of ministries, other governments, and non-governmental organizations involved
(J. Anderson, 1984). Public policy is critically important to social workers and
their clients because it is through policy that

- society's responsibilities to its citizens are defined;
- the group or individual entitlement to society's resources are identified;
- the allocation and distribution of society's resources are determined; and
- the group(s) or sector(s) that make these decisions is given the authority.

Key decisions will continue to be made by government, but there is still the
question of whether and by what means social workers will have input as the
decisions are being formulated. Significant systemic barriers certainly exist
within our governance system; however, through my own work, I recognize
that there are opportunities social workers could use to influence the system
that are not currently being used to their advantage.

Although policy development proceeds through a number of steps, the
logical linear models (J. Anderson, 1984; Brewer, 1974; Jones, 1984) do not do
justice to the realities. The linear models also do not account for globalization,
international policy convergence, society's institutional values, ideologies of
the decision makers, and the lessons drawn from past experiences. I have
experienced policy as a complicated and time-consuming strategy process
defying the logic of planning models. In this neo-conservative period, policy
is about trying to solve very complex issues in an environment characterized
by powerful transnational companies, high public expectations, confronta-
tional politics, competing and vocal stakeholders, intense media scrutiny,

and a distrustful citizenry. On any issue, the objectives being pursued are broad, with numerous considerations that must be taken into account, few reliable reference points, and a diverse range of stakeholders' interests. The "wicked" problems of contemporary policy demand continuous examination to understand the pressures and tensions acting on them and the potential solutions. Edelman argues:

The View from Inside the Policy System

> Problems come into discourse and therefore into existence as reinforcements of ideologies, not just simply because they are there or because they are important for well-being. They signify who are virtuous and useful and who are dangerous and inadequate, which actions will be rewarded and which penalized. They constitute people as subjects with particular kinds of aspirations, self-concepts, and fears, and they create beliefs about the relative importance of events and objects. They are critical in determining who exercises authority and who accepts it. They construct areas of immunity from concern because those areas are not seen as problems. Like leaders and enemies, they define the contours of the social world, not in the same way for everyone, but in the light of the diverse situations from which people respond to the political spectacle. (Edelman, 1988, pp. 12–13)

Governments and their networks maintain an ongoing discourse, articulating, interpreting, and creating public dialogue to discern the public problem. Public policies are simply the political agreements reached in the practical world where values and facts are inextricably interwoven (Fisher, 1980). Through legislation, regulation, rules, protocols, and access to media, governments not only define access to public resources, but they also attempt to gain acceptance and support for their ideological framing of problems and solutions. What constitutes legitimate need, who has authority to define the need, what government's obligations are, and what program design tools the bureaucracy will use to respond to the need are continuously being examined.

Kingdon (1984) best describes policy-making as it is practised in the working lives of governments. In his model, three "families" of simultaneous processes operate, pursuing courses largely independent of each other until critical points in time when their intersecting paths create policy windows (see Figure 5.1). First, the stream of problems gains the attention of government policy-makers through a media crisis, government question period, formal inquiries, and stakeholder pressure. Second, the community of policy specialists, including bureaucrats and their external expert contacts, is continuously contributing to the mix of the policy "stew" as they refine their understanding of the problems and available responses. Policy entrepreneurs connect and participate informally by joining the process before it formally begins. Third, the value systems of Cabinet members, proximity of an election period, party policy conventions, interest groups with access to government members, and public opinion as constructed by the media encompass the political stream (Wharf & McKenzie, 1998). Kingdon argues:

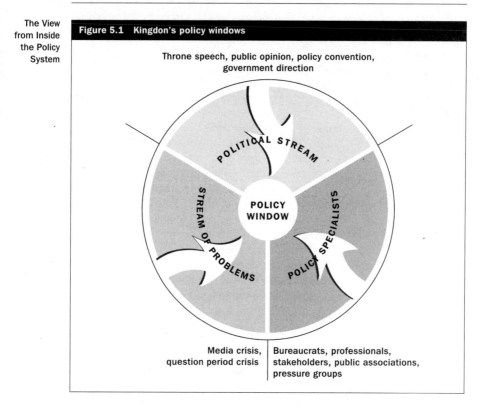

Figure 5.1   Kingdon's policy windows

Throne speech, public opinion, policy convention,
government direction

POLITICAL STREAM

STREAM OF PROBLEMS

POLICY SPECIALISTS

POLICY WINDOW

Media crisis,
question period crisis

Bureaucrats, professionals,
stakeholders, public associations,
pressure groups

> Windows are opened either by the appearance of compelling problems
> or by happenings in the political stream.... Policy entrepreneurs, people
> who are willing to invest their resources in pushing their pet proposals or
> problems, are responsible not only for prompting important people to
> pay attention, but also for coupling solutions to problems and for cou-
> pling both problems and solutions to politics. (quoted in Wharf & McKen-
> zie, 1998)

At some critical juncture, problems, policies, and politics converge; solutions
are joined to problems and both of them are joined to political forces (Kingdon, 1984). The three streams provide a first view of the opportunities for
influencing the definition of the problem, contributing to technical understanding of problems and their solutions, building linkages with policy specialists, and seeking opportunities to influence political party visions. Each is
an avenue for social workers to contribute their professional understanding
of their clients' life experiences, leadership and planning techniques, and
community building skills.

Policy windows may be triggered by regularly scheduled items such as
throne speeches, budget speeches, and estimates process, or by unplanned
external events initiated by a media crisis, pressure groups, release of inquest
findings, or a difficult question during question period. Developing policy

within the available window is increasingly complex as governments make efforts to develop solutions that cut across policy fields, government ministries, and other levels of government. One recent effort in Ontario is the creation of policy clusters that group ministries with common policy interests, enabling staff-level advisers to better work together.

From an Idea to Government Policy

Regardless of their own personal views on the issues, policy advisers are expected to serve the elected government with neutrality, anonymity, and loyalty (Kernaghan & Langford, 1990). Working in a mode of non-partisanship requires that civil servants not publicly criticize government policies or "not at any time speak in public or express views in writing for distribution to the public on any matter that forms part of the platform of a provincial or federal political party" (Kernaghan & Langford, 1990, p. 80). The traditional public service model requires that public discussion of policy be restricted to ministers; public servants are to avoid discussing "advice or recommendations tendered to Ministers" and speculating "about policy deliberations or future policy decisions" (p. 81). Gordon Robertson, a former secretary to the federal Cabinet, argued,

> anonymity... involves a substantial act of self-denial. It means an unwillingness to hint at influential association with policies or decisions; refusal to give the private briefing to a journalist; avoidance of photographs with key individuals; and eschewing the physical trappings of status that are demonstrations to the beholders of unspoken power and importance. (Robertson, 1983, p. 13)

An increased emphasis on public participation in government decision-making by bringing public servants into public forums has somewhat blurred these lines.

With the growth of policy networks, the monopoly position of career civil servants in the provision of advice to ministers is a thing of the past. At the same time, the need for quality advice founded on knowledge, research, and evaluation, tempered by informed practical experience, is even more critical given the proliferation of external sources of advice, public policy commentary, and special interest pleading by advocacy groups. The political debate that arises from claims on the public system is a struggle to give meaning to the world by defining legitimate participants, issues, and alliances. To be effective, social workers need to understand the policy system and its processes.

From an Idea to Government Policy

In a very practical way, the opportunities for social workers to be active citizens and influence public policy is largely determined by the policy infrastructure within governments and their bureaucracies. Recognizing that the systems are largely hidden to those who are outside of them, this section describes the functions within three distinct locations: the political party, the legislative structure, and the pre-legislative or bureaucratic process. Each, depending on its culture and organizational system, holds unique opportunities for social workers to contribute to the policy process.

The Political Phase

For a number of reasons, provincial and federal political parties have not made much genuine effort to develop in-house policy capacity. The two most significant reasons are that, for parties not in power, it is difficult to keep supporters politically active between elections; and for the party in power, the policy process is highly confidential and contained mostly within the caucus and the Cabinet. Weak policy capacity within the political parties has contributed to the growing influence of interest groups and independent think tanks (Baier & Bakvis, 2001). The vision and strategies of political parties are usually determined by some combination of the party leaders, executive, and members: either by the small group surrounding the party leader, or the party executive and the internal policy committees, or at conventions including the grassroots of the membership. The opinions of individual members, particularly Cabinet members, have an important bearing in formulating party positions, but this occurs behind the scenes and has little bearing on the House and its committees (White, 1997). Party leaders enjoy a dominant position and in most cases are able to impose their views on the party. In fact, almost nothing that occurs in the Legislature can be understood except through the lens of the party and the leader.

According to Robert Young (1991, p. 77), Canada's political parties "desperately need a stronger capacity to formulate policy…. In a self-reinforcing cycle, people with genuine policy concerns seek out interest groups to advance their causes, and the parties degenerate further into domination by leaders and their personal entourages, who play the politics of image and strategic vagueness." In fact, this is very descriptive of the manner in which the 1994 Ontario Conservative Party's Common Sense Revolution was crafted by a small group of the party executive, senior staff, and youth wing leaders (Jeffery, 1999). Some parties, as a means of building grassroots support, seek more inclusive methods. The Ontario Liberal Party has modelled itself after the federal party, endorsing a grassroots system of policy committees at the riding level that then contributes resolutions at policy conventions (Ontario Liberal Party, 1993). The Ontario Liberal Party policy convention in March 2001 provided opportunity for riding association representatives, party executive, and members of Parliament to hear and meet with international policy experts. Solidarity and dialogue underlie the policy resolution process of the Ontario New Democrats. The resolutions adopted at the convention held in June 2000 form the basis of party policy and direct the activities of the executive and the caucus (Ontario New Democrats, 2000). Regardless of the process and degree of inclusiveness, once a party is elected, this policy vision forms the government's direction for the next four to five years of government activity.

The Legislative Phase

From an
Idea to
Government
Policy

The most visible location of policy-making is the provincial Legislature. West-minster[1] government, as found in Canada and its provinces, is centred on ministers who are individually and collectively responsible to the House of Commons for the policies and programs of government. In the traditional Westminster model, ministers lead departments that are staffed with career civil servants. Each minister is also supported by political staff, whose job it is to advise the minister of his or her party's politics, as well as its policy preferences. On the Westminster system, White (1989, pp. 73–74) writes, "these are in the nature of zero-order beliefs—so primal as to be accepted without justification and scarcely susceptible to rational challenge. They include the concept of responsible government, the notion of a loyal opposition, party discipline, and ministerial responsibility."

In debating the issues of the day, the Legislature brings new problems to public attention, educates the public about those problems and possible solutions to them, and enables the voters to assess the positions of the political parties. The Legislature legitimizes support for government policy by providing legal authorization for laws and government spending, and it encourages people to accept measures that they dislike because of the perception that decisions made by their elected representatives reflect public opinion and public involvement as central elements (White, 1997). A brief description of the activities of the House follows.

Formal executive authority is vested in the Crown's representative, the lieutenant-governor, but exercised by the premier and the ministers of the Executive Council or the Cabinet. Ministers are accountable to the House of Commons for their exercise of executive authority, initiating legislation and administering public affairs. The throne speech, read by the lieutenant-governor at the opening of the session, details the government's plan for its agenda and policies. The subsequent budget presents the financial estimate for the new and ongoing policy initiatives and identifies the funding source.

Legislation is introduced into the House in the form of public bills (government bills are introduced by a Cabinet minister) and private bills (introduced by any other member of provincial Legislature). Government bills are the end product of processes of consensus building within Cabinet, between Cabinet and caucus, and between senior administrators and political advisers. Once a government bill is introduced to the Legislature, it is expected to pass with the full support of the caucus, barring opposition stalling, shifting government priorities, being held up in committee, or dying on the order paper when the House dissolves. Party discipline and the tendency of the electoral system to produce majority governments, combined with the considerable resources of the governing party, create a solid and predictable block of support for government initiatives.

At the introduction of new legislation, the speaker of the House moves that "leave be given to introduce the bill entitled (bill named) and the same to be read for the first time" (White, 1989). The member's brief statement explaining the bill's principles is followed by a vote on whether to accept the bill for future debate. If accepted, it is assigned a number, printed, and scheduled for second reading debate several days later. This allows MPPs time to study the proposed bill and the opposition parties to caucus on it. The second reading debate is the opportunity for the MPPs to make statements on the principles of the bill. Following the debate, a unanimous vote of all members present in the House will enable a bill to bypass the committee stage and be ordered for third reading. Other bills receiving a majority vote are referred to committee.

The decision of whether to send a bill to the committee of the whole or a standing committee is made by the minister introducing the bill, usually in consultation with the House leaders. In addition to reviewing and amending proposed legislation, standing committees, with their all-party representation, also conduct special inquiries into proposed policy changes that are not associated with a particular bill. Tradition expects that standing committees will hold public hearings, call for expert witnesses, hear directly from ministry staff, and accept submissions and oral presentations from private citizens and stakeholder groups (White, 1989). The committee also has the option of calling for public hearings before its clause-by-clause treatment or holding public hearings on specific clauses. Since meetings are less formal than House sittings and MPPs engage in real discussions among themselves and with witnesses, committees offer much greater scope for influencing policy. This is influenced by the extent to which the government members are open to advice and the degree to which committee members set aside partisan differences rather than scoring political points. Committee attention to an issue often raises public concern, which may force the government to modify a policy (White, 1997). Amendments may also arise independent of the committee process from the bureaucracy's interpretation of the public's concerns about the bill. Once the work of the standing committee is completed, the amended bill is returned to the House. Making a presentation to a standing committee and networking with government staff assigned to support the process provides an opportunity for social workers to use their expertise to reframe the problems and present concrete solutions for changes. Individual and professional credibility can and does affect the recommendations developed by the standing committee. Making formal presentations is one venue for social workers to inject social knowledge into the process.

At third reading the bill is voted on by the members without debate, or it may be returned to the standing committee with instructions to make specific amendments. Following third reading, the bill receives royal assent from the lieutenant-governor; the lieutenant-governor has the constitutional authority to withhold royal assent, but in practice this does not occur. Royal assent and proclamation dates are set by the Cabinet. The most common reason for delaying implementation is to allow the bureaucracy to put the administrative machinery in place.

Almost all government bills contain a crucial provision authorizing the government to issue legally binding "regulations" that set out details of the policy without requiring any approval from the Legislature. The consequence is that vast areas of policy-making do not come under the scrutiny of elected members (White, 1997). This is a serious weakness in the Legislature's ability to hold the government accountable.

The Pre-legislative Phase

In Westminster-style Parliaments, many critical decisions are made by the Cabinet and the bureaucracy out of the public eye during the pre-legislative phase. Although a great number of policy issues arise, many initiatives are rejected, significantly revised, or ascribed such a low priority that they fall off the policy agenda. Policy advisers work in an environment fraught with dynamic tensions: political versus administrative responsibility for policy development, values versus technically driven policy, centralized versus coordinated models of development, and, finally, closed versus participative design models.

Internal policy units, producing analysis and advice for ministers and senior public servants, are located in the central agencies and throughout the line ministries. The central agencies oversee the functions of government policy approval and coordination, fiscal planning, fiscal approval, and government human resources planning. In Ontario, these agencies include the Cabinet Office, the Management Board, the Ministry of Finance, and SuperBuild.[2] As information-seeking and processing groups, they are concerned with policy development, program planning and design, liaison, quantitative and qualitative research, and, occasionally, evaluation. The relative emphasis placed on individual functions varies among ministries and can vary within the same policy unit over time. There has been very little variation in the primary policy functions since their inception (Prince, 1979):

- problem definition: clarifying, articulating, and interpreting problem "inputs"
- policy development: defining objectives or policies, conducting priority reviews
- program design: designing concrete courses of action to achieve policy evaluation: examining policies to determine if they have or will achieve their objectives
- socio-economic research and forecasting: research projects, long-term scanning, scenario writing, and extrapolations
- policy firefighting: short-term work under pressure, "quick and dirty" studies on "hot" issues
- coordination and liaison: coordinating operational and long-term plans of a number of branches, providing liaison within the ministry, and with other ministries, the federal government, and interest groups

In addition, policy groups act as gatekeepers to the system by screening and reducing the demands made on ministries and their deputies. In some groups "firefighting," whether intended or not, dominates and may even prevent the development of planning and evaluation roles. Other constraints and considerations include insufficient resources (time, staff, position classifications, and facilities), difficulties in recruiting and retaining qualified personnel, the inexperience of some advisers, the absence of relevant data, and technical problems in the use of analytic methods. Lacking support and access to the deputy minister, some groups have remained outside the mainstream of the ministry policy processes. In a reorganization, a change in the title or location of a group often signifies changes in relations to clients, status in the ministry, intended policy roles, or an effort to reduce past bureaucratic antagonisms (Meltsner, 1976). The policy strategy is determined through an interactive process between the policy groups and their clients (clients are the minister, senior management, and members of the immediate policy network).

Understanding the dynamic tensions within the bureaucracy's role begins with the policy-administration dichotomy (Doern & Phidd, 1988). The crux of the tension is the bureaucracy's role in being sensitive to the political objectives and constraints, while initiating policy ideas and "massaging" policy proposals. During the drafting of Cabinet documents and memoranda, staff-level advisers attempt to bring the right nuance of meaning, provide the best supporting data, and develop the most cost-effective analysis while maintaining the integrity of the minister's policy vision. Advisers engage in constant discussions "up the tube" to the minister through the deputy and across ministerial lines and central agency officials. Frequently, there is also contact with outside interests and with other levels of government. Ideally, the end product of this iterative process is a polished Cabinet document, a mixture of verbal and written exchange of views, and scientific and technical rationality, bounded by a values framework. It should not come as a surprise that some ministers hold the view that their excellent ideas are sabotaged by the bureaucracy, while the bureaucracy holds the opinion that citizens may have been saved from some hare-brained schemes.

Fisher (1980) points out that the major difficulties encountered by policy-makers in policy development are inherently linked to the treatment of values. From the outset, policy advisers pay attention to the political dimensions of policy values, recruitment of political support, and accommodating contradictory goals. Dror (1968, p. 35) argued against the exclusion of the political as the technical side of the policy sciences was gaining predominance, insisting on "the need for evaluation of the probability that a policy will be sufficiently acceptable to the various secondary political decision makers, executors, interest groups and publics whose participation or acquiescence is needed for it to be translated into political action."

There are two problem-solving sequences that tend to operate parallel to each other in any policy formulation process: What is the mix required between a political or a technical response? Bureaucracy staff intent upon ascertaining the political acceptability or feasibility of a policy must evaluate whether it generates support for the particular political party that will propose it. One question becomes key: In the current environment, what solution is most likely to attain the policy goals? The technical skills that analysts bring to the process are set into this framework and define the methodologies, selection of data, analysis tools, evaluation criteria, and selection of options for determining the choice of directions. As Faludi and Voogd (1986) note, one can accept as a given that political and moral factors will be part of the policy and planning process, but that does not rule out using rationality as a decision-making rule. Rationality is the pragmatic way for policy advisers to negotiate the recognition of diverse political values, recruitment of political support, and accommodation of contradictory goals and objectives. Analysts become adept at the language of rationality and its application in well-prepared arguments to position problems, goals, and potential solutions within the ideology of the party forming the government (Fisher, 1980).

The current effort to achieve greater policy coordination is driven by pressure to reduce government expenditure, eliminate perceived duplication, ensure internal coherence, and establish consistent policy priorities. The challenging task is to find ways of making the activities of policy groups compatible with those that have similar responsibilities, while at the same time complying with the legal rules of confidentiality in very narrow time frames. Some bureaucrats argue that timely policy development is burdened by the current state-of-the-art system of stewarding policy advice through a galaxy of approval structures: central agency committees, cross-ministry deputies committees, assistant deputy minister cross-ministry committees, staff-level interministerial working groups, and third-party working groups. The problems of working across divisions and ministries are compounded when the issues of coordination across levels of government is added (Toonen, 1985), especially in federal regimes such as Canada.

From a policy perspective, the results of rights talk and cultural pluralism is that stakeholders expect to be consulted on public decisions. Putting this expectation into practice raises issues of managing public expectation of what will become of their advice. For the policy analyst, consultations are another source of information and advice contributing to the policy "stew"; however, those who are consulted want to see their contributions reflected. Considering the range of stakeholder views, this is not possible. In practice, policy advisers seek a balance between competing interests while keeping the government's vision central. Pal maintains that consultation should

> focus on the operational and programmatic level, as opposed to broad values or directions for policy development.... This distinguishes consultation as a policy management activity from broader forms of political representation, such as parliamentary committee hearings on a piece of legislation.... The objective is ongoing development and management of the policy or program in question, not the establishment of parameters for political discussion and debate. (Pal, 1987, p. 218)

From an Idea to Government Policy

From the political perspective, consultations also have their inherent dangers. Civil servants who are put in the public spotlight bleed power away from the elected ministers; in the public mind, they become the figures who seem to "really" decide (Mitchell & Sutherland, 1997). Placing mid-level policy staff in direct contact with both politicians and the stakeholders also contributes to blurring their respective roles in the minds of the public.

Social Workers as Active Citizens

This section covers the wide range of opportunities social workers can involve themselves in to influence government, particularly during the between-elections period. For social workers, the key to being active citizens is to connect the macropractice of policy to our micropractices within social work. The most important avenues of influence are the accumulation of small opportunities that arise through building networks within the broader world of our practice lives. In referring to Milbrath's work, Verba, Nie, and Kim wrote in early 1971 (p. 10) that "there are not only gladiators and non-gladiators, but different types of gladiators with different goals using different political techniques." Participation is multidimensional. Social workers can choose where to engage and also the degree of their involvement. What we bring to the policy network is our social knowledge of the everyday world, knowledge accumulated through our day-to-day work with our clients. Our first-hand experience of the impacts when conflicting and overlapping policies are operationalized and our knowledge of practical program delivery are invaluable. As we think through our commitment to participation, we must consider three decisions: whether to act or not; in which direction the act should be focused; and what should be the intensity, the duration, and the degree.

Once we decide to act, the first step is to develop an avid interest in the policy decisions being made that directly affect our work with our clients. I prefer the analogy of following a social policy field as though it is a sport. Know the issues, the players, their positions, and their playing history. Know the rules of the game and how it is being played. Understanding how decisions are reached identifies new possibilities of methods and timing of interventions. To plan strategy, social workers should begin by seeking answers to these questions:

- How "hot" is the problem?
- How has the problem evolved?
- Have there been earlier attempts at solutions?
- Is more research needed?
- Who has a vested interest in particular solutions?
- Are there limitations on possible solutions?
- Who are potential allies on all sides of the issue?

It is not enough to know what was said and done; social workers must also grasp the motives behind those actions in order to anticipate future moves.

Action in policy development must be understood as part of the complex patterns of interaction with other members of the policy community (Blumer, 1969). From the outset, it is necessary to analyze the many stakeholders both as groups and as individual players. Each has a different view of the problem and its preferred solutions and, in turn, each is attempting to use networks to see a preferred solution implemented.

Social Workers as Policy Entrepreneurs

Opportunities for Participation

In planning an action strategy, individual social workers should also consider in which arena their interests lie: family violence, child welfare, human rights, health care, homelessness, etc. Although there are similarities in the intervention required within the different environments, the actual influences on policy may be quite different. Patterns of activity meant to influence policy decision-making also have an additive characteristic. This is true in two senses: activities within one environment relate to activities in the other environment, and there is a hierarchy of involvement in that participants at one level also tend to perform many of the same actions, including those performed at lower levels of involvement. For instance, efforts to influence government policy about child welfare may well affect decision-making in the area of family violence. People who are likely to make a presentation to a standing committee are also likely to engage in lower-level activities like writing letters to their MPP or signing petitions. Participation's cumulative characteristics arise from the fact that social workers who engage in the topmost behaviours are very likely to perform those lower in the rank also.

The opportunities I propose build on the work of Milbrath (1965), Verba, Nie, and Kim (1971), and Langton (1978). (See Table 5.1.) The activities provide a great deal of flexibility for social workers to use their broad range of skills in a wide variety of contexts. While the listing is helpful, it is meant only as a starting point to examine our skills and our interests. In addition to our interpersonal skills, as social workers we bring certain skills from our practice fields: alliance building, conflict resolution, written communications, public speaking, best practices knowledge, and understanding of our clients' lives.

Social Workers as Policy Entrepreneurs

To be policy entrepreneurs, either inside or outside of government as Kingdon (1984) describes, social workers must be ready to advocate for selected problems and solutions to be given a high priority in the policy arena, prompting policy-makers to pay attention. I expect that social workers, moving in the direction of policy entrepreneurship, are motivated by a combination of several factors:

- straightforward concern about certain problems that they witness on an ongoing basis
- pursuit of benefits for their clients, profession, and/or workplaces

- the promotion of social work values within an identified policy field
- the satisfaction of participating and influencing the policy process on behalf of their clients and profession

Our claim to be heard as social workers has three sources: professional expertise, understanding of our clients, and knowledge gained from front-line service delivery. When combined with network building, negotiating skills, and political connections, the combination could be more influential than each quality taken separately. When we advocate for use of our definitions of the problems and the solutions, social work values and social knowledge gained from practice will affect the shape of social policy. To be successful policy advocates, we must be persistent and spend a great deal of time giving talks, writing papers, sending letters, attending meetings, and power lunching, all with the aim of pushing our ideas in whatever way and forum might further client-centred solutions (see Table 5.1).

The key to being successful policy entrepreneurs lies in doing continuous preparatory work and then waiting for the policy window to open (Kingdon, 1984). Our ideas, policy expertise, and proposals must be developed well in advance of the policy window opening. Early preparation and planning is critical; waiting until the policy window opens to develop our proposals is waiting too long. By continuously monitoring the policy context, we will become sensitive to subtle shifts in the environment, we will read the timing of the policy windows extremely well, and we will be in a position to move at the right moment. An important outcome of reading a changing environment is that we will be alert to the nuances and will be able to position ourselves in relation to other stakeholders.

Even though casting a single vote in an election has an extremely low influence on policy, social workers should exercise their franchise and encourage their clients to do so as well. Deciding which party to support prompts us to ask questions, discuss future policy direction, and analyze what it may mean for our work. Most parties acknowledge that their policy capacity is weak, hence social workers bringing knowledge, researched ideas, and professional best practices are likely to be well received. Advanced volunteer work within a party brings social workers in closer contact with the centre of the political system. At a minimum, social workers should be attending public meetings and using this opportunity to discuss issues and share visions with other citizens, politicians, and administrators. When politicians and/or bureaucrats engage in discussion, particularly following the initial meeting, make a concerted effort to follow up in writing, thanking them for the opportunity to speak with them and inquiring about some specific aspect that in your opinion requires change. Town hall meetings are a prime opportunity to develop a network of like-minded people who will support social workers' proposed solutions. Moving a solution to the forefront is about building opportunities and support across individuals and groups. Although it may take a number of years to build networks and move ideas ahead, fresh solu-

Table 5.1 Opportunities for participation

ENVIRONMENT	INTERVENTIONS	INFLUENCE ON POLICY
POLITICAL		
Election campaign	• Voting, pamphlet distribution, public contact on issues, discussion with candidate	• Extremely minimal, influence dependent on election outcome
Ridings association executive member	• Networking, volunteer on riding and regional policy committees, informal discussion with party members and MPPs, representation at policy conventions	• Collective outcome, encourage MPP to carry messages to caucus, coalition building, lobbying MPPs and executive
Executive position	• Strategy planning, local candidate selection, contact with Cabinet members at conventions/ meetings	• Highest influence, access to backroom, lobbying caucus; only big issues discussed at Cabinet
ADVOCACY/ADVISORY		
Citizen initiated	• Contact with politician/ bureaucrat on single issue, individual problems	• Extremely minimal, usually self-interest
Issue orientation	• Local, requires ongoing lobbying, media publicity; goal is to have politician take up the cause	• Can achieve or avert specific decisions; little influence on policy
Pressure group	• Membership in larger organiza-tion, staffed through donations, internal specialized policy exper-tise, confrontation, and/or lobbying	• Degree of influence determined by prestige, power, contacts; multiple accesses to system
Advisory group	• Invited expertise, subgovern-ment, interface with bureaucracy	• Continuous discrete influence; change in government may be detrimental
PROFESSIONAL		
Individual worker	• Contact with politician/ opposition/bureaucrat on single policy impact, letter writing, lobbying on change status, advocates for service user	• Contribution to policy stew, builds foundation for ongoing contacts with politicians, opposition, and bureaucrats, contributes from practice field
Agency representative	• Agency identifies client and organization issues, approach fits organization's decision models, coordinated through agency, letter writing, media, meetings, lobbying	• Build linkages to advisory group status, perceived as advocate for agency, networks with similar agencies
Association	• Builds coalitions across practice fields, educates membership, meetings and lobbying, position papers, presentations, briefings	• Facilitates policy discussion across practice fields and agencies, adds credibility to expert input, ongoing input to policy process

Social Workers as Policy Entrepreneurs

tions brought forward when the timing is right can have great impact. Political party participation provides many opportunities to become involved locally, regionally, and nationally in the system.

The first year of a new government is clearly the prime time for preoccupation with the subject of policy change. During a change of government, people throughout the policy communities watch to identify the political climate of the new government and anticipate the opening of policy windows. During the election campaign and throughout the transition period, policy entrepreneurs will sense the mood and seize opportunities to promote or restructure some of the items on their policy agendas. Where two or more levels of government have jurisdiction over a policy field, policy entrepreneurs may actually enhance their opportunities to move a solution ahead as the various players vie with one another for the credit and claim to jurisdiction.

As policy entrepreneurs, we must seek out opportunities to build linkages into policy networks and create support for our framing of the problems and solutions. As we build networks, we also build public profile for the problems we are concerned about. We can speak publicly, secure press coverage, and meet regularly with people who may be able to influence the policy-makers. Informal networking builds deeper linkages into our communities and governments. It requires only a minimal amount of ingenuity to create linkages into the bureaucracy by using government web sites to locate middle-level bureaucrats with policy responsibility for our fields of interest. Making contacts in a collegial manner and then sharing our concept of the problem, our research and best practices, and our thoughts on a potential solution takes our social knowledge into the policy fields. Invite policy staff for an informal visit to your agency, ask them to speak at a staff meeting, or perhaps provide an opportunity for them to hear from your clients. Staff enjoy and learn from opportunities to see and experience what they have been reading and writing about. As information packages are prepared for the deputy or the minister, the good ideas acquired from on-site visits or submitted in writing have a chance of being included. Policy analysts often network informally across ministries and will share well-researched information with their colleagues. Kingdon (1984) refers to the process as the "primeval soup" of policy. Through networking, policy analysts and social workers can become working partners. Both groups have similar objectives—to build a better system—except that policy analysts must also work within the vision of their political masters.

Social workers can further make use of networking opportunities to take ideas and float them as trial balloons, solicit reactions, revise proposals in the light of reactions, and float the ideas again. As good strategists, we can look at situations and see elements that have been there all along but were not noticed before. Making the most of an opportunity for a private meeting with the minister or senior bureaucrat responsible for the issue, perhaps at a conference, can focus the issues and contribute to moving the problem higher on the policy agenda. Often a private meeting can be formally requested through the minister's office staff after the commitment has been made for the minister to attend. Through contact with policy-makers, social workers will become more sensitive to the nuances of problem definition and will be able to seize opportunities to present their solution as the preferable option. These meetings may prompt an ongoing policy dialogue about current governmental/program performance through letters, complaints, and visits to officials.

Making contact with the Official Opposition and all the parties in opposition can be very fruitful. The members of the shadow cabinet are constantly looking for any weaknesses in the policies and administration of the party in power. In opposing the governing party, they express their own views, the views of their supporters, and the views of interest groups that may hold the balance of voter power in the next election. Briefing the opposition parties can be critical; in fact, they often welcome input in their preparation for question period and for their policies, particularly when the next election is approaching. Some opposition party members may even ask stakeholder representatives for assistance on certain legislative initiatives that they hope to move forward upon forming the new government (Sarpkaya, 1988).

Lastly, there is a vital role for social workers in softening the views of the mass public, specialized interest groups, and the policy community itself. According to Kingdon (1984), policy entrepreneurs play two different roles—advocates and brokers—both very familiar to social workers. Not only should we advocate for our ideas and solutions and soften up the process, but we should also act as brokers, negotiating among the policy actors, making critical connections, and capitalizing on opportunities as they present themselves. From our practices with individuals and communities, social workers understand that change is not achieved through a single intervention effort, and likewise significant policy change will require substantial involvement.

Briefings, Meetings, and Presentations

Most formal transfer of information between social workers and politicians and bureaucrats concerning significant problems and proposed solutions will take place in pre-arranged briefing sessions, meetings, and formal presentations. No matter how well planned, meetings with policy-makers can take a sudden turn from one subject to another, or the ebb and flow of discussion can quickly alter the intended dynamics and the tone of a meeting. Members of the public who are participating in briefings and making presentations do not always maximize face-to-face contact. Social workers attending briefings as expert witnesses are not always expert communicators. Hurried politicians and bureaucrats compound the tension by pressing for crisp information. Capitalizing on opportunities is about grasping procedural opportunities and delivering clear messages. This section sets the foundation for planning and managing presentations.

Getting on the policy agenda at the earliest stage is crucial to advancing an issue, and considering the tight schedules of policy-makers, pre-meetings

Social Workers as Policy Entrepreneurs

and briefings must be very focused. Briefing materials should be prepared and submitted in advance so there is time for the policy-makers to review and consult with staff prior to the briefing. In a short covering letter, be very clear about the issue to be addressed and what recommendations and what decisions, if any, will be sought (Fraatz, 1982). Before you actually present your information, it is important to know that there are two questions foremost in the mind of every minister or politician: Are we doing the right thing? Will this help or hurt our re-election chances? Pre-meetings may allow policy-makers to flag controversial issues, build mutual understanding on issues, and possibly make future discussions more productive.

Constantinou (1995) suggests a number of points that, in my view, are extremely helpful to social workers when preparing for a briefing session. First, understand the minister's perspective and background, and what is important to him or her about the issue. Knowing about his or her background helps to identify loyalties, values, favourite causes, and approaches to problem solving. Through talking with other people, scan the big picture related to your proposed solution so that it can be positioned with the preferred spin. Since policy-makers are often victims of information overload, consider what you think the minister needs to know to make an informed decision, including differentiation between advice and facts. Always anticipate questions and be prepared with answers. A positive approach that reveals an interest in finding answers is always more successful than a presentation that purports to have all the answers or does not consider alternative approaches. It is imperative that when seeking decisions time be allowed for consideration of what has been presented. Building effective working relations with the minister's staff can cultivate important allies and add legitimacy to your efforts in getting the minister's support. Lastly, consider whether the proposal will be well received by stakeholders, agencies, and the general public. This will weigh heavily with a minister making important choices.

We can also take advantage of the opportunities in the policy process when input on an issue or piece of legislation is invited from the public. These are royal commissions, legislative committees, task forces, appeal boards, advisory councils, public consultations, and responses to discussion papers. Although many members of the public feel that they are not listened to during the formal process, it is my experience that a creative and viable solution—well presented—will often find its way into the policy "stew," and if not used immediately, may be resurrected at a later time. Bureaucrats often provide administrative support to many public hearing procedures, so that a strong idea not picked up by the political side may surface again through bureaucratic input (White, 1997). Oral presentations and written briefs should be framed by

- clearly articulating the problem;
- specifying what is not working now and why;
- presenting the data or best-practice examples on what could be a solution;

and
* proposing well-thought-out amendments or viable alternative solutions.

In presenting briefs to committees, commissions, and task forces, the challenge is to be comfortable with the players, the process, and the rules of engagement—and using this knowledge to deliver your message in such a way as to influence decisions. As McInnes (1999, p. 2) writes, "Your 15 minutes have to stand out." The most important task in making a presentation is to make a positive impact with your remarks and your submission. No matter how well prepared you may be, appearing before a parliamentary committee can be unpredictable. There is a long list of decisions to make before actually sitting down at the committee table, such as deciding who will go, who will represent your group, the length of the brief, etc. The most important decisions involve crafting the key messages.

Regular checks of the standing committee web site will keep social workers informed about work assigned to committees, the dates, and the locations.[3] Social workers who wish to make presentations to standing committees should contact the clerk assigned to the committee about appearing, explain why they should be heard, and if possible, contact a member of the committee to advocate for them. If you are refused an invitation, look for allies in professional associations, networks of service deliverers, or local governments to form a coalition and carry your message. At a minimum, submit a written brief to the committee, the committee researchers, and the bureaucracy; they may be interested in your fresh perspective on an old problem.

Since the work of committees is to look at the big policy issues, presenters often think they have to come and address the big picture. What committee members need to hear are people's experiences and what worked in their lives—social knowledge. Hearing about individual experiences helps committee members to understand how the big picture affects "life on the ground." Most important, know your material well enough so that you will not have to read it. Remember that committee members have been sitting through many hours of presentations and you want to hold their attention. The advantage goes to the individual or group who prepares an effective and focused presentation:

* communicate well: select the spokesperson on the basis of his or her communication skills
* open the presentation distinctly: briefly introduce the spokesperson and the organization
* understand the problem: define the issue and build a supporting case
* make the issue understandable: use facts and anecdotes to help members understand the problem
* understand the needed changes: clearly articulate the required changes and why they will work
* select a few key points: reinforce the message throughout the presentation in the written submission

• respect the process: speak respectfully about the work of the committee if approached by the media. (McInnes, 1999)

In a written submission, write for quality, not for quantity. Your material should be succinct and inviting to the reader, as often politicians and their staff do not have time to read all briefs submitted to the committee. An executive summary is essential to highlight your key points. When drafting the committee's final report, staff will cull through the hearing transcripts and the submissions to find "quotable quotes," representative statements that sum up a group's position. Other items such as key statistics or the projected cost of any proposal should leap from the page. Good written presentations help readers grasp your message. Imagine reading dozens of lengthy briefs trying to determine what each group stands for on many multifaceted issues.

Moves over the number of years to decentralize the policy process have created a number of access points, and social workers should take advantage of this, particularly in view of the competition that pervades legislative debates (Fraatz, 1982). Although working with and managing coalitions of organizations making presentations can be especially challenging, the impact of cohesive groups embracing a common objective can be significant. Coalitions require additional planning as group representatives have to get positions endorsed from their respective organizations at each step along the way, all of which takes negotiation and time. If coalitions jell, a benefit is that they also demonstrate lobbying acumen to the group's broader membership. Partners in coalitions may also be called upon in the future for support in other initiatives.

It is important for social workers to be honest and straightforward in all dealings with people in government. Once an individual, agency, or organization loses credibility, and hence the ability to persuade people, they will have great difficulty in presenting their vision as viable. If a minister or senior bureaucrat is made to appear wrong, ignorant, or uninformed in front of his or her colleagues or constituents because of an error or omission on the part of a representative, the organization's credibility will always be called into question in the future. Such stories have a way of continuing to live on in the folklore of the civil service.

For governments, the questions of who to consult, how and when, about what, and for what purpose are highly sensitive questions. Discussion and consultation are equally part of a citizen's right to know about decisions being made by government and to participate in the process of government (G. Anderson, 1996). Social workers embody two very important contributions to the "policy stew": expert knowledge and grassroots input. Politicians like to reach for grassroots input by speaking to "ordinary citizens." As one committee member on a federal government panel said, "We must be careful to not let ourselves be influenced solely by very structured official lobby groups. They have their place, they are present and that is to be expected, but we must speak with ordinary Canadians" (Paul Crete, quoted in McInnes, 1999, p. 109).

Social workers must look for ways to get in the game early. The issues move up and down on organizational agendas, sometimes unpredictably. Moreover, organizations, committees, and their staffs tend to base their recommendations and decisions on the first available data and early discussions with players in the policy community. The suggestions in this section are intended merely as points of departure, largely because each policy debate is different. Not all issues call for the same kind of analysis, and not all analysis is appropriate for all audiences. Still, social workers and policy-makers can engage in more fruitful partnerships—provided, of course, that social workers take the steps to become active citizens.

Closing Comments

The responsibility to be active citizens calls social workers from our places of practice to participate in influencing public discussion and shaping the decision-making of governments. As social workers, we have an even greater responsibility because by being social workers we have accepted the responsibility of making claims on behalf of others and expanding the public domain so that more voices are heard. By bringing our professional social knowledge to the policy arena, we are focusing on securing the necessary resources for developing human capacities. Welfare is the development of human capacities and the primary concern of social workers. Policy-making is a value-laden political struggle centred on the interpretation and response to people whose voices are not present in the public arena: the poor, the homeless, and the vulnerable.

In this chapter, I endeavoured to share with my fellow professionals what I have learned over the last fifteen years of my practice. Although systemic barriers do exist in the Westminster model of governance, there are avenues of influence that social workers have left largely unused. We need to shoulder the responsibility for our own inaction and use it to push ourselves into the future. While other professions and stakeholder groups have been using the system as it exists and using it to their own ends, our voices have been largely quiet. In this neo-conservative era of decision-making, we cannot continue to be silent, but must learn to use the system as it is, with all of its inherent problems, because it is the system we have. Politicians are influenced to make decisions that their stakeholders lead them to believe will increase their public support and secure their re-election. Bureaucrats struggle to balance perceptions of the public interest and respond to the vision of their political leaders. Vocal and powerful stakeholder groups bring their resources to bear on securing decisions that benefit their interests. If we don't embark on the journey to make public claims, the powerless will continue to be subordinate and unseen.

As social workers, we take our professional identity from being advocates, networkers, advisers, counsellors, communicators, and facilitators. When combined with our social knowledge, we have something much greater than

Notes

References

only the necessary skills to be influential actors in the policy arena; we bring the knowledge and skills of responsible citizenship. Now is the time to be heard and to act.

Notes

1   Provincial parliamentary practice is a blend of written rules, British conventions, and adaptations of the British model. Underlying are the concepts of responsible government, the loyal opposition, party discipline, and ministerial responsibility (White, 1989). The Westminster model allows elected politicians to bring local interests into the parliamentary arena and the Cabinet to be held publicly accountable for decisions (Whittington & Williams, 2000).

2   The Ontario SuperBuild Corporation evaluates provincial businesses and services to determine where partnerships with the private sector can deliver higher quality services at a lower cost to taxpayers.

3   See government web sites (territorial, provincial and federal) listed in Additional Resources (below) for information about government committees.

References

Anderson, G. (1996). The new focus on the policy capacity of the federal government. *Canadian Public Administration/Administration Publique du Canada, 39*(4), 469–488.

Anderson, J. (1984). *Public policy-making: An introduction* (3rd ed.). Boston: Houghton Mifflin.

Arendt, H. (1998). *The human condition.* Chicago: University of Chicago Press. (Orig. pub. 1958).

Baier, G., & Bakvis, H. (2001). Think tanks and political parties: Competitors or collaborators? *Canadian Journal of Policy Research, 2*(1), 107–113.

Baralet, J.M. (1988). *Citizenship: Rights, struggle and class inequality.* Minneapolis: University of Minnesota Press.

Barber, B. (1984). *Strong democracy: Participatory politics for a new age.* Berkeley: University of California Press.

Blumer, H. (1969). *Symbolic interactionism.* Englewood Cliffs, NJ: Prentice Hall.

Brewer, G.D. (1974). Dealing with complex social problems: The potential of the "Decision Seminar." In G.D. Brewer & R.D. Brunner (Eds.), *Political development and change: A policy approach* (pp. 439–461). New York: Free Press.

Charih, M., & Rouillard, L. (1997). The new public management. In M. Charih & A. Daniels (Eds.), *New public management and public administration in Canada* (pp. 27–45). Toronto: Institute of Public Management.

Clarke, P.B. (1996). *Deep citizenship.* Chicago: Pluto Press.

Constantinou, P.P. (1995, May). On briefing ministers. *Policy Options, 16*(4), 45–47.

Doern, G.B., & Phidd, R. (1988). *Canadian public policy: Ideas, structure, and process.* Scarborough: Nelson.

Dror, Y. (1968). *Public policy-making re-examined.* San Francisco: Chandler.

Drover, G., & Kerans, P. (1993). *New approaches to welfare theory.* Aldershot: Edward Elgar.

Dye, T. (1972). *Understanding public policy.* Englewood Cliffs, NJ: Prentice Hall.

Edelman, M.J. (1988). *Constructing the political spectacle.* Chicago: University of Chicago Press.

Faludi, A., & Voogd, H. (1986). *Evaluation of complex policy problems.* Delft, Netherlands: Delftsche Uitgevers Maatschappij. **References**

Fisher, F. (1980). *Politics, values, and public policy.* Boulder, CO: Westview Press.

Fraatz, J.M.B. (1982). Policy analysts as advocates. *Journal of Policy Analysis and Management, 1*(2), 273–276.

Habermas, J. (1992). Citizenship and national identity: Some reflections on the future of Europe. *Praxis International, 12*, 1–19.

Held, D. (1991). Between state and civil society: Citizenship. In G. Andrews (Ed.), *Citizenship* (pp. 19–25). London: Lawrence and Wishart.

Ignatieff, M. (1991). Citizenship and moral narcissism. In G. Andrews (Ed.), *Citizenship* (pp. 26–36). London: Lawrence and Wishart.

Jeffery, B. (1999). *Hard right turn: The new face of neo-conservatism in Canada.* Toronto: HarperCollins.

Jenkins, W.I. (1978). *Policy analysis: A political and organizational perspective.* London: Martin Robertson.

Jones, C. (1984). *An introduction to the study of public policy.* Monterey: Brooks/Cole.

Kernaghan, K., & Langford, J.W. (1990). *The responsible public servant.* Toronto: Institute for Research on Public Policy.

Kingdon, J.W. (1984). *Agendas, alternatives and public policies.* Toronto: Little, Brown.

Langton, S. (1978). *Citizen participation in America.* Toronto: Lexington Books.

Lasswell, H.D. (1951). The policy orientation. In D. Lerner & H.D. Lasswell (Eds.), *The policy sciences: Recent developments in scope and method.* Stanford: Stanford University Press.

McInnes, D. (1999). *Taking it to the hill: The complete guide to appearing before (and surviving) parliamentary committees.* Ottawa: University of Ottawa Press.

Meltsner, A. (1976). *Policy analysts in the bureaucracy.* London: University of California Press.

Merriam, C. (1921). The present state of the study of politics. *American Political Science Review, 15*, 173–185.

Milbrath, L.W. (1965). *Political participation: How and why do people get involved in politics.* Chicago: Rand McNally.

Mitchell, J.R., & Sutherland, S.L. (1997). Relations between politicians and public servants. In M. Charih & A. Daniels (Eds.), *New public management and public administration in Canada* (pp. 181–197). Toronto: Institute of Public Administration in Canada.

Ontario Liberal Party. (1993). *A guide to policy development process.* Unpublished document.

Ontario New Democrats. (2000). *2000 Resolution book.*

Pal, L. (1987). *Public policy analysis: An introduction.* Toronto: Methuen.

Prince, M. (1979). Policy advisory groups in government departments. In G.B. Doern & P. Aucoin (Eds.), *Public policy in Canada: Organization, process and management* (pp. 275–300). Toronto: Macmillan.

Robertson, G. (1983, July). The deputy's anonymous duty. *Policy Options, 4*, 11–13.

Rosener, J.R. (1978). Matching methods to purpose: The challenges of planning citizen participation activities. In S. Langton (Ed.), *Citizens' participation in America* (pp. 109–112). Lexington: Lexington Books.

Sarpkaya, S. (1988). *Lobbying in Canada—Ways and means.* Don Mills: CCH Canadian.

References Schram, S. (1993). Postmodern policy analysis: Discourse and identity in welfare politics. *Policy Sciences, 26*(3), 249–270.

Sutherland, S. (1993). The public service and policy development. In M.M. Atkinson (Ed.), *Governing Canada* (pp. 81–113). Toronto: Harcourt Brace.

Toonen, T.A.J. (1985). Implementation research and institutional design: The quest for structure. In K. Hanf & T.A.J. Toonen (Eds.), *Policy implementation in federal and unitary systems* (pp. 335–354). Dordrecht: Marinus Nijhoff.

Verba, S., Nie, N., & Kim, J. (1971). *The modes of democratic participation: A cross-national comparison.* Beverly Hills: Sage.

Wharf, B., & McKenzie, B. (1998). *Connecting policy to practice in the human services.* Don Mills, ON: Oxford University Press.

White, G. (1989). *The Ontario legislature: A political analysis.* Toronto: University of Toronto Press.

White, G. (1997). The legislature: Central symbol of Ontario democracy. In G. White (Ed.), *The government and politics of Ontario* (5th ed., pp. 71–92). Toronto: University of Toronto Press.

Whittington, M., & Williams, G. (2000). *Canadian politics in the twenty-first century.* Toronto: Nelson.

Young, R. (1991). Effecting change: Do we have the political system to get us where we want to go? In B. Doern & B. Purchase (Eds.), *Canada at risk? Canadian public policy in the 1990s* (pp. 59–81). Toronto: C.D. Howe Institute.

Additional Resources

Legislative and Parlimentary websites:

Alberta: <www.assembly.ab.ca>.
British Columbia: <www.legis.gov.bc.ca>.
Manitoba: <http://www.gov.mb.ca/legislature/homepage.html>.
New Brunswick: <www.gov.nb.ca/legis/index.htm>.
Newfoundland and Labrador: <www.gov.nf.ca/hoa>.
Northwest Territories: <www.assembly.gov.nt.ca>.
Nova Scotia: <www.gov.ns.ca./legislature/>.
Nunavut: <www.assembly.nu.ca/english/index.html>.
Ontario: <www.ontla.on.ca>.
Prince Edward Island: <www.gov.pe.ca/leg/index.php3>.
Quebec: <www.assnat.qc.ca/eng/indexne3.html>.
Saskatchewan: <www.legassembly.sk.ca>.
Yukon: <www.gov.yk.ca/leg-assembly/>.
Canada: <www.parl.gc.ca>.

Program and Policy Development from a Holistic Aboriginal Perspective

Malcolm A. Saulis

> Indian cultures have ways of thought, learning, teaching, and communicating that are different than but of equal validity to those of White cultures. These throughways stand at the beginning of Indian time and are the foundations of our children's lives. Their full flower is in what it means to be one of the people. (Hampton, quoted in Battiste & Barman, 1995, p. 78)

The autonomous social welfare history of Aboriginal peoples in this country is very recent. By "autonomous," I mean that Aboriginal communities are involved in the management and provision of social welfare programs such as welfare payments (1960s), child welfare programs and agencies (1970s), addictions treatment and programs (1970s), community-based health programs and centres (1980s), and early childhood education programs and services (1990s). However, these programs and services are not autonomous in the following aspects:

- the design of the programs;
- the setting of standards or modes of delivery of the programs;
- the permanency of the programs, which are largely funded year to year in a project context, with no funding agreements designating them as permanent institutional elements of the community; and
- the policies governing the programs, agencies, or services.

With regard to operational policies, the federal funders' views of Aboriginal programming, especially in the social program arena, mirror the provincial government standard, except where caseloads are concerned. There is no clear standard for caseloads specific to Aboriginal programs. In provinces other than Ontario, which has an agreement with the federal government for social programs for First Nations, caseload standards are not applied. Furthermore, program policies are outside the purview of decision-making and, for the most part, are outside the purview of influence with regard to culture or contextualization of programs.

Even though Aboriginal communities have evolved in their comprehension and capacity to deliver and implement social welfare programs, they have not been provided with autonomy to do programming in a way that fully takes into account the culture of their people. In most cases where Aboriginal communities have taken a great deal of time to conceptualize more culturally appropriate models of program or policy delivery, the bureaucrats they work with in various government departments have not engaged in such rigorous conceptual thinking. Rather, governance issues preoccupy the discussions between Aboriginal groups and governments. In discussions of the approach to programs, practice modalities, program standards, protocol agreements, and prevention versus intervention as a strategy, the bureaucrats seem to think that there is an effective means of addressing such issues in society already—so why change when dealing with Aboriginal populations? However, Aboriginal communities would like to implement in their own way the programs that flow from the policies established by Aboriginal leaders. This would include program development (standards, protocols, and case management; program staffing and training; accountability and spending priorities). Most policy directions articulated by governments hint at the possibility of meeting the cultural needs of Aboriginal populations, but in practice the bureaucratic mindset prevails. This has been a frustrating experience for Aboriginal peoples.

Traditions and cultures are inherited elements of social groups. They come to us from our ancestors with the requirement that we work to protect the essential elements of the culture so that it has a sense of permanence. The essential elements are these:

- the nature of relationships among the people;
- the ceremonies;
- the dances, songs, drums, and gatherings; and
- the medicines, which are both physical and spiritual.

As humans, we share the responsibility to nurture our culture, and we all have cultures to draw upon if one goes back far enough in time. My sense is that prior to the Industrial Revolution, the essential natures of all people connected to a greater reality was strong.

It is important that the traditional cultures of Aboriginal peoples be expressed in the social welfare programs that we evolve for ourselves. The government of the present era has acknowledged this principle of Aboriginal programming. Examples are evident in programs such as those emerging in health transfer policies, child welfare, restorative justice and correctional initiatives, and community-based education movements. Each of these examples represents movement in the right direction, although each is at a different stage of indigenization.

What has been difficult is undoing the institutional mindset of the keepers of the Western tradition, who find it hard to grasp the scope of the change required in Aboriginal social welfare programming to make this happen. Aboriginal groups are indicating that they want to fully express their holistic world view in these programs. These programs need to have policies, standards, and modes of practice that truly reflect the reality of Aboriginal social welfare programming. This chapter will attempt to conceptualize an Aboriginal approach to program and policy development, and describe how it would work.

This chapter is about understanding. It is about reframing an existing understanding within the Canadian mindset about Aboriginal peoples and within the nature of social policy development regarding these Canadian citizens. Canadian Aboriginal peoples reside in Canada as a home territory. They do not reside here as an immigrant population, and therefore their relationship to this territory is rooted in a historical relationship, a cultural relationship, and an intimate relationship. They have, however, been the recipients of a foreign policy put into place hundreds of years ago, a policy that has not essentially changed.

An important concept for this chapter is the type of relationship that needs to emerge between Aboriginal peoples and the newcomers to enable meaningful policy and program development. I would characterize this relationship as a dialectic relationship. One would expect that such a relationship would have already developed after so many generations, but this is not the case. In social work theory, we read about the importance of establishing a dialectic relationship with the people with whom we work. This relationship is characterized as follows:

1. It is egalitarian; the helper and the helped are equal in their worth and in their importance to the relationship.
2. It permits a range of views that are not judged by either member of the relationship but that add to the knowledge of each person in better understanding where the other person comes from and what his or her experience has been.
3. It is based on the trust required to achieve the outcome. It has to be seen at many levels and experienced over a period of time. That is, it is not transitory. The statements "I mean what I say" or "I walk my talk" need to be real.
4. It not only operates on a linear or logical level but also allows and encourages the exploration of intuition, feeling, and values.

In the past, I would have concluded that it is in the hands of the newcomers to enable the development of this dialectic relationship, yet Freire takes a different view. He challenges the oppressed to be proactive on the matter: "This then, is the great humanistic and historical task of the oppressed: to liberate themselves and their oppressors as well. The oppressors, who oppress, exploit, and rape by virtue of their power, cannot find in this power the strength to liberate either the oppressed or themselves. Only power that springs from the weakness of the oppressed will be sufficiently strong to free both" (Freire, 1970, p. 28). I used to get very angry when I read this statement because it makes it the responsibility of the oppressed to find enough love and kindness to liberate themselves and others; but as with an Elder's teaching, the truth behind the thought cannot be escaped. I therefore strove to find the means of securing knowledge to underpin the action I needed to facilitate the journey to mutual freedom. This freedom would provide the basis of a good life for all concerned.

I will therefore provide insight into the knowledge base of the Aboriginal world view to help us all create a social policy process that supports a healthy dialectic relationship and a discourse that sustains the process. As a Malecite Indian (I use this term deliberately) who grew up on the Tobique Indian reserve in New Brunswick and who worked in the social service field for ten years of direct practice in setting up reserve-based agencies in the late 1970s, I have been on the front line of the development of Aboriginal services. I have influenced policy development for community-based agencies and researched Aboriginal processes and systems that are responsive to community needs. I have taught social work for over twenty years to both Aboriginal and non-Aboriginal students in a mainstream school of social work. I have come to realize that we all need to work together, all people of all races, because we all share the responsibility of keeping The Circle strong. I cherish the moment an Elder took time to teach me this knowledge and to find a place for it in my own outlook in life. Bellefeuille, Garrioch, and Ricks support this outcome when they look at the evolution of child welfare among First Nations: "Shared vision involves developing a shared vision of the future with guiding principles and practices to realize that vision. A shared vision is one that involves the skills of unearthing shared pictures of the future that foster commitment versus compliance" (1997, p. 24).

Paradigm shift may be an appropriate way to describe the work that has to be done in order to achieve the dialectic result. This view is expressed in the report of the Special Parliamentary Committee on Indian Self-Government: "The committee is strongly convinced that a major change in the orientation of federal policy must occur. There is little benefit to be gained by tinkering with the Indian Act or by adjusting the present policy of devolution (transfer of funds and authority to First Nations communities by means of funding arrangements that are not rooted in legal standing or policy authority)" (Ponting 1986, p. 339). Native writers agree that there needs to be a paradigm shift. In an Awasis Agency publication, *Mee-noo-stah-tan Mi-ni-si-win*, the point is made by Senge:

> Paradigms are the broader mental sets or world views which influence the kinds of models we develop and/or adopt. Paradigms are pictures of reality, or particular ways of constructing social realities which are shaped by our own needs and assumptions. And Thomas Kuhn ... suggested that paradigm shifts occur over time, as more and more dysfunction develops with a certain model or paradigm. Attempts to rescue the paradigm through reforms and adjustments eventually break down as the dysfunc-

tion becomes too great. (quoted in Awasis Agency of Northern Manitoba, 1997, p. 7)

Recent commitments by the federal government to increased spending for Aboriginal programs show that Canada has become aware that things have not worked for Aboriginal populations when it comes to health policies, justice policies, governance policies, social welfare polices, educational policies, or even something as basic as safe drinking water. The dysfunction of applying a mainstream paradigm of "social well-being" and its resulting programming to Aboriginal populations has become more and more evident. The oppressive nature of the existing relationship does not lead to functioning Aboriginal populations. It has not resulted in a dialectic relationship that enriches both parties.

Governments of all political parties have not been able to achieve their policy goals regarding Aboriginal populations. The implication of the constitutional entrenchment of Aboriginal rights and the creation of equal citizenship for Aboriginal peoples was that there would be an acknowledgment of the totality of Aboriginal reality. This means that there could be an expression of the Aboriginal world view within the confines of their own community. It also means that the attendant elements of the Aboriginal world view—including governance, cultural and traditional practices, and social organization—could be expressed.

However, a major obstacle in implementing the new paradigm has been the scarcity of resources. The entrenchment of Aboriginal rights in section 35 of the Canadian constitution actually limits the resources available to all Aboriginal populations. Now fiscal allocations have to be distributed among all Aboriginal populations, and not just among the Status Indians, as indicated by the Indian Act. All governments of all parties now need to operationalize their strategies toward all Aboriginal populations within this Act. The groups entitled to be recognized under the rubric "Aboriginal" now include Status Indians as defined by the Indian Act; Métis populations, as defined in relation to definitions worked out with provincial and federal governments; Inuit populations, which in the past were cared for exclusively by territorial governments; and Non-status Indians, who for reasons of marriage or enfranchisement can now reassert their Aboriginal entitlement. Thus, the available pool of resources, which originally was intended to be spent only on Status Indians living on reserves, must now be extended to cover entitlements to Indians off-reserve as well as other Aboriginal populations. Limiting such entitlements is becoming a full-time operation for governments, especially in this era of burgeoning Aboriginal populations.

Mainstream Social Policy and Social Welfare Programming

Every citizen of Canada is a social welfare recipient. Each one of us is a direct beneficiary of one or more provincial or federal programs that are part of the complex structures of Canadian social services.

In the Canadian constitution, the federal government has exclusive responsibility for social welfare matters dealing with Indians and their land and inherent rights; naturalization (immigration); criminal law; and the establishment, maintenance, and management of penitentiaries. The provinces have primary jurisdiction over social welfare issues that are not included in this specific list of federal powers.

Social policy can be defined as "action or inaction taken by public authorities to address problems which deal with human health, safety or well-being" (Westhues, 2006, p. 8). Three major groups are crucially involved in determining the outcomes of a policy process: politicians, bureaucrats, and pressure groups. The influence of each of these groups differs at various times, depending on the composition of each group and on the information and insights available to those studying the process (Wharf & McKenzie, 1998). The Cabinet is the core institution for determining priorities, however. This means that while no one part of the political system has a monopoly over the determination of priorities where new policies are concerned, the Cabinet is by far the most important institution involved (Van Loon & Whittington, 1987, p. 337).

I would like to demonstrate the distinctions in the policy-making process between the Aboriginal process and the mainstream process. It is important to underscore that social policy decision-making in the Aboriginal process is rooted in the perceptions of the people of the communities, and that they play an active role in interpreting, setting priorities for, and evaluating the directions of policy. It is not a process isolated from people and located in the bureaucracy, as we see in the mainstream process. Table 6.1 illustrates the potentially differing perspectives of Aboriginal peoples and mainstream contexts regarding the social welfare policy process. I have drawn on the thinking of George and Wilding (1985) and Douglass and Friedmann (1998) in making this analysis.

As one can see, the fundamental differences between the Aboriginal and mainstream approaches rest in the motivations for the policy process and in the planning that flows from the policy process. The people within the context are differentially considered by the two processes, with a consequent loss of citizenship and democracy in the mainstream process. The two systems are fundamentally at odds with each other. However, that does not necessarily mean that the two processes are so different that they do not make sense to each other or that the fundamental differences make it impossible to communicate with each other. The two-row wampum example given in this text alerts us that work needs to be done so that the fundamental differences between Aboriginals and non-Aboriginals do not impede achieving good results.

Table 6.1   Aboriginal and mainstream policy-making processes compared

ABORIGINAL SOCIAL POLICY AND SOCIAL WELFARE PLANNING	MAINSTREAM SOCIAL POLICY AND SOCIAL WELFARE PLANNING
1. Ideology/World View • Collectivist (collective responsibility for well-being of all); leadership is for service to the people • All people are equal • Freedom—being able to count on collective support and solidarity	**1. Ideology/World View** • Individualistic (individual and family are primarily responsible for their own well-being, with help for the "deserving"); leadership represents the interests of elites • Inequality acceptable • Freedom—limited government intervention
2. Justice and Humanism • Justice rests in the well-being of the collective and is contained within the consciousness of the collective; it is a relationship • The circle of humanity includes all people of the community, and the weakest need to be supported for the benefit of all	**2. Justice and Humanism** • Justice rests in the responsibilities of a system of justice; it is about the harm done to the state, not the harm done to the relationship with other people • All humans are as equal as is possible within a system of institutions and services, and within the confines of an economy
3. Theory of Planning/Policy-making • Inclusive, not expert driven; concerned with the equity of policies for all people, and people have a voice in what is good for them • "Circular," not linear; multidimensional and holistic; interrelated and inclusive • Intuitive as well as meaningful to the people who are concerned or affected by the outcome of the process, based on their own experience • Strength based	**3. Theory of Planning/Policy-making** • Rational and comprehensive and takes into account the views of experts in the field; may reflect the views of a representative sample of the people affected by the policy/program • Positivist and linear; not as sensitive to interconnection with a broad range of policy systems • Logical, non-intuitive, legislated; not based on experience of people affected by the outcome of the process • Deficit/medical model

The Mainstream Policy Making Process

An important observation in social policy development is that the mainstream approach is a closed system of relationships between the key power holders of the political party system, their set of interests, and the need to develop initiatives that enhance the chances of being re-elected and that a majority of voters can support through popular opinion. The players in this process need to be able to trust each other and to solicit the best views and opinions of outsiders who can be trusted. The element of trust within the system makes it operate so that the result is a workable system:

1. The perceptions of mainstream Canadians are reflected in the proposed legislation, making it acceptable to them to spend tax money on these policy initiatives.
2. It fits the agenda of the ruling party.

3. The ideas generated are vetted by people who are trusted, or at least trust-
worthy, and the views of these people will not generate too much opposition from unknown sources.

4. The measures proposed would pass through Cabinet.

The parties involved in policy development and the progressively higher
levels of the administrative process need to be able to trust each other. Therefore, they examine each other with regard to their sympatico of identity; that
is, they seem pretty much like each other. The higher the level of authority and
influence, the more like each other they become. This is not necessarily a
negative thing, but a reality that those of us who want to influence such people and processes need to know. This reality is one of the difficult elements in
introducing what seem like radically different processes, such as those rooted
in a holistic Aboriginal world view. It is difficult to influence people in positions of power because "getting to them" is a very difficult process of proving
that such perspectives and processes make sense or are workable. Yet I suggest that new perspectives influencing the Canadian policy view, such as that
contained in the "population health" perspective, provide us with hope. This
population health perspective includes the socio-economic health of Canadians, which allows us to look at factors such as poverty in health outcomes.

The governing party that holds power via elections needs to be able to
determine that its goal to be re-elected is supported by the policies set and the
antecedent processes of program design and implementation. The influence
of marginalized people with radically different world views is severely mini-
mized in this scenario. It is therefore the job of marginalized people to make
themselves understood and to make room for their paradigms in this policy
process. It would be naive to think otherwise. It is the task of this chapter to
contribute to an understanding of how that can be achieved. I have observed
that Canada has made room in recent years for such an undertaking. The
notions of "restorative," "healing," or "holistic" paradigms have gained acceptance. There has also been an effort not only to root these notions in the experience and knowledge of the mainstream, but also to apply them to settings
other than the medical/health settings. I have seen departments of Justice,
Health, Correctional Services, Indian Affairs, and Human Services grasp the
notion in a logical and linear way. It is now important to provide insights that
will set them in a holistic way into the change processes of Aboriginal Peoples.

This mainstream paradigm of social policy development and the nature
of institutional reality with regard to society are expressed in the following diagram (Figure 6.1), which I constructed as a useful tool for myself. This diagram
illustrates the independent nature of the institutions and shows that government operates as an institution unto itself. It may have a directive function
with regard to the other institutions, but the accountability of the other institutions to government is not evident. The autonomy of the institutional structures is an important element of their existence, since they need to have
autonomy to fulfill the tasks expected of them without undue interference
from other agencies.

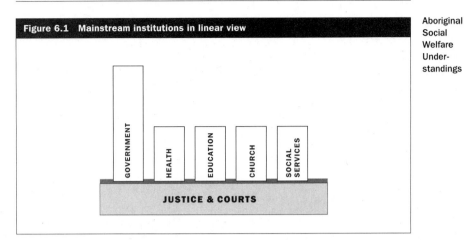

Figure 6.1   Mainstream institutions in linear view

This figure demonstrates the individualistic nature of the institutions of society. They exist for their own sake; that is, their primary goal becomes that of ensuring their existence rather than fulfilling the mission for which they were created. They compete with each other for funding, influence, impor- tance, and position, but not for service to their clientele. In fact, clientele must configure themselves to the culture of the institution.

An interesting dimension of this diagram is the place and responsibility of the institution of justice. Its place as the foundation or fabric upon which society is built, reminding society of its civilized nature, is more an illusion than a reality. The justice institution should be a reminder to society of its responsibility to its citizens. The outcomes of the dialectic relationship would inform the notion of a civil society as construed within the definition of civil law.

Aboriginal Social Welfare Understandings

Social welfare can be defined, within a capitalist paradigm and with a liberal perspective, as a complex network of legislation, policies, programs, institu- tions, professions, resources, and services that ensure for individuals access to a range of goods and services necessary to achieve their full potential in a manner acceptable to them and with due regard to the rights of others.

Aboriginal populations with a holistic world view would add to this defi- nition in the following manner: Ensuring the well-being of all people is the inherent responsibility of all people for one another, without consideration of class, gender, ability, sexual preference, or cultural orientation. In simple fact, we are all one in Creation. We fulfill our responsibility through the pro- vision of programs, institutions, professions, resources, and services that are accessible and responsive to the needs of people—not to the political viabil- ity of such elements of social order. In the holistic model, the institutions of society in Figure 6.1 would dedicate themselves to the service of meeting peo- ple's needs, the purpose for which they were created. Their efforts and work

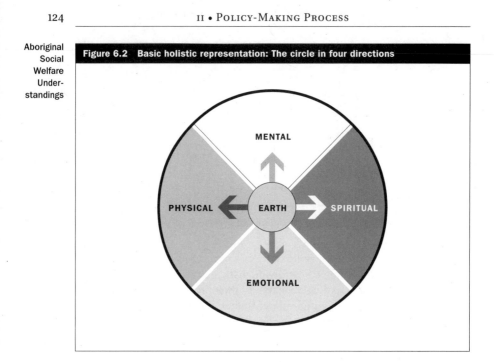

Figure 6.2   Basic holistic representation: The circle in four directions

would be an investment in the well-being of society and in the Creation that we are all a part of.

Figure 6.2 shows us the basic conceptual teachings of holistic traditions. The figure is in four parts, with each part facing in a different direction: north, east, south, west. Each direction has a concept attached to it: north is mental, east is spiritual, south is emotional, and west is physical. All of these elements are reflected in the life of each person. The important thing is that we acknowledge all the directions in others, although this may sometimes be difficult. All the directions make a whole, a one. When one part is missing, there is no longer a totality. Included is the notion of the centre as the source and driving force of the system: this is embedded in the notion of the nurturing Mother Earth or Creation.

This Circle (Figure 6.2) teaches us that we are all one. The Circle is fragile because whatever happens affects all the other components of the whole. No one is unaffected by the plight and experience of others. The centre contains our human spirit, which is the spark of the Creator from which we get our nature as people. We are provided with insight, anticipation, and understanding. Our job throughout our lives is to nurture this insight and to make the spark glow. The bond among us as elements of Creation (the whole) is our relationships and the behaviours that emerge from these relationships. The directions are all equal; no one direction is more prominent or important than another.

The notion of deserving or undeserving does not exist in this holistic scenario, as all that is provided to humans by Creation—whether it be wealth or

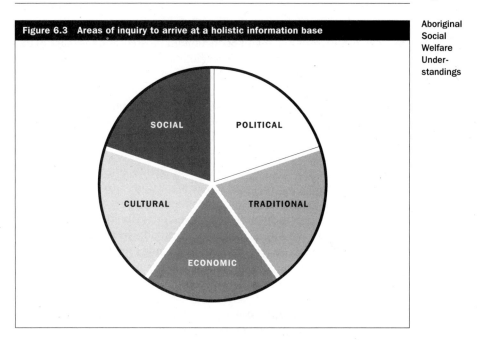

Figure 6.3   Areas of inquiry to arrive at a holistic information base

Aboriginal
Social
Welfare
Under-
standings

space or time—is for the benefit of all people. The exploitation of any people by another group of people hurts everyone. Creation and reality are made up of both tangible (empirical) and non-tangible (spiritual, for lack of a better word) aspects. Our viability as humans depends on preserving both the tangible and the non-tangible. It is through the spirit in which we carry out our work to meet the social welfare needs of others that the world remains viable and valuable. If we do not carry out our work in a good spirit, the spirit and viability of those we affect is diminished.

Figure 6.3 provides us with a useful holistic way of analyzing the consequences of our behaviour. It also provides us with an analytical tool with which to anticipate the outcomes of behaviours before we engage in them. It provides us with a way of understanding and constructing the welfare measures we hope to put into place. At the same time, it demonstrates the ripple effect of a measure applied in one component of the whole affecting the other parts of the whole. For example, if we were to consider the implementation or creation of a child welfare agency for a community, we could not simply engage in determining the organizational and staffing structure, or the fiscal requirements of the agency. The agency must be structured in ways that meet the needs of the community as defined in the holistic world view. We also could not formulate the policies and protocols under which the agency would operate without considering the implications for the social and cultural structures of a given community or context. If we were to place this agency in a perspective of holistic healing, as is required by our culture as Aboriginal peoples, then we must consider how all the elements of the agency enable that process.

This would include staffing, budgeting, planning of buildings, activities within the agency, the words and intent of documents created, and the place of traditional practices within the whole development.

Aboriginal teachings remind us that we must be contemplative about our efforts. We must be able to comprehend the impacts of our efforts not just on the tangible reality of humans but also on the non-tangible elements of Creation. A teaching that is powerful in this context is that all elements of Creation are related, and our whole reality is affected by any measures we put in place. The cultures of people are affected by measures rooted in the cultures of other people. For example, First Nations and their cultures are affected by the imposition of spiritual practices rooted in the Christian religion. The Aboriginal traditional practices honour the members of the animal and plant world as relatives, and without these relatives, our viability as humans is not possible. However, this view is judged unacceptable by the Christian traditions, even though there are similar beliefs in some Christian cultures.

In a more tangible case related to social work practice, the use of holistic healing practices could be challenged as not being rooted in the rigour of other empirically and academically based traditional practices of social work as a profession. Thus, the use of holistic healing practices in social work could be questioned. Child welfare is one area where this issue arises. In fact, though, most mainstream social work practice is not based on empirical findings at all, but on somebody's theory of how things will work best. What the mainstream social work profession has avoided considering, for the most part, is the spiritual aspect of life. This avoidance may have been in an effort to smooth over divisions among diverse cultural groups that were grounded in religious beliefs, thus creating greater "social order" or "social cohesion." The holistic perspective allows us to acknowledge spirituality once again, as spirituality is a resource that many people draw on in dealing with their troubles.

Child welfare practice is an area heavily influenced by the values, world views, and expectations of a particular class of people in mainstream society. The conclusion of policy-makers is that most middle-class Canadians favour a certain kind of child welfare practice. The aim of protecting children from imminent danger means defining imminent danger. This definition includes not just physical harm but harm arising out of a lack of parental control (understood as neglect) and children being placed in harmful situations. These situations include the conditions arising from poverty, such as unsafe housing, unsanitary conditions, or unfamiliar parenting techniques. The primary consideration of the practice of child welfare is the present and future safety of the child. However, the social worker's perception of safety and harm is determined by the culture in which the worker has been brought up and educated, and is codified in child welfare legislation, regulations, and directives. These standards and norms also determine how the worker perceives the safety of an environment. When the investigative dimension of this practice unfolds, so do the values and world views of the workers and policy-makers. The risk assessment measures now used in most parts of Canada are the way in which this is operationalized in recent years. Thus the elements of figure 6.3 that are emphasized are the social and cultural elements, which are within a specific system of values.

The element of tradition in child welfare practice is historic practice, and mainstream child welfare practice is rooted in the use of authority and judgment. Here, the immediate and the imminent take precedence over the potential of the future, and the cultural reality of the context is not considered. The practitioner as an individual with his or her own set of cultural assumptions has decision-making authority and responsibility. In contrast, in a holistic approach, which considers Aboriginal reality and the Circle analysis, the practitioner would partner with people from the context. Decision-making would be communal, and the determination of the next step would be consultative and not rooted only in the immediate and the imminent. The values of the community's culture would be respected and preserved, and the whole community would be involved in resolving the problem with the child and the family. Politics, economics, tradition, social relationship, and cultural values would all be preserved.

The Holistic Policy Process

Figure 6.4 allows us to view the relationship of the same institutions represented in figure 6.1, but within the holistic world view of Aboriginal peoples. It shows an interdependence, an interrelationship, an interconnection, that strengthens society for all people. The institutions are intended to work for a social order's healthy existence. The Aboriginal approach would attempt to be more egalitarian, more of a partnership. This perspective also looks beyond the nuclear family and even beyond the extended family to the community to determine how the child can best be cared for. The Aboriginal model is based on values and cultural practices that could be useful in mainstream contexts as well.

Within this image of institutions, people are at the centre. The people are the basis for all institutions and their functions, and have come forth from Creation, which is usually symbolized by the colour green. This Creation is embodied in our Mother Earth. The Earth provides us with all we need to live, and we have a great responsibility to respect all that Mother Earth provides. Through this respectful world view and our respectful behaviour, we sustain the Earth and it will always sustain us. Without it, we will all perish. If people are the expression and the embodiment of this Creation, then we need to be reflective people, respectful people. We need to prepare ourselves for this responsibility in various ways, but in the end, we need to understand our responsibility.

In preparing ourselves for this responsibility, we must first understand and articulate what respect is and how we might embody it. We must place ourselves in humility, so that we will be open to hearing the meaning of the

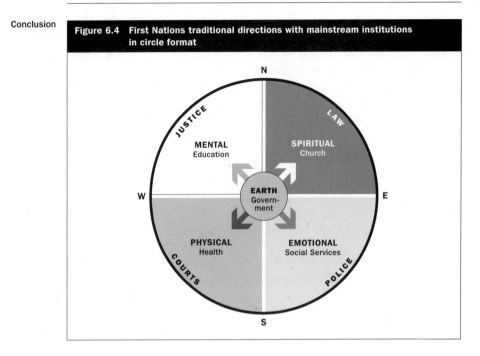

Figure 6.4 First Nations traditional directions with mainstream institutions in circle format

knowledge people give in their stories of life. We need to be reflective in the context of others who are preparing themselves so that a collective consensus will emerge that provides wise insight and mutual understanding. We must engage in ceremony and work at being loving people who are strong enough to leave behind authority and power in favour of being one of, not one above. We need to present our thoughts and considerations to the people of the community and to learn from their insights. We need to adopt a language that allows us to communicate with them and use them in our processes, so that their words have meaning and impact. We must be willing to leave the process and allow others to emerge as leaders with their skills and gifts.

Social welfare and social policy are human processes wherein humans interrelate to achieve an outcome, which constitutes policy statements and actions. We who do this work must therefore be special human beings. We must get ourselves ready and, finally, prove ourselves worthy to be participants in the process, to carry the truth of other humans, and we must be clear thinking and thoughtful as we engage in the process with other humans. It cannot be a process rooted in anger or resentment, or prejudice and racism. It must essentially be a human process.

Conclusion

We must put together all the Circles that we see above: the four directions teaching, the holistic analysis, and the holistic institutional visioning. We must pray for good direction and wisdom. We must ultimately be good leaders.

I have been told that leadership is a lonely journey, and that leaders are References recognized by people because of the spirit they carry, a spirit that is seen before their physical presence arrives. They are able to have the Eagle's vision, which sees the interconnections and the interrelationships as if from a great height. They understand responsibility and the nature of the responsibility of their vision. But these are understandings that imply an active and lifelong process to achieve. They are qualities that are not transferable. Leadership is also contextual: different people possess leadership in different ways and in different places. Therefore, ego cannot be a major element of leaders because ego will blind them to the leadership insights of other people.

We need to perceive ourselves as leaders and to behave as leaders for all of our people, regardless of whether we are Aboriginal or not. Social welfare processes are about transformations and reaffirmations of citizens and of a civilized society, as Douglas and Friedmann point out: "I see...planners passionately engaged in a transformative politics for inclusion, opportunity for self-development and social justice. It is a politics driven by the energies of a civil society that is beginning to reassert itself in all of its diversity. Its vision is for a social formation where no one is excluded from the rights and duties of full citizenship" (Douglas & Friedmann, 1998, p. 34).

Freire (1970) reminded us that "Only the power that springs from the weakness of the oppressed will be sufficiently strong to free both (the oppressor and the oppressed)." One of my teaching Elders, Dr. Danny Musqua, reminded me that the fundamental purpose of life is for us to fan the spark of the Creator, which resides in all of us at our birth. If we do not fan this spark, it is destined to remain always just a spark. In order to have it burn in our lives, the spark needs constant attention and nurturing.

By engaging in the creation of social policy processes and outcomes for the benefit of all people, we are fanning the spark. We also learn that the essential purpose of life is not how great we can make ourselves individually, but how great we can be in the context of all other people. We need to help create great human beings.

References

Awasis Agency of Northern Manitoba. (1997). *First Nations family justice: Mee-noo-stah-tan Mi-ni-si-win.* Victoria: Morriss Printing.

Battiste, M., & Barman, J. (1995). *First Nations education in Canada: The Circle unfolds.* Vancouver: University of British Columbia Press.

Bellefeuille, G., Garrioch, S., & Ricks, F. (1997). *Breaking the rules: Transforming governance in social services.* Victoria: Morriss Printing.

Freire, P. (1970). *Pedagogy of the oppressed.* New York: Seabury.

Douglass, M., & Friedmann, J. (1998). *Cities for citizens.* Toronto: John Wiley.

George, V., & Wilding, P. (1985). *Ideology and social welfare.* London: Routledge and Kegan Paul.

Ponting, R.J. (1986). *Arduous journey: Canadian Indians and decolonization.* Toronto: McClelland and Stewart.

References   Van Loon, R.J., & Whittington, M.S. (1987). *The Canadian political system.* Toronto: McGraw Hill.

Westhues, A. (2006). Becoming acquainted with social policy. In A. Westhues (Ed.), *Canadian social policy* (pp. 5–24). Waterloo, ON: Wilfrid Laurier University Press.

Wharf, B., & McKenzie, B. (1998). *Connecting policy to practice in the human services.* Toronto: Oxford University Press.

Additional Resources

Denis, C. (1997). *We are not you: First Nations and Canadian modernity.* Peterborough, ON: Broadview Press.

Joan Wharf Higgins, *John Cossom*, and *Brian Wharf*

Introduction

The objectives of this chapter are to address who participates in the development and implementation of social policy and to consider whether the current levels of participation are sufficient. We use the terms "address" and "consider" rather than "answer" since, as will become abundantly clear as the discussion proceeds, the resolution of these issues depends to a large extent on the values and perspectives of those addressing them.

The chapter is organized as follows. First, we provide our interpretation of social policy, a brief outline of our values, and a way of thinking about the levels or domains of social policy. Second, we review the various understandings of who participates in policy development, ranging from human service agencies to the federal government and the international scene. In the concluding section we consider the extent of participation and indicate our dissatisfaction with the current state of affairs.

Social Policy: What Are Its Values and Domains? What Is It?

Values are initially shaped by childhood experiences and more closely defined in adulthood. Our values have been sharply influenced by our experiences as practitioners and academics in the human services. We share a political view that espouses and cherishes social democracy. Such a philosophy holds that the state has an obligation to act for the well-being of its citizens. In turn, citizens have a responsibility to be actively involved in and to contribute to the affairs of the state. This reciprocal, beneficial arrangement exists only as long as both the state and individuals make and are able to sustain a commitment to their respective responsibilities. As we note in the section on who participates in social policy development, the state's commitment to citizen participation has waned of late with the consequence that many citizens see themselves as second-class members of an uncaring nation.

In Chapter 1, Westhues notes that "there has been a long-standing debate within the literature as to what is meant by the term 'social policy.' The central issue that frames this discussion is how inclusive the reach of social policy is" (p. 6). Some appreciation of the extent and complexity of the debate can be gained from the discussion where the attempts of eight scholars to define the term are presented (Graham, Swift, & Delaney, 2000). Westhues opts for a straightforward yet inclusive definition and claims that social policy represents "action or inaction chosen by public authorities to address an issue that deals with human health, safety, or well-being" (p. 8).

One important aspect of social policy is that of choice. Policies represent a decision to select one set of approaches from among a number available. The choice depends in large measure on the values and the ideologies of those in policy positions. Policy-making is "inevitably guided by a general conception of the role of the state" (Banting, 1987, p. 147). A second important aspect of policy is the difficulty encountered in making choices. We have always been impressed by the discussion on social problems by Rittel and Webber: "As distinguished from problems in the natural sciences which are definable and separable and may have solutions that are findable, the problems of government planning and especially those of social or policy planning, are ill defined and they rely on elusive political judgment for resolution. Not "solution." Social problems are never solved. At best they are only resolved over and over again" (1973, p. 180).

One only has to think of health care and how best to provide health services, of poverty and the various measures that have been proposed to eliminate or reduce this enduring social issue, and what to do about the puzzling dilemma of child neglect and abuse, to gain an appreciation of the slipperiness and complexity of social issues and the fragility of policies to resolve them. Hence, we suggest an addition to the definition proposed by Westhues.

Social policy is a course of action or inaction chosen by public authorities to address problems that deal with human health, safety, or well-being. This course of action represents the choices made by policy-makers, which are largely determined by their values and ideologies. Even this definition leaves out important matters such as the availability of resources, timing, and the influence brought to bear on policy-makers by interest groups.

Westhues identifies five levels or domains of policy: the organizational; the local, provincial, and federal governments; and the international scene. However, we have limited our discussion to the domains identified by Lindblom (1979) as the grand and ordinary issues of social policy. Lindblom describes grand issues as "pertaining to the fundamental structure of politico-economic life. They include the distribution of income and wealth and the distribution of political power and corporate prerogatives" (Lindblom, 1979, p. 523). We view health care and income security as of sufficient importance to qualify as grand issues. Until recently, and with the important exception of long-standing international organizations like the World Bank, national governments assumed responsibility for the grand issues. However, the locus of power for grand issues has shifted dramatically with the emergence of globalization and institutions like the World Trade Organization (WTO). Increasingly, transnational corporations seek to establish policies that allow them to move capital and workplaces without interference by national governments.

Ordinary issues are described by others (Graham, Swift, & Delaney, 2000) as the domain of social welfare policy, and these include the personal social services like child welfare, daycare, and recreation. These are dealt with mostly by provincial and municipal governments in Canada, and the precise division of responsibility varies from province to province. In addition, some provinces rely heavily on quasi-public agencies such as Children's Aid Societies and regional health organizations to actually provide services. Obviously, the two levels are closely connected, and policies established at the grand level have a decided impact on ordinary issues.

Citizens: Who Are They, and Who Participates?

Citizens: Who Are They, and Who Participates?

As concepts, citizenship and citizen participation elude precision and consensus. Citizenship not only concerns membership, but also the rights and obligations that citizens possess. Citizenship is an idea both of being and of doing (Prior, Stewart, & Walsh, 1995). The notion of "citizen" that emerged from Marshall's *Class, Citizenship and Social Development* (1977) implied equality of status and respect as a member of society, and intimated that each citizen would be accorded the same rights as every other citizen. Marshall's view assumes that all citizens are the same, stripped of any group identification or differences: "Equal citizenship is extended to people despite all their differences of birth, education, occupation, gender or race. It is a slippery slope from saying that these differences should not count, to saying that they don't even matter" (Phillips, 1993, p. 77).

Citizenship has both formal and substantive effects (Prior, Stewart, & Walsh, 1995). The distinction is between the status that provides people with the possession of formal rights and entitlements (the civil, political, and social rights as conceptualized by Marshall), and the status that enables them to have the opportunity to realize those rights and entitlements. All citizens formally possess civil, political, and social rights, but not all possess the means of realizing—and hence enjoying—the substantive benefits of citizenship.

The participation of citizens in social policy is a complex matter defying easy explanation. Canada is a democracy, but what kind of democracy? What are the expectations and opportunities for non-elected people to share in the decisions that affect them? Political philosophers have found the issues of citizen roles in the government of a democratic state and its institutions vexing ones. Indeed, the disagreements that exist today in Canada reflect the same conflicts between political philosophies that have been around for centuries.

Citizenship can be viewed on a continuum from representative to participatory democracy (Hemingway, 1999). Representative democracy, or passive citizenship, rests on the assumption that citizens themselves are not able (or perhaps willing) to become involved in the policy arena, and select representatives to look after their interests. Citizen involvement is limited to a passive role of responding to the political choices and delegating representation on issues to elected officials. Even at this end of the continuum of low citizen involvement, the dismal turnout among younger voters reflects a number of issues, including the failure to view voting as a meaningful civic responsibility (Clarke, Kornberg, MacLeod, & Scotto, 2005), feeling ill informed about and/or uninterested in the issues, declining trust in representative democracy (Abelson, Forest, Eyles, Casebeer, & Mackean, 2004; Lawton, 1979), as well as the inadequacy of traditional registration and voting mechanisms that exclude an internet-savvy population (Pammett & LeDuc, 2003). In fact, Fraser (2005) suggests that civic participation in general through electronic and technological means might be more appealing to younger citizens. The rights of citizens are emphasized at this end of the continuum, where entitlements overshadow obligations (Drover, 2000).

At the other end of the continuum, participatory democracy or active citizenship assumes that citizens can and do want to participate in the discussion and decision-making concerning social policy. Their active engagement in ongoing dialogue with fellow citizens enhances their knowledge of social issues and capacity to participate. Arai (2000) distinguishes between various forms of active citizenship—Citizen, Techno, and Labour volunteers—on the basis of the benefits experienced and contributions made. In Arai's schematic, the Technos bring specific skills and knowledge (e.g., legal, financial); Labour volunteers perform staff functions (e.g., stuffing envelopes); and it is the Citizen volunteer who debates problems and shapes solutions. Drover (2000) and Kingwell (2000) suggest that in a global era, citizenship must take an active form, include an ethic of care, transcend national boundaries, and embrace diversity.

The Principle of Affected Interests

One ambitious attempt to answer the question "Rule by what people?" has been made by Robert Dahl (1970, p. 64), who begins with the Principle of Affected Interests: "Everyone who is affected by the decisions of a government should have a right to participate in that government." He concedes that this proposition raises many thorny issues, but concludes that it is nevertheless worth pursuit. One of the problems is that different sets of people are affected by different decisions, and "the logic of the Principle of Affected Interests is that for every different set of persons affected there will be a different association or decision making unit" (Dahl, 1970, p. 64). Dahl identifies three important criteria that can be used to unravel the complications of affected interests: personal choice, competence, and economy.

Personal choice is a criterion that assesses the degree to which the decision fits one's own preference. Since it is unlikely that people will agree, the "decisions must be made in such a way as to give equal weight to the personal choices of everyone" (p. 12). In democratic systems this is usually resolved by majority decision-making that grants individuals political equality. Of course, this criterion by itself leaves democratic organizations facing complicated issues, since majority rule cannot satisfy everyone's personal choice. For example, how are the special needs of minorities protected? Too often democracy has assumed a system of commonly held values and perspectives; yet Canada is increasingly marked by sharp differences in culture, language, religion, and values. A moral consensus has become much more elusive and personal choice takes on greater significance in our society.

The criterion of competence suggests that some decisions can be accepted because they are made by people who are particularly qualified by knowledge or skill to make them. We rely on a pilot to fly the plane. Passengers do not file a flight plan by majority decision! Most of us accept higher competence as a criterion for decision-making in many areas that affect us. Some situations require choosing between personal choice and competence, resulting in decisions based on a combination of these two factors.

The criterion of economy raises the issues that have headlined in recent times—efficiency, rationality, and the preservation of scarce resources. Organizations cannot avoid addressing these variables, because time, money, and effort are certainly not unlimited when it comes to citizen input. Individuals also address the costs and benefits of participation. How much satisfaction do they get from it? How significant are the decisions they make? Will their participation make a difference? Another important economic factor is that the costs of participation in decision-making are higher for some groups and individuals than others (Warren & Weschler, 1975). For the poor, the costs of citizenship may be very high.

Each of these three criteria is important and valid, but they cannot be translated into a simple equation to produce ideal types of participation. Every situation has to be weighed on the basis of its individual needs and merits. While majority rule may be preferred in one organization, reflecting an emphasis on personal choice, competency and economy may be much more significant in another. We return to these criteria later in the chapter. Citizen participation relies on three assumptions: citizens have the right to and want to participate; citizen participation leads to better decision-making; and citizen participation is a good in and of itself. These assumptions argue that policy-making is best done by those who will be the recipients of, or will be affected by, the resulting programs or services (Bregha, 1973). In addition, participation is thought to empower the individual participant, the voluntary organization, and the community (Laverack & Wallerstein, 2001; Perlstadt, Jackson-Elmore, Freddolino, & Reed, 1998), nurture local planning skills and problem-solving abilities (Labonte & Laverack, 2001; Pivik, 2002), and contribute to social capital by strengthening citizens' trust in one another other and their connectedness to the community (Putnam, 2000; Wharf Higgins & Rickert, 2005; Ziersch, 2005). However, as we note later in the chapter, these rather optimistic views are not shared by other researchers.

In Canada, there is little opportunity for citizens to participate directly in the policy-making process, and there has been limited use of referenda, despite repeated calls by the Conservative Party to install referenda as an integral part of the policy-making process. At first glance, referenda appear to be an attractive method of including people. However, complex matters are best addressed after much thought and discussion. At the present time, the opportunity to engage in reflections and discussions is limited mostly to politicians and senior civil servants.

Participation in the Ordinary Issues of Social Policy

Ordinary issues appear to present more opportunities for citizens to participate because such issues immediately affect and are more relevant to people at the local level. Thus, while citizenship is often defined in terms of nationalistic and geographic terms and ties, its practice is most often played out in the contexts in which citizens live out their day-to-day existence (Kingwell, 2000). As Putnam (2000) points out, volunteering and participating in the life of the community are part of good citizenship, not an alternative to it. Two Canadian examples of active citizenship can be found in the Vancouver Agreement (www.vancouveragreement.ca) and Town Hall Ontario (www.townhall.ontario.com), where citizens worked with municipal and provincial governments to support community development initiatives. Rosenberg (2004) and Ball (2005) suggest that the lost youth vote does not necessarily equate to a disengaged constituency; rather, youth may turn to community service as they reject political engagement. In fact, the experience of Lifting New Voices in the US demonstrates the competency of young people in creating community change (Checkoway et al., 2003). In Canada, it has been suggested that citizens' apathy towards their democratic institutions masks their interest in "making a difference to their own lives and to the lives of their communities" (Abelson et al., 2004, p. 211). The experience with the Commission on the Future of Health Care in Canada (Romanow Commission) suggests that, when given the appropriate opportunity and access, Canadians want to take a role in shaping their public policies (Abelson et al., 2004).

The experience of the Romanow Commission is confirmed by citizen participation in the Citizens' Assembly on Electoral Reform. This assembly was established by the government of British Columbia (BC) to investigate the need for electoral reform. It was made up of 161 randomly selected individuals from all parts of BC. The assembly held fifty public hearings with 3,000 people attending: "The members of the Assembly—British Columbians who unstintingly gave their time and energy—demonstrated how extraordinary ordinary citizens are when given an important task and the resources and independence to do it right" (BC Citizens' Assembly on Electoral Reform, 2004, p. 17).

Pateman (1970) makes the point that institutions such as education, health and social agencies, trade unions, churches, workplaces, and political parties are appropriate for citizen involvement. It is in these contexts that most citizens with an inclination toward involvement cut their participatory teeth. The voluntary social agency board or the recreation commission is a good training ground that can educate citizens and prepare them to participate in larger and more complex concerns of social policy. Many important decisions affecting the lives of citizens are made outside the representative political system. The Healthy Communities / Cities projects are examples of citizens actively engaging at the local level to improve the health and quality of life of their communities (Wharf Higgins, 1992).

Typically, participants are characterized by their advanced education, income, occupation, age (Jewkes & Murcott, 1998; Lomas & Veenstra, 1995), sense of empowerment (Smith, 1995), and involvement in community life (Putnam, 2000), compared to those who do not participate. Citizens who participate enjoy the formal and substantive benefits of citizenship (Wharf Higgins, 1999). The analysis of the National Survey of Volunteering, Giving, and Participating found a similar pattern among the four fifths of Canadian adults who participate in community-oriented activities classified as "intensive community commitments" (e.g., service club, political, neighbourhood, school, or voluntary organization) (Jones, 2000).

As O'Neill (1992) has documented with respect to the Quebec experience with health care boards, community participation in health reform does not guarantee community empowerment. This certainly was the case during health reform in BC during the mid-1990s when local groups of citizens were assigned the task of developing community health plans and envisioning the future of health care delivery in their region. During the two years that participants worked to implement "New Directions for a Healthy BC," subtle and seemingly inconspicuous actions by the provincial government began to add up to what participants felt was a conspiracy against their work. In the end, the government dismissed the recommendations of the participants, who perceived the government as disavowing two years of their work and with it their committed beliefs.

In a review of the experience of citizen and community participation in health care, White (2000) concludes that participation does not lead to community control, nor does it empower individuals. Nevertheless, she asserts that health care planners and administrators continue to be enthusiastic about citizen participation. Why support a phenomenon that clearly does not achieve its stated objectives? In explaining this apparent contradiction, White notes first that the favoured form of participation is to consult citizens about established plans and, second, that having done so, administrators and planners can then present their recommendations as having the support of the public: "Lay participation as it is preached and practiced is clearly about administrative and political efficiency not democracy, consumer empowerment or community control. It derives its value principally from its role as an administrative strategy" (White, 2000, p. 477). In our view, it would be preferable to dispense with participation than to use it in such a shallow fashion.

Thus, as Wharf Higgins (1999) has documented, participants individually emerged from the health reform experience feeling empowered at the personal level; yet collectively their ability to influence the implementation of health reform decisions was negligible. As with other community participation experiences (e.g., Berry et al., 1993), this left BC citizens calculating the price of their involvement and questioning their willingness to continue. Similarly, an evaluation of citizen participation in a United Way planning process found that relatively high socio-economic status participants believed their influence had been insignificant in deciding how funds should be allocated to meet local needs (Julian, Reischl, Carrick, & Katrenich, 1997).

Second, engaging participants who reflect the diversity of the community is difficult and rarely successful. It is often assumed that because everyone has the right to participate in the decision-making process, the opportunity to do so is identical for all. However, the participation process itself can discriminate against those in the community who are not well educated, well spoken, or well off (Freedman, 1998; Wharf Higgins, 1999). While better-educated people tend to participate more, this does not necessarily imply a lower degree of interest among others in the community. The design flaws inherent in traditional participatory structure—committee meetings and public forums—often make them inconvenient, inaccessible, and intimidating to all but a few who possess the requisite professional experience and educational and discretionary resources to attend (Chrislip, 1995; Syme & Nancarrow, 1992).

For over twenty years, Rosener (1978, p. 114) has argued that participation techniques are often inconsistent with the interests and capabilities of the citizen they are intended to reach: "So while public officials claim apathy, citizens claim inequity." The circumstances that people face living in disadvantaged environments pose barriers to attending meetings or committing oneself to participating in the first place. Innovative participatory opportunities, such as citizen panels (Kathlene & Martin, 1991), and visual and practical planning experiences in malls (Anderson, Meaton, & Potter, 1994) and in neighbourhood associations and churches (Crawshaw, 1994) have been much more successful in bringing together diverse members of the community.

The power hierarchy that often exists between professionals and citizens, particularly in health and social arenas, has also hindered diverse participation (Church & Barker, 1998). Professionals are often perceived as the more knowledgeable and expert decision makers (Scanlan, Zyzanski, Flocke, Stange, & Gravagubins, 1996), whereas involving citizens in the decisions concerning social services may compromise care (Brownlea, 1997). Here, Dahl's (1970) competence criterion becomes highly influential. Tensions emerge as competing pressures between a bottom-up, community-driven process versus a more centralized, professionally driven approach collide (Foley & Martin, 2000).

Third, and much more systemic than the previous challenges, is the perception that many community members hold regarding their status as citizens. The marginalized in Canadian society—lone parents, street youth, the disabled, minorities, and the unemployed—are those who depend on the state for survival. The irony is that receiving services from the very institutions established to help these citizens—which they have the legitimate civil and political right to access—has unintended effects (Rappaport, 1985) which include dehumanization, oppression (Merzel, 1991), humiliation (Sen, 1991), a loss of independent living skills, erosion of personal dignity and self-esteem, and disempowerment (Gorham, 1995; Younis, 1995). Taking decision-making away from citizens and putting it in the hands of professionals who tend to slot people into client categories "robs citizens of their democratic standing in relation to the bureaucrat and the state" (Brown, 1994, p. 890). Hence, while in theory all citizens are created equal, some are more equal than others (Brown, 1989), generating two classes of citizenship (Gorham, 1995).

Minimizing the economic and psychological costs of participation for historically under-represented citizens demands a shift away from traditional participation structures. In addition to being convenient and welcoming, the participatory endeavour must demonstrate some reflection of citizens themselves in order to gain their involvement and trust in the process. In the absence of broad-based participation, particularly when economy of time and problems of scale restrict participation by all, experiential participation may be a step toward achieving better representation of diverse perspectives (Prior, Stewart, & Walsh, 1995). Here, the "meeting mindset" is abandoned and the context for participation takes place in schools, worksites, churches, street corners, and coffee houses, engaging citizens in a planning process that reflects their life experiences. It also demands acknowledging and respecting the diverse and non-traditional contributions of citizens to planning. In contrast to the technical and expert knowledge of professionals, citizens are recognized as having more immediate knowledge of local needs and resources (Richardson & Waddington, 1996). Meaningful participation may constitute sharing experiences as service recipients and providing input about the delivery and quality of health programs, as well as chairing meetings, interpreting statistics, and penning community plans and policies.

Participation in the Grand Issues of Social Policy

We suggest that citizen participation in the grand issues such as taxation, the distribution of income, and the development of national frameworks for income security and health care has never been extensive. In the 1950s and 1960s, the federal government attempted to secure some involvement through the establishment of advisory councils and commissions of inquiry. One review established two criteria to judge whether advisory councils had been effective in those decades: "The council is consulted by the government while policy and legislation is in the planning stage and it has to its credit at least a couple of occasions when the government altered some decision because of its intervention" (Shackleton, 1977, p. 100). On the basis of these criteria, Shackleton concluded that all of the councils had been dismal failures. We disagree with Shackleton with respect to the National Council of Welfare, which has consistently and severely criticized social policies and programs of the federal government. While it may not have succeeded in changing government policy, it has been a much-needed voice for reform and, unlike many councils, has from its inception included low-income citizens in its governing body.

Whether the federal government reached a similar conclusion to Shackleton or acted simply to save money is unknown, but most councils, including the Economic Council of Canada, have been eliminated. Ironically the National Council of Welfare, the most critical and radical of all, persists.

Another example of participation at the federal level occurred in earlier times when continuing relationships existed between senior staff of the federal government, academics, and the executive directors of major social welfare organizations. Thinkers such as Leonard Marsh, Harry Cassidy, Charlotte Whitton, C.A. Curtis, and J.J. Heagerty wrote important reports or chaired important committees, while federal civil servants such as Joseph Willard, George Davidson, and Robert Bryce helped to put these recommendations in place (Rice & Prince, 2000, p. 54).

This loose policy community was composed of like-minded professionals dedicated to the task of building a comprehensive social security and health care system. At the present time, however, this socially conscious policy group has been replaced by a fiscally conservative policy cluster that includes the Canadian Council of Chief Executives (CCCE), the Canadian Tax Foundation, and right-wing think tanks like the Fraser Institute and the C.D. Howe Institute. The resources and contacts of these organizations have enabled them to exert enormous influence on the actions of the federal government in both national and international arenas. Thomas D'Aquino, the president and chief executive officer of the Business Council on National Interests, is quoted in a bestselling book: "If you ask yourself in which period since 1900 has Canada's business community had the most influence on public policy say I would say it was in the last twenty years. Look at what we stand for and look at what all the governments, all the major parties including Reform have done, and what they want to do. They have adopted the agenda we've been fighting for in the past two decades" (Newman, 1999, p. 159). Social policies have been a particular target of the CCCE, the Fraser Institute, and the C.D. Howe Institute. Together, and with the considerable help of the media (controlled by like-minded individuals), they have taken the leadership in a campaign to radically alter the social policy scene in Canada.

Some specific changes made by the federal government include the elimination of the universal Family Allowances program; introduction of a tax clawback on Old Age Security; cancellation of the Canada Assistance Plan Act, which in return for federal contributions to the provinces insisted on a set of national standards for income assistance, and other programs; and drastic reductions in the benefits available to the unemployed.

In short, the CCCE has advocated for and has been effective in sharply limiting the role of government in grand social policy. This council has adopted an agenda that suits high-income earners who can pay for health care, send their children to private schools and summer camps, and employ nannies to look after their infant children, and who can depend on private arrangements for their recreational and cultural pursuits. They have little or no need for publicly funded schools, recreation centres, and health care. Hence their agenda is blatantly self-serving in insisting that the state limit spending on these social utilities.

Both provincial and federal governments have invited citizens to contribute to the work of Royal Commissions and other forms of state-sponsored inquiries. However, commission members have most frequently been professionals and other upper-middle-class individuals. Consumers of service and other marginalized citizens are not at the table when the agenda and work plans of the commission are set. Typically their contributions are requested as a response to plans already established—and, as noted in an earlier section of the chapter, the "meeting mindset" acts as a further barrier to these citizens. However, there are examples of voluntary organizations that have influenced social policy.

In a review of the influence of think tanks and policy advocacy groups, one author concludes that "Indeed by focusing on Ken Battle (President of Caledon) to the development of social welfare policy in Canada one might conclude and justifiably so that the President of the Caledon Institute has had a profound impact on shaping public policy" (Abelson, 2004, p. 161). The Institute has enjoyed success by employing a number of strategies: op-ed articles in major newspapers, relationships with key individuals in the federal government, and a strategy of anticipation. A favourite of the CCCE, this strategy identifies a problem faced by government, develops a number of alternative proposals, anticipates the proposal most likely to be chosen, and presents it to government.

Other examples of voluntary organizations that seek to influence national policies include the Canadian Centre on Policy Alternatives, the Canadian Council on Social Development, Campaign 2000, and the National Anti-Poverty Association. To this list we should add the National Council of Welfare. While an advisory group to the minister of Social Development, the Council has consistently produced reports critical of the actions of the federal government in social and fiscal policy.

While the influence of social policy groups pales in comparison with that exercised by the CCCE, the C.D. Howe Institute, and the Fraser Institute, one should not conclude that there are no progressive voices at the national level. Every year in response to the budget established by the federal government, the Canadian Centre for Policy Alternatives prepares an alternative budget that proposes additional spending on social programs. In a similar fashion, Campaign 2000 issues an annual report card reminding governments at national and provincial levels that they have failed to live up to the 1989 promise to eliminate child poverty by the year 2000. These reports receive extensive media coverage and remind Canadians of the dismal social policy record of governments.

Participation in the Global Issues of Social Policy

In *The Gutenberg Galaxy*, Marshall McLuhan (1962) proclaimed that "The new electronic interdependence recreates the world in the image of a global village." Surely, even this globalization prophet could not have had the vision of the "global village" we are experiencing at the beginning of the twenty-first century. We are in a dramatically different global age from the one to which McLuhan opened our eyes not so long ago.

Globalization—with its various meanings—has become a key word in defining our contemporary way of life. The pace and degree of supranational change is phenomenal. Many would say that more important activities now occur across national boundaries than within them—and not just economic transactions where international capital moves at lightning speed, manipulated by supranational corporations and organizations that operate without reference to national borders. Social, demographic, political, cultural, and environmental dimensions of globalization are in evidence everywhere (Midgely, 2000).

By no means are citizen activities on a global scale new. After all, people have long been concerned about social issues that surpass national boundaries and have participated in a multitude of ways to tackle global problems like peace, world hunger, poverty, health, the environment, and Third World development. Citizen action has long spurred the development of a myriad of both government and non-governmental organizations that attempt to ameliorate complex, transnational social problems. World citizens fulfill many functions in these organizations from financial support to volunteer service and social action and policy development.

One dramatic difference in today's global village is the capacity for simple, inexpensive, instant communication among concerned citizens. The opportunity for rapid information sharing, education, organization, mobilization, and participation in attempts to shape decisions affecting the world's citizens is available to people in the industrialized world through instant global communication—the Internet. In the last few years we have seen remarkable social action and civil disobedience responses at meetings of organizations such as the World Trade Organization (WTO), North American Free Trade Agreement (NAFTA), the General Agreement on Tariffs and Trade (GATT), and the General Agreement on Trade in Services (GATS). These large demonstrations have been marked by significant levels of information sharing, education, and sophisticated organization in preparation for gatherings.

Rarely have we seen encounters with such diverse, interconnected constituencies—Third World, labour, environmentalists of many hues, concerned young people, farmers, indigenous peoples, religious organizations, and folk from different social strata. Despite the distinct lack of commonality of concerns or agreement as to means of protest, and notwithstanding wide variation in values, a common thread of concern has emerged from the protesters and demonstrators. It is opposition to the power of a very small group of non-elected or corporate officials to alter hard-won democratic rights and attack domestic sovereignty in dealing with widely varying matters of social welfare, health care, energy, water, trade, agriculture, the environment, and natural resources. These citizen protests and challenges have become a strong voice of left-wing perspectives as traditional left-of-centre parties no longer occupy centre stage as challengers of the power elites. In Canada, citizen input on these matters has been provided, for example, through the Council of Canadians and the Canadian Centre on Policy Alternatives.

People in Western democracies have taken for granted that they have the democratic right to influence basic social policy directions for their national, provincial, and local governments. This is now cast in doubt as international negotiations and agreements seek to override national and local preference. For many, a move in the direction of world order would not be so threatening if the advantages of the First World were being sustained and distributed more equitably around the planet. Unfortunately, the evidence is quite the opposite. With globalization of the economy and trade, the disparities between the rich and poor of the world have widened, rather than receded (Klein, 2000).

The opposition to such immense international forces of global economic and cultural homogenization has taken the form of significant grassroots demonstrations designed to challenge and disrupt planning meetings. Simultaneously, one marvels at the apparent level of organization of large groups representing such diverse constituencies in the face of overwhelming economic, organizational, and oppositional odds, while despairing that this protest is the form of "participation" left to disenfranchised global citizens facing grave social problems and political choices. Klein (2000), in her international bestseller *No Logo*, describes grassroots social activism by world citizens versus transnational corporations and the monopolies they hold, while elected governments have been ignorant or impotent. While the demands of vocalizing and mobilizing around issues of personal choice are decidedly different from those made by citizens who become involved in local governance or volunteer activities, the purpose is no different: such citizens seek to effect change at the most personal of levels, with respect to the clothes we wear, the gas we use, and the non-renewable food we eat.

All around the world, parties and protests have been held in financial districts and outside stock exchanges, superstores, banks, and multinational headquarters: a collection of protectionists getting together out of necessity to fight everything and anything global. As connections have formed across national lines, however, a different agenda has taken hold, one that embraces globalization but seeks to wrest it from the grasp of the multinationals. Ethical shareholder, culture jammers, street reclaimers, McUnion organizers, human rights hacktivists, school-logo fighters, and Internet corporate watchdogs are at the early stages of demanding a citizen-centred alternative to the international rule of the brands (Klein, 2000, pp. 444–446). Citizens trying to open the doors to elite decision-making are expending an enormous amount of organizing and participatory energy.

Participation in the Global Issues of Social Policy

Conclusion   Whence citizen participation in this era of globalization? On the one hand, we see that the means of sharing information, education, organization, and participation are present in ways never before imagined. On the other, we see planetary inequality at unprecedented levels accompanying the relentless march of global capitalism. While we are at a point where the means and opportunities for global citizen participation have unbounded potential, the values and ideologies of those who dominate the world's resources represent only a fraction of the world's citizens.

Conclusion

The concluding comments of this chapter contained in earlier editions of *Canadian Social Policy* remain as relevant today as they were when they were written: namely that the participation of citizens in the development and implementation of social policy remains very much at the margin. To be sure, many middle- and upper-class citizens with the time and freedom from financial worries do participate in the affairs of health and social service agencies in the voluntary sector. Low-income citizens demonstrate enormous commitment in participating in local agencies and particularly those concerned with poverty. While the work of these agencies is important to the health and well-being of communities, they represent the ordinary issues of social policy. Indeed, from our point of view, the regrettable reality is that citizen participation in social policy is most evident where it matters the least.

There are a few, but only a few, opportunities for citizens to participate in the ordinary issues at municipal and provincial levels. In most provinces, citizens can stand for election in school boards and some provinces have created health boards composed of locally elected or appointed citizens to govern health care on a regional basis. However, as noted earlier, only the well-educated, well-spoken, and well-off are members of school and health boards. Policy development and implementation in provincial ministries or departments remains an exclusive responsibility of politicians and civil servants.

Again, from our point of view, a particularly distressing example of the absence of citizen participation occurs in public sector human service organizations. The social work profession is committed to the values of acceptance, self-determination, and respect of individuality. Social workers are dedicated to the welfare and self-realization of human beings; to the development and disciplined use of scientific knowledge regarding human and societal behaviours; to the development of resources to meet individual, group, national, and international needs and aspirations; and to the achievement of social justice for all (Canadian Association of Social Workers, 1994).

We argue that this commitment is consistent with and supports the principle of affected interests. No one is more deeply affected by the absence of social justice and by inadequate resources than those in receipt of human services. Hence, those served have a primary reason to be involved in the development and implementation of the policies that affect them. However, few public sector organizations have seen fit to honour this principle, and the social work profession has only intermittently and occasionally advocated for the inclusion of those being served in the policy process.

A hopeful example of citizen participation is occurring at the global scene where citizens have organized effective protests against the actions of multinational organizations and have forced these powerful organizations to pause in their headlong rush to establish corporations as the dominant ruling force in the world. Canada can lay claim to considerable contributions to these protests through the work of the Council of Canadians and of young activists like Naomi Klein. If multinational organizations can be throttled back through citizen action, it is theoretically possible that the same energy and commitment could be brought to bear on social policy matters that affect children and families in a most immediate fashion. Both Canada and the United Kingdom are desperately seeking ways to improve the delivery of health and social services. One path might be to finally implement the recommendations of numerous commissions of inquiry, such as the CELDIC Report (Commission on Emotional and Learning Disorders in Children, 1970) and New Directions for a Healthy British Columbia (British Columbia Ministry of Health and Ministry Responsible for Seniors, 1993) that services should be provided on a decentralized basis and governed by boards of elected citizens.

References

Abelson, J., Forest, P-G., Eyles, J., Casebeer, A., & Mackean, G. (2004). Will it make a difference if I show up and share? A citizens' perspective on improving public involvement processes for health system decision-making. *Journal of Health Services and Research Policy, 9*(4), 205–212.

Anderson, M., Meaton, J., & Potter, C. (1994). Public participation: An approach using aerial photographs at Ashford, Kent. *Town Planning Review, 6*(1), 41–58.

Arai, S. (2000). Typology of volunteers for a changing sociopolitical context: The impact on social capital, citizenship and civil society. *Society and Leisure, 23*(2), 327–352.

BC Citizens' Assembly on Electoral Reform. (2004). Making every vote count: The case for electoral reform in British Columbia. Online at <www.citizensassem bly.bc.ca/public>.

Ball, W. (2005). From community engagements to political engagement. *Political Science and Politics, 38*(2), 287–291.

Banting, K. (1987). Visions of the welfare state. In S. Seward (Ed.), *The future of social welfare systems in Canada and the United Kingdom* (pp. 147–165). Halifax: Institute for Research on Public Policy.

Berry, J.M., Kent, E.P., & Thomson, K. (1993). *The rebirth of urban democracy.* Washington, DC: Brookings Institute.

Bregha, F.J. (1973). *Public participation in planning, policy and programme.* Toronto: Ministry of Culture and Recreation.

British Columbia Ministry of Health and Ministry Responsible for Seniors. (1993). *New directions for a healthy British Columbia.* Victoria: Author.

References　Brown, C. (1989, April). Citizens' rights. *New Statesman and Society, 2*, 28.

Brown, M.P. (1994). The work of city politics: Citizenship through employment in the local response to AIDS. *Environment and Planning, 26*, 873–894.

Brownlea, A. (1987). Participation: Myths, realities and prognosis. *Social Science and Medicine, 25*(6), 605–614.

Canadian Association of Social Workers. (1994). Code of ethics. Reprinted in J. Turner & F. Turner (2001), *Canadian social welfare* (4th ed., pp. 545–555). Toronto: Allyn and Bacon Canada.

Checkoway, B., Richards-Schuster, K., Abdullah, S., Aragon, M., Facio, E., Figueroa, L., Reddy, E., Welsh, M., & White, A. (2003). Young people as competent citizens. *Community Development Journal, 38*(4), 298–309.

Chrislip, D. (1995). Pulling together—creating a constituency for change. *National Civic Review, 84*, 21–29.

Church, J., & Barker, P. (1998). Regionalization of health services in Canada: A critical perspective. *International Journal of Health Services, 28*(3), 467–486.

Clarke, H., Kornberg, A., MacLeod, J., & Scotto, T. (2005). Too close to call: Political choice in Canada, 2004. *Political Science and Politics, 38*(2), 247–253.

Commission on Emotional and Learning Disorders in Children. (1970). *One million children*. Toronto: Leonard Cranford.

Crawshaw, R. (1994). Grass roots participation in health care reform. *Annals of Internal Medicine, 120*(8), 677–681.

Dahl, R.A. (1970). *After the revolution*. New Haven: Yale University Press.

Drover, G. (2000). Redefining social citizenship in a global era. *Canadian Social Work, 2*(1), 29–49.

Foley, P., & Martin, S. (2000). A new deal for the community? Public participation in regeneration and local service delivery. *Policy and Politics, 28*(4), 479–492.

Fraser, H. (2005). Four different approaches to community participation. *Community Development Journal, 40*(3), 286–300.

Freedman, T.G. (1998). "Why don't they come to Pike Street and ask us?": Black American women's health concerns. *Social Science and Medicine, 47*(7), 941–947.

Gorham, E. (1995). Social citizenship and its fetters. *Polity, 28*(1), 25–47.

Graham, J., Swift, K., & Delaney, R. (2000). *Canadian social policy*. Scarborough: Prentice Hall/Allyn and Bacon Canada.

Hemingway, J.L. (1999). Leisure, social capital and democratic citizenship. *Journal of Leisure Research, 31*(2), 150–165.

Jewkes, R., & Murcott, A. (1998). Community representatives: Representing the community? *Social Science and Medicine, 46*(7), 843–858.

Jones, F. (2000). Community involvement: The influence of early experience. *Canadian Social Trends, 57*, 15–19.

Julian, D., Reischl, R., Carrick R., & Katrenich, C. (1997). Citizen participation—lessons from a local United Way planning process. *American Planners Association Journal, 63*(3), 345–355.

Kathlene, L., & Martin, J.A. (1991). Enhancing citizen participation: Panel designs, perspectives and policy formation. *Journal of Policy Analysis and Management, 10*(1), 46–63.

Kingwell, M. (2000). *The world we want: Virtue, vice and the good citizen*. Toronto: Viking.

Klein, N. (2000). *No logo: Taking aim at the brand bullies*. Toronto: Vintage Canada.

Labonte, R., & Laverack, G. (2001). Capacity building in health promotion, Part 1:   **References**
For whom? And for what purpose? *Critical Public Health, 11*(2), 111–127.

Laverack, G., & Wallerstein, N. (2001). Measuring community empowerment: A fresh look at organizational domains. *Health Promotion International, 16*(2), 179–185.

Lawton, D. (1979). Can communities take control of campaigns? *National Civic Review, 68,* 53–56.

Lindblom, C. (1979). Still muddling, not yet through. *Public Administration Review, 39,* 517–526.

Lomas, J., & Veenstra, G. (1995). If you build it, who will come? *Policy Options, 16*(6), 37–40.

Marshall, T.H. (1977). *Class, citizenship and social development.* Chicago: University of Chicago Press.

McLuhan, M. (1962). *The Gutenberg galaxy: The making of a typographic man.* Toronto: University of Toronto Press.

Merzel, C. (1991, Winter). Rethinking empowerment. *Health/PAC Bulletin,* 5–6.

Midgley, J. (2000). Globalization, capitalism and social welfare: A social development perspective. *Canadian Social Work, 2*(1), 13–28.

Newman, P. (1999). *Titans: How the new Canadian establishment seized power.* Toronto: Penguin.

O'Neill, M. (1992). Community participation in Quebec's health system: A strategy to curtail community empowerment? *International Journal of Health Services, 22*(2), 287–301.

Pammett, J., & LeDuc, L. (2003, March). *Explaining the turnout decline in Canadian federal elections: A new survey of non-voters.* Online at <www.elections.ca>.

Pateman, C. (1970). *Participation and democratic theory.* Cambridge: Cambridge University Press.

Perlstadt, H., Jackson-Elmore, C., Freddolino, P., & Reed, C. (1998). An overview of citizen participation in health planning: Lessons learned from the literature. *National Civic Review, 87*(4), 347–368.

Phillips, A. (1993). *Democracy and difference.* Cambridge: Polity Press.

Pivik, J. (2002). *Practical strategies for facilitating meaningful citizen involvement in health planning* (Discussion Paper no. 23). Commission on the Future of Healthcare in Canada.

Prior, D., Stewart, J., & Walsh, K. (1995). *Citizenship: Rights, community and participation.* London: Pitman.

Putnam, R. (2000). *Bowling alone: The collapse and revival of American community.* New York: Simon and Schuster.

Rappaport, J. (1985). The power of empowerment language. *Social Policy, 15,* 5–21.

Rice, J., & Prince, M. (2000). *Changing politics of Canadian social policy.* Toronto: University of Toronto Press.

Richardson, R., & Waddington, C. (1996). Allocating resources: Community involvement is not easy. *International Journal of Health Planning and Management, 11,* 307–315.

Rittel, H., & Webber, M. (1973). Dilemmas in a general theory of planning. *Policy Science, 5,* 155–169.

Rosenberg, Y. (2004). Lost youth. *American Demographics, 26*(2), 17–19.

References Rosener, J. (1978). Matching method to purpose: The challenges of planning citizen-participation activities. In S. Langton, (Ed.), *Citizen participation in America* (pp. 109–122). Lexington: D.C. Heath.

Scanlan, A., Zyzanski, S., Flocke, S., Stange, K., & Gravagubins, I. (1996). A comparison of U.S. and Canadian family physicians' attitudes toward their respective health care systems. *Medical Care, 34,* 837–844.

Sen, R. (1994). Building community involvement in health care. *Social Policy, 23*(3), 32–43.

Shackleton, D. (1977). *Power town: Democracy discarded.* Toronto: McClelland and Stewart.

Smith, D. (1995). *First person plural, a community development approach to social change.* Montreal: Black Rose.

Syme, G.J., & Nancarrow, B.E. (1992). Predicting public involvement in urban water management and planning. *Environment and Behavior, 24*(6), 738–758.

Warren, R., & Weschler, L.F. (1975). The costs of citizenship. In R. Warren & L.F. Weschler (Eds.), *Governing urban space* (pp. 10–23). Newark: University of Delaware Press.

Wharf Higgins, J. (1992). The healthy communities movement in Canada. In B. Wharf (Ed.), *Communities and social policy in Canada* (pp. 151–189). Toronto: McClelland and Stewart.

Wharf Higgins, J. (1999). Citizenship and empowerment: A remedy for citizen participation in health reform. *Community Development Journal, 34*(4), 287–307.

Wharf Higgins, J., & Rickert, T. (2005). "A taste of healthy living": Recreational opportunities and the prevention of type 2 diabetes. *Leisure Sciences, 27,* 439–458.

White, D. (2000). Consumer and community participation: A reassessment of process, impact and value. In G. Albrecht, R. Fitzpatrick, & S.C. Scrimshaw (Eds.), *Handbook of social studies in health and medicine* (pp. 465–480). London: Sage.

Younis, T. (1995). The Allende community experiment in empowerment: Participation too far? *Local Government Studies, 21*(2), 263–279.

Ziersch, A. (2005). Health implications of access to social capital: Findings from an Australian study. *Social Science and Medicine, 61,* 2119–2131.

Additional Resources

Canadian Centre for Policy Alternatives. Online at <www.policyalternatives.ca>.

Canadian Council on Social Development. Online at <www.ccsd.ca>.

Canadian Policy Research Networks. Online at <www.cprn.org>.

Council of Canadians. Online at <www.canadians.org>.

Harvey, J. (2001). *The role of sport and recreation policy in fostering citizenship: The Canadian experience.* Ottawa: Canadian Policy Research Networks.

Jenson, J., & Papillon, M. (2001). *The changing boundaries of citizenship. A review and research agenda.* Ottawa: Canadian Policy Research Networks. Online at <www.cprn.org>.

Laker, A. (2000). *Beyond the boundaries of physical education: Educating young people for citizenship and social responsibility.* London: Routledge/Falmer.

Phillips, S., & Orsini, M. (2002). *Mapping the links: Citizen involvement in policy processes.* Discussion Paper no. f21. Canadian Policy Research Network. Online at <www.cprn.org>.

Valentine, F. (2001). *Enabling citizenship: Full inclusion of children with disabilities and their parents.* Discussion Paper no. f13. Canadian Policy Research Networks. Online at <www.cprn.org>.   **References**

Anne Westhues

The Larger Political Context

Social policy is evaluated in an environment that is just as political as the one in which it is formulated. This means that evaluators have to be aware of the larger political context in which a study takes place, as well as the politics within the organizations delivering the programs intended to implement a policy. Evaluators must also be aware of how they believe knowledge is created and the implications of this perspective for their role as evaluators. The perspective taken will shape the evaluators' research design, their sampling, the means they will use to collect data, the generalizability of the findings, and any responsibility they understand themselves to have beyond carrying out research and reporting the findings. In this chapter, I will briefly review the larger political context of social policy evaluation, outline shifts in thinking over the past thirty years about the questions to be answered by evaluation, and describe the evolution of evaluation research functions since it was recognized as an essential part of the policy-making process by the federal government in Canada in the 1970s. I will show how this evolution has been influenced by both the political context and by the debates about epistemology, and I will close with a discussion of the impact that a shift to a more humanist approach to evaluation has had on the development of social policy.

The 1960s and 1970s were a time of great hope among social workers in Canada, with the passage of many progressive pieces of social policy legislation, including the Canadian Bill of Rights, the Canada Assistance Plan, the Medical Care Act, the Canada/Quebec Pension Plan, and the addition of maternity benefits to the Unemployment Insurance Act (Guest, 1985). Consequently, expenditures for health and social services increased dramatically, from $2,257 million in 1960–1961 to $61,490 million in 1982 (Guest, 1985) continuing on to $138,328 million by 2005–2006 (Statistics Canada, 2005). Spending growth increased steadily over this period, with the largest increases in times of high unemployment. This growth slowed in the 1980s when a Conservative government under Brian Mulroney replaced the Liberals federally.

The Larger Political Context

A neo-conservative policy environment gave rise to international agreements like the Free Trade Agreement in 1989 and the North American Free Trade Agreement in 1993, as well as a commitment to reduced taxation, all of which created pressure to reduce spending for health, education, and social services as the federal government attempted to "harmonize" our social policy and taxation levels with the United States. Most provincial governments during the 1990s shared this philosophy.

The perception of high levels of government spending, a more conservative political environment, and substantial growth in the number of social scientists trained to do evaluation research all contributed to the conditions that gave rise to a concern with accountability that went beyond a narrow emphasis on financial management (Muller-Clemm & Barnes, 1997). While the profit sector has the bottom line of profit and loss to tell them how well business ventures are doing, the non-profit sector has no comparable indicator to assess what is being achieved through social spending. The promise of a method that would allow the federal government to systematically measure the impact of social programs led to a commitment to program and policy evaluation.

Evaluation of programs became routine, with the Treasury Board approving its first formal policy requiring deputy heads to evaluate all programs within their jurisdiction in 1977 (Muller-Clemm & Barnes, 1997). Programs were understood to be the mechanism by which policy was implemented, so by extension, program evaluation was seen as the way to evaluate policy as well. The Nielsen Task Force review of 989 federal programs in 1984 concluded that evaluations of these programs were inadequate, in part because they were often internal evaluations and therefore seen as self-serving. They were also criticized for failing to question a program's basic rationale, focusing instead on impact (outcomes) and delivery (process). A further criticism levelled at federal program evaluations was that they were not "objective" but "political" and therefore value-laden (Sutherland, cited in Muller-Clemm & Barnes, 1997).

These critiques led to a revised policy in 1991, reaffirming a commitment to program evaluation as a mechanism for improved cost-effectiveness and for decision-making with respect to program changes, including whether a program should continue to operate (Senate of Canada, 1991). Program evaluation is now understood to be "the essential bridge from program management to policy development" (Gauthier et al., 2004). Notwithstanding a thirty-year experience with program and policy evaluation, and an apparent recommitment to an "objective" approach to evaluation by the federal government, evaluators continue to explore questions of methodology, epistemology, and the role of the evaluator (see the *Canadian Journal of Program Evaluation, Evaluation Review,* and *Evaluation and Program Planning*). Primary among these is the role of the evaluator.

Role of the Evaluator

In the early days of evaluation research, the role of the evaluator was defined as that of a detached, value-free researcher engaged in the primarily "rational" process of assessing whether a program was meeting its objectives or outcomes (Rossi & Freeman, 1982; Suchman, 1967; Weiss, 1972). Over time, researchers realized that they might discover that a program met its objectives, but not know why. They began to redefine their role to include interaction with those who had designed, delivered, and managed the programs being evaluated, to learn about the program elements and why it was thought the program would deliver the expected results; that is, there was increased recognition of the theory of the program, as well as the political and ethical aspects of evaluation (Abma, 1997; House, 1980, 1993).

More recently, the roles of program consultant or program developer have been recognized by most evaluators as appropriate practice in some cases (Patton, 1997), with the evaluator internal to the organization rather than external (Love, 1983). The "participatory" approaches advocate engagement not only with service deliverers, but with service users (Christie & Rose, 2003; Nelson, Ochocka, Griffin, & Lord, 1998; Ottier, 2005; VanderPlaat, Samson & Raven, 2001). This role requires the evaluator to be even less detached, entering, after the evaluation is completed, into in-depth discussions with service providers and service users about what should be changed based upon study findings. The politics of this relationship are clearly different and more complex than for the external evaluator.

The debate as to the appropriateness of the role of program developer within the context of evaluation research continues, and questions remain about how much responsibility the evaluator carries for ensuring that the recommendations are implemented and how neutral the researcher should be in presenting the results of a study with public policy implications (Roach & Youngman Berdahl, 1999). In addition to the discussion about internal versus external evaluators, terms like "critical evaluation" (Everitt, 1996; VanderPlaat, 1997) and "empowerment evaluation" (VanderPlaat, Samson, & Raven, 2001; Worthington, 1999) have begun to appear in the literature. This debate can be understood as the manifestation of a fundamental discussion within the social sciences: whether the researcher should adopt a philosophy of science that is positivist, or one that Maguire (1987) describes as humanist. This debate raises a number of issues that recommend different practices to the evaluator, summarized as follows by Maguire:

- objectivity versus subjectivity
- research distance versus closeness to subject
- generalizations or universality versus uniqueness
- quantitative versus qualitative
- social control versus local self-determination
- impartial advice versus solidarity and action

Role of the
Evaluator

The positivist approach posits that there are observable social facts that the researcher must discover using research methods borrowed from the natural sciences. The humanist perspective, a blend of what others have called naturalistic and transformational (Westhues, Cadell, Karabanow, Maxwell, & Sanchez, 1999), argues that human reality is socially constructed. That is, it is a consequence of the interplay between an individual's values and experience (Baum, 1987; Gergen, 1985). Hence it is critical to capture the subjective experience or perception of participants in the study. In the case of evaluation, this means not only service users but those involved in providing a social program as service deliverers, managers, and funders as well. The humanist perspective argues that meaningful insights cannot be gained without close interpersonal interchange. In this regard, the humanist perspective fits well with those wanting to privilege the experiences and perspectives of such marginalized groups as women, members of the GBLT (gay-bisexual-lesbian-transsexual-transgender) community, visible minorities, indigenous peoples, people who are differently abled, and people living in poverty (Brown & Strega, 2005; Ristock & Pennell, 1996). In contrast, associated with the positivist belief in objectivity is the need to maintain distance from the people or systems being studied.

The very purpose of research is conceptualized differently by the positivist and the humanist. For the positivist, generalization to a larger population is the intent of research, whereas for the humanist the purpose is to understand the workings of a given group or program at a specific time in history. Positivists and humanists also differ with respect to the type of data that they collect. For the positivist, the more quantifiable the data, the better. Humanists are likely to supplement qualitative data with quantitative data, or use only qualitative data, which they believe provide insight and a depth of understanding that the quantitative data alone lack. Recent discussions about mixed methods approaches have furthered our understanding of the epistemology (Greene & Caracelli, 2003; Maxcy, 2003; Teddlie & Tashakkori, 2003) and methodological issues associated with a mixed method approach (Creswell, Plano, Clark, Gutman, & Hanson, 2003; Maxwell & Loomis, 2003; Morse, 2003; Newman, Ridenour, Newman, & DeMarco, 2003).

Positivist and humanist researchers also differ with respect to their definition of the political impact of research. For the positivists, the goal is to develop understanding of human behaviour, which permits control of those behaviours by the knowledge holders: in this case, policy-makers, program developers, and managers. For the humanists, the goal is one of self-determination or empowerment. They feel that both the research process and its outcomes should put increased power in the hands of participants in the study. This understanding of the evaluation researcher's role is consistent with what Vaillancourt (1996) calls "new progressive social work" or what Brown & Strega (2005) call an anti-oppressive approach.

Finally, positivists leave it to policy-makers and politicians to decide how to use the results of the research findings: they see their job solely as providing the most objective and impartial assessment possible. By contrast, humanist researchers recognize the policy implications of their work and advocate for those changes.

Changes in evaluation practice over the past twenty-five years have moved the field away from a more purely positivist orientation toward one that fits with Maguire's conceptualization of humanist practice. This has occurred through the addition of two research functions to the field of evaluation research—evaluability assessment and needs assessment—as well as through changes in practice in the traditional research functions of process and outcome evaluation. Developments in each of the above research functions are analyzed below with respect to their contribution to the evolution of the field of evaluation research and their support of this epistemological shift.

Evolution of Evaluation Research Practice

Evolution of Evaluation Research Practice

Outcome Evaluation

The primary focus of evaluation efforts in the early years of practice was on outcome evaluation. The questions answered by an outcome evaluation are: Is the program having the desired effect? At the desired level of cost? (Pancer & Westhues, 1989). The research techniques traditionally associated with this approach are experimental (randomized, with a control group) and quasi-experimental designs (not randomized, and may not have a control group).

Reflecting the shift to a more humanist philosophy in evaluation, social workers have argued for the utility of the single case design in assessing outcomes (Bloom, Fischer, & Orme, 2006; Briar & Blythe, 1985; Jayaratne, 1978; Mutscheler, 1979; Thomas, 1978). The single case approach may use quantitative or qualitative data, but focuses upon the achievement of an individual participant's goals within the program. This shows increased concern with the unique rather than the universal or generalizable. It also shows a move toward greater subjectivity, as the assessment of whether the individual has achieved his or her goals is often a self-report measure like Hudson's self-esteem or peer relations indexes (Hudson, 1982).

Another way in which a move is seen toward the subjective is the use of client satisfaction surveys to assess the effects of participating in a social program (Atkisson & Zwick, 1982; Giordano, 1977; Nguyen, Atkisson, & Stegner, 1983). Again, the focus of these questionnaires is often upon people's experience within the program and their perception of its effects upon them. This is in contrast to a more behavioural approach, which might have the service deliverer or a trained observer assessing individual behaviours that have been defined as indicators of the program participant achieving goals such as increased self-esteem or improved peer relations. While it is now more common to collect client satisfaction data, questions are being posed about the extent to which it actually influences program design or delivery (Holosko, 1996)—an ethical challenge for evaluators.

Social impact assessments, though not yet widely used, are a means by which one can measure the effects of programs that are intended to have a community-wide impact, like a public education campaign about family violence. These effects would be clearest in small or well-defined communities experiencing few other changes (Bowles, 1981; Finterbusch & Wolf 1977; Tester & Myles, 1981). Their design is participatory and action-oriented. The findings of the assessment are fed back to the community with the intention of helping it assess whether it is meeting its goals, such as a reduction in family violence.

To determine whether the program is achieving its effects at a desired level of cost, evaluators borrowed cost-benefit and cost-effectiveness analysis from economists. Both cost-benefit and cost-effectiveness analyses involve a calculation of the costs and the benefits of a program. In cost-benefit analysis, the benefits are assigned a monetary value so that a benefit-to-cost ratio can be calculated. If a program is found to have greater benefits than costs, or a greater benefit-to-cost ratio than a specified level, then it is concluded that it is meeting its objectives at an acceptable level of cost (Stokey & Zeckhauser, 1978; Yates, 1985).

A further refinement of the cost question is the development of cost-outcome analysis (McCready & Rahn, 1983, 1986). With this approach, costs are calculated for the program, a determination is made of what proportion of clients are successfully treated within the program, and then a cost-per-successful outcome figure is calculated. Thus, if a program is expensive for each person served, but has a high success rate, it would have a higher cost-outcome benefit than a program that was less expensive on a per capita basis but which also had a lower level of successful outcomes.

Process Evaluation

It soon became evident to evaluation researchers that the programs they were asked to assess were often "black boxes." That is, the actual service delivered was not clearly articulated, and there was little or no monitoring to ensure that it was implemented as it had been designed (Weiss, 1972). This meant that if the evaluator found that the program was meeting its objectives, it wasn't clear how to replicate that program in another setting. If the finding was that it was not meeting its objectives, it wasn't clear if this was a failure of theory or a failure of implementation. The response to this realization was to invest in developing the aspect of evaluation research that is called process evaluation, or monitoring (Rossi & Freeman, 1982) or auditing (Posavac & Carey, 1997).

A process evaluation answers the primary question: Is the program operating as planned? More specifically, is the quantity of service intended being delivered, and is the quality of service intended being delivered? (Pancer & Westhues, 1989). Information systems, peer review ratings, and client satisfaction surveys are the research techniques most often utilized in process evaluation. To determine whether the quantity of service is sufficient, data would be gathered on how many clients are being served; whether they are the intended client group; and whether they are receiving the intended types of service (Caputo, 1986; Hanbery, Sorenson, & Kucic, 1981). All these questions are routinely answered with data from a well-constructed information system.

To answer the question of whether the intended quality of service is being provided is more complex. Data sources might include periodic case reviews like those that are now common with children in foster care (Backus, 1978; Chappell, 1975; Claburn & Magura, 1978); comparison to standards that have been set by the program funder or a professional body (Ontario Ministry of Community and Social Services, 1981); judicial reviews to determine the constitutionality of a policy or whether it has been implemented according to principles of due process and accepted administrative law (Howlett & Ramesh, 1995); or a quality-assurance approach that relies upon peer review to determine whether the appropriate service was provided (Frankel & Sinclair, 1982; Sinclair & Frankel, 1983). Observational techniques might also be used, as in an evaluation of a distress line where quality of service was assessed by means of pseudo-calls made to the distress line by an actress (Crocker, 1983). Observation through a one-way mirror might be possible to assess the quality of counselling being offered. Client satisfaction surveys may also focus on process as well as outcomes, providing insight into how people who use services experience them (Williams et al., 2001). The health care and education "report cards" now being issued in many provinces are an example of a fairly comprehensive process evaluation that draws upon a mix of the approaches outlined above.

While process evaluation was recognized early as important to the understanding or interpretation of the results of an outcome evaluation (Suchman, 1967), the argument is now made that process evaluation is useful in and of itself when the purpose of the evaluation is formative (Posavac & Carey, 1997). This position reinforces the legitimacy of the evaluator's role as program developer. As such, it reflects a humanist perspective because it recognizes the uniqueness of each program, and its potential to unfold in a way that is unlike any other program. Process evaluation also emphasizes the importance of qualitative data such as client comments about their experience in the program, as well as quantitative data such as how many clients are being served, and whether they are demographically the same as the intended group.

Evaluability Assessment / Program Logic Models

From the beginning, evaluators encountered difficulties regarding program objectives when undertaking evaluations: program and policy objectives were often implicit rather than explicit; or they had in fact shifted from what was explicitly written when the program was first begun a number of years earlier; or there were different understandings among service providers, managers, funders, and program participants as to program objectives. If evaluators selected objectives for the program, or if they took as objectives what was stated in the original program description, those choices could well be at variance with the current focus of program activities. As a consequence, the program would be evaluated against objectives that were no longer valid in the perception of service providers, service recipients, or perhaps funders. When this happened, or was perceived to happen, the research findings were not utilized (Patton, 1997). To address this problem of non-utilization, evaluators began to write about "pre-evaluation work" (Suchman, 1967), "developing a program model" (Weiss, 1972), evaluability assessment (Rutman, 1980; Wholey, Nay, Scanlon, & Schmidt, 1975), or, more recently, program logic models (McLaughlin & Jordan, 1999; Montague, 2000; Petrosino, 2000; Rush & Ogborne, 1991; Wong-Rieger & David, 1993). All of these are frameworks to organize thinking; they support what came to be known as theory-based evaluation (Chen, 1990, 1994; Finney & Moos, 1989).

Rutman, a Canadian who played a major role in developing these ideas, suggested that the purpose of the evaluability assessment is twofold: to determine what kind of evaluation is appropriate for the program at this time; and to ensure that the program managers and the evaluator have agreed upon realistic, measurable objectives with respect to process and outcomes, appropriate performance indicators, and intended uses of the information prior to the evaluation (Rutman, 1980). The evaluability assessment answers these questions: What are the components of the program? Are the intended effects (goals) and unintended effects of the program clearly specified? Can the program realistically achieve the specified goals or produce the anticipated effects? (Pancer & Westhues, 1989). The technique associated with this aspect of evaluability assessment is called a program logic model (Rush & Ogborne, 1991), and in addition to telling the evaluator whether it is reasonable to proceed with an outcome evaluation and what to focus on in a process evaluation, it can also be used to help explicate the theory of the program (McLaughlin & Jordan, 1999) and to define outcome objectives for performance measurement (McEwan & Bigelow, 1997).

A second aspect of the evaluability assessment is to complete what Rutman calls a purpose analysis. This addresses another difficulty that evaluators experienced—the recognition that evaluation can be carried out for many reasons, including a desire to whitewash a poorly functioning program, or to torpedo a well-functioning one (Suchman, 1967). By purpose analysis, Rutman means that the evaluator should attend to the political concerns pertaining to the evaluation, answering these questions: Why is this evaluation being proposed at this time? Who are the various stakeholders, or interest groups? Whose interests are primary, that is, which of the stakeholders is pushing for the evaluation right now—the managers, the consumers, or the funders? (Rutman, 1980).

It can be seen from the above description that the development of the research function called evaluability assessment rests upon an acceptance of humanist principles. It builds upon the assumption that program objectives are socially constructed and thus can be identified only in discussion with program providers and program participants. The process of reaching agreement on the objectives of the program creates a trust and closeness in the working relationship between the evaluator and program staff that is unlikely to occur if the evaluator remains distant from them in an attempt to retain objectivity. The literature is full of articles outlining the tensions between practitioners and researchers, an indication of the pervasiveness of this problem (Carrilio, 1981; Casselman, 1971/72; Davies & Kelly, 1976; Fanshel, 1966; Gordon, 1984; Saleeby 1979; Stiffman, Feldman, Evans, & Orme, 1984). The use of an evaluability assessment also recognizes that when a program is delivered in a number of sites, the sites share common objectives, but they may have additional unique ones. This shift may be at variance with the funders' expectations if they are interested in "apolitical" assessments against predetermined outcomes, a reversion back to the thinking in the early days of program evaluation, which we see being articulated by neo-conservative governments today (Muller-Clemm & Barnes, 1997).

The intent of the staff and service user consultation with respect to specification of objectives and input into the design of the research is to empower those involved in delivering and using the program by giving them the opportunity to have questions asked in the data collection that will be helpful to them in program development. Finally, it is argued that an evaluation that is based upon an evaluability assessment is more likely to be used by program managers and staff because they understand the research process and have had input into its design. This is congruent with the humanist position that a researcher has responsibility for ensuring that the results of his or her work are utilized.

Using the Logic Model

The work of "evaluability assessment" has come to be identified with the use of program logic models to articulate the program components, the activities expected to be associated with each component, the shorter-term outcomes associated with delivery of the components, and the longer-term outcomes associated with the program as a whole (Rush & Ogborne, 1991; Wong-Rieger & David, 1993). A recent article by Nelson, Ochocka, Trainor, and Lauzon (2004) develops a comprehensive evaluation framework for mental health consumer/survivor initiatives using a logic model to identify components, activities, and outcomes succinctly; showing how outcome and process evaluations are related; and demonstrating how a logic model makes these linkages transparent.

Outcomes associated with the various program components, as can be seen in Figure 8.1, include an increased sense of belonging, increased volunteering, increased skills among consumer/survivors, increased opportunities for social interaction, increased awareness of mental health issues and supports, increased opportunities for social interaction, an increased sense of well-being, increased networks of support, and reduced hospitalization.

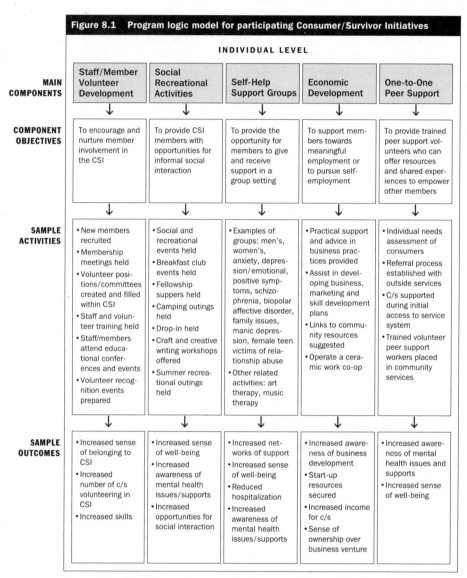

Figure 8.1   Program logic model for participating Consumer/Survivor Initiatives

INDIVIDUAL LEVEL

	Staff/Member Volunteer Development	Social Recreational Activities	Self-Help Support Groups	Economic Development	One-to-One Peer Support
MAIN COMPONENTS	Staff/Member Volunteer Development	Social Recreational Activities	Self-Help Support Groups	Economic Development	One-to-One Peer Support
COMPONENT OBJECTIVES	To encourage and nurture member involvement in the CSI	To provide CSI members with opportunities for informal social interaction	To provide the opportunity for members to give and receive support in a group setting	To support members towards meaningful employment or to pursue self-employment	To provide trained peer support volunteers who can offer resources and shared experiences to empower other members
SAMPLE ACTIVITIES	• New members recruited • Membership meetings held • Volunteer positions/committees created and filled within CSI • Staff and volunteer training held • Staff/members attend educational conferences and events • Volunteer recognition events prepared	• Social and recreational events held • Breakfast club events held • Fellowship suppers held • Camping outings held • Drop-in held • Craft and creative writing workshops offered • Summer recreational outings held	• Examples of groups: men's, women's, anxiety, depression/emotional, positive symptoms, schizophrenia, biopolar affective disorder, family issues, manic depression, female teen victims of relationship abuse • Other related activities: art therapy, music therapy	• Practical support and advice in business practices provided • Assist in developing business, marketing and skill development plans • Links to community resources suggested • Operate a ceramic work co-op	• Individual needs assessment of consumers • Referral process established with outside services • C/s supported during initial access to service system • Trained volunteer peer support workers placed in community services
SAMPLE OUTCOMES	• Increased sense of belonging to CSI • Increased number of c/s volunteering in CSI • Increased skills	• Increased sense of well-being • Increased awareness of mental health issues/supports • Increased opportunities for social interaction	• Increased networks of support • Increased sense of well-being • Reduced hospitalization • Increased awareness of mental health issues/supports	• Increased awareness of business development • Start-up resources secured • Increased income for c/s • Sense of ownership over business venture	• Increased awareness of mental health issues and supports • Increased sense of well-being

Source: Adapted from A comprehensive evaluation approach for mental health consumer-run organizations: Values, conceptualization, design, and action, by G. Nelson, J. Ochocka, R. Janzen, J. Trainor, & S. Lauzon, 2004, *Canadian Journal of Program Evaluation, 19*(3), 41.

While Nelson et al. (2004) have used an ecological perspective to conceptualize these outcomes as individual level outcomes, they may also be understood to be program goals; that is, they are goals for all participants in a particular consumer/survivor initiative organization, or they can be understood to be shared goals across consumer-survivor initiatives. Goals, or outcomes, specific to individuals can also be identified. For example, an individual participating in a self-help support group might set a personal goal of improving his or her housing situation, or completing a postsecondary degree.

Figure 8.1 shows us indicators that could be used to measure process, as well as outcomes—to answer whether the quantity and the quality of service intended has been delivered. The number of the various activities to be provided that are identified under the heading "Sample Activities" could be quantified in an annual service plan, for instance, and then monitored to see if the goals were achieved. Again, this could be done on an organization-specific basis, or across a number of organizations with a similar mission. For example, the intention might be that three groups of an eight-week duration be offered each year for people diagnosed with bipolar disorder, or two groups of an eight-week duration for female teen victims of relationship abuse. If the evaluation purpose is to assess policy, it is more likely to be a multi-site evaluation, however. Quality of service in a self-help organization might best be assessed through consumer feedback. With this in mind, a goal could be added to each of the component objectives that reads "To attain a high level of consumer/survivor satisfaction with the services offered, and the way in which they are offered."

In Figure 8.2, program components typically associated with consumer/survivor organizations that are intended to "have an impact on the human service system, the broader community, and social policy" (Nelson et al., 2004, p. 39) are also articulated. Activities like public education, political advocacy, community planning, and action research are intended to increase awareness of and sensitivity to the consumer/survivor perspective, broaden the discourse regarding mental health issues, increase participation of consumer/survivors in mental health reform and planning, have a greater consumer/survivor perspective in mental health policy and planning documents, produce more appropriate community supports, increase involvement of consumer/survivors in action research, and increase the information gathered to support education, advocacy, and planning activities. It would be relatively easy to engage in a process evaluation looking at the amount of effort expended in these various activities, but fewer studies have attempted to measure system level outcomes than individual level outcomes.

Needs Assessment

The final evaluation research function that has evolved since the 1960s is needs assessment. Needs assessments were first developed to answer the question, can we justify our claim that we require a service or a program in this community? (Pancer & Westhues, 1989). With community expectations that are often greater than our resources, it has become necessary to demonstrate in a more evidence-based way that there is a need for a service, and to show the magnitude and nature of that need. As program developers became sensitive to the fact that the specific form of the program needed in one community might vary from that in another community because of resource availabil-

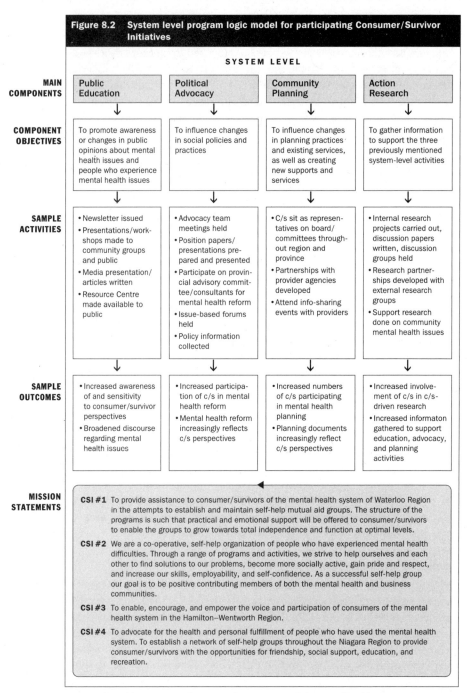

Figure 8.2 System level program logic model for participating Consumer/Survivor Initiatives

SYSTEM LEVEL

MAIN COMPONENTS	Public Education	Political Advocacy	Community Planning	Action Research
COMPONENT OBJECTIVES	To promote awareness or changes in public opinions about mental health issues and people who experience mental health issues	To influence changes in social policies and practices	To influence changes in planning practices and existing services, as well as creating new supports and services	To gather information to support the three previously mentioned system-level activities
SAMPLE ACTIVITIES	• Newsletter issued • Presentations/workshops made to community groups and public • Media presentation/articles written • Resource Centre made available to public	• Advocacy team meetings held • Position papers/presentations prepared and presented • Participate on provincial advisory committee/consultants for mental health reform • Issue-based forums held • Policy information collected	• C/s sit as representatives on board/committees throughout region and province • Partnerships with provider agencies developed • Attend info-sharing events with providers	• Internal research projects carried out, discussion papers written, discussion groups held • Research partnerships developed with external research groups • Support research done on community mental health issues
SAMPLE OUTCOMES	• Increased awareness of and sensitivity to consumer/survivor perspectives • Broadened discourse regarding mental health issues	• Increased participation of c/s in mental health reform • Mental health reform increasingly reflects c/s perspectives	• Increased numbers of c/s participating in mental health planning • Planning documents increasingly reflect c/s perspectives	• Increased involvement of c/s in c/s-driven research • Increased informaton gathered to support education, advocacy, and planning activities

MISSION STATEMENTS

CSI #1 To provide assistance to consumer/survivors of the mental health system of Waterloo Region in the attempts to establish and maintain self-help mutual aid groups. The structure of the programs is such that practical and emotional support will be offered to consumer/survivors to enable the groups to grow towards total independence and function at optimal levels.

CSI #2 We are a co-operative, self-help organization of people who have experienced mental health difficulties. Through a range of programs and activities, we strive to help ourselves and each other to find solutions to our problems, become more socially active, gain pride and respect, and increase our skills, employability, and self-confidence. As a successful self-help group our goal is to be positive contributing members of both the mental health and business communities.

CSI #3 To enable, encourage, and empower the voice and participation of consumers of the mental health system in the Hamilton–Wentworth Region.

CSI #4 To advocate for the health and personal fulfillment of people who have used the mental health system. To establish a network of self-help groups throughout the Niagara Region to provide consumer/survivors with the opportunities for friendship, social support, education, and recreation.

Source: Adapted from A comprehensive evaluation approach for mental health consumer-run organizations: Values, conceptualization, design, and action, by G. Nelson, J. Ochocka, R. Janzen, J. Trainor, & S. Lauzon, 2004, *Canadian Journal of Program Evaluation*, 19(3), 40.

ity, the religious and ethnic culture of the community, or the size of the community, for instance, it became clear that we needed to communicate with the community in some way to determine what they see as necessary (Batsche, Hernandez, & Montenegro, 1999; Weaver, 1999).

Milord (1976) and McKillip (1987) identify three approaches to assess community need: the social indicators approach, the survey approach, and the community impressions approach. The social indicators approach involves the use of statistics like age distribution within a geographic area to project the need for a service. You might be trying to assess the need for child care, for instance. Agreement would have to be reached on a reasonable standard of service provision, for instance, that group child care facilities be able to accommodate 25% of children between the ages of three and five. These standards, to be widely accepted, must be created in consultation with service providers and consumers of services. The number of children in this age group, multiplied by the proportion specified in the standard, is then used to determine the number of daycare spots that should be available in that area.

Another social indicators approach that is commonly used is based upon the demand for service. Estimates of need are based upon the number of families that have requested child care but could not be accommodated and are therefore on a waiting list. The difficulty with this approach is that it may not provide a valid indicator of need. If resources are limited, people may fail to leave their names on a list anywhere, resulting in an underestimate of need. Conversely, they might have their names on every available waiting list, with the result that the need for service would be overestimated.

It is generally more expensive to use the second approach to needs assessment—the survey—than the social indicators approach. It is also often difficult to generate a random sample of potential users of service for the study. This approach has the advantage, however, of providing detailed information about people's need for service. It can tell you, for instance, how many parents would use group child care, the ages of their children, what they would be willing to pay, and which hours of service are preferred. The answers to these questions would permit program development to proceed in a way that is based more upon the needs identified by potential users of the service than upon the best guesses of program planners.

The community impressions approach can provide similar information to the survey, but at a lower cost. Its primary drawback is that the opinions of those who come out to a community forum may be less representative of the broader community than are those who respond to a survey, especially if the response rate is high. Recent calls for multi-perspectual, multi-methods approaches to research would offset this bias, though with the trade-off of a greater cost for the research (Tashakkori & Teddlie, 2003).

An example of a multi-method, multi-persepctual needs assessment is one conducted by Grant and Westhues (2005) on the need for respite supports for carers of people with serious mental health issues in the Region of Waterloo, Ontario. A grounded theory approach was used to allow a program model to be built that honoured the voices of participants, as opposed to approaching the research with preconceived ideas about the nature of a possible model (Creswell, 1998; Strauss & Corbin, 1998). Qualitative methods were used because the research questions focused on understanding individual experiences, specifically perceptions of need for respite and the reasons behind these perceptions. Using open-ended, semi-structured methods, interview data were collected through focus groups and individual interviews. Interviews were conducted with service providers (individual interviews), carers (focus groups), and consumers (individual interviews). Questions used for all interviews were similar and included the following: "What are the challenges facing individuals with mental health issues?"; "How do they face those challenges?"; "What are the challenges facing carers?"; "How do they face those challenges?"; "Do you think there is a need for respite services for mental health in our community?"; and "What would be the most helpful type of respite service?"

A convergent analysis of participants' responses was used to identify a possible model of respite, while a divergent analysis elucidated the program and value dilemmas for potential planners of programs directed at multiple stakeholders. Frustrations with the current services varied among the different stakeholders, a reminder to mental health service providers and researchers of the importance of consulting with all stakeholders as programs are evaluated and developed.

The development of the needs assessment research function is an important indicator of the shift toward a humanist philosophy of science within the program evaluation field. Where once the need for a new service was defined only by service delivery "experts," the people who are potential users of the service are now also seen as "expert" for this purpose. Further, all of the approaches outlined by Milord (1976) recognize that need is defined by the opinions and preferences of potential consumers of service, not by a standard created by a planner in isolation from consumers.

Needs assessments recognize the uniqueness of each community, as they do not attempt to generalize their findings beyond the community where they are conducted. They also support local self-determination by permitting the opinions and preferences of community members to define which services should be provided. Finally, needs assessments are quintessentially action-oriented; their purpose is to provide data that will help decide whether a program is needed in a given community, and what form that program should take.

Effects of the Shift toward Humanism
on Social Policy Development

I have argued that there has been a shift toward humanism in the philosophy of science guiding the practice of program evaluation over the past twenty years. This means that evaluators have added qualitative and participatory research approaches to their tool kit, and they understand that they may become engaged in program development and advocacy activities that result from their evaluation studies. Feminist, anti-racist, and anti-oppressive language has been adopted to bring attention to issues of privilege and power between researchers and those being researched, and to focus attention on the experiences of marginalized groups such as women, members of the GBLT community, visible minorities, indigenous peoples, people who are differently-abled, and people living in poverty. Needs assessment is now an integral part of evaluation research, sometimes at the program development stage and sometimes as a "zero-based approach" to determine whether a program is continuing to meet the needs of service users. Program logic models are commonly used, again, sometimes in the program development stage and sometimes as a means of helping service deliverers articulate the theory of the program they are offering and reach agreement on what the program is intended to achieve. Multi-perspectual research designs, including the service user perspective, are common. Research processes that are shaped by service users are less common, but beginning to occur; and multimodal or multiple method studies are understood to assess a program in ways that are useful not only to managers but also to service deliverers and to service users (Church, 1995).

Effects of the Shift toward Humanism on Social Policy Development

The effect on policy development of this shift toward humanism has been fourfold. The greatest impact has been what might be called the democratization of the process. Where once policy development was the domain of politicians and a small number of bureaucrats, the input of the service provider and the consumer is now a greater consideration in the decision-making process. In Ontario, for instance, the Social Assistance Review Committee (Ontario Ministry of Community and Social Services, 1988) held twenty-three public hearings in fourteen communities. They received more than 1,500 submissions and briefs, many from individual citizens. The input from this broad array of citizens shaped the recommendations of the Review Committee, and ultimately the policy that was passed by the Peterson government with regard to social assistance. At the federal level, this same pattern appeared in the work of the Royal Commission on Aboriginal Peoples (1996). While some recently elected governments have shown less regard for the input of what they define as "interest groups," the tradition of consultation remains strong with others. The report of the Commission on the Future of Health Care (also known as the Romanow Report) (Romanow, 2002), headed by Roy Romanow and charged with identifying how to maintain a public, universal health care system, is an example of continued broadly based consultations as a precursor to policy change.

A second effect of the shift toward humanism has been to provide policymakers with a perspective that was not heard, or was given much less credence in the policy-making process in earlier times. The subjective experience of the individual is captured through the use of qualitative data—the actual words used by people in written submissions or in presentations to the task force at community meetings. *Transitions* (Ontario Ministry of Community and Social

In Conclusion

Services, 1988) captures this effectively in the sections titled "Voices," which appear throughout the report. Both the Royal Commission on Aboriginal Peoples (1996) and the Romanow Report (2002) used a similar approach, with powerful effect. The consequence of hearing these experiences as a policy-maker is to give a sense of urgency to the policy-making process—to tear oneself away from the detachment traditionally associated with it. Policy-makers are more likely to then become advocates for change.

A third effect of the shift toward humanism is to make clearer the link between policy and program, what some describe as "thinking globally, but acting locally" (Health and Welfare Canada, 1990). In recognizing the link between policy objectives and program objectives, it becomes possible not only to assess how well we are realizing policy objectives, but also to identify the programs that are intended to realize them and the extent to which programs make differential contributions to the achievement of the objectives. This provides us with guidance as to which programs should be continued or expanded and which might reasonably be discontinued.

The final effect of the shift toward humanism is the provision of a framework that makes it possible to recognize the uniqueness of each program, and the uniqueness of each community's objectives within the context of that program, while still seeing that program as part of a larger policy direction. This permits a community to address its own particular needs with respect to its cultural or religious values or ethnic and racial makeup while still permitting the community to be connected with the broader policy initiatives of its province or country. Another way of saying this is that the humanist perspective allows us to meld the rational focus on common outcomes with the more subjective or political focus on the needs of a specific community.

In Conclusion

In spite of the progress made in developing a perspective that allows us to make multimodal, multi-perspectual evaluations that provide a more comprehensive understanding of the effects of a given policy, challenges remain for the evaluator. Some are more technical/rational and others more political. None are easily addressed, but perhaps most challenging is the pressure exercised by politicians like Erik Nielsen (who headed a review of all federal programs in 1984 and demanded that evaluations be less "political" and more "objective") at a time when we have come to a postmodern understanding that there is a plurality of opinions about what constitutes a good and just society (Abma, 1997).

We are now seeing governments emphasize performance measurement, outcomes, and results. Who defines which outcomes will be measured, and how? Who defines whether they are symptomatic of success or failure? Is placement in a job a success indicator even if the person is earning below the poverty line, for instance? Is a program successful if service users are satisfied with their experience, but show no change in "objective" measures like reading scores, parenting skills, or knowledge of community resources? The evaluator is more likely to be able to ask these questions and utilize a humanist perspective to influence the design of evaluations at the agency or local level than at the provincial, federal, or international level. But given the essentially political nature of evaluation, some perspective will always be missing or not given sufficient emphasis. Our job as social workers committed to furthering social justice is to bring a critical perspective to the design or reading of evaluation studies with a view to identifying these omissions and advocating for their inclusion in our judgments of which policies work.

References

Abma, T.A. (1997). Voices from the margins: Political and ethical dilemmas in evaluation. *Canadian Review of Social Policy, 39*, 41–53.

Atkisson, C.C., & Zwick, A. (1982). The client satisfaction questionnaire: Psychometric properties and correlations with service utilization and psychotherapy outcome. *Evaluation and Program Planning, 5*(3), 233–237.

Backus, T.K. (1978). Foster care review: An Ohio example. *Child Welfare, 57*(3), 156–164.

Batsche, C., Hernandez, M., & Montenegro, M.C. (1999). Community needs assessment with Hispanic, Spanish-monolingual residents. *Evaluation and Program Planning, 22*, 13–20.

Baum, G. (1987). Humanist sociology: Scientific and critical. In K. Westhues (Ed.), *Basic principles for social science in our time* (pp. 77–91). Waterloo: University of St. Jerome's Press.

Bloom, M., Fischer, J., & Orme, J.G. (2006). *Evaluating practice: Guidelines for the accountable professional* (5th ed.). Englewood Cliffs, NJ: Prentice-Hall.

Bowles, R.T. (1981). *Social impact assessment in small communities.* Toronto: Butterworths.

Briar, S., & Blythe, B.J. (1985). Agency support for evaluating the outcomes of social work services. *Administration in Social Work, 9*(2), 25–36.

Brown, L., & Strega, S. (Eds.). (2005). *Research as resistance: critical, indigenous, and anti-oppressive approaches.* Toronto: Canadian Scholars' Press.

Caputo, R.K. (1986). The role of information systems in evaluation research. *Administration in Social Work, 10*(1), 67–77.

Carrilio, T.E. (1981). The impact of research in a family service agency. *Social Casework, 62*(1), 87–94.

Casselman, B. (1971–72). On the practitioner's orientation to research. *Smith College Studies in Social Work, 42*, 211–233.

Chappell, B. (1975). Organizing periodic review in foster care: The South Carolina story. *Child Welfare, 54*(7), 477–486.

Chen, H.T. (1990). *Theory-driven evaluation.* Newbury Park, CA: Sage.

Chen, H.T. (1994). Theory-driven evaluations: Need, difficulties and options. *Evaluation Practice, 15*, 79–82.

Christie, C.A., & Rose, M. (2003). The language of evaluation theory: Insights gained from an empirical study of evaluation theory and practice. *Canadian Journal of Program Evaluation, 18*(2), 33–45.

References   Church, K. (1995). *Forbidden narratives: Critical autobiography as social science.* New York: Routledge.

Claburn, W.E., & Magura, S. (1978). Administrative case review for foster children. *Social Work Research and Abstracts, 14*(1), 34–40.

Cresswell, J.W. (1998). *Qualitative inquiry and research design: Choosing among five traditions.* Thousand Oaks, CA: Sage.

Creswell, J.W., Plano Clark, V.L., Gutman, M.L., & Hanson, W.E. (2003). Advanced mixed methods research designs. In A. Tashakkori & C. Teddlie (Eds.), *Handbook of mixed methods in social and behavioral research* (pp. 209–240). Thousand Oaks, CA: Sage.

Crocker, P. (1983). *An evaluation of the quality of service at a volunteer-run telephone distress line.* Unpublished master's thesis, Wilfrid Laurier University, Waterloo, ON.

Davies, M., & Kelly, E. (1976). The social worker, the client and the social anthropologist. *British Journal of Social Work, 6*(2), 213–231.

Everitt, A. (1996). Developing critical evaluation. *Evaluation: International Journal of Theory, Research and Practice, 2*(2), 173–188.

Fanshel, D. (1966). Sources of strain in practice-oriented research. *Social Casework, 47*(3), 357–362.

Finney, J.W., & Moos, R.H. (1989). Theory and method in treatment evaluation. *Evaluation and Program Planning, 12,* 307–316.

Finterbusch, K., & Wolf, C.P. (Eds.) (1977). *Methodology of social impact assessment.* Stroudsberg, PA: Dowden, Hutchison, and Ross.

Frankel, M., & Sinclair, C. (1982). Quality assurance: An approach to accountability in a mental health centre. *Professional Psychology, 13,* 79–84.

Gauthier, B., Barrington, G., Bozzo, S.L., Chaytor, K., Cullen, J., Lahey, R., Malatest, R., Mason, G., Mayne, J., Myers, A., Porteous, N.L., & Roy, S. (2004). The lay of the land: Evaluation practice in Canada today. *Canadian Journal of Program Evaluation, 19*(1), 143–178.

Gergen, K.J. (1985). The social constructionist movement in modern psychology. *American Psychologist, 40,* 266–275.

Giordano, P.C. (1977). The clients' perspective in agency evaluation. *Social Work, 22*(1), 34–39.

Gordon, J.E. (1984). Creating research-based practice principles: A model. *Social Work Research and Abstracts, 20*(1), 3–6.

Grant, J., & Westhues, A. (2005). Mental health respite services: A grounded model. *Canadian Journal of Community Mental Health, 24,* 63–78.

Greene, J.C., & Caracelli, V.J. (2003). Making paradigmatic sense of mixed methods practice. In A. Tashakkori & C. Teddlie (Eds.), *Handbook of mixed methods in social and behavioral research* (pp. 91–110). Thousand Oaks, CA: Sage.

Guest, D. (1985). *The emergence of social security in Canada.* Vancouver: University of British Columbia Press.

Hanbery, G.W., Sorensen, U., & Kucic, A.R. (1981). Management information systems and human resource management. *Administration in Social Work, 5*(3/4), 27–41.

Health and Welfare Canada. (1990). *The report of the special advisor to the minister of National Health and Welfare on child sexual abuse in Canada: Reaching for solutions.* Ottawa: Author.

Holosko, M. (1996). Service user input: Fact or fiction? *Canadian Journal of Program Evaluation, 11*(2), 111–126.   **References**

House, E.R. (1980). *Evaluating with validity.* Beverly Hills: Sage.

House, E.R. (1993). *Professional evaluation, social impact and political consequences.* Newbury Park, CA: Sage.

Howlett, M., & Ramesh, M. (1995). *Studying public policy: Policy cycles and policy subsystems.* Don Mills: Oxford University Press.

Hudson, W.W. (1982). *The clinical measurement package: A field manual.* Homewood, IL: Dorsey Press.

Jayaratne, S. (1978). Analytic procedures for single subjects designs. *Social Work Research and Abstracts, 14*(4), 30–40.

Love, A.J. (1983). *Developing effective internal evaluation.* San Francisco: Jossey Bass.

Maguire, P. (1987). *Doing participatory research: A feminist approach.* Amherst: Center for International Education, University of Massachusetts.

Maxcy, S.J. (2003). Pragmatic threads in mixed methods research in the social sciences: The search for multiple modes of inquiry and the end of the philosophy of formalism. In A. Tashakkori & C. Teddlie (Eds.), *Handbook of mixed methods in social and behavioral research* (pp. 51–90). Thousand Oaks, CA: Sage.

Maxwell, J.A., & Loomis, D.M. (2003). Mixed methods design: An alternative approach. In A. Tashakkori & C. Teddlie (Eds.), *Handbook of mixed methods in social and behavioral research* (pp. 241–272). Thousand Oaks, CA: Sage.

McCready, D.J., & Rahn, S.L. (1983). *The feasibility of cost-outcome analysis in Ontario social services: Six case studies.* Toronto: Ontario Economic Council.

McCready, D.J., & Rahn, S.L. (1986). Funding human services: Fixed utility versus fixed cost. *Administration in Social Work, 10*(4), 23–30.

McEwan, K.L., & Bigelow, D.A. (1997). Using a logic model to focus health services on population health goals. *Canadian Journal of Program Evaluation, 12*(1), 167–174.

McKillip, J. (1987). *Needs analysis: Tools for the human services and education.* Beverly Hills: Sage.

McLaughlin, J.A., & Jordan, G.B. (1999). Logic models: A tool for telling your program's performance story. *Evaluation and Program Planning, 22*, 65–72.

Milord, J.T. (1976). Human service needs assessment: Three non-epidemiological approaches. *Canadian Psychologist, 17*, 260–269.

Montague, S. (2000). Focusing on inputs, outputs, and outcomes: Are international approaches to performance management really so different? *Canadian Journal of Program Evaluation, 15*(1), 139–146.

Morse, J.M. (2003). Principles of mixed methods and multimethod research design. In A. Tashakkori & C. Teddlie (Eds.), *Handbook of mixed methods in social and behavioral research* (pp. 189–208). Thousand Oaks, CA: Sage.

Muller-Clemm, W.J., & Barnes, M.P. (1997). A historical perspective on federal program evaluation in Canada. *Canadian Journal of Program Evaluation, 12*, 47–70.

Mutscheler, E. (1979). Using single case evaluation procedures in a Family and Children's Services agency. *Journal of Social Service Research, 3*(1), 115–133.

Nelson, G., Ochocka, J., Griffin, K., & Lord, J. (1998). Nothing about me without me: Participatory action research with self-help / mutual aid organizations for psychiatric consumer / survivors. *American Community Psychology Journal, 26*, 881–912.

References Nelson, G., Ochocka, J., Janzen, R., Trainor, J., & Lauzon, S. (2004). A comprehensive evaluation approach for mental health consumer-run organizations: Values, conceptualization, design, and action. *Canadian Journal of Program Evaluation, 19*(3), 29–53.

Newman, I., Ridenour, C.S., Newman, C., & DeMarco, Jr., G.M.P. (2003). A typology of research purposes and its relationship to mixed methods. In A. Tashakkori & C. Teddlie (Eds.), *Handbook of mixed methods in social and behavioral research* (pp. 167–188). Thousand Oaks, CA: Sage.

Nguyen, T.D., Atkisson, C.C., & Stegner, B.L. (1983). Assessment of patient satisfaction: Development and refinement of a service satisfaction questionnaire. *Evaluation and Program Planning, 6*, 299–314.

Ontario Ministry of Community and Social Services. (1981). *Foster care: Proposed standards and guidelines for agencies placing children.* Toronto: Author.

Ontario Ministry of Community and Social Services. (1988). *Report of the Social Assistance Review Committee: Transitions.* Toronto: Author

Ottier, A. (2005). Participatory evaluation in the context of CPBD: Theory and practice in international development. *Canadian Journal of Program Evaluation, 20*(1), 123–148.

Pancer, M., & Westhues, A. (1989). A developmental stage approach to program planning and evaluation. *Evaluation Review, 13*(1), 56–77.

Patton, M.Q. (1997). *Utilization-focused evaluation: The new century text.* Thousand Oaks, CA: Sage.

Petrosino, A. (2000). Answering the why question in evaluation: The causal-model approach. *Canadian Journal of Program Evaluation, 15*(1), 1–24.

Posavac, E.J., & Carey, R.G. (1997). *Program evaluation: Methods and case studies.* Englewood Cliffs, NJ: Prentice-Hall.

Ristock, J., & Pennell, J. (1996). *Community research as empowerment practice. Feminist links, postmodern interruptions.* Don Mills, ON: Oxford University Press.

Roach, R., & Youngman Berdahl, L. (1999). Lessons from the field: Surveying hard-to-reach populations. *Canadian Review of Social Policy, 43*, 101–110.

Romanow, R.J. (2002) *Building on values: The future of health care in Canada— Final report.* Ottawa: Minister of Supplies and Services.

Rossi, P.H., & Freeman, H.E. (1982). *Evaluation: A systematic approach* (2nd ed.). Beverly Hills: Sage.

Royal Commission on Aboriginal Peoples. (1996). *Report.* Ottawa: Minister of Supplies and Services.

Rush, B., & Ogborne, A. (1991). Program logic models: Expanding their role and structure for program planning and evaluation. *Canadian Journal of Program Evaluation, 6*(2), 95–106.

Rutman, L. (1980). *Planning useful evaluations.* Beverly Hills: Sage.

Saleeby, D. (1979). The tension between research and practice: Assumptions of the experimental paradigm. *Clinical Social Work Journal, 7*, 267–284.

Senate of Canada. (1991). *Report of the Standing Senate Committee on National Finance: The program evaluation system in the Government of Canada.* Ottawa: Minister of Supplies and Services.

Sinclair, C., & Frankel, M. (1983). The effect of quality assurance activities on the quality of mental health services. *Journal of Quality Assurance, 8*, 7–15.

Statistics Canada. (2005). *Consolidated provincial and territorial government revenue and expenditures.* Online at <www40.statcan.ca/101/csto1/govt55a.htm?sdi=social%20services>.

Stiffman, A.R., Feldman, R.A., Evans, D.A., & Orme, J.G. (1984). Collaborative research for social agencies: Boon or bane? *Administration in Social Work, 8*(1), 45–57.

Stokey, E., & Zeckhauser, R. (1978). *A primer for policy analysis.* New York: W.W. Norton.

Strauss, A., & Corbin, J. (1998). *Basics of Qualitative Research* (2nd ed.). Thousand Oaks, CA: Sage.

Suchman, E.A. (1967). *Evaluative research: Principles and practice in public service and social action programs.* New York: Russell Sage Foundation.

Tashakkori, A., & Teddlie, C. (Eds.). *Handbook of mixed methods in social and behavioral research.* Thousand Oaks, CA: Sage.

Teddlie, C., & Tashakkori, A. (2003). Major issues and controversies in the use of mixed methods in the social and behavioral sciences. In A. Tashakkori & C. Teddlie (Eds.), *Handbook of mixed methods in social and behavioral research* (pp. 3–50). Thousand Oaks, CA: Sage.

Tester, F.S., & Myles, W. (Eds.). (1981). *Social impact assessment: Theory, method and practice.* Calgary: Detselig.

Thomas, E.J. (1978). Research and service in single case experimentation: Conflicts and choices. *Social Work Research and Abstracts, 14*(4), 20–31.

Vaillancourt, Y. (1996). Remaking Canadian social policy: A Quebec view. In J. Pulkingham & G. Ternowetsky (Eds.), *Remaking Canadian social policy* (pp. 81–99). Halifax: Fernwood.

VanderPlaat, M. (1997). Emancipatory politics, critical evaluation and government policy. *Canadian Journal of Program Evaluation, 12*(2), 143–162.

VanderPlaat, M., Samson, Y., & Raven, P. (2001). The politics and practice of empowerment evaluation and social interventions: Lessons from the Atlantic Community Action Program for Children regional evaluation. *Canadian Journal of Program Evaluation, 16*(1), 79–98.

Weaver, H.N. (1999). Assessing the needs of Native American communities: A Northeastern example. *Evaluation and Program Planning, 22,* 155–161.

Weiss, C.H. (1972). *Evaluation research: Methods of assessing program effectiveness.* Englewood Cliffs, NJ: Prentice Hall.

Westhues, A., Cadell, S., Karabanow, J., Maxwell, L., & Sanchez, M. (1999). The creation of knowledge: From paradigm to practice. *Canadian Social Work Review, 16*(2), 129–154.

Wholey, J.S., Nay, J.N., Scanlon, J.W., & Schmidt, R.E. (1975). Evaluation: When is it really needed? *Evaluation Magazine, 2,* 89–93.

Williams, A.M., Caron. M.V., McMillan, M., Litkowich, A., Rutter, N., Hartman, A., & Yardley, J. (2001). An evaluation of contracted palliative care home care services in Ontario, Canada. *Evaluation and Program Planning, 24,* 23–31.

Wong-Rieger, D., & David, L. (1993). *A hands-on guide to planning and evaluation.* Ottawa: National AIDS Clearinghouse.

Worthington, C. (1999). Empowerment evaluation: Understanding the theory behind the framework. *Canadian Journal of Program Evaluation, 14*(1), 1–28.

Yates, B.T. (1985). Cost-effectiveness analysis and cost-benefit analysis: An introduction. *Behaviour Assessment, 2*(3), 271–82.

References   **Additional Resources**

Canadian Evaluation Society. Online at <www.evaluationcanada.ca/site.cgi?s=4&ss =2&_lang=an>.

Knox, C. (1996). Political context and program evaluation: The inextricable link. *Canadian Journal of Program Evaluation, 11*(1), 1–20.

Tortu, S., Goldsamt, L.A., & Hamid, R. (2002). *A practical guide to research and service with hidden populations.* Toronto: Allyn and Bacon.

Tyson, K. (1995). *New foundations for scientific social and behavioral research: The heuristic paradigm.* Toronto: Allyn and Bacon.

Weiss, C. (1987). Where politics and evaluation research meet. In D.J. Palumbo (Ed.), *The politics of program evaluation* (pp. 100–145). Beverly Hills: Sage.

Westhues, K. (1987). *Basic principles for social science in our time.* Waterloo: University of St. Jerome's College Press.

III   Current Social Policy Issues

Introduction to Part III

The major policy issues currently under debate in Canada are introduced and discussed in this section. A range of theoretical perspectives, identified in the chapter descriptions that follow, is used by the authors in making their analyses. Each chapter addresses the following questions:

- What is the nature of the problem?
- How are the key concepts used to describe the problem defined, and how have they changed over time?
- Who is experiencing the problem, and what are their characteristics?
- What social values are being threatened by the problem?
- What efforts have been taken to address the problems of, for instance, legislation, funding allocation, or advocacy?
- Who defines the conditions as a problem?
- What are the causes of the problem, including relevant theoretical considerations and political, social, and economic factors historically?
- What are the gender, class, and ethno-racial considerations necessary to understand the problem?

The section opens with Garson Hunter addressing the critical issue of child poverty. He shows us that child poverty rates in Canada remain high in spite of a series of attempts, which go back to 1975, to restructure the way in which we transfer income to families with children. He argues that the explanation for this failure to alleviate child poverty rates, in spite of an all-party resolution to do this in 1989, is that any commitment to reducing child poverty has been tempered by a more strongly held value: that any transfer of funds to families with children should not impede the incentive to work. He concludes that a different strategy is needed if we are to be successful in reducing child poverty—a strategy that focuses on the inadequacy of current minimum wages.

Marilyn Callahan and Karen Swift contribute a new chapter to the fourth edition that explores the question of "risk" and "risk assessment" in child welfare. They explain the managerial, medical, and legal influences that have fostered the development of the risk assessment measures that are now widely used in child welfare in Canada, the UK, the US, and Australia. They argue that these tools have not kept their promise of reducing workloads for child welfare workers or increasing the safety of children. They continue to be used because they protect organizations and individual workers from litigation. They also make the job of supervisors—who must train and supervise many newly graduated social workers—easier. Workers report liking the sense of order that the risk assessment measures bring to the complex, stressful task of assessing whether a family is in need of support or if a child is in sufficient danger that he or she should be removed from the home.

In chapter 11, Barbara Waterfall challenges the reader to think about the impact of colonization on Native peoples. She argues that the effects of historical and ongoing colonial processes permeate the social work profession and social work education. She uses the case example of child welfare practice with Native peoples to substantiate this argument, tracing the roots of colonial practice to the Indian Act of 1876. The profession of social work is called on to disengage from current neo-colonial and constitutional colonial politics in favour of advocating and supporting anti-colonial initiatives. Schools of social work are viewed as one site for mapping and developing strategies to move the profession toward relations of equality and respectful coexistence.

Geoff Nelson contributes the second new chapter to the fourth edition, addressing a substantive policy issue. Geoff provides a rich blend of a historical review of the evolution of mental health policy in Canada with an evidence-based perspective on what we know about how best to support people with "serious mental health issues" and "mental health problems." He concludes that a value-based, systems approach to policy reform is needed if resources are to be shifted from our previous emphasis on hospital care toward mental health programs that are community-based, consumer-directed, recovery-oriented, and sensitive to class, race, ethnicity, and gender.

Lea Caragata ably illustrates a constructivist perspective with the issue of homelessness in chapter 13. She identifies and analyzes the three major perspectives that have been used to understand homelessness and to shape policy solutions to address it. These include the liberal perspective, the structural perspective, and the more recent social exclusion perspective. She outlines the beliefs associated with each of these perspectives, and the social expectations that result from them. Lea argues that there appears to be agreement across the spectrum that homelessness exists, and that it is time to address the issue. Depending upon one's construction of the problem, a sufficient response may be as minimal as providing temporary services like emergency shelters or as comprehensive as finding ways to re-engage people in the economy, socially and politically.

In chapter 14, Iara Lessa uses a postmodern perspective to analyze the changes in what we understand to be role expectations for single mothers since Mother's Allowance legislation was first introduced in Manitoba in 1916. Using Foucauldian concepts like governmentality, she shows how motherhood was once seen as a sufficient responsibility to make a woman "deserving" of social assistance. While eligibility was extended to a larger group of single mothers in the post–World War II period, she demonstrates how single mothers came to be defined as "unemployable" for family reasons, establishing a connection between single mothers and the labour force. Once children were of an age that they no longer needed a mother's care full-time, these women were considered employable. She argues that the Canada Health and Social Transfer has shifted our definition of single mothers to that of potential labour force participants first, with their mothering role clearly secondary. These role definitions shape eligibility for social assistance.

Linda Snyder identifies herself as working from a social democratic perspective in chapter 15. This positions her as a critic of the current shift in public policy from seeing social assistance as an entitlement for people who are not able to support themselves to requiring that welfare recipients participate in work and related activities in order to receive financial assistance. She demonstrates how these policies, known as "workfare," are inconsistent with social democratic values, and reviews the research literature, which shows that an exit from social assistance under workfare programs is not necessarily enduring and often fails to result in the recipient finding work that raises his or her standard of living above the poverty line.

Brian O'Neill offers us a useful introduction to the concepts associated with same-sex sexual orientation in chapter 16. He then provides a historical perspective on heterosexism in Canada, explaining how this belief system has led to oppressive policies pertaining to gay men and lesbians over the years. The belief that same-sex acts were unacceptable was sufficiently pervasive that they remained in the Criminal Code until 1969, and were classified as a psychiatric disorder until 1973. There has been a shift to greater tolerance of gays and lesbians within the past decade, as reflected in opinion polls and a revision to the Canadian Human Rights Act in 1996 to include gays and lesbians as a protected group. He argues that the next big challenge for social workers is to make the mainstream services we provide sensitive to the needs of people with a same-sex sexual orientation. O'Neill's perspective could be described as anti-heterosexist, or anti-oppressive.

Using an anti-racist, anti-oppressive perspective, Usha George provides a sobering historical overview of our racist immigration and refugee policies in chapter 17. She outlines how the major policy shifts in 1967 and 1976 addressed the most blatant of these inequities, but failed to address others. The newest legislation, Bill C-11 was passed in June 2001, and has been criticized by social justice groups like Amnesty International and the Canadian Council for Refugees for its continued lack of transparency, its potential for human rights abuse, and its failure to address gender and class biases. She tells us that this shortcoming can be explained by the valuing of economic objectives in setting policy rather than more humanitarian considerations, even in the case of refugees.

In chapter 18, Mike Burke and Susan Silver identify the normative foundations of Canadian medicare that have shaped the challenges we now face in the provision of medical services. They argue that the legacies of equity of access through national standards and strong federal leadership in the making of health care policy, along with public opinion, which strongly supports the maintenance of these values, help prevent the erosion of our health care system. The neo-conservative policy environment nonetheless presents us with challenges such as renewed interest in user fees, delisting of services, private clinics, and the privatization of home care. They challenge the argument that the current system is inefficient, an argument frequently heard from critics of publicly funded health care.

In chapter 19, Sheila Neysmith stimulates our thinking about how we can best meet the caring needs of an aging population. Working from a feminist, constructivist perspective, she reminds us that most of the elderly people requiring care are women, and that most of the care they receive is through the informal care system of family and friends. The majority of these carers are also women. She is particularly effective in illustrating the relationship between how we define a problem and the policy alternatives that we are likely to generate.

Finally, in chapter 20, Peter Dunn gives us a comprehensive overview of the policies that affect the lives of people with disabilities. Using a constructivist, anti-oppressive perspective, he describes how the UN declaration of 1981 as International Year of the Disabled Person served as a catalyst in Canada to put in place a range of policies that would promote a shift from an institutionally based, expert-driven model of service delivery for people with disabilities to one that is community-based and consumer-driven. While this new model is still more an ideal than a reality in many contexts, the ideas have been identified that would make its realization possible. The challenge is to continue to implement the model in the face of reduced government spending.

Garson Hunter

The Problem of Child Poverty in Canada

To address the problem of child poverty in Canada, the federal minister of Finance, Paul Martin, presented the new Canada Child Tax Benefit (CCTB) program on February 18, 1997, as part of the 1997–1998 Federal Budget. The federal, provincial, and territorial governments negotiated an agreement known as the National Children's Agenda to advance the income and living standards of families with children (National Council of Welfare [NCW], 1999a). Certainly, it was with good reason that a program to address child poverty was introduced in Canada. A comprehensive household survey of twenty-three industrialized nations, based upon data from the *Luxemburg Income Study*, ranked Canada's relative[1] child poverty level at seventeenth out of twenty-three industrialized nations in the 2000 report (UNICEF, 2000, p. 3) and nineteenth out of twenty-five industrialized nations in the 2005 report (UNICEF, 2005, p. 6). Canada's child poverty rate is higher than the child poverty rate in countries such as the Czech Republic, Hungary, Greece, and Poland.

A high child poverty rate in rich nations such as Canada is a serious issue, as solid research exists that identifies the correlation between lack of an adequate income and negative impacts on families and children. The Innocenti Research Centre's *League Table of Child Poverty in Rich Nations* (UNICEF, 2000) noted this basic fact:

> Such statistics represent the unnecessary suffering and deprivation of millions of individual children. They also represent a failure to hold faith with the developed world's ideal of equality of opportunity. For no matter how many individual and anecdotal exceptions there may be, the fact remains that the children of the poor simply do not have the same opportunities as the children of the non-poor. Whether measured by physical or mental development, health and survival rates, educational achievement or job prospects, income or life expectancies, those who spend their childhood in poverty of income and expectation are at a marked and measurable disadvantage. (UNICEF, 2000, p. 3)

How Child
Poverty Is
Defined and
Measured

Research on child poverty in Canada demonstrates that the disadvantages for children in poor families include being more likely to grow up in substandard housing, live in neighbourhoods with drug dealing and vandalism, suffer health problems such as vision, hearing, mobility, and cognition impairments, and have less participation in organized sports or in arts program (Ross, Scott, & Smith, 2000, pp. 1–2). Obviously addressing child poverty is a serious issue. However, analyzing child poverty is not an easy task, as "the political landscape is already littered with political rhetoric about children, broken promises and token efforts that provide very little real help to families or help only a minuscule number of the families who are in dire straits" (NCW, 1999a, p. 1).

The year 2000 marked the eleventh anniversary of the House of Commons' unanimous resolution to achieve the goal of eliminating child poverty by the year 2000. As the data[2] indicate, the federal and provincial governments failed to achieve that goal by 2003. Campaign 2000, an organization of over ninety national, provincial, and community partners dedicated to seeing the government of Canada adhere to its resolution of eliminating child poverty, found that almost one in six children in Canada were still living in poverty in 2003 (2005, p. 2). When discussing child poverty, however, we need to remember that we cannot discuss children in isolation from the economic situation of their parents. All children except those who live in an institutional setting live in some definition of a family.[3] Joan Grant-Cummings incisively apprised the audience at the Eighth Conference on Canadian Social Welfare Policy (Regina, June 25, 1997) that child poverty is being presented to the public as if it fell from an impartial sky to settle among us as a gentle rain. She reminded the audience of what is obvious: poor children live in poor families. Any attempt to try and separate poor children from their poor families is a circuitous diversion from the class and gender issues of child poverty. This chapter will examine the key concepts used to describe the definition and measurement of child poverty: Who are the poor? Who experiences child poverty and what are their characteristics? What social policy measures exist to address child poverty? What causes child poverty, and what are the political, social, and economic factors involved? The chapter ends by considering social policy suggestions to address child poverty in Canada.

How Child Poverty Is Defined and Measured

Canada actually has no official poverty line (including the Low Income Cut-Off [LICO] measure), and there is no general agreement in Canada on what constitutes poverty (Fellegi, 1997). On the issue of poverty lines, Ternowetsky comments, "We have come to understand, for example, that even the concept of poverty is elusive. It is difficult to define, hard to measure and it is seemingly impossible to obtain a level of agreement on what it means to be poor in Canada" (2000, p. 1). Poverty is a political issue, and especially so in Canada since the House of Commons resolution to eliminate child poverty. Canada is also a signatory to the United Nations Convention on the Rights of the Child, where Article 27 speaks directly to the material needs of children and the obligations of parents and governments to meet those needs. The United Nations Innocenti Report Card on *Child Poverty in Rich Countries* (2005) contains an individual section titled "Canada: Children Still Waiting," which focuses on Canada's commitment to end child poverty by the year 2000. The report discusses how Canada continues to use and develop different poverty lines, and concludes that "Canada's target year 2000 came and went without agreement on what the target means, or how progress towards it is to be measured, or what policies might be necessary to achieve it" (p. 21). The debate about child poverty in Canada has become a debate about "duelling poverty lines," and one way to avoid dealing with poverty is for governments to continually challenge how it should be measured. Consequently this chapter will spend some time exploring the substance of the poverty line debate.

How Child Poverty Is Defined and Measured

In reporting child poverty numbers, Campaign 2000 relies on the Statistics Canada Low Income Cut-Off measure (LICO), the most common unofficial poverty line used in Canada. LICO is used to calculate the incidence of poverty represented by the number of economic families that are measured against a definition of low-income.[4] The LICO calculation is a relative measure of poverty. It measures relative deprivation based upon income compared to a defined community standard. In other words, a relative measure of poverty is informed from the position that "peoples' experience of hunger and poverty is directly related to the societies in which they live and the standards of living which are customarily enjoyed" (Riches, 1997, p. 10). LICO is based upon the average family or individual expenditures for food, shelter, and clothing: "The LICOs represent levels of gross income where people spend disproportionate amounts of money for food, shelter, and clothing. Statistics Canada has decided over the years—somewhat arbitrarily—that 20 percentage points is a reasonable measure of additional burden (NCW, 1999b, p. 3). Most income data from Statistics Canada contains one of two base years, the 1986 base or the 1992 base. Using the 1986 base, the average Canadian family spent 36.2% of gross income on food, shelter, and clothing; therefore, with the addition of 20 points, low-income Canadians spent 56.2% or more on these necessary items. If the 1992 base is used, then a low-income Canadian spent 54.7% or more on these necessary items (NCW, 1999b, p. 3). When using LICO to measure the child poverty rate, the Statistics Canada measure takes into account family size and differing costs of living by size of community. Table 9.1 lists the LICOs for 2003.

A number of criticisms have been made about LICO since its development in 1961. Perhaps the most common is that although it is widely used, it is not a poverty line. The political nature of the debate about poverty was not lost on Statistics Canada when it commented that it was partly due to the government commitment to eliminate child poverty that the LICO measure was under a great deal of public scrutiny (Webber, 1998, p. 7).

Table 9.1　Low-income cut-offs before-tax income for 2003 using LICO 1992 base				
SIZE OF FAMILY UNIT	URBAN AREAS				RURAL AREAS

SIZE OF FAMILY UNIT	500,000 and over	100,000 to 499,000	30,000 to 99,999	Less than 30,000*	RURAL AREAS
1 person	19,795	16,979	16,862	15,690	13,680
2 persons	24,745	21,077	21,077	19,612	17,100
3 persons	30,774	26,213	26,213	24,390	21,268
4 persons	37,253	31,952	31,731	29,526	25,744
5 persons	41,642	35,718	35,469	33,004	28,778
6 persons	46,031	39,483	39,208	36,482	31,813
7 persons	50,421	43,249	42,947	39,960	34,847

* Includes cities with a population between 15,000 and 30,000 and small urban areas (under 15,000).
Source: *Poverty lines*, Canadian Council on Social Development, 2004 (Ottawa: Author).

Statistics Canada, which produces the LICO data, entered into the debate about using LICO as a poverty measure and reported, "At the heart of the debate is the use of the low income cut-offs as poverty lines, even though Statistics Canada has clearly stated, since their publication began over 25 years ago, that they are not" (Fellegi, 1999, p. 36). As well, "Statistics Canada continues to correct media commentary that portrays low income estimates as a measure of poverty. The Agency often repeats that they are not intended as such" (Webber, 1998, p. 9). Statistics Canada argues that LICO is not actually a poverty measure; rather, it is a measure of low income. However, a reading of Podoluk's writing indicates that at least to him as the developer of LICO, low income and poverty were synonymous.[5] No distinction is made between low income and poverty in his work, and the words are often used interchangeably.

Another important concern with the LICO measure is that the level of low-income cut-offs rises over time. The reason the low-income cut-off level rises with time is that in recent years the ratio of expenditures on necessities is less than the growth in income, and therefore people spend, on average, less of their yearly income on necessities. As the amount of the family's income spent on necessities declines, the low-income cut-off levels rise. For example, in 1961 when the LICO measure was developed, the average family expenditure on necessities was approximately 50% of their pre-tax income. With the 20 percentage points added to the average, low income was defined as families who spent 70% or more on necessities. As incomes have increased and the average ratio of expenditures on necessities as a proportion of income has decreased, the low-income cut-off levels have risen. The most current rebasing (1992) of the LICO measure calculated on the average family expenditures on necessities was established at 35% of pre-tax income. If the 20 percentage points are added to that average, low income would be defined as families who spend 55% or more on necessities. The decline from 70% of income spent on necessities to be considered low income in 1961 to 55% of income spent on necessities to be considered low income in 1992 has caused concern (Kerstetter, 2000, pp. 6–8).

How Child Poverty Is Defined and Measured

However, the developers of LICO were aware that their poverty measure was relative, and that the level at which people would be considered poor would climb over time. Commenting on the issue, Podoluk wrote, "It is because poverty is a relative concept that poverty or low income does not diminish as much as might be expected in view of the real income growth of a country. The extent of change can be evident only if contemporary standards are applied to the income structure of an earlier day" (1968, p. 183). Explaining why poverty or low income does not decrease as would be expected in terms of income growth that is adjusted for the inflation rate, Podoluk noted, "Thus, even though the level of living of the poor improves through time, poverty never seems to be eliminated because a wide gap persists between the level of living attained by some segments of the population and those enjoyed by the majority of the community" (p. 184). The developers of LICO also knew that the low-income or poverty rate would not remain fixed at 70%; rather, if the income of the majority grew over time then the level of what was considered low income would grow as well. They believed that if the standard of the community changes, then low income should be evaluated in the context of the rising (or possibly, falling) community standard.

Statistics Canada has made a major change to the way it reports low income in its publications. In its major publications used to evaluate low income such as *Incomes in Canada*, Statistics Canada now only reports after-tax LICO. Much debate has revolved around the use of LICO based upon the before-tax Total Income variable and the after-tax Total Income variable to calculate low-income rates. It is an important discussion. At the essence of this argument is the poverty rate in Canada. Using LICO on the after-tax Total Income variable dramatically reduces the poverty rate. For example, if the before-tax Total Income LICO is used with the 2003 Survey of Labour and Income Dynamics (SLID) data, the poverty rate for children in 2003 is 17.6% (Campaign 2000, 2005); however if the after-tax Total Income LICO is used the poverty rate for children in 2003 falls to 12.4% (Statistics Canada, 2005).

The argument presented by Statistics Canada for the drop in poverty rates is that using the LICO measure based upon after-tax Total Income reflects the progressive income tax structure of Canada whereby the income disparity in Canada becomes more compressed (Statistics Canada, 2002, p. 135). Some consider that the after-tax method may be a truer standard of poverty than the before-tax method (Graham, Swift & Delaney, 2003, p. 76). Others see problems with the after-tax method. For instance, the after-tax method only adjusts income for provincial and federal income taxes, and not for all the other taxes such as provincial sales tax, GST, EI premiums, and so on (Ross, Scott, & Smith, 2000, pp. 35–36); and taxation rates differ across provinces.[6] It has also been argued elsewhere that the major problem with using LICO with after-tax Total Income is methodological (Hunter & Miazdyck, 2004). The methodological argument focuses on the additional 20 points added to the average expenditures.

The LICO measure was developed when only before-tax income figures were available; Podoluk's decision to add 20 points was intended to included room for taxation. If Statistics Canada wishes to measure LICO with after-tax income that is fine, but it is "double counting" to use income after tax and then still add 20 points as if before tax income was still being used to measure low income. To be methodologically sound, the 20 points needs to be reduced by some amount. I would suggest that if after-tax income is used, then the 20 points should be reduced by the rate of taxation. If one third of income is taxed, then 14–15 points should be added. In doing so, the after-tax LICO rate comes out to be more similar to the before-tax LICO rate.

Although LICO is the most commonly used measure of poverty, there are other poverty measures used in Canada. Additional *relative* measures of poverty include the Low Income Measure (LIM) from Statistics Canada, the Toronto Social Planning Council measure, the Canadian Council on Social Development measure, the measure devised by the 1971 Senate Committee on Poverty known as the Croll, and the Gallup Poll measure. Others argue that provincial welfare rates are implicit poverty lines, with welfare rates serving as the minimum income a family or person should receive (Ross, Scott, & Smith, 2000). In reporting on child poverty in rich countries, UNICEF's *Child Poverty in Rich Countries* uses 50% of the national median income (2005, p. 6). There are also three *absolute* measures of poverty that are commonly used in Canada: the Montreal Diet Dispensary measure, the Fraser Institute's Sarlo poverty line, and Statistics Canada's new Market Basket Measure (MBM).

Absolute poverty measures differ from relative measures of poverty in that they are not linked to an average standard of living. Rather these measures examine what is the absolute minimum an individual or a family needs to survive.[7] In actuality, however, absolute poverty measures are always relative measures because of the decisions that are made as to what constitutes an absolute minimum. How many socks, how many shoes, and how much milk to buy each year are all relative judgements—judgments that are made by the developers of absolute poverty measures.

In May 2003, Statistics Canada introduced its own absolute low-income measure: the Market Basket Measure (MBM). The MBM was not produced as a result of requests from a large number of advocacy groups and researchers. Rather, the measure was developed in response to a 1997 request of the Federal/Provincial/Territorial Ministers Responsible for Social Services (Human Resources Development Canada [HRDC], 2003, p. 1). As an absolute measure, the MBM approach is an attempt to determine how much disposable family income[8] is required for a pre-determined, specific basket of goods and services. The HRDC market basket measure includes five types of expenditures: (1) food; (2) clothing and footwear; (3) shelter; (4) transportation; and

(5) other household needs (e.g., school supplies, personal care products, telephone, furniture).

The MBM is calculated with a referent family, comprised of two adults (one male and one female) aged 25–49, and two children (a girl aged 9 and a boy aged 13). All other household configurations are calculated using a formula based on the Low Income Measure (LIM) equivalence scale. A family of four has an equivalence scale value of 2. A single person has an equivalence value of 1. Therefore it is postulated by Statistics Canada that a family of four requires twice as much income as a single adult (HRDC, 2003, pp. 34–35). The MBM then establishes thresholds, which are the sum of costs for the predetermined basket of goods and services for the selected communities and community sizes across the ten provinces. Economic families that are below the MBM thresholds are considered low income.

Several issues with the MBM approach should be raised in the context of the LICO measure. First, although the MBM is considered an absolute approach to poverty measurement, it is actually a relative measure because it must be decided what constitutes a basket of goods and services. Any number of subjective opinions comprises what should and should not be in the market basket. All measures of poverty, in this sense, are relative. However, the larger problem is that the MBM approach does not account for the growing disparity of income between the rich and the poor. The income and wealth of the rich recede from scrutiny when consideration is focused on what constitutes a reasonable MBM basket of goods and services. The methodology behind relative measures of poverty has the advantage of employing all sources of income and therefore reflecting the growth of income disparity.

To illustrate why it matters to policy-makers and advocates which measure is used to assess child poverty, the figures for the MBM, the after-tax LICO and the before-tax LICO, and their corresponding poverty rates are presented. For the year 2000, the incidence of low income for children in Canada was 16.9% using the MBM (Giles, 2004, p. 34); 13.8% using after-tax LICO (Statistics Canada, 2005b, p. 126); and 16.5% using before-tax LICO (Campaign 2000, 2000, p. 1). Only the year 2000 is used for comparison, as there are no other data currently available for the MBM.

Using Income Measures to Define the Condition of Child Poverty

We can see from the above figures that using either of the Statistics Canada LICO measures,[9] high levels of child poverty have persisted up to and including 2003 in Canada. In 1989 (year of the declaration to end child poverty in Canada by 2000), the child poverty level in Canada was 14.4%. Disturbingly, the incidence of child poverty in Canada increased to 17.6% for the year 2003 (Campaign 2000, 2005, p. 2). The clear and disconcerting outcome from an analysis of the data is the continuous high incidence of child poverty in Canada.

A concept related to the incidence of poverty is the depth of poverty. Depth of poverty refers to how far below a poverty line an income falls (Ross,

Who
Experiences
the Problem
of Poverty?
Class and
Gender Issues
Scott & Smith, 2000, p. 103). The average low income gap is calculated by determining the sum of all of the income amounts that are below the income cut-off level for any given category (see Table 9.1), and dividing that sum by the number of units (individuals, families). The measure is useful as it provides some idea of how much is needed to bring up the income of people to a pre-determined low-income cut-off level. For example, in 1989, the average depth of poverty for all families with children was $7,300, which has risen to $8,000 for the year 2003.[10] Another useful statistic is the proportion of Canada's real (constant dollar) Gross Domestic Product (GDP)[11] that is devoted to social spending. The increase in child poverty in Canada from 14.4% in 1989 to 17.6% in 2003 has corresponded to a decrease in the proportion of Canada's GDP devoted to social spending, from 18.6% in 1990 to 17.3% in 2000 (UNICEF, 2005, p. 26).

Who Experiences the Problem of Poverty?
Class and Gender Issues

There are four major sources of income available to people: (1) private material resources such as dividends, savings, insurance, and property; (2) employee compensation from a job; (3) family and community support; and (4) state subsidies in the form of pensions, unemployment insurance, welfare, and other income assistance. The poor obviously do not have private material resources for a source of income. The poor either do not have employee compensation, or if they do it is barely adequate to meet basic needs. The poor often rely on family and friends for support, or the services of charities such as food banks; the poor often have to rely on social income programs to survive.

Unlike those who have private material resources, the threat to working people and the poor is income insecurity. Those who can work are utterly dependent on securing and maintaining waged labour, and therefore are constantly faced with the threat of unemployment. The unemployable who are poor and the poor who cannot obtain decent employment, must rely upon state subsidy programs. The threat to these programs is similar to that represented by waged labour. They are constantly faced with the exigency of program elimination, program cutbacks, and being denied services from these programs. The lesson is very clear. If you are not wealthy, then you had better have a good job or a responsible government (Hicks, 1999).

Thousands of Canadian children are poor and live in families without private wealth, families where parents do not have a decent steady job and where there are no wealthy and generous relatives or neighbours. The highest incidence of child poverty is among female single-parent families at 38.4% (Statistics Canada, 2005b),[12] or 208,000 families out of the total of 541,667 female lone-parent families. Aboriginal children are especially vulnerable to poverty, as almost 46% of Aboriginal children under fifteen live with a lone parent (Anderson, 2003). Aboriginal children under fifteen had a poverty rate of

41.1% for the year 2000, while the total child poverty rate for Canada was 19.1% (Statistics Canada, 2005a). This number is especially alarming as, for the total national population, 77.1% of income comes from employment while the Aboriginal population earns 75.1% of their income from employment. Aboriginal peoples are obviously receiving far lower wages and salaries for their employment than the total population in Canada. Race also appears to be a factor when minority status is examined for 2003. Youth aged 15–17 years who are not from a visible minority experienced a poverty rate of 10.9%, but visible minority youth experienced a poverty rate of 30.1%.[13]

When the data were last examined in 1998 (Statistics Canada, 2005b),[14] the highest incidence of poverty using the LICO cut-off was among female lone-parent families with no earner: 52.2% (132,000 families of the total of 253,000 female lone-parent families below 1992 LICO). Female lone-parent families with one earner[15] had a poverty incidence level of 45.8% (116,000 families of the 253,000 female lone-parent families). The overall incidence of poverty for female-headed families in 1998 was 42.9%. In 1998, the figures indicated two things: (1) the inadequacy of social income programs (e.g. welfare; CTB and its replacement, the CCTB) in bringing female lone-parent families with no earner anywhere near the LICO cut-offs; and (2) a female lone-parent family with one earner reduces the incidence of poverty (using the 1992 LICO measure) by only 6.4% when compared with female lone-parent families with no earner. Employment for this group did reduce the incidence of poverty but not substantially. In 2003, the situation for no earner and one earner female lone-parent families *has reversed.*

For 2003, the highest incidence of poverty using the LICO cut-off is among female lone-parent families at 38.4% (or 208,000) of the total number of female lone-parent families (541,667 for 2003). Among female lone-parent families, the highest poverty rate is among families with one earner at 53.8%, or 112,000 families of the total of 208,000 female lone-parent families below 1992 LICO. Female lone-parent families with no earner have a poverty incidence level of 39.4%, or 82,000 families of the 208,000 families. For 2003, the figures indicated two things: (1) the continued inadequacy of social income programs (e.g. welfare; CTB and its replacement, the CCTB) in bringing all female lone-parent families with no earner anywhere near the LICO cut-offs; and (2) a female lone-parent family with one earner does not reduce the incidence of poverty (the 1992 LICO measure). Indeed, having earnings *increased* the poverty rate by 14.4% between 1998 and 2003.

At first, the concept of employment increasing the poverty rate does not make sense. With provincial welfare rates well below minimum wages across Canada, how can families with no earners have a lower poverty rate than those with income? Indeed, the reversal is quite dramatic. In 1996, the year the Canada Assistance Plan (CAP) was replaced by the Canada Health and Social Transfer (CHST), the poverty rate was 64.3% (195,000) for female lone-parent families with no earners and 33% (100,000) for female lone-parent families

Who
Experiences
the Problem
of Poverty?
Class and
Gender Issues
with one earner (Statistics Canada, 2005b, p. 147).[16] The best explanation of the data is workfare. Many of these women are now participating in workfare schemes across the country. The type of employment most likely to be found is temporary contract work at or near minimum wage levels. Many more women are now participating in these various workfare programs, but their participation does not raise them and their children out of poverty.

The group experiencing the next highest levels of child poverty are two-parent families with children. For 2003, there are 3,045,454 two-parent families with children in Canada. Of that total, 201,000 (6.6%) are below the low-income cut-off for 2003. Among two-parent families with children in this group, 20% (40,000 of the total of 201,000 families) have no earner, 37.3% (75,000) have one earner, and 33.8% (68,000) have two earners. The obvious fact that can be observed from the data, especially for female lone-parent families, is that having a job is not an assurance of escaping poverty.

Jackson, Robinson, Baldwin, and Wiggins (2000) write that Canada has experienced a continuing increase in wage inequality with employment becoming polarized into streams of good jobs and bad jobs. It is not just employment that employable people need—it is employment with a decent salary that is required. Evidence from the research of Jackson et al. (2000) indicates that collective bargaining raises employment remuneration for union workers as compared to non-union workers doing similar jobs. In fact, the advantage of unionization is greatest for those who would otherwise be low-wage[17] earners. The union advantage for women can clearly be seen in the fact that almost one half of women who are not unionized are in low-wage employment, while less than 10% of women who are unionized are in low-wage employment (Jackson et al., 2000, p. 101). Many other factors affect the quality of life outside of wages, and many union positions also provide for holidays, sick days, dental plans, maternity leave provisions, and occupational pensions that are not available to women in low-wage non-unionized employment.

A study by Statistics Canada sheds further light on employment and low-income in Canada (Janz, 2004). Less than one-half of Canadian workers (47%) who had low-paying jobs[18] in 1996 had managed to climb out of poverty by 2001. Those most likely to rise above low income were young university-educated men in professional occupations and industries. Most often they worked full-time in large unionized firms in Ontario or Alberta. The 53% trapped in low-paid work from 1996 to 2001 tended to be older women, those with high school education or less, and those working part-time for small, non-unionized organizations.

Wages are obviously important when examining the characteristics of poverty. Data published by the Canadian Council on Social Development (Jackson, 2001) demonstrates that a household with a single earner working forty hours per week for the *median salary* of $13.86 per hour is unlikely to be defined as low-income using the LICO measurement. A full-time job at the

Who
Experiences
the Problem
of Poverty?
Class and
Gender Issues

Table 9.2 Child poverty rate and low wages in rich nations		
COUNTRY (Rich Nations)	CHILD POVERTY (%)	LOW WAGES (%)
Sweden	2.8	5.2
Finland	4.3	5.9
Belgium	4.4	7.2
Netherlands	7.7	11.9
France	7.9	13.3
Germany	10.7	13.3
Japan	12.2	15.7
Spain	12.3	19
Australia	12.6	13.8
Canada	15.5	23.7
Ireland	16.8	18
United Kingdom	19.8	19.6
Italy	20.5	12.5
USA	22.4	25

Source: *The league table of child poverty in rich nations*, by UNICEF, 2000 (Florence: UNICEF Innocenti Research Centre).

minimum, or near minimum wage (low wage) is not enough to bring a single parent family with one child above the LICOS, however. Comparative data from the 2005 Innocenti Research Centre's report card in Table 9.2 show that countries that have been successful in reducing the percentage of families with low wages also have lower child poverty rates (UNICEF, 2005).

Also important when studying poverty is the length of time one is poor. The Survey of Labour and Income Dynamics (SLID) data from Statistics Canada provides information on issues such as duration of unemployment and duration of poverty but this data set is not yet available. The SLID data would provide demographic and longitudinal information about households, such as labour market and income characteristics. The data that are now available indicate that on average 41% of the poor escape poverty within one year of becoming poor. Over a ten-year period a family remains poor for an average of five years (Ross, Scott & Smith, 2000, pp. 121–122). The likelihood of escaping poverty varies according to different years, which suggests that economic factors play some part in the incidence and depth of poverty. Additionally, the number of employable people on welfare appears to follow seasonal variations as well as economic factors.

In summary, the factors that are most important in answering the question of who is poor are the level of support from social income programs, the type of wages that can be secured in the labour market, the unionization of employment, and economic cycles.

What Are the Causes of Child Poverty?

One method of approaching theories about the causes of poverty is to use the classification system of Townsend (1979), which encompasses sociological, economic, and political domains. This classification system is useful in examining poverty, as "Peter Townsend's work follows the Fabian tradition in so far as its object of scrutiny is poverty and its strategy is redistribution, but at the same time it goes beyond the tradition in identifying structural problems whose solution requires structural transformations" (Dunn, 1999, p. 296).

One of the sociological theories of poverty described by Dunn (1999) as particularly salient among the general public in Canada is the "culture of poverty" theory: "Poverty is seen as a way of life passed on from one generation to another. The poor have similar value systems, spending patterns, and time orientations. They buy as their needs arise, are heavy drinkers, and live in crowded quarters. The solution to these problems is to have social workers change the values and patterns of the poor and break their cycle of poverty" (Dunn, 1999, p. 296).

Katz (1989) explains that the culture of poverty theory originated among liberals who wanted to advocate for generous and active programs to help the poor. According to Katz (1989), their arguments were developed from the work of Oscar Lewis and his ethnographic descriptions of Mexicans and Puerto Ricans. In Lewis's work, the behaviours of the poor were viewed as common adaptations to common problems of being poor (Katz, 1989, p. 17). However, during the 1970s the culture of poverty theory shifted, and in that process came to support a conservative perspective (Katz, 1989, pp. 16–17), with the culture of poverty now understood as the cause of continued poverty.

In its substance, the culture of poverty theory is grounded in the idea of deferred gratification; that is, the poor wish to have immediate gratification of rewards while the prudent middle-class person can wait and therefore obtain long-term rewards (Ryan, 1976, pp. 117–141). Summing up the debate about the merits of the culture of poverty theory, Ryan writes:

> A related point—often the most overlooked point in any discussion of the culture of poverty—is that there is not, to my knowledge, any evidence whatever that the poor perceive their way of life as good and preferable to other ways of life. To make such an assertion is to talk pure nonsense. To avoid making such an assertion is to admit, at least implicitly, that the culture of poverty, whatever else it may be (if, indeed it is anything more than a catch phrase approximately as respectable intellectually as the concept of The Pepsi Generation) is, in no conceivable sense, a cultural phenomenon.
>
> Lee Rainwater has developed perhaps the most broadly acceptable formulation of these issues. He notes that there is relatively little difference in descriptions of the *behavior* differences that characterize the poor and suggests that, from a policy point of view, the crucial issue is to view this behavior as adaptive, adaptive to a state of being deprived, excluded, and demeaned. (1976, p. 134, italics in the original)

The culture of poverty theory is an *individual* theory of poverty: the cause of poverty is found within the individual.

What Are the Causes of Child Poverty?

Another sociological theory of poverty identified by Dunn (2000) develops from the feminist theory formulation of patriarchy. This perspective expands upon theories of poverty, introducing the concept of active discrimination that is beyond general structural accounts as usually presented in the poverty literature. Commenting upon Townsend's (1979) analysis of poverty and women, Williams observes that Townsend sets his analysis in class terms (1989, p. 135). Although within his class analysis Townsend (1979) identifies the underclass as comprising different groups, including the low paid, lone parents, and older people, many in those groups are women. Townsend does not identify an interaction between class and gender, however (Williams, 1989, p. 135).

Economic and political theories of poverty suggest that the economy is the cause of poverty. Classical economists would find the cause of poverty in a deficit of human capital, including education, skills, ability, and experiences that separately or in aggregate lead to poverty (Dunn, 1999, p. 297). This theory of poverty would suggest that structural unemployment leads to job loss and perhaps poverty if adjustments are not made to combat the changing needs of the labour force (Ternowetsky & Thorn, 1991, p. 164). Dealing with structural unemployment necessitates years of retraining workers, and results in ongoing job vacancies and unemployment.

A short-term type of unemployment that is derived from the economic system is the pattern of cyclical unemployment. Cyclical unemployment is tied to the cycles of the market economy and represents the difference in the incidence of unemployment between the peak and trough years of a business cycle. Periods of economic growth produce lower unemployment levels whereas recessionary periods result in higher levels of unemployment and the need for social income programs. Unfortunately, during recessionary periods, fewer tax revenues are collected that can be devoted to social programs just when the demands for these programs are at the highest.

More recently, the federal and provincial governments and territories have suggested that social income programs create dependency among the recipients and therefore actually harm recipients by keeping them from paid employment. The familiar argument is that people are poor because they do not have a job, and if they are moved off welfare by supports such as the Canada Child Tax Benefit (CCTB) program and into employment, then employment will lead them out of poverty. Even writers who present themselves as progressive state that social income programs like welfare contain disincentives from taking employment and create dependency among social income program recipients:

> Paradoxes of intervening in the economic life of some Canadians have long been recognized: financial assistance programs may sometimes decrease the incentive to paid work for some recipients, that is, they contain inherent labour force participation disincentives. Authors of this

textbook, like other progressive observers, insist on the need for plenti-
ful jobs offering meaningful employment and decent wages. More than
any other factor, decent jobs would alleviate much of the problem of
labour force participation disincentives. (Graham, Swift, & Delaney, 2003,
p. 57)

As these authors and others suggest that the creation of decent jobs and
meaningful employment is a way to overcome the disincentives of social
income programs, should not then the argument about welfare dependency
be revised? Rather than creating programs such as the CCTB to help working
poor families, the focus should shift to concentrate on labour market disincentives to employment. Should it not be argued that it is the labour market
that creates the disincentives to employment and that the labour market
needs to change to create meaningful employment, unionized workplaces,
decent wages, and decent jobs? In doing so, attention would be refocused
from the individual poor and individual solutions for poverty, to examining
the market system as a cause of unemployment and poverty, requiring solutions based upon universal social and economic policies.

Although government programs for the poor concentrate on lack of
employment skills (e.g., how to look for work, resumés, personal behaviours
at work) or work discipline (e.g., poor who have lost the skills of work such
as being on time, being rested for work, proper work deportment) or lack
of moral responsibility among the poor, the structural and cyclical nature of
unemployment and poverty are not easy to ignore. The market cycles of expansion and contraction in the economy require attention if the issue of child
poverty is going to be addressed in a serious manner.

The neo-liberal perspective that now dominates all political parties in
Canada and the Western world defines the modern welfare state as a major
offender in creating poverty. Current changes to public policy to address
poverty, as viewed by their advocates, are a break from the mistakes of the old
welfare state. Public policy during the modern welfare state was "passive"
and based mostly upon the concept of entitlement with little to say about
responsibility; that is, the state has a duty to offer assistance to citizens who
have no other resources or options for support. The policy of entitlement did
little to stimulate employment. Reflecting a neo-liberal perspective, the Organization for Economic Cooperation and Development (OECD) advocates for
what it terms an "active society," which is characterized by a wide range of
reforms that include linking cash benefits (welfare) to work-orientated incentives across a broad range of options (Gilbert, 2004).

The Scandinavian countries, Britain, Australia, New Zealand, the United
States, and Canada have all taken up this perspective and developed somewhat different work-orientated welfare policies. In tandem with the transition
from passive to active policies, programs have moved from a needs-based
approach (the financially destitute have a right to social benefits) to a focus
on the responsibilities of recipients to find work, to be self-sufficient, and to

lead productive lives. The continuation of entitlement-based public policy without responsibilities is seen to be unworkable. Canada, as well as the rest of the world, we are told, must face and adjust to the new global economy: "Social programs must change to keep up with new realities—realities around a changing economy, around unmanageable public debt and around problems with the programs themselves" (Gilbert, 2004, p. 283). **What Are the Causes of Child Poverty?**

Within the "New Economy" welfare state it is not material benefits that matter. What is important is a different concept, one that is thin in tangible benefits, and vague in definition, and has a pleasant ring in media sound bites—social exclusion. Social exclusion (again not poverty) has come to join welfare dependency as the enemy. The supposed wreckage to society and the New Economy brought by social exclusion is to be overcome by means of government policies of labour-market inclusion. It is not the labour market that needs to change. Instead, the excluded (the poor, including the disabled) should be rendered employable in response to the shifting nature of the economy and employment. To be without employment, apparently unless one is wealthy, idle, and living in a gated neighborhood, is to be outside of the community. The idea that people on welfare and the disabled are excluded from full citizenship has its genesis in conservative ideology. Jones and Novak (1999) comment, "The primary aim of social inclusion and cohesion is therefore to bind the excluded back into the labour market as a solution to the problem. That this may result in their continuing poverty is conveniently overlooked, since it is their exclusion (whether self-imposed or structural) that is the problem rather than their poverty" (p. 188).

Within the logic of active welfare state public policy, citizenship for individuals and families is defined as having a "job, [being] self-sufficient, contributing to society with access to education, health care and security" (Saskatchewan Social Services, 1999). As welfare state programs among industrialized countries with both conservative and social democratic governments, poverty policies "are increasingly wrapped in the elaborate rhetoric of social inclusion (in the labor force), empowerment (to earn wages), activation (to find a job), and responsibility (to take the job)" (Gilbert, 2004, p. 67).

Much of the debate about welfare reform has come to focus on whether the "active" programming changes should adopt a labour force attachment (LFA) model, wherein the government considers any employment to be better than welfare provision. Increasingly, the LFA approach to welfare has been the model most favoured by Canada and the provinces: "Welfare has increasingly shifted from being an 'entitlement' program designed to help fight poverty, to a temporary support intended to promote individual self-sufficiency through labour force attachment strategies" (HRDC, 2000). The other model is the human resources development (HRD) or human capital development (Peck, 2001, p. 78) model most identified with the Scandinavian social democratic welfare states. The HRD model is, in the short term, a more costly approach because it emphasizes education and training leading to labour force entry above the minimum wage. Over the long term, the HRD model is

Alleviating
Child Poverty
and the
Canada Child
Tax Benefit
Legislation
viewed as beneficial to workers and the labour market because individual and overall wages increase with this approach.

Especially disheartening in discussions about labour force attachment versus human capital development models is the lack of any serious debate. The labour force attachment model can be criticized for placing people in temporary at-or-near-minimum-wage employment with few if any benefits. However, the more progressively viewed human capital development model is not without its flaws. As the economist James K. Galbraith (1998) notes, the skills-mismatch idea deflects attention from the fact that the roots of income inequality lie in monopoly power rather than educational deficiency (Katz, 2001, p. 352). Galbraith observes, "What the existing economy needs is a fairly small number of first-rate technical talents, combined with a small super-class of managers and financiers, on top of a vast substructure of nominally literate and politically apathetic working people" (Galbraith, 1998, pp. 34–35; cited in Katz, 2001, p. 352). Perhaps that explains why so many countries have adopted the labour force attachment model in their "active welfare states." When the causes of poverty are examined, the lack of money and / or wealth is the simplest explanation.

Alleviating Child Poverty and the
Canada Child Tax Benefit Legislation

The major piece of legislation enabling the social income transfer program in Canada designed specifically to address child poverty is the Canada Child Tax Benefit (CCTB), which is administered by the Canada Revenue Agency (CRA) using filed income tax returns. The predecessor to the CCTB (1997) was the New Integrated Child Tax Benefit (CTB) (1993). The social income programs that existed for families with children before the CTB were the universal Family Allowance program and income tax based measures including the refundable child tax credit, the non-refundable child tax credit, the-equivalent-to married credit, and the child care expense reduction. Under the Integrated CTB there were now three components: the Child Tax Benefit, the equivalent-to-married credit and the child-care deduction. The previous non-refundable and refundable tax credits and the Family Allowance program were aggregated into the income-tested CTB. The elimination of the Family Allowance program represented a fundamental rethinking about children in Canada: children were no longer viewed as the responsibility of society as a whole as well as parents, children were now seen as part of the budget and expenses for family after-tax income spending (Kitchen, 2001, p. 240). Family Allowances allowed all children access to some portion of the social wage; with the CTB program, the social wage was only available to families who were economically vulnerable. The CTB program clawed back benefits as family incomes increased. Additionally, the program did not have scheduled adjustments for inflation.

In 1997, the CTB program was replaced with the CCTB legislation. Both programs are somewhat similar in their underlying values. The major difference between them is that the CCTB program includes all of the provinces and territories, while they were not part of the CTB program, which was solely federally funded. The Canada Child Tax Benefit (CCTB) program is divided into two benefits. One is the Basic Benefit that is provided to all families with children contingent upon their level of income. The other benefit is provided under the cost-shared National Child Benefit program (NCB), a program that the federal government shares with the provinces and territories and that is intended for low-income families with children. The federal contribution to the NCB is the National Child Benefit Supplement (NCBS), which is similar to the previous Working Income Supplement (WIS) program. The WIS Program replaced the universal Family Allowance program and was a *per family benefit* provided to low-income families with children, while the NCBS is a *per child benefit* (as was the Family Allowance program) provided to low-income families with children.

The NCBS has been integrated into the basic allowance component of provincial social assistance programs in the provinces and territories (Kitchen, 2001, p. 241). The NCBS program can be used to remove children from the basic allowance component of the provincial welfare rolls, with those payments now coming from the federal government's NCBS contribution to the NCB. The provincial, territorial, and First Nations contribution to the NCB is to provide programs that support low-income working families with children, whether or not the families receive welfare. Programs that can be provided by the provinces to low-income families with children could include pharmacare or dental care, child care services, child credit for low-income families (British Columbia, Quebec), an earned income credit (Alberta), a combination of programs (Saskatchewan, New Brunswick), and early prevention programs for children at risk (Ontario). The provincial and territorial contributions to the NCB go under a dazzling array of various names and programs (some having a shorter life span than others) in the different provincial/territorial, and First Nations jurisdictions.[19]

The provincial savings from reduced welfare expenditures under the CCTB are quite substantial, and these "reinvestment funds" created through provincial clawbacks of the increased federal spending under the CCTB have gone into programs that supplement low-income wages. The provincial savings on welfare expenditures due to increased federal contributions through the CCTB do not need to go to increased spending on families with children on welfare who have no other source of income, presumably the poorest children in Canada. Rather, the money can be used to fund social income programs for the working poor, as has happened in a number of provinces. Retaining the funds saved by not passing on the increase in federal expenditures to the poorest families on welfare with no source of income, and using those funds to support families with low incomes, is entirely in keeping with the intent of

Alleviating Child Poverty and the Canada Child Tax Benefit Legislation the CCTB program. An Enriched Canada Child Tax Benefit will "pave the way for provinces and territories to redirect their resources towards improved child services and income support for low-income working families" (Canada, 1997a, p. 2) and further "to promote attachment to the workforce—resulting in fewer families having to rely on social assistance—by ensuring that families will always be better off as a result of finding work" (Canada, 1997b, p. 1).

The savings incurred by the provinces under the NCB program of the CCTB are to be directed toward children's services and income support programs for low-income families with children. Lightman writes of the NCB program, "The central intent of this change was to reward families in the low-paid workforce and, by extension, to penalize those on social assistance. In other words, the program was now structured to provide a strong work incentive; and arguably, the focus was more on work incentives than on support for children" (pp. 156–157).

Conclusion

The continuing high rates of child poverty suggest that the rewards aspect of the NCB need closer investigation. The focus of the NCB policy initiative on the workplace attachment of the recipient is a fundamental flaw in the NCB portion of the CCTB program. If the program were designed to eliminate child poverty, benefits would increase according to the financial need of families with children (Pulkingham & Ternowetsky, 1997, pp. 206–207). There is no extra money for families whose only source of income is social assistance. Rather, the federal government has used the CCTB program to alleviate some of the provincial welfare expenditures related to children to gain provincial support for the program.

An examination of the program criteria and the income effects of the "active welfare state" federal / provincial child poverty program could lead to a conclusion that the new CCTB initiative is not about reducing poverty for the poorest children in Canada. The initiative appears to be designed within the framework of citizenship theory and the right to make it more attractive to work than to receive assistance. Beyond just distinguishing between worthy and unworthy poor, the program is therefore also entrenching the poor law concept of "less eligibility." It also follows that rather than the main benefactor of the CCTB being children, the business sector will gain the most from the program because it tends to subsidize low-wage labour. Research evidence indicates that the consequences of the cuts made during the 1990s to the welfare system in Canada have been to impoverish further the poor on welfare, and to depress the wages of the working poor (Klein & Montgomery, 2001, p. 5).

Current job growth in Canada is mainly in the service sector, where many of the jobs are low paying with no benefits (Broad, 2000). What the CCTB program has achieved in application is to implement a program that could subsidize employers by distributing small income gains and limited health benefits to their employees. Now, there are obviously some businesses that cannot afford high wages; however, the government could have chosen to help these workers through a more progressive structure in the income tax system. Lower paid workers in marginal industries and services identified through the income tax system could be taxed at a reduced rate while top income earners, consistent with the principles of a progressive tax system and a desire to reduce inequality, would be taxed at a higher rate. As well, the program could also be funded from a variety of taxes that could be placed on businesses profits (Mackenzie, 1998, pp. 335–358). That way, a program to assist workers who are vulnerable to job elimination and who receive lower wages would be funded by a vertical transfer of benefits from the wealthy rather than the horizontal transfer system introduced by the CCTB program.

Under the current structure of the CCTB, any business, including large businesses, can hire taxpayer-subsidized employees at minimum wage and continue to provide little or no health benefits or decent salaries and wage increases to their employees. Commensurate with neo-liberal ideology, the government, rather than use the tax system in a progressive manner to assist low-income earners, has decided to assist businesses by subsidizing low wages and has, therefore, firmly entrenched the concept of less eligibility and worthy and unworthy poor within the welfare system. The CCTB, as it is presently designed and delivered, is not a children's benefit. It is an enriched Working Income Supplement (WIS) program for working poor families with children (Pulkingham & Ternowetsky, 1997, p. 206). By introducing the Canada Child Tax Benefit in its current form, governments are acknowledging that, for a growing group of people, the economic system will not provide a surplus wage and / or social wage, and subsequently inequality of income, inequality of opportunity, and inequality of condition for the poorest in Canada will continue to grow.

Notes

1 UNICEF uses a relative measure of poverty based upon households with incomes below 50% of the national median. This measure differs from the LICO measure used by Statistics Canada, which is based upon the community average spent on essentials.

2 The year 1997 is the last year Statistics Canada produced the *Survey of Consumer Finances*, the data set that has been used on a yearly basis to examine child poverty. The *Survey of Labour and Income Dynamics* (SLID) has replaced it. There are currently strict criteria on access to the SLID data. The longitudinal nature of the SLID data has raised concerns of possible identification of respondents. Only a cross-sectional version of SLID is available to the public.

3 Statistics Canada defines a family economic unit as all occupants of a dwelling unit who are related by blood, marriage, or adoption, and couples living together in common-law relationships.

4 When using Statistics Canada data, a family's income can be calculated using income from either Wages and Salaries, or Total Income including government transfers or income after tax. The researcher should identify which income variable was used in the

study. In creating the data sets, Statistics Canada does not include families living in First Nations communities (reserves) and children living in institutions.

5   For more on Podoluk and the development of LICO see Hunter & Miazdyck (2004, pp. 34–46).

6   For a more complete discussion of issues with after-tax incomes and the LICO measure see Cotton and Webber (2000).

7   For a more thorough discussion of poverty lines in Canada, see the second edition of John Graham, Roger Delaney, and Karen Swift, *Canadian Social Policy: An Introduction* (2003, 74–86); and David Ross, Katherine Scott, and Peter Smith (Eds.), *The Canadian Fact Book on Poverty* (2000).

8   The MBM defines disposable family income as the sum remaining after deducting from the total household income the following: total income taxes paid; the personal portion of payroll taxes; other mandatory payroll deductions such as contributions to employer-sponsored pension plans, supplementary health plans, and union dues; child support and alimony payments made to another household; out-of-pocket spending on child care; and non-insured but medically prescribed health-related expenses such as dental and vision care, prescription drugs, and aids for persons with disabilities (HRDC, 2003, p. 4). As such, the MBM definition of disposable household income would appear to more closely reflect available funds than the after-tax LICO.

9   In Income in Canada 2003, Statistics Canada Low Income Cut-Offs (LICO) are used as the benchmark to identify poor children and their families. The data for poor children under eighteen exclude those who are unattached individuals, those that are the major income earner, or those who are the spouse or common-law partner of the major income earner. In creating these survey data sets, Statistics Canada does not include families living in First Nation communities (reserves).

10   Data calculated by Canadian Council on Social Development using Statistics Canada's *Survey of Labour and Income Dynamics 2003*, masterfile.

11   Real GDP is the value of all final goods and services produced in Canada for a given year in constant prices. Constant prices, or constant dollars, are used rather than only reporting nominal values so that comparisons can be made across different years accounting for the rise in prices measured by the Consumer Price Index (CPI).

12   The figures are calculated using LICO 1992 total income *after tax*. The totals are not equal due to rounding estimates provided in the publication.

13   From data prepared by the Canadian Council on Social Development using SLID masterfile.

14   The figures are calculated using LICO 1992 total income *after tax*. The totals are not equal due to rounding estimates provided in the publication. Also, Statistics Canada continually revises previously released data; therefore values often vary somewhat even for the same year using later published data.

15   Statistics Canada defines an earner as a person who received income from employment (wages and salaries) and/or self-employment during the reference year (Statistics Canada, 2005b).

16   The reader must be careful when looking at data figures in the *Income in Canada* documents. For example, *Income in Canada* (2005b, 120, 146) lists low-income rates of 86% for female lone-parent families with no earners. What that value represents however, is that 86% (82,000) of all female lone-parent families with no income were below LICO. The reader must calculate what the values represent in relation to all female lone-parent families below LICO.

17   Less than two thirds of median income.

18   Low wages based upon the before-tax LICO. To calculate "low-paid work" threshold, the appropriate LICO was divided by 52.14 (weeks/year), which provides the dollars per week needed to reach a LICO low-income cut-off line in 1996. Earning at 10% above the applicable LICO low-income cut-off is defined as "moving up" out of low-paid work.

19 For further information on provincial programs see Canada Revenue Agency, *Your*   **References**
    Canada Child Benefit, online at <www.cra-arc.gc.ca/E/pub/tg/t4114/t4114-e.html>.

References

Anderson, J. (2003, March). *Aboriginal children in poverty in urban communities: Social exclusion and the growing racialization of poverty in Canada.* Ottawa: Canadian Council on Social Development. Online at <www.ccsd.ca/pr/2003/aboriginal.htm>.

Broad, D. (2000). *Hollow work, hollow society? Globalization and the casual labour problem in Canada.* Halifax: Fernwood.

Campaign 2000. (2000). *Child poverty in Canada: Report card 2000.* Toronto: Author.

Campaign 2000. (2005). *Child poverty in Canada: Report card 2005.* Toronto: Author.

Canada. (1997a). *Towards a national child benefit system.* Online at <www.fin.gc.ca/budget97/pamph/childpae.pdf>.

Canada. (1997b). *Working together towards a national child benefit System: Budget 1997.* Online at <www.fin.gc.ca/budget97/child/childe.pdf>.

Canada Revenue Agency. (2005). *Your Canada Child Tax Benefit.* Online at <www.cra-arc.gc.ca/E/pub/tg/+4114-e.html>.

Canadian Council on Social Development (2004). *Poverty lines.* Ottawa: Author. Online at <www.ccsd.ca/factsheets/fs_lico03_bt.htm>.

Cotton, C., & Webber, M. (2000, September). Should the Low Income Cut-Offs be updated? *A summary of feedback on Statistics Canada's discussion paper* (Catalogue no. 75F0002MIE-00011). Ottawa: Income Statistics Division, Statistics Canada.

Dunn, P. (1999). Poverty issues. In F. Turner (Ed.), *Social work practice: An introduction* (pp. 291–305). Scarborough: Prentice Hall Allyn and Bacon Canada.

Fellegi, I. (1997, September). *On poverty and low income* (Catalogue no. 13F0027XIE). Ottawa: Statistics Canada.

Fellegi, I. (1999, December). On poverty and low income. In *Should the Low Income Cut-Offs be updated? A discussion paper* (Catalogue no. 75F0002MIE–99009). Ottawa: Income Statistics Division, Statistics Canada.

Galbraith, J. (1998). *Created unequal: The crisis in American pay.* New York: Simon and Schuster.

Gilbert, N. (2004). Transformation of the welfare state: The silent surrender of public responsibility. London: Oxford University Press.

Giles, P. (2004, December). *Low income measurement in Canada* (Catalogue no. 75F0002MIE). Ottawa: Statistics Canada.

Graham, J., Swift, K., & Delaney, R. (2003). *Canadian social policy: An introduction* (2nd ed.). Toronto: Prentice Hall.

Hicks, A. (1999). *Social democracy and welfare capitalism.* Ithaca: Cornell University Press.

Human Resources Development Canada. (2000, March). *Reconnecting social assistance recipients to the labour market: Lessons learned.* Evaluation and Data Development (Catalogue no. SPAH123E-03-00). Online at <www11.hrdc-drhc.gc.ca/pls/edd/v_report.a?p_site=EDD&sub=SARLM>.

Human Resources Development Canada. (2003, May). *Understanding the 2000 low income statistics based on the market basket measure* (Catalogue no. SP-569-03-03E). Ottawa: Author.

References   Hunter, G., & Miazdyck, D. (2004). *Current issues surrounding poverty and welfare programming in Canada: Two reviews*. Ottawa: Canadian Centre for Policy Alternatives. Online at <www.policyalternatives.ca/documents/Saskatchewan_Pubs/poverty_welfare.pdf>.

Jackson, A. (2001). *Low income trends in the 1990s*. Canadian Council on Social Development. Online at <www.ccsd.ca/pubs/2000/lit/>.

Jackson, A., Robinson, D., Baldwin, B., & Wiggins, C. (2000). *Falling behind: The state of working in Canada*. Ottawa: Canadian Centre for Social Policy.

Janz, T. (2004, March). *Low-paid employment and "moving up": 1996–2001* (Catalogue no. 75F0002MIE–no. 003). Ottawa: Statistics Canada.

Jones, C., & Novak, T. (1999). *Poverty, welfare and the disciplinary state*. London: Routledge.

Katz, M. (1989). *The undeserving poor*. New York: Pantheon.

Katz, M. (2001). *The price of citizenship: Redefining the American welfare state*. New York: Henry Holt.

Kerstetter, S. (2000). LICOs and LIMs. In M. Goldberg & J. Pulkingham (Eds.), *Defining and measuring poverty: Prince George Forum, April 3, 2000*. Prince George: Child Welfare Research Centre, University of Northern British Columbia.

Kitchen, B. (2001). Poverty and declining living standards in a changing economy. In J. Turner & F. Turner (Eds.), *Canadian social welfare* (4th ed., pp. 232–249). Toronto: Pearson Education Canada.

Klein, S., & Montgomery, B. (2001). *Depressing wages: Why welfare cuts hurt both poor and working poor*. Ottawa: Canadian Centre for Policy Alternatives.

Lightman, E. (2003). *Social policy in Canada*. Toronto: Oxford University Press.

Mackenzie, H. (1998). Tax relief for those who really need it. In Canadian Centre for Policy Alternatives, *Alternative federal budget papers: 1998* (pp. 335–358). Ottawa: Canadian Centre for Policy Alternatives.

National Council of Welfare. (1999a). *Children first: A pre-budget report by the National Council of Welfare*. Ottawa: Minister of Public Works and Government Services Canada.

National Council of Welfare. (1999b). *Poverty profile 1997*. Ottawa: Minister of Public Works and Government Services Canada.

Peck, J. (2001). *Workfare states*. London: Guilford Press.

Poduluk, J. (1968). *Income of Canadians*. Ottawa: Census Monograph, Dominion Bureau of Statistics.

Pulkingham, J., & Ternowetsky, G. (1997). The new Canada Child Tax Benefit: Discriminating between "deserving" and "undeserving" among poor families with children. In J. Pulkingham & G. Ternowetsky (Eds.), *Child and family policies: Struggles, strategies and options* (pp. 204–208). Halifax: Fernwood.

Riches, G. (1997). Hunger and the welfare state: Comparative perspectives. In G. Riches (Ed.), *First world hunger: Food security and welfare politics* (pp. 1–13). London: Macmillian.

Ross, D., Scott, K., & Smith, P. (2000). *The Canadian fact book on poverty*. Ottawa: Canadian Council on Social Development.

Ryan, W. (1976). *Blaming the victim* (Rev. ed.). New York: Vintage.

Saskatchewan Social Services. (1999). *Information: Social assistance handbook* [Brochure].

Statistics Canada (2002, November). *Income in Canada 2000* (Catalogue no. 75–202 **References**
  XIE). Ottawa: Statistics Canada,.
Statistics Canada. (2005a). *2001 Census* (Catalogue no. 97F0011XB2001047). Ottawa:
  Author.
Statistics Canada. (2005b, May). *Income in Canada 2003* (Catalogue no. 75–202-XIE).
  Ottawa: Statistics Canada.
Ternowetsky, G. (2000). *Poverty and corporate welfare.* Regina: Social Policy
  Research Unit, Faculty of Social Work, University of Regina.
Ternowetsky, G., & Thorn, J. (1991). *The decline in middle incomes: Unemployment,
  underemployment and falling living standards in Saskatchewan.* Regina: Social
  Policy Research Unit, Faculty of Social Work, University of Regina.
Townsend, P. (1979). *Poverty in the United Kingdom.* Harmondsworth: Penguin.
UNICEF. (2000). *The league table of child poverty in rich nations.* Florence: UNICEF
  Innocenti Research Centre.
UNICEF. (2005). *Child poverty in rich countries 2005.* Florence: UNICEF Innocenti
  Research Centre.
Webber, M. (1998, May). *Measuring low income and poverty in Canada: An update*
  (Catalogue No. 98–13). Ottawa: Statistics Canada, Income Statistics Division.
Williams, F. (1989). *Social policy: A critical introduction.* Cambridge: Polity Press.

Additional resources

Campaign 2000 website. Online at <www.campaign2000.ca/>.
Canada, National Child Benefit website. Online at <www.nationalchildbenefit.ca/
  ncb/govtofcan4.shtml>.
Fraser Institute website. Online at <www.fraserinstitute.ca/>.
Paul, E., Miller, F., Jr., & Paul, J. (Eds.). (1997). *The welfare state.* Cambridge: Cambridge University Press. A useful set of resources that present neo-liberal ideology on the welfare state, poverty lines, etc.
Seguin, Giles. (n.d.). Personal website: <www.canadiansocialresearch.net/>. A vast
  number of resources on social policy in Canada, including numerous references to child poverty.

Marilyn Callahan and *Karen Swift*

Introduction

Risk assessment measures have been introduced into provincial child welfare systems within the last decade, at a time when child welfare "failures" were featured prominently in the media and when several formal reviews of child welfare systems were undertaken as a response to media coverage.[1] This trend was not limited to Canada but appeared in the United States, United Kingdom, Australia and other Euro-western countries (Parton, Thorpe, & Wattam, 1997; Schene & Bond, 1989; Saunders & Goddard, 1998). The promise of risk assessment was considerable. Among other attributes, it appeared to provide tangible evidence that governments were taking action on child protection, using tools designed to predict which children were in danger of maltreatment. It also seemed to provide a way to screen the important cases from those of less concern, triaging the scarce resources of child welfare. The intent of this chapter is to examine why risk assessment has largely failed to live up to its dual promise of improving the protection of children and better managing the ever-greater workload of child welfare workers. We consider the underlying intentions of risk assessment and suggest other approaches to meet the challenge of child protection in the concluding section of the chapter.

The Evolution of Canadian Child Welfare:
Medical, Legal, and Managerial Influences

In Canada, provincial rather than federal governments are responsible for health, education, and welfare, including child welfare. All ten provinces and three territories have their own child protection legislation, as well as organizational structures designed to protect children. Although child welfare in Canada cannot be described as a single, unified system, some common traditions and understandings across the country provide the basis for describing Canadian child welfare. Generally speaking, child welfare services are residual, or "last chance," services and are highly regulated.

The Evolution
of Canadian
Child Welfare:
Medical,
Legal, and
Managerial
Influences

Since its inception in the early twentieth century, formal child welfare work in Canada has been driven in large measure by complaints made by individuals about particular children and parents. Archival documents show that the everyday responsibilities for child protection were carried out mainly by women, some trained as social workers, some not. They received complaints of reportedly irresponsible parents and unruly children, wrote copious case notes on what they observed, and intervened—sometimes quite actively—in the lives of families brought to their attention (Chen, 2001; Swift, 1995a). Although these women gradually became more professional, records suggest a strong leaning toward British moral traditions of individual responsibility, the nuclear family, and at least the appearance of propriety and morality as central to the style and direction of much child welfare work during the early period (Swift, 1995b).

By the middle of the twentieth century, a series of changes to child welfare legislation and focus occurred. One in particular, the "discovery" of the battered child (Kempe, Silverman, Steele, Droegemuller, & Silver, 1962), led to changes in provincial legislation, the most notable being the addition of mandatory reporting requirements in child welfare legislation. This change compelled professionals and community and family members to report their suspicions about child maltreatment to child welfare organizations. Other significant events included the release of the Badgley Report (1984) on sexual abuse of children and the introduction of the Canadian Charter of Rights and Freedoms (1982). Both of these policy influences increased attention to legal issues in child welfare and intensified relationships between child protection workers, police, and the court system. At the same time, the idea of least intrusive action—always a thread in Canadian child protection practice— was encoded in protection legislation, imposing a requirement for child welfare intervention to be at the least intrusive level consonant with protecting children from harm. This stands in contrast to the approach of pioneer child welfare workers who intervened without much compunction into the lives of families, offering advice and services wherever they deemed necessary.

In the 1990s a series of high profile media reports of deaths of children known to child protection authorities led to several formal reviews of child welfare (Bennet, 1998; Bridge Child Care Consultancy, 1991; Gove, 1995; Porter, 1998). These cases and subsequent reviews have prompted policy shifts in several provinces and jurisdictions (Parton et al., 1997; Swift, 2001). In general, formal reviews have occurred after a child has been killed by a parent or caregiver and have focused on the actions of individual workers and the practice and policies governing their work. As a result, recommendations emerging from these reviews have tended to lower the threshold of risk required to intervene to protect a child and also to expand definitions of abuse and neglect in order to ensure that cases are identified. For instance, changes to child welfare legislation in British Columbia included the phrase "has been or is likely to be" when defining child maltreatment, where previous legislation made no mention of future harm.[2] This inclusion in many child welfare statutes gave legislative authority for risk assessment designed to predict the future safety of children. Other recommendations have included the development of training programs for child welfare workers, the installation of computer-based information systems, and tougher mandatory reporting clauses in legislation. Taken together, these changes are sometimes referred to as a "child-centred" approach. This approach stands in contrast to a "family-centred" one where services are offered to families in need of support without requiring intensive investigations into their care of children.

The introduction of risk assessment measures occurred following rapid increases in complaints to child welfare organizations, in part as a result of media coverage and formal inquiries. Not all complaints are investigated. Some are screened out because they are deemed frivolous, because the family lives in an area outside the jurisdiction of the agency, or because the complaint does not fall within the definition of child maltreatment in the legislation. However, a recent Canadian study documents a startling increase in the numbers of investigations that child welfare organizations carry out each year. From 1998 to 2003

> across the whole country the estimated rate of investigations increased 78%, from a rate of 21.52 per 1,000 children to 38.33 per 1,000. During the same period the estimated number of investigations grew from 135,573 to 235,315. Excluding Quebec, the increase was even more pronounced, with the incidence of investigations growing by 86%, from 24.55 to 45.68 per 1,000 children. (Trocmé, MacLaurin, Fallon, Black & Lajoie, 2005, p. 95)

The introduction of risk assessment and other policy changes came at a time when governments of all political stripes were making strenuous efforts to reduce expenditures on social programs, child welfare included. Thus risk assessment, while it promised to take seriously the goal of child protection, also offered hope that costs could be contained by limiting worker involvement to only those cases where children were likely to be harmed. It was a tall order.

Throughout the decades, child welfare workers have always undertaken some kind of assessment to determine whether individual children are safe in their homes. The most recent iteration has been a concerted attempt to change these assessments from ones governed largely by Euro-Christian values about traditional families to assessments based upon medical or other scientific knowledge that would meet the test of legal evidence.

Risk Assessment: A Tool and a Work Process

A survey of child welfare jurisdictions in Canada in 2000 (Federal / Provincial Working Group on Child and Family Services Information, 2001) found that six of ten provinces presently use formal risk assessment instruments, the majority favouring the New York Risk Assessment Model (Newfoundland and Labrador, New Brunswick, some parts of Quebec, Ontario, and BC, with PEI giving consideration to it). All provinces and territories use some form of immediate safety assessment in their investigations of child maltreatment. Some of these safety assessments are part of the overall risk assessment instrument while others are stand-alone assessment forms.

Underpinning risk assessment is, of course, the notion of risk and a society that embraces it. We are reminded daily about the risks around us and what we should do to avoid them. Good citizens are increasingly defined as those who manage their risks. Those who cannot are viewed more and more as irresponsible and a drain on the public purse if they need help or if the public must take action to protect itself from their activities. Of course, this attention on individual responsibility to manage an increasing number of risks fits with neo-liberal thinking about citizenship and achieving reductions in the welfare state apparatus. Attention has been shifted from the "needs" of the vulnerable to the "risks" they create for themselves and others. The solution arising from risk thinking is to shore up the commitment and skills of individuals so that they are self-managing citizens or to segregate them if they will not comply.

Our confidence in the validity of "risks" is shaken regularly. We find ourselves confronted with new "scientific" facts making old risks redundant and new risks visible. Yet we cling to the notion of risk management in spite of the evidence that many risks are socially constructed and differ across time and cultures.

In child welfare, risk assessment is first and foremost "a process of predicting whether or not a child will be maltreated at some future point in time" (Jones, 1994, p. 1037) and is based primarily upon actuarial rationales that make predictions of behaviour according to statistical computations of particular characteristics shared by groups within the population at large (Silver & Miller, 2002).[3] Many of these characteristics have emerged from social workers, who draw upon their experience with parents and caregivers reported to child welfare. Most risk assessment instruments include measures of present safety, but all focus upon making some prediction of future harm. Previously, child welfare investigations were largely limited to assessing the present safety of children and did so by examining individual and family conditions as more or less unique cases.

While risk assessments vary in their length and rating criteria, the New York model[4] in most frequent use in Canada requires workers to score parents and children in two major areas: child specific factors (age of child, number of children in home) and caretaker factors (caretaker abilities, age). Twenty-two or twenty-three items are scored on a four-point scale with descriptors provided for each item and level. The assessment of the likelihood of risk to children is based upon tallied scores for each of these items.

Administering these tools requires a substantial investment in time, including training of workers and their supervisors. Workers are urged to collect "objective" data to validate their scores, data that are frequently obtained

Table 10.1 Risk assessment: How it works	
While risk assessment processes vary, the following example illustrates how the New York model generally plays out in practice in two provinces, BC and Ontario.	
Making a complaint	A school teacher phones the local child welfare office, stating that one of her pupils regularly comes to school late, without breakfast or a packed lunch, and seems withdrawn and unhappy. School progress is poor and parents have not returned the teacher's calls.
Assessing the complaint	The worker listens to the complaint, all the while scanning her form that determines whether this is a valid complaint under child welfare legislation and policies. Once this is established the worker fills out a complaint form, assesses its urgency given other criteria, and passes it along to her supervisor, who signs it off and then passes it to the investigating social worker.
Investigating the complaint	The investigating social worker immediately opens the information system to determine whether the family is known to the agency and the nature and disposition of previous contacts. The teacher may be interviewed along with others mentioned in the file, the child, and parents. The worker uses a 13-point safety assessment (part of the risk assessment document) to determine whether the child is in immediate danger, the nature of the problems, and their urgency. At this point the worker may find other problems beyond those mentioned by the teacher. For instance, the mother may be leaving the child alone after school.
	If necessary, after completion of the safety assessment and consultation with the supervisor, the worker will complete a full risk assessment, scoring the parent on 23 items. In this process, more items may be found to be addressed. The decision whether the child is in need of protection is made with the supervisor. The worker prepares a summary of the risks, weaving them together to make a coherent story about the family and identifies risks to be reduced.
Reducing risk	The file is then passed to a family service worker who examines the risk assessment forms and identifies those risks that can be addressed by the agency. Some, such as past events (parent was maltreated as a child or whose marital relationship has broken down) or current circumstances (age, marital status, number of children), are not usually selected.
	Most commonly, those risks having to with parental behaviour will be the focus of the risk reduction plan. The worker will identify risks to be reduced, actions required of the parent, and timelines for completion of the tasks. A contract will be drawn up between the mother and social work, explicating the plan, which the supervisor will approve. Further contracts will be established between the child welfare agency and community agencies identified to address the risks with the mother, again with timelines and roles identified. The family service worker will review the contracts and repeat the risk assessment at regular intervals to document changes.
	Parents work throughout the risk assessment process, with their most intense activities taking place during the risk reduction phase.
This outline of the work does not include the activities around court procedures that may occur if children are removed from their parents.	

Risk
Assessment:
Managing
Work,
Protecting
Children
from files and opinions of other professionals and community workers. The risk assessment may be completed without the involvement of parents and children. These assessments are filed on computer and become part of the client's permanent record.

Risk assessment also defines a work process moving through a series of stages from evaluating the initial complaint, to an immediate safety assessment, to a risk assessment and risk reduction plan (see Table 10.1). Although the process is not exactly a linear one, nonetheless the activities of each stage are outlined in detail through practice standards and agency policy. Each phase of the assessment may be completed by a different worker, particularly in large urban offices, and the file is passed from one staff member to the next. In some provinces, particularly Ontario, the time allotted to complete tasks is specified and child welfare organizations receive funding on the basis of a formula determining the amount and nature of the work completed.

The above account portrays the worker as something of a cog in a machine, carrying out various tasks according to well-defined policies and instructions. This is true in part, but it misses the point that social workers in child protection are individuals with their own histories and values shaped by their experience and education, among other things. While the documents and policies direct workers to act in specific ways and demand that workers complete paperwork to demonstrate that they have taken these actions, workers nonetheless devise their own systems for completing the work using different techniques for different occasions.

Risk Assessment: Managing Work, Protecting Children

The next section of the chapter explores two important impacts of risk assessment: its effect on the nature and volume of the work of child welfare, and its capacity to identify and protect children in need of assistance.

Risk Assessment and Workload

One of the clearest attributes of risk assessment is that it makes visible and precise the work process that social workers must undertake in child protection. As the above illustration indicates, there is a set pattern to the work, governed by detailed policies and procedures. While these policies differ from jurisdiction to jurisdiction, there is a general consensus that risk assessment adds to the work of child protection in significant ways and for unexpected reasons. Reports from child welfare workers continue to raise complaints about the overwhelming volume of the work. It is useful to examine carefully the use of risk assessment measures and its contribution to that volume.

A Screen with Few Holes

The profile of people who are reported to child welfare has remained consistent over the years. Most often, they have limited economic means and are disproportionately female single parents and women of colour (Callahan, 1994;

Swift, 1995a; Trocmé et al., 2005). Poverty frequently leads to poor housing, more frequent moves, and limited social networks. Risk assessment scores parents on most of these characteristics, thus making it a self-fulfilling prophecy that poor parents who are reported will exhibit risk characteristics. Risk assessment also requires workers to fill out all items on the assessment, and therefore it is likely that further risks besides the ones named in the initial complaint will be found. A fundamental weakness of risk assessment is its initial focus on "risks" and its lack of attention to strengths that may offset these risks. It is difficult to set aside a case where at least some risks are rated high.

A Powerful Instrument

Parents and caregivers reported to child welfare organizations have little opportunity to refuse to participate in the risk assessment process. Those from other cultures may be totally unfamiliar with the process and potential outcomes of investigations. Others who have been through it before know that workers will complete the risk assessment whether they cooperate or not. They may therefore decide that compliance is their best strategy. Risk assessment, as a "scientific instrument," makes it difficult for either parents or social workers to dispute its findings. At the same time, it makes visible the work process so that steps that social workers omit or do not undertake fully will be evident to supervisors and auditors. Workers must protect themselves.

A Complex Administrative Process

Following a comprehensive study of the Ontario Risk Assessment Model, Parada (2004) identifies three ways in which the model intensifies the work of child protection. First, it is heavily based upon documentation guided by computer programs that demand completion of one screen before another can be tackled. Workers in his study and others (Lu, 2000) report that these demands for documentation and administrative tasks are so great (up to 70% of their time) that little time is left over for contact with families and children. Building a case based upon evidence from informants and files has become the central activity of protection.

Second, the model places sharp limits on the time that can be expended on specific tasks. In many cases, these limited time frames are a result of legislation to ensure that complaints are responded to in a timely fashion and that children are not adrift in the child welfare system. In the face of many steps and procedures to be tackled and many cases waiting for attention, workers must triage their time, focusing on the work that must be done within specific time frames (the paperwork) and putting aside optional tasks (such as relationship building with families and community members).

Risk assessment also demands constant consultation between supervisors and workers about making decisions and taking next steps. Any variations from time frames and policies also require consultations. The focus of supervision tends to be directed to the policies and procedures of the risk assessment work process and not on the interaction of social workers with their clients.

Finally, at least in the initial stages of the work process, risk assessment shifts workers' views of children and families from unique individuals to scores on a series of factors (Parada, Swift & Callahan, 2005), further removing workers from a sense that they are "doing social work." Taken together, shifts in practice that respond to risk assessment require social workers to view their work as a series of largely administrative tasks that must be done quickly and that are completed, not when the family or child is "helped" but when the file is turned over to the next worker or managed in some fashion. Given the disjuncture that occurs for some workers who enter social work to work with "people not paper," the work seems even more demanding.

Risk Assessment and Child Protection

Although the work of child protection may have expanded, intensified, and become less like social work, this would seem to be a justifiable outcome if children benefited from the changes. The next section of the chapter examines the evidence as to whether the expected benefits have been realized.

A search of recent literature reveals no studies demonstrating that the incidence of abuse and neglect of children has been reduced since the introduction of risk assessment measures in North America and elsewhere. The most serious form of harm to children, and of most concern to child protection authorities, is death, often occurring at the hands of parents or caregivers. Over the past thirty years, there has been no significant change in the number of children killed by family members in Canada, and no pattern of change or decrease in the years since a risk assessment approach was introduced (Statistics Canada, 2005, p. 51).

As mentioned before, statistics kept by provinces do show a sharp increase in cases reported and investigated by child welfare authorities. In Ontario, for example, the number of investigations carried out has increased 23% since 1998, from 66,759 to 82,137 in 2004–05. The number of children in care has also risen dramatically in that province, from 11,260 in 1997 to 18,830 in 2005, an increase of 67% (Federal Provincial Working Group, 2001; Ontario Association of Children's Aid Societies, 2005). In BC the proportion of Aboriginal children in care, already very high at 31–33% of all children in care, jumped to 37% between 1998 and 2000 after the introduction of risk assessment (Foster & Wright, 2002, p. 124), and now stands at over 49% in August 2005 (Foster, unpublished ms). It might seem from this increased level of surveillance and intervention that more children have been rescued from dangerous situations. However, there is substantial evidence that is not the case.

In almost half of the cases reported and investigated by child welfare workers, the case is "unsubstantiated," and of those cases that have been substantiated, only 44% received any ongoing attention (Trocmé et al., 2005,

p. 56). Thus we have the situation that for many of the families investigated by child welfare workers, little else occurs, at least until another complaint is lodged.

There are also indications that workers are making decisions based on risk assessment that could be harmful for children (Rycus & Hughes, 2003). One Ontario study showed that workers' ratings of risk have become higher as the tool has become entrenched in practice (Leslie & O'Connor, 2002) because workers feel more secure themselves rating risk levels as high. Higher ratings, of course, mean an increased likelihood that children will come into care.

Further, it is not clear that children coming into care are at risk of immediate harm. The Canadian Incidence Study (Trocmé et al., 2005, p. 108) found that only 3% of investigated cases in Canada involved harm to a child sufficient to require treatment. It was also found that children in families designated as neglectful were more likely to be brought into care than children who had been abused (Trocmé et al., 2005, p. 114).[5] The study demonstrated in fact that in at least 40% of reported child protection cases, the primary issue is neglect (p. 114).

It is well established that the indicators of child neglect are very similar to issues of poverty (Swift, 1995a). In cases in which poverty is a substantial issue, two things can happen. One is that poverty may be viewed by protection workers as neglect. In this case the parent, usually the mother, will be asked to address problems of deprivation that she may not have resources to correct. She will be scrutinized and supervised, but neither the agency nor the worker has the mandate to ameliorate her poverty, and children may be brought into care as a result. A study on housing by Chau, Fitzpatrick, Hulchanski, Leslie, and Schatia (2001) showed that for up to 20% of children brought into care in Ontario, one precipitating factor is lack of acceptable housing. The other possible response is that the case may be accurately assessed as poverty and closed since no resources to address this issue are available. In any event, the case-by-case nature of child welfare work ensures that issues of poverty will only become visible when an individual referral is made. Families living in communities suffering widespread poverty, for example on First Nation reserves, will receive no attention for this issue from child protection authorities.

One of the chief attributes of risk assessment, especially the more complex kinds, is that it is "front-end loaded." That is, the intensive amount of investigative work at the front end consumes a substantial amount of the total time and resources that will be devoted to working on any given case. Further, given the increase in numbers of children being brought into care, substantial child protection resources will go to supporting alternate care arrangements.[6] The drastic cuts in services and levels of income support across North America during the past decades of neo-liberal rule have resulted in a context of extreme scarcity for the most vulnerable families. Child welfare workers report that many of the programs they found helpful in supporting and helping families to heal have been cut or are underfunded. Long waiting lists for existing programs mean that when children are assessed as requiring significant kinds of help, they often don't receive it because supporting programs are not available. What is available, and most often recommended, are programs to "fix" the family, for instance, parenting skills programs.

A critique of risk assessment instruments has emerged from research challenging modernist notions of the unlimited potential of science. This research suggests that although risk assessment measures appear to be empirical instruments, there is no research-based evidence that they actually predict risk (Camasso & Jagannathan, 1995; Doueck, English, DePanfilis, & Moote, 1993; Michalski, Alaggia, & Trocmé, 1996; Pecora, 1991; Wald & Woolverton, 1990). Unclear conceptualization (English & Pecora, 1994), inconsistency of operational definitions (DePanfilis, 1996), debates about appropriate definitions of "risk events," and inconsistencies among laws, policies, mission and training (Berkowitz, 1991) raise important questions about what is being measured. Further, questions about whether risk assessment models are effectively and consistently implemented have been raised by Doueck et al. (1993) and Pecora (1991). Conflicting expectations about what such measures can produce (Cicchinelli, 1989) use of associated factors rather than causal links (Pecora, 1991), and questionable predictive value, especially concerning the all-important issue of child death (Lyons, Doueck, & Wodarski, 1996; Trocmé & Lindsey, 1996), all appear in the literature of the 1990s. Moreover, the research problems in testing these instruments are substantial. For instance, each assessment tool may contain many items, but trying to isolate how scores on the variables interact in the particular situation is extremely difficult. Does a high score (unfavourable) on alcohol and drug abuse overshadow a low score on child's response to parent? Under what conditions? In the most wide-ranging review of the literature sponsored by the North America Resource Centre on Child Welfare, the authors examine the issues of predictability in risk assessment and state that

> The preponderance of research literature continues to raise serious questions about the reliability and validity of most of the risk assessment models and instruments currently used by child welfare agencies. In practice, many child welfare professionals are making decisions about children and families with little more accuracy than flipping a coin, while believing they are using technologies that reduce subjectivity and bias, and that increase the quality of their decisions. (Rycus & Hughes, 2003, p. 23)

What Has Risk Assessment Accomplished?

If risk assessment has failed to reduce the workload and cannot be shown to increase protection to children, then it is interesting to speculate about why it persists as a policy direction in many jurisdictions in Canada and beyond.

Several reports evaluating risk assessment claim that one reason for its ongoing appeal rests in its ability to protect organizations (Saunders & Goddard, 1998; Parton et al., 1997):

> under the guise of protecting children, and even of protecting workers from potential litigation, risk assessment instruments may essentially be attempts by bureaucratic, managerialist organisations to protect themselves from blame when tragedies occur. Ill-equipped to ensure the prompt delivery of services to all those in need, organisations have adopted risk assessment instruments "in lieu of pushing political system[s] for more resources." (Wald & Woolverton, 1990, p. 504)

While this may appear cynical, there may be some truth to the claim. Should a child be harmed or killed while under the protection of an organization, it can be argued that all possible actions have been undertaken to ensure the child's safety. Should individual workers fail to complete the procedures as required, then they could be held personally responsible for the tragedy.

For managers, risk assessment narrows and specifies the range of skills necessary for social workers and enables them to hire novices who can be quickly trained into risk assessment processes and thinking. Given the chronic problems of social work turnover in child protection, this is no small benefit. Further, risk assessment organizes the work into clear stages with specific goals, making it more possible to "contract out" portions of it. Much of the work of "risk reduction" is accomplished through contracts with profit and non-profit organizations, reducing the need for public employees.

Risk assessment holds some appeal for child protection workers. They state that while it has added to their paperwork and increased their vulnerability, it has also brought a welcome order to their practice (Callahan & Swift, **in press**). There is a beginning and an end to their work. Risk assessment brings some standardized practice to the chaotic work of child protection, ensuring that most workers follow the same procedures and cover the same material in their investigations. Risk assessment instruments help social workers raise difficult matters with parents and children that they may have ignored in the past, for instance, questions pertaining to sexual abuse. The authority of risk assessment, with its scientific aura, has also assisted workers in making clear presentations in court with evidence to support their statements.

For these reasons, risk assessment may be difficult to dislodge from child welfare organizations in spite of evidence that it has not fulfilled its promise. It is also difficult to challenge risk assessment because it occupies sacred turf: predicting harm to children and taking action to prevent it. To be opposed to risk assessment would appear indefensible.

Policy Alternatives to Risk Assessment

We began this chapter with the observation that risk assessment was introduced into child welfare to meet two major and challenging goals: protecting children from harm and managing the increasing workload facing child welfare organizations. It is not surprising that it has been found wanting. It is difficult to address such daunting problems with one policy initiative (Rycus & Hughes, 2003). Moreover, the limitations of risk assessment made it a doubtful policy option in the first place.

It is timely to suggest policy alternatives to risk assessment. Risk assessment is now firmly entrenched in child welfare practice in Canada, but it seems to have lost some of its lustre. The sharp rise in removals of children from their families has not found favour with the many governments that are introducing other policies to counteract this trend. Two of these include "differential response," where only some cases are investigated[7] with risk assessment tools, and "kinship care," including family group conferencing, where children are placed with extended family members rather than coming into government care. Yet these policies are not without problems that should be addressed openly. Differential response returns some opportunities for judgment to social workers, yet leaves intact the assumptions about risk assessment. Kinship care offers potential for children and their families, but it cannot be simply a measure to cut costs and offload care onto family members (Callahan, Brown, MacKenzie, & Whittington, 2005).

Our overarching conclusion is that risk assessment has shifted the balance of child welfare efforts and expenditures so that most are now spent in investigation and in out-of-home placements of children. Risk assessment has altered the fundamental tension between building a case for child protection and providing supportive services to parents who often struggle on their own. There is little room for supportive efforts by social workers trained to provide these services. We need to restore balance, a conclusion reached by many others, including the authors of a review of "reviews" of child deaths in many countries (Axford & Bullock, 2005). In the last section of the paper we examine how this may be achieved and what social work perspectives could offer to the task.

Revamping Funding Policies

Funding for child welfare emanates from the Canada Social Transfer between the federal government and the provinces. This agreement sets no demands upon the provinces about how funds should be spent, aside from some very broad parameters. Provincial governments develop funding formulas for child welfare based upon the number of protection investigations and children in care. In Aboriginal communities where the federal government has direct responsibility for funding, the number of children in care determines the amount of money transferred to a particular band or nation. Under these conditions, the funding in child welfare envelopes diminishes if there is a reduction in investigations and out-of-home placements—the very direction that many advocates recommend. Funding formulas that are based upon the number of children in the jurisdiction hold much more promise, providing child welfare agencies with the resources to develop many of the key family support programs required by parents.

Transforming Some Individual Complaints into Community Actions

While legislative changes have paid attention to expanding the definitions of child maltreatment and introducing and reinforcing mandatory reporting clauses, we think it is timely to acknowledge the resources that are spent and the harm that may be done in investigating the large number of unsubstantiated complaints. Moreover, many families, particularly those reported for neglecting their children, are investigated again and again (Trocmé et al., 2005, p. 55). A more sensible course is to provide first-level responses in communities, so that those with concerns about children and their parents have local resources to call upon. Several studies demonstrate that meeting concrete needs (Chaffin, Bonner & Hill, 2001) and providing other preventive resources can be the most effective approach in reducing risk (Gambrill & Shlonsky, 2001; Gilgun, Klein, & Pranis, 2000; Wharf, 2002). Social workers skilled in group and community work can mobilize community efforts to tackle at least in part the daunting problems of poverty and neglect.

Nowhere is the need for transforming complaints into community actions more apparent than in the situation where children witness violence in their homes. The rate of exposure of children to such situations increased 259%, from 1.72 to 6.17 substantiated cases per 1,000 children, and such exposure was the second most likely type of complaint to be substantiated (after neglect). Most situations involve children witnessing violence in their home between a male person and their mother (Strega, 2004, in press). Mothers suffer double jeopardy: injury to themselves and the potential loss of their children because they did not protect them from the sight of their beating. It is likely that changes to reporting and investigating procedures are documenting many more situations than before, particularly since workers in women's shelters may be required to report such situations to child welfare workers. We need imaginative responses that direct attention and resources away from reporting these incidents as our only response and instead toward approaches that offer protection and healing for mothers and children. We should build upon the sparsely funded efforts of women's shelters to undertake such actions. Instead, cutbacks to these organizations have resulted in the elimination of many of their programs designed to address the effects of violence on women and children.

In many parts of the country, Aboriginal peoples are taking hold of their own child welfare systems although in most cases they are required to replicate the existing child welfare system and govern themselves by existing child welfare laws. This requirement works against their long traditions of extended family and community responsibilities for child rearing. Clearly, many Aboriginal peoples and social workers are working together to find ways to shape child welfare services to respect traditions and yet acknowledge the limited resources and loss of traditions that exist in many communities (Brown, Haddock, & Kovach, 2002). This should be the highest priority of child welfare at the present time, given the large numbers of children in care that are of Aboriginal origin.

Refocusing on Social Work Principles in Child Protection Investigations

A risk assessment approach places the responsibility for diagnosing the problem and recommending the solution squarely with child protection authorities, a highly disempowering process that reduces parents' motivation and ignores their knowledge. In a spirited examination of the social work shortage in the UK, Harlow (2004) argues that the incursion of managerialism into social work practice, evident by such work processes as risk assessment, is a significant force driving the predominantly female social workers out of the field and preventing others from entering. She argues that what attracts people to social work are relationships with others and the opportunities to make change, features of the work that are sharply curtailed under risk assessment. In the process, both parents and social workers can be disenfranchised.

Building upon this analysis, Krane and Davies (2000) suggest that we return to investigations that focus upon parents,' children's, friends,' and families' narratives about what is happening, and build bridges among these stories and our own understanding of the situation. The challenges facing parents, children, and social workers are often deeply confounding and contradictory, change at a rapid pace, and are not captured in the precise and stationary instrument of risk assessment (even if it is repeated on several occasions). Approaches to accountability that incorporate parents' and children's views of their circumstances and what they think makes a difference to their lives is indeed possible (Weller & Wharf, 2002). These are not pie-in-the-sky suggestions. The violence against women movement has used such methods as a staple approach. Police involved in family violence units are trained in dispute resolution based upon these principles. Indeed, family group conferences offer a beginning opportunity to return these approaches to child welfare, albeit they usually occur after the investigation is well underway or completed (Pennell & Anderson, 2005).

One of the most poignant observations of risk assessment is that it directs attention to future harm that may occur, taking the worker's gaze away from what has already happened to the child and what must be done to repair the damage (Saunders & Goddard, 1998). Once immediate safety is addressed, many files are closed even though children and parents have been through very difficult and destructive experiences. Given the fallacy of ignoring harm, the frailty of the science in predicting risk for children, and the finite resources available for child welfare, it seems sensible to turn our attention to the present instead of the future. What are the needs of the child and their parents in the present time, beyond immediate safety, and how might these be addressed?

Conclusion

This chapter identified risk assessment as an important and pervasive policy in child welfare and marshalled evidence to assess how this policy addresses two of child welfare's most confounding problems: an increasing workload and its apparent failure to protect children. On these issues, risk assessment simply does not measure up. However, we also suggest that risk assessment provides a highly valued approach to redefining and reorganizing the volatile and unruly work of child welfare so that politicians, managers, and social workers can argue that they are doing what needs to be done. We also note that risk and risk assessment in child welfare are part and parcel of larger discourses that redefine the relationship between citizens and government, favouring one that defines good citizens as those who manage their own risks. Given these realities, dislodging the notion of risk and the value of risk assessment will be a formidable task.

Yet it is our contention that social work responses have a great deal to offer the challenges facing child protection at the present time. We do not shrink from a recognition that some children are in grave danger within their families and must be protected. We do challenge the notion that the best way to protect these children is to use scarce resources trying to predict the future while paying scant attention to the present circumstances that confront them, their families, and their neighbourhoods.

Notes

1 This chapter arises from a study on risk assessment in child welfare that aims to examine the work processes of risk assessment in two provinces, BC and Ontario and how these processes affect the organization of social work and other human service professions in the social and economic conditions of globalization. Data has been collected through a series of interviews with key informants, social workers, and parents who have been through the risk assessment process. We also analyzed the many documents related to risk assessment in these two provinces. The study is funded by the Social Science and Humanities Research Council of Canada.

2 Section 13(1) a,b,c, and d of the Child, Family and Community Service Act (FCSA) of British Columbia, 1996.

3 At least two types of risk assessment items have been identified in child welfare: actuarial (based upon research such as those used for car insurance) and consensus (based upon the views of professionals about which are the most important items). However, regardless of the means of identifying variables to be assessed, all risk assessments are expected to predict future harm to children.

4 The New York Risk Assessment Model has been imported almost without changes into several Canadian jurisdictions although developed in a jurisdiction with a very different policy context, population and history. Recently the State of New York has made significant changes to the model, reducing the number of items in the instrument because many did not predict future child maltreatment.

5 The Canadian Incidence Study reported that 11% of neglect investigations resulted in out of home placement, compared to 6% of abuse investigations (Trocmé et al., 2005, 58–59, 114).

6 In Ontario, the budget for child welfare services has increased 56% since 2000, to a total of $1.174 billion. Almost exactly half of this amount is allocated to substitute care.

References   7 Several authors question the use of risk assessment for situations based primarily on neglect where parents simply don't have the resources to care for their children (key informant; Weller & Wharf, 2002). These cases usually represent about half of the complaints coming to child welfare. In many situations risk assessment is scarcely necessary as it is obvious that continued deprivation would be harmful to children. Others also wonder about the usefulness of risk assessment in obvious and egregious cases of abuse where the outcomes are clear.

References

Axford, N., & Bullock, R. (2005). Child death and significant case reviews: International approaches. Dartington, UK: Dartington Social Research Unit.

Badgley, R. (1984). *Sexual offences against children: Report of the Committee on Sexual Offences against Children and Youth.* Ottawa: Justice Canada.

Bennet, R. (1998). *Verdict, recommendations, synopsis and summary of responses regarding the inquest into the death of Shanay Jami Johnson.* Toronto, ON: Ministry of the Solicitor General.

Berkowitz, S. (1991). *Key findings on definitions of risk to children and uses of risk assessment by state CPS agencies from the state survey component of the study of high risk child abuse and neglect groups.* Paper prepared by Westat, Inc., and presented to the National Center on Child Abuse and Neglect Symposium on Risk Assessment in Child Protective Services, Washington, DC.

Bridge Child Care Consultancy. (1991). *Sukina: An evaluation report of the circumstances leading to her death.* London: Bridge Child Care Consultancy.

Brown, L., Haddock, L., & Kovach, M. (2002). Watching over our families and children: Lalum'utul' Smun'eem Child and Family Services. In B. Wharf (Ed.), *Community approaches to child welfare* (pp. 131–151). Peterborough, ON: Broadview Press.

Callahan, M. (1994). Feminist approaches: Women recreate child welfare. In B. Wharf (Ed.), *Rethinking child welfare* (pp. 172–209). Toronto: McClelland and Stewart.

Callahan, M., Brown, L., MacKenzie, P., & Whittington, B. (2005). Catch as catch can: Grandmothers raising grandchildren. *Canadian Review of Social Policy, 54,* 58–78.

Callahan, M., & Swift, K. (in press). Great expectations and unintended consequences: Risk assessment in child welfare in BC. In L. Foster & B. Wharf (Eds.), *people, politics and child welfare in BC.* Vancouver: University of British Columbia Press.

Camasso, M., & Jagannathan, R. (1995). Prediction accuracy of the Washington and Illinois Risk Assessment Instruments: An application of receiver operating characteristics curve analysis. *Social Work Research, 19*(3), 174–183.

Chaffin, M., Bonner, B.L., & Hill, R.F. (2001). Family preservation and family support programs: Child maltreatment outcomes across client risk levels and program types. *Child Abuse and Neglect, 25,* 1269–1289.

Chau, S., Fitzpatrick, A., Hulchanski, D., Leslie, B., & Schatia, D. (2001). *One in five… housing as a factor in the admission of children to care: New survey of Children's Aid Society of Toronto updates 1992 study.* Toronto: Central for Urban and Community Studies, University of Toronto.

Chen, X. (2001). *Tending the gardens of citizenship: Child protection in Toronto, 1880s–1920s.* Unpublished thesis. Toronto: Faculty of Social Work, University of Toronto.

Child, Family, and Community Services Act, R.S.B.C. 1996, c.46.

Cicchinelli, L. (1989). Risk assessment models: CPS agencies and future directions. In *CPS risk assessment conference proceedings: From research to practice; Designing the future of Child Protective Services*. Burlington, VT; Washington, DC: American Public Welfare Association.

DePanfilis, D. (1996). Implementing child mistreatment risk assessment systems: Lessons from theory. *Administration in Social Work, 20*(2), 41–59.

Doueck, H., English, D., DePanfilis, D., & Moote, G. (1993). Decision-making in child protective services: A comparison of selected risk assessment systems. *Child Welfare, 72*(5), 441–452.

English, D., & Pecora, P. (1994). Risk assessment as a practice method in child protective services. *Child Welfare, 73*(5), 451–473.

Federal/Provincial Working Group on Child and Family Services Information. (2001). *Child welfare in Canada 2000*. Ottawa: Human Resource and Social Development Canada. Online at <www.hrsdc.gc.ca/en/cs/sp/sdc/socpol/publications/reports/2000-000033/page01.shtml>.

Foster, L. (in press). The more things change, the more they stay the same. In L. Foster & B. Wharf (Eds.), *People, politics and child welfare in British Columbia*. Vancouver: University of British Columbia Press.

Foster, L., & Wright, M. (2002). Patterns and trends in children in the care of the Province of British Columbia: Ecological, policy and cultural perspectives. In M. Hayes & L. Foster (Eds.), *Too small to see, too big to ignore: Child health and well-being in British Columbia* (pp. 103–140). Victoria, BC: Western Geographical Press.

Gambrill, E., & Shlonsky, A. (2001). The need for comprehensive risk management systems in child welfare. *Children and Youth Services Review, 23*(1), 79–107.

Gilgun, J.F., Klein, C., & Pranis, K. (2000). The significance of resources in models of risk. *Journal of Interpersonal Violence, 15*(6), 631–650.

Gove, Thomas J. (1995). *Report on the Gove inquiry into child protection*. Victoria: British Columbia Ministry of Social Services.

Harlow, E. (2004). Why don't women want to be social workers any more? New managerialism, post-feminisim and the shortage of social workers in social service departments in England and Wales. *European Journal of Social Work, 7*(2), 167–179.

Jones, D. (1994). Assessing and taking risks in child protection work. *Child Abuse and Neglect, 18*, 1037–1038.

Kempe, C.H., Silverman, F.N., Steele, B.F., Droegemuller W., & Silver H.K. (1962). The battered child syndrome. *Journal of the American Medical Association, 181*, 17–24.

Krane, J., & Davies, L. (2000). Mothering and child protection practice: Rethinking risk assessment. *Child and Family Social Work, 5*, 35–45.

Leslie, B., & O'Connor, B. (2002). What are the products of the Ontario Risk Assessment Tool? *Journal of the OACAS, 46*(4), 2–9.

Lu, V. (2000, August 24). CAS to resume talks with social workers. *Toronto Star*, A1.

Lyons, P., Doueck, H., & Wodarski, J. (1996). CPS risk assessment: A review of the empirical literature on instrument performance. *Social Work Research, 20*(3), 143–155.

References   Michalski, J., Alaggia, R., & Trocmé, N. (1996). *A literature review of risk assessment models.* Toronto: Centre for Applied Social Research, Faculty of Social Work, University of Toronto.

Ontario Association of Children's Aid Societies. (2005). *CAS Facts: April 1, 2004–March 31, 2005.* Online at <http://www.oacas.org>.

Parada, H. (2004). Social work practices within the restructured child welfare system in Ontario: An institutional ethnography. *Canadian Review of Social Policy, 21*(1), 67–86.

Parada, H., Swift, K., & Callahan, M. (2005, June 16–18). *Forging social futures: Illuminating the interaction of housing and risk assessment in child protection.* Paper presented to the Canadian Social Welfare Policy Conference: Forging Social Futures. Fredericton, NB: University of New Brunswick.

Parton, N., Thorpe, D., & Wattam, C. (1997). *Child protection, risk and the moral order.* Basingstoke: Macmillan.

Pecora, P. (1991). Investigating allegations of child maltreatment: The strengths and limitations of current risk assessment systems. In M. Robin (Ed.), *Assessing child maltreatment reports: The problems of false allegations* (pp. 73–93). New York: Haworth Press.

Pennell, J., & Anderson, G. (Eds.). (2005). *Widening the circle: The practice and evaluation of family group conferencing with children, youths, and their families.* Washington, DC: NASW Press.

Porter, B. (1998). *Report on inquests into the death of children receiving services from a Children's Aid Society.* Toronto: Ontario Ministry of the Solicitor General.

Rycus, J.S., & Hughes, R.C. (2003). *Issues in risk assessment in child protective services.* Policy White Paper. Columbus: North American Resource Center for Child Welfare, Center for Child Welfare Policy.

Saunders, B., & Goddard, C. (1998). *A critique of structured risk assessment procedures: Instruments of abuse?* Ringwood, Victoria: Australian Childhood Foundation and the National Research Centre for the Prevention of Child Abuse, Monash University.

Schene, P., & Bond, K. (1989). *Research issues in risk assessment for child protection.* Denver: American Humane Association.

Silver, E., & Miller, L. (2002). A cautionary note on the use of actuarial risk assessment tools for social control. *Crime and Delinquency, 48*(1), 138–161.

Statistics Canada. (2005). *Family violence in Canada: A statistical profile.* Online at <www.statcan.ca/english/freepub/85-224-XIE/free.htm>.

Strega, S. (2004). *The case of the missing perpetrator: A cross-national investigation of child welfare practice, policy and discourse in cases of mother battering.* Unpublished PhD dissertation, School of Social Work Studies, University of Southampton, England.

Strega, S. (2006). Failure to protect? Child welfare interventions when mothers are being battered. In R. Alaggia and C. Vine (Eds.), *Cruel but not unusual: Violence in Canadian families* (pp. 650–690). Waterloo: Wilfrid Laurier University Press.

Swift, K. (1995a). *Manufacturing "bad mothers": A critical perspective on child neglect.* Toronto: University of Toronto Press.

Swift, K. (1995b). "Missing persons": Women and child welfare. *Child Welfare, 74*(3), 486–502.

Swift, K. (2001). The case for opposition: An examination of contemporary child **References** welfare policy directions. *Canadian Review of Social Policy, 47*, 59–76.

Trocmé, N., & Lindsey, D. (1996). What can child homicide rates tell us about the effectiveness of child welfare services? *Child Abuse and Neglect, 20*(3), 171–184.

Trocmé, N., MacLaurin, B., Fallon, B., Black, T., & Lajoie, J. (2005). *Canadian incidence study of reported child abuse and neglect 2003 data.* Toronto: Centre of Excellence for Child Welfare.

Trocmé, N., & Wolfe, D. (2001). *Canadian incidence study of reported child abuse and neglect.* Ottawa: National Clearinghouse on Family Violence. Online at <www.phac-aspc.gc.ca/publicat/cissr-ecirc>.

Wald, M., & Woolverton, M. (1990). Risk assessment: The Emperor's new clothes? *Child Welfare, 69*(6), 483–511.

Weller, F., & Wharf, B. (1997). *From risk assessment to family action planning.* Victoria: University of Victoria School of Social Work, Child, Family and Community Research Program.

Wharf, B. (2002). *Community work approaches to child welfare.* Peterborough, ON: Broadview Press.

Native Peoples and Child Welfare Practices: Implicating Social Work Education [1]

Barbara Waterfall

This chapter is intended to begin a discussion about the relationships between child welfare practices, social work education, and Native peoples.[2] It is located within social policy discourse pertaining to the accreditation of social work education in Canada. I am arguing that schools of social work have an ethical and professional responsibility to create centred spaces for the articulation and development of Native systems and methods of helping.[3] I also assert that schools of social work must create core curricula that construct colonialism as problematic and support the efforts and objectives of Native grassroots self-determined agency.

It must be understood that this examination does not take place within a vacuum. Any discussion that concerns Native peoples takes place within the context of a history of colonialism, imperialism, and the predominance of Eurocentric thought. Informed by feminist anti-colonial thought, I will thus speak to this history, to the implications of Eurocentrism, and to ongoing imposing colonial processes. In so doing, I will be implicating the profession of social work through the apparatus of child welfare as a colonizing practice. I am asking social workers and social work educators to reflect seriously on the problematics embedded within the current neo-colonial child welfare system. I am also challenging the reader, wherever we are located, to ask broader questions. That is, how can social work practice in general work toward the objectives of Native peoples' self-determined agency? In particular, how can the social work profession support Native-centred helping practices that are based upon traditional, life-sustaining axiological, ontological, and epistemological foundations?

This chapter is not intended to be an exhaustive inquiry but rather to begin to ask critical questions for the purposes of encouraging the development of decolonizing methodologies. It was originally written for Native peoples who have been working in the Native social work field and for Native social work educators. However, the contents of this discussion have far-reaching implications, not just for Native peoples and for Native social workers but for the profession of social work as a whole and for the broader objectives of social work education in Canada. It is thus intended that this chapter

will influence the development of policy through accreditation criteria for
social work education.

Location of Author

I am a Métis Anishnabe-Kwe.[4] For the last ten years, I have been a social work
educator. I have also been trained as a social worker and worked in the child
welfare system within the context of Native communities. I am very cognizant
of my privileged middle-class positioning. In this paper, I problematize social
work's relationship to Native peoples. It is important to acknowledge that I
implicate myself and my own past social work practices within this politic. It
is my intent that this chapter can serve in part as an amends to the Native families that I inadvertently harmed in my past social work practice. It is also my
aspiration that this work will stimulate further discussion, and in particular
create space for Native voices that have been marginalized and silenced
through colonial oppression.

Discursive Framework

I am employing a feminist, anti-colonial discursive framework to guide this
discussion on the relationship between child welfare practices, social work
education, and Native peoples. In accordance with Dei (2000b, pp. 23–24) I
am identifying this framework as "discursive" rather than "theoretical" to
provide space for the reality that academic and political questions are continually changing, reflective of "social realities as well as the narration of different histories and experiences." Informed by Adams (1999), Akwesasne Notes
(1981), Alfred (1999, 2005), Allen (1986), Anderson (2000), Dei (2000a), Dei &
Asgharazadeh (2000), Fanon (1995), Graveline (1998, 2004), Maracle (1996),
Puja (2001), Smith (1999), and Trask (1991), I define feminist anti-colonialism as committed to a future with the absence of colonial imposition and
colonial influences, with the agency to govern oneself, and the practice of
such agency based on gynocentric and gynocratic[5] Native traditional practices.

I contextualize a feminist anti-colonial perspective as one located outside of the imposed colonial system. The framework that I am proposing
assumes that the objectives of the Canadian constitution and the Canadian
state are counterproductive to an anti-colonial cause. Hence, it assumes that
efforts to assert Native rights for self-determination through the apparatus of
the Canadian constitutional agenda are counterproductive to a feminist anti-
colonial objective. Informing a prescriptive course for action, this framework
does not look to the Indian Act or any other colonial policy for legitimacy or
direction. Nor are Eurocentric theories, models, practices, professional discourses, and ethics sought out as the first order of practice with Native peoples. Native self-determined agency is viewed as stemming from outside of the
parameters of the Canadian state, and is embedded in the foundational wisdoms of our Native ancestors. This practice is grounded in Native traditional

axiological, ontological, and epistemological standpoints enabling the resurgence of our Native traditional networks, systems, and methodological understandings (Alfred, 2005). It thus informs Native-centred practice.

This framework problematizes the profession of social work when its practices are embedded in and reinforced by the apparatus of the colonial state. From a practical standpoint this means that one of the primary objectives for Native self-determined agency is the work of building upon Indigenous traditional networks and methods of practice. It is recognized that colonialism has imposed patriarchal values and a patriarchal ordering of social relations within present Native systems. Along with Anderson (2000), and Maracle (1996), I argue that our current understanding of Native "traditions" must be interrogated for patriarchal and other imposed colonial influences. A feminist anti-colonial perspective assumes that most Native cultures were matriarchal or matri-focal prior to colonization (Allen, 1986). Thus, a feminist anti-colonial discursive framework functions to revitalize Native governance systems based on the values of gynocentric nurturance and gynocratic life-giving principles.

It needs to be clearly acknowledged that traditional gynocratic social practices are about meeting the everyday needs of all members of Native societies. Furthermore, systems of accountability are an essential part of gynocratic governance systems. Humanistic, compassionate, or any other grounds do not justify colonial policy imposing foreign or dominating systems and practices within traditional gynocratic structures. I argue that social work practice and social work education could prudently be guided by a feminist anti-colonial discursive framework. I contend that only such a framework enables us both to map colonialism in all of its guises and to develop strategies that support, rather than hinder, the objectives of traditional Native self-determined agency.

Eurocentrism as Rationale for the Colonial Agenda

Eurocentrism as Rationale for the Colonial Agenda

Battiste and Youngblood Henderson (2000), and Blaut (1993) state that Eurocentric thought informs the theories, the opinions, and the laws that relate to Native peoples. Eurocentric discourses serve the purpose of justifying the colonial agenda. Smith (1999) states that there is a direct relationship between the expansion of knowledge, the expansion of trade, and the expansion of the British empire. The colonial objective on Turtle Island was and continues to be that of gaining access and control of the land's resources. The Native populations were a threat and still are a threat to this objective. In the present-day context, global economic forces continue to exploit the natural resources of this land, such as water, oil, gas, and uranium (Adams, 1999; Alfred, 2005).

Battiste (2005, p. 124) argues that Eurocentrism "is an ultra-theory in modern thought" that informs standard or legitimated theoretical formulations. Eurocentric theories influence research and policy development concerning Native peoples. In turn, Eurocentric theories inform the nature of the structures that exist in Native communities. They are based on the biased notion that European peoples are culturally and politically superior to all other peoples of the world (Adams, 1999; Battiste & Youngblood Henderson, 2000). Related to this understanding is the concept of diffusionism. Battiste (2005), Battiste and Youngblood Henderson (2000), and Blaut (1993) assert that diffusionism is based on the premise that most human people are uninventive and those who are inventive should be the permanent centres for cultural change and progress. Eurocentric ideology assumes that Europeans are superior because they are inventive. Conversely, this thinking assumes that Native people require the diffusion of European characteristics such as creativity, imagination, invention, innovation, rationality, and a sense of ethics in order for Native peoples to progress (Battiste & Youngblood Henderson, 2000). This theorizing justifies a view of Native peoples as primitive and inferior.

For the most part Eurocentrism has dominated the profession of social work and thus social work practices. Indeed, Graveline (2004) and Hart (2002) describe a dominating and imposing notion that all legitimate social work practice must ascribe to the rules and standards of Eurocentric social work discourse. While there are many paradigms for helping and offering social assistance among various cultures, Eurocentrism operates by centring Euro-Western theories and practices as the dominant social work paradigm. Indeed as de Montigny (1995) argues, the activities of social work are about engaging in the socially organized practices of power from the standpoint of ruling relations.

In the following pages, I will speak to the neo-colonial child welfare context in which some social work practice with Native peoples is located. In spite of Native peoples having our own historic systems and methods of practice, Euro-Western case management models are operative within most of today's Native social welfare systems. The Eurocentric social work processes of intake, case recording, clinical assessment, clinical treatment (such as individual, group, and family therapy), referral, and the termination of case files have become the hegemonic and taken for granted way of managing Native social work practices and Native social welfare systems. Indeed, Eurocentric assumptions about what counts as legitimated case recording and accountability procedures are operative in what has otherwise been defined as a unique Native cultural perspective (Swinomish Tribal Mental Health Project, 1991). So too, Eurocentric theories of practice such as functionalist family, systems, ecological, brief solution-focused, and narrative therapies take precedence over Native-centred perspectives (Graveline, 2004; Hart, 2002).

In the recent past, government audits routinely ensured that the dominant paradigm was carried out in child welfare social work practice (de Montigny, 1995; Parada, 2000). In response to Native militancy, currently only Crown ward files are audited in the Ontario child welfare system. However, I remember practicing social work in the early 1990s when all files were audited. This created a highly stressful working environment, as failure to comply with

Eurocentric paradigms and methods of practice often meant the loss of government funding and thus the failure of the government-funded initiative. As a result, the need to meet the imposed government objectives easily took precedence over meeting the needs of people the social work profession is intended to serve. During my work as a social worker within agency settings, I spent 80% of my time involved in documenting daily activities and writing reports for the clinical files. De Montigny (1995) states that the socially organized practice of social work case recording silences the actual voices and lived realities of clients. Adding to de Montigny's understanding, I also contend that social work case recording often functions as a dehumanizing and a colonizing practice. Frustrated by this reality and by the paternalistic power differential embedded in social work case recording activities, I worked with a Native Elder to create a culturally appropriate method for conducting clinical assessments based on the medicine wheel paradigm (Nabigon & Waterfall, 1995). This effort did facilitate the development of a Native-centred practice. However, it did little to rupture what was still a dominant Eurocentric systemic paradigm.

The Problematic of Historic and Ongoing Colonial Imposition

The Problematic of Historic and Ongoing Colonial Imposition

Stuckey and Murphy (2001) assert that colonialism characterizes not only our historic past but also our present reality. Dei & Asgharzadeh (2000) provide a broad definition, stating that colonialism is anything that is imposing or dominating. From this perspective, we can contextualize that colonialism can encompass the cognitive (Battiste, 1997; Smith 1999). These authors further propose colonialism as a living system that continually changes and reformulates itself. Colonialism in its imperialist form originally meant the direct control of Native peoples, Native systems, and Native lands by colonial officials. After World War II, Native peoples began resisting this direct control. A new colonial system was put in place to appease this resistance. This new system has come to be defined as neo-colonialism (Adams, 1999; Akwesasne Notes, 1981; Alfred, 2005). Instead of non-Native officials administering programs for Native peoples, the system of neo-colonialism enables programs such as child welfare, income assistance, job training, health, education, and the maintenance of Indian bands and Métis villages to be administered by Native peoples. However, the major decision-making and the control of finances of these programs remains within the hands of colonial forces (Adams, 1999; Alfred, 2005). New to Native relations has been the bringing of provincial governments into direct relationship with Native systems. Enforced through the British North America Act (1867), the areas of Native education, social assistance, child welfare, and some justice issues[6] came under the direct control of the provincial governments. As a result, Native communities now have to negotiate with both the federal and provincial governments. Battiste (1997) refers to these new provincial relationships as an example of how colonialism has reformulated itself.

The
Problematic
of Historic
and Ongoing
Colonial
Imposition

Adams (1999), a Métis academic, now deceased, was heavily influenced by Marxist thought.[7] His analysis of neo-colonialism in Canada highlighted the fact that a new Native middle-class structure was created through the creation of jobs for administrators and workers within these programs. A core outcome resulted in a shift away from relying on Indigenous domestic and traditional land-based economies to a dependence on the capitalist system (Adams, 1999; Akwesasne Notes, 1981). A debilitating consequence has been that very few Native people can support the traditional ceremonies that serve as the basis of traditional societies (Akwesasne Notes, 1981). Adams (1999) further argued that a minority of Native people achieve economic benefits from this new neo-colonial schema. While a very few are able to access jobs, the majority of the people live in abject poverty. Indeed, Alfred (2005) determines only 10% of the Canadian Native population are favorably advantaged by neo-colonialism.

Today, many refer to those Native peoples who are given jobs in these programs as the Native middle-class elite (Adams, 1999; Alfred, 1999, 2005; Maracle, 1996).[8] The elite class gains economic benefits and social status from these positions. While Alfred (2005, p. 30) acknowledges the hard work involved in gaining education as a means of climbing out of poverty, he also argues that "in the midst of all the apparent progress, there is a nagging sense among many people that something is wrong even with these supposed solutions." Indeed, a fundamental problematic is that the system that we middle-class people find ourselves working in is inherently neo-colonial. Adams (1999, p. 131) specifically took issue with the fact that our authority within this schema stems from the colonial state, rather than "from the will of the people." Adams (1999) and Alfred (1999) also argued that that for the most part the Native elite have come to function as collaborators of what are still imperial structures and policies. From a Native community grassroots perspective, Native peoples not only have to deal with external colonial imposition but also internal collaborative colonial processes. Alfred (1999) helps to explicate this dynamic by stating that there are two value systems at work in Native communities. One value system is rooted in traditional cultural practices while the other has been imposed by the colonial state. He contends that these two value systems create disunity and factionalism in Native communities, making it difficult to effect change.

Adams (1999) and Alfred (1999) further explicate that the Canadian state has created a more subtle form of colonialism through the constitutional agenda. The modern-day practices of "First Nations"[9] treaty negotiations take place within the context of the Canadian constitution. The objectives of the Canadian constitution are not and have never been about affording a fair deal to the Native peoples of this land. When Native peoples signed treaties with the colonial government, they did not know the details of what were contained in these legal documents. They were verbally told that they would be given a reserve land base to live on so that they could continue to live their lives without interference from the colonial government. From a Native perspective the word "reserve" was understood to come from the French word "reservoir." The reserves were perceived as a place where Native people could protect and maintain their traditional Native way of life.[10] The Native peoples who signed the treaties were not cognizant of the fact that they had signed a legal document that stated that they had agreed "to cede, release, surrender, and yield up to the government of the dominion of Canada, forever, all their rights, titles, and privileges whatsoever" (Adams, 1999). They did not know that the reservation system was to be an institutionalized form of apartheid serving imperial and colonial interests.

Colonial Imposition and the Disruption of Native Extended Family Systems

We are now living in a time when the rhetoric of Native self-government, including Native economic development, is being realized; yet these initiatives are couched within the neo-colonial and constitutional colonial agendas. They are designed to serve not only the interests of colonial governments but also the interests of multinational corporations.[11] Today, this translates into multinational corporations gaining access to the natural resources that exist in Native territories. As indicated above the dominant model of self-government applied today merely grants a few Native elites the right to act as puppets for agendas that serve both the colonial state and multinational interests (Adams, 1999; Alfred, 1999, 2005). Furthermore, the rhetoric of Native economic development initiatives merely positions Native peoples as representatives, or stakeholders. Foreign industry inevitably controls the strings, making the ability to work within a framework based on Native traditional life-sustaining principles impossible to accomplish (Alfred, 1999).[12] Alfred (1999) states that these supposed self-governing processes do not help Native peoples in Canada. They merely further embed us deeper into colonial structures.

Colonial Imposition and the Disruption of Native Extended Family Systems

There is a great deal of diversity among the varied Native nations. However, commonalities do exist. I contend that this is particularly true in relation to child-rearing practices. Native peoples traditionally believe that children represent the means through which a culture can preserve its tradition, heritage, and language (Miller, 1996; Thomas & Learoyd, 1990). Traditionally, Native child rearing was valued as a sacred responsibility. Within this context, child abuse was not a problem. Children were nurtured in a community sense of belonging. Children were encouraged to develop mastery in skills that were needed for survival. They were also encouraged to develop their own unique sense of autonomy while at the same time being taught the value of generosity (Brokenleg & Brendtro, 1989). Punishment was not a concept that was used traditionally by Native peoples. Rather, techniques such as modelling, group influence, discussion, and positive expectations were employed (Miller, 1996; Thomas & Learoyd, 1990).

Native communities are made up of extended family systems. Traditionally, families functioned within community systems by being responsible to

Colonial
Imposition
and the
Disruption
of Native
Extended
Family
Systems
and for each other. Within this context everyone within the community was responsible for the well-being of the children (Antone, Miller, & Myers, 1986). Traditionally, Native societies were based on a preventive medicine that focused on maintaining an intricate balance within an ecology that was constantly in flux or change (Battiste & Youngblood Henderson, 2000). These societies were based on a cosmology that understood and respected our connectedness and kinship with all of Creation. Problems and issues that arose traditionally in daily life were immediately dealt with through clan systems of governance.[13] Decision-making was based on a consensual paradigm. Citing Mi'kmaw traditional thought, the welfare of the group was valued over the individual, as was the extended family over the immediate family. This ensured that peace and good order would be preserved within Native community life (Battiste & Youngblood Henderson, 2000).[14] Due to colonial interference, the ability to maintain a sense of peace and good order has been difficult to accomplish.

By the authority of the Indian Act (1876), Native children were forcibly removed from their homes and placed in Christian-run residential or day schools. The purpose of these schools was an assimilationist strategy. The children who attended these schools were taught racist ideologies about their own traditional cultures and were encouraged to adopt Euro-Western values and practices (Haig-Brown, 1989). Bennet & Blackstock (2003) comment that residential schools were developed in direct response to prior failed colonial attempts to assimilate Native people. Armitage (1995) further states that it was assumed that assimilation would be successful if Native children were removed from their families. Children were forbidden to speak their own Native languages. If they were caught speaking their own languages, they were punished (Milloy, 1999).[15] Physical punishment was severe and was used extensively (Assembly of First Nations, 1994; Knockwood, 1992). Many survivors of residential schools have reported being subjected to what they considered torture by staff within these schools.[16] The principal methods of behaviour management used were control, domination, shame, and intimidation. As a result, we now see these negative uses of power displayed by Native peoples within Native community contexts (Assembly of First Nations, 1994; Whiteye, 2002).

The curriculum did not support children learning English and other skills that would help them participate as equals among the mainstream societies. Rather, the curriculum focused on Christian teachings. Most of the time spent in these schools was dedicated to prayer and hard physical labor. The children provided most of the labour to maintain these schools, such as laundering, cooking, cleaning, and gardening (Assembly of First Nations, 1994; Knockwood, 1992). However, these students did not receive the benefits of their work. It was the staff in these schools that used the cream separated from the milk in their morning porridge. The staff dined well with three-course meals while the children were not adequately fed. The typical diet for children in these schools was beans, porridge, rancid meat, and rotten potatoes

(Assembly of First Nations, 1994; Knockwood, 1992). The experience of seeing first-hand that some live in luxury while others live meagrely taught these children to accept unequal class relations as a taken for granted way of doing things.[17]

The effects of the residential school system severely disrupted the traditional Native way of life. Imagine waking up to a community whose children have all been taken away. The results of the forced removal of Native children were devastating. The adults who were left behind fell into feelings of despair and apathy (Antone, Miller, & Myers, 1986; Waterfall, 1992). It is not surprising that many of the people picked up alcohol in an effort to cope. In many cases, the children in residential schools were only allowed to go home two times during the year. When these children returned to their home communities, they often found family members intoxicated and unable to take care of them. Furthermore, these children were speaking the colonizer's language, making it difficult for their communication to be understood. The children no longer felt at home and safe in their own communities (Assembly of First Nations, 1994; Whiteye, 2002).

The early 1970s marked the beginning of the end of mandatory residential schooling for Native children in colonial Canada. While these schools are no longer in operation, they remain as vivid memories in the minds of those who attended them. Antone, Miller and Myers (1986, pp. 24–25) assert that we live with an intergenerational legacy of residential school. They further state, "while our relatives who experienced the despair of the boarding school (residential school) system passed away … their beliefs live on." Traditionally, Native peoples possessed profound child care wisdom. Thomas and Learoyd (1990) documented the fact that the European immigrants might have been better to have adopted this wisdom. Given the distress caused by residential school and the interruption of traditional child-rearing practices, we now see a multitude of child abuse cases in Native communities (Antone, Miller, & Myers; 1986, Waterfall, 1992). In response, the social work profession working within the structures of children's aid societies became involved with Native families and Native communities. The Canadian Welfare Council and the Canadian Association of Social Workers delivered a presentation to a Special Joint Committee of the House of Commons, arguing that Native people were being denied child protective services in the early 1940s. Accordingly, the Indian Act was amended in 1951, giving the provinces jurisdiction over reserve communities in certain areas such as child welfare. However, it was not until the 1960s that funding was provided for child welfare services to become engaged in child protection on Native territories.[18]

Native Peoples and the Profession of Social Work

Through the above-stated colonial apparatus, the profession of social work became involved with Native peoples (Alcoze & Mawhiney, 1988; Yellow Bird & Chenault, 1999). The prevalence of Eurocentric discourses about Native

Native
Peoples
and the
Profession
of Social
Work

peoples prevented a critique of colonialism and a discussion of the adverse effects that colonization had on Native peoples and Native family systems. Influenced by Eurocentrism and diffusionism, Native people were presumed by social workers employed within children's aid societies to be unfit to raise their own children. In response, a disproportionate number of Native children were apprehended and were placed in white foster homes (Johnston, 1983). Indeed, Fournier & Crey (1997) report that while Native peoples represent less than 4% of the population, Native children comprised approximately 30–40% of the legal wards of the colonial state. Social workers failed to recognize the effects of residential schools on Native families, or other debilitating consequences of oppression. They therefore did not respond fairly and appropriately by encouraging the teaching of Native traditional child care practices. Instead, the social workers intervened when incidents of child abuse were reported, by taking children from their families and their communities. Many of these children did not return to their home communities and were adopted into white families (Fournier & Crey, 1997; Waterfall, 1992).

In the literature, this time period is referred to as the "sixties scoop" as it predominantly took place during the 1960s (Johnston, 1983). As indicated above, Native residential schools were closing; Native children had returned to their families. It is therefore not surprising that there was an increase in the number of reported cases of child abuse in Native communities. This time it was neither the federal government nor the Christian churches who intervened by taking children from their homes. The provincial governments intervened through the legal apparatus of child protection legislation. We thus see another example of how colonization keeps reformulating itself. Indeed Hudson and McKenzie (1980) argued that the child welfare system was an active agent in the colonization of Native peoples. Maracle (1996) stated that the act of apprehending children from their homes is tantamount to kidnapping and inflicts terror on children. It is a violent act, and one must wonder how this can be justified in the name of child safety? A social worker who did this dirty work of kidnapping was not well received within Native communities. Indeed, this is still the case. A social worker armed with a child protection mandate from the state is both feared and hated.[19]

One would assume therefore that Native peoples would be hesitant to pursue social work as a profession or to work in agencies with a child protection mandate. However, one only needs to look at the predominant neo-colonial context to realize that there are very limited options available. I do admit that Native social workers do a great deal of good for individuals, groups, and families. I also readily acknowledge that many Native social workers are working from Native-centred perspectives. However, I contend that we must understand that the profession and its relationship to Native peoples are fundamentally problematic for two reasons. These reasons relate to what I have discussed earlier. That is, the characteristics of Eurocentrism and diffusionism make it difficult to bring Native methodologies to the center of a social work practice. Furthermore, the actual practices of Native social work are embedded within a neo-colonial context. I will speak to the case of Native Child Welfare to explicate my point.

Examining the Case of Native Child Welfare Initiatives

In the 1980s, Native leaders in the form of elected chiefs, Elders, lawyers, administrators, and social workers were concerned about the interference and devastating impact that the child welfare system had in their communities (Assembly of First Nations, 1989; Native Council of Canada, 1989; Ontario Native Women's Association, 1982). They were primarily concerned with finding ways to control the problem of Native children being apprehended from their communities. A not-so-surprising correlation existed at this time. That is, provincial governments were changing their legislation, enabling Native peoples to inform the direction of foster-care placements for children who were band members within their communities. In 1984, the Ontario Child and Family Services Act was passed, enabling this to take place. Using the Native traditional discourse of "customary care," the Act was amended to enable Native children at risk to be placed with extended family members within their own communities.[20]

This new provision in the Child and Family Services Act was perceived by Native leaders as a window of opportunity to prevent the further interference of children's aid societies in Native communities (Soloman, 1999). In response, some Native territories developed their own child protection agencies. From a Native grassroots perspective, these agencies are often viewed as "brown" children's aid societies. Many of these agencies began with a vision of offering programs based on Native traditional values.[21] However, the explicit focus of these agencies was not about ridding Native peoples of colonial imposition; nor was the focus concerned with revitalizing our Native languages, laws, systems, and cultural practices.[22] Rather, the inevitability of colonial imposition was assumed. Part of the baggage of assuming, or accepting the inevitability of colonial imposition was that of accepting Eurocentric social welfare practices.[23]

I speak from my own experience as a Native social worker and to a dynamic that appeared to be apparent in the Native contexts where I was employed. That is, many Native peoples who worked within these Native agencies, including me, often accepted the Eurocentric and hegemonic assumption that Native parenting was problematic within Native communities. Native people were thus the problem and the ones who needed to be fixed. Furthermore, the funding criteria for these agencies ensured that standard provincial guidelines were followed. The result was that Native peoples were now doing the dirty work of apprehending Native children from their families. Even though it was now called "customary care," Native children were forcibly removed from their homes and placed in other settings. Furthermore, through time Native workers began placing Native children within White foster homes, as they were deemed to be the most appropriate placements.[24] We can see how, although well intentioned, we as Native people can inadvertently end up perpetuating an assimilationist agenda.

One current debilitating child welfare practice has been the imposition of the Ontario risk assessment model (Ontario Association of Children's Aid Societies, 2000) to determine whether children are in need of child protective services. It has been designed to include broad issues in the examination of risk, such as parents' past histories with family violence, child sexual abuse, and addictions. For workers, the method of employing this model involves having clients answer required and predetermined questions through a "checking of the box" system. Answers given are then used to assess the level of perceived risk. For novice or unseasoned workers, what can factor into whether a child is determined to be at risk, and thus requires placement in a foster home, can be informed by this inhumane coding system. That is, rather than being guided by the knowledge, skill, intuitive insight, and common sense of the worker, the rating system can determine which children are at risk without contexualizing the root causes of the issues.

I argue that the predominant usage of the risk assessment approach has very debilitating consequences for Native people, as it negatively skews Native parents to be assessed as at risk of abusing their children. The reality is that many Native people have histories with abuse and addictions. Are we to assume that people who were sexually abused in residential school are at high risk of abusing their own children? Furthermore, even when Native children are being abused at home, we need to understand that this problem is a direct consequence of experiences of colonial oppression. What a bitter poison it is to have a foreign child welfare system impose and enforce practices that do not reflect our Native foundational values, systems, and methods of practice!

It is at this juncture that I believe we must ask a critical question of Native child protective services. That is, how can we presume to say that we are offering culturally relevant or appropriate services under a child protection mandate? Being reminded of Maracle's (1996) understanding pertaining to apprehension, where in our Native traditions, laws, or values was the terrorizing or kidnapping of children acceptable? We need to seriously reflect on this question. This is not to say that Native peoples who work within these Native agencies do not offer some culturally appropriate services. Indeed Native Healers and Elders are being recruited and funded to offer "culturally appropriate" services such as sweat lodge ceremonies, healing circles, and other Native traditional practices. However, our Native Healers and Elders are usually not positioned as full-time staff within these agencies. Furthermore, there is often a large discrepancy between what Eurocentric practitioners are paid within these agencies and what our own traditional Native experts and specialists, who are defined as "paraprofessionals," are offered. That is, the Eurocentric practitioners are given much greater salaries. The prominence of Eurocentrism justifies and ensures that this is so. Therefore, while we may see some "culturally appropriate" programs, they are embedded within a neo-colonial bureaucracy where Euro-Western values and methods of practice predominate. I thus contend that we need to seriously interrogate what is presumed to be Native self-determined child welfare programs.

I also believe that we need to interrogate our current objectives in the devolution or transfer of services to Native communities. Indeed, we live in a political climate where buzz terms such as devolution and transfer of services are being readily utilized (Browning & van de Sande, 1999; Timpson & Semple, 1997). However, I contend that we need to seriously interrogate how these buzz terms are really being taken up and by whom. That is, we need to question whether we are merely moving what is a Eurocentric service from a main office model to a decentralized Native context. Are we merely allowing the few Native elites, such as the elected leadership, to be responsible for administering these programs while the majority of the people living within the community are alienated from the processes of decision-making? If this is indeed the case, we are merely changing the players in what are still bureaucracies.

Alfred (1999) states that the terms "brown" and "bureaucrat" are not compatible. While appearing to be moving toward the objectives of Native peoples' self-determined agency, these modern-day initiatives are merely reformulations of neo-colonial structures (Alfred, 2005). I contend that Native initiatives will remain colonizing as long as they are couched within the parameters of the constitutional colonial agenda.[25] In the case of Native child welfare initiatives, the provincial governments still ultimately wield the power. The change merely means decentralizing services. It does not change the nature of the services. Native peoples are still positioned to carry out the child protection mandate of the colonial state. We thus must not delude ourselves by what appears to be encouraging discourses about Native self-government, devolution, or the transfer of services.

We also need to seriously reflect on the positioning of Native social workers within neo-colonial schemas. I contend that being positioned as a Native social worker within these contexts presents a very specific and difficult dilemma. If we have accepted Eurocentric practices as a taken-for-granted way of doing things, we may not feel the dilemma. However, if we are traditionally sensitized to see the great value in our own Native knowledges and methodological practices, we find ourselves in a very difficult position. That is, we are being asked to bridge the gap between the perspectives, values, and methods used and recommended by Elders and Healers and the demands imposed by Eurocentric discourses and Eurocentric social work processes. As Native social workers who have been positioned as full-time staff within these contexts, we are automatically put in this position. I contend that without an appropriate prescriptive course for action, such as the feminist anti-colonial one delineated above, we will not know how to navigate around ongoing neo-colonial impositions.

Implications for Social Work Education

Alfred (2005, p. 268) asserts that neo-colonial structures and processes will not help Native peoples. He further states that "the only hope for indigenous peoples to survive as Nations is in the power of movements outside of the established political structures, and beyond the paths provided by state law and government policies." I contend that whether we are Native or non-Native, we are all personally implicated. It is thus critically important for social workers, for the profession of social work, and for social work education to disengage from neo-colonial dynamics. A key way that we can accomplish this task is by working with and in support of Native traditionalists in grassroots contexts. I want to clarify for the reader that I do not consider community-based, government-funded structures or services as composites of the grassroots. Rather, I am asserting that grassroots activity is more organic. It requires that supporters or allies in grassroots struggles take time to develop relationships with Native people in community capacities, such as traditional societies and informal networks or circles. Pivotal in this endeavour is making meaningful connections with persons who have been the most marginalized through colonial oppression, such as traditionalists, women, people on income assistance, Métis and non-Status peoples, persons with differences in ability, and two-spirited people. What I am calling for here is more than token gestures. I argue that it is crucial to create space for the centring of marginalized voices and perspectives.

In the course of my doctoral thesis journey, I have spent substantial time thinking through how social work education can serve the interests of traditional Native self-determined agency (Waterfall, forthcoming). While this is not an extensive account of this work, I offer the following as guidelines for a prescriptive course for action. As a starting point, curricula must create core space for the articulation and exploration of resurgent traditional Native helping systems and methods of practice. Crucial in this endeavour is the involvement of grassroots traditionalists in social work education. Following this important area of study, social work curricula must investigate the organization and effects of colonialism in its historic and ongoing guises. To serve this end, colonialism, rather than Native persons or behaviours, must be problematized. This will enable the development of fair and responsive Native-centred practices that adequately attend to social problems that are in existence within Native families and communities.

In addition, social work curricula must give ample space for the inclusion of Native theories or discursive frameworks for practice, such as the feminist anti-colonial perspective that I have delineated. Rather than teaching predominantly Eurocentric theories that perpetuate Native peoples' oppression, schools of social work must be open to multi-centric perspectives and methods[26] inclusive of Native formulations. Finally, social work education must encourage the articulation and development of decolonizing methodologies. I recognize that this is a relatively new field and thus a new area of study.

Alfred (2005, p. 278) asserts the importance of Native peoples' "release from dependency on the colonial state and regaining our independence in every form possible: financial, political, physical, and psychological." I contend that crucial in obtaining this objective is resurgent Native spiritual ceremonies and traditional economies that foster the development of sustainable technologies. Decolonization will require a new relationship between Native and non-Native peoples. I assert that ethical social work practice has a responsibility to help develop these new relationships. This will require our returning to the original, pre-colonial Treaty or Wampum agreements made between various First Peoples and European Peoples. In these original treaty relationships, each agreed not to interfere but to live in support of each other as autonomous Nations (*Royal Commission on Aboriginal Peoples*, 1996, vols. I & II). Informed by Bishop's (2002) notion of becoming an ally and by these early treaty arrangements, I challenge the social work profession and social work education to become beacons and co-creators in the implementation of a fundamental Native value—respectful coexistence with all of Creation.

Conclusion

Conclusion

Alfred (1999) states that the primary problem with the profession of social work is that Native peoples' lives continue to be controlled by others. In controlling the lives of Native peoples, the profession of social work remains a colonizing practice. This all too often is a sad fact, whether we are located as Native or non-Native social work professionals. Many Native peoples who have been trained in Eurocentric universities have not been given a chance to adequately define what Native helping consists of outside of the parameters of mainstream theories. Even when we do understand what Native helping encompasses, the current neo-colonial politic impedes our ability to work with our people based on our own Native foundational understandings. It is imperative thus that the profession of social work develop effective strategies to rupture the dominant colonial paradigm.

Alfred (1999) further states that colonialism is not an abstract notion. It is a real set of people, relationships, and structures that can be resisted and combatted by placing our respect and trust where it belongs: in Native peoples, relationships, and structures. This necessarily encompasses the project of Indigenous decolonization. Alfred (2005, p. 34) defines the work of decolonization as a social and political resurgence. In this chapter, I have challenged the profession of social work to actively work toward the Indigenous grassroots objective of self-determined agency. The Canadian Association of Social Workers (CASW, 1994) gave a clear direction for the profession of social work to follow. During a presentation to the Royal Commission on Aboriginal Peoples, the CASW acknowledged Native people's inherent right to self-determination, autonomy, self-sufficiency, and the preservation of culture. At that time, it also recognized that social work education must become culturally relevant. I challenge the social work profession in Canada not merely to cite these words as empty promises but to implement strategies that will lead to far-reaching and life-sustaining change.

Notes

1 This chapter has been adapted from an essay entitled "Native People and the Social Work Profession: An Examination of Colonizing Problematics and the Development of Decolonized Thought" that was earlier published in the *Journal of Educational Thought* 36(3), 2002.

2 I am using the term peoples here as intended by Smith (1999, p. 114) to acknowledge Native peoples' right to self-determination and also to acknowledge the reality of Native peoples as diverse.

3 My thinking about Native-centrism has been informed by African scholars such as Asante (2003) and Dei (1996). Following Asante (2003), I conceptualize Native-centrism as a mode of thought and action where the centrality of Native interests, values, and perspectives predominate.

4 The term Anishnabe-Kwe refers to being a woman of the Anishnabec Nation.

5 The terms gynocentric and gynocratic were used by Allen (1986, p. 2) to refer to traditional Native systems as matriarchal or woman-centred.

6 Within the structures of colonial Canada, the provincial governments are responsible for judicial convictions and sentencing of two years less a day. Other sentences are within the jurisdiction of the federal justice system.

7 Some Indigenous people involved in nationalist movements find problematic the usage of critical Marxist thought within Indigenous discourses. One reason given has been that the language presented has been largely framed within "oppositional discourse" (Smith, 1999, p. 69). However, I find insightful and particularly illuminating Adam's (1999) writings as he has had the courage to speak what had been the unspeakable within internal Native circles.

8 The author acknowledges that she is part of the middle class within Native societies.

9 The term First Nations is prominently used by treaty chiefs to refer to Native communities that fall under the jurisdiction of the Indian Act. People such as Adams (1999) contend that it is an exclusionary term that serves a constitutional colonial agenda where Non-Status Indians and Métis have been left out of the politic. Adams (1999, p. 64) refers to this as a problematic that serves colonial interests of dividing and conquering Native peoples. For this reason, I am not using the term First Nations in this text in favour of using the inclusive term of Native peoples.

10 As told by a very respected Anishnabe Elder. Due to Anishnabe protocol and the expressed wishes of this Elder, I will not cite his name. Many Anishnabec who read this text will easily be able to identify the origins of this statement.

11 The 2002 deal signed between Hydro-Québec and the James Bay Cree is an example of corporate interests superceding the interests and values of traditional Cree land-based people. Through this deal, the James Bay Cree relinquished their rights to their land and the land's resources.

12 This is a very sad reality, given the nature of how Native peoples feel about the land. Traditionally, the land is understood to be our Mother. As Indigenous peoples of this land, we believe that we have been given the responsibility from the Creator of Life to be stewards and thus caretakers of the land. Multinational interests will prevent us from being able to continue to act in this capacity. Alfred (1999, p. 97) contends that the choices for Native peoples today are two-fold. Either they are about gaining immediate economic benefits or they are about refusing to comply with imposed corporate and neo-colonial structures in favour of preserving the long-term goal of Native self-determination on terms that are based on our own cultural values. This is not an easy choice, given the nature and extent of poverty in Native communities.

13 This information has been obtained through our Native oral tradition. It has been pre-
    cisely passed down to me through my associations with many respected Native Elders
    and traditional teachers.

14 Traditionally, the notion of power over was never used. Rather the model of power tra-
    ditionally used is that of power from within. One gains power and holds power through
    life experience and from directed learning from Elders. If a convincing argument needs
    to be employed, it can be achieved by way of oration or verbal persuasion (Alfred, 1999,
    pp. 48–51; Maracle, 1992, p. 87)

15 I acknowledge the influence of Lori Hill, a doctoral candidate in the Faculty of Social
    Work at Wilfrid Laurier University, in obtaining this information.

16 I heard numerous stories about residential school survivors being tortured throughout
    my social work practice.

17 I contend that this is one reason why the Native middle class does not speak out in
    outrage concerning the deplorable conditions that the majority of Native people live in.

18 This information was obtained from Lori Hill, a doctoral candidate in the Faculty of
    Social Work at Wilfrid Laurier University.

19 I am aware of this perception from my own experience of working as a social worker in
    a Native agency that had a child protection mandate. While the work that I did was
    essentially clinical, my clients were very aware that I carried a big stick and could report
    child abuse cases to the investigation unit within this agency.

20 The term "customary care" refers to the extended family as the locus of support for
    children within the community. It was thus not unusual for children to live with
    extended family members. This notion does not equate easily within the context of
    the Eurocentric nuclear family system where one would go to live with extended fam-
    ily members in times of extreme need. Traditionally, everyone within the community
    was responsible for the caregiving of all the children in the community (Thomas &
    Learoyd, 1990, pp. 21–22). Colonial interference through residential school and the
    imposition of Christian marriages changed the fabric of Native community life (Allen,
    1986, pp. 41–42). Based on my own observations of Native communities, I can see that
    today there is the hegemonic assumption that if children go live with extended family
    members, it is defined as symptomatic of there being a problem.

21 My thinking about this has been influenced by Dennis McPherson, a Native lawyer
    who was one of the people whose work enabled the term customary care to be included
    in the amended Ontario Child and Family Services Act. From a Native perspective, the
    motivation for having the provision of customary care included in the Act was to enable
    Native communities to deal with incidents of child abuse in a traditional Native, or
    customary, fashion. In practice, the new provision merely provided an opportunity to
    place Native children at risk in other Native homes. It did not enable Native peoples to
    deal with the problem of child abuse in Native communities according to their own tra-
    ditional laws, cultures, and values. That is, the area of Native child welfare was still
    bound by the legislation of the Eurocentric child welfare legislation.

22 I am purposefully not including the names of these agencies because I do not have
    their expressed permission to do so, nor do I intend to create any kind of harm for
    these agencies, or for the people who work within them.

23 In fairness, I must say that the interventions used in a Native agency where I was
    employed were very much leading edge in terms of going beyond the surface of the
    observable dysfunctional behaviours by dealing with internalized pain and trauma.

24 Provincial foster care guidelines found many Native homes unfit for foster care place-
    ments. One reason was that a foster home could not contain firearms; yet hunting is a
    very common practice in Native communities, and thus guns are often found in Native
    homes. Another issue was that the impoverished conditions that many Native peo-
    ples lived in were deemed to be unacceptable for foster care placements.

References 25 The First Nations and Inuit Home and Community Care Program (2000) funded by the federal government's First Nations Indian Health Branch is a concrete example of how Indigenous self-governed initiatives are being organized and structured according to Eurocentric standards. St. Germaine (2001) indicates that the rhetoric of this program is one of being "community-based" and "community-paced." However, she also states that "First Nations are subject to Eurocentric/hegemonic thought, through the imposition of contribution arrangements that include goals and objectives, deadlines, work plans and budgets." She also says, "to add insult to injury a policy template has been developed for ease of implementation by First Nations without regard for culture or community ownership of the document" (see Saint Elizabeth Health Care, 2000, for a copy of the template).

26 My knowledge of multi-centric curricula has been influenced by Dei (1996).

References

Adams, H. (1999). *Tortured people: The politics of colonization.* Penticton: Theytus.

Alcoze, T., & Mawhiney, A.M. (1988). *Returning home. A report on a community-based Native human services project.* Sudbury: Laurentian University.

Akwesasne Notes. (Ed.). (1981). *A basic call to consciousness.* Summertown, TN: Native Voices.

Alfred, T. (1999). *Peace power righteousness: An indigenous manifesto.* Don Mills: Oxford University Press.

Alfred, T. (2005). *Wasase: Indigenous pathways of action and freedom.* Toronto: Broadview Press.

Allen, P.G. (1986). *The sacred hoop: Recovering the feminine in American Indian traditions.* Boston: Beacon Press.

Anderson, K. (2000). *A recognition of being: Reconstructing Native womanhood.* Toronto: Secondary Press.

Antone, R., Miller, D., & Myers, B. (1986). *The power within people: A community organizing perspective.* Deseronto: Peace Tree Technologies.

Armitage, A. (1995). Canada: First Nations family and child welfare policy. In A. Armitage, *Comparing the policy of Aboriginal assimilation: Australia, Canada and New Zealand* (pp. 100–135). Vancouver: University of British Columbia Press.

Assante, M.K. (2003). *Afrocentricity: The theory of social change.* Chicago: African American Images.

Assembly of First Nations. (1989). *National inquiry into First Nations child care.* Ottawa: Author.

Assembly of First Nations. (1994). *Breaking the silence: An interpretive study of residential school impact and healing as illustrated by the stories of First Nations individuals.* Ottawa: Author.

Battiste, M. (1997, June 8–11). *Enabling the autumn seed: Framing a decolonized curricular approach toward Aboriginal knowledge language and education.* Paper presented at the CSAA Learned Society Conference, St. John's, NF.

Battiste, M. (2005). You can't be the global doctor if you're the colonial disease. In P. Tripp & L. Muzzin (Eds.), *Teaching as Activism: Equity Meets Environmentalism* (pp. 121–133). Montreal: McGill-Queen's University Press.

Battiste, M., & Youngblood Henderson, J.S. (2000). *Protecting indigenous knowledge and heritage: A global challenge.* Saskatoon: Purich Publishing.

Bennet, M., & Blackstock, C. (2002). *A literature review and annotated bibliography focusing on aspects of Aboriginal child welfare in Canada.* First Nations Research

Site of the Centre for Excellence for Child Welfare. Winnipeg: Faculty of Social Work, University of Manitoba.

Bishop, A. (2002). *Becoming an ally: Breaking the cycle of oppression in people.* Halifax: Fernwood.

Blaut, J. (1993). *The colonizer's model of the world: Geographical diffusionism and Eurocentric history.* New York: Guilford Press.

Brokenleg, M., & Brendtro, L. (1989). *The circle of caring: Native American perspectives on children and youth.* Paper presented to the Child Welfare of America International Conference, Washington, DC.

Browning, R., & van de Sande, A. (1999). Long-term evaluation of health-transfer initiatives: Major findings. *Native Social Work Journal, 2*(1), 153–162.

Canadian Association of Social Workers (1994, December). The social work profession and the Aboriginal peoples: CASW presentation to the Royal Commission on Aboriginal Peoples. *The Social Worker, 158.*

Dei, G.J.S. (2000a). Rethinking the role of indigenous knowledges in the academy. *International Journal of Inclusive Education, 4*(2), 111–132.

Dei, G.J.S. (2000b). Towards an anti-racism discursive framework. In G.J.S. Dei (Ed.), *Power, knowledge and anti-racism education: A critical reader* (pp. 23–40). Halifax: Fernwood.

Dei, G.J.S. (1996). *Anti-racism education: Theory and Practice.* Halifax: Fernwood.

Dei, G.J.S., & Asgharzadeh, A. (2000). The power of social theory: The anti-colonial discursive framework. *Journal of Educational Thought, 35*(3), 297–323.

De Montigny, G. (1995). The power of being professional. In M. Campbell & A. Manicom (Eds.), *Knowledge, experience and ruling relations* (pp. 209–220). Toronto: University of Toronto Press.

Fanon, F. (1995). National culture. In B. Ashcroft, G. Griffiths, & H. Thiophene (Eds.), *The post-colonial studies reader* (pp. 153–157). New York: Routledge.

First Nations and Inuit Health Branch. (2000). *First Nations and Inuit home and community care: Planning resource kit.* Ottawa: Government of Canada.

Fournier, S., & Crey, D. (1997). *Stolen from our embrace: The abduction of First Nations children and restoration of Aboriginal community.* Vancouver: Douglas and McIntyre.

Graveline, F.J. (1998). *Circle works: Transforming Eurocentric consciousness.* Halifax: Fernwood.

Graveline, F.J. (2004). *Healing wounded hearts.* Halifax: Fernwood.

Haig-Brown, C. (1988). *Resistance and renewal: Surviving the Indian residential School.* Vancouver: Arsenal Pulp Press.

Hart, M.A. (2002). *Seeking mino-pimatisiwin: An Aboriginal approach to helping.* Halifax: Fernwood.

Hudson, P., & McKenzie, B. (1985). Native children, child welfare and the colonization of Native people. In K. Levitt & B. Wharf (Eds.), *The challenge of child welfare* (pp. 125–141). Vancouver: University of British Columbia Press.

Johnston, P. (1983). *Native children and the child welfare system.* Ottawa: Canadian Council on Social Development.

Knockwood, I. (1992). *Out of the depths: The experiences of Mi'kmaw children at the residential school at Shubenacadie, Nova Scotia.* Lockeport: Roseway.

Maracle, L. (1996). *I am woman: A Native perspective on sociology and feminism.* Vancouver: Press Gang.

References Miller, J.R. (1996). *Shingwauk's Vision: A History of Native Residential Schools.* Toronto: University of Toronto Press.

Milloy, J. (1999). *A national crime: The Canadian government and the residential school system: 1879–1986.* Winnipeg: University of Winnipeg Press.

Nabigon, H., & Waterfall, B. (1995). An assessment tool for First Nations individuals and families. In Francis Turner (Ed.), *Social work treatment: Interlocking theoretical approaches* (4th ed.) (p. 32). New York: Free Press.

Native Council of Canada. (1989). *Report on the National Day of Native child care: Challenges into the 1990s.* Ottawa: Author.

Ontario Association of Children's Aid Societies. (2000). *Risk assessment model.* Toronto: Queen's Printer for Ontario.

Ontario Native Women's Association. (1982). *Remove the child and the circle is broken: A response to the proposed Children's Act Commission paper.* Thunder Bay: Author.

Parada, H. (2000). *The social organization of power within Children's Aid societies.* Paper presented at the May 2000 Institutional Ethnography Conference, Ontario Institute for Studies in Education of the University of Toronto, Toronto.

Puja, G.K. (2001). *Moving against the grain: Expectations and experiences of Tanzanian female undergraduates.* Unpublished doctoral thesis. Toronto: OISE/ University of Toronto.

Royal Commission on Aboriginal Peoples. (1996). *Report of the Royal Commission on Aboriginal Peoples. Vol. 1: Looking forward, looking back; Vol. 2: Restructuring the relationship.* Ottawa: Canada Communications Group.

Saint Elizabeth Health Care. (2000). *First Nations and Inuit home and community health care policies template manual.* Markham: Author.

Smith, L. (1999). *Decolonizing methodologies: Research and indigenous peoples.* New York: Zed Books.

Soloman, A. (1999). Interview notes, Toronto, November 15.

St. Germaine, J. (2001). *Home and community care policy development.* Unpublished paper. Sudbury: Native Human Services, Laurentian University.

Stuckey, M.E., & Murphy, J.M. (2001). Rhetorical Colonialism in North America. *American Indian Culture and Research Journal, 25,* 73–78.

Swinomish Tribal Mental Health Project. (1991). *A gathering of wisdoms: Tribal mental health; A cultural perspective.* Swinomish Tribal Community: LaConner.

Thomas, L., & Learoyd, S. (1990). *Native child care: In the spirit of caring.* Unpublished masters thesis. Ottawa: Carleton University.

Timpson, J., & Semple, D. (1997). Bringing home Payahtakenenmowin (Peace of mind): Creating self-governing community services. *Native Social Work Journal, 1*(1), 87–101.

Trask, H.K. (1991). Natives and anthropologists: The colonial struggle. *The Contemporary Pacific, 3*(1), 159–167.

Waterfall, B. (1992). *Mending the circle: Healing from the effects of family violence.* Unpublished master's thesis. Ottawa: Carleton University.

Waterfall, B. [forthcoming]. *Decolonizing Native social work education: A reflexive study.* Doctoral thesis, Ontario Institute for Studies in Education of the University of Toronto.

Whiteye, B. (2002). *A dark legacy: A primer on Indian residential schools in Canada.* Self-published.

Yellow Bird, M.J., & Chenault, V. (1999). The role of social work in advancing the   **References**
practice of Indigenous education: Obstacles and promises in empowerment-
oriented social work practice. In K.G. Swisher and J.W. Tippeconnic III (Eds.),
Next steps: Research and practice to advance Indian education (pp. 201–235).
Charleston: ERIC Clearinghouse on Rural Education and Small Schools.

Additional Resources

Allen, P.G. (1998). *Off the reservation: Reflections on boundary-busting, border crossing, loose canons.* Boston: Beacon Press.

Baskin, C. (2003). Structural social work as seen from an Aboriginal perspective. In
Shera, W. (Ed.), *Emerging perspectives on anti-oppressive practice* (pp. 65–70).
Toronto: Canadian Scholars' Press.

Battiste, M. (2002). *Reclaiming Indigenous voice and vision.* Vancouver: University
of British Columbia Press.

Cajete, G. (1999). *Igniting the sparkle: An Indigenous science education model.* Skyland, NC: Kivaki Press.

Cajete, G. (1994). *Look to the mountain: An ecology of indigenous education.* Skyland,
NC: Kivaki Press.

Dumont, J. (1993). *Justice and Aboriginal people.* Ottawa: Ministry of Supply and
Services Canada.

Duran, E.D., Duran, B., Brave Heart, M., & Yellow Horse-Davis, S. (1998). Healing the
American Indian soul wound. In Y. Danieli (Ed.), *International handbook of
multigenerational legacies of trauma* (pp. 341–354). New York: Plenum Press.

Laduke, W. (1999). *All our relations: Native struggles for land and life.* Cambridge,
MA: South End Press.

Lawrence, B. (2004). *"Real" Indians & Others: Mixed-blood urban Native People
and Indigenous nationhood.* Vancouver: University of British Columbia Press.

McIvor, S.D. (1999). Self-government and Aboriginal women. In E. Dua & A. Robertson (Eds.), *Scratching the surface: Canadian anti-racist feminist thought*
(pp. 167–186). Toronto: Women's Press.

Mihesuah, D.A. (2003). *Indigenous American women: Decolonization, empowerment, activism.* Lincoln: University of Nebraska Press.

Mihesauh, D.A., & Wilson, A.C. (Eds.). (2004). *Indigenizing the Academy: Transforming scholarship and empowering communities.* Lincoln: University of
Nebraska Press.

Monture-Angus, P. (2001). In the way of peace: Confronting "whiteness" in the university. In R. Luther, E. Whitmore, & B. Moreau (Eds.), *Seen but not heard: Aboriginal women and women of colour in the academy* (pp. 29–49). Ottawa: CRIAW.

Monture-Angus, P. (1995). A first journey in decolonized thought: Aboriginal women
and the application of the Canadian Charter. In P. Monture-Angus (Ed.), *Thunder in my soul: A Mohawk woman speaks* (pp. 131–151). Halifax: Fernwood.

Ouellette, G.J.M.W. (2002). *The fourth world: An Indigenous perspective on feminism
and Aboriginal women's activism.* Halifax: Fernwood.

Ricks, F., Wharf, B., & Armitage, A. (1990). Evaluation of Indian child welfare: A different reality. *Canadian Review of Social Policy, 25,* 41–47.

Royal Commission on Aboriginal Peoples. (1996). *Report of the Royal Commission
on Aboriginal Peoples. Vol. 1: Looking forward, looking back; Vol. 2: Restructuring the relationship; Vol. 3: Gathering strength; Vol. 4: Perspectives and realities;*

References   *Vol. 5: Renewal: A twenty-year commitment.* Ottawa: Canada Communications Group.

Stevenson, W. (1999). Colonialism and First Nations women in Canada. In E. Dua & A. Robertson (Eds.), *Scratching the surface: Canadian anti-racist feminist thought* (pp. 49–80). Toronto: Women's Press.

Wane, N., & Waterfall, B. (2005). Hoops of spirituality in science and technology. In P. Tripp & L. Muzzin (Eds.), *Teaching as activism: Equity meets environmentalism* (pp. 46–63). Montreal: McGill-Queen's University Press.

Geoffrey Nelson

Overview

The purpose of this chapter is to review and analyze mental health policy in Canada. I concentrate on adult mental health rather than children's mental health, because policy initiatives and reforms across Canada have focused primarily on the adult population.

The Canadian Context

Canada is a vast, bilingual nation, composed of ten provinces and three northern territories with a population of about 32 million people in 2005. Almost two thirds of Canadians reside in Ontario and Québec (Latimer, 2005a), and the majority of citizens live close to the southern border with the US. English and French are the first languages of about 61% and 24% of the population, respectively (Lakaski, Wilmot, Lips, & Brown, 1993). Canada is also rapidly becoming more culturally diverse, with 18% of the current population being foreign born and over 200 ethnic groups residing in Canada (Statistics Canada, 2005), and there is a population of roughly one million Aboriginal people.

In 1961, under the leadership of Premier Tommy Douglas, the government of Saskatchewan implemented a provincial health care system (Freeman, 1994). Five years later, in 1966, the federal government passed the Medical Care Act, which brought health care to all Canadians. While the federal government has set principles (accessibility, universality, portability, comprehensiveness, government administration) and provides funding to the provinces, planning and decision-making in health care are the responsibility of provincial governments (Goering, Wasylenki, & Durbin, 2000). Perhaps since the provinces have so much responsibility for health care, Canada is the only G8 nation without a national mental health policy (Latimer, in press). The federal government is responsible, however, for the mental health care of Aboriginal people and veterans.

Recently, there have been calls for a national action plan on mental health and mental illness (Kirby, 2005). Senator Michael Kirby, Chair of the Standing Senate Committee on Social Affairs, Science and Technology, has led a multi-pronged investigation into mental health reform in Canada. According to Kirby (2005), the recently released report of the Senate committee was guided by the vision "of a consumer-centred system with a focus on recovery and access to personalized care" (p. S9). The process of developing this report has created some momentum for mental health policy reform across Canada. Another federal initiative is the Canadian Community Health Survey, a large survey of the Canadian population conducted by Statistics Canada, which included for the first time in 2001 some questions related to mental health (e.g., depression, contact with mental health professionals).

Federal funding for health care is a contentious issue between the federal and provincial governments. The federal portion of health care funding was reduced from 42% to 10% from the mid-1970s to the turn of the century, although it is now rising under the current government (Barlow, 2005). At the same time, there has been an increase in privatized health care and pressures for further privatization, trends that are fuelled by the current context of economic globalization, and reduced taxes and government spending on social programs (Barlow, 2005; Morrow, 2004b).

Within the framework of national health care, the mental health system consists of provincial psychiatric hospitals, general hospital psychiatric units, reimbursement to physicians (including psychiatrists) for mental health services, and, more recently, community mental health programs (Goering et al., 2000). These services typically come under the control of provincial health ministries. The provinces have moved or are moving to decentralized, regional administration of health services, which includes planning, decision-making, funding, and coordination/integration of mental health services (Latimer, 2005a). In terms of human resources, mental health specialists in private practice from disciplines other than medicine/psychiatry (psychologists, social workers, occupational therapists, psychiatric nurses) cannot receive reimbursement from government sources for mental health services. Individuals who have the financial means or supplementary private health insurance (typically through their workplaces) can obtain therapeutic services from these mental health professionals, who are private practitioners. As well, individuals can receive help from professionals from disciplines other than psychiatry who work for publicly funded agencies (e.g., hospitals, community mental health services). Historically, mental health services in Canada have been controlled by government, the medical profession, and, in Québec, the Catholic church up until the 1960s (Boudreau, 1987; Simmons, 1990).

"Mental Illness" and Mental Health

Since the late 1800s, the biomedical perspective of psychiatry has dominated the mental health field. Medical superintendents and psychiatrists have run mental hospitals and general hospital psychiatric units, and, as noted earlier, only medical doctors are eligible to receive reimbursement from government for mental health services provided in the context of private practice. With the advent of psychoactive drug treatments beginning in the 1950s, the pharmaceutical industry has become a major partner to medicine and psychiatry in the promotion of the medical model of mental illness. The *Diagnostic and Statistical Manual* (DSM), now in its fourth edition, is *the* tool for the diagnosis of mental illness. Today many mental health professionals adhere to a broad biopsychosocial framework to understand mental health issues that includes multiple interacting causes of mental illness (e.g., genetic, biochemical, hormonal, psychological traits, family factors, environmental trauma, economic conditions). However, it is the biological component of the framework that continues to receive the strongest emphasis in research and practice.

The biomedical perspective and the concept of "mental illness" as a disease have been contested. Psychiatrist Thomas Szsaz (1961) argued that mental illness is a myth, that there are no known lesions, defects, or diseases of the nervous system that underlie any of the conditions that are called mental illness. Rather, he argued that the labelling of problems in living by psychiatrists is a social act that involves value judgements. What is judged to be normal or abnormal depends upon one's values and the social context. Are individuals abnormal or is there something wrong with the social conditions in which people live?

The case of sexual orientation illustrates the contested nature of the concept of mental illness. Prior to 1973 "homosexuality" was included in the DSM as a mental disorder. Values and social context, not scientific evidence, were the reasons for the inclusion of homosexuality as a disorder and for its eventual removal from the DSM. Psychologist Paula Caplan (1995) argued that the DSM has both a cultural and gender bias with white, male, North American psychiatrists deciding who and what is viewed as "crazy." There are numerous other criticisms of the medical model and the DSM, including the emphasis on deficits, the lack of attention to environmental conditions that contribute to mental health problems (especially poverty, racism, sexism, homophobia); the "stickiness" of diagnostic labels that can lead to stigma, discrimination, and negative self-fulfilling prophecies; the power imbalance between psychiatrists and patients; iatrogenic illnesses (problems created by professional treatments, such as tardive dyskinesia, a disorder resulting from psychoactive drug treatment); and others (Cohen, 1990).

In the federal report *Mental Health for Canadians: Striking a Balance*, former minister of Health and Welfare Jake Epp (1988) distinguished between mental disorder and mental health, which he argued exist on separate continua. Mental health was broadly defined as "the capacity of the individual, the group and the environment to interact with one another in ways that promote subjective well-being, the optimal development and use of mental abilities (cognitive, affective and relational), the achievement of individual and collective goals consistent with justice and the attainment and preservation of conditions of fundamental equality" (Epp, 1988, p. 7). To address mental disorders effectively and to promote mental health, the report advocated reducing inequities, increasing prevention, and enhancing coping.

How widespread are mental health problems in Canada? Bearing in mind the criticisms of the DSM and the concept of mental illness as a disease, there is epidemiological research that suggests that mental health problems, whether conceived as problems in living or illness, are widespread. In 1990–91, an epidemiological study of adult mental disorders was conducted with nearly 10,000 Ontario residents (Offord et al., 1994). The researchers found that the one-year prevalence rate for any disorder was 30%; the lifetime prevalence rate was 48%; and the prevalence rate for severe mental illness was 2%. Thus, almost half of all adult Ontarians will experience a mental health problem at some time in their lives. The most prevalent disorders were anxiety and mood disorders and substance abuse, while the most disabling mental disorder, schizophrenia, is less common, affecting 1% or less of the population (Arboleda-Florez, 2005). Stephens and Joubert (2001) have estimated the economic costs of mental health problems in Canada to be $14 billion in 1998.

Mental health policy in the Canadian provinces has focused on the population of individuals with "serious mental illness," which encompasses diagnosis, disability resulting from the disorder, and duration of the disorder. People with serious mental illness typically have diagnoses of schizophrenia, severe depression, or bipolar disorder; the majority are unemployed and have major problems coping with daily living; and their problems are long-term in nature. In contrast, those with more moderate mental health issues typically have diagnoses of anxiety, minor mood disorder, or substance abuse; the majority are employed but have significant problems coping with the stressors of daily living; and their problems are often short-term or episodic in nature. One of the historical problems in mental health policy is that people with moderate mental health issues are more likely to receive psychotherapy than those with more serious mental health issues (Hollingshead & Redlich, 1958). Schofield (1964) wrote that mental health professionals prefer to work with clients who are young, attractive, verbal, intelligent, successful, and female, and that many people who seek help are not mentally ill but lonely and looking for friendship.

Serious Mental Health Issues

In their review of the evolution of mental health policy in Canada for people with serious mental health issues, Trainor, Pape, and Pomeroy (1997) argued that mental health policy has passed through several stages: (a) the institutional consensus, (b) deinstitutionalization, (c) community mental health services, and (d) the community process approach. In this section, we review these stages.

From Institutionalization to Deinstitutionalization

In the early 1800s in Canada, as elsewhere, people with significant mental health issues were placed in poorhouses and jails. The first mental hospital in Canada opened in 1836 in New Brunswick, and by the mid-1860s there were eleven provincial mental hospitals (Rochefort, 1992). US mental health crusader Dorthea Dix was influential in establishing some of the first institutions in the Canadian maritime provinces. Foucault (1965) and Scull (1977) have argued that these institutions were developed to confine people with mental health problems who did not fit into the industrial labour market in the growing capitalist economies of western nations. Power was vested in the hands of psychiatry, with tremendous power imbalances between psychiatrists and other institutional staff, on the one hand, and people who were institutionalized, on the other hand (McCubbin & Cohen, 1996), sometimes resulting in both subtle and blatant abuse of patients (Burstow & Weitz, 1988). One of the most egregious examples of patient abuse occurred at the Allan Memorial Institute in Montreal in the 1950s and early 1960s under the direction of Dr. Ewan Cameron. His CIA-funded research included subjecting roughly 100 patients to sensory deprivation, drugging, and massive shock treatments. In mental hospitals, patients were "out of sight and out of mind" with little chance of returning to their families and home communities. Moreover, the mental hospital was *the* mental health system for most people; few other options existed. A number of valuable first-person accounts and some historical research chronicle the many problems inherent in institutionalization from the perspective of Canadians who were patients in such settings (Burstow & Weitz, 1988; Chamberlin, 1978; Reaume, 2000).

There were periodic efforts to reform mental health policy and move to a more community-based approach, but until the past few decades, these efforts never gained enough momentum to have an impact (Simmons, 1990). Clarence Hincks, a physician, founded what is now known as the Canadian Mental Health Association (CMHA) in 1918. Through Hincks and other reformers, the CMHA brought to light the deplorable conditions of mental hospitals and advocated for community-based care. However, it was not until much later in the century that progressive reform took root.

Deinstitutionalization in Canada began in the 1960s with the bed capacity of provincial mental hospitals dropping from 69,128 in 1965 to 20,301 in 1981, a 70% reduction (Sealy & Whitehead, 2004). This change occurred in part due to economic reasons: psychiatric hospitals were becoming expensive to maintain, and the development of a public welfare system provided a (very) minimal support system for people with mental health problems to live in the community (Bloche & Cournos, 1990; Lewis, Shadish, & Lurigio, 1989; Scull, 1977). Recognition of the limitations of institutions, an increasing focus on human rights, and a new vision that support and treatment would be more effective in the individual's home community were other reasons for deinstitutionalization (McCubbin, 1994). In the early years of deinstitutionalization, funding was transferred to local general hospital psychiatric units rather than community mental health services. From 1960 to 1976, the number of general hospital psychiatric beds increased seven-fold from 844 to 5,836 (Wasylenki, Goering, & MacNaughton, 1994). One of the more innovative approaches was the famous "Saskatchewan Plan," which created eight regional mental health centres in Saskatchewan with an emphasis on providing services within the person's home and community (Lafave & Vanden Ham, 1979).

Many discharged individuals were and continue to remain isolated from communities of support, often living in "psychiatric ghettoes" consisting of boarding homes, other poor-quality housing, or homelessness (Capponi, 1992; Dear & Wolch, 1987; Rochefort, 1993). Aftercare support often consisted primarily of medication with little in the way of psychosocial support, even though many of the problems faced in the community are social, economic, or interpersonal in nature (Harris, Hilton, & Rice, 1993). In their 1981 study on psychiatric aftercare in Toronto, Goering, Wasylenki, Farkas, Lancee, and Freeman (1984) found that six months after discharge from psychiatric facilities in Toronto, one third of the sample was readmitted to hospital; only 38% were employed; 68% reported moderate to severe difficulties in social functioning; and 20% were living in inadequate housing.

Within this context of institutional abuse and community neglect, people with mental health problems formed their own mutual aid organizations. In Vancouver, ex-patients formed the Mental Patients Association (MPA), which provided respite housing and mutual aid and which engaged in advocacy to protect the rights of people with mental health problems (Chamberlin, 1978). Inspired by Vancouver MPA, a group in Toronto formed On Our Own, a radical anti-psychiatry group that operated a "mad market," engaged in political action (e.g., opposition to electroconvulsive therapy (ECT) and psychoactive drug use in hospitals), and produced a periodical called *Phoenix Rising* for several years (Weitz, 1984). These early self-help, social movement organizations of ex-patients set the stage for the expansion of self-help alternatives that have received government support more recently.

Community Mental Health and Mental Health Reform

Since the late 1980s, most of the provinces have pursued an agenda of mental health reform. Like deinstitutionalization before it, mental health reform in Canada, and elsewhere, has been driven both by governments' concerns for cost containment and by visions of more effective community supports for people (Fisher, 1994; Morrow, 2004b; Shera, Aviram, Healy, & Ramon, 2002). Mental health reform has included efforts to reallocate resources from institutional services to community mental health supports and programs. During the late 1980s, all of the provinces except Saskatchewan spent 68% or more of their mental health budgets on institutional services (Saskatchewan spent 48%) (MacNaughton, 1991). However, from the late 1980s to 1998, provincial spending on community mental health increased thirteen-fold from $8 million to $113 million (Sealy & Whitehead, 2004), with several provinces making significant progress in reallocating resource from hospitals to community-based services.

In 1988, New Brunswick created a Mental Health Commission, which made significant reforms, including the development of more than thirty self-help groups and activity centres, and a variety of alternatives to hospitalization (Niles & Ross, 1992). British Columbia dramatically scaled down the number of beds in the province's main mental hospital and reallocated resources to community mental health services (Berland, 2001). From the late 1980s to the mid-1990s, Ontario made significant reforms, including the development and funding of more than sixty Consumer/Survivor Initiatives and a provincial umbrella organization called the Ontario Peer Development Initiative (OPDI), more than ten consumer-run businesses, and a provincial umbrella organization called the Ontario Council of Alternative Businesses (OCAB), supportive housing options, and a variety of other community-based case management and psychosocial programs (Hartford, Schrecker, Wiktorowicz, Hoch, & Sharp, 2003; Nelson, Lord, & Ochocka, 2001; Trainor, Shepherd, Boydell, Leff, & Crawford, 1997; Trainor & Tremblay, 1992).

During the late 1990s and more recently, Ontario doubled the number of supportive and supported housing spaces, focusing on people with serious mental illness who were homeless or at-risk for homelessness, and the province has funded more than sixty Assertive Community Treatment (ACT) teams across the province (Latimer, 2005a; Sylvestre et al., under review). Quebec has undergone a number of major changes in recent years, including regionalization of mental health services, the integration of mental health services into Centres de santé et services sociaux, the development of more than 100 alternative supports and consumer advocacy groups (Regroupement de ressources alternatives en santé mentale au Québec [RRASMQ], l'Association des groupes d'intervention en défense de droits en santé mentale au Québec [AGIDD-SMQ]), all with an emphasis on partnership between professionals and people with mental health problems and their family members in planning community supports (Boudreau, 1991; Fleury, 2005; Latimer, 2005a; Mercier & White, 1994).

Simply reallocating resources from institutions to community mental health services, however, does not ensure that there is a fundamental transformation of mental health policy and services. Some institutional programs may be repackaged in the community, yielding "old wine in new bottles." Many community treatment and rehabilitation approaches have retained the character of the institutional paradigm (see Table 12.1). For example, case management and ACT teams (e.g., Stein & Test, 1980), as they were originally conceived, are often professionally driven services that aim to prevent hospitalization, reduce symptoms, and promote life skills. While located in the community, programs like ACT have historically been guided by much the same values as the institutional approach, function like a "hospital without

Table 12.1 Changing paradigms in community mental health		
KEY VALUES	COMMUNITY TREATMENT AND REHABILITATION PARADIGM	RECOVERY AND EMPOWERMENT PARADIGM
Health	• Emphasis on symptom reduction and prevention of hospitalization • Focus on psychosocial deficits and social skills training	• Focus on whole person • Recognition of strengths • Emphasis on recovery and quality of life
Stakeholder participation and empowerment	• Dependence on professionals • Client role • Professional as expert • Professionally prescribed treatment	• Consumer choice and control • Autonomous consumer and family organizations • Citizen role • Professional role focuses on enabling and collaboration
Community support and integration	• Professional, paraprofessional, and volunteer services • Community-based	• Self-help/mutual aid • Individualized support • Informal supports • Integration in community settings and social networks
Social justice and access to valued resources	• Group homes, halfway houses, and supervised apartments, often with many people with mental health challenges living in the same setting • Vocational training and placement • Sheltered workshops	• Independent housing chosen by residents from normal housing stock in the community, with portable and flexible support • Supported employment and education

Source: Adapted from *Shifting the paradigm in community mental health: Towards empowerment and community*, by G. Nelson, J. Lord, & J. Ochocka, 2001 (Toronto: University of Toronto Press).

walls," maintain a power imbalance between staff and clients, and use some coercive methods (Spindel, 2000). While clients are *in* the community, they are not a part *of* the community, often being isolated in segregated settings, such as group homes, boarding homes, and sheltered workshops.

Approaches like ACT and psychiatric rehabilitation have been widely disseminated and adopted. Lewis et al. (1989) warned the mental health field about the perils of "guild innovationism" in community mental health, which benefits professionals more than service-users. Planning and policy in mental health often uses the progressive language of "partnership" between mental health professionals, individuals with mental health problems, and their family members. In practice, however, researchers and activists have argued that the power imbalances between professionals, service-users, and family members continue to plague community partnerships and to undermine more radical reform (McCubbin, 1994; Mercier & White, 1994; Morin, 1992). In a qualitative study of service-user participation in mental health reform in Ontario, Everett (2000) described the participation of service-users as a "fragile revolution."

Since the 1990s, however, an alternative vision and values of community mental health have been articulated by both professionals and people who use mental health services (who refer to themselves as "consumers" or "survivors"). Some of the key themes of this emerging, alternative paradigm are recovery, empowerment, community integration, peer support, informal support, self-help, and social justice (see Table 12.1). Whereas the community treatment and rehabilitation paradigm focuses on ameliorative change (moving from hospitals to the community), this recovery and empowerment paradigm focuses on transformative or fundamental change in the values and power arrangements of mental health policy and practice (Nelson & Prilleltensky, 2005). Trainor et al. (1997) make a similar distinction between what they call community mental health services and a community process approach.

In the US, Patricia Deegan (1988), who is both a consumer/survivor activist and a mental health professional, introduced the idea of recovery as an alternative vision to the dominant professional view of the "chronic mental patient." One of the founders of psychiatric rehabilitation, William Anthony (1993), has further promoted recovery as the "guiding vision of the mental health service system." Both Deegan and Anthony emphasize that recovery is a process that involves movement towards a more positive quality of life. Paul Carling (1995) has brought a disability rights perspective to the mental health field, advocating for inclusion of people with mental health concerns in typical community settings and informal networks of support (i.e., community integration). Carling has also argued that the traditional emphasis on changing people with mental health problems so that they can function better in society needs to be accompanied by community change to make society a more welcoming place for people who have experienced mental health struggles. Finally, Carling has articulated an approach called "supported" housing, education, and employment, in which mental health consumers are assisted to "choose, get, and keep" the basic resources that they want.

In Canada, Trainor, Pomeroy, and Pape (1999) articulated a "framework for support" for people with serious mental health problems under the auspices of the National Office of the Canadian Mental Health Association. This framework, first conceived during the early 1980s, elaborates the community process approach (Pomeroy, Trainor, & Pape, 2002). There are several key features of the framework. First, not only is the consumer at the centre of the framework, but the consumer also controls and directs the sources of support that surround him or her. Second, while mental health services are part of the framework, there is a strong emphasis on other sources of support, including family, friends, social networks, peer support, self-help, and community groups and agencies. Third, the framework includes access to the basic resources that are needed to promote a desirable quality of life, including housing, income, work, and education. Fourth, the framework asserts that while medical science and social science are valuable ways to understand mental illness, they are not the only sources of knowledge. Experiential knowledge and the knowledge of lay persons are also valuable and need to be incorporated into mental health policy and programs. Finally, implicit in the framework is a strong emphasis on the participation of mental health consumers and family members in mental health policy-making, planning, service delivery, and the creation of self-help approaches.

This framework has been very influential and was adopted by the governments of New Brunswick and Ontario as the centrepiece guiding their mental health reform processes. The progressive changes that have been achieved in New Brunswick (Niles & Ross, 1992) and Ontario (Bezzina, 1998; Nelson et al., 2001) point to the importance of having a framework that clearly outlines an alternative vision and values, as well as strategies for change (Carling, 1995). While the vision and values are necessary for the implementation of new paradigm practices, there are often many obstacles to implementation of such practices, as Townsend (1998) found in a study of occupational therapy settings in mental health in Nova Scotia.

Today, the lines between the community treatment and rehabilitation paradigm and the recovery and empowerment paradigms, between community mental health services and community process, have become blurred. While there are clear examples of more traditional programs and more innovative programs, many programs are hybrids that straddle the two paradigms. One example is changes within ACT programs. For example, the Pathways program in New York City uses ACT as the support component for its supported housing, and ACT staff is committed to the "practice of radical acceptance of the consumer's point of view" (Tsemberis & Eisenberg, 2000, p. 489). Moreover, "unlike the traditional ACT model, the Pathways supported housing program allows clients to determine the type and intensity of services or refuse them entirely" (Tsemberis & Eisenberg, 2000, p. 489). Research on ACT teams in Ontario has shown that while clients have some concerns about ACT (e.g., conflict over medications and money), most are very satisfied with their relationships with staff and the program (Krupa et al., 2005; Redko, Durbin, Wasylenki, & Krupa, 2004). There is also a growing trend of peer support within case management and ACT programs, and research has found that consumer case managers achieve the same beneficial outcomes as professional case managers (Solomon, 2004). Another example is the mix of supported, independent housing and some congregate or group living arrangements with on-site staff for consumers with greater needs (Sylvestre et al., under review).

Evidence-based Mental Health Policy and Practice

Historically, mental health policy has relied very little on research. With the advent of community mental health programs, there has been an increasing emphasis on research informing mental health policy (Latimer, 2005b). The Health Systems Research and Consulting Unit of the Centre for Addiction and Mental Health completed a review of best practices in mental health for the federal government in 1997 (Health Canada, 1998). The review included research evidence regarding the core services of a comprehensive mental health system, including case management, ACT teams, crisis intervention, supportive and supported housing, inpatient and outpatient care, consumer self-help and consumer initiatives, family self-help, and vocational services. Recently in Ontario, government partnered with the Centre for Addiction and Mental Health, the Ontario Division of CMHA, and the Ontario Mental Health Foundation (a research funding organization) in the creation of a Community Mental Health Evaluation Initiative (CHMHEI). The CHMHEI involved a coordinated set of studies, including several with common measurement tools and assessment intervals, that longitudinally examined the effectiveness of crisis services, intensive case management, ACT, family self-help, and Consumer/Survivor Initiatives. The results of this set of studies have been reported in a document entitled *Making It Happen* (Ontario Ministry of Health and Long-term Care, 2004). Such linkages between policymakers, researchers, and service providers are being made in other provinces as well (Berland, 2001; Latimer, 2005b). At the federal level, the Canadian Institutes of Health Research, the major national funding body for health research, now has several institutes that fund mental health research: (a) neurosciences, mental health, and addiction, (b) health services and policy research, (c) Aboriginal people's health, (d) human development and child and youth health, (e) gender and health, and (f) population and public health.

(margin note: Moderate Mental Health Issues)

Moderate Mental Health Issues

Dewa, Rochefort, Rogers, and Goering (2003) have argued that, in focusing on people with serious mental illness, mental health reform has neglected a large population of people with moderate mental health issues. They define moderate mental illness as a condition that is "diagnosable, sufficiently severe to impede functional abilities, and considered to require, and could likely benefit from, mental health treatment under broadly established professional norms" (p. 45). The main types of moderate mental health problems are anxiety disorders, mood disorders, and personality disorders. These disorders cause significant distress to the individuals afflicted and to members of their family and social network, and they are quite costly to society.

In the previously mentioned epidemiological study of adult mental health problems in Ontario (Offord et al., 1994), it was found that 75% of those who were judged to have a disorder did not seek treatment from a mental health professional (including 76% of those with an anxiety disorder and 40% of those with a mood disorder). When asked why they had not sought help, 81% said they didn't believe they had a problem; 57% were too embarrassed to ask for help; and 42% were uncomfortable asking for help. Denial and stigma are barriers to help seeking. Also, the researchers found that 42% of those who did seek help from a professional did not have a mental disorder! Clearly the mental health system is not working when the majority of those with moderate mental health problems do not seek treatment, while nearly half of those who do not have mental health problems receive mental health treatment.

Other research has shown that those experiencing mental health problems often turn to their family doctors, counsellors, or clergy for help (Kulka, Veroff, & Douvan, 1979), although people are turning to doctors less frequently than they have in the past (Swindle, Heller, Pescosolido, & Kikuzawa, 2000). Because of their training in medicine rather than psychotherapy, physicians are likely to rely on psychoactive drugs for treatment. While drug treatments can be effective for a variety of moderate mental health problems, like anxiety or depression, many people need more than what drugs have to offer. They often need help with their marriages and families, their other relationships, work-related stressors, traumatic experiences, coping and social skills, self-esteem, and a variety of complicated life problems. Clergy often have some training in counselling, but physicians, clergy, and other counsellors and helpers who are not specialists in mental health issues typically do not have training in current evidence-based treatment approaches for moderate mental health issues.

The question then for moderate mental health issues is how to bring the most effective mental health treatments to people with mental health problems. There are now a number of well-established psychotherapeutic and pharmacological treatments for anxiety and depression (Dewa et al., 2003). Moreover, clinical researchers have developed a number of different self-directed treatments that can be used by people with emotional disorders, such as anxiety and depression, including bibliotherapy, audiotape programs, multimedia computer packages, interactive voice response systems, web-based systems, stepped care approaches, etc. (Vincent, Walker, & Katz, in press). Not only is there evidence that these approaches are effective, but much of the research indicates that these approaches are as effective as traditional face-to-face professional treatment (den Boer, Wiersnia, & van den Bosch, 2004; Vincent et al., in press). Finally, it has been shown that primary care patients and their physicians are receptive to the use of these types of treatment (Vincent et al., in press). Shared care arrangements between mental health professionals and primary care physicians, and training of physicians, clergy, and other helpers, are some possible ways of bringing evidence-based treatments to people with moderate mental health problems (Dewa et al., 2003).

To reform mental health policy for people with moderate mental illness, there also needs to be a re-examination of what professionals and what type of treatments should be reimbursed for private practice. Since many of the most effective psychotherapeutic treatments for anxiety and mood disorders have been developed by psychologists and social workers, there need to be policy changes that would tap into the resources of such non-medical professionals for private practice. Finally, as is the case for serious mental illness, policy and practice for people with moderate mental health problems should not be viewed exclusively in terms of professional treatment. Across Canada, self-help/mutual aid groups for people facing a variety of life issues have developed (Gottlieb & Peters, 1991), and there is a growing body of research attesting to the effectiveness of such groups in improving the mental health and quality of life of a number of different populations (Kyrouz, Humphreys, & Loomis, 2003).

Prevention of Mental Health Problems and Mental Health Promotion

The prevention of mental health problems for adults has not received a great deal of attention in Canadian mental health policy. For example, in a 1979 mental health planning report, the BC government based its position on prevention on an article by two US psychiatrists who asserted that mental health problems are genetically caused and thus not preventable and that there is no evidence that "mental illness" can be prevented (Nelson, Potasznik, & Bennett, 1983). Twenty-five years later, a great deal of evidence has accumulated regarding the effectiveness of prevention and promotion programs in mental health (Nelson, Prilleltensky, & Peters, in press). In spite of an emphasis on prevention/promotion in federal policy documents (Epp, 1988), this has not translated into prevention/promotion policies. For example, in a survey of the provinces and territories, Nelson, Prilleltensky, Laurendeau, and Powell (1996) found that funding for prevention is very low (less than 1% of health budgets).

There are, however, some encouraging signs about policy related to prevention/promotion. First, the federal government created a mental health promotion unit in 1995 within its public health agency, whose mandate is knowledge and policy development regarding mental health promotion from a population health perspective that considers a broad range of determinants of mental health. Second, the provinces, with federal funding for early childhood education, have invested in prevention programs focused on preschool children, including family support and centre-based programs (Nelson et al., in press). Such programs can prevent later mental health problems as the children mature into their youth and adult years (Nelson, Westhues, & MacLeod, 2003). Further policy work on mental health promotion is needed to build on these positive developments.

Class, Ethnoracial, and Gender Considerations

To what extent has an analysis of class, race, and gender been used to inform mental health policy? While social class and poverty are sometimes mentioned in mental health policy documents, actions to address the problem of poverty are lacking. In an early study, Hollingshead and Redlich (1958) found that those in the lowest social class are most likely to receive a diagnosis of serious mental illness, while those in the higher social classes were more apt to receive a diagnosis indicating moderate mental illness. This finding has been replicated many times, and poverty is clearly a major problem for people with serious mental illness and a risk factor for the development of mental health problems. Canadian survivor and advocate David Reville (2005) cautioned mental health reformers not to "lose sight of the issue of poverty" (p. S65). Wilton (2004) documented the deleterious impacts of chronic poverty on the quality of life of people with serious mental illness. Moreover, he found that social assistance benefits in Ontario declined by 13% from 1994 to 2001, and that this decline was directly attributable to changes in government policy. People with serious mental illness who are on social assistance receive a personal needs allowance of a mere $112 per month, a sum that has not been increased since 1992. There is a great need for mental health policy to be linked with income support and with employment policies and programs towards the goal of poverty reduction. Krupa, Kirsch, Gewurtz, and Cockburn (2005) have outlined a number of strategies that could be used to improve the employment of people with serious mental illness.

With regard to ethno-racial status, the federal government commissioned a Canadian Task Force on Mental Health Issues Affecting Immigrants and Refugees in the 1980s. The reports of this task force (Health and Welfare Canada, 1988a, 1988b) and a subsequent review (Beiser, 2005) found that certain aspects of the migration experience (e.g., drop in socio-economic status, language challenges, separation from family, isolation, etc.) and pre-migration catastrophic stress experiences (e.g., exposure to or victim of war, violence, torture, or natural disasters) are risk factors for mental health problems; the reports underscored the importance of measures to prevent mental health problems, including language and job-training programs and settlement services. Poverty, poor housing, and racial discrimination have also been found to contribute to poor mental health of racialized groups in Canada (Access Alliance Multicultural Community Health Centre, 2005).

In their review of factors influencing people's utilization of mental health services in Canada, Beiser, Gill, and Edwards (1993) noted that treatment approaches are based on Euro-North American values, which are often incongruent with the beliefs of immigrants and refugees and lead to their underutilization of mental health services. Different cultural concepts of mental illness, the strong stigma and shame associated with mental illness that exists in many cultures, racism, and language are all barriers to the use of mental health services (Beiser et al., 1993; Health and Welfare Canada, 1988b). The need to incorporate traditional healers from different ethno-racial groups and to provide training in cultural competence to mental health service providers were recommendations of the report. While there have been some mental health policy documents (Lieber, 1993) calling for changes in mental health organizations to take specific actions to address the needs of ethno-racial groups, mental health services are just beginning to scratch the surface of this issue.

Mental health services for Aboriginal people, which is primarily the responsibility of the federal government, are a major concern. As Lafave and

Vanden Ham (1979) stated, "In Canada as a whole, and Saskatchewan is no exception, services to the [sic] Indian population are abominable" (p. 14). Bennett (1982) has argued that the power loss, culture loss, residential schooling, poverty, and racism experienced by Native communities have led to a host of health and mental health problems. Schmidt (2000) has shown that geographic and economic factors pose major barriers to psychiatric rehabilitation programs in remote Aboriginal communities. A transformative approach is needed to address the mental health needs of Aboriginal people in their historical, cultural, social, political, and economic context.

Class, Ethnoracial, and Gender Considerations

A great deal of work has documented sexist practices in the mental health system. Women have historically been viewed as more irrational and vulnerable to emotional problems than men, and this has been linked to women's biological makeup (e.g., attributions of hysteria to a woman's "wandering uterus") (Morrow, under review). In her book *Women and Madness*, Phyllis Chesler (1972) argued that women are diagnosed with disorders for over-conforming or under-conforming to stereotypical female gender roles. In support of this argument, Broverman, Broverman, Clarkson, Rosencrantz, and Vogel (1970) found in a study of clinicians that if women conform to traditional female qualities, they are judged as unhealthy people, but if they do not conform to such a role, they are judged as unhealthy women. As well, for many years, mental health professionals ignored many of the social stressors that disproportionately affect women, including child sexual abuse, sexual assault, rape, sexual harassment, psychological and physical violence, single motherhood, and poverty. Women from ethno-racial minorities and Aboriginal women are particularly at risk for these stressors (Morrow, under review).

While feminist therapies and other alternative approaches have been developed that are sensitive to the gendered nature of mental health and illness, public mental health policy and programs have, for the most part, taken a gender-neutral approach (Morrow, under review). Some notable exceptions that exemplify a women-centred approach to mental health include the Women's Mental Health and Addiction Section of the Centre for Addiction and Mental Health and the Women's Mental Health Program in the Department of Psychiatry, University of Toronto, both in Toronto. A conference in 2003 in Quebec entitled Women, Psychiatry, Secondary Victimization brought the concerns of women into the mental health consumer movement, and several reports on women's mental health by the BC Centre of Excellence for Women's Mental Health, including a policy document on the creation of a national strategy for women's mental health (Morrow, 2004a), have also brought women's mental health concerns to the attention of practitioners and policy-makers. More attention needs to be paid to how women and men with serious mental health problems view their service needs. Scheyett and McCarthy (in press) found that while women and men have many similar perceptions of service needs, women tend to place more emphasis on the need for relationships with mental health support workers to be based on caring, understanding, and mutuality.

In answer to the question about the extent to which mental health policy
in Canada has been informed by an analysis of class, race, and gender, the
available evidence suggests that all of these critical issues have been in the
background of mental health policy. While there have been some excellent
policy documents dealing with some of these considerations, there have been
few strategic policy decisions in the provinces addressing issues of oppression
due to poverty, ethno-racial background, and gender.

Conclusion

While there is still pervasive social stigma with regard to mental health problems, some progress has been made with regard to mental health over the
past fifty years. Issues of mental health and "mental illness" are now much
more visible; witness the number of TV talk shows and self-help books that
touch upon mental health issues. Psychiatric terminology like "ADHD," "bipolar disorder," and "eating disorders" have become common place in public discourse. In Canada, provincial governments have made people with serious
mental illness the priority of mental health policy reform. While progress has
been uneven, all of the provinces have created community mental health
programs and have begun to shift resources from hospitals to communities.
Moreover, in many communities, mental health consumers and survivors
and family members are now much more visible and active in the creation of
mental health policy and the provision of community mental health services
and supports.

In spite of these advances, there are many issues that have been neglected in current policies, including the population of people with moderate
mental health issues, supportive and supported housing, poverty, ethno-
racial and gender considerations, and the need for more emphasis on prevention. To address these issues, a value-based, systems approach to policy
reform is needed, since many policies and systems outside of the traditional
domain of mental health are important for the promotion of mental health
reform (McCubbin & Cohen, 1999). In keeping with Epp's (1988) report and the
recent work of the Kirby (2005) commission, social policies that promote
social justice and social inclusion are needed to broaden the vision of mental health, to address the biopsychosocial factors and processes that promote
or undermine the mental health of Canadians, and to further develop
approaches to mental health that are community-based, consumer-directed,
recovery-oriented, and sensitive to class, race, ethnicity, and gender.

Note

1   I would like to thank Paula Goering, Michael McCubbin, Marina Morrow, John Trainor,
and Anne Westhues for their helpful comments on an earlier draft of this chapter.

References

Access Alliance Multicultural Community Health Centre of Toronto (2005). *Racialised groups and health status: A literature review exploring poverty, housing, race-based discrimination and access to health care as determinants of health for racialised groups.* Online at <www.ceris.metropolis.net/events/seminars/2005/August/LiteratureReviewRGHS.pdf>.

Anthony, W. (1993). Recovery from mental illness: The guiding vision of the mental health service system in the 1990s. *Psychiatric Rehabilitation Journal, 16*(4), 11–24.

Arboleda-Florez, J. (2005). The epidemiology of mental illness in Canada. *Canadian Public Policy, 31*, S13–16, Special Electronic Supplement on Mental Health Reform for the 21st Century. Online at <www.economics.ca/cpp/en/special issue.php>.

Barlow, M. (2005). *Too close for comfort: Canada's future within fortress North America.* Toronto: McClelland and Stewart.

Beiser, M. (2005). The health of immigrants and refugees in Canada. *Canadian Journal of Public Health, 96*(Suppl. 2), S30–44.

Beiser, M., Gill, K., & Edwards, R.G. (1993). Mental health care in Canada: Is it accessible and equal? *Canada's Mental Health, 41*(2), 2–7.

Bennett, E.M. (1982). Native persons: An assessment of their relationship to the dominant culture and challenges for change. *Canadian Journal of Community Mental Health, 1*(2), 21–31.

Berland, A. (2001). Mental health reform in British Columbia. *Administration and Policy in Mental Health, 29*, 89–93.

Bezzina, A. (1998). *ACCESS: A framework for a community based mental health service system.* Toronto: Canadian Mental Health Association/Ontario Division.

Bloche, M.G., & Cournos, F. (1990). Mental health policy for the 1990s: Tinkering in the interstices. *Journal of Health Politics, Policy, and Law, 15*, 387–411.

Boudreau, F. (1987). The making of mental health policy: The 1980s and the challenge of sanity in Québec and Ontario. *Canadian Journal of Community Mental Health, 6*(1), 27–47.

Boudreau, F. (1991). Stakeholders as partners: The challenge of partnership in Québec mental health policy. *Canadian Journal of Community Mental Health, 10*(1), 7–28.

Broverman, I.K., Broverman, D.M., Clarkson, F.E., Rosencrantz, P.S., & Vogel, S.R. (1970). Sex-role stereotypes and clinical judgements of mental health. *Journal of Consulting and Clinical Psychology, 34*, 1–7.

Burstow, B., & Weitz, D. (Eds.). (1988). *Shrink resistant: The struggle against psychiatry in Canada.* Vancouver: New Star Books.

Caplan, P. (1995). *They say you're crazy: How the world's most powerful psychiatrists decide who's normal.* Reading, MA: Addison-Wesley Longman.

Capponi, P. (1992). *Upstairs in the crazy house: The life of a psychiatric survivor.* Toronto: Penguin.

Carling, P.J. (1995). *Return to community: Building support systems for people with psychiatric disabilities.* New York: Guilford Press.

Chamberlin, J. (1978). *On our own: Patient-controlled alternatives to the mental health system.* New York: McGraw-Hill.

Chesler, P. (1972). *Women and madnesss.* New York: Avon Books.

References   Cohen, D. (Ed.). (1990). Challenging the therapeutic state: Critical perspectives on psychiatry and the mental health system [special issue]. *Journal of Mind and Behavior, 11*(3/4).

Dear, M.J., & Wolch, J.R. (1987). *Landscapes of despair: From deinstitutionalization to homelessness.* Oxford: Polity Press.

Deegan, P. (1988). Recovery: The lived experience of rehabilitation. *Psychosocial Rehabilitation Journal, 11*(4), 11–19.

den Boer, P.C.A.M., Wiersnia, D., & van den Bosch, R.J. (2004). Why is self-help neglected in the treatment of emotional disorders? A meta-analysis. *Psychological Medicine, 34,* 959–971.

Dewa, C.S., Rochefort, D.A., Rogers, J., & Goering, P. (2003). Left behind by reform: The case for improving primary care and mental health system services for people with moderate mental illness. *Applied Health Economics and Health Policy, 2,* 43–54.

Epp, J. (1988). *Mental health for Canadians: Striking a balance.* Ottawa: Minister of Supply and Services.

Everett, B. (2000). *A fragile revolution: Consumers and psychiatric survivors confront the power of the mental health system.* Waterloo: Wilfrid Laurier University Press.

Fisher, D.B. (1994). Health care reform based on an empowerment model of recovery by people with psychiatric disabilities. *Hospital and Community Psychiatry, 45,* 913–915.

Fleury, M.-J. (2005). Québec mental health services networks: Models and implementation. *International Journal of Integrated Care, 1.* Online at <www.ijic.org/>.

Foucault, M. (1965). *Madness and civilization: A history of insanity in the age of reason.* New York: Vintage Books.

Freeman, S.J.J. (1994). An overview of Canada's mental health system. In L.L. Bachrach, P. Goering, & D. Wasylenki (Eds.), *Mental health care in Canada* (pp. 11–20). San Francisco, CA: Jossey-Bass.

Goering, P., Wasylenki, D., & Durbin, J. (2000). Canada's mental health system. *International Journal of Law and Psychiatry, 23,* 345–359.

Goering, P., Wasylenki, D., Farkas, M., Lancee, W., & Freeman, S.J.J. (1984). From hospital to community: Six-month and two-year outcomes for 505 patients. *Journal of Nervous and Mental Disease, 172,* 667–673.

Gottlieb, B.H., & Peters, L. (1991). A national demographic portrait of mutual aid group participants in Canada. *American Journal of Community Psychology, 19,* 651–666.

Harris, G.T., Hilton, N.Z., & Rice, M.E. (1993). Patients admitted to psychiatric hospital: Presenting problems and resolution at discharge. *Canadian Journal of Behavioural Science, 25,* 267–285.

Hartford, K., Schrecker, T., Wiktorowicz, M., Hoch, J.S., & Sharp, C. (2003). Four decades of mental health policy in Ontario, Canada. *Administration and Policy in Mental Health, 31,* 65–73.

Health Canada (1998). *Review of best practices in mental health reform.* Prepared for the Federal/Provincial/Territorial Advisory Network on Mental Health.

Health and Welfare Canada (1988a). *After the door has been opened.* Ottawa: Minister of Supplies and Services.

Health and Welfare Canada (1988b). *Review of the literature on migrant mental health.* Ottawa: Minister of Supplies and Services.

Hollingshead, A., & Redlich, F. (1958). *Social class and mental illness: A community study.* New York: Wiley.

Kirby, M. (2005). Mental health reform for Canada in the 21st century: Getting there from here. *Canadian Public Policy, 31,* S5–11, Special Electronic Supplement on Mental Health Reform for the 21st Century. Online at <www.economics.ca/cpp/en/specialissue.php>.

Krupa, T., Eastabrook, S., Hern, L., Lee, D., North, R., Percy, K., Von Briesen, B., & Wing, G. (2005). How do people who receive Assertive Community Treatment experience this service? *Psychiatric Rehabilitation Journal, 29*(1), 18–24.

Krupa, T., Kirsch, B., Gewurtz, R., & Cockburn, L. (2005). Improving the employment prospects of people with serious mental illness: Five challenges for a national mental health strategy. *Canadian Public Policy, 31,* S59–63, Special Electronic Supplement on Mental Health Reform for the 21st Century. Online at <www.economics.ca/cpp/en/specialissue.php>.

Kulka, R.A., Veroff, J., & Douvan, E. (1979). Social class and the use of professional help for personal problems: 1957 and 1976. *Journal of Health and Social Behavior, 20,* 2–17.

Kyrouz, E.M., Humphreys, K., & Loomis, C. (2003). A review of the effectiveness of self-help/mutual aid groups. In B.J. White & E.J. Madara (Eds.), *A review of research on the effectiveness of self-help/mutual aid groups* (7th ed.) (pp. 71–86). Cedar Knolls, NJ: American Self-Help Clearinghouse.

Lafave, H., & Vanden Ham, M.T. (1979). Mental health in Saskatchewan: A look at the past, present, and future. *Canada's Mental Health, 27*(1), 13–16.

Lakaski, C.M., Wilmot, V., Lips, T.J., & Brown, M. (1993). Canada. In D.R. Kemp (Ed.), *International handbook on mental health policy* (pp. 45–66). Westport, CN: Greenwood Press.

Latimer, E. (2005a). Community-based care for people with severe mental illness in Canada. *International Journal of Law and Psychiatry, 28*(5), 561–573.

Latimer, E. (2005b). Organizational implications of promoting effective evidence-based interventions for people with severe mental illness. *Canadian Public Policy, 31,* S47–52, Special Electronic Supplement on Mental Health Reform for the 21st Century. Online at <www.economics.ca/cpp/en/specialissue.php>.

Lewis, D.A., Shadish, W.R., & Lurigio, A.J. (1989). Policies of inclusion and the mentally ill: Long-term care in a new environment. *Journal of Social Issues, 45,* 183–186.

Lieber, H.M. (1993). *Multicultural access within a national organization: Report on a Canadian Mental Health Association Initiative.* Vancouver: Canadian Mental Health Association/British Columbia Division.

MacNaughton, E. (1991). *Community reinvestment—Vol. 2: Towards rebalancing Canada's mental health system.* Toronto: Canadian Mental Health Association/National Office.

McCubbin, M. (1994). Deinstitutionalization: The illusion of disillusion. *Journal of Mind and Behavior, 15*(1/2), 35–54.

McCubbin, M., & Cohen, D. (1996). Extremely unbalanced: Interest divergence and power disparities between clients and psychiatry. *International Journal of Law and Psychiatry, 19,* 1–25.

McCubbin, M., & Cohen, D. (1999). A systemic and valued-based approach to strategic reform of the mental health system. *Health Care Analysis, 7,* 1–21.

References Mercier, C., & White, D. (1994). Mental health policy in Québec: Challenges for an integrated system. In L.L. Bachrach, P. Goering, & D. Wasylenki (Eds.), *Mental health care in Canada* (pp. 41–52). San Francisco, CA: Jossey-Bass.

Morin, P. (1992). Québec's mental health policy: A sign of hope or a false start? *Canada's Mental Health, 40*(1), 19–24.

Morrow, M. (2004a). *Mainstreaming women's mental health: Creating a national mental health strategy.* Vancouver: BC Centre of Excellence in Women's Health.

Morrow, M. (2004b). Mental health reform, economic globalization, and the practice of citizenship. *Canadian Journal of Community Mental Health, 23*(2), 39–50.

Morrow, M. (in press). Women's voices matter: Creating women-centred mental health policy. In M. Morrow, O. Hankivsky, & C. Varcoe (Eds.), *Women's health in Canada: Critical perspectives on theory and policy.* Toronto: University of Toronto Press.

Nelson, G., Lord, J., & Ochocka, J. (2001). *Shifting the paradigm in community mental health: Towards empowerment and community.* Toronto: University of Toronto Press.

Nelson, G., Potasznik, H., & Bennett, E.M. (1983). Primary prevention: Another perspective. *Canadian Journal of Community Mental Health, 2*(1), 3–12.

Nelson, G., & Prilleltensky, I. (Eds.). (2005). *Community psychology: In pursuit of liberation and well-being.* Basingstoke, UK: Macmillan.

Nelson, G., Prilleltensky, I., Laurendeau, M.-C., & Powell, B. (1996). The prevention of mental health problems in Canada: A survey of provincial policies, structures, and programs. *Canadian Psychology, 37,* 161–172.

Nelson, G., Prilleltensky, I., & Peters, R. DeV. (in press). Prevention and mental health promotion in the community. In P. Firestone & D. Dozois (Eds.), *Abnormal psychology: Perspectives* (3rd ed.). Scarborough, ON: Prentice-Hall.

Nelson, G., Westhues, A., & MacLeod, J. (2003, December). A meta-analysis of longitudinal research on preschool prevention programs for children. *Prevention and Treatment, 6,* online at <www.journals.apa.org/prevention/volume6/toc -dec18–03.html>.

Niles, E., & Ross, K. (1992). Putting policy in practice: Mental health in New Brunswick. *Canada's Mental Health, 40*(1), 15–19.

Offord, D., Boyle, M., Campbell, D., Cochrane, J., Goering, P., Lin, E., Rhodes, A., & Wong, M. (1994). *Mental health in Ontario: Selected findings from the Mental Health Supplement to the Ontario Health Survey.* Toronto: Ministry of Health.

Ontario Ministry of Health and Long-term Care (2004). *Making a difference: Ontario's Community Mental Health Evaluation Initiative.* Toronto: Centre for Addiction and Mental Health, Canadian Mental Health Association/Ontario Division, Ontario Mental Health Foundation, and Ontario Ministry of Health and Long-term Care.

Pomeroy, E., Trainor, J., & Pape, B. (2002). Citizens shaping policy: The Canadian Mental Health Association's framework for support project. *Canadian Psychology, 43,* 11–20.

Reaume, G. (2000). *Remembrance of patients past: Patient life at the Toronto Hospital for the Insane, 1870–1940.* Oxford: Oxford University Press.

Redko, C., Durbin, J., Wasylenki, D., & Krupa, T. (2004). Participant perspectives on satisfaction with Assertive Community Treatment. *Psychiatric Rehabilitation Journal, 27*(3), 283–286.

References

Reville, D. (2005). Mental health reform: Still saying the same thing after all these years. *Canadian Public Policy, 31,* S65–68, Special Electronic Supplement on Mental Health Reform for the 21st Century. Online at <www.economics.ca/cpp/en/specialissue.php>.

Rochefort, D.A. (1992). More lessons, of a different kind: Canadian mental health policy in comparative perspective. *Hospital and Community Psychiatry, 43,* 1083–1090.

Rochefort, D.A. (1993). *From poorhouses to homelessness: Policy analysis and mental health care.* Westport, CT: Auburn House.

Scheyett, A.M., & McCarthy, E. (in press). Women and men with mental illnesses: Voicing differing service needs. *Affilia.*

Schmidt, G. (2000). Barriers to recovery in a First Nations community. *Canadian Journal of Community Mental Health, 19* (2), 75–87.

Schofield, W. (1964). *Psychotherapy: The purchase of friendship.* Englewood Cliffs, NJ: Prentice-Hall.

Scull, A.T. (1977). *Decarceration: Community treatment and the deviant—A radical view.* Englewood Cliffs, NJ: Prentice-Hall.

Sealy, P., & Whitehead, P.C. (2004). Forty years of deinstitutionalization of psychiatric services in Canada: An empirical assessment. *Canadian Journal of Psychiatry, 49,* 249–257.

Shera, W., Aviram, U., Healy, B., & Ramon, S. (2002). Mental health system reform: A multi country comparison. *Social Work in Health Care, 35* (1/2), 547–575.

Simmons, H.G. (1990). *Unbalanced: Mental health policy in Ontario, 1930–1989.* Toronto: Wall and Thompson.

Solomon, P. (2004). Peer support/peer provided services: Underlying processes, benefits, and critical ingredients. *Psychiatric Rehabilitation Journal, 27,* 392–401.

Spindel, P. (2000). Polar opposites: Empowerment philosophy and Assertive Community Treatment (ACT). *Ethical Human Sciences and Services: An International Journal of Critical Inquiry, 2,* 93–100.

Statistics Canada (2005). *Canadian statistics—Tables by subject: Population and demography.* Online at <http://www40.statcan.ca/l01/cst01/popula.htm>.

Stein, L.I., & Test, M.A. (1980). Alternative to mental hospital treatment: 1. Conceptual model, treatment program, and clinical evaluation. *Archives of General Psychiatry, 37,* 392–397.

Stephens, T., & Joubert, N. (2001). The economic burden of mental health problems. *Chronic Diseases in Canada, 22.* Online at <www.phac-aspc.gc.ca/publi cat/cdic-mcc/22–1/d_e.html>.

Swindle, R., Heller, K., Pescosolido, B., & Kikuzawa, S. (2000). Responses to nervous breakdowns in American over a 40-year period: Mental health policy implications. *American Psychologist, 55,* 740–749.

Sylvestre, J., Nelson, G., Durbin, J., George, L., Aubry, T., & Ollenberg, M. (in press). *Housing for people with serious mental illness: Challenges for system-level development.*

Szasz, T.S. (1961). *The myth of mental illness: Foundations of a theory of personal conduct.* New York: Dell.

Townsend, E. (1998). *Good intentions overruled: A critique of empowerment in the routine organization of mental health services.* Toronto: University of Toronto Press.

References   Trainor, J., Pape, B., & Pomeroy, E. (1997). Critical challenges for mental health policy. *Canadian Review of Social Policy, 39,* 55–63.

Trainor, J., Pomeroy, E., & Pape, B. (Eds.). (1999). *Building a framework for support: A community development approach to mental health policy.* Toronto: Canadian Mental Health Association / National Office.

Trainor, J., Shepherd, M., Boydell, K.M., Leff, A., & Crawford, E. (1997). Beyond the service paradigm: The impact and implications of consumer/survivor initiatives. *Psychiatric Rehabilitation Journal, 21,* 132–140.

Trainor, J., & Tremblay, J. (1992). Consumer/survivor businesses in Ontario: Challenging the rehabilitation model. *Canadian Journal of Community Mental Health, 11*(2), 65–71.

Tsemberis, S., & Eisenberg, R.F. (2000). Pathways to housing: Supported housing for street-dwelling homeless individuals with psychiatric disabilities. *Psychiatric Services, 51,* 487–493.

Vincent, N., Walker, J.R., & Katz, A. (in press). Self-help approaches in primary care. In P.L. Watkins & G.L. Clum (Eds.), *Handbook of self-help therapies.* Mahway, NJ: Lawrence Erlbaum Associates.

Wasylenki, D., Goering, P., & MacNaughton, E. (1994). Planning mental health services: Background and key issues. In L.L. Bachrach, P. Goering, & D. Wasylenki (Eds.), *Mental health care in Canada* (pp. 21–29). San Francisco, CA: Jossey-Bass.

Weitz, D. (1984). "On our own": A self-help model. In D.P. Lumsden (Ed.), *Community mental health action: Primary prevention programming in Canada* (pp. 312–320). Ottawa: Canadian Public Health Association.

Wilton, R. (2004). Putting policy into practice? Poverty and people with serious mental illness. *Social Science and Medicine, 58,* 25–39.

Lea Caragata

Homelessness touches the lives of many Canadians, and most urban Canadians have some direct experience with homeless people. It might be passing a homeless person on a street corner, or exchanging an occasional word with a panhandler; however, current levels of homelessness also mean that those on the streets or without adequate housing are increasingly likely to be the brother, sister, son, or daughter of someone you know. Research done in Kitchener-Waterloo found a surprisingly high rate of personal connections to the homeless among those randomly selected to participate in a focus group on the issue (Jeffrey, 1999). It is widely acknowledged that there are homeless people and that they exist in greater numbers than ever. This is perhaps the limit of a common understanding of the issue. Why homelessness occurs and its causes are a matter of intense debate with important implications for public policy. This chapter will discuss these issues and their policy ramifications.

Notwithstanding a debate about cause, there has been strong societal agreement that homelessness is a social problem. This accord probably stems from the frequency of contact between those who are homeless and the rest of the population. The Canadian public is unused to being confronted with our social ills—the problems of the poor, domestic violence, slum housing—as they are usually removed from our everyday world. Because contact with the homeless is largely unavoidable, public discomfort may explain the consequent public concern. This, as we shall further discuss, does not necessarily translate into the policy responses that might address the problem. There is an unusual level of agreement among the public, governments, and homeless people themselves that homelessness is a problem. Given the nature of such accord, one might justifiably ask why so little has been achieved in resolving the issue since it first came to the public's attention over fifteen years ago (Burt, 1992; City of Toronto, 1995; Dear & Wolch, 1987; Greve, 1971; McLaughlin, 1987). This query returns us to the question of cause, because our understanding of the nature and severity of the problem determines the scope and nature of the policy response. If we incorrectly assess the cause, if our commitment is limited and/or our willingness to spend is weak or inconsistent, we will have (as in the case of homelessness) policies and programs at every

level of government and a continuation of the problem. Such is the policy
minefield related to those who are homeless.

Social Problems as Social Constructions

Before identifying the homeless, a point about how we construct and define
a social problem is in order. Blanco (1994), Hacking (1999), and many others
have discussed the social construction of social issues, so these debates will
not be replicated here. It is, however, important to note that disagreements
over who counts among the homeless are not mere quibbles over numbers;
these debates say much about our social expectations and the ideologies on
which they are based. Our constructions include more than the "facts" of the
issue. Facts are determined by the nature of the inquiry into a problem, which
is in part determined by our suppositions about it. In our suppositions, we
have various ideas or notions about an issue that may or may not be strictly
relevant. Over time, a framework of associations, images, and attitudes cluster around a term and reinforce its ideological reproduction. In this way,
social problems become "metaphors" (Blanco, 1994). We think we know what
we mean by homelessness, and this causes, as Blanco suggests, "goals and
strategies for action to be quickly accepted, often by-passing a comparison of
causal structures, functional, temporal and other aspects of the situations"
(1994, p. 185). Because a term comes to have a varying and often pejorative
subtext, the term "deconstruction" has come to signal a de-layering or un-
masking of these other meanings.

As an illustration of the social (and political) significance of our definitions,
if we include among the homeless welfare recipients who spend more than
30% of their incomes on housing (and are therefore at least statistically at
risk of homelessness), we acknowledge that such a level of impoverishment
is a social issue and therefore a matter of public, rather than individual or
private, concern. The kind of definition we employ directs us toward certain
kinds of policy choices and obscures others. For example, it appears that
street homelessness causes greater public concern than "doubling up," that
is, people sharing accommodation. Why? Is our concern only for the welfare
of those on the street? Or is there a mixture of concern for them and middle-
class self-interest in not wishing to confront beggars as we leave a store or
restaurant? Making efforts to genuinely appraise what drives the identification of an issue as a social problem helps to deconstruct or tease out unspo-
ken associations, such as that between street homelessness and alcoholism
or—in another social policy area—associations between teenage pregnancy
and welfare dependency. Such associations affect our policy choices; if we
think young women are having babies in order to be eligible for welfare, we
will put in place a different set of welfare regulations (as has occurred in the
United States and more recently, in Canada) than we would if we believed that
teen pregnancies are unplanned. If we think that the street homeless are alco-
holics, we may decide that these people are undeserving and offer fewer serv-

ices or even punitive responses such as vagrancy laws. Alternatively, services may be oriented to treatment (which assumes individual pathology) rather than addressing structural failings. While the evidence of a linkage between alcoholism and homelessness is not so obvious in the Canadian case, in Finland the word for "homeless" combines two other Finnish words meaning "lacquer" (drunk by people on the street) and "man" (Glasser, 1994). Aware of the problems engendered by such language, the Finnish government made an attempt to de-label the homeless. Summa (quoted in Glasser, 1994) refers to the new language as "coded." The associations with alcoholism are no longer explicit but still endure, which likely remains the case in Canada as well as in the United States.

Both underpinning and deriving from these associations are our notions of the deserving and undeserving poor. These distinctions are especially influential in policy choices with regard to the homeless. Given the presence of shelters and other services (but not housing), the street homeless are often perceived as "choosing" to stay on the streets, rather than stay in available hostels. The debate is falsely based on the notion that the choice to be on the street is freely made, whereas in fact the "choice" is severely constrained by the very limited range of available options. The following is illustrative of the policy direction that can result when homelessness is viewed as self-caused, a matter of "choice": "We have travelled in the wrong direction for far too long. We must face the reality that vagrancy is against the law and proceed accordingly with formulating public policy. People do not have a right to live on our streets and in our parks" (San Francisco mayoralty candidate, quoted in Daly, 1996, p. 179).

The Government of Ontario provided another example of a punitive policy response in introducing the Safe Streets Act (1999). The Act banned panhandling in certain circumstances and also prohibited "squeegee" kids from approaching motorists at busy intersections. These policies (and there are similar ones at various levels of court challenge in other Canadian jurisdictions, although in Ontario the law has thus far been upheld [Canadian Civil Liberties Association, 2005]) acknowledge more directly that part of the policy goal is saving "taxpayers" from the nuisance of beggars and homeless people. Policies of this nature are in stark contrast to those facilitating social housing construction (which acknowledge structural or at least market failures).

Who Is Homeless and Why?

Definitions

Canadian governments and other key housing players utilize "core housing need" as a common measure of the number of people in Canada who have a housing "problem" of significant severity. Core housing need measures the adequacy of the household unit (having a full bathroom and not in need of major repairs); its suitability (having sufficient bedrooms, generally no more than two people per room and no sharing of bedrooms between opposite-sex children or between a parent and a child older than twelve years); and affordability (shelter and utility costs are not more than 30% of household income) (Canada Mortgage and Housing Corporation, 1996). Households whose housing does not meet one or more of these standards and whose income is insufficient to obtain housing without such deficits are considered to be in core housing need. The definition and its application are generally considered adequate for assessing housing need in Canada. As will be evident, it is possible to have an adequate government-sanctioned assessment tool and still experience the sort of definitional debate revealed below. Such disjuncture is a consequence in part of the many players who are involved in problem definitions, technical specifications, needs assessments, treasury allocations, policy development, and the raw politics that inform all of these decisions.

In spite of the seemingly clear determination of "core housing need," an enormous debate continues over where to draw the definitional line. The British literature makes such distinctions as single homelessness or "sleeping rough," referring to street homelessness (Pleace, 1998), while the Canadian and American literature (Daly, 1996; Springer, Mars, & Dennison, 1998; Turcotte & Renaud, 2004) identifies categories like hostel users, people who live on the street, and those "at risk," or alternatively, "absolute" or "relative" to describe who is being spoken of among the homeless. People who live on the street are one of the most difficult groups to count. They are not generally amenable to being counted, nor is it easy to determine real numbers. A significant number of people whom many would regard as homeless live in shelters for what are usually two-week residencies. While most engaged in defining the homeless include hostel users among that group, there is a neo-conservative view that hostel users are not without shelter and are already in receipt of services. Even more contentious and hard to count are those who are "doubling up," staying with friends or family, often on a rotational long-term basis. One such family of six reported staying with friends on this basis for several months, although they acknowledged, "it can't last" (Caragata & Hardie, 1999). Another group that homeless advocates claim must be counted are those at imminent risk of homelessness. To be assessed as "at risk," one must meet the federal government's own definition of core housing need. Risk is assessed on the basis of the cost of the housing relative to the family income, in situations of a pending eviction, or where there are significant rent arrears. Advocates argue that people in these "at risk" situations have often been homeless before, and periods of housing and homelessness become cyclical as each housing situation is likely to be unaffordable or inadequate in the long run, triggering a further incident of homelessness. Clearly, this definitional move dramatically increases the numbers identified as homeless. Another group sometimes included in this "at risk" category are those who have qualified to be on waiting lists for subsidized housing but have not yet received a housing unit. Advocates argue that because such applicants must demonstrate both financial and housing need, they are at risk of homelessness until they obtain secure, affordable housing. Recent data confirm that a high percentage of social housing applicants are currently homeless, have been homeless before, and/or have housing situations that put them at imminent risk (Caragata & Hardie, 1999). Thus, social housing waiting lists are a reliable way to tally at least a portion of the "at risk" group. Who Is Homeless and Why?

In the UK, there has been a focus on identifying who the homeless are in order to ascertain eligibility for services. The definition is broad and inclusive, is written in an accessible manner, and even delineates the elements of being at risk that can constitute homelessness (Shelter, 2005). This represents some of the changes being made in the European context to address homelessness, including fully acknowledging its differing forms. In a similar vein, there are emerging efforts to clarify our understanding of cause. Oberlander and Fallick suggest that:

> homelessness involves more than simply the presence or absence of shelter. The search for the nature and scale of homelessness in Canada rests on the definitional problems. Is homelessness an issue of poverty? Or employment? Is it an issue of discrimination? Or of location? Of education? Or is it primarily an issue of measurement? Varied evidence increasingly points to the answer: It is all of these factors and more; no single causal factor can be used to define homelessness exclusively or successfully. (quoted in Layton, 2000, p. 32)

This view, while instructive, has not resolved questions of who is homeless and how many people are indeed homeless (using whatever definition might be in vogue) in any region at a given time. Reliable estimates of the numbers of homeless are difficult to obtain because of potential double counting and the logistical issues of counting those who are doubling up and living on the streets. However, many efforts have been made to profile the homeless in Canada, and a brief summary of these data will follow.

Much of what follows in this review of homelessness in Canada will be, if not familiar, then at least not surprising. The category of homeless people encompasses the full range of human needs in all their variation. Perhaps the only constant among the homeless is the absence of a secure affordable home. Most homeless people are poor; as a group, they are less well educated; sometimes they have histories of abuse; some have addictions or mental health issues, while others may have been in trouble with the law. These issues act in combination with the largely private housing market and very limited availability of low-end rental accommodation to explain most homelessness in Canada. This is a critical point: many people with personal or behavioural issues or problems do not become homeless if their housing is secure and readily affordable for their income level. Rather, competition in a tight housing market renders many individuals who were already vulnerable unable to compete. In the absence of a housing safety net, homelessness results.

More Definitions and Categorization: Attempts to Understand

A number of major studies have been done across Canada over the last 10 years that provide a picture of homelessness. Beginning in Toronto, the Mayor's Action Task Force on Homelessness submitted a report in 1999 and funded several research studies. More recently, also in Ontario, the Ontario Non-Profit Housing Association (ONPHA) has updated their earlier study done in conjunction with the Cooperative Housing Federation of Canada, Ontario Region (CHF). The 2005 study, "Where's Home: A Picture of Housing Needs in Ontario" claims that in spite of improvement in rental housing production and higher vacancy rates in most Ontario housing markets, there is still insufficient affordable rental housing to meet the need. British Columbia has completed a large review of issues related to homelessness, and the cities of Ottawa and Edmonton have also done studies. Nationally, the Federation of Canadian Municipalities (FCM) also completed a report on homelessness. The number of studies supports the assertion that the problem is one of significance and concern to a broad range of interests.

Conservative estimates from 1998 suggest there were at least 200,000 homeless people in Canada—people with no private spaces in which to live, people existing day to day, twenty-four hours a day, in public places. While there are no very reliable new estimates, all of the evidence points to this number having increased. In Ontario, rental housing construction has faced a serious decline, in spite of recent very modest gains. There were only 3,600 rental unit construction starts in 2004, compared with an average of more than 12,000 per year in the early 1990s. In this same period, Ontario also lost over 14,000 rental units to conversions and demolitions (ONPHA, 2005). In Toronto, estimates suggest that the number of homeless people likely ranges between 60,000 and 70,000 people (CBC, 2004). These estimates are supported by the fact that almost 32,000 different individuals used shelters in Toronto in 2002, an increase of over 21% since 1990 (City of Toronto, 2003). At the end of October 2001, hostel occupancy levels were reported to be 97% (Toronto Disaster Relief Committee [TDRC], 2001); effectively all shelter beds were full.

The fastest-growing groups of homeless in Toronto are women and children. There were more than 122,426 households (perhaps representing as many as 300,000 people) on the waiting list for social housing in Ontario, and over 43% of those waiting were families (ONPHA, 2005). In Montreal, estimates suggest there are more than 15,000 homeless people and almost 25% of tenant households pay more than 50% of their income in rent. In Canada almost one million households are paying more than half of their incomes on rent (National Homelessness Initiative, 2004).

Calgary is one of the only Canadian cities to do an annual count of the homeless. From 1996 to 1998 there was an increase of 61% in the number of homeless, and the number doubled between 1994 and 2000 (National Homelessness Initiative, 2004). Rental housing in Calgary is also disappearing at an alarming rate. In Vancouver, more than 2,000 people sleep on the street every night, an increase of more than 100% between 2002 and 2005. Estimates place over 126,000 people as homeless or at risk of homelessness in the Greater Vancouver area. Vancouver's spiralling housing costs, exacerbated by a paucity of rental and social housing construction, are contributing to increasing homelessness (Greater Vancouver Regional District, 2005). Who Is Homeless and Why?

Homelessness is generally higher in urban settings, although it is not only a big city problem. Barrie, Ontario, is a case in point. An hour north of Toronto, Barrie has become a commuter town and one of the fastest-growing communities in Ontario. Although its vacancy rate has recently eased from 1 to 2%, there has been a ten-fold increase in the number of people using shelter beds since 1995 (ONPHA, 2005; Layton, 2000, p. 80). The small city of Peterborough east of Toronto has had a 100% increase in people occupying shelter beds during the same period and unlike in other rental markets where vacancy rates have eased slightly, the vacancy rate has remained very low at only 1.4% (ONPHA, 2005). Overall, vacancy rates have improved in many cities across Canada, largely due to low mortgage interest rates, which have enabled many renters to purchase homes and condos. In spite of this, rents have not declined in many rental markets, with 75% of Ontario renters having endured rent increases beyond the rate of inflation (ONPHA, 2005).

Estimating the numbers of homeless is, of course, subject to the variety of issues previously discussed. Homelessness is often hidden. If there is less social tolerance, homeless people are more likely to stay out of busy commercial areas. If, however, there is tolerance and even sympathy, the prospect of handouts makes it more likely that homeless people will be visible in busy neighbourhoods. The absence of obvious street sleepers is not an indication that a community does not have a homelessness problem.

Keyes (as cited in Mulroy & Lane, 1992) classifies the homeless population into a continuum of three major groups that accord with most analyses of homelessness and identification of who is homeless. The first group is "needs housing only," the economic homeless, those who cannot compete in a private rental market to secure adequate affordable housing. Homelessness in this case derives from both an income and a housing stock problem. Increasing the income of one individual will enable him or her to compete, but overall the presence of a group of economically homeless suggests that there is not enough rental housing at the low end of the market. Developers concede that this is a group in whom they have little interest (Daly, 1996, p. 184), because the profitability of low-end market rental properties is poor. For this reason, all of the industrialized countries have had some level of postwar government intervention in the housing market for low-income people.

The second group Keyes identifies are the "situational homeless," who require housing but also face additional difficulties such as domestic violence or medical problems. For some members of this group, homelessness was likely triggered by an acute incident, and so they may not fit the profile of those we usually associate with homelessness. During some previous research (Caragata & Hardie, 1999), I interviewed a sixty-five-year-old grand-mother who had lived all her married life in a home owned with her now-deceased spouse. He had died suddenly and she had no financial compe-tence ("I could always rely on him"). By accepting the well-meaning but ill-advised help of a neighbour, she lost her house and was living in a shelter. She was too humiliated to make contact with her family. Such stories are more common than might be imagined. There are many people who cope quite well as long as nothing extreme happens, but when and if it does, they have few resources—personal, social, or financial. For many members of this group, once homeless, the resources necessary to secure and return to per-manent housing are difficult to marshal. In a very tight rental market, these individuals can find it very difficult to escape from homelessness as land-lords can pick and choose among prospective tenants and inevitably select those with more resources. (The targeted services discussed later are useful for this group. However, the availability of housing stock remains an issue.)

Keyes's third group is the "chronic homeless," who include those with chronic mental health and substance abuse issues. As Mulroy and Lane (1992) point out, this latter group's presence among the homeless is quite directly attributable to state deinstitutionalization policies and the lack of viable com-munity-based alternatives. They are often the very visible street homeless.

Profiles of the Homeless

Following are brief summary descriptions of some population groups who together comprise the homeless. Hundreds of books and journal articles pro-vide in-depth analyses of each subgroup. These descriptions are meant to show the scope of homelessness and to highlight some of the less-visible populations (Glasser, 1994). I have not provided more detail on the single homeless because most often they are who we assume the homeless to be. As discussed, our constructions of homelessness and the associations we have on hearing the word usually evoke a picture of a homeless man, often with substance abuse issues. Appreciating the pervasiveness and scale of the issue requires a fuller understanding of its impact on other sectors of the popula-tion.

People of Colour

In Canada, which prides itself on being multicultural and at least quasi-egalitarian, homelessness is not colour-blind. As in most industrialized countries, people of colour make up a disproportionate percentage of the homeless population. In the United States, Blacks and Hispanics are dispro-portionately represented. This correspondence between homelessness and people of colour is also apparent in the countries of Western Europe, although there it is an immigrant (largely from the countries of North Africa) rather than native-born population who are homeless and marginalized. In Canada, most of the people of colour disproportionately affected are Aboriginal, but the degree of racialization is much the same. Using the Canadian Mortgage and Housing Corporation's (CMHC) definition of core housing need, 52% of Aboriginal households fall into this category compared to only 32% of non-Aboriginal households (CMHC, 1996). One quarter of on-reserve households lack a functioning bathroom. In urban areas, Aboriginal households are almost twice as likely as non-Aboriginal households to be in core need (CMHC, 1996, p. 2). Aboriginal peoples are part of that same stream of rural-urban migration that is occurring worldwide. In 1961, only 14% of all Aboriginals in Canada were urban dwellers; by 1981, it was more than half. Because of the poverty endemic in Native communities, most of those relocating to Canada's urban centres (primarily the prairie cities) are poor. Consider, for example, the 50,000 Aboriginals in Winnipeg. According to Murphy (2000), they have the worst housing (three quarters have problems with housing conditions), the lowest incomes (of which half is spent on rent), and are frequent victims of discrimination by landlords. Estimates suggest that half of Winnipeg's homeless are Native. In all of Canada's prairie cities, night after night, Aboriginal peoples are dramatically overrepresented among the homeless.

It is not only Aboriginal peoples who experience discrimination based on notions of "race." In recent research examining social housing waiting-list applications, immigrants felt they experienced discrimination in trying to obtain market housing. One man said, "No matter whether I see the apartment first, [or] how I fill in the application, they always call back and say, 'Sorry, the apartment has gone to another applicant.'" While many applicants appeared reluctant to claim that they felt discriminated against, one man said gently, "It's the same in my country—we put my country's people first" (Caragata & Hardie, 1999). The need for larger units and the desirability of living in a community with others from their native country create further obstacles for many immigrants and refugees in the housing market. These issues are in addition to the struggle they face as a result of differences in language, customs, and culture (such as family size), as well as discrimination.

Further data have been well presented by Murphy (2000) and Daly (1996), as well as the more extensive work on issues of "race" and poverty. In summary, in most White-dominated societies, a disproportionate number of those experiencing homelessness are the racialized "other."

Families with Children

Caplow, Bahr, and Sternberg (quoted in Glasser, 1994) cite a classic conception of homelessness as a "detachment from society." Glasser (1994, p. 84) contrasts this with the notion of family: "the very act of being a family is an affirmation of the ability to bond." Glasser's view and the data on homeless families confirm that the issue of family homelessness derives from poverty and inadequate affordable housing. Homeless families have reason to remain

Profiles
of the
Homeless

less visible. In addition to trying to ensure some level of safety and security for their children—which is not usually possible on busy thoroughfares—they also face the constant threat of losing their children to child protection authorities (Caragata & Hardie, 1999; Glasser, 1994). In the United States, the phrase the "new homeless" is often used to distinguish homeless families from the "old" or traditional skid-row homeless male (Glasser, 1994). There is widespread agreement that the cause of homelessness for families with young children is primarily attributable to the increased numbers of poor, usually woman-headed households and to the lack of affordable low-income housing (Blau, 1992; Choi & Synder, 1999; Rossi, 1989). Thus, families remain largely in the category of the "deserving" poor, and we are more likely to suggest macro-level issues as the causes of this widespread and growing rupture in family life. This macro-analysis, if it might be called that, is very superficial as our approaches to family homelessness have differed only marginally from programs for singles.

In all three of Keyes's categories of homelessness (quoted in Mulroy & Lane, 1992), the numbers of mothers with children are increasing. Canadian studies have found this to be the fastest-growing group among the homeless (Caragata & Hardie, 1999; Golden et al., 1999). In a review of social housing waiting-list data in Toronto, 48% of all applicants were families with children. The number of applicant households tripled between the periods 1991–93 and 1994–96. In 2005, 64,000 people remain on a wait-list for subsidized housing (Lewington, 2005). These data from Toronto mirror the circumstances of low-income families across Canada, in the United States, and to a lesser degree, in Western Europe. In Canada, the income levels of Canadian women show that for single-mother-led families, obtaining affordable housing and other necessities of life will be extremely difficult. Over 90% of poor lone parents are women (National Council of Welfare, 2002) and 15.1% of Canadian families are headed by lone mothers (Statistics Canada, 2006). Almost 40% of poor children in Canada live in a single-parent, mother-led family (Freiler & Cerny, 1998). This number has grown from 31% in 1980. Together, women and children account for 70% of Canada's poor (Canadian Centre for Policy Alternatives, 1998, p. 33).

These statistics have both a personal face and enduring implications. Children suffer from homelessness in ways that will affect their adult lives through poor nutrition, stress, transience, and poor school attendance. As well, their lives tend to be less carefully supervised, thus putting them at greater risk of accidents and abuse. One single mother reported having to leave her children alone while she attended a community college program. She had asked for help and been refused because her program was "too intensive" (Caragata & Hardie, 1999). A family who, while homeless, lived in a shelter, reported that

> the whole family found it easier—no constant worry over rent. We could just live. There was no space, we were on top of each other, but there

was less stress. I knew I'd get the money for food and we could spend it on food.... When I [have] got a place, like now, I always worry, "Don't buy so much, don't buy meat, save the money for the rent," and there's never enough [money] for both [food and rent]. I feel like I'd rather die than tell my kids there isn't any more [food].

Deprivation also extends to homeless parents as they routinely give up things—including food—for the sake of their children. Burt and Cohen (1989) report that adults in homeless families consistently eat less and eat less well than single homeless people. In their study, a full 88% of the homeless adults with children were women.

This points to an important and less well understood aspect of home-lessness. Because those "sleeping rough" are more likely to be men, women's homelessness is often hidden. However, women's gendered and precarious labour market roles (Caragata, 2003; Vosko, 2002), their continued economic and social reliance on male partners and their continuing victimization from partner abuse cause them, and their children, to be among the most vulner-able to homelessness, as most hostel and evictions data demonstrate (Centre for Equality Rights in Accommodation, 2005).

Two additional subgroups among the homeless warrant mention. Due to space limitations, it is not possible to describe appropriately the growing numbers of seniors and youth who are homeless. Welfare state retrench-ment, combined with a very tight housing market, have forced seniors into unprecedented levels of homelessness. In the case of youth, causal factors also include welfare state retrenchment; most provinces deny benefits to those under eighteen and to "single employables" beyond that age. Family breakdown—fleeing violence or abuse—is often cited as the reason youth leave home. A possible explanation for the increasing numbers of youth on the street is that low-income families face heightened stress from their increased poverty—directly or indirectly forcing their children to leave home—an eerie and not-too-distant parallel with poor families in Brazil or India.

Money and Housing Stock

Whatever the divergence of opinion about the causes of homelessness, there is agreement that homelessness is a problem of, in part, affordability related to housing stock and the housing market, which determines what "stock" is available and for how much money. A number of factors combine to make rental housing beyond what is affordable for many people.

Declining incomes for those at lowest income levels

As we have seen, in Vancouver one in four tenants pays more than 50% of his or her income on rent (Layton, 2000). In 1996, 44% of Ontario tenants had an affordability problem (defined as those paying more than 30% of their income on housing). This situation has worsened continually over the past four census periods (Canada Mortgage and Housing Corporation as quoted in ONPHA & CHF, 1999). An impact of the "new economy" has been the much-reported polarization of jobs and incomes (Sassen, 1998). For those with low incomes, these changes have occurred in combination with significant welfare benefit cuts (Yalnizyan, 1997), further reducing the incomes of the already poor.

Rising rents

Rents go up with increased demand when there are fewer rental units on the market and more people wanting them, which happens when potential buyers can't afford to buy and there is an influx of new residents (growth and new household formation). Average rents in Ontario have increased about 20% since 1995 (Shapcott, 2001).

Reduced vacancy rates

Vacancy rates are very low in many urban centres across Canada because of a combination of high demand and limited supply. They are particularly low in Ontario—below 3%—and 3% or greater vacancy is considered a marker of a healthy rental market. In Toronto, Canada's largest city, the vacancy rate has fluctuated from a low of 1% (ONPHA & CHF, 1999) to a high of 4.3% in 2004. It has since fallen to about 3.5%; however the average rent for a one-bedroom apartment remains high at almost $900 and is unchanged over the past year (CMHC, 2005).

High prices for purchased homes

If the price of home ownership goes up because house prices, interest rates, and the costs of borrowing rise, fewer people leave the rental market. Thus, the rising cost of home ownership affects the rental stock available. Because landlords discriminate against the poor, especially those on social assistance, middle-income earners do better in a tight rental market; landlords will choose tenants with more resources. Builders cite increasing building code standards as one reason for increased housing costs. They query whether we can really afford the construction standards now in place (Murphy, 2000).

Declining rental stock construction

In Canada, 30,000 rental units were begun in 1986. In 1999, only 7,000 units were begun in all urban centres across the country (Murphy, 2000, p. 104). In Ontario, rental housing construction comprised 27% of all housing starts in 1989 and only 6% in 1998 (ONPHA & CHF, 1999). The reasons for this dramatic decline are complex. Murphy likens it to a strike, private sector developers citing income tax changes, lot levies, property tax issues, rent controls, and increasing building code variance and standards as all contributing to an environment in which investment in rental accommodation is simply not profitable. In reviewing these issues, Murphy concludes that although the building industry's lobby group, the Canadian Homebuilders Association, is pressing for government reductions in regulation and taxation, they make no promises about the private sector's ability to provide rental housing for low-income people (Murphy, 2000).

Non-profit housing construction stops

The year 1945 marked the beginning of the construction of public housing in Canada with the Wartime Housing Act. Thousands of small "wartime houses" can be found in cities across the country. These were followed by the now infamous large-scale public projects such as Regent Park in Toronto. In 1973, there was a further change to the National Housing Act to enable the construction of non-profit housing co-operatives. The 1970s and early 1980s saw the development of many municipal non-profit housing developers and the growth of small non-governmental organizations (NGO) building specialized social housing. Overall, there has been small but continuous growth of housing stock specifically geared for those tenant households who might otherwise be at risk in a competitive rental market. Social housing has ensured housing security to those outside the home ownership market. In Canada, state intervention in the housing market effectively ended in 1993 when the federal government withdrew all new funding; Ontario and other provinces followed this federal lead. In Britain, Margaret Thatcher was well known for her contentious selling off of many "council houses" or municipally owned non-profit stock. In this same period—during which the Canadian federal government stopped funding social housing—other industrialized countries did the same. In much of Western Europe and, to a lesser extent, even in the United States, this policy has now been reversed and governments have re-entered the social housing arena.

The Canadian government has committed limited matching funds for new social housing on a province-by-province basis. For a five-year period from 2001 to 2006, the federal commitment was $136 million dollars, a sum that would build only about 5,000 new units per year in a country of 11 million households (Hulchanski, 2002). These federal resources have leveraged some new housing although it is largely identified as "special needs" and at a scale not beginning to approach either what is needed or even what was being built prior to 1993. The federal initiative on homelessness, created in 1999 to address the national concerns on homelessness, has focused the majority of its efforts on research and emergency shelter provision (Neal, 2004).

Policy Responses

Jobs

Policies of "full employment," increases in the minimum wage, and public sector employment were over the past forty years the labour market policies that helped Canadians avoid unemployment and poorly paid employment, which contribute to homelessness. These were, of course, augmented by a social safety net without the gaping holes of today. Unemployment insurance and welfare programs combined to keep most people out of extreme poverty when labour market solutions were unavailable. In both of these areas, benefits have been cut and eligibility narrowed. For example, from 1989 to 1994, the number of unemployed parents without Employment Insurance protection increased from 28% to 41% (Novick & Shillington, 1996), and average weekly benefits fell by $6 (Battle, 1996).

These policy changes have been accompanied by dramatic changes in the nature of paid work. Current labour market options for less skilled workers tend to be low-paid employment with irregular hours, shift work, and on-call demands (Caragata, 2003; E. Smith & Jackson, 2002). Among Canadian women workers, 69% of those earning low wages (low-wage earners are those earning less than 10% above the LICO) earn less than $8 per hour (Maxwell, 2002), and among the Organisation for Economic Co-operation and Development (OECD) nations, Canada is only exceeded by the US in the proportion of its labour force in low-wage employment (Caragata, 2003). As data on women's earnings demonstrate, these labour market changes are profoundly gendered but are also inflected by the now increasingly familiar intersection of race, class, and immigration status as additional determining factors.

While unemployment rates have fallen consistently over the last ten years (Statistics Canada, 2005), the nature of work has changed to reflect a now common phenomenon in the industrialized West: insecure or precarious employment consisting of part-time, low-waged work without benefits and without the legislated employment protections of our former welfare state has become the norm for many workers. The very precariousness of work and the absence of protections, including reduced levels of unionization, reveal why homelessness may so readily result.

Housing

A variety of models are in place around the world whereby governments support the construction of housing units for the poor. These models vary from direct government construction and ongoing ownership to funding of non-governmental organizations to build and manage units, to support for the private market to build housing for this constituency. Early manifestations of "public" or government-developed housing tended to be large projects that congregated the poor and gave such interventions a bad name. Later, many Canadian municipalities began to develop housing, usually on a smaller scale and in better-integrated forms. Funding for these developments was shared and reliant on high levels of federal support. Although there were real issues of scale and lack of integration with some government-developed housing, even these provided stable, affordable housing for many tenant households who might otherwise be on the street. Cooperative housing and supported housing developed by religious organizations and NGOs (usually for seniors or special-needs groups) are models of housing construction that remain non-profit and are an enduring part of Canada's housing stock. A number of such projects were built on a small scale specifically to house the homeless and have been very successful.

The private sector also used to build housing for low-income Canadians, supported by public programs, including mortgage subsidies, tax breaks, tax shelters, and loan agreements wherein some percentage of the rental units would be available at lower rents for a given number of years. Private sector developers claim that the end of these incentives and overregulation, municipal lot levies, increasing building code standards, and rent controls drove them from building rental accommodation (Murphy, 2000). The advantage of these federally initiated new-construction programs is that they produced new housing stock that, some twenty to forty years later, continues to house low-income households. While some of these programs were expensive, they produced a good of lasting value. Unfortunately, both governments and the private sector increasingly plan on short-term cycles—the upfront costs are assessed at the expense of considering the long-term benefits.

The major policy competitor to public or social housing construction has long been the shelter allowance. Simply put, the shelter allowance gives extra money to eligible individuals so that they can afford private market rents. The arguments for and against shelter allowances can be complex and are well detailed (Murphy, 2000) and thus are discussed here only briefly. A benefit of the shelter allowance is its portability, which enables the tenant to choose where he or she wishes to live. The subsidy can be given directly to the tenant so that the landlord need not know that the household is being subsidized. The program is easily expandable in tight housing markets, and can be readily contracted when markets ease. The level of subsidy too can be easily adjusted to take account of changes in household income or average market rents. The downside of shelter allowances is that they do not add any housing units to the marketplace. Thus, they tend to have an escalating effect on rents as more tenants compete for the same rental units. The benefits of a tight housing market and low vacancy rates continue to accrue to private market landlords. Proponents of expanded shelter allowance programs have become very active as pressure to deal with homelessness increases.

The "New" Focus: Services

As homelessness has become both widespread and accepted, a range of new policy measures have been directed to it. These interventions, as we have seen, have done little to ameliorate the numbers of homeless people. What has developed is an industry of services for homeless people that do little, if anything, to address the problem of homelessness itself. If one subscribes to a macro or structural view, this will be of little surprise as real structural change confronts the ideology of the marketplace. What has been put in place is a range of extensive—but still inadequate—secondary or emergency services. The US McKinney Act (1987) is a useful illustration. It represented a national commitment to homelessness and was wide ranging, providing fiscal incentives and planning requirements for state implementation: "Unfortunately, however, most programs funded by the McKinney Act were meant only as short-term, emergency responses and were directed at ameliorating or managing the symptoms instead of ending homelessness by addressing systemic causes of homelessness, poverty and the lack of low income affordable housing" (Choi & Snyder, 1999, p. 26). In 1997, there was a modest amendment to the Act directed to permanent housing, but the primary emphasis remained emergency services (Choi & Snyder, 1999).

Canada has no national policy on homelessness. Instead we once had a modest national program of social housing construction. After the federal government withdrew funding for new social housing construction and most provinces followed suit, homelessness became a matter largely for municipalities to deal with using their limited resources. The downloading of this responsibility has caused policy on homelessness in Canada to mirror that of the United States. Where there are policies and programs to address the needs of the homeless, they are emergency services. Over the course of the 1980s, the US Department of Housing and Urban Development (HUD) reduced housing expenditures by over 70% (Daly, 1996, p. 174).

In Canada, Layton (2000), a Toronto city councillor and now (2006) leader of the New Democratic Party, discusses his response and strategy, prompted by the death of a homeless man who froze near his own home. Layton and others sought city council support for an emergency phone line for homeless people in trouble, expanded cold-night street patrols, expanded drop-ins and shelter beds, and formed a committee to work to prevent freezing deaths (Layton, 2000, p. 11). Other new services for homeless people support job and apartment hunting. These services are useful, but unlikely to make a difference as adequate responses to homelessness. The housing market and vacancy rates are such that if one low-income person manages to find an affordable apartment with the aid of such support services, that person is better off, but another low-income person has lost the opportunity to occupy that unit. The funding of emergency services may also give the public a sense that government is responding and may even minimize the number of homeless people visible on the streets.

The Role of Theory in Understanding Homelessness

The theory of why people are homeless is, of course, critical to developing an adequate policy response. While some would argue that all levels of government in Canada have failed to substantively address the problem of homelessness, imagine that government was committed to eliminating homelessness in Canada. What might the "right" policies be to eradicate homelessness in Canada? An adequate answer requires research that can build theory, or (depending on one's level of adherence to positivism) the testing of theory through research. This has, of course, given rise to much research on homelessness—how many people are homeless and who they are (Burt & Cohen, 1989; Golden et al., 1999; Kozol, 1988); what causes or triggers homelessness (Golden et al., 1999; Layton, 2000; Marcuse, 1987; Rossi, 1989); the behaviours of homeless people (Carlen, 1996); their health and health histories (Bines, 1994; Pleace & Quilgars, 1996); and their stories (Kozol, 1988; Ralston, 1996). This research has produced what are seemingly quite thorough studies, but most findings have remained focused on some combination of the two theoretical perspectives described below.

Two Major and Competing Theories

It's Their Fault

> To most observers, poor people, particularly men and women not attached to family constellations, are either the "undeserving" or "unworthy poor" of old or (using the new "medicalized" vocabulary of the late twentieth century) people with severe personal pathologies. (Wagner, 1997, p. 55)

This view includes a wide range of perspectives, including the most extreme and largely ideological conviction (emanating from a liberal world view) that we are individuals responsible for our own well-being, to the extent that we are able to make choices about it. Thus, if we are hit by a car or severely disabled, our level of responsibility for the consequences will be tempered by society accepting some responsibility. However, if someone is unable to find work (and there are deemed to be jobs available) or doesn't want to work at these available jobs, the economic and social consequences facing that person are seen to be of his or her own making. The extreme liberal view of absolute self-reliance has been tempered over time by extending public responsibility, but usually only to those perceived as needy and/or deserving of public help.

The critical question is how far such public or social responsibility extends and to whom. Usually such need is established on the basis of the vulnerability or helplessness of the claimant—the notions of the "deserving" and "undeserving" poor. Historically, the "deserving" poor included children and single parents, although this view has begun to change, as those with indisputable illness or disability are inconsistently seen as deserving. Thus, the person who is ill may warrant some form of social support, while the person who does not want to work would warrant none. This range of views is associated with characterizing homelessness as deriving from individual pathology, i.e., it is the individual's fault that he or she is in this circumstance. Because no rational person would voluntarily opt for such circumstances, he or she therefore must have some deficit or shortcoming that, as Wagner suggests in the above citation, is often now medicalized. Thus, it follows for some that the homeless are made up of two groups: those who have some personal problem that makes them unable to function "properly," and those who are on the streets by choice. For the former group, services are already in place although they may need some adjustment to make them better suited to the particular kinds of problems the homeless have. The basic belief is that help is available to those who really want help. The notion of choice or intentionality is given legal status in Britain, where the Housing (Homeless Persons) Act of 1977 mandates local governments to provide housing for homeless people except those who are homeless as a result of "intentionality." This notion is variably interpreted sometimes to include those who lose their housing because of rent arrears—that is, they have become homeless by "intention" (Daly, 1996).

Structural Failing

The other widely held view can be classified as the structural view: homelessness is caused by failings in our economic and social systems that leave some people without adequate money to "purchase" housing in the marketplace in which it is a commodity like any other. Our economic system needs what Galbraith (1992) refers to as the "functional underclass": "All industrial countries have one.... As some of its members escape from deprivation and its associated compulsions, a resupply becomes essential" (Galbraith, 1992, p. 412). The holders of these structural views may argue about whether a first priority in addressing the issue is jobs, or the level of public assistance, or the construction of non-market housing. They are, however, in general accord that homelessness is a function of the capitalist marketplace, and that increasing neo-conservatism has slowed our collective willingness to intervene in the market. Because our housing system is a "market" system, we have an insufficient supply of specialty housing—public or social or supported housing— to meet the needs of all those who can't function sufficiently well in the marketplace to afford the market rates for housing.

These two views are, of course, not mutually exclusive, and there are many subscribers to some mix of the two perspectives. More recently, there are some who have begun to contend that neither of these theories adequately and satisfactorily accounts for the problem. One such perspective is that of Springer (2000), at the United Nations Center for Human Settlements, who proposes that we abandon the use of homelessness as a term because it combines both structural and individual issues, permitting the structural policy issues to be overlooked in favor of an emphasis on individual pathology. Springer (2000) suggests instead, that we refer to "houselessness" as the determining categorization as all homeless people have this in common— they are without housing. She suggests that we can further refine the term by referring to "absolute houselessness," or those on the streets; "concealed houselessness," or those doubling up or in shelters; and at "at risk of houselessness," referring to those facing eviction, deinstitutionalization, or the termination of other forms of residence (shelters, social service programs, etc.). This work is indeed promising of a shift in how we understand and consequently address the problem—no matter what else may be required, the "houseless" require housing. So, while the use of "houselessness" may advance a social housing agenda, it needs to be combined with a continuing analysis that focuses on who is "houseless" and why, and whether the provision of housing will be sufficient to effect their full public and social engagement. This begs, I suggest, a consideration of another theoretical view.

An Alternative or Modified Theory: Social Exclusion

In the European literature (Pitts & Hope, 1997; Pleace, 1998; D. Smith & Stewart, 1997), there is a broadening acknowledgement of a phenomenon, or a set of phenomena, that have been labelled social exclusion. Perhaps the use of this term might come about only in a European context where there remains at least a history (if not more) of expectation that, at some level, the homeless population was to be included as part of the public realm. Thus, when evidence suggests that there is a systematic, classifiable process of exclusion, it comes to society's attention. The theory being developed to explain these phenomena argues that homelessness is a symptom of another more complex set of problems. Thus, we hearken back to Blanco's (1994) notion of social problems as social constructions and the need to deconstruct or tease out what the "real" problem might be.

In a North American context, the focus of policy attention is more narrowly on homelessness and tends toward the individual pathology end of the spectrum—the increasing number of services already described. What is meant by the phrase "social exclusion"? Does it have merit as a way of thinking about what we call homelessness?

Bryne (1995, p. 95) suggests that the term "underclass"—used to characterize a broad group that would include the homeless—has increasingly been utilized (to explain both the phenomenon and the particular people in it) to infer a "combination of the 1960s concept of the culture of poverty and the identification of the dependence-inducing character of income maintenance programmes." This usage by the new right has caused others to abandon the term, not wishing to invoke these same associations. In querying the term and what it signifies, Bryne and others do not wish to suggest that this phenomenon—a group seemingly without critical ties to the social and economic system, often even without enduring personal ties—is not real or in need of research. Quite the contrary. The change in our social and economic structures—that there is a large, seemingly permanent group relegated not only to the economic sidelines but the social and political as well—has warranted further scrutiny. The European literature has settled on "social exclusion" as a descriptor that is now utilized by governments as well as academics and activists.

What does such exclusion look like? What are its implications? There have always been people who don't work, for whom jobs are difficult to get or hang on to. Some of these people—largely men, as for most of the period of industrialization women were not expected to work outside the home—were the traditional inhabitants of skid row, occupying the offices of casual labour pools when economic necessity required it. Most often, such people drifted in and out of work. They may have been, in the "medicalized" parlance of today, "poorly attached," usually single, and sometimes without permanent housing. Others, though, followed these same work patterns, but were strongly established in their working-class neighbourhoods, where they may have boarded or rented a room. Except during the Depression of the 1930s, they were in relatively small number. What appears to have happened now is that such minimal attachment, the lack of a meaningful stake in the community, is experienced by a diverse range of people of all ages, many different backgrounds, and even levels of education (Choi & Snyder, 1999). This exclusion is not *just* from the labour force, although that aspect is critical. Much of our social engagement stems from having money; it affects the neighbourhood we live in, the schools our children attend, where we shop, and what we buy. All of these things are more spatially segregated by income than was the case fifty years ago. In the cities of forty and even thirty years ago, for example, we all shopped in the stores located "downtown." Think now of the strategically located shopping malls and the stores in them, which target the neighbourhood income level. No dollar stores will be found in the malls of exclusive neighbourhoods. Our jobs also determine our social locations, which, in part because of this spatial separation, are much less integrated. Our social networks are very likely to be based in these residential or work communities, and these have been demonstrated to be important in helping us maintain our social and economic position—staying "included." Our social activities too are more market-based. Thus, those describing social exclusion claim that it is both powerful and self-reinforcing (Caragata & Skau, 2001). Central to the notion of social exclusion are social and spatial separation, not only by class, money, status, etc., but also by a more profound exclusion from the social order of things: "It is not simply a matter of the group being poor but it is separated from mainstream society so that it cannot access general social life and crucial social goods, especially education in schools, on the same terms as the rest of us" (Bryne, 1995, p. 97). As education has historically been the door to upward mobility (Kaus, 1992), without such access the permanence of these divisions is reinforced.

Concluding Thoughts: Combined, Multilevel Responses

We must consider what might be adequate policy solutions. They must address the structural elements—housing and income—but also pay attention to social inclusion, social engagement. Because this, too, has become structurally and spatially shaped, it will not be an easy task.

Continued demands must be made of the federal government in Canada to resume its leadership role in supporting the construction of affordable housing. Part of this role must be creating incentives for provincial involvement. All types of housing models should be explored; many NGOs have developed innovative, cost-effective examples. Private sector involvement should also be encouraged, and building codes must be re-examined. In the postwar housing crisis, many families built their own homes and were given time to bring them up to building code standards.

Job creation is critical, and the role of job creation programs and public sector employment should be re-examined. Many of those who are currently homeless do work or have worked when other support services were in place to facilitate their getting to work. A national daycare policy, such as has been promised and is in place in Quebec, would do much to enable families, including those who are mother-led, to earn incomes. Skills upgrading and training are essential to improving employment prospects beyond low skilled precarious work and recent findings on Canada's failing productivity ("Forgotten Issue," 2006) point to our reluctance to invest significantly in creating the high-value work force that we talk about.

Social assistance levels must be high enough to enable recipients to secure housing that will be sustainable in the long run. A single mother of three I interviewed paid over $900 per month for rent out of a benefit cheque of under $1,400 (Caragata & Hardie, 1999). She had been homeless before, and with that percentage of expenditure on rent, it was clear she would be again.

An emergency service in Vancouver caught my attention recently because it offered courses to its users—not in life skills or resumé preparation but in philosophy and the classics, taught voluntarily by university professors. These are unlikely offerings because we assume a hierarchy of human needs—that those on the streets are unlikely to want intellectual engagement. Such assumptions reinforce the exclusion of the already marginalized. If living on the street is now part of one's ongoing expectations, then every possible enrichment would seem in order. The Vancouver experience seems successful, as are other diverse efforts at re-engaging those who are excluded. These include political and social action (an Ontario example is Low Income Families Together (LIFT), which demonstrates the impact of such activity on participants as they gain voice and confidence and focus attention on the needs of low-income families). Other efforts include neighbourhood associations that have been successful in regaining control of what were once violent or unsafe areas, and various self-help housing associations in which homeless people contribute their skills to developing their own housing solutions.

Many other examples could be provided, but instead I will reiterate the principle issue. If we recognize homelessness to be symptomatic of this larger problem of social exclusion, then we have a new set of considerations to undertake in planning a policy response.

References

Battle, K. (1996). *Precarious labour market fuels rising poverty.* Ottawa: Caledon Institute.

Bines, W. (1994). *The health of single homeless people.* York: Centre for Housing Policy, University of York.

Blanco, H. (1994). *How to think about social problems.* Westport, CT: Greenwood Press.

References Blau, J. (1992). *The visible poor: Homelessness in the United States.* New York: Oxford.

Bryne, D. (1995, February). Deindustrialization and dispossession: An examination of social division in the industrial city. *Sociology, 29*(1), 95–115.

Burt, M. (1992). *Over the edge: The growth of homelessness in the 1980s.* New York: Russell Sage Foundation.

Burt, M.R. & Cohen, B.E. (1989). *America's homeless: Numbers, characteristics, and the programs that serve them.* Washington, DC: Urban Institute Press.

Canadian Broadcasting Corporation (CBC). (2004, November 25). News Online at <www.cbc.ca/news/background/municipalities/squatters.html#toronto>.

Canada Mortgage and Housing Corporation (CMHC). (1996, August). *Research and Development Highlights, 27.*

Canada Mortgage and Housing Corporation (CMHC). (2005, December). *Rental market survey.*

Canadian Centre for Policy Alternatives. (1998). *Alternative federal budget papers 1998.* Ottawa: Author.

Canadian Civil Liberties Association (CCLA). Online at <www.ccla.org/news/01–12_safestreets.shtml>.

Caragata, L. (2003). Neoconservative realities: The social and economic marginalization of Canadian women. *International Sociology, 18,* 559–580.

Caragata, L., & Hardie, S. (1999). *Social housing waiting list analysis: A report on quantitative and qualitative findings.* Prepared for the Mayor's Action Task Force on Homelessness, City of Toronto, ON.

Caragata, L., & Skau, B. (2001). A chip in the Canadian veneer: Family and child poverty as social exclusion. *Social Work and Social Science Review, 9*(1), 36–53.

Carlen, P. (1996). *Jigsaw: A political criminology of youth homelessness.* Buckingham, UK: Open University Press.

Centre for Equality Rights in Accommodation (CERA). (2005). *Submission to the United Nations Human Rights Committee Fifth Periodic Review of Canada, October 17, 2005.* Toronto: Author.

Choi, N.G., & Snyder, L.J. (1999). *Homeless families with children.* New York: Springer.

City of Toronto. (1995). *Report of the alternative housing subcommittee.* Toronto: Author.

City of Toronto. (2003). *Toronto report card on housing and homelessness.* Toronto: Author.

Daly, G. (1996). *Homeless.* New York: Routledge.

Dear, M., & Wolch, J. (1987). *Landscapes of despair: From deinstitutionalization to homelessness.* Cambridge: Polity Press.

The forgotten issue: The productivity gap. (2006, January 3). *Globe and Mail,* p. A12.

Freiler, C., & Cerny, J. (1998). *Benefiting Canada's children: Perspectives on gender and social responsibility.* Ottawa: Status of Women Canada.

Galbraith, J.K. (1992). The functional underclass. *Proceedings of the American Philosophical Society, 136*(3), 411–415.

Glasser, I. (1994). *Homelessness in global perspective.* Toronto: Maxwell Macmillan International.

Golden, A., Currie, W., Greaves, E., & Latimer, E.J. (1999). *Taking responsibility for homelessness: An action plan for Toronto.* Report of the Mayor's Homelessness Action Task Force. Toronto: City of Toronto.

Greater Vancouver Regional District (GVRD). (2005). *Homeless Count 2005,* Bulletin. Online at <www.gvrd.bc.ca/homelessness/>.

Greve, J. (1971). *Homelessness in London.* Edinburgh: Scottish Academic Press.   **References**

Hacking, I. (1999). Teenage pregnancy: Social construction? In J. Wong & D. Check-land (Eds.), *Teen pregnancy and parenting: Social and ethical issues* (pp. 71–80). Toronto: University of Toronto Press.

Hulchanski, D. (2002). *Housing policy for tomorrow's cities* (Discussion paper F/27). Ottawa: Canadian Policy Research Networks (CPRN), December.

Jeffrey, H. (1999). *The construction of homelessness as a social problem: Linking contributing factors, mediating factors, and interventive strategies.* Unpublished MSW thesis. Wilfrid Laurier University.

Kaus, M. (1992). *The end of equality.* New York: Basic Books.

Kozol, J. (1988). *Rachel and her children: Homeless families in America.* New York: Crown.

Layton, J. (2000). *Homelessness: The making and unmaking of a crisis.* Toronto: Penguin/McGill Institute.

McLaughlin, M.A. (1987). *Homelessness in Canada: The report of the national inquiry.* Ottawa: Canadian Council on Social Development.

Marcuse, P. (1987, April 4). Why are they homeless? *The Nation,* 426–429.

Maxwell, J. (2002). *Working for low pay.* Presentation to Alberta Human Resources and Employment December 4, 2002. Ottawa: Canadian Policy Research Networks.

Mulroy, E.A., & Lane, T.S. (1992). Housing affordability, stress and single mothers: Pathway to homelessness. *Journal of Sociology and Social Welfare, 19*(3), 51–64.

Murphy, B. (2000). *On the street: How we created the homeless.* Ottawa: J. Gordon Shillingford.

National Homelessness Initiative. (2004). Business plan. Online at <www.home lessness.gc.ca/publications/businessplan/businessplan_e.pdf>.

National Council of Welfare. (2002). *Welfare incomes.* Ottawa: Author.

Neal, R. (2004). *Voices: Women, poverty and homelessness in Canada.* National Anti-Poverty Organization. Online at <www.napo-onap.ca/en/resources/Voices_English_04232004.pdf>.

Novick, M., & Shillington, R. (1996). *The progress of Canada's children.* Ottawa: Canadian Council on Social Development.

Ontario Non-Profit Housing Association (ONPHA) & Co-operative Housing Federation of Canada (CHF). (2005). *Where's home? A picture of housing needs in Ontario.* Toronto: ONPHA.

Ontario Non-Profit Housing Association (ONPHA) & Co-operative Housing Federation of Canada (CHF). (1999). *Where's home? A picture of housing needs in Ontario.* Toronto: ONPHA.

Pitts, J., & Hope, T. (1997). The local politics of inclusion. *Social Policy and Administration, 31*(5), 37–58.

Pleace, N. (1998). Single homelessness as social exclusion: The unique and the extreme. *Social Policy and Administration, 32*(1), 46–59.

Pleace, N., & Quilgars, D. (1996). *Health and homelessness in London: A review.* London: King's Fund.

Ralston, M. (1996). *Nobody wants to hear our truth.* Westport, CT: Greenwood Press.

Rich, D.W., Rich, T.A., & Mullins, L.C. (1995). *Old and homeless—double jeopardy.* Westport, CT: Auburn House.

Rossi, P.H. (1989). *Down and out in America: The origins of homelessness.* Chicago: University of Chicago Press.

References   Safe Streets Act, S.O. 1999, chap. 8.

Sassen, S. (1998). *Globalization and its discontents*. New York: Free Press.

Shapcott, M. (2001). *Housing and the 2001 Ontario Budget*. Toronto: Co-operative Housing Federation of Ontario.

Shelter. (2005). Home page. Online at < england.shelter.org.uk/home/index.cfm >.

Smith, D., & Stewart, J. (1997). Probation and social exclusion. *Social Policy and Administration, 31*(5), 96–115.

Smith, E. & Jackson, A. (2002). *Does a rising tide lift all boats?* Ottawa: Canadian Council on Social Development.

Springer, S. (2000). Homelessness: A proposal for a global definition and classification. *Habitat International, 24*, 475–484.

Springer, J.H., Mars, J.H., & Dennison, M. (1998). A profile of the Toronto homeless population. In A. Golden et al. (Eds.), *Background papers*, Vol. II. Toronto: City of Toronto.

Statistics Canada. (2005, December 2). *Labour force survey*. Ottawa: Author.

Statistics Canada. (2006). Persons in low income before tax, by number (2000–2004). Online at < www40.statcan.ca/101/cst01/famil41b.htm?sdi >.

Toronto Disaster Relief Committee (TDRC). (2001). *Toronto's shelter system: Overcrowded, dangerous and not enough beds*. Online at < www.tdrc.net/Report-01-12-TDRC.htm#PartA >.

Turcotte, P., & Renaud, V. (2004, November). *Towards possible changes to the census recommendations on families and households: Statistics Canada*. Presented at the Joint ECE-Eurostat Work Session on Population Censuses Session 6: Families and Households Working Paper no. 12. Geneva, Switzerland.

Vosko, L. (2002, April 11). *Re-thinking feminization: Gendered precariousness in the Canadian labour market and the crisis in social reproduction*. Robarts Canada Research Chairholders Series, York University, Toronto, Ontario.

Wagner, D. (1997). Reinterpreting the undeserving poor. In M.J. Huth & T. Wright (Eds.), *International critical perspectives on homelessness* (pp. 55–68). Westport, CT: Praeger.

Yalnizyan, A. (1997). *The growing gap*. Toronto: Centre for Social Justice.

Single Motherhood in the Canadian Landscape: Postcards from a Subject[1]

Iara Lessa

Motherhood carries such consensual approval that the word is commonly used to represent issues that convey undisputable support and acceptance. But what does this consensual approval bring with it? A detailed look at motherhood in Canada, as in other parts of the Western world, requires a careful examination of the most vulnerable group of mothers: single mothers. Changes in family form and the redefinition of the family as an institution have been at the core of the discussions regarding the nature of these societies. Single mothers are, in these locations, central to the discussion about the future of the nation and its social welfare system. As enduring and controversial as the welfare system itself, the single mother is one of that system's most popular images. She can be considered a threat to the assumptions of the traditional family, a promise of women's independence from male control, or even a challenge to the universalization of the wage-worker subject. Consequently, social interventions addressing single mothers, directly or indirectly, have been at the centre of discussions regarding the public management of a future society and the socialization of its members.

In this chapter, I will discuss how the group of women called single mothers assumed this position of importance in Canadian social policy. Although these women come from a variety of social locations and life circumstances, through many processes, their social identity becomes essentialized as mothers raising children alone, and their contributions to society are interpreted and valued differently at various times. This discussion calls attention to the nature of single motherhood and its relationship with social welfare, and focuses on the ways society problematizes certain population groups and makes them the object of collective provision. The topic's conceptual underpinnings can be situated in a body of literature inspired by Foucault's work and loosely called governmentality for its interest in exploring the contexts in which government of self and others take place (Dean, 1999; Rose, 1999). The chapter starts with a classification of the various issues associated with single mothers to arrive at a rather broad definition of this group. It then proceeds to examine the several policies that contributed to shaping and defining single motherhood in Canada. Finally, it describes and discusses contemporary policies and issues associated with single mothers and their relationship with dignity, commitment to social justice, and the inequitable distribution of resources in society.

Defining Perspectives

The term "single or lone mother" gained currency during the 1960s, unifying a variety of situations that until then were understood as different and isolated: for example, the death of the father, the abandonment of the family by the husband, a birth out of wedlock, a divorce, or a separation. The term consolidated within one group the war widow with young children, the deserted mother, the divorced mother, the separated or married mother with absent husband, the displaced homemaker, the battered wife, the adolescent mother, and multiple other characterizations of many women's lives, which had been, throughout the twentieth century, the focus of particular social policies and strategies. This large group of women, independent of their class, race, religion, sexual preference, country of birth, physical and mental abilities, or any other descriptor, became defined by one sole aspect of their lives: the absence of a father in their family unit. While in the United States the term is also highly racialized, in Western societies in general, single motherhood in itself implies a set of social attributes and makes the lives of poor women raising children alone the subject of public scrutiny and attention.

The ideal of the male breadwinner, dependent wife, and children as the basic unit of society has inspired a system that reproduces and reinforces this form of family through a complex of ideas and practices. The social organization of Western societies and the functioning of their capitalist economic systems assume a basic family unit that has been shaped according to specific class, race, gender, and heterosexual assumptions as the core of production and reproduction of resources (e.g., Cossman, 1997). Families that deviate from it, such as the one constituted by the woman who is raising children alone, are considered incomplete and problematic. Single mothers become the feared others, outside the idealized norm, problematized through reference to social expectations regarding the private family responsibility for maintenance, care, and upbringing of their children (Gordon, 1994).

In the face of this normalized family ideal, the mention of single mothers in the Western world invokes a variety of tightly woven social traditions, values, and judgments. These are both echoed and fuelled by professional and scientific discourses that cast this group of women as a social problem (Harding, 1993a, 1993b). The problems they seem to represent are as diverse as the many individual portraits of single mothers themselves. They seem, nevertheless, to converge around three general arguments—individual characteristics, structural circumstances, and moral imperatives (Seccombe, James, & Walters, 1998)—which, although not mutually exclusive, characterize the common discourses regarding single motherhood.

A first set of arguments sees single motherhood as a problem characteristic of particular individuals or groups, such as Blacks in the United States, who, as argued by Amott (1990), were forced into a tradition of customary family separations under slavery. This association persists despite the fact that in 1996 African Americans constituted only 36% of welfare recipients (Seccombe, James, & Walters, 1998, p. 850). Another group currently associated with single motherhood is comprised of teenage unwed mothers and young divorcees. In Canada, there are reports that this group is growing, and increasingly these mothers are choosing to raise their children themselves rather than pursuing adoption or abortion (Clark, 1993). This group is widely assumed to be unprepared for motherhood and doomed for dependency on state support despite evidence to the contrary (Davis, McKinnon, Rains, & Mastronardi, 1999; Lessa, 2005). They are commonly pathologized (Horowitz, 1995) and portrayed in the media as deviant and as symbols of the decline of social order and discipline (e.g., Hewlett, 1986; Schamess, 1990). As part of these arguments, some authors have constructed an explanation of single motherhood in which certain families have developed a set of "sub-cultural" (Seccombe, James, & Walters, 1998) or "underclass" values (Leung, 1998) as a result of living for prolonged periods in social marginalization. Therefore, single-mother families are not only a problem for the present but also a reminder of the exponential growth of these problems with their intergenerational consequences for the future. Some arguments propose that offspring from single-mother families are "more likely to drop out of school, be unemployed, and themselves form mother only families than are children who grow up with two parents" (Garfinkel & McLanahan, 1986, p. 11–12).

The structural argument invokes the prevalence of poverty and associated stresses among single mothers (e.g., Lero & Brockman, 1993; McDaniel, 1993). Although not all single mothers are poor, a large group of the poor seem to be single mothers. Resting on feminist and political economy explanations, authors using this argument (e.g., Kitchen, 1992) discuss the structural barriers to women obtaining stable, well-paid jobs; the demands of contemporary standards of living that require, most often, two incomes per family; the domestic division of labour; and women's disadvantaged situation in the labour market. Consequently, single mothers are associated with low income, housing difficulties, and dependency on state support (e.g., Milar, 2000). Single mothers' poverty is also seen as significantly affecting their children's academic, behavioural, and emotional situation (e.g., Hetherington, Camara, & Featherman, 1983), as well as being a risk to adolescents' health and adaptation (Hamburg, 1993; Russell & Ellis, 1991). These arguments are variously explained by a combination of less parenting time, extreme stress and duress, absence of father figure, impoverished living environment, and less than adequate housing situations (Amato, 1999; Gringlas, 1995).

The third set of general arguments regarding the problematics of single motherhood—the moral arguments—proposes that fatherless families are a problem to the institution of the family, threatening to break down and disorganize this basic unit of society (Morgan, 1995). In the United Kingdom, Green (1993, p. vi) suggests that the traditional family is the foundation of

Defining Perspectives

freedom because in it children "learn voluntary restraint, respect for others and sense of personal responsibility." Reflecting the deep patriarchal roots of Western society, single-mother families, in this argument, embody the fears and concerns about the changes in the family and the relationships between the genders (see discussion in Eichler, 1997). In this sense, lone mothers are portrayed as a growing threat to the foundation of liberal societies and constitute the preferred target for groups advocating the return to traditional ways (e.g., Richards, 1997). Single motherhood, thus, has been used as one of the reasons to attack sex education, divorce laws, abortion, obscenity, homosexuality, and contraceptives (see Somerville, 1992).

These understandings of single motherhood as a problem for social organization have generated an urgency for change and heated discussions throughout the affluent West, significantly linking single motherhood with the welfare state. The state and the market were accorded particular roles in the allocation of resources and in the formulation of solutions to the problems associated with it. For the Western idea of welfare, single mothers embody a particularly conflicting combination of roles in modern societies: they are responsible for children's upbringing and socialization, but at the same time they are also responsible for supporting the family. In other words, they are mothers and workers or caregivers and breadwinners (Evans, 1992). On the one hand, as mothers nurturing the future generation, they should be supported in order to adequately carry out their social reproduction functions. On the other hand, they must be socially discouraged in order to discourage the numbers of those entering single motherhood and to limit the costs to the system. Ellwood (1988) has argued that availability of financial and other benefits tends to encourage single parenthood and consequently just increases the problem. More conservative commentators have charged that the support of single mothers is a disincentive to marriage and family life (Gilder, 1982; Murray, 1984) and actually causes single motherhood (Richards, 1997). Many feminist authors argue in favour of an extensive web of supports for single motherhood, citing evidence that as many as 40% of Canadian women may experience single motherhood at some time in their lives (Desroisiers, le Bourdais, & Lehrhaupt, 1994) and while 67% of lone-parent women with children at home were employed in 2001 (Statistics Canada, 2002), paid employment was not sufficient to meet the basic needs of many of their families (Stephenson & Emery, 2003, p. 26). To map the nature of what we call single mother is, hence, to touch on the very processes that constitute the complex set of relations and interactions embedded in the implementation of social care—the welfare system and our society as a whole.

I propose that we approach single motherhood as an assemblage of ideas, knowledges, expectations, beliefs, judgments, and assumptions about women raising children without a male partner. This assemblage represents relations of power; that is, it represents ways of acting upon these women that bring about relations among individuals. Some women become socialized into single motherhood through a series of rationalities and practices directed at poor women raising children alone but also aimed at the well-being of the population of a nation as a whole. As such, single mothers are not a given, ahistorical or universal. They are located in a specific time and place, in constant change, and profoundly bound to collective values, social policies, and practices.

Three Broad Periods

Thus, discussing single motherhood in Canada necessarily involves reviewing the policies that help to create a variety of power relations to produce a concrete group of women who, despite their various circumstances, represent a challenge to the social ethics of care. This discussion involves not only the actual policies but also their motivations and intentions, as well as the contexts and practices that help to translate those into actions. The next section proposes a broad periodization of policies addressing single motherhood in Canada and discusses how they shaped contemporary understandings of women who raise children alone. Its starting point is not who single mothers are or what their needs are but how they were made to be; how it became thinkable to support mothers in their child-raising activities; and what forms these practices took. The focus, thus, is not on a coherent and simplified statistical profile but on an intricate way of governing social well-being that creates particular ways of life with implications for society as a whole.

Three Broad Periods

Paying for Mothers' Caring Work

While single motherhood is not specific to an economic class, it is primarily mothers who are poor and single who became a social concern and in need of financial support. Support to mothers constituted, both in Canada and in the United States (e.g., Gordon, 1994; Mink, 1998), the first experience with direct public financial aid for a group. Previously there was no concerted social policy addressing women who raised children without a male partner, but a series of traditions and conventions with old roots undertaken by individuals, institutions, organizations, and local governments. In Britain, the Poor Laws called for different treatment for widows and deserted or unmarried mothers, and these traditions, although not implemented throughout Canada, influenced the charitable approaches to these women during the nineteenth and early twentieth century until the institution of Mother's Allowance by the provinces after World War I.

Many factors contributed to the widespread acceptance of supporting poor mothers. Paid motherhood was one of the various reforms advocated by the late nineteenth and early twentieth-century women's movement across Western nations, which also included women's suffrage, birth control, sexual freedom, child welfare, labour reform, civil rights, and other demands (Comacchio, 1999; Gordon, 1994). Paid motherhood was proposed as a way of preventing the dissolution of family ties and attending to the plight of dependent poor children. It stressed the importance of enabling women to dedicate

Three Broad
Periods
themselves to child socialization. As articulated at the time, these arguments implied support for a gender division of labour with the male worker being paid a family wage, and defined motherhood by White middle-class standards of citizenship, class relations, gender differences, race, and national identity (Little, 1995).

By World War I in Canada, the growth of slums, infant mortality, crime, and disease became increasingly associated with the instability of the family, and support for motherhood received widespread sanction. Suffragists such as Nellie McClung argued for greater appreciation of women's maternal qualities and more humane values, while Leacock, for example, emphasized female weakness, questioning women's ability to support themselves and their families on their own (Strong-Boag, 1979). Mother's Allowance legislation in Canadian provinces was also influenced by events during the 1914–1918 war: the images of poor widows and their children popularized the need for the propagation of a physically and morally fit generation to inherit the nation. Examples of public interventions were provided by the implementation of the mothers' aid programs in some of the American states and, as well, by support provided by the Canadian Patriotic Fund and local experiments by Local Councils of Women.

Mother's Allowance (1916–1964)

Mother's Allowance was the first instance of provincial governments accepting responsibility for the welfare of a specific group of people and committing themselves to their support (Struthers, 1994). Manitoba (in 1916) was the first province in Canada to pass legislation granting an allowance to poor widows. By 1920, the western provinces and Ontario had similar legislation in place, and by the 1950s, all provinces had some form of support for these mothers (Little, 1998). Particularly important is the fact that provinces and municipalities were paying mothers without means of support to stay at home to look after their children, thus supporting caring work and family life, and recognizing the importance and value of motherhood and its effects on a healthy citizenship. From the onset, as we shall see next, they were characterized by restricted domestic supervision, categorical eligibility, rigorous moral requirements, and meagre financial support.

Grounded in their White, middle-class Protestant origins, women's organizations and social service leaders modelled the program on their own charitable initiatives, insisting on stringent eligibility criteria and enforcing their own values as standards. While supporting poor mothers, women in these organizations also saw for themselves a role in the public world defined by a career in family management using professional tools for the direction of mothers of the lower classes, whom they regarded as deviant and distressed. They initially supported primarily poor widows with at least two dependent children, but gradually eligibility criteria were extended to include various categories of excluded poor mothers alone: wives of incapacitated men, deserted women, foster mothers, mothers with only one child, divorcees and officially separated mothers, wives of criminals in prison, unmarried mothers, as well as previous residents of other provinces and immigrants. These sequential enlargements of eligibility criteria were the result of struggles by the excluded group and those who spoke for them (social workers and women's groups). This process of negotiation left its mark on the program by simultaneously maintaining its categorical nature and increasing the total number of beneficiaries. By the 1960s, most provinces did not place restrictions on the causes of single motherhood, but arguments regarding fathers' or male partners' responsibility for their families continued to be important mechanisms of exclusion from benefits.

Three Broad Periods

In addition, mothers were subjected to strict tests of destitution and thriftiness, as well as moral investigations in order to be admitted and to continue in the program (Strong-Boag, 1979). Supervision of mothers regarding their motherhood expertise, their household management, and their moral fitness were central characteristics of Mother's Allowance programs throughout their existence. They incorporated an understanding of individual circumstances of the families, but imposed on them a grid of priorities elected by the program values and objectives: healthy habits, children's upbringing, satisfactory home environment, budgeting and management, and moral fitness (Lessa, 1999). In so doing, the programs defined these priorities as indicators of good motherhood, shaping it according to the class, race, religion, sexuality, and gender of investigators and administrators.

The type and amount of support varied, but, with the caseloads soaring, financial support maintained one constant aspect: provincial obsession with cost containment. The provinces only reluctantly accepted the responsibility for the well-being of families with a female head, and the programs were residual and partial. The women and their families were kept in the most abject poverty. In-kind and tagged benefits consisted of medical and dental assistance, support for fuel, and winter clothing, and, in some cases, emergency funds were incorporated into the allowance as a discretionary practice resulting from advocacy and the recognition of inadequacy of benefits. Financial support, reflecting a fear of discouraging industriousness, was contingent on assessments of need and constrained by strict ceilings. The allowance was never sufficient to raise a family, even by the most modest standards, and women were expected, initially, to supplement it with approved work. The major real supplementation to Mother's Allowance, however, was the Family Allowance, a universal benefit established by the federal government in 1944 (Kitchen, 1987).

In sync with the development of Western capitalism, a focus on work, during the Mothers' Allowance period (1916–1964), grew to dominate the discourse of the programs, gradually eroding their initial valuing of caring activities. In the process of building the Canadian post-World War II welfare state, transfer of federal funds for provincial social programs became contingent on the employable–unemployable dichotomy (Hum, 1987), and existing provincial programs were adapted to benefit from these funds. Consequently, mothers raising children without men were recast under this dichotomy: rather than being seen as important to the nation because of their mother-hood role, they started to be defined (in the different policy proposals of the time) primarily in relation to their participation in the labour market. Their motherhood duties, until then seen as a necessary job, were reinterpreted as an obstruction to entering the labour force. Although in earlier periods the Mother's Allowance beneficiary was prompted to work to supplement the allowance, in the postwar period she gradually become a category of the unemployable because of her family responsibilities. Mother's Allowance ceased to be an enabler for the ability to do child raising with employment supplementation and supervision, and became essentially a provision attend-ing to a deficiency impeding full-time employment (Lessa, 1999). Through these transformations, poor mothers' activities and duties became under-stood differently from those of other mothers: that is, they began to be rede-fined as workers first and as mothers secondarily. Her employability was, however, rigidly constrained by the programs through a limit in the number of hours she was permitted to work, forcing her into a life of poverty.

Canada Assistance Plan (1966–1996)

The introduction of the Canada Assistance Plan (CAP) in the mid-1960s is a marker for the consolidation of the transformations in social policy approaches to poor women raising children alone. It captured and crystallized a change in the understanding of the importance of motherhood, a change reflected in Mother's Allowance and the eligibility for social support of women raising children alone. Many of these mothers were, in fact, "unemployable" not only because of motherhood obligations but also because of their lack of paid work experience, limited skills, the cumulative effect of living in poverty for years, and the structural results of devaluing traditional women's jobs. While some of these trends also affected married women, who by the 1960s began to enter the labour force in large numbers, in the two-parent family, the mother's income from work was but a complement to her husband's. Within the families of women raising children alone, earnings from work were the sole source of support, and when they supplemented the allowance, these earn-ings were controlled and deducted from the benefit received. Faced with ben-efits eroded by inflation, an economic recession that made supplementation through paid work very difficult, and extremely high shelter costs, women raising children alone became the main image of the newly discovered fem-inization of poverty.

Under the CAP umbrella, provincial Mother's Allowance programs were integrated into the national system of welfare, consolidating a number of federal and provincial programs—Unemployment Assistance, Old Age Assis-tance, Blind Person's Allowance, Disabled Person's Allowance, and Mother's Allowance—into a single 50/50 cost-sharing arrangement between the gov-ernments. Provincial residency requirements were dropped and standard responsibilities were imposed on all provinces. Reflecting contemporary progressive discussions regarding poverty amid postwar wealth (Struthers, 1994), Three Broad Periods benefits were proposed in terms of human rights and their calculation conditioned to a particular definition of needs. CAP gave women who raise children alone the legal right to benefits, thus empowering different groups of mothers and individuals to demand dignity and adequate living standards (Evans, 1996).

The discourse of needs and rights, however promising, carried only a rhetorical weight. CAP turned away from the causes of poverty as the justification for support and supported all groups of women raising children alone under the generic financial need of the unemployable subject, reflecting a universalization of formulation of deservedness. Implementation of the program, however, maintained the traditions of the Mother's Allowance program: eligibility under categorical definitions, similar definition of needs, and emphasis on supervision of mothers. The discourse of rights was further eroded when considering the promised mechanisms of appeal, which were not consistently or independently established in all provinces.

Paradoxically, accompanying the discourse of rights and dignity of the poor, the implementation of programs for poor single mothers under CAP was marked by low levels of benefits and increasingly intrusive practices. The support provided by the provincial programs was below the poverty line in all provinces. The paltry amounts of the benefits (constantly eroded by inflation) and the regulation (not only of home life but also of the type and hours of work) maintained single mothers' marginal status in society. Through home visiting by welfare caseworkers, CAP incorporated the racial and class assumptions embedded in the supervisory activities of Mother's Allowance, and the judgments regarding the morality and the respectability of the recipients (Little, 1994). As the number of divorced mothers increased with the Divorce Act of 1968, Little (1998) points out, the lives of women raising children alone were scrutinized, their contacts with men were carefully monitored, and cohabiting mothers became the target of extreme regulations.

Under CAP, preventive services and employment training also received federal cost sharing, and the social services sector expanded enormously through the provision of personal services to poor mothers. Preventive services, provided primarily by a variety of dispersed, private, non-profit social services agencies, delivered what is known as personal services in a model that made integration and coordination difficult. In addition, many of these services were conceptualized through individualistic assumptions, which dissociated them from general poverty measures and drove a wedge between financial and personal needs of poor mothers (Lessa, 2004). Furthermore, professional discourses, as well as the increased costs in standards of living and consumption of goods, created additional barriers to poor mothers' ability to care adequately for their children by raising child-rearing requirements (Callahan, 1991). These circumstances—hopeless poverty, intrusiveness of benefits, the individualistic nature of preventive services, and the changes in child-rearing practices—combined to establish a common set of individual characteristics attributed to mothers receiving preventive services funded under CAP: low self-esteem, anxiety, guilt, and inability to manage their families under increasingly demanding child care requirements.

CAP also emphasized employability, which constituted, perhaps, its most striking legacy for single motherhood. Provincial governments seized upon this opportunity and experimented with a variety of different training and support programs varying from education advice to significant supports for voluntary participation in employment schemes (Evans, 1992; Snyder, 2000). The latter could include providing benefits such as housing subsidies, dental care, and daycare, which were substantial contributions to poor women's standard of living and gave strong encouragement to join the labour force. By the end of the 1980s, these programs occupied an increasingly central place in the government agenda in an attempt, as discussed by Evans (1996), to transform the single mother into a worker modelled after the ideal of the independent male breadwinner. The programs overlooked the structural forces that locked women in low-paying jobs, and, in fact, few poor mothers could escape poverty even with full-time employment. These women were in a weak position in the marketplace since the already low salaries and the number and quality of entry-level jobs were declining, as well as the chances for improvement through training, individual mobility, or collective bargaining. In addition, the absence of a child care program made it impossible for women to work for the low wages offered to the abundant pool of unskilled labour. The possibilities for training were reduced due to the devaluation of professions and tasks traditionally dominated by women, which were performed under deteriorating conditions. While employment constituted a banner of the women's movement and has substantially improved the lives of middle-class professional mothers, their sisters raising children alone in poverty found in the banner of employment just another mechanism for transferring the responsibility for structural inequalities to them.

The failure to transform poor single mothers into self-sufficient workers resulted in them being further pathologized and blamed. They were increasingly seen under the influence of neo-conservative arguments as difficult to employ, incompetent learners, and unable to keep a job for a lengthy period. However, as of the mid-1980s, despite the failure of the employment programs, work requirements grew increasingly mandatory and the amount of time women could stay on benefits was reduced (Baker, 1997). Conditions for single mothers deteriorated even further with an economic depression that devalued benefits through inflation and a wave of government reforms that cut expenditures. In addition, the universal Family Allowance, which, since World War II, had complemented Mother's Allowance, was, in 1993, replaced by the Child Tax Benefit, which privileges those in employment. Finally, after many changes, CAP was finally eliminated in 1996 and replaced by the Canada Health and Social Transfer (CHST).

The CAP installed a different approach to supporting women raising children alone: a language of rights to benefits based on needs that were, however, implemented through regulations and practices derived from Mother's Allowance; an attention to labour market issues through employment programs, which, although transferring to poor mothers much of the burden of employment, helped to bring attention to gender inequities; and an expansion of preventive personal services grounded in individualistic assumptions. The mothers' own understanding of themselves and their situation was also radically changed from the supplicant and grateful widow of the early twentieth century. Single mothers, living in public housing projects, receiving benefits as a single category of unemployable for family reasons, and being bombarded with professional and media discourses that harmonized their predicaments, gained a sense of group identity and became the centre of gender discourses. They achieved priority in public housing waiting lists (Lessa, 2002), consultation status in support services, a voice in the movements against injustices and inequality, and leadership roles in organizations and campaigns (McKeen, 2001). Their image became the symbol of social inequity and a catalyst for struggles regarding the issues of social citizenship and the right to form an independent household without the risk of poverty, violence, or marginalization (Orloff, 1993).

Shaping the Present

The CHST comes in the form of block funds for health, post-secondary education, and social assistance while continuing the trend of reducing federal contributions to social programs (Baker & Tippin, 1999). It belongs to a political landscape in which a neo-liberal social and economic agenda has installed a version of globalization based on the mobility of capital and labour through privatization, deregulation, and technological innovations. Together, these mechanisms implemented radical changes on the nature and management of national states. The neo-liberal state emphasises individual responsibilities, targets service delivery to facilitate integration into the labour force, and revisits the role of the family and caring in contemporary society (McDaniel, 2002; Peck, 2001; Vosko, 2000). The CHST gave the provinces the leeway to spend federal funds without national standards and allowed the provinces to establish their own eligibility criteria for social welfare. The result was a profound "shift from welfare-oriented to workfare-driven social assistance" in Canada (Vosko, 2002, p. 35): cuts to benefits, a redefinition of "employable" persons, and the requirement to work for a specific number of hours in a designated job for basic welfare benefits. In most provinces, benefits to single mothers became conditional upon acceptance of specific types of training, low-paying, unattractive work or workfare entrenching the punitive and rash measures many provinces had been experimenting with.

Eight years after the introduction of the CHST, in April 2004, new changes were introduced and the federal transfer payments to provinces and territories were split: those for health services were delivered under the new Canada Health Transfer, and those for post-secondary education and social assistance and services under the new Canada Social Transfer. The new CST continued the imperative of integrating single mothers into the labour force initiated during the CHST. In 2001, women headed 83.6% of all lone-parent families, representing 13% of all census families. Their total number (1,111,116 families) grew by 3.1% in 2000–2001, compared to 0.9% for all census families (Statistics Canada, 2001). The low income rate for female lone-parent families in 2003 (38%) was about four times the average for all families. While this rate was even higher in 1996 at 53%, and the percentage of persons in these families living in low income decreased from 56% to 41% since then (Statistics Canada, 2005c), lone parent families gained comparatively little in this period of economic rebound in most provinces.

Under the CHST/CST, a mother who was a sole breadwinner continues to face bleak employment prospects. For example, in 2003 the national median income for lone-parent families was $28,600, compared to that of couple families at $62,600 (Statistics Canada, 2005d). Although their labour force participation has grown significantly since 1995, in 2001 women raising children alone were less likely than mothers in two-parent families to be employed (only 67% of single mothers were employed, compared with 71% of mothers in two-parents families) (Statistics Canada, 2002). Single mothers are getting jobs, but they can survive on their market income only for short periods of time and continue to live in poverty (Frennette & Picot, 2003; Michalopoulous et al., 2002). Occupying insecure, part-time, temporary, low-paying, precarious jobs shaped by deregulation and erosion of employment relations (Vosko, 2000, 2002), many women raising children alone maintain a pattern of moving from welfare to work and back to welfare again, being especially overrepresented among the chronically unemployed (Statistics Canada, 2005f) and low-paid workers (Statistics Canada, 2005a).

While earnings of single/lone mothers as a group rose, the economic position of those who remained in low income deteriorated. Consistent with Canadian studies of concentration of low income (e.g., Myles & Picot, 2005; Statistics Canada, 2005a), Kapsalis & Tourigny (2002) report that being a recent immigrant or of Aboriginal origin, or having a work-limiting disability are among the strongest factors associated with high risk for low income and social exclusion among lone mothers. These three groups together represent 30% of all low income lone mothers, and 52% of all single mothers in this groups are in low income. The increased racialization of poverty in Canada can be evidenced in the two first categories. Poverty among people who immigrated in the last decade is rapidly growing: 36% in 2000 in comparison to 14% among Canadian-born people (Myles & Picot, 2005). Cranford, Vosko & Zukewich (2003, p. 16) report that while 10% of women of colour are in part-time temporary jobs and 17% are in part-time permanent jobs, only 7% of White men are in these precarious forms of work (see also Smith & Jackson, 2002, p. 2). In 2001, one in five Aboriginal households living in eleven Canadian metropolitan areas was headed by a lone parent. In the western centres alone, the proportion of all Aboriginal households headed by a lone parent was at least double that of their non-Aboriginal counterparts, and in Winnipeg, Regina, and Saskatoon, over half of Aboriginal children lived in lone-parent families (Statistics Canada, 2005e). While women with disabilities were only slightly more likely than women without disabilities to live as a lone parent in 1996, over one third of them reported running out of money to buy food compared to one fifth of lone-parent women without disabilities (Fawcett, 2000).

Among the primary obstacles to sustained employment is the lack of access to child care (Stephenson & Emery, 2003) which, in Canada, is delivered, except in Quebec, in a patchwork of programs under declining subsidies (Breitkreuz, 2005). Child care and various other supports around child rearing represent not only a barrier to entering paid employment but also to keeping it since child emergencies are inevitable (Mason, 2003). In addition, under the banner of preventing crime and violence, children and youth came under increased surveillance, bringing to the fore an emphasis on effective parenthood, which further blamed mothers for the lack of options society offers for its future generations (Chen, 2000). Housing, especially in large cities, has become a particular challenge for these mothers (Jackson, Schetagne & Smith, 2001), who are taken to court over minor rent issues (Monsebraaten, 2005; Philp, 2001) and are increasingly constituting the ranks of the homeless. One third of all single-mother households reported food insecurity, in comparison to 9% of people who were partners in a couple without children (Statistics Canada, 2005b). Their lives are made miserable: single mothers have debts, restricted expenditure on basic items, and lack of choice in housing and neighbourhood; they are unable to have things that other families take for granted, such as holidays, toys, new clothes, and sports equipment (McMullin, Davis & Cassidy, 2002).

These conditions are accompanied by the institutionalization of demeaning everyday practices, such as Ontario's snitch line, finger printing of welfare recipients, the forced disclosure of the father's name, a public discussion of the cost of single motherhood to the public purse (Little, 1999), and, rather than social transfers or programs, staying married or entering a marital relationship has become the best guarantee against poverty for women and their children (Lochhead & Scott, 2000; Statistics Canada, 1999). All of these are damaging to a person's dignity, self-esteem, and public image, and they define women raising children alone as incompetent mothers who produce children costly to society. Their treatment by social systems is permeated with suspicion, disrespect, and the utmost contempt, making these women feel shame, concealment, and chronic depression. Negative stereotypes are frequently associated with them: they are alleged to be lazy, unmotivated, and dependent; they are accused of getting pregnant to qualify for benefits and sitting idly at home (Little, 1998).

Understanding single motherhood not as the problematic characteristic of a group of people but as a web of relations of power allows an analytical emphasis on the social policies and practices that shape the lives of women

Note

References

in this marginalized location. From their marginal social location, women raising children alone are used as postcard images for the rest of society to enforce and normalize assumptions about individual opportunities, to erode commitment to collective responsibility, and to discourage challenges to a social organization based on the nuclear family, a gendered division of labour, and income exclusively based on employment. They have, therefore, a paradigmatic importance for social policies: talking about single mothers is also talking about how society is organized and structured. Addressing single motherhood involves, hence, combining ways to confront the ingrained effect of structural forces, with prioritizing the value of caring work and the different situations, preferences, and concerns of these mothers. Some alternatives have urged the definition of a new citizenship (Lister, 1997) or of entitlement based on human rights (Pearce, 2000), which, having the single mother as a barometer, encompass not only work issues—jobs, education, and training articulated with a wage policy—but a variety of conditions to care for children and a diversity of housing options. While these calls may be ambitious, they may prompt alternatives in the form of programs and supports that, as proposed by Lister (1997), promote women's independence, in the context of relationships of interdependence, allowing women raising children alone to signal welcome news of the ethics of collective care and social justice.

Note

1 Different parts of the research for this chapter were supported by a National Welfare Fellowship from the government of Canada, the Dean of the Faculty of Community Services at Ryerson University, and a SSHRC standard grant.

References

Amato, P.R. (1999). Parental involvement and children's behaviour problems. *Journal of Marriage and the Family, 61*(2), 375–385.

Amott, T.L. (1990). Black women and AFDC: Making entitlement out of necessity. In L. Gordon (Ed.), *Women, the state, and welfare* (pp. 280–98). Madison: University of Wisconsin Press.

Baker, M. (1997). Women, family policies and the moral right. *Canadian Review of Social Policy, 40*, 47–64.

Baker, M. & Tippin, D. (1999). *Poverty, social assistance, and the employability of mothers: Restructuring welfare states.* Toronto: University of Toronto Press.

Breitkreuz, R.S. (2005). Engendering citizenship? A critical feminist analysis of Canadian welfare to work policies and the employment experiences of lone mothers. *Journal of Sociology and Social Welfare, 32*(2), 147–165.

Callahan, M. (1991). A feminist perspective on child welfare. In B. Kirwin (Ed.), *Ideology, development and social welfare: Canadian perspectives* (pp. 137–156). Toronto: Canadian Scholars' Press.

Chen, X. (2000). Is it all neoliberal? Some reflections on child protection policy and neo-conservatism in Ontario. *Canadian Review of Social Policy, 45/46*, 237–247.

Clark, S.M. (1993). Support needs of the Canadian single parent family. In J. Hudson & B. Galaway (Eds.), *Single parent families: Perspectives on research and policy* (pp. 223–237). Toronto: Thompson Educational.

Comacchio, C.R. (1999). *The infinite bounds of family: Domesticity in Canada, 1850–1940.* Toronto: University of Toronto Press.

Cossman, B. (1997). Family inside/out. In M. Luxton (Ed.), *Feminism and families: Critical policies and changing practices* (pp. 124–141). Halifax: Fernwood.

Cranford, C.J., Vosko, L.F., & Zukerwich, N. (2003, Fall). Precarious employment in Canadian labour market: A statistical profile. *Just Labour, 3,* 6–22.

Davis, L., McKinnon, M., Rains, P., & Mastronardi, L. (1999). Rethinking child protection practice through the lens of a voluntary service agency. *Canadian Social Work Review, 16*(1), 103–116.

Dean, M. (1999). *Governmentality: Power and rule in modern society.* London: Sage.

Desroisiers, H., le Bourdais, C., & Lehrhaupt, K. (1994). *Vivre en famille monoparentale et en famille recomposée: Portrait des Canadiennes d'hier et d'aujourd'hui.* Montréal: Institut National de la Recherche Scientifique.

Eichler, M. (1997). *Family shifts: Families, policies, and gender equality.* Toronto: Oxford University Press.

Ellwood, D.T. *(1988). Poor support: Poverty in the American family.* New York: Basic Books.

Evans, P. (1992). Targeting single mothers for employment: Comparisons from the United States, Britain, and Canada. *Social Services Review, 66*(3), 378–398.

Evans, P. (1996). Single mothers and Ontario's welfare policy: Restructuring the debate. In J. Brodie (Ed.), *Women and public policy* (pp. 151–171). Toronto: Harcourt.

Fawcett, G. (2000). *Bringing down the barriers: The labour market and women with disabilities in Ontario.* Ottawa: Canadian Council on Social Development.

Frenette, M., & Picot, G. (2003). *Life after welfare: The economic well being of welfare leavers in Canada during the 1990s.* Ottawa: Statistics Canada.

Garfinkel, I., & McLanahan, S. (1986). *Single mothers and their children.* Washington, DC: Urban Institute Press.

Gilder, G. (1982). *Wealth and poverty.* London: Buchan and Enright.

Gordon, L. (1994). *Pitied but not entitled.* New York: Free Press.

Green, D.G. (1993). Editor's foreword to the second edition. In N. Dennis & G. Erdos (Eds.), *Families without fatherhood* (2nd ed., pp. vi–vii). London: IEA Health and Welfare Unit.

Gringlas, M. (1995). The more things change: Single parenting revisited. *Journal of Family Issues, 16*(1), 29–53.

Hamburg, D.A. (1993). The American family transformed. *Society, 30*(2), 60–69.

Harding, L.F. (1993a). "Alarm" versus "liberation"? Responses to the increase in lone parents—Part 1. *Journal of Social Welfare and Family Law, 2,* 101–112.

Harding, L.F. (1993b). "Alarm" versus "liberation"? Responses to the increase in lone parents—Part 2. *Journal of Social Welfare and Family Law, 2,* 174–184.

Hetherington, E.M., Camara, K.A., & Featherman, D.L. (1983). Achievement and intellectual functioning of children in one parent households. In J. Spence (Ed.), *Achievement and achievement motives* (pp. 205–284). San Francisco: W.H. Freeman.

Hewlett, S.A. (1986). *A lesser life: The myth of women's liberation in America.* New York: William Morrow.

References Horowitz, R. (1995). *Teen mothers: Citizens or dependants?* Chicago: University of Chicago Press.

Hum, D. (1987). Working poor, the Canada Assistance Plan, and provincial response in income supplementation. In J.S. Ismael (Ed.), *Canadian social welfare policy* (pp. 120–138). Kingston: McGill-Queen's University Press.

Jackson, A., Schetagne, S., & Smith, P. (2001). *A community growing apart: Income gaps and changing needs.* Ottawa: Canadian Council on Social Development.

Kapsalis, C., & Tourigny, P. (2002). *Profiles and transitions of groups at risk of social exclusion: Lone parents.* Ottawa: Humans Resources and Development Canada, Applied Research Branch, Strategic Policy.

Kitchen, B. (1987). The introduction of family allowance in Canada. In A. Moscovitch & J. Albert (Eds.), *The benevolent state* (pp. 222–241). Toronto: Garamond Press.

Kitchen, B. (1992). Framing the issues: The political economy of poor mothers. *Canadian Woman Studies, 12*(4), 10–15.

Lero, D., & Brockman, L.M. (1993). Single parent families in Canada: A closer look. In J. Hudson & B. Galaway (Eds.), *Single parent families* (pp. 91–114). Toronto: Thompson Educational.

Lessa, I. (1999). *Restaging the welfare diva: Case studies of single mothers and social policy.* Unpublished PhD dissertation, Wilfrid Laurier University.

Lessa, I. (2002). Unravelling a relationship: Single motherhood and the practices of public housing. *Affilia, 10*(3), 314–331.

Lessa, I. (2004). "Just don't call her a single mother": Shifting identities of women raising children alone. *Atlantis: A Women's Studies Journal, 29*(1), 43–51.

Lessa, I. (2005). Discursive struggles within social welfare: Restaging teen motherhood. *British Journal of Social Work, 36,* 283–298.

Leung, L.C. (1998). *Lone mothers, social security and the family in Hong Kong.* Aldershot, UK: Ashgate.

Lister, R. (1997). *Citizenship: Feminist perspectives.* London: Macmillan Press.

Little, M.H. (1994). "Manhunts and bingo blabs": The moral regulation of Ontario single mothers. *Canadian Journal of Sociology, 19*(2), 233–247.

Little, M.H. (1995, Summer). The blurring of boundaries: Private and public welfare for single mothers in Ontario. *Studies in Political Economy, 47,* 89–109.

Little, M.H. (1998). *No car, no radio, no liquor permit: The moral regulation of single mothers in Ontario, 1920–1997.* Toronto: Oxford University Press.

Little, M.H. (1999). Limits of Canadian democracy: The citizenship rights of poor women. *Canadian Review of Social Policy, 42,* 59–76.

Lochhead, C., & Scott, K. (2000). *The dynamics of women's poverty in Canada.* Ottawa: Status of Women Canada.

Mason, R. (2003). Listening to mothers: Paid work, family life and child care. *Journal of Children and Poverty, 9*(1), 41–54.

McDaniel, S.A. (1993). Single parenthood: Policy apartheid in Canada. In J. Hudson & B. Galaway (Eds.), *Single parent families* (pp. 203–212). Toronto: Thompson Educational.

McDaniel, S.A. (2002). Women's changing relations to the state and citizenship: Caring and intergenerational relations in globalized western democracies. *Canadian Review of Sociology and Anthropology, 39*(2), 125–150.

McKeen, W. (2001). Writing women out: Poverty discourse and feminist agency in the 1990s National Social Welfare policy debate. *Canadian Review of Social Policy, 48,* 19–33.

References

McMullin, J.A., Davis, L., & Cassidy, G. (2002). Welfare reforms in Ontario: Tough times in mothers' lives. *Canadian Public Policy, 38*(2), 297–314.

Michalopoulos, C., Tattrie, D., Miller, C., Robins, P., Morris, P., Gyarmati, D., Redcross, C., Foley, K., & Ford, R. (2002). *Making work pay: Final report on the self-sufficiency project for long-term welfare recipients.* Ottawa: Social Research and Demonstration Corporation.

Milar, J. (2000). Lone parents and the new deal. *Policy Studies, 21*(4), 333–345.

Mink, G. (1998). *Welfare's end.* Ithaca: Cornell University Press.

Morgan, P. (1995). *Farewell to the family?* London: Institute of Economic Affairs.

Monsebraaten, L. (2005, September 27). Tenant act ruled discriminatory: Working single mother of three faced eviction; Activists hail unprecedented decision. *Toronto Star*, A04.

Murray, C. (1984). *Losing ground.* London: Basic Books.

Myles, J., & Picot, G. (2005). *Trends in income inequality in Canada from an international perspective.* Ottawa: Statistics Canada, Analytical Studies Branch–Research Paper Series.

Orloff, A.S. (1993). Gender and the social rights of citizenship: The comparative analysis of gender relations and welfare states. *American Sociological Review, 58*, 303–328.

Pearce, D. (2000). Rights and wrongs of welfare reform: A feminist approach. *Affilia, 15*(2), 133–152.

Peck, J. (2001). *Workfare states.* New York: Guilford Press.

Philp, M. (2001, April 30). Public housing landlord gets tough: Emphasis on corporate bottom line means more tenants threatened with eviction. *Globe and Mail*, A16.

Richards, J. (1997). *Retooling the welfare state.* Toronto: C.D. Howe Institute.

Rose, N. (1999). *Powers of freedom: Reframing political thought.* London: Cambridge University Press.

Russell, C.D., & Ellis, J.B. (1991). Sex-role development in single parent households. *Social Behavior and Personality, 19*(1), 5–9.

Schamess, G. (1990, March). Toward an understanding of the etiology and treatment of psychological dysfunction among single teenage mothers: Part 1, A review of the literature. *Smith College Studies in Social Work, 60*(2), 153–168.

Seccombe, K., James, D., & Walters, K.B. (1998). "They think you ain't much of nothing": The social construction of the welfare mother. *Journal of Marriage and the Family, 60*(4), 849–865.

Smith E., & Jackson, A. (2002). Does a rising tide lift all boats? *The labour market experiences and incomes of recent immigrants, 1995–1998.* Ottawa: Canadian Council on Social Development.

Somerville, J. (1992). The new right and family politics. *Economy and Society, 21*(2), 100–120.

Snyder, L. (2000). Success of single mothers on social assistance through a voluntary employment program. *Canadian Social Work Review, 17*(1), 49–68.

Statistics Canada. (1999a, April 24). Low income among children. *The Daily*.

Statistics Canada. (2001). *Annual demographic statistics* (Catalogue no. 91–213). Ottawa: Statistics Canada.

Statistics Canada. (2002). *Women in Canada: Work chapter updates* (Catalogue no. 89F0133XIE). Ottawa: Statistics Canada.

Statistics Canada. (2005a, April 25). Study: Low paid work and economically vulnerable families. *The Daily*.

References   Statistics Canada. (2005b, May 3). Food insecurity in Canadian households. *The Daily*.

Statistics Canada. (2005c, May 12). Family income. *The Daily*.

Statistics Canada. (2005d, May 20). Family income. *The Daily*.

Statistics Canada. (2005e, June 23). Study: Aboriginal people living in urban areas. *The Daily*.

Statistics Canada. (2005f, September 21). Study: Trends and conditions in census metropolitan areas: Final Assessment. *The Daily*.

Stephenson, M., & Emery, R. (2003). *Living beyond the edge: The impact of trends in non-standard work on single/lone parent mothers*. Ottawa: Status of Women Canada.

Strong-Boag, V. (1979). "Wages for housework": Mothers' allowances and the beginnings of social security in Canada. *Journal of Canadian Studies, 14*(1), 24–34.

Struthers, J. (1994). *The limits of affluence: Welfare in Ontario, 1920–1970*. Toronto: University of Toronto Press.

Vosko, L. (2000). *Temporary work: The gendered rise of a precarious employment relationship*. Toronto: University of Toronto Press.

Vosko, L. (2002). *Rethinking feminization: Gendered precariousness in Canadian labour market and the crisis in social reproductions*. Monograph in Annual Robart's Lecture Series. Toronto: Robarts Centre for Canadian Studies.

Additional Resources

Canadian Social Research Links: <www.canadiansocialresearch.net>. This website offers a comprehensive array of links to policy and discussions about children, families, and youth in Canada.

Childcare Resource and Research Unit: <www.childcarecanada.org>. This website provides a link to online policy and research documents with a very good search engine.

Statistics Canada's website and *The Daily* are the most important sources of empirical data about single mothers in Canada. In addition to census data, they publish periodical booklets addressing specific groups, among which single mothers figure prominently: <www.statcan.ca> and <www.statcan.ca/ Daily>.

Linda Snyder

Workfare arrived as a relatively new and highly controversial policy alternative in Canada during the 1990s. The term "workfare" is a contraction of "work for welfare" and refers to programs that require welfare recipients to participate in work and related activities in order to receive financial assistance (Evans, 1993). Welfare attempts to address the problem of insufficient income for individuals and families to meet their basic needs. Workfare, as a contemporary form of welfare tied to work, has arisen from a neo-conservative ideology that reformulates welfare assistance as a disincentive to employment. Controversy has arisen precisely because of this shift away from the problem of meeting people's basic needs to addressing what some policy-makers believe is a pervasive disincentive to work. Ontario, in 1997, was the first Canadian province to formally introduce workfare; however, Quebec's practice, since the early 1990s, of providing lower benefits to recipients not participating in employment programs, as well as Alberta's rate reductions in 1993, were earlier examples of the same eligibility restriction policy.

Key Concepts

Several concepts important to an understanding of the topic of workfare need to be clarified at the outset.

Social assistance, more commonly known as "welfare," is the government program that provides a minimal income to people "in need." Eligibility requirements are specified in relation to reasons for being "in need"—reasons such as lack of employment, family breakdown, and inability to work. For example, employable people applying for assistance due to lack of employment have always been required to actively seek employment and to accept any work that they are physically capable of doing. Social assistance is an important component of Canada's social safety net along with universal programs (such as Old Age Security) and insurance programs (such as Employment Insurance). However, it is the "program of last resort" after recourse to the market and all other legitimate sources of income have been sought. Provincial and territorial governments are responsible for the provision of social assistance, although in some provinces this responsibility is delegated to municipalities and First Nations' councils.

Employment strategies to reduce welfare expenditures have been conceptualized by Martin Rein (1974) as comprising three fundamental approaches. The income incentives strategy promotes employment by exempting a portion of earned income in the calculation of social assistance benefits. The service strategy encourages independence through direct services such as job search assistance and training programs and through indirect supports such as help with child care and transportation costs. The third strategy of eligibility restrictions, which uses sanctions such as loss of benefits for non-compliance, is the strategy underlying workfare. More recent conceptualizations distinguish between "carrots" and "sticks." The carrots are human resources strategies, sometimes called human capital development models, that parallel Rein's incentives and services strategies; the sticks are workfare programs, sometimes referred to as "active" labour force attachment models, that parallel Rein's restrictive strategies (Lightman, 2003; Torjman, 1996). Another useful typology is offered by Morel (2002), who distinguishes between the insertion model used in France that seeks to combat exclusion and the workfare model epitomized by the American objective of combating dependency.

The term "workfare" has come to have a very elastic meaning (Peck, 2001). Its strictest definition is "work for welfare" referring to programs that require welfare recipients to perform unpaid work for designated organizations in order to receive financial assistance (Gorlick & Brethour, 1999). A broader definition is commonly used, however, which implies mandatory participation in a range of designated employment-related activities along with sanctions, such as reduced assistance, for non-compliance (Pulkingham & Ternowetsky, 1998; Torjman, 1996).

The "employable" category of social assistance eligibility refers to able-bodied, working-age recipients who must actively seek employment in order to qualify for assistance. The definition of "employable" is particularly relevant to single parents receiving social assistance who, in earlier days, were exempt from job search requirements because of their child care responsibilities but who, with the advent of eligibility restriction strategies such as workfare, are now considered employable unless they have young or disabled children.

Social Assistance Recipients and Their Realities

The number of people across Canada who were receiving social assistance in 2004 is estimated to be 1.7 million (National Council of Welfare, 2005). However, the total numbers include dependent children, disabled people, and others who would not be categorized as "employable" and, therefore, should not be included in a count of Canadians subject to workfare expectations. The "other" category includes people with temporary medical conditions that prohibit employment, foster parents, elderly people who don't meet residency requirements for Old Age Security, and refugees who have not been granted permission to work in Canada.

Employable recipients without work or without full-time work at a level of earnings to meet their families' needs must continue to search for gainful employment in the competitive labour market. Income from social assistance varies by province and other factors such as family size, but, in all cases, leaves people living well below Statistics Canada's Low Income Cut-Off (LICO). For example, in Ontario, Canada's largest province, the estimated 2004 welfare income (including basic assistance plus other "income-tested" benefits provided through the tax system, such as the federal Child Tax Benefit, the GST credit, and provincial tax credits) for a single employable person was $6,973 and for a single parent with one child was $14,251; in comparison, the 2004 Statistics Canada LICO, for a city with a population of 500,000 or more, for a single person was $20,337 and for a family of two was $25,319 (National Council of Welfare, 2005).

In addition to the economic deprivation of poverty, people living on social assistance live with the stigma and stereotypes associated with receipt of welfare. This stigma has been heightened through the public vilification of the poor by politicians attempting to persuade the electorate of the necessity of the workfare policy (Lightman, 2003). Two of the most popular myths propagated are the misconception of laziness and the fallacy of dependency (Handler, 2005). Providers of employment services, meanwhile, have been well aware of clients' desire to find work and become independent of social assistance and of the reality that employment programs are usually oversubscribed (Lalonde, 1997). Furthermore, analysis of longitudinal data reveals that lone mothers' decisions about paid employment and social assistance are influenced more by the labour market than by the level of welfare benefits (Dooley & Finnie, 2001). These economic and social assaults affect physical and emotional well-being, relationships within the family, child development, and opportunities to participate fully as citizens within the social and political life of the community.

Social Values at Stake

Judgments concerning what values are at stake depend upon one's ideological perspective. Mullaly (1997) has illuminated the core values in the various paradigms (neo-conservative, liberal, social democratic, and socialist) across the ideological spectrum.

The dominant ideology, evident globally in the discourse concerning international trade and locally in policy decisions favouring workfare, is the neo-conservative perspective. The neo-conservative position upholds the values of freedom, individualism, and inequality, and it advocates a minimalist role for the state (Mullaly, 1997). Freedom is held to be a natural right and an absolute principle, more important than other ideals such as distributive justice. Individualism leads to the conceptualization of many conditions, which would otherwise be considered social issues, as problems with individual causes that are best managed through self-reliance and family responsibility. Inequality is an essential incentive for innovation and effort. The most important role of the state, in this perspective, is to ensure the freedom of the market.

From the neo-conservative ideology emanate the neo-liberal economic policies that include elimination of trade barriers, decreased public spending, and deregulation (World Bank, 1995). Transnational corporations and international investors benefit enormously, under the "free-market" model, from this reduction in both the costs and constraints to their operations. Through their relocation and investment leverage, they have pressured governments worldwide to adopt the neo-liberal policies. Thus, we find, in many of the nations that had developed advanced welfare state programs in the postwar period, the imposition of workfare programs and the residualizing of welfare (Peck, 2001).

The emphasis of the neo-conservative perspective upon individual responsibility and culpability is unmistakable in the rhetoric promoting workfare. As Peck notes in his cross-national study, "Discourses of 'welfare dependency' that construct the causes of poverty and un(der)employment in terms of individual failings and that legitimate distinctively antiwelfare restructuring strategies are fast becoming staples of the political orthodoxy ... particularly where neo-liberal economic orthodoxies are most heavily entrenched" (Peck, 2001, p. 11). These models highlight the individual duty of the poor, rather than the collective duty of society (Morel, 2002) and focus on the deficiencies of a 'moral underclass' rather than on structural unemployment or inequality (Mitchell & Shillington, 2002).

In Canada, Jim Struthers (1996) finds the same emphasis in four recurring themes throughout workfare's history: that workfare follows major structural change in the economy, that it occurs in response to high welfare caseloads, that it is "part of a wider campaign of suspicion and punitive administrative practices directed against those on welfare," and that it "represents an attempt to shift the causal location of persistently high levels of unemployment away from structural changes within the economy and towards the inner moral character or values of the victims of these changes" (Struthers, 1996, p. 7).

Similarly, in relation to the United States, Nancy Rose (1995, p. 1) identifies the rationale for the workfare initiatives as "drawing on negative stereotypes of recipients ... and justified by arguments that 'welfare dependency' should be replaced by the 'independence' that comes from working for wages." Describing the 1990s as an intensification of processes begun in the 1980s, Rose (1995, p. 150) writes, "Ignoring structural causes of poverty, a 'culture of poverty' analysis diagnosed 'welfare dependency' as a disease that could be cured by absorbing American values of 'work, self-reliance, and family.'" Even the title of the 1996 legislation, the Personal Responsibility and Work Opportunity Reconciliation Act (PRWORA) is very telling.

The "work ethic" and "family values" are central to the neo-conservative emphasis on individual responsibility. The preservation of the "work ethic" has been paramount in social assistance policies since their origin in the Elizabethan Poor Laws. Limbert & Bullock (2005, p. 259) describe the United States' "work first" approach as "promoting work as a source of personal redemption ... regardless of the labour being performed, the inadequacy of the pay, or the lack of benefits," and Bloom & Kilgore (2003) compare this moral judgmentalism to the assumed superiority of colonizers. Mink (1998, p. 4) criticizes the preeminence of "family values," and documents the fact that "the broad support for disciplinary welfare reform is rooted in the view that mothers' poverty flows from moral failing." She finds the reforms that followed Clinton's promise to "end welfare as we know it" an outrageous assault on women's equality and citizenship rights, and claims, "We do indeed need to end welfare—but as poor single mothers experience it, not as middle-class moralizers imagine it" (Mink, 1998, p. 134).

Social democracy, with its emphasis on the values of equality, freedom, and collectivism (Mullaly, 1997) stands in stark contrast to the ideology of neo-conservatism. It is the paradigm that is most closely aligned with the core values and principles of the social work profession, including respect for human dignity and people's right to self-determination (Canadian Association of Social Workers, 2005). Clearly, workfare policies that are based on negative misconceptions of social assistance recipients and that enforce compliance with mandatory participation requirements through sanctions are at odds with social work principles and responsibilities. An examination of outcomes of various employment strategies including workfare will reveal, as Lightman (1995, p. 153) has pointed out, that the promotion of workfare "has more to do with values, norms, and ideology than any rational or empirical assessment."

Alternatives Attempted

Policy alternatives to encourage independence from social assistance through employment have been attempted as voluntary programs emphasizing incentives and services and as mandatory programs using the eligibility restrictions of workfare. Examples of voluntary programs in Canada will be described before looking at examples of workfare programs in Canada and other countries.

Voluntary Employment Programs

In Canada, an extensive social safety net was woven during the twentieth century. Numerous social and economic rights ratified by the United Nations were enshrined in Canadian legislation, such as the Canada Assistance Plan, which guaranteed the right to income when in need and the right to work that is freely chosen (Morton, 1998). Workfare strategies were ineligible for federal cost sharing until the repeal of the Canada Assistance Plan in 1996. Thus, from 1966 to 1996, primarily incentive and service strategies were prevalent.

Incentive strategies were exemplified in British Columbia and New Brunswick in a federally funded experiment managed by the Social Research and Development Corporation (SRDC). The Self-Sufficiency Project provided a substantial supplement (equal to half the difference between the participant's earnings and approximately $37,000) for up to three years to single parents who left social assistance for full-time employment (SRDC, 2005). Incentive strategies have been utilized in other Canadian provinces, although none to the scale of the Self-Sufficiency Project. In fact, the Supports to Employment Program (STEP) introduced in Ontario in the 1980s has been downscaled under Ontario Works—with the basic exemption removed and 50% of full earnings being deducted from the social assistance payment (Ontario Ministry of Community and Social Services [OMCSS], 2005a).

Service strategies were abundant in Canada prior to the implementation of workfare. Ontario's Employment Support Initiative (ESI), a voluntary program begun in 1983, assisted single parents with a range of pre-employment programs and with the cost of child care and transportation. A provincial evaluation in 1988, using matched comparison groups, found that ESI participants were less likely to be on social assistance, more likely to be in school or job training, more likely to work full-time, and received higher hourly rates of pay than the comparison group (OMCSS, 1988). A later evaluation of ESI conducted a four-year follow-up of clients who entered the program in 1985–1986, and found a small but positive impact: "57.6% of ESI clients were off [social assistance] by December 1989 compared to 54.3% of the adjusted comparison group—a net impact of +3.3%" (Porter, 1991, p. 39). The researcher makes a very interesting comparison with seven US studies, where mandatory elements were being introduced, which also found a net impact of 3.3%.

In one Ontario municipality, a longitudinal study was conducted of a voluntary employment program that assisted single parents with employment preparation as well as child care and employment-related expenses. Outcomes of participants who completed up to five years by 1995 were examined. The study found that involvement in the program and, in particular, participation in the program's career planning and job search components, along with the clients' previous employment experience, were more significant in predicting employment and/or exiting social assistance than personal demographics or child factors (Snyder, 2000).

Workfare Strategies

An international survey completed under the auspices of the Organisation for Economic Co-operation and Development (OECD, 1999a) identified the introduction of welfare-to-work programs in several member countries during the 1990s with considerable differences in the measures introduced. Peck (2001, pp. 74–75) notes, "In the 'liberal' welfare states, such as the United States, Canada, Australia, Switzerland, and the United Kingdom, where means

testing and limited social transfers reflect a vision of welfare as necessarily sub- **Alternatives**
ordinate to market allocation, workfare strategies have been at their most **Attempted**
developed." It is interesting to note, however, that Australia, in contrast with
other OECD countries emphasizing work expectations for single mothers, has
high rates of social assistance receipt and low levels of employment for lone
parents (Whiteford, 2005).

The European Union has adopted a coordinated approach, known as the
European Employment Strategy, which has been characterized as "a strategy for the re-commodification of labour," actively promoting the employability of workers as human capital for the labour market (Dean, Bonvin,
Vielle, & Farvaque, 2005, p. 4). Although less extreme than the American
approach, few European countries share France's focus on inclusion and solidarity that gives primacy to citizen rights rather than freedom of the market.
France attends to the demand side of the labour market, promotes equality
in the labour market, and fosters the balancing of family and work (Mitchell &
Shillington, 2002).

Scandinavian countries, similarly, have retained their commitment to
citizen welfare by adapting to global competition through negotiated pacts
involving labour, employers, and government (Benner, 2003). The United
States introduced mandatory participation in employment services in the
1980s and work-for-welfare expectations in the 1990s. However, the harshest
of restrictive eligibility strategies to date is found in the Personal Responsibility and Work Opportunity Reconciliation Act (PRWORA) of 1996 (Straits, 1999).
It ended the Aid to Families with Dependent Children (AFDC) program, as
well as the federal entitlement to welfare, and replaced it with a system of
block funding to the states under the new Temporary Assistance to Needy
Families program (Rose, 2000). Some claim that, with the work requirements
and the lifetime limit of sixty months of social assistance, US public assistance policy has now been transformed into labour policy (Karger, 2003).

In Canada, the implementation of workfare strategies became more widespread with the repeal of the Canada Assistance Plan and its replacement
with the Canada Health and Social Transfer block funding regime in 1996.
Although there are some parallels with the legislative and funding changes
in the United States in the same year, it is important to discern that while
Canadian legislation now permits workfare, US legislation now requires it.

Strategies in place across Canada have been documented by Gorlick and
Brethour (1998a, 1999). In their overview document, Gorlick and Brethour
(1998b) distinguish between "welfare-to-work" and "workfare" programs,
indicating that the provinces and territories appear to have defined workfare
as requiring a recipient to work in an unremunerated job (not primarily
intended as on-site training) in order to continue receiving social assistance.
The researchers note that most of the provinces and territories insist that
their welfare-to-work programs are not workfare programs, with the exception of Ontario, which describes its Community Participation component as
workfare. However, across the country, a much more coercive approach is

apparent than was evident in the earlier employment programs. Most of the provinces and territories now have active employment strategies, emphasizing "the shortest route to paid employment," based on the belief that "any job is a good job," with requirements for mandatory participation and sanctions for non-compliance (Gorlick & Brethour, 1998b, pp. 6–7). The more restrictive strategies were frequently accompanied by substantial cuts to social assistance benefits rates—19.0% for single, employable Albertans in 1993 (Boessenkool, 1997) and 21.6% for all non-disabled recipients in Ontario in 1995 (National Council of Welfare, 1997).

In most Canadian provinces, single parents with dependent children are now considered employable depending on the age of their youngest child. The age-of-youngest-child criterion varies considerably across the country. British Columbia sets this age at seven years; Manitoba uses the age of six years; Ontario exempts single parents with preschoolers, and Quebec is similar with its criterion of five years; Saskatchewan, the Yukon, and Newfoundland set the age at two years; Nova Scotia and Prince Edward Island use one year; Alberta, however, considers single parents employable when their child reaches six months of age (Gorlick & Brethour, 1998b; Morel, 2002; National Council of Welfare, 2005).

The OECD's (1999b) comparative study of Canada and Switzerland reported that Ontario was the only province of the four Canadian provinces studied that had a workfare program. New Brunswick and Saskatchewan were specifically cited as emphasizing a long-term reintegration strategy to improve clients' employability, holding the view that as long as job search expectations were met, forcing recipients into employment programs would be counterproductive. Although Alberta is similar to Ontario in its political tone and in the use of a retrenchment strategy such as cutting benefit rates, Alberta policy-makers stressed that the workfare strategy is not used.

Quebec's approach reflects the influence of France's post-revolutionary egalitarianism in policies such as child care at a universal price of $5 a day. However, its reductions in benefits for those who refused to participate in employability programs reflect adoption of a "soft-core" version of workfare, in comparison with Ontario's "hard-core" version (Morel, 2002, p. 115).

In Ontario, the Progressive Conservative (PC) party, elected in June 1995, reversed the direction of the earlier reform. As Mike Harris (1995, p. 36), former leader of the PC party stated, "Our proposals are intended to mark a fundamental change in the direction of the welfare system … an acknowledgement of mutual responsibility through the mandatory requirements of workfare." The Ontario workfare strategy is detailed in the initial government publication (OMCSS, 1996) and on the government website. As noted above, it is the Community Participation component placing social assistance recipients in not-for-profit organizations where they "work for welfare" that distinguishes Ontario Works as fitting the strict, formal definition of workfare. The sanctions for non-compliance—reduction or cancellation of social assistance for refusing to participate in any component of Ontario Works—are consistent with broader definitions of workfare. Work-related obligations are now stipulated as a condition of eligibility for social assistance, and there is no longer an exemption from employment expectations for single parents in recognition of their child care responsibilities (Ontario Legislative Assembly, 1997).

By the end of 1999, as a condition of eligibility, sixteen- and seventeen-year-old mothers were required to attend school without regard for the age of their children—within the Learning, Earning, and Parenting (LEAP) program and, later, drug testing and literacy testing as additional mandatory elements of social assistance eligibility were introduced (OMCSS, 2001). Although the Ontario Liberal Party defeated the Progressive Conservative Party in the fall 2003 election and claims to be "delivering on their commitment to treat social assistance recipients with dignity and respect" (OMCSS, 2004, p. 1), the welfare-to-work strategy remains intact and nothing more than a 3% rate increase in each of 2004 and 2005 has been provided.

Outcomes of Workfare Strategies

It has been about a decade since workfare strategies gained pre-eminence, and outcome data are now available. The European experience is interesting, given the variations in their "coordinated" approach. In the Netherlands and in France, despite a stronger emphasis on inclusion in France, immigrants did not fare well in welfare-to-work programs; and generally throughout Europe, the socially excluded did not benefit from more active labour market strategies (Handler, 2003). A study of the "work first" strategy in the UK's New Labour program suggests that for people with multiple barriers, a "life first" approach would be more effective—one that would prioritize their total life needs including their need to work (Williams, 2001). It is especially noteworthy that the Scandinavian countries, where negotiated adaptation rather than full adoption of the workfare strategy took place, were "among the 10 countries considered the most conducive to economic growth" (Benner, 2003, p. 132).

In the United States, the number of families on welfare has decreased by over 50% since the implementation of PRWORA, from about 4.5 million in 1996 to 2 million in June 2003 (United States Department of Health and Human Services [USDHHS], 2005). Most of this decline occurred during the first five years during a lengthy period of strong economic growth (SRDC, 2005). In the past few years, with the worsening of the economy, fewer of those who leave welfare are finding and retaining jobs (Loprest, 2003; USDHHS, 2004). Research reports are now available that provide meta-analyses of state level studies and these reviews conclude that most families who leave welfare have low income. The analysis completed by Acs and Loprest (2004) found that "about two in five leaver families live in poverty" (p. 96). When examining the incomes of only the mothers who left welfare for employment, Moffitt (2002) discovered that their incomes increase only modestly, and Brown (2003) found that some women were worse off, with those in the lowest quin-

tile of earnings experiencing a 4% decline in their income. Lower employment rates and incomes tended to be experienced by women who were less
educated and in poorer health (Moffitt, 2002).

The programs that were most effective in assisting participants to obtain
employment were those that allowed for short-term education or training; and
"only programs that supplemented the income of parents who went to work
consistently increased income" (Michalopoulos, 2004, p. 20). Unfortunately,
if the supplement is provided through continuing receipt of social assistance
with enhanced earnings exemptions, the recipient is using up time-limited
assistance. Other hardships after leaving welfare were experienced in paying for housing (Boushey & Gundersen, 2001) and for health care (Bitler, Gelbach, & Hoynes, 2004). Researchers remain very tentative in comments about
outcomes for children since impacts may not be immediate and the results of
the current downturn in the economy remain to be seen (Besharov & Rossi,
2003). However, there is some evidence that programs with earnings supplements enhanced children's behaviour, health, and academic achievement
(Morris & Duncan, 2002), and that children of families who lost benefits due
to non-compliance were more likely to experience hunger and hospitalization
(Children's Defense Fund, 2004). Even a government report acknowledges
that parents who leave welfare for work often lack supports such as quality
child care, transportation, and training to succeed in the workforce (USDHHS,
2004).

Some Canadian data are now available that begin to reveal the impacts of
workfare and other eligibility restriction strategies; however this is despite
an obvious lack of interest on the part of provincial governments in evaluating their programs (Quaid, 2002). The numbers of social assistance beneficiaries Canada-wide decreased from 3.1 million in 1994 to 1.7 million in 2004, or
by 45% (National Council of Welfare, 2005). Finnie, Irvine and Sceviour (2005)
have now completed a useful analysis of caseload dynamics during the 1990s
based on the Longitudinal Administrative Data (a 10% sample of Canadian tax
filers, followed over time as individuals and families). Social assistance usage
as well as entry rates peaked in 1993–1995 and then declined dramatically to
the end of the decade. Exit rates increased for families with children but
decreased for others. The utilization rates for lone mothers are lowest in
Alberta at 22% in 2000 and most radically changed in Ontario from 56% in 1995
to 33% in 2000.

Although findings about the precise interaction of social assistance policy with economic recovery and federal income security programs are yet to
be released, it is noteworthy that striking changes in the Ontario caseload
dynamics began before the PC election victory and the implementation of
workfare. Frenette and Pinot (2003) examined the same longitudinal data
and determined that although "the average outcomes of welfare leavers were
favourable, income declined (sometimes substantially) for about one-third of
welfare leavers" (p. 19) and that former recipients in Ontario experienced the
greatest declines. Another study benefitting from national longitudinal data

compared the school readiness of preschool children both before and after the welfare reforms began in the mid-1990s and found that children living in poverty had lower scores than their non-poor peers regardless of whether the income was from social assistance or employment (Williamson & Salkie, 2005).

Alternatives Attempted

In Ontario, where Ontario Works was introduced in 1997, a remarkable social assistance caseload decline is apparent—from 1.3 million in March 1995 to 672,000 in March 2004 (National Council of Welfare, 2005). Most of this decline occurred in the Ontario Works caseload (with around 390,000 beneficiaries in 2005) rather than in the Ontario Disability Support Program (with around 290,000 beneficiaries in 2005) (OMCSS, 2005b, 2005c). Quaid (2002) notes, however, that this reduction is less attributable to workfare than to tightening eligibility requirements and moving students to a different program. She found that only about 2% of recipients were engaged in the workfare component of Ontario Works—mandatory work in community placements—despite the government's prescribed rate of 15%. Interestingly, Quaid observes, neither the government (which announced meaningless participation rates of 30% in 2000) nor community activists (who did much to block community placements) want pressure to force the issue. A report by TD Economics (2005) notes that it is extremely difficult to get on welfare with the low benefit levels since 1995 because the earnings exemptions are not applied in the first three months for new applicants. They, in agreement with Finnie et al. above, suggest that low entry levels, not simply workfare policies, are an important explanation for the decline in caseloads. In other words, it is possible that there are now less people receiving social assistance because fewer applicants are eligible. For example, applicants' earnings, although inadequate, may still exceed the current low benefit rates and lone parents are no longer eligible if enrolled in post-secondary education or if living with a partner, no matter how brief a duration. Thus, workfare policies, which are intended to increase exits from social assistance, may not be the sole or even primary explanation for the caseload decline.

The Levy-Coughlin Partnership (1996), contracted by the Ontario government to survey a sample of people who left social assistance in May 1996, found that 46% withdrew because they founds jobs; however, among sole support parents as many left because of a change in living arrangements as found jobs (about 1/3 for each reason)—quite likely because women living with boyfriends were no longer eligible. A federally funded study that looked specifically at the impact of Ontario's welfare reforms on single parents found that "while the proportion of lone mothers with paid work went up, some of those who found jobs may have been financially better off in 1994 than they were in 1996" (HRDC, 1998). A longitudinal study of a panel of ninety people receiving social assistance in Toronto in the fall of 2001 has yielded some early findings from interviewers with the forty-three panelists they were able to locate after two years. The data differentiated nine leavers, five mixers (who require social assistance to top-up earnings), four cyclers (who spend some time working and then cycle back onto assistance), and twenty-five stayers who remained on assistance (Lightman, Mitchell, & Herd, 2004). Leavers, mixers, and cyclers were struggling to make ends meet, relying on food banks, and feeling pressured to leave welfare even though it may have been unrealistic in their circumstances. Stayers wanted to work but couldn't given their significant barriers; they "reported a daily struggle to eke out an existence" (p. 6). Sole support parents found "the lack of accessible and afford-able childcare and the demands of juggling work and care responsibilities combine to direct mothers into low wage, precarious jobs that do not make them any more self-sufficient or independent" (p. 7).

Some useful information is also available regarding the results of the eli-gibility restriction strategy in Alberta. A study by Boessenkool (1997) notes that the number of social assistance beneficiaries in Alberta was nearly halved (in rounded numbers, from 95,000 to 50,000) between 1993 and 1996. The greatest reduction was a result of the decrease in first-time applicants—gen-erally young people who were refused access to assistance. Many of those potential clients, as well as some existing clients, were diverted to employa-bility enhancement and skill-training programs as well as job-creation proj-ects. These human resources strategies were expensive, with an average annu-alized cost per participant of over $10,000 for university education and over $18,000 for job creation. Job growth in a robust economy is also acknowl-edged as contributing to the caseload reduction. Concern is raised about the evidence that some people may have returned to abusive relationships. A further question is posed as to whether the low caseload levels can be main-tained in the next economic downturn.

A separate evaluation of outcomes in Alberta was completed by Elton, Sieppert, Azmier, and Roach (1997), who conducted a follow-up study of peo-ple who left social assistance between September 1993 and October 1996. Although they found that about two thirds had found either full-time or part-time work, an equivalent proportion reported "not having enough money to meet their basic needs (food and shelter) at least once since leaving welfare" (Elton et al., 1997, p. 86). As in many other applications of eligibility restrictions, the concern remains that although people are exiting social assistance, many are not escaping poverty.

Final results are also now available from the voluntary Self-Sufficiency Project implemented in British Columbia and New Brunswick. As noted ear-lier, from the large review of North American programs, Michalopoulos (2004) found that only this type of earnings supplement program consistently resulted in increased incomes for families. Although, at the end of the fol-low-up period, control group members were as likely as program group mem-bers to find jobs, the program group members had higher incomes and less poverty (Michalopoulos et al., 2002). When the supplement option was intro-duced to new applicants, the financial benefits were even greater (Ford, Gyarmati, Foley, & Tattrie, 2003). In considering members of the program group who were not working at the time of the follow-up, the researchers

point out that less capable or resilient single parents may initially need supportive work environments that would allow them to gain a sense of competency (SRDC, 2004). Another follow-up study notes the positive effects of the
Self-Sufficiency Project for early school-aged children, but calls for accessible,
quality child care services for preschool children as well as after-school programs for adolescents (SRDC, 2005).

To conclude the discussion of policy alternatives attempted and workfare strategy outcomes, it is instructive to look at an international review
encompassing a broader range of strategies. Maureen Baker (1996) found
government support and statutory protections to be more important in alleviating poverty than strategies that focus on employment requirements for
mothers:

> Instead of being influenced by the employability of mothers, family
> poverty is influenced by the generosity and scope of government bene-
> fits (including the level of cash benefits and tax concessions for families
> with children), the availability of jobs with statutory protection (such as
> pay equity, parental benefits, and leave for family responsibilities), the
> availability and affordability of child care, and the existence of universal
> social programs such as health insurance and unemployment insurance.
> (Baker, 1996, p. 486)

Whose Problem Definition?

The governments implementing workfare strategies generally hold a neo-
conservative political philosophy consistent with the view of the business
communities and social elites that support them. From their perspective,
lack of income and lack of employment are seen first and foremost as responsibilities of the individual and not of the government. The problem of insufficient individual or family income is considered to be best remedied through
earnings from employment or through support from one's primary community; government expenditures and resultant taxes are thought to be a hin-
drance to business competitiveness in the global market. Unemployment
and underemployment are seen as the fault of the individual and not related
to structural problems in the economy and the labour market; the market is
thought to be best left "unfettered." In addition, provision of social assistance
is believed to be a serious disincentive to seeking employment and likely to
create dependency amongst those of weak moral character (Morel, 2002).
The primacy of the political agenda, despite evidence from research about the
ineffectiveness of workfare strategies, was clear in the government choices
made during the design of Ontario Works (Gorlick & Brethour, 1998a) and
remains apparent in subsequent decisions such as the increase in Community Participation targets (Quaid, 2002).

The social work profession, as well as other humanitarian groups and
individuals operating from a more social democratic philosophy, see the
problem of inadequate income as stemming from structural flaws. Unem-

ployment and underemployment are related to global changes in the economy and the nature of work as well as to systemic disadvantages for particular groups (Mitchell & Shillington, 2002). From this perspective, the workfare strategy itself is seen as a problem that further punishes and excludes those who are the victims of larger forces.

The Context of the Problem

My analysis of the problem and its context are situated within the framework of a social democratic ideology. Thus, consistent with the humanitarian and egalitarian values of the social work profession and many other progressive social organizations, I see the problem as one of insufficient income rather than insufficient effort on the part of social assistance recipients. Lack of sufficient income is related to inequitable distribution of wealth, a decrease in the number of stable, well-paying jobs, and barriers to employment for marginalized groups. Economic, political, and social factors contribute to the creation and maintenance of these problems.

The primary economic force is the globalization of the market through advances in communications and transportation technology, resulting in heightened competition for best product prices and increased mobility of production. In this environment, producers seek a low-cost, flexible labour force and are able to relocate in order to find it. Wages remain low and jobs become more precarious (e.g. part-time, limited-term) while wealth becomes concentrated among the owners of capital and the means of production (Swift, 1997).

Political decision-making is strongly influenced by the business elites who hold considerable leverage in their ability to move their revenue-producing operations to other jurisdictions. The political policies that favour business support neo-liberal (free market) economic measures, which minimize costs and constraints to production. These include low taxation and minimal government spending, limited regulations (e.g., employment standards, environmental controls), and freedom for trade. The congruent neo-conservative philosophy, with its emphasis on individual responsibility for one's own well-being, promotes a break from Canada's historical development of programs expressing a collective sense of responsibility (Baker & Tippen, 1999). One example of this is the alteration of unemployment insurance in Canada from a program that provided insurance-based benefits to 88% of unemployed workers in 1990 to the new Employment Insurance Act, which covered only 43% of unemployed workers by mid-1997 (National Council of Welfare, 1997). Consistent with policies favouring lower government costs and the location of culpability with the individual, we witness in the workfare strategy the current preference for labour force attachment programs rather than human capital development strategies (Peck, 2001), "propping up the flexible labour market to the direct benefit of employers' profit margins" (Hartman, 2005, p. 67).

Some of the social factors that have contributed to more restrictive social assistance policies are the increases in numbers of people receiving social assistance, the high rate of poverty among female-headed, single-parent families, and the general increase in women's participation in the labour force. The number of Canadians receiving social assistance climbed from 1,334,000 in 1980 to a high of 3,100,200 in 1994; the numbers continued to climb even after the end of the recession in 1991 because of persistently high unemployment (National Council of Welfare, 1998). The 2001 census identified over 1.3 million single-parent families, which represents one quarter of families with children in Canada (Statistics Canada, 2004). Over 80% of single parent families are headed by women; a large percentage of them (38.4% in 2003) have incomes below the Statistics Canada LICO, and generally about one third report receiving some social assistance (Finnie et al., 2005; National Council of Welfare, 2004; Statistics Canada, 2004). Finally, the increase in women's participation in the labour force (from 30% in 1961 to 62% in 2004) has been a factor in the redefinition of women on social assistance as employable (Baker, 2001; Statistics Canada, 2005).

Implications for Oppressed Groups

Implications for Oppressed Groups

The workfare strategy has particularly poignant impacts for members of groups that have already been marginalized through the historical processes of patriarchy, capitalism, and colonialism. Nancy Rose (1995), in her historical overview of women, welfare, and government work programs, uses a conceptual framework based on the importance of gender, class, and race.

Abramovitz (1988) was one of the first feminists to highlight the imposition of the family ethic and the maintenance of patriarchy through social welfare policy. Gender biases are more evident in the social assistance policies of the United States since their programs were constructed initially to assist single-parent families only (Sorensen, Mincy, & Halpern, 2000). Heterosexist and patriarchal assumptions underlie the framing of single motherhood as problematic (Limbert & Bullok, 2005). Hence, it is not surprising to find that the PRWORA and the Temporary Assistance to Needy Families (TANF) program explicitly promote marriage to end dependency on social assistance (Rose, 2000).

In Canada, where single mothers constitute a much smaller portion of the welfare caseload (27% in 1997 [National Council of Welfare, 1998]), there is a similar redirection of single mothers to "become either economically self-sufficient or the responsibility of any 'male bread-winner'" (Mayson, 1999, p. 107). Single mothers are expected to participate in welfare-to-work programs with exemptions only for parents of young or disabled children (Gorlick & Brethour, 1998a). In addition, single mothers cohabiting with unrelated males are considered to be in a spousal relationship and are no longer eligible for social assistance in their own right.

An important change in the conceptualization of employability has occurred with the advent of workfare programs. From the initiation of Mother's Allowance in Manitoba in 1916 to the end of the 1950s, women's labour market participation was considered "incompatible with their duty to their children" (Evans, 1996, p. 153). Women on social assistance in Ontario during this period were fearful of losing their children to the child welfare authorities if they sought employment in order to improve their economic well-being (Strong-Boag, 1979). The traditional view began to give way in the 1970s and 1980s in response to both feminist pressures for greater choices for women and economic pressures for additional income in two-parent families (Morel, 2002). Women's choices regarding parenting or work outside the home and regarding their economic dependence on male friends are more circumscribed under workfare regimes. Bloom and Kilgore (2003) describe workfare programs as negating the caregiving role of single mothers and converting participants' "mothering" identities to "employable" identities with a colonial zeal.

According to a Marxist analysis of capitalism, the owners of capital and of the means of production have higher profits when there is a ready supply of cheap labour. The cost of labour is reduced through the application of workfare policies, as Rose explains: "Workfare programs are congruent with the logic of production-for-profit. In fact, they lower wage costs and boost profits in the short run by channelling the poor into low-wage labor markets, where the increased supply of labor makes it more difficult for workers to demand higher wages and better working conditions" (Rose, 1995, p. 14). Workfare and other restrictive eligibility policies in Canada similarly fit the strategy of present-day "owners of capital" who seek a flexible, yet disciplined, low-cost labour market (Broad, 1997; Pinder, 2004). Peck (2001, p. 6), who describes workfare as a labour force regulator, notes that "workfare is not about creating jobs for people who don't have them; it is about creating workers for jobs that nobody wants."

The reality of oppression based on race in Canada has been documented by Christensen (1999), who shows that discrimination in employment keeps non-White workers in lower paying, less secure employment and, therefore, at greatest risk of needing social assistance and facing workfare measures—which, in turn, ensures their ties to an unrewarding job market. Immigrant women are disadvantaged right from the application process, which requires families to designate a principal applicant (the member most likely to score the highest points in the rating system) and others as dependents, who then are less likely to receive language instruction and other preparation for employment (Mann, 2004). Foreign credentials are often not recognized in Canada and, most shamefully, race rather than place of birth outside of Canada has been found to be a more reliable predictor of how foreign education is valued (Reitz, 2001).

Historical patterns of race, class, and gender discrimination are embedded in social structures and policies, including workfare (Lindhorst & Mancoske, 2003). As Caragata (2003) notes, the resultant exclusion of women Conclusion who are poor and, particularly, poor women of colour, makes it more difficult for their claims to be brought into public discourse. References

Conclusion

Workfare has reformulated the problem of insufficient income, formerly addressed (albeit only partially) by welfare programs, into an ill-founded fear of pervasive disincentives to work, which purportedly must be addressed through restrictive strategies. It is a social policy that is firmly rooted in neo-conservative ideology, holding individuals and families responsible for the causation and solution of their poverty. Workfare meets the neo-liberal economic objectives of limiting government spending and maintaining a ready supply of workers for a flexible, low-cost labour market. Thus, many advanced welfare states, yielding to the pressures of globalized capitalism, have chosen to impose workfare programs.

Although much of the political rhetoric attempts to suggest that workfare gives "a hand up" to social assistance recipients, empirical evidence reveals that, while social assistance caseloads have decreased, the economic well-being of many former recipients has worsened. Many people are no longer eligible for social assistance and have found employment in the precarious low-paying, part-time, and temporary job market. Their earnings and benefits, minus their employment-related expenses for such costs as child care and transportation, frequently provide less than what they were receiving earlier in welfare benefits. The social consequences of this poverty are borne disproportionately by groups already experiencing oppression due to gender, race, and class. Women are particularly disadvantaged in the provisions that require them to work, but that do not recognize the realities or the importance of their child care responsibilities.

Clearly, economic objectives take precedence over social goals in the neo-conservative world of workfare. Government spending on social assistance has been reduced and a more flexible workforce has been created. Poverty, with its disabling consequences, has worsened for many who left social assistance. An ideology congruent with the interests of the architects of global capitalism undergirds workfare strategies, an ideology that is not in keeping with Canada's tradition of liberalism and collective concern for well-being.

References

Abramovitz, M. (1988). *Regulating the lives of women: Social welfare policy from colonial times to the present.* Boston: South End Press.

Acs, G., & Loprest, P. (2004). *Leaving welfare: Employment and well-being of families that left welfare in the post-entitlement era.* Kalamazoo, MI: W.E. Upjohn Institute for Employment Research.

Baker, M. (1996). Social assistance and the employability of mothers: Two models from cross-national research. *Canadian Journal of Sociology, 21*(4), 483–503.

References

Baker, M. (2001). *Families, labour and love*. Vancouver: University of British Columbia Press.

Baker, M. & Tippen, D. (1999). *Poverty, social assistance, and the employability of mothers: Restructuring welfare states*. Toronto: University of Toronto Press.

Benner, M. (2003). The Scandinavian challenge: The future of advanced welfare states in the knowledge economy. *Acta Sociologica, 46*(2), 132–149.

Besharov, D., & Rossi, P. (2003). Conclusion. In D. Besharov (Ed.), *Family and child well-being after welfare reform* (pp. 279–298). New Brunswick, NJ: Transaction.

Bitler, M., Gelbach, J., & Hoynes, H. (2004). *Welfare reform and health*. Cambridge, MA: National Bureau of Economic Research.

Bloom, L.R., & Kilgore, D. (2003). The colonization of (m)others in welfare-to-work education. *Educational Policy, 17*(3), 365–384.

Boessenkool, K. (1997, April). Back to work: Learning from the Alberta welfare experiment. *C.D. Howe Institute Commentary, 90*, 1–29.

Boushey, H., & Gundersen, B. (2001). *When work just isn't enough: Measuring hardships faced by families after moving from welfare to work*. Washington, DC: Economic Policy Institute.

Broad, D. (1997). The casualization of the labour force. In A. Duffy, D. Glenday, & N. Pupo (Eds.), *Good jobs, bad jobs, no jobs: The transformation of work in the 21st century* (pp. 53–73). Toronto: Harcourt Brace.

Brown, M. (2003). Ghettos, fiscal federalism, and welfare reform. In S. Schram, J. Soss, & R. Fording (Eds.), *Race and the politics of welfare* (pp. 47–71). Ann Arbor: University of Michigan Press.

Canadian Association of Social Workers. (2005). *Code of ethics*. Ottawa: Author.

Caragata, L. (2003). Neo-conservative realities: The social and economic marginalization of Canadian women. *International Sociology, 18*(3), 559–580.

Children's Defence Fund. (2004). *New findings show direct link between loss of TANF benefits and children suffering*. Online at <http://www.childrensdefence.org/familyincome/welfare/tanflink.aspx>.

Christensen, C. (1999). Multiculturalism, racism, and social work: An exploration of issues in the Canadian context. In G. Lie & D. Este (Eds.), *Professional social service delivery in a multicultural world* (pp. 293–310). Toronto: Canadian Scholars' Press.

Dean, H., Bonvin, J-M., Vielle, P., & Farvaque, N. (2005). Developing capabilities and rights in welfare-to-work policies. *European Societies, 7*(1), 3–26.

Dooley, M., & Finnie, R. (2001). *Differences in labour force participation, earnings and welfare participation among Canadian lone mothers: A longitudinal analysis*. Hull: Human Resources Development Canada, Applied Research Branch.

Elton, D., Sieppert, J., Azmier, J., & Roach, R. (1997). *Where are they now? Assessing the impact of welfare reform on former recipients*. Calgary: Canada West Foundation.

Evans, P. (1993). From workfare to the social contract: Implications for Canada of recent U.S. welfare reforms. *Canadian Public Policy, 19*(1), 54–67.

Evans, P. (1996). Single mothers and Ontario's welfare policy: Restructuring the debate. In J. Brodie (Ed.), *Women and Canadian public policy* (pp. 151–172). Toronto: Harcourt.

Finnie, R., Irvine, I., & Sceviour, R. (2005). *Social assistance use in Canada: National and provincial trends in incidence, entry and exit*. Ottawa: Statistics Canada.

Ford, R., Gyarmati, D., Foley, K., & Tattrie, D. (2003). *Can work incentives pay for themselves: Final report on the Self-Sufficiency Project for welfare applicants.* Ottawa: Social Research and Demonstration Corporation.

Frenette, M., & Pinot, G. (2003). *Life after welfare: The economic well being of welfare leavers in Canada during the 1990s.* Ottawa: Statistics Canada.

Gorlick, C., & Brethour, G. (1998a). *Welfare-to-work programs: A national inventory.* Ottawa: Canadian Council on Social Development.

Gorlick, C., & Brethour, G. (1998b). *Welfare-to-work programs: An overview.* Ottawa: Canadian Council on Social Development.

Gorlick, C., & Brethour, G. (1999). *Welfare-to-work—Provincial summaries.* Ottawa: Canadian Council on Social Development.

Handler, J. (2003). Social citizenship and workfare in the US and Western Europe: From status to contract. *Journal of European Social Policy, 13*(30), 229–243.

Handler, J. (2005). Myth and ceremony in workfare: Rights, contracts, and client satisfaction. *Journal of Socio-Economics, 34,* 101–124.

Harris, M. (1995). Welfare should offer a hand up, not a hand-out. *Policy Options, 16*(4), 33–36.

Hartman, Y. (2005). In bed with the enemy: Some ideas on the connections between neo-liberalism and the welfare state. *Current Sociology, 53*(1), 57–73.

Human Resources Development Canada (HRDC). (1998). Welfare cuts may lead to more paid work for lone mothers—but not necessarily to higher incomes. *Applied Research Bulletin, 4*(1), 25–26.

Karger, H. (2003). Ending public assistance: The transformation of US public assistance policy into labour policy. *Journal of Social Policy, 32*(3), 383–401.

Lalonde, L. (1997). Tory welfare policies: A view from the inside. In D. Ralph, A. Regimbald, & N. St-Amand (Eds.), *Mike Harris's Ontario: Open for business; closed to people* (pp. 92–102). Halifax: Fernwood.

Levy-Coughlin Partnership. (1996). *A survey of people who have left social assistance.* Toronto: Ontario Ministry of Community and Social Services.

Lightman, E. (1995). You can lead a horse to water, but ...: The case against workfare in Canada. In J. Richards et al. (Eds.), *Helping the poor: A qualified case for workfare* (pp. 151–183). Toronto: C.D. Howe Institute.

Lightman, E. (2003). *Social policy in Canada.* Don Mills, ON: Oxford University Press.

Lightman, E., Mitchell, A., & Herd, D. (2004). *One Year On: Leavers, mixers, cyclers and stayers; Tracking the experiences of a panel of Ontario Works recipients* [Social Assistance in the New Economy project]. Toronto: University of Toronto Faculty of Social Work.

Limbert, W., & Bullock, H. (2005). "Playing the fool": US welfare policy from a critical race perspective. *Feminism and Psychology, 15*(3) 253–274.

Lindhorst, T., & Mancoske, R. (2003). Race, gender and class inequities in welfare reform. *Race, Gender and Class, 10*(2), 27–40.

Loprest, P. (2003). *Fewer welfare leavers employed in weak economy.* Washington, DC: Urban Institute.

Mann, G. (2004). Gender, work and migration: Deskilling Chinese immigrant women in Canada. *Women's Studies International Forum, 27,* 135–148.

Mayson, M. (1999). Ontario Works and single mothers: Redefining "Deservedness and the social contract." *Journal of Canadian Studies, 34*(2), 89–109.

References   Michalopoulos, C. (2004). *What works best for whom: Effects of welfare and work policies by subgroup.* Online at <www.acf.hhs.gov/programs/opre/welfare_employ/what_wksbest>.

Michalopoulos, C., Tattrie, D., Miller, C., Robins, P. K., Morris, P., Gyarmati, D., Redcross, C., Foley, K., & Ford, R. (2002). *Making work pay: Final report on the Self-Sufficiency Project for long-term welfare recipients.* Ottawa: Social Research and Demonstration Corporation.

Mink, G. (1998). *Welfare's end.* Ithaca: Cornell University Press.

Mitchell, A., & Shillington, R. (2002). *Poverty, inequality and social inclusion.* Toronto: Laidlaw Foundation.

Moffitt, R. (2002). From welfare to work: What the evidence shows. In I. Sawhill, K. Weaver, R. Haskins, & A. Kane (Eds.), *Welfare reform and beyond: The future of the safety net* (pp. 79–86). Washington, DC: Brookings Institute.

Morel, S. (2002). *The insertion model or the workfare model? The transformation of social assistance within Quebec and Canada.* Ottawa: Canada, Status of Women.

Morris, P., & Duncan, G. (2002). Which welfare reforms are best for children? In I. Sawhill, K. Weaver, R. Haskins, & A. Kane (Eds.), *Welfare reform and beyond: The future of the safety net* (pp. 71–78). Washington, DC: Brookings Institute.

Morton, B. (1998). No cap in hand: The government has virtually eliminated universal social programs. *Briarpatch, 26*(10), 9–10.

Mullaly, R. (1997). *Structural social work: Ideology, theory and practice.* Toronto: McClelland and Stewart.

National Council of Welfare. (1997). *Another look at welfare reform.* Ottawa: Public Works and Government Services Canada.

National Council of Welfare. (1998). *Profiles of welfare: Myths and realities.* Ottawa: Public Works and Government Services Canada.

National Council of Welfare. (2004). *Poverty profile 2001.* Ottawa: Public Works and Government Services Canada.

National Council of Welfare. (2005). *Welfare incomes 2004.* Ottawa: Public Works and Government Services Canada.

Ontario Legislative Assembly. (1997). *Bill 142: An act to revise the law related to social assistance by enacting the Ontario Works Act and the Ontario Disability Support Program Act.* Toronto: Author.

Ontario Ministry of Community & Social Services. (1988). *Towards independence: Highlights of the evaluation of the Employment Opportunities program.* Toronto: Queen's Printer.

Ontario Ministry of Community & Social Services. (1996). *A summary of the Ontario Works program.* Toronto: Queen's Printer for Ontario.

Ontario Ministry of Community & Social Services. (2001). *Ontario Works.* Online at <www.gov.on.ca/css/page/services/ontworks.html>.

Ontario Ministry of Community & Social Services. (2004). *Improving Ontario's social assistance programs.* Online at <www.cfcs.gov.on.ca/CFCS/en/newsRoom/backgrounders/041215A.htm>.

Ontario Ministry of Community & Social Services. (2005a). *Ontario Works: What are the earnings exemptions?* Online at <www.cfcs.gov.on.ca/CFCS/en/programs/IES/OntarioWorks/FAQS/q-ow-earningsexemptions.htm>.

Ontario Ministry of Community and Social Services. (2005b) *Ontario Works: Quarterly statistical report.* Online at <www.cfcs.gov.on.ca/CFCS/en/programs/IES/OntarioWorks/Publications/owCaseload.htm>.

Ontario Ministry of Community and Social Services. (2005c). *Ontario Disability Support Program: Quarterly statistical report.* Online at <www.cfcs.gov.on.ca/ cfcs/en/programs/ies/OntarioDisabilitySupportProgram/Publications/odsp Caseload.htm>. *References*

Organisation for Economic Co-operation and Development (oecd). (1999a). *The local dimension of welfare-to-work: An international survey.* Paris: Author.

Organisation for Economic Co-operation and Development (oecd). (1999b). *The battle against exclusion: Social assistance in Canada and Switzerland.* Paris: Author.

Peck, J. (2001). *Workfare states.* New York: Guilford Press.

Pinder, S. (2004). *Welfare, workfare, single mothers and their re-entry into the workforce: Canada and the United States.* Unpublished PhD dissertation, New School University, New York.

Porter, E. (1991). *The long-term effects of three employment programs for social assistance recipients.* Toronto: Ministry of Community and Social Services.

Pulkingham, J., & Ternowetsky, G. (1998). *A state of the art review of income security reform in Canada.* Ottawa: International Development Research Council.

Quaid, M. (2002). *Workfare: Why good social policy ideas go bad.* Toronto: University of Toronto Press.

Rein, M. (1974). The welfare crisis. In L. Rainwater (Ed.), *Social problems and public policy* (pp. 89–102). Chicago: Aldine.

Reitz, J.G. (2001). Immigrant skill utilization in the Canadian labor market: Implications of human capital research. *Journal of International Migration and Integration, 2*(3), 347–378.

Rose, N. (1995). *Workfare or fair work: Women, welfare, and government work programs.* New Brunswick, NJ: Rutgers University Press.

Rose, N. (2000). An analysis of welfare reform. *Journal of Economic Issues, 34*(1), 143–157.

Snyder, L. (2000). Successes of single mothers on social assistance through a voluntary employment program. *Canadian Social Work Review, 17*(1), 49–68.

Social Research and Demonstration Corporation. (2004). Making the transition from welfare to work. *Learning What Works, 4*(2), 1–2.

Social Research and Demonstration Corporation. (2005). Whither welfare? *Learning What Works, 5*(1), 6–7.

Sorensen, E., Mincy, R., & Halpern, A. (2000). *Redirecting welfare policy toward building strong families.* Washington, DC: Urban Institute.

Statistics Canada. (2004). *Census families in private households by family structure.* Online at <http://www40.statcan.ca/l01/cst01/famil54d.htm>.

Statistics Canada. (2005). *Labour force and participation rates by sex and age group.* Online at <http://www40.statcan.ca/l01/cst01/labor05.htm>.

Straits, R. (1999). Issues raised by welfare reform in the United States. In Organisation for Economic Co-operation and Development (Ed.), *The local dimension of welfare-to-work: An international survey* (pp. 177–196). Paris: OECD.

Strong-Boag, V. (1979). Wages for housework: The beginnings of social security in Canada. *Journal of Canadian Studies, 14*(1), 24–34.

Struthers, J. (1996). *Can workfare work? Reflections from history.* Ottawa: Caledon Institute of Social Policy.

References   Swift, J. (1997). From cars to casinos, from work to workfare: The brave new world of Canadian employment. In A. Duffy, D. Glenday, & N. Pupo (Eds.), *Good jobs, bad jobs, no jobs: The transformation of work in the 21st century* (pp. 35–52). Toronto: Harcourt Brace.

Torjman, S. (1996). *Workfare: A poor law.* Ottawa: Caledon Institute of Social Policy.

TD Economics (2005). *From welfare to work in Ontario: Still the road less travelled.* Toronto: TD Bank Financial Group.

United States Department of Health and Human Services. (2004). *FY 2003 annual performance report.* Online at <www.acf.hhs.gov/programs/opre/acf_perfplan/ann_per/apr2005/apr2005.pdf>.

United States Department of Health and Human Services. (2005). *TANF caseloads reported as of 12/02/03.* Online at <www.acf.hhs.gov/news/press/2003/mar03_jun03.htm>.

Whiteford, P. (2005). *The welfare expenditure debate: Economic myths of the left and right revisited.* Delivered at the Social Policy Research Centre Conference, University of New South Wales, Sydney, 21 July. Online at <www.sprc.unsw.edu.au/ASPC2005/papers/Paper7.pdf>.

Williams, F. (2001). In and beyond New Labour: Towards a political ethics of care. *Critical Social Policy, 21,* 467–493.

Williamson, D., & Salkie, F. (2005). Welfare reforms in Canada: Implications for the well-being of preschool children in poverty. *Journal of Children & Poverty, 11* (1), 55–76.

World Bank. (1995). *World development report 1995: Workers in an integrating world.* Oxford: Oxford University Press.

Toward Inclusion of Gay and Lesbian People:
Social Policy Changes in Relation to
Sexual Orientation

16

Brian O'Neill

One of the most striking social changes in Canada and much of the world over the past three decades has been the increased acceptance of gay and lesbian people, and the decrease in discrimination based on sexual orientation. This change, though contentious and hotly debated, represents a shift in Canadian values evident in social policies at various levels. Four developments have been pivotal: decriminalization of sexual acts between members of the same sex by changes to the Criminal Code in 1969; declassification of homosexuality as a mental disorder by the American Psychiatric Association in 1973; recognition of the rights of gay, lesbian, and bisexual people under the 1982 Canadian Charter of Rights and Freedoms and federal and provincial human rights codes beginning in the late 1970s; and increased awareness of human service needs related to same-sex sexual orientation, due in part to advent of the HIV/AIDS pandemic since the 1980s. This chapter first discusses heterosexism, the ideology that underlies the oppression encountered by gay, lesbian and bisexual people. It then introduces concepts related to sexual orientation and highlights features of the gay and lesbian communities. The remainder of the chapter traces changes in the expression of heterosexism in public policies and identifies directions for future development.

Heterosexism

Historically, the response in Canada to same-sex sexual orientation has been shaped by heterosexism. Analogous to racism and sexism, heterosexism is "the cultural ideology that perpetuates sexual stigma by denying and denigrating any nonheterosexual form of behavior, identity, relationship, or community" (Herek, 2004, p. 16). Heterosexist discourses promulgate stereotypes of gay men and lesbians as dangerous sex offenders, threats to the family, and mentally ill (C.A. O'Brien & Goldberg, 2000). As with other oppressive ideologies (Mullaly, 2002), heterosexism is reproduced at the structural, cultural, and personal levels, privileging those who conform to the dominant sexual orientation, heterosexuality, and disadvantaging those who show signs of same-sex orientation. Because heterosexuality is presented as natural and universal, oppression related to sexual orientation has been widely supported at least

Intersection of
Heterosexism
with Racism
and Other
Oppressive
Ideologies

Sexual
Orientation

tacitly, and, for the most part, gone unrecognized. However, the emergence of gay and lesbian communities, and challenges to heterosexism by members of these communities and their allies have led to social changes that are reflected in legislation, organizational policies, and public attitudes.

The term "homophobia," coined by Weinberg in 1972 to identify the irrational fear of same-sex sexual orientation, is commonly used to refer to prejudice against gay men and lesbians. The term is not used in this chapter in that way because to do so obscures the systemic nature of oppression based on sexual orientation, creating the impression that discrimination against gay people is related solely to individuals' attitudes and psychological problems (Williamson, 2000). Rather, following Herek (2004), "internalized homophobia" is employed here more narrowly to refer to the negative impact on people who are sexually attracted to members of their own sex, when they internalize heterosexism.

Intersection of Heterosexism with Racism and Other Oppressive Ideologies

It is an oversimplification to assume that gay people are subject only to heterosexism and homophobia. The intersectional model recognizes that any one person may have more than one social location and that the various forms of exclusion based on race, ethnicity, class, gender, age, and ability may interact, producing complex and harsh experiences of oppression (Beck, Williams, Hope, & Park, 2001). Thus, gay men and lesbians who are members of other minority groups may be simultaneously disempowered by several ideologies in both the general and ethnic minority communities as well as the gay and lesbian communities (Boodram, 2003; Diaz, Ayala, Bein, Henne, & Marin, 2001).

In the past, individuals who did not conform to conventional gender roles were accepted and honoured in some North American Aboriginal societies (Brotman, Ryan, Jalbert, & Rowe, 2002a). However, due in large part to colonialism, modern First Nations communities incorporated many of the values that inform the dominant culture. Thus, Aboriginal people may encounter heterosexism within their indigenous communities as well as the dominant culture. The term "two-spirited" has been taken up by many Aboriginal people as a more culturally appropriate way to identify their gender and sexual identities (Cameron, 2005).

Sexual Orientation

Terms related to gender and sexuality are often confused despite their distinct meanings (Todd, 2006). "Gender identity" is the sex individuals believe they are, usually male or female, based on their primary physical sex characteristics. Despite stereotypes to the contrary, most gay men think of themselves as male and most lesbians consider themselves to be female. It is transgendered people, including transsexuals, who have gender identities different than those ascribed to them based on their physical characteristics, for instance, people with male genitalia who consider themselves to be female (Shapiro, 2005). Transgendered individuals may have either heterosexual or same-sex sexual orientation. "Gender roles" are behaviours deemed appropriate for each sex, and they vary across cultures. They may be defined loosely or rigidly, and they extend to all areas of life, including not only speech and behavioural mannerisms, but also choices of occupation, family roles, and sexual partners. Heterosexism shapes gender roles in our culture to exclude same-sex sexual behaviour. Policies specifically focused on transgendered people are not addressed in this chapter because most commonly the oppression they may encounter is related to their gender identity and performance of gender roles rather than their sexual orientation per se.

The common sense understanding of "sexual orientation" in the northern European traditions that have shaped the dominant cultures of Canada is that heterosexuality refers to attraction between males and females, homosexuality to attraction between members of the same sex, and bisexuality to attraction to people of both sexes. In other cultural contexts, classification of sexual orientation may also be based on the age and roles of participants in addition to their gender (Elliston, 2005).

Clearly, it is an oversimplification to assume that sexual orientation is a clear-cut and stable trait. Kinsey's pioneering investigations of sexuality suggested that 5–10% of males (Kinsey, Pomeroy, & Martin, 1948), and 3–5% of females (Kinsey, Pomeroy, Martin, & Gebhard, 1955) participate in sex primarily with members of their own sex for a period of three or more years during their adult lives. However, these studies also revealed that in addition, at least as many people are bisexual, do not act on their same-sex attractions, or experience changes in the focus of their sexuality during their lives. Although more recent studies in the United States (e.g., Lauman, Gagnon, Michael, & Michaels, 2000) and Canada (Statistics Canada, 2004b) found that lower proportions of respondents identify as gay, lesbian, or bisexual, data continue to indicate that a significant proportion of the population is sexually interested in members of their own sex for at least a period of their adult lives (Kinsey Institute, 2005).

Theories about the causes of variation in sexual orientation abound (Murphy, 1997). Some explanations focus on biological factors such as differences in brain structures, prenatal hormonal influences, and genetic heredity (Stein, 2001). There is some empirical support for these propositions, but it is not conclusive. A second set of theories points to social environmental influences. For instance, some interpretations of psychoanalytic theory hold that same-sex sexual orientation is an aberration in psychosexual development due to deficiencies in parent–child relationships (Drescher, 2002). Yet a third line of thinking holds that sexuality is socially constructed; influenced by cultural values and circumstances, people have the potential for sexual involvement with others regardless of sex, and may or may not identify as gay, lesbian, or bisexual (Vance, 2005; Weeks, 2001). The fact that some people who have

Sexual
Orientation

previously been exclusively heterosexual participate in sexual behaviour with members of their own sex when in sex-segregated environments or when they meet a particular individual supports the argument that human sexuality is extremely flexible. However, there is no evidence supporting claims that sexual orientation can be changed by means of behavioural, psychological, or other forms of therapy.

Knowledge about Same-Sex Sexual Orientation

In the development and analysis of policy, information is needed about the population affected by the problem. Unfortunately, there is a lack of accurate knowledge about the lives of those most seriously affected by heterosexism, those who are, or are perceived to be, sexually attracted to members of their own sex. A multitude of characteristics have been thought to be associated with same-sex sexual orientation (J. O'Brien, 2001). These include behaviours such as gender atypical mannerisms and speech patterns, and aptitudes for certain artistic and athletic endeavours. Of more serious concern in relation to social policy are stereotypes that those who are oriented to their own sex are likely to be sexual predators, mentally disturbed, and unable to form stable mature relationships.

Despite concerted efforts by social scientists as well as the police and military, a valid and reliable method of detecting and categorizing people according to their sexual orientation has not been developed (Archer, 1999; Kinsman, 2000). This limitation impedes research in the area, as it is not feasible to draw representative samples of people who are oriented to their own sex. However, studies conducted over the past thirty years based on samples of gay, lesbian, and bisexual people drawn from non-clinical populations discredit earlier negative beliefs about same-sex sexual orientation (Minton, 2002). Nevertheless, this body of knowledge does not provide information about the lives of those who have some degree of same-sex sexual orientation but do not identify as gay, lesbian, or bisexual or who are unwilling to come out.

Identities Based on Sexual Orientation

The terms "sexual identity" and "sexual orientation" are often used interchangeably in referring to sexual attraction and behaviour. However, although there is evidence of same-sex sexual behaviour occurring in numerous cultures throughout history (Churchill, 1967; Crompton, 2003; Scasta, 1998), until relatively recently, having particular sexual interests, whatever their cause, was not necessarily the basis for ascribing identity. Rather, sexual contact with another person of the same sex has had diverse meanings across time and in various social contexts. In some cultures, it was considered simply to be a behaviour, though often censured; for instance, in Europe during the middle ages, same-sex sexuality may have been disapproved of as immoral in much the same way that heterosexual adultery was, but it was not seen as a marker of identity. In contrast, in certain cultures, same-sex activity was a highly valued aspect of the process of taking on an adult identity, though not necessarily seen as erotic (Elliston, 2005). As noted earlier, in some cultures sexual orientation, and subsequently sexual identity, may be defined more in terms of roles in sexual encounters than the genders of the people involved. For instance, in Latin cultures, the man who is penetrated during anal intercourse may be considered homosexual, while the man who penetrates may retain his identity as heterosexual (Irvine, 1995).

Gay and Lesbian Communities

Until the Kinsey studies, it was thought that same-sex sexual orientation was relatively rare because its expression was largely covert due to its stigmatization. It was not until the late nineteenth century that the concept of homosexuality as a defining characteristic of identity appeared primarily within medical discourse, and people who were attracted to others of their own sex came to be known as homosexuals (Weeks, 2001). In reaction to the creation of the "homosexual" as a stigmatized category of person, during the second half of the twentieth century people who were sexually attracted to members of their own sex began to define themselves as gay, lesbian, or bisexual, but gave these identities a positive connotation (Altman, 2001). Although the term "gay" may refer to both men and women, more recently it has been used to refer specifically to males who are sexually attracted to males. In contrast, although the term "lesbian" alludes to sexual and emotional attraction between women, it may be used without necessarily inferring a sexual element (Meyer, 2001).

The process of becoming aware of and disclosing one's gay, lesbian, or bisexual identity is referred to as "coming out." There are various models of coming out, with some differences in the pattern for men and women (Tully, 2000). The number of people who come out is smaller than those who experience same-sex sexual orientation in part because of fear of discrimination, but also because not all people who are attracted to or participate in sex with members of their own sex identify as gay, lesbian, or bisexual. However, sizable gay and lesbian communities have emerged around the world, exerting considerable influence on the development of social policies, particularly in Canada (Adam, Duyvendak, & Krouwel, 1999).

Gay and Lesbian Communities

There are well-developed, but largely unnoticed, social networks among people who are attracted to members of their own sex throughout rural Canada (Warner, 2002). However, it is the communities that have developed in the centres of large Canadian cities, in part due to migration from rural and suburban areas, that have shaped public images of gay and lesbian people. These communities originated primarily around commercial establishments catering to gay men, such as bars, baths, and restaurants, but over time have come to include organizations focusing on the needs of both men and women. Gay and lesbian communities include businesses that provide various products and services, newspapers and magazines, cultural organizations, religious groups, sports and recreational clubs, political associations and social change movements, support groups for youth and seniors, as well as health care and counselling services. The advent of HIV in the 1980s stimulated the development of AIDS service organizations based largely in gay communities (Cain, 1997). In addition to their participation in communities dominated by gay men, lesbians have also developed separate communities within the context of the women's movement (Altman, 2001). No comparable bisexual communities have emerged.

Media coverage has contributed to a distorted image of gay and lesbian populations. In current movies and television shows, gay men and to a lesser extent lesbians are portrayed as relatively wealthy, youthful, white, middle class, and able-bodied. Gay men in particular are presented as being unencumbered by family responsibilities and focusing mainly on achieving sexual and social satisfaction (e.g., Cooper, 2003). In reality, there is diversity within the gay population with respect to race/ethnicity, age, social class, physical and intellectual ability, and religion (Greene, 1997; O'Neill, 1999), and many lesbians and gay men care for their children as well as support aging parents (O'Brien & Goldberg, 2000). Members of various ethnic minority groups and religions as well as people with disabilities have organized to counter discrimination against them within the gay and lesbian communities (Warner, 2002).

Increasing Canadian Acceptance of Gays and Lesbians

Individuals' opinions about sexual orientation are correlated with their social locations and belief systems (Herek, 2000). In general, prejudice toward gays and lesbians is associated with being male, older, less educated, and living in rural areas. Negative beliefs are also stronger among those who have authoritarian personalities, hold conservative religious beliefs, and support traditional gender roles. In contrast, attitudes are more positive among those who have had personal contact with gay men and lesbians. Since 1975, when only 28% of Canadians were accepting of same-sex sexual orientation (Bibby, 1995), attitudes have consistently become more positive. For instance, a 1994 national survey indicated that 61% of respondents had at least some degree of tolerance for same-sex sexuality (Widmer, Treas, & Newcomb, 1998) and a more limited 1998 survey by Altemeyer (2001) indicated the majority of respondents were non-homophobic. In part, this change may be related to more gay and lesbian people coming out, as 50% of respondents in a 1998 poll indicated that they were aware that some of their friends, co-workers, and relatives were gay or lesbian (Canadian Press, 2000). However, although attitudes have become more positive, a 1999 poll by the British Columbia Human Rights Commission (2001) found that gays and lesbians were the least tolerated minority group in the province.

Canadian Social Policies

Public policy in Canada has evolved from outright denunciation of same-sex sexual behaviour, to requirements for tolerance of differences of sexual orientation, to the currently emerging recognition of the equality rights of gay and lesbian people. Given the diverse meanings of sexual behaviour and identity, and the lack of a value consensus in relation to human sexuality, developing social policies relevant to sexual orientation is a challenge. This section of the chapter discusses key changes in legislation, professional guidelines, and organizational policies that have reduced the stigmatization of same-sex sexual orientation and increased the accessibility and responsiveness of human services.

Criminal and Immigration Law

Historically, the most direct and wide-reaching expression of heterosexism has been in criminal law. As early as 1533 in England, sex between men was punishable by death, and it remained an offence there until 1967 (Kinsman, 1996). Although the criminalization of same-sex sexuality has decreased, sexual activity between people of the same sex is still an offence in over forty countries around the world (International Lesbian and Gay Association [ILGA], 2001). The death penalty continues to be the punishment in nine countries. As Canada's Criminal Code was based on that of Britain, it included gross indecency and anal intercourse as sexual offences. Although there was no definition of gross indecency in the Code, until 1954 the offence could be laid only in relation to acts between males (Casswell, 1996). In practice, these offences were prosecuted primarily against men who had consenting sex with men, and repeated conviction could lead to being declared a dangerous sexual offender and indefinite incarceration. In 1969, the Criminal Code was amended to allow these acts between married couples and consenting adults in private. Subsequently, in 1988, the offence of gross indecency was deleted from the Code and the age of consent for anal intercourse was lowered to eighteen.

Another significant expression of heterosexism in federal law was found in the Immigration Act that barred gay people from entering Canada (Willms, 2005). Although this provision was dropped in 1977, Canadian residents were unable to sponsor their same-sex partners as immigrants whereas those in male-female relationships were able to do so. In 2002, the Immigration Act was replaced by the Immigration and Refugee Protection Act (Bill C-11) with regulations allowing sponsorship of same-sex partners. In addition, individuals who claim to have been persecuted on the basis of their sexual orientation are admitted as refugees under the Act. This practice is consistent with the interpretation of the United Nations High Commissioner for Refugees: the UN recognizes gay men and lesbians as social groups that can suffer persecution (ILGA, 2001).

The heterosexist provisions of the Criminal Code and the Immigration Act continue to influence discourse about sexual orientation even though for the most part they have been repealed. The impression persists among many that same-sex sexuality is illicit and that gay men and lesbians are somewhat disreputable. This perception subtly shapes the administration of justice, so that gay men and lesbians are treated more harshly than heterosexuals (Mac-Dougall, 2000). Nevertheless, the most serious implication of the stigmatization of same-sex sexual orientation is that it provides a rationale for discrimination and violence perpetrated against those perceived to be gay or lesbian (Richardson & May, 1999). Data from Canadian police forces indicate that hate crimes related to sexual orientation comprise 10% of all those reported, and that those perpetrated against gay men and lesbians are twice as likely to be violent as those against other groups (Statistics Canada, 2004a). Furthermore, studies suggest that more than one third of gay men and lesbians have experienced anti-gay attacks (Casswell, 1996, p. 8; Trussler et al., 2000). The positive evolution in public values, however, is evident in the addition to the Criminal Code in 1995 of stiffer sentences for hate crimes including those committed against gay men and lesbians.

Psychiatric Classification

After its decriminalization, the declassification of homosexuality as a mental disorder was the next significant step in the evolution of policies regarding same-sex sexual orientation. With the development of psychiatry in the late nineteenth century, homosexuality had come to be considered a mental illness (Murphy, 1997). This theory was buttressed by research conducted largely on samples drawn from mentally ill and incarcerated populations and informed by the assumption that same-sex sexual orientation was a problem in itself. However, studies conducted in the latter half of the twentieth century with appropriate research designs did not detect any differences in mental health or cognitive abilities related to sexual orientation (American Psychological Association [APA], 2001). Nevertheless, homosexuality remained classified as a disorder by the APA until 1973 (Murphy, 1997) and by the World Health Organization until 1991. These guidelines shaped the provision of mental health services in Canada, with serious repercussions for clients as well as care providers (Kinsman, 1996). Clients who revealed their same-sex sexual orientation were diagnosed as mentally ill and often subjected to abusive and ineffective interventions aimed at changing their sexuality. Furthermore, health and social service workers who were gay or lesbian were reluctant to reveal their sexual orientation, depriving clients of the benefits of their knowledge and experience.

Although no longer endorsed by professional bodies, the psychiatric classification of homosexuality continues to shape the perception of same-sex sexual orientation as an illness. Influenced by the previous criminalization of same-sex sexual behaviour and the more recent advent of HIV/AIDS, gay men and lesbians are frequently portrayed in popular culture as strange, dangerous, and contaminated. The declassification of homosexuality as a mental illness allowed the possibility of the development of health and social services that could be supportive to gay and lesbian people. However, health care and social service providers have continued to hold negative beliefs regarding same-sex sexual orientation (Brotman, Ryan, Jalbert, & Rowe, 2002b), contributing to the lack of accessibility and responsiveness of services.

Canadian
Social
Policies

Human Rights Legislation and the Charter

Following the achievement of changes in the Criminal Code, and supported by the depathologization of homosexuality, the focus of Canadian gay and lesbian activism turned to gaining protection from discrimination through the inclusion of sexual orientation in human rights codes. Human rights legislation identifies grounds on which discrimination is prohibited in areas such as housing, services, employment, and membership in organizations, and applies in both the public and private spheres (Casswell, 1996). In addition to harassment and violence, people perceived to be gay or lesbian have frequently encountered discrimination in areas addressed by human rights legislation (Warner, 2002). An example is the 1991 termination of a gay teacher in Alberta, where sexual orientation was not included in the human rights code. Since 1977, Canadian public opinion has consistently supported inclusion of sexual orientation in human rights legislation. For instance, 84% of respondents in the above-noted 1998 national poll advocated protection of gays and lesbians from discrimination (Canadian Press, 2000). As a result of a concerted campaign of political action and court challenges, sexual orientation was added to the Quebec Charter of Human Rights and Freedoms in 1977 and subsequently incorporated into all other provincial and territorial human rights codes (Egale Canada, 2003b). Furthermore, The Canadian Human Rights Act was amended in 1996 to include protection for gays and lesbians (Casswell, 1996). In contrast, sexual orientation discrimination is proscribed in only twenty-one other countries (ILGA, 2001) and is not addressed in the Universal Declaration of Human Rights. Although Canadians generally disapprove of overt discrimination, policy-makers have been more reluctant to affirm same-sex sexual orientation by explicitly extending to gay and lesbian people the same rights enjoyed by heterosexuals (Carter, 1998).

With discrimination on the basis of sexual orientation prohibited by human rights laws, the achievement of full equality became the focus of attention. The Charter of Rights and Freedoms (the Charter), part of the 1982 Canadian constitution, addresses the right of Canadians to equal treatment by public services, regardless of ethnicity, gender, or other differences (Casswell, 1996). Subsequent to the introduction of the Charter, gay men and lesbians successfully mounted court challenges to policies that denied same-sex partners access to public services such as benefits under the Old Age Security Act. As a result, although it does not refer explicitly to sexual orientation, since 1996 the Charter has been interpreted by the Supreme Court as apply-

ing to sexual orientation. This interpretation was widely supported by public opinion; a national poll taken in 2001 suggested that 75% of Canadians
believed that gay and lesbian people should have the same rights as heterosexuals (McInnes, 2001). These developments had far-reaching implications
for the legal recognition of same-sex couples and policies regarding employment benefits, pensions, taxes, inheritance, and family life. In 2000, the federal government passed the Modernization of Benefits and Obligations Act
(Bill C-23), requiring that federal laws apply equally to both same-sex and
heterosexual common-law couples (Willms, 2005). Provincial governments
also amended their laws similarly (Egale Canada, 2002).

The most contentious developments related to sexual orientation were
legal changes allowing same-sex couples to marry. The federal law restricting
the right to marry to male-female couples was struck down in a British Columbia court in 2003 (Egale Canada, 2003a) and subsequently in most other
provincial courts. Although national polls indicated a majority of Canadians
supported same-sex marriage (Egale Canada, 2004), there was vigorous debate across the country. In 2005, the Canadian Parliament passed the Civil
Marriage Act (Bill C-38) omitting reference to the sex of individuals, effectively making same-sex marriages lawful in all provinces and territories.

Despite these successes in the courts and legislatures, some gay men and
lesbians have reservations about being included in policies that formerly
applied only to heterosexuals (Donovan, Heaphy, & Weeks, 1999; Smith, 1999).
They fear that inclusion of gay and lesbian people in mainstream social institutions may reinforce the status quo rather than advance social changes in
relation to sexuality and gender that have been goals of the gay liberation
and feminist movements. For instance, the achievement of same-sex spousal
benefits privileges only those involved in long-term relationships, particularly if they are in higher tax brackets. In addition, there are concerns about
same-sex couples being able to marry, given that this institution has historically been an unequal relationship, usually benefiting the male partner at
the expense of the woman (Antoniuk, 1999). In any case, a significant implication of the recognition of the rights of gay and lesbian people to equal treatment is that human services are required to provide services that are accessible and appropriate regardless of sexual orientation.

Impact of HIV/AIDS

A major impetus to addressing issues related to same-sex sexual orientation
in human service policies has been the HIV/AIDS epidemic. Although the rate
of infection among men who have sex with men declined during the 1990s, this
group still accounts for 77% of Canadian AIDS cases (Public Health Agency of
Canada, 2005). Thus, health and social services have been called on to respond
to the needs of gay and bisexual men and their families and friends. The initial appearance of the illness in North America primarily among gay men
buttressed the stereotype of same-sex sexual orientation as a dangerous
pathology (Herringer, 1996). However, the response to the epidemic also had

positive impacts because it mobilized the gay and lesbian communities (Warner, 2002), bringing them closer together (Stoller, 1998), and stimulated the development of community-based AIDS service organizations. The need to develop policies for the prevention of HIV infection and to address the complex medical and social needs of those already living with the disease (Cadwell, 1998) forced mainstream services to address issues related to same-sex sexual orientation in more supportive ways (Adam, 1995). One of the barriers to accessing services for people with HIV/AIDS is the stigma attached to the disease because of its association with same-sex sexuality, a stigma some agencies have attempted to avoid by downplaying their connections to the gay community (Cain, 1997).

Policies of Social Services and Professional Education

In addition to having the same health and social service needs as heterosexuals, gay, lesbian, and bisexual people may have needs specifically related to the pervasive social stigmatization attached to their sexual orientation. In particular, they may need help in coping with discrimination and harassment (McCreary Centre Society, 1999; Richardson & May, 1999; Warner, 2002), integrating their sexuality into their lives and developing a positive identity (Gochros & Bidwell, 1996; O'Neill, 1999; Shernoff, 1998; Tully, 2000), and establishing and maintaining supportive relationships (Appleby & Anastas, 1998; Frederiksen, 1999; McVinney, 1998). Despite the progressive policy developments described earlier in relation to same-sex sexual orientation, heterosexism continues to present barriers to accessing services that respond adequately to these needs.

A lingering effect of the history of criminalization and pathologization of same-sex sexuality is that health and social services are slow to respond to the rights of gay people to equitable services (Mule, 2005). Although agency policies proscribe direct discrimination on the basis of sexual orientation, for the most part they do not provide for services that support the lives of gay and lesbian people. The intent of this omission may be to provide services equally to all (Brotman et al., 2002b); however, another purpose may be to avoid the controversy that officially addressing gay and lesbian issues could provoke. Unfortunately, because of the pervasiveness of heterosexism, the effect is to silence discussion of sexual orientation, impeding the development of accessible and responsive programs, and leaving decisions regarding service delivery to individual workers. This approach may not only prevent clients from receiving adequate service, but also leave workers without guidance and support in their practice (Mallon, 2000).

When differences of sexual orientation are not comprehensively addressed throughout organizational policies, heterosexist assumptions subtly shape practices. Most health and social services do not gather information regarding the sexual orientation of clients (Harris & Licata, 2000). However, if they did, in the absence of official statements affirming respect for gay, lesbian, and bisexual people, clients may not feel safe enough to reveal their sexual orientation, withholding information that could be crucial in their care (Brotman et al., 2002b). The result is that agencies remain for the most part unaware of the presence of people who are oriented to their own sex in the populations they serve and do not recognize their unique needs (Daley, 1998). For example, child welfare services and schools may fail to protect youth who are questioning their sexual orientation from abuse and harassment, and may not support them in integrating their sexuality into their identities (Mallon, 1998; C.A. O'Brien, 1994). Similarly, geriatric services may overlook the needs of elderly gays and lesbians (Jacobs, Rasmussen, & Hohman, 1999), who may fear that they will have to conceal their sexual orientation when living in long-term care facilities, thus increasing their isolation. The presupposition that battering occurs only in male-female relationships may contribute to services being unresponsive to the needs of those abused by same-sex partners (Lutz, 1998; Merrill & Wolfe, 2000). Unawareness of the pervasiveness and impact of heterosexism may cause addiction services to disregard the stress of coping with anti-gay discrimination in their programs (Travers & Schneider, 1996). Finally, lack of acknowledgement of same-sex relationships by health care providers may result in exclusion of the partners of gay patients from involvement in their care (Mule, 1999).

In the absence of affirmative policies, agency personnel may also conceal their sexual orientation, contributing to the impression that all service providers are heterosexual, and denying colleagues and clients the benefit of their knowledge and experience (Hidalgo, 1995). Furthermore, the lack of attention to heterosexism leaves undisturbed the knowledge deficiencies and negative attitudes of many helping professionals (Brotman et al., 2002b). Although there is evidence that inclusion of issues of sexual orientation in professional education has improved the quality of services to gay and lesbian clients (Liddle, 1999), there are still educational policy and curriculum gaps in this area (O'Neill, 1995; Stainton & Swift, 1996). Similar to the policies of many service providers, while the Canadian Association of Schools of Social Work (CASSW, 2004) prohibits discrimination on the basis of sexual orientation, it does not specify that content regarding heterosexism and same-sex sexual orientation be included in curricula.

The first step in addressing the lack of attention to sexual orientation in mainstream social services is to acknowledge that gay, lesbian, and bisexual people are among the clients of the agency (Mule, 2005). Subsequently, gay and lesbian people can be involved in the systematic review and development of policies to comprehensively address issues related to sexual orientation. A successful approach to the development of services is collaboration between mainstream agencies and the plethora of social services that have developed within gay and lesbian communities (Poverny, 1999). In particular, it would be useful for non-gay community organizations that focus on countering discrimination to join with gay and lesbian organizations in addressing heterosexism.

Conclusion

This overview of social policy developments in Canada relevant to sexual orientation reveals a steady movement toward respect for gay and lesbian people and recognition of their rights to equitable access to social resources. This trend is consistent with Canadian ideals regarding acceptance of diversity and the achievement of social justice. It seems inevitable that the process will continue and that gay and lesbian people will eventually achieve full participation in social institutions. With changes well underway at the legislative level, the focus now shifts to challenging heterosexism at the program level. Health and social services will need to systematically examine their policies and practices to determine how they subtly silence, ignore, and disadvantage people who are oriented to members of their own sex. This process will require openness, sensitivity, and courage, as addressing issues related to sexuality touches on strongly held values that are integral to identity. At the same time, it needs to be recognized that heterosexism is but one oppressive ideology. To successfully advance social justice, policies at each level simultaneously need to address the expression of all forms of marginalization.

References

Adam, B.D. (1995). *The rise of a gay and lesbian movement* (Rev. ed.). New York: Twayne.

Adam, B.D., Duyvendak, J.W., & Krouwel, A. (Eds.). (1999). *The global emergence of gay and lesbian politics: National imprints of a worldwide movement.* Philadelphia: Temple University Press.

Altman, D. (2001). Gay/lesbian movements. In *International encyclopedia of the social and behavioral sciences* (pp. 5895–5899). Online at <www.sciencedirect.com/science/referenceworks/>.

Altemeyer, B. (2001). Changes in attitudes toward homosexuals. *Journal of Homosexuality, 42*(2), 63–75.

American Psychological Association (APA). (2001). *Guidelines for psychotherapy with lesbian, gay and bisexual clients.* Online at <www.apa.org>.

Antoniuk, T. (1999). Policy alternative for a diverse community: Lesbians and family law. *Journal of Gay & Lesbian Social Services, 10*(1), 46–70.

Appleby G.A., & Anastas, J.W. (1998). *Not just a passing phase: Social work with gay, lesbian, and bisexual people.* New York: Columbia University Press.

Archer, B. (1999). *The end of gay (and the death of heterosexuality).* Toronto: Doubleday Canada.

Beck, E., Williams, I., Hope, L., & Park, W. (2001). An intersectional model: Exploring gender with ethnic and cultural diversity. *Journal of Ethnic and Cultural Diversity in Social Work, 10*(4), 63–80.

Bibby, R. (1995). *The Bibby report: Social trends Canadian style.* Toronto: Stoddart.

Boodram, C. (2003). *Building the links: The intersection of sexual orientation and race.* Online at <www.egale.ca>.

British Columbia Human Rights Commission. (2001). *1999 public opinion survey.* Online at <www.bchrc.gov.bc.ca>.

References Brotman, S., Ryan, B, Jalbert, Y., & Rowe, B. (2002a). Reclaiming space-regaining health: The health care experiences of two-spirited people in Canada. *Journal of Gay and Lesbian Social Services,* 14(1), 67–87.

Brotman, S., Ryan, B., Jalbert, Y., & Rowe, B. (2002b). The impact of coming out on health and health care access: The experiences of gay, lesbian, bisexual and two-spirited people. *Journal of Health and Social Policy,* 15(1), 1–29.

Cadwell, S.A. (1998). Providing services to gay men. In D.M. Aronstein & B.J. Thompson (Eds.), *HIV and social work: A practitioner's guide* (pp. 411–429). New York: Harrington Park Press.

Cain, R. (1997). Environmental change and organizational evolution: Reconsidering the niche of community-based AIDS organizations. *AIDS Care,* 9(3), 331.

Cameron, M. (2005). Two-spirited Aboriginal people: Continuing cultural appropriation by non-aboriginal society. *Canadian Woman Studies,* 24(2/3), 123–127.

Canadian Association of Schools of Social Work (CASSW). (2004). *Standards of accreditation.* Online at <www.cassw-acess.ca>.

Canadian Press. (2000, February 9). [Excerpts from 1998 Angus Reid poll on homosexual rights]. *Canadian Press Newswire.*

Carter, D.D. (1998). Employment benefits for same-sex couples: The expanding entitlement. *Canadian Public Policy,* 24(1), 107–117.

Casswell, D.G. (1996). *Lesbians, gay men, and Canadian law.* Toronto: Emond Montgomery Publications.

Churchill, W. (1967). *Homosexual behavior among males: A cross-cultural and cross-species investigation.* New York: Hawthorn Books.

Cooper, E. (2003). Decoding Will and Grace: Mass audience reception of a popular network situation comedy. *Sociological Perspectives,* 46(4), 513–533.

Crompton, L. (2003). *Homosexuality and civilization.* Cambridge, MA: Harvard University Press.

Daley, A. (1998). Lesbian invisibility in health care services: Heterosexual hegemony and strategies for change. *Canadian Social Work Review,* 15(1), 57–71.

Diaz, R.M., Ayala, G., Bein, E., Henne, J., & Marin, B.V. (2001). The impact of homophobia, poverty, and racism on the mental health of gay and bisexual Latino men: Findings from 3 US cities. *American Journal of Public Health,* 91(6), 927–932.

Donovan, C., Heaphy, B., & Weeks, J. (1999). Citizenship and same sex relationships. *Journal of Social Policy,* 28(4), 689–709.

Drescher, J. (2002). Causes and becauses: On etiological theories of homosexuality. *Annual of Psychoanalysis,* 30, 57–68.

Egale Canada. (2002). *Provincial same-sex bills.* Online at <www.egale.ca/index.asp?lang=E&menu=65>.

Egale Canada. (2003a, July 8). *Same-sex marriage now legal in British Columbia.* Online at <www.egale.ca/index.asp?lang=E&menu=50&item=109>.

Egale Canada. (2003b, November 5). *Nunavut passes Human Rights Act.* Online at <www.egale.ca/index.asp?lang=E&menu=2003&item=485>.

Egale Canada. (2004, July 1). *Survey finds huge increase in support for equal marriage.* Online at <www.egale.ca/index.asp?lang=E&menu=2004&item=1055>.

Elliston, D.A. (2005). Erotic anthropology: "Ritualized homosexuality" in Melanesia and beyond. In J. Robertson (Ed.), *Same-sex cultures and sexualities: An anthropological reader* (pp. 91–115). Malden, MA: Blackwell.

Frederiksen, K.I. (1999). Family caregiving responsibilities among lesbians and gay men. *Social Work, 44*(2), 142–155. References

Gochros, H.L., & Bidwell, R. (1996). Lesbian and gay youth in a straight world: Implications for health care workers. *Journal of Gay and Lesbian Social Services, 5*(1), 1–17.

Greene, B. (Ed.). (1997). *Ethnic and cultural diversity among lesbians and gay men.* Thousand Oaks, CA: Sage.

Harris, H.L., & Licata, F. (2000). From fragmentation to integration: Affirming the identities of culturally diverse, mentally ill lesbians and gay men. *Journal of Gay and Lesbian Social Services, 11*(4), 93–103.

Herek, G.M. (2000). The psychology of sexual prejudice. *Current Directions in Psychological Science, 9*(1), 19–22.

Herek, G.M. (2004). Beyond "homophobia": Thinking about sexual prejudice and stigma in the twenty-first century. *Sexuality Research and Social Policy, 1*(2), 6–24.

Herringer, B. (1996). A clash of knowledges: Toward an analysis of the social organization of AIDS "suicide." *Canadian Social Work Review, 13*(1), 39–52.

Hidalgo, H. (1995). The norms of conduct in social service agencies: A threat to the mental health of Puerto Rican lesbians. *Journal of Gay and Lesbian Social Services, 3*(2), 23–41.

International Lesbian and Gay Association (ILGA). (2001, July 13). *ILGA world legal survey.* Online at <www.ilga.org>.

Irvine, J.M. (1995). *Sexuality education across cultures: Working with differences.* San Francisco: Jossey-Bass.

Jacobs, R.J., Rasmussen, L.A., & Hohman, M.M. (1999). The social support needs of older lesbians, gay men, and bisexuals. *Journal of Gay and Lesbian Social Services, 9*(1), 1–30.

Kinsey, A.C., Pomeroy, W.B., & Martin, C.E. (1948). *Sexual behavior in the human male.* Philadelphia: W.B. Sanders.

Kinsey, A.C., Pomeroy, W.B., Martin, C.E., & Gebhard, P. (1955). *Sexual behavior in the human female.* Philadelphia: W.B. Sanders.

Kinsey Institute. (2005). *Frequently asked sexuality questions: Homosexuality.* Online at <www.indiana.edu/~kinsey/>.

Kinsman, G. (1996). *The regulation of desire: Homo and hetero sexualities* (2nd ed.). Montreal: Black Rose Books.

Kinsman, G. (2000). Constructing gay men and lesbians as national security risks, 1950–1970. In G. Kinsman, D.K. Buse, & M. Steedman (Eds.), *Whose national security? Surveillance and the creation of enemies in Canada* (pp. 143–153). Toronto: Between the Lines.

Laumann, E.O., Gagnon, J.H., Michael, R.T., & Michaels, S. (2000). *The social organization of sexuality: Sexuality practices in the United States.* Chicago: University of Chicago Press.

Liddle, B.J. (1999). Recent improvements in mental health services to lesbian and gay clients. *Journal of Homosexuality, 37*(4), 127–137.

Lutz, J. (1998). *Support services for lesbians experiencing relationship abuse: Barriers to healing.* Unpublished graduating essay, UBC School of Social Work, Vancouver.

MacDougall, B. (2000). *Queer judgments: Homosexuality, expression, and the courts in Canada.* Toronto: University of Toronto Press.

References Mallon, G.P. (1998). *We don't exactly get the welcome wagon: The experience of gay and lesbian adolescents in child welfare systems.* New York: Columbia University Press.

Mallon, G.P. (2000). Gay men and lesbians as adoptive parents. *Journal of Gay and Lesbian Social Services, 11*(4), 1–22.

McCreary Centre Society. (1999). *Being out: Lesbian, gay, bisexual and trangendered youth in B.C.: An adolescent health survey.* Burnaby, BC: Author.

McInnes, C. (2001, July 17). B.C. quits same-sex challenge. *Vancouver Sun,* p. A3.

McVinney, L.D. (1998). Social work practice with gay male couples. In G.P. Mallon (Ed.), *Foundations of social work practice with lesbian and gay persons* (pp. 209–227). New York: Haworth Press.

Merrill, G.S., & Wolfe, V.A. (2000). Battered gay men: An exploration of abuse, help seeking, and why they stay. *Journal of Homosexuality, 39*(2), 1–30.

Meyer, L.D. (2001). Lesbians: Historical perspectives. In *International encyclopedia of the social and behavioral sciences* (pp. 8720–8725). Online at <www. science direct.com/science/referenceworks/>.

Minton, H.J.L. (2002). *Departing from deviance: A history of homosexual rights and emancipatory science in America.* Chicago: University of Chicago Press.

Mule, N. (1999). Social work and the provision of health care and social services to sexual minority populations. *Canadian Social Work, 1*(1), 39–55.

Mule, N. (2005). Beyond words in health and well-being policy: "Sexual orientation"—from inclusion to infusion. *Canadian Review of Social Policy, 55,* 79–98.

Mullaly, R.P. (2002). *Challenging oppression: A critical social work approach.* Don Mills, ON: Oxford University Press.

Murphy, T.F. (1997). *Gay science: The ethics of sexual orientation research.* New York: Columbia University Press.

O'Brien, C.A. (1994). The social organization of the treatment of lesbian, gay and bisexual youth in group homes and youth shelters. *Canadian Review of Social Policy, 34,* 37–57.

O'Brien, C.A., & Goldberg, A. (2000). Lesbians and gay men inside and outside families. In N. Mandell & A. Duffy (Eds.), *Canadian families: Diversity, conflict, and change* (2nd ed., pp. 115–145). Toronto: Harcourt Brace Canada.

O'Brien, J. (2001). Heterosexism and homophobia. *International encyclopedia of the social and behavioral sciences* (pp. 6672–6676). Online at <www.science direct.com/science/referenceworks/>.

O'Neill, B.J. (1995). Canadian social work education and same-sex sexual orientation. *Canadian Social Work Review, 12*(2), 159–174.

O'Neill, B.J. (1999). Social work with gay, lesbian and bisexual members of racial and ethnic minority groups. In G. Lie & D. Este (Eds.), *Professional social service delivery in a multicultural world* (pp. 75–91). Toronto: Canadian Scholars' Press.

Poverny, L. (1999). It's all a matter of attitude: Creating and maintaining receptive services for sexual minority families. *Journal of Gay and Lesbian Social Services, 10*(1), 95–113.

Public Health Agency of Canada. (2005, May). *HIV/AIDS Epi Updates.* Online at <www.phac-aspc.gc.ca>.

Richardson, D., & May, H. (1999). Deserving victims? Sexual status and the social construction of violence. *Sociological Review, 47*(2), 308–332.

Scasta, D. (1998). Historical perspectives on homosexuality. *Journal of Gay and Lesbian Psychotherapy, 2*(4), 3–17.

Shapiro, J. (2005). Transsexualism: Reflections on the persistence of gender and the mutability of sex. In J. Robertson (Ed.), *Same-sex cultures and sexualities: An anthropological reader* (pp. 138–161). Malden, MA: Blackwell.

Shernoff, M. (1998). Individual practice with gay men. In G.P. Mallon (Ed.), *Foundations of social work practice with lesbian and gay persons* (pp. 77–103). New York: Haworth Press.

Smith, M. (1999). Lesbian and gay rights in Canada: Social movements and equality seeking, 1971–1995. Toronto: University of Toronto Press.

Stainton, T., & Swift, K. (1996). "Difference" and social work curriculum. *Canadian Social Work Review, 13*(1), 75–87.

Statistics Canada. (2004a, June 1). Pilot survey of hate crime. *The Daily.* Online at <www.statcan.ca/Daily>.

Statistics Canada. (2004b, June 15). Canadian Community Health Survey, 2003. *The Daily.* Online at <www.statcan.ca/Daily>.

Stein, E. (2001). Sexual orientation: Biological influences. *International encyclopedia of the social and behavioral sciences* (pp. 13995–13998). Online at <www.sciencedirect.com/science/referenceworks/>.

Stoller, N.E. (1998). Lesbian involvement in the AIDS epidemic: Changing roles and generational differences. In P.M. Nardi & B.E. Schneider (Eds.), *Social perspectives in lesbian and gay studies: A reader* (pp. 366–376). London: Routledge.

Todd, S. (2006). Social work and sexual diversity: Celebrating human diversity. In S.F. Hick (Ed.), *Social work in Canada: An introduction* (2nd ed., pp. 273–295). Toronto: Thompson Educational.

Travers, R., & Schneider, M. (1996). Barriers to accessibility for lesbian and gay youth needing addictions services. *Youth and Society, 27*(3), 356–378.

Trussler, T., Barker, A., Buchner, C., Dolan, T., Granger, P., Jagosh, J., Marchand, R., Mo, E., Peralta, V., & Perchal, P. (2000). *Gay health in Vancouver: A quality of life survey.* Vancouver: Community-Based Research Centre.

Tully, C.T. (2000). *Lesbians, gays, and the empowerment perspective.* New York: Columbia University Press.

Vance, C.S. (2005). Anthropology rediscovers sexuality: A theoretical comment. In J. Robertson (Ed.), *Same-sex cultures and sexualities: An anthropological reader* (pp. 15–32). Malden, MA: Blackwell.

Warner, T. (2002). *Never going back: A history of queer activism in Canada.* Toronto: University of Toronto Press.

Weeks, J. (2001). Sexual orientation: Historical and social construction. *International encyclopedia of the social and behavioral sciences* (pp. 13998–14002). Online at <www.sciencedirect.com/science/referenceworks/>.

Weinberg, G.H. (1972). *Society and the healthy homosexual.* New York: St. Martin's Press.

Widmer, E.D., Treas, J., & Newcomb, R. (1998). Attitudes toward nonmarital sex in 24 countries. *Canadian Journal of Human Sexuality, 7*(4), 349–59.

Williamson, I.R. (2000). Internalized homophobia and health issues affecting lesbians and gay men. *Health Education Research: Theory and Practice, 15*(1), 97–107.

Willms, M. (2005, Spring). Canadian immigration law and same-sex partners. *Canadian Issues,* pp. 17–20.

References **Additional Resources**

American Psychological Association. (2001). Guidelines for psychotherapy with lesbian, gay, and bisexual clients. Online at <www.apa.org>.

Canadian Journal of Human Sexuality. Online at <www.sieccan.org/cjhs.html>.

Coalition for Lesbian and Gay Rights in Ontario. Online at <www.web.ca/~clgro>.

Egale Canada. Online at <www.egale.ca>.

International Lesbian and Gay Association. Online at <www.ilga.org>.

Journal of Gay and Lesbian Social Services. Online at <www.haworthpress.com/web/JGLSS/>.

Usha George

Canada is one of the few countries in the world that has an active immigrant and refugee admission policy and program. Even before 1860, when figures on immigration became available, immigrants and refugees from different countries made Canada their home. The 1990s can be described as the decade of immigration, as the average number of arrivals per annum exceeded 200,000, the highest in Canadian history (George & Fuller-Thompson, 1997). The numbers of newcomers and source countries have depended on the immigration policies and practices in effect at particular times. Immigration has become an enduring feature of Canada's policy milieu; however, this does not imply that immigration is an uncontested topic in Canada. As Freeman (1995, p. 882) points out, in liberal democracies such as Canada, the political economy model of policy-making, with a constitution based on individual rights, competitive party systems, and periodic elections, influences the direction of immigration policy: "The politics of immigration in such systems can be analyzed at the level of individual voters, organized groups, and state actors."

The inevitable question is: Why immigration? The question can be answered at a general theoretical level or by examining factors specific to Canada. At the theoretical level, push-and-pull factors can explain immigration. Push factors operate when individuals decide to leave their country of origin because of worsening economic conditions, including high levels of unemployment. Pull factors operate when people are attracted to a country because of the opportunities it offers for economic betterment and social mobility. The distinction between push and pull factors is not always clear (Isajiw, 1999). Simmons (1998) argues that economic globalization leads to greater income inequality between developed and developing countries, and thus creates pressure for emigration in less developed countries. In the context of increased international competition, producers in wealthy nations get immigrant workers to work for low wages, resulting in conflicting views about immigration in those countries.

There are two explanations specific to the Canadian situation. First, Canada's natural population growth "has declined steadily in recent decades from 3 percent in the 1950s to less than 1 percent in the late 1990s" (Knowles,

2000, p. 4). Mackenzie King's 1947 statement in the House of Commons clearly indicated the population-enhancing goal of Canada's immigration policy: "The policy of the government is to foster the growth of the population of Canada by the encouragement of immigration. The government will seek by legislation, regulation, and vigorous administration, to ensure the careful selection and permanent settlement of such immigrants as can advantageously be absorbed in our national economy" (Knowles, 2000, p. 67).

The main reason for the decline in population growth is the drop in the fertility rate as a result of women entering the workforce, as well as the general growing tendency for couples to have fewer or no children at all. The fertility rate declined from four children per woman in 1959 to less than two per woman by 1998. As Knowles (2000, p. 4) has observed, "should this low fertility rate continue—and all the indications are that it will—immigration will become essential for this country's healthy growth and even, perhaps, for its survival." Canada also has an aging population because people are living longer. The number of seniors has steadily increased over the last century. In 1991, 12% of the population was sixty-five years and older. Estimates are that by the year 2011, one quarter of the population will be older than sixty-five years (Grant, 2000). Young immigrants thus offset the growing dependency ratio.

Second, there is the need for skilled labour. In fact, early immigration was spurred by the demand for labour to build railways and support industries such as mining, fishing, and lumber. As the supply of manual labour from the United States and Europe began to dwindle in the 1880s, over 1,500 labourers were recruited from China to lay the track for the Canadian Pacific Railway (Bolaria & Li, 1988; Henry, Tator, Mattis, & Rees, 2000). In more recent times, the need for skilled labour for Canada's expanding industrial and high-tech fields has been well recognized. Currently, the temporary worker program is designed to address the acute labour shortages in high-tech, building trades, and other areas identified by the private sector, in conjunction with the federal Human Resources Department (Thompson, 2001).

This chapter provides a brief overview of Canada's immigration and refugee policy and practice. Due to the extensive amount of scholarship on this topic, only a summary review is possible. The first section defines key terms such as immigrants, refugees, and newcomers. The next section provides a brief overview of the history of immigration in Canada, followed by an examination of the provisions in the new Immigration Act, which came into effect in 2002. In order to illustrate the workings of the Immigration Act, a summary of the annual plans for 2005 and 2006 follows along with an analysis of the directions of immigration and refugee policies in Canada. The final section provides a brief review of the impact of Canadian immigration policy.

The term "immigrant" generally refers to anyone from another country who is legally admitted to live in a country. In Canada, these people are also called permanent residents or landed immigrants. Landed immigrants can apply to become Canadian citizens after three years. Canadian citizenship is granted to any landed immigrant, provided the person meets residency requirements, has no criminal record, and passes a simple citizenship test. A landed immigrant is entitled to all the privileges of a citizen, except the right to vote in provincial and federal elections; however, once a citizen, regardless of the country of origin, a person is entitled to all rights and privileges.

In practice, however, immigrants experience landed immigrant status and citizenship differently because of discrimination and prejudice in Canadian society. While each group of immigrants has its own experiences of discrimination and prejudice, people from visible minority backgrounds generally continue to be perceived as immigrants, regardless of their length of stay in Canada. A great deal of scholarship has developed around the notion of the "social construction of immigrants and refugees." Li (1997) calls this "bench marking," as the term "immigrant" is used as a folk, bureaucratic, and analytical concept.

As Isajiw (1999, p. 71) observes, "refugees are people who have to leave a country because they are denied a human existence and are accepted by another country on account of this country's humane or humanitarian concerns." These refugees are also called convention refugees, as per the United Nations Convention Relating to the Status of Refugees, 1951, to which Canada is a signatory. Two distinct groups of refugees are recognized in Canadian policy and practice circles: sponsored refugees, and asylum seekers or refugee claimants. Sponsored refugees can be either government or privately sponsored. Privately sponsored refugees are those sponsored by religious or other non-profit groups. Once in Canada, sponsored refugees receive landed immigrant status and all related entitlements. Asylum seekers or refugee claimants, in contrast, are people who arrive in Canada as visitors and apply for refugee status for fear of persecution in their countries of origin. Asylum seekers must undergo a lengthy process of hearings and appeals with the Immigration and Refugee Board (IRB). Once accepted by the IRB, these people acquire the status of convention refugees, but they have to go through the immigration process to become landed immigrants. Canada's domestic law integrates its international obligation by stipulating that convention refugees legally in Canada cannot be deported unless they pose a threat to national security or commit serious crimes (Christensen, 1999).

Asylum seekers / refugee claimants as a separate refugee group are mostly invisible, mainly because they are excluded from receiving many of the entitlements awarded to landed immigrants and citizens. Most claims come from refugee-producing countries (Adelman, 1991; Richmond, 1994), yet because of its distance from refugee-producing regions, Canada receives fewer refugee claimants than, for example, European countries (Macklin, 2001). Currently an estimated 150 million people are on the move worldwide, fleeing civil strife, ethnic conflict, natural disasters, and economic and political upheaval (Citizenship and Immigration Canada, 2001a).

In recent times, the term "newcomer," which does not distinguish people on the basis of their legal status, has been used by academic, bureaucratic, and social service communities because it is considered more inclusive. This term distinguishes individuals based on their length of time in Canada, and this distinction serves an instrumental purpose for the federal Department of Citizenship and Immigration settlement services, which are generally available to landed immigrants who have been in the country for less than five years. Service providers, however, contend that the term "newcomer" masks the ongoing problems faced by immigrants in general, regardless of the length of their stay in Canada. Discrimination in employment, stereotyping faced by visible minorities, and family and youth issues faced by second-generation immigrants are examples of such problems.

Another important term in Canadian immigration policy is "family class." Generally, family-class or family-related immigrants are those who migrate to another country to join immediate relatives. Family-class relatives may include lineal relatives such as spouses, parents, children, and grandparents, as well as lateral relatives such as brothers, sisters, and uncles (Isajiw, 1999). Although, historically, Canadian immigration policy and practice have allowed a mix of lineal and lateral relatives, the current policy restricts family class to lineal relatives.

History of Canadian Immigration Policy and Practice

Canadian immigration policy and practice have attracted a great deal of scholarly attention. Bolaria and Li (1988) examine the experiences of different visible minority ethnic groups in Canadian society in terms of Canada's attempts at capital accumulation for the development of a capitalist state. Other scholars have divided the history of Canadian immigration into stages or phases, often according to major policy changes (Abu-Laban, 1998; Christensen, 1999; Green & Green 1996; Henry, Tator, Mattis, & Rees, 2000; Isajiw, 1999; Knowles, 2000). Isajiw (1999) divides the history of settlement, colonization, and immigration in Canada into eight stages. For the purpose of providing a brief overview of Canadian immigration, we turn to Isajiw (1999), as he provides a chronologically comprehensive account of Canada's immigration history.

The original settlers of Canada were the ancestors of today's First Nations or Native peoples. When European settlers arrived, about 220,000 Indians and Inuit were living on the land. Isajiw describes the years 1600–1759 as the period of French immigration to Canada. The British defeat of the French in 1759 marked the next phase of colonization and immigration, when large numbers of English, Scottish, and German immigrants, along with many Loyalist refugees and exiles from the American Revolution, settled in Canada. In the latter half of the eighteenth century, the basic "pattern of continuous annual immigration was set." Isajiw adds, "Another pattern, however, was also being established, that of migrant subordination of other ethnic and racial groups who were beginning to immigrate to Canada. This pattern was enormously reinforced in the next period of Canadian history" (Isajiw, 1999, p. 80).

The beginning of the 1880s was unique: people from many parts of the world started coming to Canada because the country needed additional labour not only for its farms but also for the industries that were being built by the expanding railway system. Among workers recruited to Canada for the Canadian Pacific Railway, prominent were groups of Chinese, Japanese, and East Indians. Between 1880 and 1914, many refugees and immigrants arrived in Canada: Jews, Hungarians, Mormons, Ukrainians, Sikhs, Japanese, and Italians, as well as people from Britain and America. While Canada had immigration laws since 1869, the first Immigration Act of 1906 established formal policies and gave power over national borders (Knowles, 2000).

History of Canadian Immigration Policy and Practice

The period between the two world wars was one of immigration restriction and reduction. The Canadian government took specific measures to prevent immigration from non-European countries and to limit the arrival of the families of the immigrants already here. Concern about the ethnic composition of the Canadian population was foremost in the minds of policymakers. The continuation of the Head Tax for the Chinese, the limitation of Japanese immigration to 400 per year, introduction of the Continuous Passage rule, and restriction of Black immigration are all examples of how policymakers handled such concerns. At the end of World War II there was large-scale immigrant and refugee movement to Canada; however, the restrictions on Asian immigration remained, as it was believed that large-scale immigration from the Orient would alter the "fundamental composition" of the Canadian population (Isajiw, 1999).

Government policy began to change during the first half of the 1960s, signalling a movement toward the removal of restrictions on nationality-based immigration, although preference remained for Caucasian immigrants. For example, in 1961, British immigration was only 17% of the total immigration for the year; in 1966, it rose to 37% (Isajiw, 1999). The number of immigrants from other ethnic groups, including Asian and Black, also increased during this period.

The white paper on immigration, released in 1966, formed the basis for the new immigration regulations of 1967 (Isajiw, 1999). Through regulatory changes, racial discrimination was eliminated as the basis for selecting immigrants; in addition, the point system was introduced in an attempt to bring justice and fairness to the immigration process, as well as to meet the needs of the country. Under the new merit-point structure, applicants in the category of "independent immigrants" were to be assessed on the basis of a number of characteristics, each of which was assigned a range of merit points. The characteristics included education and training; personal qualities such as adaptability, motivation, and initiative; demand for the individual's occupation in Canada; occupational skill; arranged employment; knowledge of English or French; relatives in Canada; and employment opportunities in the area of destination (Isajiw, 1999). Beginning in 1968, the ethnic composition of immigrants changed as a result of this non-racist immigration policy. The period 1968–1976 "represented the reversal of the proportion of the white to non-white immigrants to Canada" (Isajiw, 1999; p. 85). Furthermore, Canada's endorsement of the United Nations' Convention on Refugees in 1970 led to refugees from Czechoslovakia, Tibet, Uganda, Chile, Vietnam, and Cambodia being admitted to Canada.

The volume of immigration became more of a concern in 1974, the year in which Canada had one of the largest influxes in the postwar period. A government study of immigration—the green paper on immigration—was tabled in the House of Commons and became the Immigration Act of 1976, which took effect in 1978. The changes introduced in the new legislation resulted from a number of factors: internal pressure for a multiculturalism policy that would recognize the racial and ethnic diversity in Canada, increasing politicization and mobilization of minority immigrant groups demanding a fair immigration policy, pressure by human rights activists, pressure from the international community to eliminate open racism, and, most importantly, economic need. Faced with dwindling European immigration, the shortage of highly educated and skilled workers was a major government concern (Henry et al., 2000).

The 1978 Act was a piece of framework legislation that included only the main provisions, leaving most of the details to regulations. The Immigration Act and Regulations were based on such fundamental principles as non-discrimination, family reunion, humanitarian concern for refugees, and the promotion of Canada's social, economic, demographic, and cultural goals (Citizenship and Immigration Canada, 2001a). Major features of the Act included linking immigration to economic conditions and demographic needs. It also required the minister of Immigration to announce annual immigration plans, which would estimate the number of immigrants Canada could absorb comfortably each year. These plans were to be presented to Parliament after mandatory consultations with both provincial and territorial governments, and private and voluntary sectors. The Act stipulated four basic categories of individuals eligible for landed immigrant status: (1) family class; (2) humanitarian class consisting of refugees defined in the 1951 United Nations' Convention relating to refugees and a designated class of displaced persons who do not qualify as refugees under the UN definition; (3) independent class, selected on the basis of the point system; and (4) assisted relatives who are distant relatives sponsored by a family member in Canada and who meet some of the selection criteria of the independent class (Knowles, 2000). It also established the Immigration and Refugee Board and required immigrants and visitors to obtain visas from abroad. The Act protected the civil rights of immigrants and visitors through a quasi-judicial inquiry and provided short-term alternatives to permanent deportation for cases involving violation of the Immigration Law (Citizenship and Immigration Canada, 2001a).

In the next twenty-eight years of its operation, the Act was changed through a number of regulations (Simmons, 1998). By the end of 1980s, there was new criticism of immigration because of an economic recession and an increased number of asylum seekers. In 1993, the Immigration Act was amended to link it to population and labour market needs. The 1993 amendments introduced three classes of immigrants: family class, refugees, and independent immigrants consisting of business immigrants, skilled workers, and assisted relatives. Since then, more of Canada's immigrants have been arriving from non-traditional source countries (Isajiw, 1999). For example, the top ten source countries during 2000 were China, India, Pakistan, Philippines, South Korea, Sri Lanka, United States, Iran, Yugoslavia, and Great Britain (Citizenship and Immigration Canada, 2001a).

Live-In Caregiver Program

Live-In Caregiver Program

The review of Canadian immigration policy and practice would not be complete without noting another significant initiative, the domestic worker program or Live-in Caregiver Program, as it is known today. Since its inception, this program has undergone a number of changes, and Cohen's (1994) account of the evolution of the domestic worker program is summarized below.

During the late nineteenth century, when settlement in the Canadian prairies was expanding, Canada recruited domestic workers from rural areas in England, Scotland, Ireland, and Wales to perform various household tasks. In the 1920s, under the Servant-Turn-Mistress Program, Northern European women were recruited for the Canadian Northwest. However, during the Depression and World War II, the modification of exclusionary immigration laws and shortage of domestic workers from Britain compelled Canada to recruit domestics from countries such as Germany, Italy, and Greece. Between 1950 and 1954, 15,000 Central European domestics arrived in Canada.

In 1955, in response to the great need for domestics, Canada and the United Kingdom signed an agreement called the West Indies Domestic Scheme. Consequently, between 1955 and 1967, 3,000 Black women were allowed to enter Canada. The point system introduced in 1967 applied to domestics as well, although the criteria were different. In 1973, a new policy called the Employment Authorization Program was introduced. Under this policy, domestic workers were not allowed to apply for landed status. As a result of the lobbying efforts by organizations supportive of domestic workers in Canada, the then-minister of Immigration appointed a task force to review this policy, and the government introduced a new policy called the Foreign Domestic Movement in 1979. The main provision of the policy was that domestics could apply from within Canada to be permanent residents after two years of continuous service if they also demonstrated self-sufficiency or the potential to achieve self-sufficiency. The new policy detailed the salaries and benefits for workers, as well as employers' responsibilities. In 1988, the government introduced new guidelines to evaluate each applicant, and in 1992, the program was revised to become the Live-in Caregiver Program. Two sets of conditions apply to any candidate: one for admission to the program, and the other for eligibility for landed status. The program has

attracted a great deal of criticism (e.g., Calliste, 1991; Cohen, 1994; Cunningham Armacost, 1995; Intercede, 1992; Stasiulis & Bakan, 1997a, 1997b; Villasin &
Phillips, 1994) for its sexist and classist regulations such as the "live-in" requirement.

Bill C-11: The Immigration and Refugee Protection Act, 2002

In 1994, the federal government held public consultations to decide future
directions for immigration and refugee policy. A non-partisan advisory group
set up by the federal government reviewed legislation, programs, and policies
relating to immigrants and refugees, and in 1998 the group produced a report
entitled *Not Just Numbers: A Canadian Framework for Future Immigration*.
The report, with its 172 recommendations, was to form the basis for a new
immigration law, replacing the 1978 Immigration Act. Originally proposed as
Bill C-31, it was then revised and renamed Bill C-11 when it was presented to
the House of Commons in February 2001. The House passed the Act Respecting Immigration to Canada and the Granting of Refugee Protection to Persons
Who Are Displaced, Persecuted or in Danger on June 13, 2001.

The Act is framework legislation, similar to the 1978 Immigration Act;
however, it incorporates some core principles previously intended to be
included in the regulations. These include the principles of equality and freedom from discrimination, of detaining a minor child only as a last resort and
in the "best interests of the child," and of equality of status for both official languages. The Act specifies separate objectives for immigration and refugee
admission (s. 3.1 and 3.2). The Act and regulations consist of provisions regarding consultations with provinces, the volume and selection criteria of immigrants, definition and processing of refugees, sponsorship rights, fees, and
appeals and deportation. Although it does not specify each covenant to which
Canada has subscribed, the Act does refer to the Canadian Charter of Rights
and Freedoms and states that immigration policy must fulfill Canada's international legal obligations. Such obligations include the Convention on the
Rights of the Child, the Convention Relating to the Status of Refugees, the
Convention Against Torture, the Convention on the Reduction of Stateless-
ness, and the Universal Declaration of Human Rights.

The Act recognizes three categories of foreign nationals for permanent
resident status: family class; economic class, to be selected on the basis of
each applicant's ability to become economically self-sufficient in Canada;
and convention refugees to be selected inside or outside Canada. Family class
is established for the first time in the Act, and parents are now included in the
definition of family class. Family class also includes common-law and same-
sex partners. The Act also broadens the definition of dependent child from
under age nineteen to under age twenty-two.

Government can now collect from a sponsor the amount of social assistance given to a sponsored family member. The length of sponsorship requirement has been reduced from ten to three years for spouses and common-

law partners, both opposite and same-sex. The age at which Canadian citizens and permanent residents can sponsor has been reduced from nineteen to eighteen. The Act has also created an in-Canada landing class for sponsored spouses and partners of both immigrants and refugees, and it exempts sponsored spouses, partners, and dependent children from inadmissibility on the basis of excessive demand on health and social services (Citizenship and Immigration Canada, 2001c). Family reunification provisions are mostly left to regulations (Canadian Council for Refugees, 2001, p. 48). Sponsorship obligations have been strengthened for people who default on court-ordered child-support payments, and individuals who have been convicted of domestic abuse and not demonstrated rehabilitation do not have sponsorship privileges. People on social assistance, except in cases of disability, also do not have sponsorship privileges. Through legislative provisions, the Act strengthens the federal government's ability to recover the cost of social assistance in cases of sponsorship default.

The Act sets up criteria for permanent residents. Permanent residents have to meet the physical residency requirement of being present in Canada for a cumulative period of two years for every five working years. Exceptions are allowed for people who have to spend time outside Canada to accompany a Canadian citizen, to work for a Canadian company, or for humanitarian reasons. All permanent residents are to have fraud-resistant permanent resident cards. Loss-of-status cases can present an oral appeal to the Immigration and Refugee Board (Citizenship and Immigration Canada, 2001c).

In selecting skilled workers in the economic class, perhaps one of the most unique features of the Act is its movement away from using an occupation-based model to using a model based on flexible and transferable skills. The proposed human capital model will replace the general occupation list and intended occupation concepts. Education and knowledge of an official language are given more weight; however, language is no bar to admission. An in-Canada landing class has been created for temporary workers, including recent graduates who have a permanent job offer and have been working in Canada. The temporary worker program will be expanded to meet the immediate needs of employers. The Act also proposes to establish objective criteria to assess the business experience of both investor and entrepreneur programs, and to establish a net worth for entrepreneurs (Citizenship and Immigration Canada, 2001c).

The Act defines two classes of refugees: convention refugees and people in need of protection. The Act proposes to strengthen refugee protection and overseas resettlement by ensuring that people in need of urgent protection are brought to Canada within days and by pursuing agreements with non-governmental organizations to locate and pre-screen refugee applications in areas where refugees are most in need of protection. It also proposes to amend the criteria for claimants' ability to establish themselves in Canada to include social as well as economic factors. To facilitate family reunification of refugees, overseas families (including extended family members) are to be processed

Bill C-11: The Immigration and Refugee Protection Act, 2002

as a unit whenever possible. Dependants of a refugee, whether living in Canada or abroad, will be processed as part of the same application within one year of the refugee's obtaining permanent status. Another feature of the Act is its provision for faster and fairer refugee processing inland. Referral to the Immigration and Refugee Board is to be made within three working days, with single interviewers supported by paper appeal being the norm. A single hearing is to examine all risk grounds, such as the Geneva Convention, the Convention Against Torture, and the risk of cruel and unusual punishment. The waiting period for landing in Canada for undocumented refugees, who are unable to obtain documents from their country of origin, has been reduced from five to three years. A security check is to be initiated when a person makes a refugee claim; merit will be determined by an independent adjudicator. Perhaps the most controversial provisions of the Act concern enforcement: the Act increases penalties for existing offences and creates a new offence for human trafficking. The penalty for migrant smuggling and trafficking is life in prison.

The Immigration and Refugee Protection Act empowers the minister to enter into agreements with provinces and territories on sharing responsibility for immigration. The Canada–Quebec Accord, signed in 1991, is the most comprehensive one. It gives Quebec selection powers and control over its own settlement services. The federal government retains responsibility for defining immigration categories, setting immigration levels, and providing enforcement. CIC has signed agreements with British Columbia, Saskatchewan, Manitoba, New Brunswick, Newfoundland, the Yukon, and Prince Edward Island. According to the agreements, British Columbia and Manitoba are given funds and responsibility for settlement services, a greater say in planning, and an agreement to attract more business immigrants. Alberta, Saskatchewan, Manitoba, New Brunswick, Newfoundland, and Nova Scotia have signed provincial nominee agreements that allow them to select a small number of immigrants to meet labour market needs. In November 2005, the Canada–Ontario Immigration Agreement was signed. Under the terms of this agreement, Canada will invest an additional $920 million over the next five years in Ontario. This first comprehensive agreement between Ontario and Canada is intended to offer settlement services to help newcomers reach their full potential by increasing federal funding from $800 to about $3,400 per immigrant (Citizenship and Immigration Canada, 2005c). The agreement is the first of its kind to involve municipalities in discussions on immigration. In addition, a provincial nominee program and a temporary worker program will be developed. The Ontario government will also launch its first website to provide potential newcomers with timely information related to all aspects of settlement.

Many organizations, such as Amnesty International, the Canadian Bar Association, the Canadian Council for Refugees, the Maytree Foundation, and the United Nations High Commissioner for Refugees, along with provincial and citywide advocacy groups, have raised significant concerns about the new Act. Criticisms of the two documents leading to the new Immigration Act (Bill C-11 and its precursor Bill C-31) can be grouped into three main areas: the framework legislation's lack of transparency, human rights, and class and gender concerns.

Bill C-11: The Immigration and Refugee Protection Act, 2002

Lack of Transparency

Like previous legislations, the current Act is framework legislation, in that many important details are left to regulations. Consequently, Citizenship and Immigration Canada can implement immigration policy changes without having to face the House of Commons or public scrutiny. This latitude allows the government to say one thing but, in effect, do another (Green & Green, 1996). Although it is recognized that this structure allows the system to be more flexible and responsive, such wide powers of discretion are seen as problematic (Amnesty International, 2001; Canadian Council for Refugees, 2001; Maytree Foundation, 2001). For example, family unification provisions, the selection of independent immigrants, and the definitions of terms such as "international rights" and "terrorism" are all left to regulations; the artic- ulation of these will have serious implications for many individuals and fam- ilies.

Human Rights and Humanitarian Concerns

The potential for human rights abuse, evident from the tone and substance of the Act, is a major concern for many (Amnesty International, 2001; Cana- dian Bar Association, 2001; Canadian Council for Refugees, 2001; Maytree Foundation, 2001; United Nations High Commissioner for Refugees [UNHCR], 2001). The Act bestows expanded privileges on immigration officers and is more restrictive toward asylum seekers and permanent residents. Overall, the Act emphasizes economic objectives. Admissibility criteria—such as the ability to settle, find work, and become independent—are also applied to refugees (Hyndman, 1999). Similarly, the Act's emphasis on finding refugees resettlement close to their own country is more of a political strategy to reduce the numbers of refugees who are asylum seekers in Canada (UNHCR, 2001).

Class and Gender Issues

The class and gender biases in the 1976 Immigration and Refugee Act have received much attention (Bolaria and Li, 1988; Boyd, 1995; Das Gupta, 1994). Similar observations have been made of the new Immigration Act and the consultations that preceded it. Since 1976, the Canadian government has held consultations with various stakeholders to determine immigration pol- icy. However, despite the government's espousal of democratic ideals, the framing of questions and issues in immigration consultations reaffirms sex- ist and racist ideology (Thobani, 2000). The requirement for official language competence for independent immigrants is bound to have a gendered impact (Hyndman, 1999). The relative positioning of the family class and the independent immigrants in relation to the latter's potential for self-sufficiency is seen as "a new problematization of the immigrant family. More specifically, because immigrant women typically come under the family class, the plan also reflects a problematization of immigrant women" (Abu-Laban, 1998; p. 200). The Act will have differential negative consequences for women and racialized minorities (Canadian Council for Refugees, 2001).

Bill C-11 Immigrant and Refugee Protection Act (IRPA) became law on June 28, 2002, but the provisions relating to immigrant selection are not yet implemented, due to the backlog in the immigrant application processing system.

Annual Immigration Plans 2005–2006

As previously mentioned, immigration policy since 1976 has required the minister of Immigration to announce annual plans for immigration. The year 2001 saw the beginning of multi-year planning, consisting of three major components: outcomes, analysis, and activities. The outcomes are related to the goals and results of the immigration program; analysis uses the tools of research and consultation to increase the efficiency of the program; and activities are based on the outcomes and analysis in order to set future priorities and directions that will, in turn, warrant a review of existing policies and programs. Multi-year planning is to focus on issues related to the processing and selection of immigrants, refugees, temporary workers, and students; and the settlement of immigrants and refugees. Instead of presenting the annual plan for only one year, the 2001 plan proposed annual targets for a minimum of two years.

In the 2001 Annual Immigration Plan presented to Parliament, the stated objectives of the immigration program are "to ensure that the movement of people into Canada contributes to Canada's social and economic interests and that it meets Canada's humanitarian commitments" (Citizenship and Immigration Canada, 2001b, p. 3). The long-term plan is to "move toward immigration levels of approximately one percent of the population" (p. 4). The plan states that the factors considered for planning immigration levels are constantly shifting domestic and global environments, operational capacities, the consequences of legislative and policy changes, and the capacity of provinces and territories to absorb and integrate new immigrants.

The multi-year planning process takes into consideration international and domestic trends and challenges. The major international trends affecting Citizenship and Immigration Canada's (CIC) selection and integration programs include an increase in the non-government movement, global labour shortages in certain key economic sectors, competition in the global market, a shift in source countries, and growing numbers of people in transit. The major domestic trends are an aging population, a shrinking labour force, and ever increasing settlement in urban centres. The CIC document also lists international and domestic challenges arising from these trends. At

Table 17.1   Immigration overview: Permanent and temporary residents

CANADA: PERMANENT RESIDENTS BY CATEGORY (NO BACKLOG REALLOCATION)

Category	1995	1996	1997	1998	1999	2000	2001	2002	2003	2004
					NUMBER					
Spouses & partners	30,151	31,562	29,774	28,064	32,789	35,294	37,761	32,767	38,748	43,985
Parents & grandparents	32,998	24,545	20,153	14,165	14,481	17,768	21,340	22,228	19,384	12,732
Others (including children)	13,306	11,617	9,611	8,370	7,957	7,550	7,691	7,304	6,993	5,529
Family class	76,455	67,724	59,538	50,599	55,227	60,612	66,792	62,299	65,125	62,246
Skilled workers*	80,823	97,125	104,924	80,814	92,382	118,567	137,197	122,705	105,220	113,442
Business immigrants	19,417	22,452	19,924	13,777	13,018	13,665	14,589	11,021	8,100	9,764
Provincial/ territorial nominees	0	228	47	0	477	1,252	1,275	2,127	4,418	6,248
Live-in caregivers	5,414	4,723	2,718	2,867	3,260	2,783	2,625	1,985	3,304	4,292
Economic immigrants	105,654	124,528	127,613	97,458	109,137	136,267	155,686	137,838	121,042	133,746
Government-assisted refugees	8,179	7,856	7,661	7,387	7,443	10,671	8,697	7,505	7,505	7,411
Privately sponsored refugees	3,244	3,063	2,580	2,140	2,330	2,922	3,571	3,036	3,252	3,115
Refugees landed in Canada	12,350	13,240	10,430	10,060	11,779	12,993	11,897	10,547	11,265	15,901
Refugee dependants**	3,420	3,938	3,194	2,919	2,805	3,492	3,749	4,021	3,959	6,258
Refugees	27,193	28,097	23,865	22,506	24,357	30,078	27,914	25,109	25,981	32,685
Retirees	304	147	46	8	9	0	0	1	0	0
DROC & PDRCC***	314	3,274	3,233	2,486	1,020	460	205	125	79	53
Temporary resident permit holders	0	0	0	0	0	0	0	9	97	148
Humanitarian & compassionate cases****	0	0	0	0	0	0	0	3,626	9,019	6,945
Other immigrants	618	3,421	3,279	2,494	1,029	460	205	3,761	9,195	7,146
All immigrants & refugees	209,920	223,770	214,295	173,057	189,750	227,417	250,597	229,007	221,343	235,823
Backlog cases	2,949	2,303	1,743	1,143	216	48	41	33	12	1
Total permanent residents	212,869	226,073	216,038	174,200	189,966	227,465	250,638	229,040	221,355	235,824

* Includes independents and assisted relatives.
** Dependants of refugees landed in Canada including spouses and partners.
*** Deferred removal orders and post-determination refugee claimants.
**** Note: The figures for "Humanitarian and compassionate grounds" have been adjusted since the publication of the Annual Report to Parliament on Immigration, as the manner in which final numbers for these cases are calculated has been further refined for increased accuracy. This newer method has been applied to previous years, resulting in a modification of these numbers. As a result, numbers reported for certain categories of immigrants in Facts and Figures 2003: Immigration Overview—Permanent and Temporary Residents have been revised in this edition.

Source: Facts and figures 2004: Immigration overview permanent and temporary residents, by Citizenship and Immigration Canada, 2004 (Ottawa: Minister of Public Works and Government Services Canada). Online at <www.cic.gc.ca/english/pub/facts2004/index .html>.

Table 17.2 Immigration levels plan 2006		2006 RANGES Lower–Upper	RATIO (%)
IMMIGRANT CATEGORY		**2006 RANGES** Lower–Upper	**RATIO** (%)
Skilled workers		105,000–116,000	
Business		9,000–11,000	
Entrepreneur			
Self-employed			
Investor			
Live-in caregiver		3,000–5,000	
Provincial nominees		9,000–11,000	
TOTAL ECONOMIC		**126,000–143,000**	**56%**
Spouses, partners, and children	44,000–46,000		**44%**
Parents and grandparents*	17,000–19,000		
TOTAL FAMILY	**61,000–65,000**		
Government-assisted refugees	7,300–7,500		
Privately sponsored refugees	3,000–4,000		
Inland protected persons	19,500–22,000		
Dependants abroad	3,000–6,800		
TOTAL REFUGEE	**32,800–40,300**		
Humanitarian and Compassionate/ Public Policy	5,100–6,500		
Permit holders	100–200		
TOTAL NET ECONOMIC	**99,000–112,000** →	**99,000–112,000**	
TOTAL		**225,000–255,000**	

* This number includes 12,000 parents and grandparents as announced by the Minister on April 18, 2005.

Source: *Annual report to Parliament on immigration, 2005*, 2005, by Citizenship and Immigration Canada. Online at <www.cic.gc.ca/english/pub/annualreport2005/section1.html>.

the international level, challenges include managing processing demands, remaining competitive, and maintaining client service and program integrity. At the domestic front, the key challenges are ensuring that all parts of Canada share in the benefits of immigration and removing barriers to successful settlement and integration. The 2001 Annual Immigration Plan lists the indicators of successful integration and acknowledges the difficulties faced by immigrants in gaining recognition of foreign credentials so as to obtain appropriate employment.

Table 17.1 provides the number of permanent residents by category from 1995–2004 and Table 17.2 provides details of the immigration plan for 2006. In 2004, 57% were economic immigrants and their dependants, as compared to 55% in 2003. Overall, 57% of the new permanent residents were in the economic class, while 43% were in the non-economic class. The proportion 57:43 is very close to the 60:40 balance desired between the economic and non-economic components of the immigration program (Citizenship and Immigration Canada, 2005b).

Review of Immigration and Refugee Policy Directions

Immigration policy is influenced by a number of considerations, such as national goals and the cost of achieving these goals (Simmons, 1998); market, non-market, and international considerations (Timmer & Williamson, 1998); and the politics of liberal democracies (Freeman, 1995). These factors do not operate in isolation: their influence at a particular time depends also on the immigration history of a country, as evidenced clearly in the evolution of Canadian immigration policy and practices. Green and Green (1996, p. 1) note that the defining feature of Canadian immigration policy is its flexibility, and that the goals of immigration policy in Canada are often difficult to determine as the policy is "a complex entity consisting of an interconnected set of guidelines, regulations and actual actions by government agents," mostly outside the realm of public scrutiny. Since the 1910 Immigration Act, Parliament has entrusted a great deal of power to the Cabinet, and thereafter to the minister of Immigration. Such flexibility has been a useful feature in times of emergency.

Canadian immigration policy until 1967 was highly discriminatory, with a strong preference for people from European backgrounds (Abu-Laban, 1998; Green & Green, 1996; Henry et al., 2000; Isajiw, 1999). The same is true of Canada's refugee history (Adelman, 1991; Richmond, 1994). Historically, Canadian immigration policy was driven by short- and long-term economic objectives, absorptive capacity, family reunification, demographic needs, and cultural factors (Abu-Laban, 1998; Christensen, 1999; Green & Green, 1996). During the 1970s and 1980s, recession and high levels of unemployment led to economic factors dominating immigration policy. For example, as a result of the economic downturn in the 1980s, the independent worker category was reduced to only 14% of all immigration, the lowest level in postwar history. Major policy initiatives were launched for immigration policy to focus more on family class and the increasing number of refugees and asylum seekers (Simmons, 1998). During the 1970s and 1980s, there was also immigration policy interest in issues of social, economic, and cultural incorporation. During the late 1980s and 1990s, policy changes arose when the government recognized how international immigration could improve Canada's productivity and lower the public cost from all categories of immigration (Abu-Laban, 1998; Simmons, 1998). The category of economic-class immigrants, consisting of independent workers, business immigrants, and entrepreneurs, was carefully revised and its allotted proportion increased alongside a reduction to the family class proportion. In 1994, economic class accounted for 43% of all immigration, and this figure increased to 53% in 2000. Family class was reduced from 51% in 1984 to 44% by 1997 (Simmons, 1998).

In order to contain the costs of immigration and reduce immigrants' and refugees' dependence on public funds, a landing fee was introduced in 1994. Refugee claimants were also allowed to work while their claims were being processed. Sponsoring relatives were given financial responsibility for their sponsored relatives for ten years. Bill C-44 was also introduced to respond to public concern over rising rates of crime involving immigrants and refugees (Simmons, 1998).

Canadian immigration policy has paid a great deal of attention to absorptive capacity. During the postwar period, immigration levels were reduced during periods of high unemployment. Selecting immigrants to fill specific occupations that are in high demand also illustrates this concern. However, recent evidence suggests that absorption is no longer a key issue in policy-making (Green & Green, 1996).

During the 1990s, there was also a clear and new preference for "integration" as a policy objective (Abu-Laban, 1998). The 1994 Immigration Working Group noted that it accepted the notion of integration as a policy objective in Canada. Distinct from assimilation and segregation, integration "ideally involves a two-way process of accommodation between newcomers and Canadians" (quoted in Abu-Laban, 1998, p. 202). This shift addressed one of the criticisms of Canadian multiculturalism policy, which was that it undermined Canadian unity by promoting a multiplicity of cultures without a shared core of Canadian values. In fact, in 1996, the revised multiculturalism program incorporated integration as the framework and emphasized the themes of identity, civic participation, and social justice (Abu-Laban, 1998). The trend toward encouraging integration is also evident in the Annual Immigration Plan, as well as the stated goals of the new Immigration Act.

Recent Developments

Following the transfer of enforcements and intelligence functions from CIC to the newly created Canada Border Services Agency (CBSA) in 2003, CIC has developed new vision and mission statements that provide the basis for an integrated package of programs and services. Three strategic outcomes are identified to guide CIC's activities. These are: maximum contribution to Canada's economic, social, and cultural development from migration; reflection of Canadian values and interests in the management of international migration, including refugee protection; and successful integration of newcomers and promotion of Canadian citizenship. Integration is thus a central goal of the new immigration framework.

On December 29, 2004, Canada implemented the safe third country agreement with the United States. This agreement stipulates that refugee claimants are required to request asylum in the first safe country they arrive in. This agreement applies to refugee claims made at land borders. Refugee claimants accessing Canada from the Canada–US land border are not eligible for refugee determination hearing with the Immigration and Refugee Board, unless they qualify for an exception. Implementation of this agreement has reduced the number of land border refugee claims by 40% (CIC, 2005).

In April 2005, the Minister of Citizenship and Immigration announced the tripling of the target for parents and grandparents to 18,000 to address the backlog within the system. Visa students were allowed to obtain employment provided they are outside the major cities—Toronto, Montreal and Vancouver.

In pursuance of the strategic outcome of the successful integration of newcomers to the Canadian labour market and society, all the settlement programs are strengthened. In addition, a coordinated strategy to integrate foreign-trained Canadians and immigrants into Canadian labour market was developed in 2004 as part of a government-wide initiative focusing on four areas: foreign credential assessment and recognition, enhanced language training and bridge-to-work initiatives, labour market information, and research. The 2005 budget provides for increased spending over the next four years for settlement and integration (CIC, 2005b).

Impact of
Immigration
Policies:
1967 to
Present

Impact of Immigration Policies: 1967 to Present

Overall, Canadian society has experienced three major trends in relation to the post-1967 changes to immigration policies. The first is the continuous increases in the diversity of the population due to immigration from non-traditional source countries. The second is that immigration is recognized more and more as the source of labour supply in Canada. The third, although not attributable to immigration policy per se, is the growing social inequality between newcomers and native-born Canadians.

Increasing Diversity

Although the elimination of racist immigration policies in 1967 resulted in increased immigration from non-traditional source countries, the introduction of three immigrant classes in 1993 spurred even further growth in inflows from non-European nations (Isajiw, 1999). In 2004, the top ten source countries (China, India, Philippines, Pakistan, United States, Iran, United Kingdom, Romania, South Korea and France) provided over 52.5% of Canada's newcomers (CIC, 2005b). China, India, Pakistan, and the Philippines have been the top four source countries of newcomers to Canada since 1999, accounting for 15%, 11%, 6%, and 5% respectively in 2004. Due primarily to the changes in source countries and regions and sustained high levels of immigration, the population has become increasingly ethnically heterogeneous. In 2001, 13.4% of the population was "visible minorities"[1] (Statistics Canada, 2003a, p. 10). However, it is projected that by 2017 19 to 23% of the population will be "visible minorities" and immigrants will comprise 22% of Canada's population (Statistics Canada, 2005). Over half of all newcomers settle in Ontario, with Toronto and surrounding regions becoming home to the largest number of arrivals, particularly of those who are "visible minorities." Toronto's population in 2001 included 44% foreign-born individuals and 36.8% "visible minorities," with 79% of those who arrived in the 1990s being "visible minorities" (Statistics Canada, 2003a). The majority of immigrants to Canada settle in the three largest cities: Toronto, Vancouver and Montreal. It is predicted that

over half of both Toronto and Vancouver's populations will be "visible minorities" by 2017 (Statistics Canada, 2005).

The diversity of languages spoken by immigrants has also increased dramatically, with almost half of all those admitted in 2003 speaking neither of
the country's official languages (CIC, 2004). In the same year, 45.4% of newcomers spoke English, 3.3% spoke French, 3.0% spoke both official languages,
and a full 48.3% spoke neither. Finally, religious affiliations have also changed
over time. Prior to 1961, 83.5% of immigrants belonged to a Christian denom-
ination, whereas by the period 1991–2001 this was the case for only 45.3%,
with increases in admissions of those reporting Muslim, Hindu, Buddhist,
and Sikh religious affiliations, as well as for those reporting no religious affil-
iation (Statistics Canada, 2003b).

Supplying Labour Needs

Historically, immigration has been the major source of supplying labour
needs within Canadian society. More recently, labour shortages have been
identified as a major business constraint. Labour shortages are likely to
become a challenge as baby boomers retire during the next two decades. It is
predicted that without immigration, the size of the Canadian labour force
will decline. By the end of the decade, immigration will account for all the
net growth in the labour force. Currently, immigration accounts for an estimated 70% of Ontario's net population growth, but will account for all of the
net labour force growth within the next six years (CIC, 2005c). Approximately
70% of Ontario's working-age (25–64 years-old) immigrants are highly educated and trained and, of this group, 23% are professionals (Ontario Ministry
of Training, Colleges and Universities, 2005).

Inequalities in Access and Outcomes

Inequality between newcomer and native-born populations is evident in a
number of spheres, including employment, housing, civic and political participation and representation, and human services. These inequalities in
access and outcomes exist in areas related to primary settlement needs and,
thus, impede the ability of newcomers to successfully integrate into Canadian
society. Although racism is difficult to measure, many scholars assert that
disparate outcomes in spheres such as those outlined above are evidence of
the racial discrimination that is pervasive and embedded in Canadian society (Castles, 1997; Henry & Tator, 2005; Kunz, Milan, & Schetagne, 2000; Ornstein, 2000).

A number of studies have documented racial prejudice and employment
disparities in Canada (Boyd, 1995; Galabuzi, 2001; Li, 1997; Reitz & Breton,
1994, quoted in Reitz, 2004). Income disparities between newcomers and the
native-born have increased as more and more newcomers belong to non-
dominant racial groups (Jackson & Smith, 2002), leading to the phenomenon
of racialized poverty. Earning differentials between visible minority new-

comers and White Canadian-born citizens because of unrecognized credentials and direct discrimination toward the former (Harvey, Siu, & Reil, 1999; Ornstein, 2000) cost the Canadian economy about $55 billion a year (Reitz, cited in Siddiqui, 2001) and create a highly stratified society. The average newly arrived male immigrant earned roughly 80% of the average native-born salary in 1980; however, by 2000 he earned only 60% (Reitz, 2004). In 1980, 86% of immigrant men and 91% of native-born men were employed. In contrast, by 2000 only 68% of newcomers were working, in comparison with 85% of the native-born population. It is argued that the barriers to employment for newcomers, such as the requirement for Canadian employment experience and the non-recognition of foreign credentials and experience, can be directly attributed to racism and/or other forms of discrimination (Cabral, 2000; Galabuzi, 2001; Henry & Tator, 2005; Integrated Settlement Planning Research Consortium, 2000). The systemic barriers associated with credential evaluation and licensing for trades and occupations are well documented (Basran & Zong, 1998; Brouwer, 1999; Calleja, 2000). Newcomers to Canada have higher levels of education on average than Canadian-born citizens, yet the newcomers find it more difficult to find jobs (Badets & Howatson-Leo, 1999; McDonald & Worswick, 1997). Although Canada does not have the extensive empirical studies of housing discrimination available in the US, there is evidence that newcomers face numerous barriers to accessing housing in both the private and social housing markets (Housing New Canadians, n.d.), with many disadvantaged in the housing market on the basis of race, ethnicity, class, and/or gender (Murdie, Chambon, Hulchanski, & Teixeira, 1999). Newcomers often reside in the least desirable housing units in the least desirable areas (Sparks & Wolfson, 2001) and are increasingly over represented in Toronto's high-poverty neighbourhoods; in 1980, 24.4% of low-income neighbourhood residents were recent immigrants, whereas by 2000, 39.1% were recent immigrants (United Way of Greater Toronto & Canadian Council on Social Development, 2004). Furthermore, "visible minorities" frequently reside in unsafe, rundown buildings, but typically pay nearly the same amount for housing as their neighbours with higher incomes and better housing (Ornstein, 2000).

Newcomers are increasingly represented in the category of "absolute homelessness" (residing outdoors and using community shelters) (Ballay & Bulthuis, 2004, P. 119). In Toronto in 1999, refugees comprised 24% of families requiring emergency shelters (City of Toronto, 2001a, quoted in Ballay & Bulthuis, 2004) and 23% of singles who used a shelter more than five times in the year (City of Toronto, 2001b, quoted in Ballay & Bulthuis, 2004, P. 120). In 2001, 800 refugee claimants were accommodated in Toronto's shelters at any given point (City of Toronto, 2001a, quoted in Ballay & Bulthuis, 2004).

Although civic and political participation is an integral component of democracy, proportionate representation of diversity remains lacking in Canada's political life (Biles & Tolley, 2004). The proportionality index for "visible minorities" on Toronto's municipal council is 0.3 (Bird, 2004); this

Impact of Immigration Policies: 1967 to Present

means that they are represented at only one third of the level required for proportionate representation. The proportionality index for "visible minorities" in the House of Commons is slightly higher at 0.4. However, defining political participation as only participation in electoral and party politics excludes numerous other forms of political activism, such as involvement in social and protest movements, trade unions, and "homeland politics" (Stasilius, 1994, quoted in Stasilius 1997, p. 1). Newcomers also participate politically through a large number of organizations, agencies, and coalitions aimed at improving their chances for success, as well as through charitable giving and volunteering.

Newcomers underutilize human services due to lack of access to appropriate programs and services (Henry & Tator, 2005). Lack of access for members of non-dominant racial and cultural groups is caused by lack of information about the services, unavailability of services, service providers' lack of knowledge of the linguistic and cultural needs of different groups, and inappropriate service models. A number of studies have demonstrated the existence of barriers to services for newcomers (Neufeld, Harrison, Stewart, Hughes, & Spitzer, 2002; Reitz, 1995, quoted in George & Ramkissoon, 1998; Truelove, 2000).

Access and equity for newcomers has increasingly become an item on the agendas of communities and various levels of government. Employment-oriented disparities appear to have received the most attention thus far and, within this area, the majority of advocacy and initiatives has occurred for foreign-trained professionals. While such work represents a step forward, it is important to note that foreign-trained professionals comprise only a small portion of the pool of highly educated newcomers.

Broadly, programs and initiatives for foreign-trained professionals can be categorized as those that provide information, assessment of international credentials and/or work experience, specialized advisement and/or counselling, bridging, coordination and/or integration of service provision, policy advocacy, and employer incentives. In April 2005, the federal government launched the Internationally Trained Workers Initiative, which includes the Integration of Internationally Trained Health Professionals, the Foreign Credential Recognition (FCR) program, the Going to Canada Immigration Internet Portal; and the Enhanced Language Training (ELT) and Bridge to Work (CIC, 2005b). The government of Ontario has introduced a plan to speed the entry of internationally trained professionals and tradespersons into the labour market (Ontario Ministry of Training, Colleges and Universities, 2005). This plan focuses on making information on Ontario's labour market needs and the criteria for licensure, registration, or certification available to prospective immigrants; expanding access to higher-level language training; offering an assessment service that evaluates international credentials and compares them with those earned in Ontario; increasing skill upgrading opportunities; and increasing opportunities to gain the equivalent of Canadian work experience.

At the community level, a number of agencies, coalitions, networks, and other organizations have increasingly advocated for access and equity in employment for foreign-trained professionals and tradespersons and have introduced training and other employment-oriented initiatives to achieve their goal. To cite only one example, the Toronto Region Immigrant Employment Council (TRIEC) is a multi-stakeholder council that works to improve access to employment for immigrants in the Toronto region through six major initiatives (TRIEC, n.d.). These initiatives cover territory such as the bridging of occupational and licensing gaps, employment mentoring, paid internship provision, informational assistance, building knowledge about employer promising practices, and public awareness.

Conclusion

Notes

References

Conclusion

The success of the immigration and refugee program should not be judged only by the achievement of annual immigration targets. Although there is no overall evaluation of Canadian immigration policy, academic and practice communities have consistently raised critical issues for research and debate. Some of the academic debates centre on questions such as the annual number of immigrant and refugee admissions; the proportions of family, economic, and refugee classes; and immigration's role in economic growth (DeVoretz, 1995). Immigrant and refugee advocates have raised concerns about issues such as the landing fee, criminalization of racial minorities, processing delays, and lack of access to trades and professions for newcomers.

This chapter should have been titled "Social Policy in Relation to Newcomers to Canada" rather than "Immigration and Refugee Policy in Canada" because while the current immigration and refugee policy enables Canada to meet its overall goal of population growth, there is a major policy vacuum concerning the adaptation and integration of newcomers to Canada. As economic goals are high on the agenda for immigration, an important question is whether immigrants to Canada, especially those in the economic class, have adequate opportunities to become contributing members of Canadian society. Reitz (1998) argues that four institutions—immigration, labour market structure, educational institutions, and the welfare state—should work together to form an institutional approach to immigration and immigrant adjustment in Canada.

Notes

1   The term "visible minorities" is defined in the Employment Equity Act (1995) as "persons, other than Aboriginal peoples, who are non-Caucasian in race or non-white in colour."

References

Abu-Laban, Y. (1998). Welcome/stayout: The contradiction of Canadian integration and immigration policies at the millennium. *Canadian Ethnic Studies, 30*(3), 190–211.

References Adelman, H. (1991). Canadian refugee policy in the postwar period: An analysis. In H. Adelman (Ed.), *Refugee policy: Canada and the United States* (pp. 173–223). Toronto: York Lanes Press.

Amnesty International. (2001). *Brief on Bill C-11: An act respecting immigration to Canada and the granting of refugee protection to persons who are displaced, persecuted or in danger.* Online at <www.amnesty.ca/Refugee/Bill_C-11.pdf>.

Badets, J., & Howatson-Leo, L. (1999, Spring). Recent immigrants in the workforce. *Canadian Social Trends, 52,* 16–22.

Ballay, P., & Bulthuis, M. (2004, Spring). The changing portrait of homelessness. In C. Andrew (Ed.), *Our diverse cities, 1,* 119–123.

Basran, G., & Zong, L. (1998). Devaluation of foreign credentials as perceived by visible minority professional immigrants. *Canadian Ethnic Studies, 30*(3), 6–23.

Biles, J., & Tolley, E. (2004, spring). Getting seats at the table(s): The political participation of newcomers and minorities in Ottawa. In C. Andrew (Ed.), *Our diverse cities, 1,* 174–179.

Bird, K. (2004, Spring). Obstacles to ethnic minority representation in local government in Canada. In C. Andrew (Ed.), *Our diverse cities, 1,* 182–186.

Bolaria, B.S., & Li, P.S. (1988). *Racial oppression in Canada* (2nd ed.). Toronto: Garamond Press.

Boyd, M. (1995). Immigrant women: Language and socio-economic inequalities and language issues. In S.S. Halli, F. Trovato, & L. Driedger (Eds.), *Ethnic demography: Canadian immigrant, racial and cultural variations* (pp. 275–296). Ottawa: Carleton University Press.

Brouwer, A. (1999). *Immigrants need not apply.* Ottawa: Caledon Institute of Social Policy.

Cabral, V. (2000). *Settlement services for newcomers and access to family services.* Toronto: Integrated Settlement Planning Research Project and the Multicultural Coalition for Access to Family Services.

Calleja, D. (2000). Right skills, wrong country: Why is Canada making it next to impossible for talented newcomers to practice in their fields of expertise? *Canadian Business, 73*(12), 34–39.

Calliste, A. (1991). Canada's immigration policy and domestics from the Caribbean: The second domestic scheme. In J. Vorst et al. (Eds.), *Race, class, gender: Bonds and barriers* (pp. 136–168). Toronto: Garamond Press.

Canadian Bar Association. (2001). New bill is "unfair" to immigrants says CBA's immigration section. Online at <www.cba.org/cba/news/2001>.

Canadian Council for Refugees. (1998). *Best settlement practices: Settlement services for refugees and immigrants to Canada.* Montreal: Author.

Canadian Council for Refugees. (2001). Bill C-11 brief.

Castles, S. (1997, June). *Globalisation and migration. Some pressing contradictions.* Keynote address presented at the UNESCO-MOST Intergovernmental Council, Paris. Online at <www.unesco.org/most/igc97cas.htm>.

Christensen, C.P. (1999). Immigrant minorities in Canada. In F. Turner (Ed.), *Social work practice: A Canadian perspective* (pp. 179–211). Scarborough: Prentice Hall.

Citizenship and Immigration Canada. (2001a). *Appendix B: Immigrant arrivals, 2000. 2001 Annual Immigration Plan.* Ottawa: Minister of Public Works and Government Services Canada.

Citizenship and Immigration Canada. (2001b). *Appendix C: Immigration plan, 2001 and 2002.* Ottawa: Minister of Public Works and Government Services Canada.

Citizenship and Immigration Canada. (2001c, February). *Immigration and Refugee Protection Act introduced*. News release. Ottawa.

Citizenship and Immigration Canada. (2004). *Facts and figures 2004: Immigration overview permanent and temporary residents*. Ottawa: Minister of Public Works and Government Services Canada. Online at <www.cic.gc.ca/english/pub/facts 2004/index.html>.

Citizenship and Immigration Canada (CIC). (2005a, April 25). *Government of Canada announces internationally trained workers initiative*. News Release. Online at <www.cic.gc.ca/English/press/05/0513-e.html>.

Citizenship and Immigration Canada (CIC). (2005b). *Annual report to Parliament*. Ottawa: Minister of Public Works and Government Services Canada.

Citizenship and Immigration Canada (CIC). (2005c) *Ontario immigration facts*. Ministry of Citizenship and Immigration. Online at <www.citizenship.gov.on .ca/english/about/f211105.htm>.

Cohen, R. (1994). A brief history of racism in immigration policies for recruiting domestics. *Canadian Woman Studies, 4*(2), 83–86.

Cunningham Armacost, N. (1995). Gender and immigration law: The recruitment of domestic workers to Canada, 1867–1940. *Indian Journal of Gender Studies, 2*(1), 25–43.

Das Gupta, T. (1994). Political economy of gender, race and class: Looking at South Asian women in Canada. *Canadian Ethnic Studies, 26*, 70–71.

DeVoretz, D.J. (1995). *Diminishing returns: The economics of Canada's recent immigration policy*. Ottawa: C.D. Howe Institute.

Employment Equity Act, S.C. 1995, c. 44.

Freeman, G.P. (1995). Modes of immigration politics in liberal democratic states. *International Migration Review, 29*(4), 881–903.

Galabuzi, G.E. (2001). *Canada's creeping economic apartheid: The economic segregation and social marginalization of racialized groups*. Toronto, ON, Canada: Centre for Social Justice and Foundation for Research and Education.

George, U., & Fuller-Thompson, E. (1997). To stay or not to stay: Characteristics associated with newcomers planning to remain in Canada. *Canadian Journal of Regional Science, 1*(2), 181–193.

George, U., & Ramkissoon, S. (1998). Race, gender, and class: Interlocking oppressions in the lives of South Asian women in Canada. *Affilia, 13*(1), 102–119.

Grant, K. (2000). Health care in an aging society: Issues, controversies, and challenges for the future. In B. Singh Bolaria (Ed.), *Social issues and contradictions in Canadian society* (3rd ed., pp. 363–390). Toronto: Harcourt Canada.

Green, A., & Green, D. (1996). *The economic goals of Canada's immigration policy, past and present*. (Research on Immigration and Integration in the Metropolis, Working Paper Series, no. 96–04). Burnaby: Simon Fraser University.

Harvey, E.B., Siu, B., & Reil, K.D.V. (1999). Ethnocultural groups, period of immigration and socioeconomic situation. *Canadian Ethnic Studies, 31*(3), 94–103.

Henry, F., Tator, C., Mattis, W., & Rees, T. (2000). *The colour of democracy: Racism in Canadian society* (2nd ed.). Toronto: Harcourt Canada.

Henry, F., & Tator, C. (with Mattis, W., & Rees, T.) (2005). *The colour of democracy: Racism in Canadian society* (3rd ed.). Toronto: Thomson Canada.

Housing New Canadians. (n.d.). *Introduction: Research theme #1: The "housing trajectory" of newcomers*. Online at <www.hnc.utoronto.ca/intro/theme1.htm>.

References Hyndman, J. (1999). Gender and Canadian immigration policy: A current snapshot. *Canadian Woman Studies, 19*(3), 6–10.

Immigration and Refugee Protection Act, S.C. 2001, c. 27 (Bill C-11).

Integrated Settlement Planning Research Consortium. (2000). *Re-Visioning the newcomer: Settlement support system.* Toronto: Author.

INTERCEDE (1992, February). *Response to the proposed reform of the Ontario Labour Relations Act.* Toronto: Author.

Isajiw, W.W. (1999). *Understanding diversity: Ethnicity and race in the Canadian context.* Toronto: Thompson Educational.

Jackson, A., & Smith, E. (2002). Does a rising tide lift all boats? Recent immigrants in the economic recovery. *Horizons, 5*(2), 1–30. Online at <www.policyresearch.gc.ca/v5n2_e.pdf>.

Knowles, V. (2000). *Forging our legacy: Canadian citizenship and immigration, 1900–1977.* Public Works and Government Services Canada.

Kunz, J.L., Milan, A., & Schetagne, S. (2000). *Unequal access: A Canadian profile on racial differences in education, employment and income.* (Report prepared for the Canadian Race Relations Foundation by the Canadian Council on Social Development). Online at <www.amachi.biz/diversfiles/en/pub/rep/ePubRep UneqAcc.pdf>.

Li, P.S. (1997). Biases in benchmarking immigrants. In B. Abu-Laban & T.M. Derwing (Eds.), *Responding to diversity in the metropolis: Building an inclusive research agenda* (pp. 112–118). Proceedings of the First Metropolis National Conference on Immigration. Edmonton: Prairie Centre of Excellence for Research on Immigration and Integration.

Macklin, A. (2001). New directions for refugee policy: Of curtains, doors and locks. *Refuge, 19*(4), 1–4.

The Maytree Foundation. (2001). *Brief to the Standing Committee on Citizenship and Immigration regarding Bill C-11, Immigration and Refugee Protection Act.*

McDonald, J.T., & Worswick, C. (1997). Unemployment incidence of immigrant men in Canada. *Canadian Public Policy, 23*(4), 353–373.

Murdie, R.A., Chambon, A.S., Hulchanski, J.D., & Teixeira, C. (1999). *Differential incorporation and housing trajectories of recent immigrant households: Towards a conceptual framework.* Toronto, ON: Housing New Canadians Research Working Group.

Neufeld, A., Harrison, M.J., Stewart, M.J., Hughes, K.D., & Spitzer, D. (2002). Immigrant women: Making connections to community resources for support in family caregiving. *Qualitative Health Research, 12*(6), 751–768.

Ontario Ministry of Training, Colleges and Universities. (2005). *Opening doors: An investment in prosperity.* Online at <www.edu.gov.on.ca/eng/document/reports/getresults/index.html>.

Ornstein, M. (2000). *Single and multi-dimensional disadvantage. Ethno-racial inequality in the City of Toronto: An analysis of the 1996 census.* Prepared for the Access and Equity Unit, Strategic and Corporate Policy Division.

Reitz, J.G. (1998). *Warmth of the welcome: The social causes of economic success of immigrants in different nations and cities.* Boulder: Westview Press.

Reitz, J.G. (2004). Canada: Immigration and nation-building in the transition to a knowledge economy. In W.A. Cornelius, T. Tsuda, P.L. Martin, & J.F. Hollifield (Eds.), *Controlling immigration: A global perspective* (pp. 97–133). Stanford, CA: Stanford University Press.

Richmond, A. (1994). *Global apartheid: Refugees, racism and the new world order.* **References** Toronto: Oxford University Press.

Siddiqui, H. (2001, January 14). Immigrants subsidize us by $55 billion per year. *Toronto Star*, A13.

Simmons, A.B. (1998). Economic globalization and immigration policy: Canada and Europe. *Journal of Contemporary International Issues, 1*(1).

Sparks, R.J., & Wolfson, W.G. (2001). *Settlement in the workplace: The settlement needs of employed newcomers.* Toronto: COSTI Immigrant Services.

Stasiulis, D.K. (1997, November). *Participation by immigrants, ethnocultural/visible minorities in the Canadian political process.* Paper presented at the Second National Metropolis Conference, Montreal, Quebec, Canada. Online at <http://canada.metropolis.net/events/civic/dstasiulis_e.html>.

Stasiulis, D.K., & Bakan, A.B. (1997a). Regulation and resistance: Strategies of migrant domestic workers in Canada and internationally. *Asian and Pacific Migration Journal, 6*(1), 31–57.

Stasiulis, D.K., & Bakan, A.B. (1997b, Autumn). Negotiating citizenship: The case of foreign domestic workers in Canada. *Feminist Review, 57*, 112–139.

Statistics Canada. (2003a). *Canada's ethnocultural portrait: The changing mosaic.* Ottawa: Minister of Industry.

Statistics Canada. (2003b). *Religions in Canada* (2001 Census: analysis series) (Catalogue no. 96F0030SIE2001015). Ottawa: Minister of Industry.

Statistics Canada. (2005). *Population projections of visible minority groups, Canada, provinces and regions: 2001–2017.* Ottawa: Minister of Industry.

Thobani, S. (2000). Closing ranks: Racism and sexism in Canada's immigration policy. *Race and Class, 42*(1), 35–55.

Thompson, A. (2001, June 27). Ottawa to open door for "temp" workers. *Toronto Star*, A1.

Timmer, A.S., & Williamson, J.G. (1998). Immigration policy prior to the 1930s: Labor markets, policy interactions, and globalization backlash. *Population and Development Review, 24*(4), 739.

TRIEC Home Page. (n.d.). Online at <www.triec.ca/>.

Truelove, M. (2000). Services for immigrant women: An evaluation of locations. *The Canadian Geographer, 44*(2), 135–151.

United Nations High Commissioner for Refugees (UNHCR). (2001, March 5). *Comments on Bill C-11 "An Act respecting immigration to Canada and the granting of refugee protection to persons who are displaced, persecuted or in danger."* Submission to House of Commons Standing Committee on Citizenship and Immigration.

United Way of Greater Toronto & Canadian Council on Social Development. (2004). *Poverty by postal code: The geography of neighbourhood poverty; City of Toronto, 1981–2001.* Online at <www.unitedwaytoronto.com/who_we_help/pdfs/Poverty byPostalCodeFinal.pdf>.

Villasin, F.O., & Phillips, A.M. (1994). Falling through the cracks: Domestic workers and progressive movements. *Canadian Woman Studies, 14*(2), 87–90.

Additional Resources

Canadian Council for Refugees. Online at <www.web.net/~ccr>.

Ceris. Online at <www.ceris.metropolis.net>.

References   Citizenship and Immigration. Online at <www.cic.gc.ca>.

Driedger, L. (1996). *Multi-ethnic Canada: Identities & inequalities.* Toronto: Oxford University Press.

Maytree Foundation. Online at <www.maytree.com>.

Ontario Ministry of Citizenship. Online at <www.gov.on.ca/mczcr>.

Universal Health Care: Normative Legacies Adrift

Mike Burke and *Susan Silver*

Introduction

Canada's national health care system, known as medicare, is a source of immense collective achievement. Unlike other facets of Canadian social policy, it sets out a vision of distributive justice based on the principle of "equity." Equity as a distributive principle requires that "need," not ability to pay, be the sole determinant of access and distribution of health services. Equity based on need alone means that no one has a prior entitlement based on status, wealth, race, or other social differences (Churchill, 1987, p. 94). Medicare escaped the "residual trap" (Taylor, 1978), characteristic of other social policy measures, by adopting a universal, one-tier, publicly financed model of insurance covering hospital services and physician services for all Canadians, rich and poor alike. Though aggressively contested, the founding principle of "equity of access" has endured as a normative legacy in relation to "medically necessary" hospital services and doctor's services. Medicare has remained an egalitarian institution in an otherwise inegalitarian society.[1]

While escaping this residual trap, we have not succeeded in quelling privatization pressures that are inevitable in a nation that allows the private market, with its inherent inequities, to prevail as the dominant mechanism for allocating income and other scarce resources. These privatization pressures, while a mainstay of capitalist society, have been increasingly fuelled by the current neo-liberal political climate. Neo-liberalism, as a political ideology, calls for a profound reconfiguration of social welfare responsibilities among the public sector, the private sector, the family, and the non-profit sector (Burke, Mooers, & Shields, 2000). It seeks to minimize the social role of the state by recommodifying public services and, consequently, to expand the space available for the market provision of such services. It justifies this reconfiguration by an appeal to a narrow and distorted discourse of "efficiency" that equates efficiency with cutting public expenditures on social services.[2] In the case of health care, neo-liberalism identifies efficiency as the predominant if not sole criterion of health policy evaluation, asserts that publicly funded systems of health care are inefficient by definition, and concludes that the state's role in health care must be severely curtailed in order to contain public costs. This definition of efficiency threatens to undermine the *quality* of our medicare system, disrupt considerations of equity, and exacerbate disparities in the health of Canadians.

These issues are critical, and the stakes are high for Canadians in general and for vulnerable populations such as Aboriginal peoples and racialized immigrant groups specifically. However, with total health care expenditures exceeding $130 billion in 2004 alone (Canadian Institute for Health Information [CIHI], 2004), proponents of privatization stand to achieve huge financial rewards. As expressed by an American health care firm, medicare is "one of the largest unopened oysters in the Canadian economy" (quoted in Canadian Centre for Policy Alternatives [CCPA], 2000, p. 4).

These are the fundamental choices facing policy-makers. Do we reaffirm and strengthen the public system and thereby the equity principle, or seek to further accelerate the neo-liberal program of privatization and the inevitable erosion of accessibility and quality? The health care debate is, however, not explicitly framed in terms of choices, but as a fiscal imperative obligating privatization.

This chapter begins with the assumption, borrowed from Richard Titmuss, that values are central to policy debates. Titmuss contends that "policy is all about values" (1974, p. 132), and he defines policy as the "principles that govern action directed towards given ends" (p. 23). Titmuss further argues that the goal of policy analysis is to "expose more clearly the value choices confronting society" (p. 136). Using this framework for policy analysis, this chapter initially examines the normative foundations or dominant values that framed the original intentions of medicare. The chapter then briefly reviews the early successes and the political shift from a concern with equity to a concern with cost control. Recent federal and provincial commissions and health policy initiatives are reviewed in relation to their contribution to the debate over the future of medicare. Three challenges to the normative foundations are then examined. These challenges, central to the neo-liberal project, are (1) the retrenchment of the federal role in relation to national standards; (2) the privatization thrust, and with it the increasing commodification of health care services; and (3) the relegation of responsibility from the public sector to the family and the community. These challenges threaten to erode the normative foundations of medicare and widen the gap between the "promise of citizenship and the reality of exclusion" (Galabuzi, 2004, p. 246) experienced by members of vulnerable populations such as racialized groups and immigrants.

Medicare's accomplishments extend far beyond the field of health care. Medicare is a beacon, a constant reminder of the possibilities of equality and inclusiveness within Canadian society. The ties that bind Canadians together are the shared and common experiences that result from a consistent interpretation of our fundamental national values. The chapter concludes with a rallying call to progressive social work activists to add their voices and values to the social policy debate, clearly articulating the normative possibilities of collective action.

Normative Policy Framework

A normative analysis attempts to expose and clarify the values that influence policy debates and policy outcomes (Titmuss, 1974). Values are conceptions of the desirable within every individual and society and serve as standards or normative criteria to guide action, attitudes, and judgments. A primary objective of a normative analysis is to clarify and understand the values that represent a nation's policy choices (Silver, 1993). Public policies, thus, constitute choices among alternative normative intentions, among competing perceptions of the common good (Kronick, 1982). Normative choices are fundamentally distributive, defining what constitutes a "social" as opposed to a "private" good, and setting out the conditions of allocation.

Titmuss distinguished between residual/selective and institutional/universalist modes of distribution (1968). Services delivered on a residual/selective basis almost always involve means tests that foster "both the sense of personal failure and the stigma of a public burden" (Titmuss, 1968, p. 134). With residually delivered services or programs, state responsibility begins only when the private realms of the family and the market fail. In contrast, universalist services are distributed as a social right, accessible to all citizens in a manner that does not involve any "humiliating loss of status, dignity or self respect" (Titmuss, 1968, p. 129). There is no assumption of personal blame or failure. The service or program in question is considered an appropriate institutional, and not residual, function of the state. Mediating this universalist discourse of institutional function, Ife (1997) has introduced a relativist understanding of need. Responding to the postmodern critique of universalism, Ife has offered a humanist vision in which social justice is both an expression of universal understandings of human rights, and an endorsement of contextualized and culturally appropriate definitions of need (Ife, 1997, p. 126).

Esping-Andersen (1989) maintains that the essence of a welfare state is its capacity to grant "social rights," rights that are embedded in citizenship and distributed outside of the market. The concept of decommodification is used to refer to the degree to which a service or basic good is detached from the market as the distributive mechanism. Social rights cease being commodities, emancipating individuals from their market dependence (Esping-Andersen, 1989, p. 21). Commodification in health care refers generally to an increasing reliance on the market for either the financing or delivery of health care services (Esping-Anderson, 1989; Offe, 1984).

With this framework, we will now explore the normative foundations of medicare, specifically examining the set of social rights and allocative principles that were established.

Normative Foundations of Medicare

Medicare originated with two pieces of legislation: the Hospital Insurance and Diagnostic Services Act of 1957, insuring hospital services; and the Medical Care Act of 1966, insuring doctor's services. Four federal–provincial cost-sharing conditions were imposed:

1. Universal coverage: every provincial resident must be covered under uniform terms and conditions
2. Portability: requires that all Canadians can receive health care services across Canada
3. Comprehensiveness: all medically necessary hospital services and physician services are to be covered
4. Public administration: each provincial plan must be publicly administered on a non-profit basis without the involvement of the private sector.[3]

By the end of 1971, every province had taken advantage of the federal cost-sharing incentive and approximately 100% coverage was attained in Canada.[4] The national plan was achieved through interlocking ten provincial plans, all of which shared certain common features. Canadians are free to choose their own physician and hospital. There is no limit on the benefits payable as long as medical need is determined. There are no limits on the number of days of hospital care or the number of visits to physicians. With respect to the scope of coverage, benefits are intended to be virtually complete. There is no distinction between basic and non-basic services. Instead, all medically necessary physician and hospital services are covered by all provincial plans.

From the onset, physician and acute-care hospital services have been the defining national aspects of our health care system. Specifically excluded from coverage were psychiatric hospitals, tuberculosis sanatoria, and institutions providing custodial care, such as nursing homes. These categories were excluded on the grounds that care in such hospitals was already being provided by the provinces, virtually without cost to provincial residents (LeClair, 1975). Other services not covered under the cost-shared agreement were home care services, ambulances services, drugs administered outside hospitals, dentists, and any health care services not provided by physicians. These omissions have resulted in an over-emphasis on doctors and hospitals, resulting in the lack of comparable national standards across these other health care services.[5]

With medicare, a right to "medically necessary" health care services was established and medical services were "de-commodified." Access to these services was determined solely on the basis of medical need and not on one's ability to pay. The doctor's office and the acute care hospital ward became "public" spaces where all Canadians shared common experiences of citizenship. Consequently, the principle of equal access became the normative foundation of medicare. The principle of equal access was further embedded by the stipulations that over 90% of residents must be covered by provincial plans and that each provincial plan was to operate on a non-profit basis and be administered by a public agency. These two conditions essentially elimi- Normative Foundations of Medicare nated any incentives for private insurers and, with it, a private tier of coverage. Our one-tier system has successfully precluded an "exit option" for Canadians wishing to "jump the queue." The lack of an exit option requires that the system meet the expectations of all Canadians, a necessary prerequisite for high-quality public services.

Medicare further established a dynamic, and often tense, federal–provincial relationship that has remained a mainstay of the continuous health policy debates. Canadian constitutional practice has evolved to make the provision of health care services primarily a provincial responsibility. The Constitution further generated a fiscal imbalance in which the pre-eminent ability to raise money resides with the federal government while the significant obligations to spend money for health, education, and other social services reside with the provincial governments (Van Loon & Whittington, 1971). Many provinces initially resisted or otherwise disagreed with trading their jurisdictional powers for federal funds. Through the federal conditional grant and the cost-shared program, the federal government gained access to areas of health and social assistance. However, the degree of "shared" responsibility in medicare was unparalleled in Canadian social policy at the time.[6]

Much to the dismay of reluctant provincial governments and medical associations, the four program conditions for cost sharing resulted in a substantive set of national standards that were uniformly implemented across all provincial plans. The federal government's pivotal role as the guardian of national standards was indelibly etched in the foundations of medicare.

Early Success

By the end of 1971, every province had been in medicare for at least one full year, and 100% coverage was achieved in virtually every province. Canada experienced marked changes in many vital statistics. Prior to the introduction of the Hospital Insurance Program, Canada's infant mortality rate was approximately 40% higher than Australia's, 30% higher than that of England, and 5% higher than that of the United States. By the end of 1971, Canada's infant mortality rate was almost identical to Australia's and England's and 10% lower than that of the United States. Maternal mortality rates also dropped by a third towards the end of 1971, and studies indicated that pregnant women were seeking medical attention a few months earlier than they had been (LeClair, 1975, p. 43)

With respect to utilization rates, hospital admission rates increased from 143.4 per 1,000 in the mid-fifties to 165.9 per 1,000 in 1970 (Taylor, 1987, p. 417). By enacting the hospital insurance program ten years before the physicians' services insurance program, Canadians became accustomed to using hospitals wherever possible. During the mid-1970s Canada had the highest hospital admission rate in the world and spent 60% of all health care expenditures on institutional care (Van Loon, 1978, p. 457). Physician utilization patterns also reflected an initial spurt of about a 4% increase within the first year of medicare (LeClair, 1975, p. 47). By 1975, it was also recognized that adding a new physician to the system costs an additional $200,000 to $250,000 per year in health services utilization (Van Loon, 1978, p. 457).

By 1974, medicare had successfully replaced income-based access with needs-based access, with consumption patterns more closely aligned with health care risks (Manga, 1987). The association between income and health care utilization was inversed, with the lowest income groups consuming more than double the health care services of the higher groups (National Council of Welfare, 1982, p. 23). Total government spending on health services by 1976 accounted for 7.2% ($7.1 billion, or 10.8 billion in current dollars as derived by CIHI) of the GNP in Canada. At that time the United States was spending at 8.6% of GNP on health care, while England was spending 5.4% of GNP (Van Loon, 1978, p. 456).

With these early successes, the politics of medicare quickly moved from a concern with equal access to issues of cost containment. More recently, a social rights analysis has been eclipsed by a preoccupation with controlling, and significantly reducing, the public role in the financing and delivery of health care to Canadians. We will now more closely examine the current debate and the related challenges to medicare's normative legacies.

Current Challenges

Canadians are reminded, on an almost daily basis, of the fragility of the health care system and warned of the pressure points that are destined to destroy it. Newspaper headlines are replete with stories of insured services being delisted; increasing numbers of private, for-profit clinics and hospitals; ever-growing waiting lists for medical treatment and diagnostic services; over-crowded emergency departments; escalating conflicts between health care providers and governments; shortages of nurses and physicians; shorter hospital stays coupled with decreasing home care budgets; an increasing expectation that families and friends assume responsibility for care in the home; and the repeated posturing of federal and provincial governments, each accusing the other of funding shortfalls.

Recently, there has been an intensification of the debate on the future of health care in Canada, exemplified by the explosion of intergovernmental negotiations on health and the proliferation of federal and provincial health reports. This debate centres on two related issues: (1) securing and allocating sufficient resources to ensure the sustainability of the health care system and the respective roles of the public and private sectors in the funding and delivery of health care; and (2) constructing adequate and transparent mechanisms of public accountability, and the relative weight of federal and provincial priorities in those mechanisms. The continuous intergovernmental acrimony and deal making over the past decade can be understood in this light. The provinces have been struggling to recover the health funds lost in the initial cuts in the mid-1990s, and some of the difficulty that delayed full

intergovernmental agreement on health care was related to substantial differ-　
ences over both the level of federal funding for health and extent of federal
control of accountability mechanisms.

The questions of sustainability and accountability also figure prominently
in major federal and provincial reports on health care. In his interim report
in February 2002, Roy Romanow noted that Canadians' concerns with the
fiscal sustainability of health care were undermining public confidence in
the system (Commission of the Future of Health Care in Canada, 2002a;
2002b). He framed his final report in November in an expanded conceptualization of sustainability and remarked that "The changes I am proposing are
intended to strengthen and modernize medicare, and place it on a more sustainable footing for the future" (Commission on the Future of Health Care
in Canada, 2002c, p. 3). The final report calls for a strong federal role in a
national, transparent, and accountable health care system. It recommends
that a new "Canadian Health Covenant" be established, in part to clarify the
responsibilities of governments in the funding and delivery of health care;
that accountability be added as a sixth principle of the Canada Health Act; and
that a new institutional means—the Health Council of Canada—be created
to implement accountability (Commission on the Future of Health Care in
Canada, 2002d).

Within the context set by sustainability and federal-provincial dispute,
the Canadian health care debate is insistently fuelled by parallel forms of
neo-liberal welfare state dismantling, three of which will be examined here:
the decentralization of the federal system of government, the commodification of health care, and the relegation of health care. Taken together, these
forms of dismantling constitute an unmistakable shift from collective to individual responsibility and from universal to residual modes of distribution,
as health care increasingly becomes a private commodity.

Decentralization

The debate about the decentralization of the Canadian federation is inti-
mately linked to the debate about national standards in social policy. Arguments for and against decentralization are often arguments about which level
of government should take the primary fiscal and legislative responsibility
for social policy. Although the provinces have primary constitutional jurisdiction for the general area of health care policy, the historical use of federal
spending power has given Ottawa a large role in determining the resources
available for health and in setting the broad conditions of health care provision.

Subsequent to the establishment of medicare in the 1960s, the use of the
federal spending power in relation to national standards reached a pinnacle
with the Canada Health Act (CHA), passed in 1984. The purpose of the CHA
was to consolidate the Hospital Insurance and Diagnostic Services Act of 1957
and the Medical Care Act of 1966, and to define more precisely the terms and

conditions upon which federal payments would continue to be made. The Act
reaffirmed the four program conditions that had been previously included in
the Medical Care Act of 1966 and added a fifth: reasonable access. The most
controversial aspect of the Act pertained to Section 12(1), in which the conditions relating to the criterion of accessibility were specifically operationalized. The Act stated that provincial plans "must provide for insured health
services on uniform terms and conditions and on a basis that does not impede
or preclude, either directly or indirectly whether by charges made to insured
persons or otherwise the reasonable access to those services by insured persons." For every dollar of extra-billing or hospital user fees, the federal government would withhold one dollar from its cash contribution. With the CHA,
"equity of access" was affirmed as a national standard, and with the elimination of user fees, the CHA did succeed in harnessing efforts at privatizing
physician and hospital services.

A decade later, the trend towards decentralization of power or "provincialism" is unmistakable and is supported by both Ottawa and the provinces.
The passage of the Canada Health and Social Transfer (CHST) in 1996 clearly
signalled this trend. The CHST consolidated funding into a single block transfer for health, post-secondary education, social assistance, and social services.
According to Ottawa, one purpose of the fundamental restructuring of social
policy arrangements embodied in the CHST was to decentralize power by providing provinces with "greater flexibility in determining priorities and in
designing programs to meet local needs" (Canada, 1996, p. 10). Battle and
Torjman regard the CHST as "a watershed in the history of Canadian social
policy" that consolidates "a withdrawal of both federal *dollars* and federal
presence from the provincially run welfare, social services, post-secondary
education and health programs that constitute a significant part of Canada's
social security system" (Battle and Torjman, 1995, p. 1). They also point out that
it represents a declining federal commitment to maintaining national standards in social policy.[7] Others have likewise suggested that strengthening the
federal presence is the only way to prevent the erosion of national standards
in health care and other areas of social policy (Barlow, 2002; Begin, 1999;
Osberg, 1996; Silver, 1996).

The creation of the CHST, with the announcement that Ottawa was
decreasing federal transfer payments to the provinces by $7 billion over two
years, underlined a key dimension of the decentralization debate: What is the
appropriate federal-provincial balance between the level of responsibility for
health care and the level of control over the fiscal resources necessary to fund
health care?[8] From the moment the federal government announced the CHST
cuts, provincial governments have been lobbying Ottawa to reverse them. As
a result of this intense private bargaining and heated public disputation,
Ottawa has regularly increased health funds to the provinces since 1996.

The Social Union Framework Agreement (SUFA) of February 1999 between
the federal government, all provincial governments except Quebec, and the
territories was in no small part about health care funding. SUFA was accom-

panied by a side agreement on health care that saw Ottawa increase CHST Current Challenges funding by $11.5 billion over five years (Canada, 1999a; Canada, 1999b, Canada, 1999c, chap. 4). SUFA is also a prime example of the linkages between decentralized federalism and declining federal interest in maintaining national standards. In the Agreement, Ottawa reconfirmed its policy not to introduce any new national initiatives in health care, post-secondary education, and social assistance without the agreement of a majority of provincial governments; recognized the provincial role in identifying the national priorities and objectives of such initiatives; and acknowledged the authority of the provinces and territories to determine the details of program design and mix.

SUFA evoked much negative comment from social policy advocates and other observers. Recalling the opposition to the CHST, critics noted that the Social Union discussions indicated a weakening of federal support for enforceable national standards in health care and social assistance. They also noted that the requirement of gaining majority provincial support for new initiatives would probably prove to be an insurmountable obstacle to the creation of new programs in pharmacare, home care, and child care (Council of Canadians, 1999; PovNet, 1999; Walkom, 1999).

The three intergovernmental health agreements reached since 1999 committed Ottawa to increase health funding by a total of $23.4 billion over five years (2000), $34.8 billion over five years (2003), and $41.3 billion over ten years (2004) (Canadian Intergovernmental Conference Secretariat, 2000; Canada, 2003a; Canada, 2004b).[9] The 2003 accord also resulted in the creation of two new transfers, formed from the partition of the CHST: the Canada Health Transfer (CHT) for health and the Canada Social Transfer (CST) for post-secondary education, social assistance, and social services, including early childhood development (Canada, 2003b, p. 83). Establishing the CHT was consistent with the Romanow Commission's call for the creation of a separate transfer dedicated to health (Commission on the Future of Health Care in Canada, 2002d, p. 65).

In his final report on Canadian health care in November 2002, Roy Romanow stated that the "medicare bargain" committed the federal government to provide a cash contribution equal to 25% of provincial–territorial expenditures on publicly insured health services. He found that, in fiscal year 2001–02, the federal cash share was only 18.7% of relevant provincial–territorial expenditures. To meet its commitment of paying a 25% share, Ottawa would be required to spend an additional $15 billion between 2003 and 2006 (Commission on the Future of Health Care in Canada, 2002d, p. 64; 2002c). The Romanow Gap became the popular term used to describe this shortfall in federal funding of provincial–territorial health expenditures. A major part of provincial dissatisfaction with the 2003 health accord was that it did not provide sufficient federal funds to eliminate the Gap (Laghi & McCarthy, 2003).

The 2004 Health Agreement closed the Gap by providing additional federal funds, more money in fact than the Romanow Commission had recommended. Part of that funding included an annual 6% CHT escalator, of the kind Romanow had proposed, to ensure predictable growth in the federal share of provincial–territorial expenditures under the Canada Health Act; but if the funding gap disappeared, another Romanow Gap emerged in the accord's vague provisions on conditionality, accountability, and enforcement.

In an article published on the eve of the intergovernmental accord, Romanow warned of the need to address "unresolved obstacles to a truly renewed health care system" by developing clear accountability structures that ensure additional monies are spent on effecting positive change in the system and by expanding coverage under the Canada Health Act (Romanow, 2004). It was in precisely these areas that the provisions of the 2004 health accord fell significantly short of the recommendations of the Romanow Commission.

On the question of accountability, the Romanow Commission envisioned a strong and vibrant Health Council playing a crucial role in (1) sustaining effective federal involvement in health care to ensure similar levels of quality and service around the country; and (2) developing a new approach to national leadership founded on the cooperation of federal, provincial, and territorial governments (Commission on the Future of Health Care in Canada, 2002d, chap. 2). The Health Council described in the 2003 and 2004 accords may prove to be that kind of institution, but the early prognosis is not promising. The Klein government in Alberta, for instance, has refused to cooperate with the Health Council and has not yet named a councillor to sit on it.

The 2004 agreement's provisions on wait times are another instructive example of the governments' ambivalent position on accountability and enforcement. The issue of wait times is crucial. The first ministers themselves agree in the accord "that access to timely care across Canada is our biggest concern and a national priority" (Canada, 2004b, n.p.). It is the issue on which the Supreme Court of Canada rendered its highly controversial and potentially far-reaching judgment in the Chaoulli case (*Chaouli v. Quebec*, 2005). The accord's section on reducing wait times contains some of the strongest governmental commitments on accountability. It talks of the need for developing indicators, establishing targets, and reducing wait times. It sets numerous deadlines by which these tasks should be accomplished. Importantly, however, it fails to specify any consequences for missing deadlines. There was much speculation that at least three provincial governments would fail to meet the deadline of December 31, 2005, for formulating evidence-based benchmarks for medically appropriate wait times for selected medical and diagnostic services (Bueckert, 2005a). It now appears that the deadlines may be met, but in a restricted way that offers limited help to patients (Galloway, 2005). The failure to establish extensive benchmarks by the agreed date puts other wait-time deadlines in jeopardy.

The accord's separate and specific arrangements for Quebec, in which the Quebec government states that it will follow its own health plans and objectives in accordance with its fiscal capacity, may simply be an example of Current
Challenges Ottawa's formal recognition of the need for "asymmetrical federalism" (Canada, 2004a); but, given the tenor of the accord's accountability provisions, such arrangements may also be an indication of the federal government's abiding lack of interest in enforcing national standards in health care.

If the 2004 accord fails to heed Romanow's warning on the need to develop meaningful structures of accountability and enforcement, it likewise fails to respond to his call for expanding health care coverage under the Canada Health Act. The final report of the Romanow Commission foresees that home care, prescription drugs and diagnostic services will be included in the Act. The 2004 accord does not bring these health care sectors into medicare nor does it attempt to modernize or expand the Canada Health Act in any way, with the result that the accord's provisions are not enforceable under the Act and stand entirely outside its criteria and conditions.

The 2004 intergovernmental agreement on health is an example of "decentralizing federalism": the absence of meaningful structures and processes of accountability, the lack of conditionality and the failure to strengthen the Canada Health Act point to ineffective federal engagement and declining national standards. As Boismenu and Jenson suggest, though, this debate goes beyond the question of decentralizing power from Ottawa to the provinces:

> despite often being presented in the language of "decentralizing federalism," and sometimes vaunted as a solution to the constitutional tangle of Quebec–Canada relations, the social union concept is more than that. The model of the social union involves decentralization to be sure. It is *not a shift within federalism* of decision-making power going from one level of government to the other, however. Rather, the power that is being decentralized is going from states to markets, and from public to private. The private sector, communities, families, and individuals are being exhorted to take more responsibility, as governments scale back their roles. At the same time ... the nine provinces acting together assert themselves as *co-managers* of the social union, seeking to establish institutional guarantees that they will be consulted and involved in Ottawa's actions in their areas of constitutional jurisdiction. (Boismenu & Jenson, 1998, pp. 60–61)

Commodification

This shift from states to markets and from public to private brings us to the second challenge to medicare, that of intensified commodification. In the process of commodification, health care service itself becomes a commodity, that is, it becomes a "unit of output" that is produced and packaged for sale in the sphere of capital accumulation (Leys, 2001, p. 84). The intricate and ever-changing mix of public and private principles in Canadian health insurance obscures some of the trends towards commodification (Deber, 2000;

Deber et al., 1998; Naylor, 1986), but there are identifiable trends whose recognition is made easier by explicit comparisons that policy-makers draw between the proper roles and responsibilities of the public and private sectors.

First, the discourse of health care reform is becoming increasingly characterized by the language, meanings, values, and assumptions of the market. Deber et al. (1998) capture the generality of, and tensions between, the old and new paradigms in health:

> In general, every industrialized country, with the exception of the United States, espouses the principle of universal health coverage for its people as a right of citizenship, rather than as a commodity to be bought and sold in the open market. Historically, principles of universality and equity of access have been the driving force behind decisions about financing health. These principles have recently been challenged as the general social and economic climate has turned to questions of efficiency and cost-effectiveness. (Deber et al., 1998, p. 504)

In the neo-liberal conception of efficiency, to decrease waste and increase sustainability, public expenditures on social policy must be curtailed by expanding the role of the market and diminishing the role of the state.

The tensions between the binaries of public-private and state-market are well illustrated by the different positions taken by the final reports of the Romanow Commission and the Senate Committee on Social Affairs, Science and Technology, chaired by Michael Kirby. While both reports recommend the continuation of government as the single payer for publicly insured hospital and doctor services, they diverge sharply on the question of the private delivery of health care.[10] The Romanow Commission is not only strongly opposed to the expansion of private provision but suggests that current levels be curtailed: "Rather than subsidize private facilities with public dollars, governments should choose to ensure that the public system has sufficient capacity and is universally accessible" (Commission on the Future of Health Care in Canada, 2002d, p. 9). The Kirby report, in contrast, is much more favourable to the commodification of health care. It recommends that government be neutral or indifferent on the question of public versus private delivery, and proposes the development of internal competitive markets among service providers that would, in all likelihood, see a steady expansion of private delivery (Canadian Health Coalition, 2002; Courchene, 2003; Kirby, 2002; Kirby & Keon, 2004; Senate, 2002).

Another example of commodification is the process of "privatization by default" or "passive privatisation" in which the private share of health care spending has been slowly creeping up over time, until very recently (Tholl, 1994, p. 61). In virtually each year from 1984 to 1997, private health spending increased faster than did public expenditure. In this period, the private share of health expenditures rose from under 24% to almost 30%. The discrepancy in public and private annual growth rates was particularly wide from 1992 to 1996, years in which governmental restraint measures held the average annual rate of growth of public health spending to only 0.6%, the lowest in twenty years. In the late 1990s, the situation was reversed, with public growth higher than private growth, reflecting particularly heavy governmental spending on capital projects and drugs. By 2002, private sector growth had recovered and the private share of spending stood at 30.3% (CIHI, 2001, 2004). Current Challenges

The commodification of health care is, however, a much more vigorous, explicit, and purposeful process than is suggested by the term "passive privatisation." To be sure, the passive privatization of health care that characterized most of this period was partly the result of technological change. Increasingly, health care was moving out of sectors dominated by public insurance, like hospital and medical services, and into sectors in which private financing played a much larger role, like home care and drug therapy outside hospitals. This kind of privatization was not simply passive, however. It was also the result of proactive governmental decisions that constrained the growth of public health expenditures, removed health services from coverage under the public insurance plan, encouraged a kind of asymmetrical competition that marginalized not-for-profit health care providers and privileged for-profit providers, and failed to reinvest in community care the resources that were saved by closing and restructuring hospitals (Baranek, 2000; Browne, 2000; Epps & Flood, 2001; Fuller, 1998; Tuohy, Flood, & Stabile, 2001).

Pat Armstrong uses the phrase "cascading privatization" to describe the process in which decisions made by different health care players interact to reinforce the privatization of the heath care system: the federal government adopts the neo-liberal project and slashes social spending; neo-liberal provincial governments justify their own project of cutting costs, downloading services, and closing hospitals by pointing to federal cutbacks; the community health care sector, which remains seriously under-resourced, is overwhelmed by the spiralling demands for its services; these engineered problems in the publicly funded system are used as evidence that medicare is not working and become a rationale for further privatization; the principle of universality is eroded as the wealthy pay for private health services; and the publicly funded system becomes increasingly vulnerable to additional privatization (Browne, 2000; CCPA, 2000).

The recent Supreme Court decision in the Chaoulli case gives new impetus to the already vibrant dynamic of privatization. In a 4–3 ruling on June 9, 2005, the Court invalidated those sections of Quebec's laws that disallow private health insurance for medically necessary services delivered under the publicly funded plan. The ruling affects only Quebec's laws, and the Court suspended the effect of its judgement for one year, but the implications of the case are potentially far reaching.[11] In a scathing critique of the questionable legal, political, and evidentiary bases of the majority opinion, the three dissenting justices point out the likely devastating consequences of the ruling: (1) it is the policy of the Canada Health Act and its provincial offspring "to provide health care based on need rather than on wealth or status"; (2) "it cannot be contested that as a matter of principle, access to private health care based on wealth rather than need contradicts one of the key social policy objectives expressed in the Canada Health Act"; (3) "it is Quebeckers who have the money to afford private medical insurance and can qualify for it who will be the beneficiaries" of the Court's decision; and (4) "the proposed constitutional right to a two-tier health system for those who can afford private medical insurance would precipitate a seismic shift in health policy for Quebec" that could frustrate the realization of the objectives of the Canada Health Act (*Chaouli v. Quebec*, 2005).

In an article written the day after the ruling, Roy Romanow concluded that the Chaoulli decision "certainly creates the appearance that the slide to privatization has increased in the province of Quebec" (Romanow, 2005). Two weeks later, he had stiffened his opposition to the ruling and warned that it could undermine medicare (Bueckert, 2005b). Certainly, the Court's decision helped prepare the ideological and policy ground for the Klein government's enthusiasm for increasing the weight of private health insurance in Alberta and the Canadian Medical Association's recent policy resolutions in favour of the privatization of health care (Friends of Medicare, 2005; Picard, 2005).

Relegation

Relegating health care is a third challenge to medicare. Relegation refers to the direct or indirect transfer of responsibility for health care to the family and the non-profit sector.[12] It involves shifting the provision and costs of care to family and friends, volunteer labour, and organizations that rely disproportionately on volunteer labour or are otherwise in the non-profit sector. There is an observable trend towards relegating health care, with more and more patients receiving informal care at home from friends and relatives or in the community from volunteers and voluntary organizations (Armstrong & Armstrong, 1996). Governments certainly see relegation as an attractive policy option. For some years, both the federal and provincial levels of government have been calling for increased voluntarism and developing initiatives to encourage donations and enhance the resources available to charitable organizations (Canada, 1997; Ontario, 1995).

Governments often use the progressive language of health promotion, community development, social empowerment, and mutual support to justify this shift in the responsibility for health care; but the predominant concerns of the neo-liberal agenda in health care demand that relegation be used to contain or externalize costs. This view of the economic rationale for relegating health care is consistent with the conclusion of a recent study of home care in Ontario: it is likely that the "real driving force of the shift to home care has been governments' desire to reduce costs" (Browne, 2000, p. 82).[13] The transfer of funds to the family and community sector usually lags behind the transfer of responsibility. Governments are not generally willing to make a substantial financial commitment to home care and, consequently, have been reluctant to become the champion of the 1997 recommendation of the National Forum on Health that home care be considered "an integral part of publicly funded health services" (National Forum on Health, 1997, p. 21).[14]

Overcoming the Challenges

Paradoxically, the pressure for privatization continues to grow in the face of overwhelming and incontrovertible evidence that undermines virtually all the assumptions and conclusions of privatized health care. Recent examinations of the Canadian health care system show that the sustainability of the system is not in question (Friends of Medicare, 2002; Murnighan, 2001) and that there is no fiscal crisis in health, although public opinion polls show that there is a popular perception of crisis (Deber et al., 1998; Evans, Barer, Lewis, Rachlis, & Stoddart, 2000; Rachlis, Evans, Lewis, & Barer, 2001). Increasing the role of the private sector in health will expand, not contain, costs and jeopardize equity of access, the quality of care, and the comprehensiveness of coverage (Deber et al., 1998; Evans et al., 2000; Tuohy, Flood, & Stabile, 2002). Downloading responsibilities and offloading costs to the family and nonprofit sector will place a disproportionate burden on women because of their social role as primary caregiver. This will threaten the quality of care, as informal caregivers are increasingly asked to provide sophisticated kinds of care requiring skills that they do not have. It will further increase total costs to the system in the form of increased stress on caregivers and inadequate care of patients, and lead to a debilitating transformation of the non-profit sector as it loses government support and competes with for-profit providers (Browne, 1996; CCPA, 2000; Hall & Reed, 1998).

Direct comparisons of the relative benefits of publicly and privately financed health care systems end with the endorsement of the public system. One such review suggests "the evidence generally points away from increased private financing as a means to achieve effective health care reform," and it concludes that "In order to achieve the goals of a publicly funded health care sector (to allocate care on the basis of need and not ability to pay) requires that the *funding* of the system remain concentrated within the realm of the public and quasi-public (social insurance systems)" (Flood, Stabile, & Tuohy, 2001, p. 42).

Government failure to expand public coverage under the Canada Health Act and to attach meaningful conditions to the infusion of federal funds has put the entire system of medicare at risk by affording enhanced legitimacy to proposals that privilege private over public health care. This marginalization of arguments supporting medicare occurs partly because the health care debate is, in its essentials, a political matter. Just as the so-called fiscal crisis in health is less an economic trend than a political construction, so the case for privatization is based more on political myth than reasoned argument.

Further, mounting evidence of the disparities in health, disproportionately experienced by vulnerable and racialized populations (see Beiser & Stewart,

2005; Galabuzi, 2004; Raphael, 2004) signify the human casualties of an eroding health care system combined with the neo-liberal social policy agenda. As examined by Galabuzi, "other determinants such as income, gender, race, immigrant status and geography increasingly define the translation of universality as unequally differentiated" (2004, p. 246). Groups particularly vulnerable to low health status include Aboriginal peoples, immigrants, refugees, the disabled, the poor, the homeless, and other groups in precarious life circumstances. For example, Aboriginal babies in Canada are three times more likely to die in their first year of life than non-Aboriginal babies (Beiser & Stewart, 2005, p. S4). While immigrants make up 18% of Canada's population, they account for almost 60% of all cases of tuberculosis (Beiser, 2005, p. S32).

Meeting these challenges to medicare and to growing health disparities requires that health care analysts and social work activists do things differently. They need to do a better job at popular education by engaging and mobilizing social constituencies in support of progressive political change. The battle for medicare and for the health of all Canadians will not be won in academic journals, although it may be lost there. It will be won by constructing a political coalition to oppose the disproportionate and debilitating political influence wielded by neo-liberalism.

Notes

1 This conception of "equity" was formulated in Silver (1993).

2 This argument is based on the analysis in Burke (2000).

3 Reasonable access subsequently became the fifth independent program condition in the 1984 Canada Health Act.

4 When the program began on July 1, 1968, only Saskatchewan and British Columbia were operating schemes that were eligible for cost-sharing.

5 The earlier proposals contained in the Heagerty report on Health Insurance in 1945 had included the full range of benefits such as dental, pharmaceutical, and nursing services, but were then omitted, to be implemented in the next series of health care reforms which, due to costs, never did materialize (Guest, 1985).

6 In contrast, with the Canada Assistance Plan, also passed in 1966, the federal government neither specified the precise eligibility conditions nor the level of benefits. Consequently, very little in the way of national standards of assistance have emerged. The amount of provincial discretion permitted by the legislation has resulted in a social assistance system that is extremely complex, treats similar cases of need differently, relies on an intrusive and stigmatizing determination of need, and sets assistance rates well below the most conservative poverty lines (National Council of Welfare, 1987, p. 7).

7 In recent budgets, Ottawa has increased the cash component of the CHST, but the money restored to health does not equal the money taken from health.

8 In the 1995 federal budget that announced the restructuring of social transfer payments, the CHST was originally called the Canada Social Transfer (CST).

9 CHST funding increases support not only for health but also for post-secondary education, social assistance, and social services.

10 Earlier Kirby reports seemed to contemplate a much larger role for private insurance than did the final report (Canadian Labour Congress, 2002; Senate, 2001a; Senate, 2001b).

11 See the useful caveats in CUPE's analysis of the Chaoulli decision (CUPE, 2005).

12   This definition is similar to but broader than what Brodie calls refamilialization: "the
     growing consensus among policy-makers that families (whatever their form) should
     look after their own and that it is up to the neo-liberal state to make sure that they do"
     (Brodie, 1996, 22–23).

13   The quoted phrase is emphasized in the original.

14   As Health minister, Allan Rock showed a rhetorical commitment to home care and
     pharmacare but did not transform the rhetoric into public policy (Canada, 1998).

References

Armstrong, P., & Armstrong, H. (1996). *Wasting away: The undermining of Canadian health care.* Toronto: Oxford University Press.

Baranek, P.M. (2000). *Long term care reform in Ontario: The influence of ideas, institutions and interests on the public/private mix.* PhD dissertation, Department of Health Administration, Faculty of Medicine, University of Toronto.

Barlow, M. (2002, February). *Profit is not the cure.* Ottawa: Council of Canadians.

Battle, K., & Torjman, S. (1995). *How finance re-formed social policy.* Ottawa: Caledon Institute of Social Policy.

Begin, M. (1999, September). *The future of medicare: Recovering the Canada Health Act.* Ottawa: Canadian Centre for Policy Alternatives.

Beiser, M. (2005, March/April). The health of immigrants and refugees in Canada. *Canadian Journal of Public Health: Reducing Health Disparities in Canada, 96,* S30–S44.

Beiser, M., & Stewart, M. (2005, March/April). Reducing health disparities. *Canadian Journal of Public Health:Reducing Health Disparities in Canada, 96,* S4–S5.

Boismenu, G., & Jenson, J. (1998). A social union or a federal state? Competing visions of intergovernmental relations in the new Liberal era. In L.A. Pal (Ed.), *How Ottawa spends, 1998–99; Balancing act: The post-deficit mandate* (pp. 57–79). Toronto: Oxford University Press.

Brodie, J. (1996). Canadian women, changing state forms, and public policy. In J. Brodie (Ed.), *Women and Canadian public policy* (pp. 1–28). Toronto: Harcourt Brace Canada.

Browne, P.L. (1996). *Love in a cold world? The voluntary sector in an age of cuts.* Ottawa: Canadian Centre for Policy Alternatives.

Browne, P.L. (2000). *Unsafe practices: Restructuring and privatization in Ontario health care.* Ottawa: Canadian Centre for Policy Alternatives.

Bueckert, D. (2005a, October 13). Health accord promise will be broken, provincial officials say. *Globe and Mail,* p. A9.

Bueckert, D. (2005b, June 17). Romanow says Supreme Court ruling may kill Canada Health Act. Canadian Press.

Burke, M. (2000). Efficiency and the erosion of health care in Canada. In M. Burke, C. Mooers, & J. Shields (Eds.), *Restructuring and resistance: Canadian public policy in an age of global capitalism* (pp. 178–193). Halifax: Fernwood.

Burke, M., Mooers, C., & Shields, J. (2000). Critical perspectives on Canadian public policy. In M. Burke, C. Mooers, & J. Shields (Eds.), *Restructuring and resistance: Canadian public policy in an age of global capitalism* (pp. 11–23). Halifax: Fernwood.

Canada. (1996). *Renewing the Canadian federation: A progress report.* Background document for the First Ministers' meeting, June 20–21, 1996.

References   Canada. (1997). *Budget 1997: Budget plan.* Department of Finance. Ottawa: Public Works and Government Services Canada.

Canada. (1998, February 4). *Minister marks first anniversary of National Forum on Health report.* Health Canada news release. Online at <www.hc-sc.gc.ca/english/media/releases/1998/98_07e.htm>.

Canada. (1999a, February 4). *The federal-provincial-territorial health care agreement.* Prime Minister's Office. News release.

Canada. (1999b, February 4.) *A framework to improve the social union for Canadians.* Online at <www.socialunion.ca/news/020499_e.html>.

Canada. (1999c, February 16). *Budget plan 1999.* Ottawa: Department of Finance.

Canada. (2003a). *2003 First Ministers' accord on health care renewal.* Ottawa: Health Canada.

Canada. (2003b). *Budget plan 2003.* Ottawa: Department of Finance.

Canada. (2004b, September 16). *10-year plan to strengthen health care.* Ottawa: Health Canada.

Canada. (2004a, September 15). *Asymmetrical* [*sic*] *federalism that respects Quebec's jurisdiction.*

Canada Health Act, R.S. 1985, c. C-6.

Canadian Centre for Policy Alternatives (CCPA). (2000, November). *Health care, limited: The privatization of medicare.* Synthesis report prepared by the CCPA for the Council of Canadians. With guidance from CCPA research associates P. Armstrong, H. Armstrong, and C. Fuller, and in collaboration with the Canadian Health Coalition.

Canadian Health Coalition. (2002, October 25). *A recipe for commercialization and privatization.* News Release. Online at <www.healthcoalition.ca/kirby-release.html>.

Canadian Institute for Health Information (CIHI). (2001). *National health expenditure trends, 1975–2001: Report; Executive Summary.* Online at <www. secure. cihi.ca>.

Canadian Institute for Health Information (CIHI). (2004). *National health expenditure trends, 1975–2004.* Online at <www. secure. cihi.ca>.

Canadian Intergovernmental Conference Secretariat. (2000, September 11). News Release. First Ministers' Meeting: Communiqué on Health.

Canadian Labour Congress. (2002, October 29). *CLC analysis of the Standing Senate Committee on Social Affairs, Science and Technology report; Vol. 6: The health of Canadians—the federal role.*

Chaoulli v. Quebec (*Attorney General*), S.C.C. 35. (2005).

Churchill, L.R. (1987). *Rationing health care in America: Perceptions and principles of justice.* Notre Dame: University of Notre Dame Press.

Commission on the Future of Health Care in Canada. (2002a, February 6). Statement by Roy J. Romanow, QC, Commissioner, on the release of the interim report of the Commission on the Future of Health Care in Canada at the National Press Theatre, Ottawa.

Commission on the Future of Health Care in Canada. (2002b). *Shape the future of health care: Interim report* (Romanow report). Saskatoon: Author.

Commission on the Future of Health Care in Canada. (2002c, November 28). Statement by Roy J. Romanow, QC, Commissioner, on the release of the final report of the Commission on the Future of Health Care in Canada at the National Press Theatre, Ottawa.

Commission on the Future of Health Care in Canada. (2002d, November 28). *Build-* **References** *ing on values. Final report* (Romanow report). Saskatoon: Author.

Council of Canadians. (1999, January). Power game: Five problems with the current social union talks. Online at <www.canadians.org>.

Courchene, T.J. (2003). Medicare as a moral enterprise: The Romanow and Kirby per-spectives. *Policy Matters, 4*(1), 1–20.

CUPE. (2005, September 1). *Inside the Chaoulli ruling: A CUPE backgrounder.* Online at <www.cupe.ca/www/insidechaoulli>.

Deber, R. (2000). *Getting what we pay for: Myths and realities about financing Canada's health care system.* Background paper prepared for the Dialogue on Health Reform: Sustaining confidence in Canada's health care system.

Deber, R., Narine, L., Baranek, P., Sharpe, N., Duvalko, K.M., Zlotnik-Shaul, R., Coyte, P., Pink, G., & Williams, A.P. (1998). The public-private mix in health care. In National Forum on Health (Ed.), *Canada health action: Building on the legacy; Papers commissioned by the National Forum on Health,* vol. 4 (pp. 423–545). Sainte-Foy: Editions MultiMondes.

Epps, T., & Flood, C. (2001). *The implications of the NAFTA for Canada's health care system: Have we traded away the opportunity for innovative health care reform?* Working draft.

Esping-Andersen, G. (1989). The three political economies of the welfare state. *Canadian Review of Sociology and Anthropology, 26*(1), 10–35.

Evans, R.G., Barer, M.L., Lewis, S., Rachlis, M., & Stoddart, G.L. (2000). *Private high-way, one-way street: The deklein and fall of Canadian medicare?* Centre for Health Services and Policy Research, University of British Columbia. Online at <www.chspr.ubc.ca>.

Flood, C., Stabile, M., & Tuohy, C.H. (2001, September). The borders of solidarity: How countries determine the public/private mix in spending and the impact on health care. *Health Matrix, 12*(2), 277–356.

Friends of Medicare. (2002, January 9). Real reform or road to ruin: Friends of Medicare analysis of the Premier's Health Advisory Council report. Online at <www.hsaa.ca/news_and_media/reports_submission/fom.pdf>.

Friends of Medicare. (2005, July 26). *Premier's third way evolves into a two-tier health care monster.* News Release. Online at <www.keepmedicarepublic.ca/medicare/news.shtml>.

Fuller, C. (1998). *Caring for profit: How corporations are taking over Canada's health care system.* Vancouver: New Star.

Galabuzi, G.E. (2004). Social exclusion. In D. Raphael, (Ed.), *Social determinants of health: Canadian perspectives* (pp. 235–250). Toronto: Canadian Scholars' Press.

Galloway, G. (2005, October 24). Deal set on waiting times. *Globe and Mail.* Online at <www.theglobeandmail.com/servlet/story/RTGAM.20051024.wxhealth24/BNStory/National/>.

Guest, Dennis. (1985). *The emergence of social security in Canada.* Vancouver: University of British Columbia Press.

Hall, M.H., & Reed, P.B. (1998, Spring). Shifting the burden: How much can govern-ment download to the non-profit sector? *Canadian Public Administration, 41,* 1–20.

Hospital Insurance and Diagnostic Services Act, S.C. 1957, c. 28.

Ife, J. (1997). *Rethinking social work.* Australia: Longman.

References   Kirby, M. (Chair of the Senate Standing Committee on Social Affairs, Science and Technology). (2002, December). Response to the Romanow Report.

Kirby, M.J.L., & Keon, W. (2004, September). Why competition is essential in the delivery of publicly funded health care services. *Policy Matters, 58*, 1–32.

Kronick, J. (1982). Public interest group participation in congressional hearings on nuclear power development. *Journal of Voluntary Action Research, 11*, 45–59.

Laghi, B., & McCarthy, S. (2003, February 6). Premiers grumble, but PM gets deal on health. *Globe and Mail*, p. A1.

LeClair, M. (1975). The Canadian health care system. In A. Spyros (Ed.), *National health insurance: Can we learn from Canada?* (pp. 11–88). Malabar: Krieger.

Leys, C. (2001). *Market-driven politics: Neo-liberal democracy and the public interest.* New York: Verso.

Manga, P. (1984). Preserving medicare: The Canada Health Act. *Perception, 70*, 12–15.

Medical Care Act, S.C. 1966, c. 64.

Murnighan, B. (2001, April). *Selling Ontario's health care: The real story on government spending and public relations; Ontario Alternative Budget* (Technical Paper no. 11). Canadian Centre for Policy Alternatives.

National Council of Welfare. (1982). *Medicare: The public good and private practice.* Ottawa: Supply and Services Canada.

National Council of Welfare. (1987). *Welfare in Canada: The tangled safety net.* Ottawa: Supply and Services Canada.

National Forum on Health. (1997). *Canada health action; Building on the legacy. Vol. 1: The final report of the National Forum on Health.* Ottawa: Minister of Public Works and Government Services.

Naylor, D.C. (1986). *Private practice, public payment: Canadian medicine and the politics of health insurance, 1911–1966.* Montreal: McGill-Queen's University Press.

Offe, C. (1984). *Contradictions of the welfare state.* (John Keane, Ed. and Introd.). Cambridge: MIT Press.

Ontario. (1995). *1995 fiscal and economic statement.* Toronto: Queen's Printer for Ontario.

Osberg, L. (1996, January). *The equity, efficiency and symbolism of national standards in an era of provincialism.* Ottawa: Caledon Institute of Social Policy.

Picard, A. (2005, August 18). Private health care should be available to all, doctors say. *Globe and Mail*, p. A4.

PovNet. (1999, February 4). *Social union framework heartless say social justice groups.* PovNet social union press release and backgrounder. Online at <www.povnet .web.net/socialunion.html>.

Rachlis, M., Evans, R.G., Lewis, P., & Barer, M.L. (2001, January). *Revitalizing medicare: Shared problems, public solutions.* A study prepared for the Tommy Douglas Research Institute. Online at <www.tommydouglas.ca>.

Raphael, D. (2004). Introduction to the social determinants of health. In D. Raphael (Ed.), *Social determinants of health: Canadian perspectives* (pp. 1–18). Toronto: Canadian Scholars' Press.

Romanow, R. (2004, September 13). Scrutiny is the best medicine. *Globe and Mail*, p. A15.

Romanow, R. (2005, June 10). Now is the time to stand up for medicare. *Globe and Mail*, p. A17.

References

Senate. Standing Committee on Social Affairs, Science and Technology. (2001a, September). *The health of Canadians: The federal role. Vol. 1: The story so far.* Interim report on the state of the health care system in Canada (Kirby report). Ottawa: Government of Canada.

Senate. Standing Committee on Social Affairs, Science and Technology. (2001b, September). *The health of Canadians: The federal role. Vol. 4: Issues and options* (Kirby report). Ottawa: Government of Canada.

Senate. Standing Committee on Social Affairs, Science and Technology. (2002, October). *The health of Canadians: The federal role. Vol. 6: Recommendations for reform; Final report* (Kirby report). Ottawa: Government of Canada.

Silver, S. (1993). *Universal health care: The Canadian definition.* PhD dissertation, Bryn Mawr College, Philadelphia.

Silver, S. (1996). The struggle for national standards: Lessons from the federal role in health care. In J. Pulkingham & G. Ternowetsky (Eds.), *Remaking Canadian social policy: Social security in the late 1990s* (pp. 67–80). Halifax: Fernwood.

Taylor, M. (1987). *Health insurance and Canadian public policy: The seven decisions that created the Canadian health insurance system.* Montreal: McGill-Queen's University Press.

Tholl, W.G. (1994). Health care spending in Canada: Skating faster on thinner ice. In J. Blomqvist & D.M. Brown (Eds.), *Limits to care: Reforming Canada's health system in an age of restraint* (pp. 53–89). Toronto: C.D. Howe Institute.

Titmuss, R. (1968). *Commitment to welfare.* London: George Allen and Unwin.

Titmuss, R. (1974). *Social policy.* London: George Allen and Unwin.

Tuohy, C.H., Flood, C.M., & Stabile, M. (2001, June). *How does private finance affect public health care systems? Marshalling evidence from OECD nations.* Working paper.

Van Loon, R.J. (1978). From shared cost to block funding and beyond: The politics of health insurance in Canada. *Journal of Health Politics, Policy and Law, 2* (Winter), 454–478.

Van Loon, R., & Wittington, M. (1971). *The Canadian political system.* Toronto: McGraw-Hill.

Walkom, T. (1999, February 9). Social union deal a step backward for Canadians. *Toronto Star,* p. A2.

Additional Resources

Badgely, R., & Wolfe, S. (1967). *Doctor's strike.* Toronto: Macmillan of Canada.

Begin, M. (1988). *Medicare: Canada's right to health.* Ottawa: Optimum.

Canadian Association for Community Care. Online at <www.cacc-acssc.com/page2.html>.

Canadian Centre for Policy Alternatives. Online at <www.policyalternatives.ca/>.

Canadian Council on Social Development. Online at <www.ccsd.ca/>.

Canadian Health Coalition. Online at <www.healthcoalition.ca/>.

Canadian Home Care Association. Online at <www.cdnhomecare.on.ca/e-index.htm>.

Canadian Institute for Health Information. Online at <secure.cihi.ca/cihiweb/dispPage. jsp?cw_page=home_e>.

Canadian Public Health Association. Online at <www.cpha.ca/english/index.htm>.

References   Centre for the Study of Living Standards. Online at <www.csls.ca/>.

Evans, R., & Stoddart, G. (Eds.). (1986). *Medicare at maturity.* Calgary: University of Calgary Press.

Hall, E.M. (1980). *Canada's national-provincial Health Insurance Program for the 1980s: A commitment for renewal.* Ottawa: Department of National Health and Welfare.

Health Action Lobby (HEAL). Online at <www.cna-nurses.ca/heal/healframe.htm>.

Health Canada. Online at <www.hc-sc.gc.ca/ >.

Lalonde, M. (1974). *A new perspective on the health of Canadians.* Ottawa: Supplies and Services.

National Council of Welfare. Online at <www.ncwcnbes.net/>.

National Council of Welfare. (1990). *Health, health care and medicare.* Ottawa: Supply and Services.

Tommy Douglas Research Institute. Online at <www.tommydouglas.ca/>.

World Health Organization. Online at <www.who.int/home-page/>.

Sheila Neysmith

As people age, the quality of their lives is affected by a range of social policies. However, it is long-term care policy that the public generally associates with aging. In Canada and the United States, finding ways of meeting the forecasted health care needs of old people has taken centre stage as the policy concern of an aging population. It is anticipated that this demographic phenomenon will make heavy demands on the health care system, necessitating a growth in services that will be costly. The Canadian population is aging, albeit still quite young when compared to those of European countries. Causally linking population aging to rising health costs has been repeatedly challenged by research (for example, Evans, McGrail, Morgan, Barer, & Hertzman, 2001; Gilleard & Higgs 1998; Robertson, 1997), but this is routinely ignored as correlations between health care costs and utilization data are proclaimed as "obvious." The power of this demographic crisis discourse remains quite unabated and seems to reappear in a new guise as soon as one form is discredited. This dynamic is part of the political economy within which twenty-first century Canadian social policy is being developed. Understanding the relationship between an aging population, the distribution of caring responsibilities, and health costs—the focus of this chapter—means engaging with varied research and policy debates.

The shape and content of health care literature reflects the presence of professions and organizations that are powerful players in, and thus definers of knowledge about, the health care services used by elderly people. The discourse that permeates this literature tends to position old women in particular, because of their higher morbidity and longevity rates, as a caring problem (Gibson, 1996), a problem that will get worse and will be costly to address. An aging population does present different policy challenges than that of a demographically young nation. Whether this translates into a "caring problem" depends on how the issue is taken up—how this demographic fact is incorporated into social policy. Older people do have more chronic health conditions than younger people. The aging process within Canadian society frequently means that people need help with some of the activities of daily living. An important policy issue is how to ensure that the resources, and types and amounts of service needed are available and provided. The complexity of meeting this policy objective cannot be reduced to media sound bites that assert that Canadians are committed to universal health care or that seniors want to remain in their own homes. Such statements gloss over important controversies about where responsibility lies for guaranteeing that needed services exist and are accessible. At present, families, not the health care system, do the lion's share of caring for relatives who are in need of daily assistance. We know that this proves costly to many women as they age; yet our social policies and health care services seem unable to ameliorate, let alone eliminate, these costs. In many cases it seems that existing policies actually perpetuate inequities (Grenier, 2005).

The population of older Canadians, like younger age cohorts, is marked by diversity. Recent figures released by Statistics Canada (2005) confirm that this will increase dramatically in the next decade. Along with this diversity come social disparities based on gender, class, ethno-racial differences, ability, and sexuality, to name but those most visible. These differences are as important as age in determining how social policies affect the quality of people's lives as they age (see Dilworth-Anderson, Williams, & Gibson, 2002 for a twenty-year review of these issues in caregiving research). In the following pages, I consider how several key concepts are used in defining the "caring problem." This will be followed by an examination of some of the stakeholders. The next section will step back to consider what it is that Canadians envision for the aging members of our society. The final part of the chapter assesses several existing programs and points to directions that Canadian social policy needs to pursue to start realizing a future where groups of aging citizens are not excluded.

The Power of Concepts in Defining Reality

Language is important—it shapes our thoughts and communicates meaning. Concepts and theories used in social policy are not neutral. They emphasize what is important to consider, and consequently what can be ignored. For instance, what is often called "long-term care" policy varies across provinces, and attendant policy statements are littered with ambiguous references to health, community, and caring. Long-term care policy is usually seen as part of health care policy. Although the concept of health seems to be used in a very broad sense in policy statements such as the preamble to the Canada Health Act of 1985 (CHA), when operationalized in terms of services covered, it is narrowed to hospitals, physician fees, drugs, and lab tests. This effectively means that most of the services needed by elderly people in the community are excluded. Similarly, policy concepts such as community care, managed care, and the mixed economy of care reverberate with service delivery implications; yet most actual care occurs in peoples' homes, delivered informally by family members where the minimal formal services that are available are not covered by the CHA. Finally, "caring" is a word that carries positive overtones, but it also is used ambiguously. One is never sure exactly what it covers, so its meaning needs to be investigated in each setting. The now-considerable feminist literature on the topic of caring defines the concept as the physical, mental, and emotional activities involved in looking after, responding to, and supporting others (see for example, Baines, Evans, & Neysmith, 1998). It includes both paid and unpaid work.

Another much-used, yet ephemeral, policy concept is that of community. The term will probably always be ambiguous, but the challenge is to determine how the idea is being employed today in long-term care policy. The concept of community-based care both captures a range of services that exist and expresses a policy goal for what we would like to exist. Not surprisingly, once we start to operationalize it, we discover some very contradictory ideas. On the one hand, the term seems to invoke a nostalgia for simpler times, reflecting idealizations of what family and community were like in some imagined past. On the other hand, there is an alternative discourse—that which stresses how to make communities inclusive rather than exclusive. The use of the plural here is important. The challenge is around how to build alliances that recognize differences but can deal with conflicts as part of the process of pursuing desired goals (McBride, 2005).

Canadian civil society at any given historical moment is made up of individuals who belong to multiple communities, and these memberships will change over a life course. A pressing question is "What ideas of community inform our current models of community-based care?" At present, at least in long-term care policy, the idea of community support seems to be limited to shoring up families and encouraging the use of volunteers as ways of meeting need (Hughes, 1998, pp. 98–99). Furthermore, as programs based on universal entitlements shrink, services get more and more targeted. The definitions that guide narrowing service categories are based on expert definitions of need (Fraser, 1989). Enforcing these definitional guidelines is not an option; it is a necessity if local managers are to stay within their budgets. This being said, all of us, in our respective roles as professionals, administrators, users, researchers, and advocates, use language that can reinforce rather than challenge how caring labour is thought about. With this in mind, I want to consider some of the assumptions behind the concept of "community" that are being enacted on the long-term care policy/program stage at this particular historical hour.

The drama is supposedly about providing services that can help people remain engaged in the life of their families and communities even as physical abilities decline. The plot line, however, is unclear. Indeed at points the players seem to be reading from different scripts. In the current production, the character of "Client" has disappeared. The "Consumer/Customer" has taken her place. Rather oddly, sometimes this role is played by an old person, but just as often "Family" is cast in the role. Either way, these actors speak quietly. Indeed, their microphone seems to have been usurped by service providers and industry reps who march around the stage loudly proclaiming "consumer choice" and "customer satisfaction." There are times when this chorus line is so loud one can hardly make out the dialogue, let alone follow the story. Hovering in the wings is a tattered character called "Citizen," who can be most charitably defined as having an identity crisis. When she or he occasionally says something, there is silence for an instant, and then the chatter continues as if Citizen had never spoken. It is worth stopping to consider what is going on here.

Community-based care policy is ambiguous because contradictory language and concepts are at play. The market language of consumer/customer is about choice and purchase power, not need and access, the language of citizen-based claims. In the last edition of this book, I wrote, "It is ironic that in the mixed economy of care models (Baldock, 1997; Evers, 1993) operating across countries today, if choice exists at any point it is where a designated access agency tenders contracts to provide services. An old woman, or family member, gets little choice—they receive service from a designated provider. Granted, for those with sufficient resources, there is the option to purchase from commercial firms, if these exist where one lives. Like all market transactions, however, it is a case of 'buyer beware.'" In the intervening years these trends have intensified. For instance, in Ontario for-profits provided 18% of home nursing services before contract bidding was introduced in 1997. By 2001, this had increased to 48% (Ontario Health Coalition [OHC], 2005). The Ontario Community Support Association reports that prior to the introduction of competitive bidding, there were twenty-four small, non-profit agencies servicing local markets in Ontario; only three were left by the time the report was released in 2004.

In sum, receiving services in one's own home does not mean that one is part of a community, or that the services are developed by or in a community, yet the use of the term carries both these overtones. Ambiguous and contradictory concepts are not just the result of fuzzy policy thinking or poor program planning. They arise from competing priorities among long-term care policy players.

Who Are the Stakeholders in the "Caring Problem"?

A quick tabulation suggests that the stakeholder list would include hospitals, home care agencies, federal and provincial governments, businesses, families, and old people themselves. Equally important to recognize is that some of these players are more powerful than others and that there are tensions between family, state, market, and voluntary sector; between cash and services as modes of delivery; between carer and person cared for; between caring and the type of paid work done by women and men; and between nations in the growing global care chain.

It seems obvious to claim that the well-being of elderly persons is the primary concern because they are the ones experiencing the conditions that give rise to the service debate. It can be argued, however, that they are the weakest stakeholder because the problem is in fact a creation of the health care system. The discourse casts the former as needy and resource users; the latter is positioned as a service provider with limited resources that are being inundated by ever-increasing demands. In this scenario, the old person is depicted as a dependent rather than a senior citizen with attendant entitlements. The image projected is actually that of a poor old woman. As I have argued elsewhere, aging is a gendered process, so women experience old age differently than do men. One of these differences is that old women inhabit an aging body in a culture that devalues both. To be old, non-White, disabled, or female is not only to be different but also to be inferior (Neysmith & McAdam, 1999). The implications of this for the well-being of women as they age have not received a lot of attention in gerontology. Certainly, there has been much written about the state of the aging female body. Unfortunately, much of it reflects a continuation of the tradition wherein the female body is a site for regulation and control (for a feminist assessment of this literature, see Shildrick, 1997). Professional concerns connect the deteriorating condition of this body to service use implications. That is, the effects of physical frailty on an elderly person's ability to perform certain tasks are not taken up in policy discourse as problematic because they are a threat to a person's sense of identity, nor are they seen as an indicator that the health care system is failing to meet need. Rather persons are categorized as "at risk," bearing warning signs of potential demands on service budgets. Ironically, research has consistently demonstrated that these are in fact poor predictors of service use, and that it is the presence or absence of informal carers that is most critical: "The finding that the majority of Manitoba's Home Care clients are older and not married is in keeping with other studies that age and marital status are important factors in home care use" (Mitchell, Roos, & Shapiro, 2005 p. 66).

The social construction of aging as a problem of physical deterioration allows certain conditions to be named and appropriated as treatable while others are not. These defined medical problems fall under the authority of the CHA, which covers hospital and physician costs. Most conditions, however, fall outside the acute care focus of these services. As such, once a hospital treatment regime is completed, the case is handed to a social worker to do discharge planning. Plans assume that there is a family that will be able to provide most of the care and manage what limited community services are available. In this current version of community-based services, the old person and their family are considered a service unit for assessment of service purposes. In other words, what an old person needs is conflated with what family can provide at the point of assessment. Front-line workers are aware of this dynamic but see few options except to factor in family caring potential as they ration the very limited services available. No matter how understandable, given front-line realities, such practices are built on dangerous assumptions. First, there is no evidence that family members can provide the type of care delivered by a qualified nursing assistant or home care worker. This off-

What
Approaches
Have Been
Tried to
Address the
"Caring
Problem"?
loading onto families also results in services being moved off the public stage and rendered invisible by relocating them in the private sphere of family responsibility. The item is effectively removed from public scrutiny, avoiding the debate that occurs when responsibilities are moved from one column in the health care ledger to another. Second, as well documented in the caring literature (Hooyman & Gonyea, 1995; Neysmith, 2000), the emotional, mental, and physical costs to both parties are ignored. Third, little attention is paid to what is happening to home care staff and how the discourse of scarcity pits professional and para-professional personnel (most of whom are women) against each other (Aronson & Neysmith 2006; Denton, Zeytinoglu, & Davies, 2002). In my own research, I have documented the racial tensions that are sparked in a stratified labour force where women of colour hold the poorest jobs (Neysmith & Aronson, 1997). However, this is just the tip of the iceberg.

The mental health of women as they age has been largely neglected in health care research. However, it has been associated with the stress and financial implications of caring across the life cycle. Milne and Williams (2000), in a wide-ranging assessment of what literature is available, came to the conclusion that social inequality was a much neglected but powerful determiner of the mental health of aging women. The emphasis of health care research and aging literature needs to be watched to ensure that knowledge needed to develop equitable policies is not undercut by current health care priorities.

What Approaches Have Been Tried to Address the "Caring Problem"?

Policies can be thought of as providing resources directly in the form of services or indirectly through the tax system. In this section, four policy approaches tried in Canada, two of each type, are briefly discussed (Neysmith, 2005). These are relief services such as respite, caregiver payment schemes, caregiver tax credits, and compassionate leave. The discussion comes with a major caveat, however. Since kin provide most of the care to people as they age, the programs discussed in the following paragraphs are only minor players in accomplishing the task of caring for people who need help with the activities of daily living, even though they seem to occupy centre stage. Furthermore, while each province has some form of community-based care legislation, Canada does not have a national home and community care program like, for example, what exists in Australia—a country with many similar state structures (Neysmith, 1995).[1] Consequently, there is not the same guarantee of funding as results from the funding formula for hospitals and physician fees covered by the Canada Health Act. Federal funding comes via the Canada Health Transfer (CHT), an amendment to the Federal Provincial Fiscal Arrangements Act in 2004 that imposes few restrictions on provinces as to how the funds are to be allocated among competing health care priorities.

Home care has grown rapidly in the last decade and will expand in the future, not because it is a preferred service approach (although most endorse it) but because hospital budgets and changes in the financing of acute care dictate early discharge. Since the mid-nineties this trend has intensified dramatically. For instance, after documenting the great increase in post-acute and end-of-life service hours, the Ontario Association of Community Care Access Centres (OACCAC) was sufficiently concerned about the effects on supportive home care that they made the following recommendation in their pre-budget submission to the Ontario government (OACCAC 2005, p. 5):

What Approaches Have Been Tried to Address the "Caring Problem"?

> While continued investment in post-acute home care services is important to ensure that patients can be diverted home from hospital emergency rooms and discharged from inpatient beds as soon as possible, there is even greater potential to expand the effectiveness of chronic disease management and preventative maintenance services in the community to prevent hospitalization in the first place. The recent emphasis on investing in post-hospital services has sometimes resulted in a diversion of resources from clients with long-term health care needs.

In most provinces, public agencies are not the providers of services; rather, regional bodies are mandated to oversee the contracting out of service delivery to competing non-profit and for-profit home and public sector care providers. I will go no further on the problems of this model; there has been considerable ink spilled on it already (Aronson & Neysmith, 1997, 2006; Canadian Association of Retired Persons, 1999; Light, 2001; Ontario Health Coalition, 2005; Williams, Barnsley, Legatt, Deber, & Baranek, 1999). What is important is that this model of health care funding and delivery and the discourse of scarce resources that accompanies it are the context within which case managers are deciding how to ration their very tight budgets. One consequence is that assessments of need in practice take into account the seeming availability of family to provide care and/or the possibilities for families to obtain additional services from commercial home care services. Such practices reinforce gender and class inequities as they contribute to the expansion of the for-profit service market. This trend is also troubling because the pay level and conditions of employment are poor (Aronson et al., 2004). Using a national probability panel sample in the US and England, Budig and Folbre (2002) were able to show statistically how care workers systematically suffered what they called a pay penalty. Using Canadian data, Denton et al. (2002) documented how working conditions negatively affected the mental health of visiting home care workers. The service crunch to supportive home care has encouraged researchers to undertake a closer examination of other approaches to providing care.

One response has been the development of respite services. Respite relieves caregivers by providing them with temporary relief through in-home or out-of-home care. Understanding what respite is and a commitment to providing it—because it is the one service consistently requested by users—

What
Approaches
Have Been
Tried to
Address
the "Caring
Problem"? does not mean that there is agreement on what is meant by the call for respite. We all use language that is available to us. This relief service has been named respite. The pressing question is why carers are experiencing burden to the point that they need respite? Respite may provide relief, but perhaps prevention should be the focus of our enquiries. Thus, it is important to know under what conditions the cry for respite arises. What does respite mean to users, providers, and policy-makers? How important is respite compared to other services in the highly political health care priority list? These questions are not directly answered in the available research, but studies can throw light on how we might start to address them.

Much of this research is based on caring for aging persons with Alzheimer-types of cognitive impairment (Cotrell & Engel, 1998; Feinberg & Whitlatch, 1998; Gill, Hinrichsen, & DiGuiseppeet, 1998). The later stages of this disease frequently mean that carers are coping with cognitive and behavioural changes. Respite services come in various forms, the three most common being in-home, out-of-home day care, and short-term stays in an institutional setting. These respite programs are seldom set up primarily to provide respite. Rather, they are existent services with some spaces set aside for respite care. In other words, respite users look like other users of such services. Respite is what the caregiver experiences, but the service is the regular package of services that make up home or institutional care. Respite users are either not regular home care clients or clients who need more service than they regularly get.

The existence of respite services is one of the few concrete indicators of recognition of who is doing most of the caring work. Respite is not being called for by those who are employed to do caring work, that is, by formal care providers. No matter how large the disparities between the salaries and working conditions of doctors, nurses, social workers, and home care workers, respite is built into the organization of their work through the institutional structures of a workday, benefits, vacation, etc. Not so for those who do most of the caring work: family members. Study after study shows that kin carers want some relief. Respite is one word used to describe services that might address this well-documented need; but does the word challenge assumptions around kin-based care that make respite necessary? The current concept of respite puts it in the same type of service model as food banks and shelters. They are necessary to the survival of users, but at the same time their use implies a certain weakness on the part of users and questions their ability to cope. Thus respite is a good temporary response, but in and of itself will not address the basic issue. If caring labour needs such services, then it is an indicator of a problem, not the answer—much as food banks and shelters are indicators of policy, not family, failure. Now, we can confine ourselves to the equivalent of building more shelters and developing more food banks, or we can ask the policy question—how do we eliminate the need for respite?

Another approach to increasing the supply of caring labour is the development of carer allowances, which are available to relatives in a number of countries. This policy option is not well developed in Canada—in fact, only four provinces have some form of it in place (Guberman, 1999). This attempt to undergird the care provided by kin is fraught with dubious outcomes for many women. There continues to be debate about its merits in the international literature, so it seems prudent to post huge "Proceed with caution" signs along this policy road (for a recent assessment of various approaches to paying for informal care in European countries see Ungerson, 2004). The money available is usually more of a compensation (allowance) rather than payment for work done. Kin carers cannot negotiate pay scales or working conditions. Perhaps most worrisome are the types of differences between women who use such programs and those who do not. For instance, Janice Keefe in Nova Scotia has undertaken a series of studies that compare those who use carer allowances with those who use home care services (Keefe & Fancey, 1997). The former are non-urban, and they live in areas where services are scarce and where unemployment is high. Thus, any choice that such programs might theoretically make available come up against the stark reality that women make decisions under conditions where few options in fact exist. In such circumstances, programs can reinforce rather than decrease disparities in the larger society. In this case, home care becomes only an urban option because it is uneconomical to provide it beyond the city—a situation that will be exacerbated if the delivery of service is based on competitive bidding. Such considerations are important when examining what is happening to elderly people and their families in the mixed economy of care.

What Approaches Have Been Tried to Address the "Caring Problem"?

Turning to the use of the tax system as an avenue for increasing the resources available to old people and their families, the Caregiver Tax Credit is the most visible. Introduced in 1998, the current credit can be up to $3,784 annually. However, you must live in the same residence as the person cared for, the person must be a direct relative, and it does not apply if the dependent person has an income over $16,705. The credit has numerous shortcomings, the most obvious of which are that the amount is low; it does not reflect the amount of work done; and it is of no value if the caregiver is not employed, if his or her income is just over the allowed amount (often the case where elderly spouses provide care), or if the elderly person needing care does not live in the home of the caregiver—a norm for many Canadian households. Like all tax deductions, this means that those living in higher income households benefit more than low-income women. From a somewhat different perspective, in 1999 the Canadian National Advisory Council on Aging recommended that the work of caring be recognized through pension adjustments rather than rather than allowances (NACA, 1999). Whatever the limitations of these schemes, not the least of which is the low monetary value attached to the work done whether conceived of as a deduction or a benefit, it is argued that it puts resources in the hands of carers who could then determine for themselves how best to use them.

What
Approaches
Have Been
Tried to
Address
the "Caring
Problem"?

Another tax route policy introduced in 2004 is Compassionate Care Leave (Canada, 2005). It provides employees with up to six weeks of leave from their job with benefits protected. To qualify, the employee must be in a job covered by Employment Insurance and have at least 600 hours of earnings. A person must obtain a certificate from a physician stating that the individual needing care, who must be a direct family member, is at risk of death within twenty-six weeks. This policy had a very low take-up rate in the year following its introduction. In fact, only 5–6% of those expected to use it did so. One immediate problem was the restrictive definition of who was eligible. Another was the reluctance by physicians to "certify" the life expectancy of a patient. One can imagine that family members were equally unwilling to hear such predictions. At the time of writing, the Bill is being reviewed, but in the short term, rather than addressing some of the above problems, the amount budgeted for benefits has been substantially reduced (Goar, 2005)!

I do not want to leave this examination of efforts taken to address the "caring problem" without mentioning one other sector that is getting a lot of publicity in policy documents these days—the volunteer. A discourse on volunteering emerged in the 1990s that could not have been imagined during the decades that marked the reign of the welfare state (Hughes 1998). Then the word "volunteer" was avoided because it conjured up images of charity that were quite at odds with ideas of citizen entitlements and state obligations; yet today volunteers have become players in a wide array of social programs. At least at the level of official policy, their presence is articulated as essential to the achievement of both program and organizational goals. Volunteers may be positioned in policy documents as critical for ensuring that services reflect community concerns. Nevertheless, the work of volunteers is also becoming increasingly essential to the capacity of organizations to carry out their mandates. Thus, we can add volunteers to profit and non-profit organizations, families, and public services that make up the mixed company of players who deliver home care. In policy documents, the volunteer is assigned an array of responsibilities, but there is limited understanding of what the work means to those who are doing the volunteering. In fact, existing literature is mainly written from the perspective of organizations that use volunteers and funding bodies that seek to ensure the presence of community representatives in programs (Fischer, Mueller, & Cooper, 1991; Horch, 1995; Pearce, 1993).

In summary, we cannot avoid the paid/unpaid labour dilemma by reinventing the volunteer. The contributions that seniors make as volunteers are noted in many policy documents (Chappell & Prince, 1997; Fischer et al., 1991; National Advisory Council on Aging, 1999). They do indeed, but the question is "How is the discourse on volunteering developing in a rhetoric of scarce resources?" A pressing concern is the implications of this renewed emphasis on volunteerism in a hollowed-out welfare state (Aronson & Neysmith, 1997; Jessop, 1993; Reitsma-Street & Neysmith, 2000).

These sketches of what is happening to different sectors of the caring labour force together paint a picture that formal and informal carers have much to be concerned about. In the mixed economy of care that character-izes what we call community care policy today, the much-discussed restruc-turing of health care is not resulting in the transfer of resources from institu-tional to home care—but rather the transfer of costs. In addition, as they are jettisoned from the health care budget period, at home women pick up the responsibilities with no say as to the terms and conditions under which car-ing is done.

Developing Policy That Recognizes Caring Labour

One of the underlying causes of the "caring problem" is that family-based caring is not recognized as labour, and when it is provided by non-kin a low value is ascribed to it. Getting both of these issues into the policy-making agenda has been, and continues to be, an uphill struggle. We talk about old people who need care as users or consumers (or sometimes even customers), on the one hand. On the other, we refer to family carers as service providers. The former take; the latter give. In this scenario, the actors are positioned in ways that guarantee conflict, guilt, and resentment. The setting is disem-powering for all. What are the possibilities if we change the script? Let me suggest that perhaps the problem is the image we have that normally people are not carers. Certainly many aspects of social life are organized without regard to the caring responsibilities that citizens carry. Employment prac-tices do not build in caring as a normal and expected responsibility of adults, a responsibility that requires work schedules that accommodate the demands of caring (Lewis & Guillari, 2004). Most jobs are regulated by employment standards and minimum wage schedules; many also have pension benefits and supplementary health insurance. In the last few years, some unions and progressive employers have even brought in family care benefits, but these are concessions from the "normality" of paid employment. They are defined as fringe benefits, suggesting that they are not central to paid employment, even though the demands made on the employee may be anything but fringe-like in their impact. Of course, for those who provide unpaid care, this is not even regarded as work. Thus, those family members who take up the responsibil-ity of providing care suffer the economic consequences of doing so. Behind this is the continued existence of a framework that separates the public and the private lives of citizens. This assumption that family life and its responsi-bilities are a private matter is rooted in nineteenth-century industrial mod-els yet continues to dominate policy thinking at the beginning of the twenty-first century.

It might help to shake up assumptions if we asked ourselves how long-term care programs would be described if we took out all references to fam-ily providing care. One approach to crossing the public/private sphere divide that is so costly to women is to ungender caring labour and institutionalize what Nancy Fraser (1997), an American political scientist, terms a universal caregiver model. Such a model would assume that all adults carry caring

Developing
Policy That
Recognizes
Caring Labour

responsibilities; the ebb and flow of these may change over the life cycle of individuals but caring responsibilities are a social given. Under such a model, employment policies and job descriptions would have caring-related rights and benefits that complement the health and pension benefits today. Promotion ladders that do not allow for caring responsibilities could be challenged as discriminatory. Doing so is pivotal if women's citizenship claims are to be realized. This will happen only if caring for others is seen as central to the lives of all citizens, as central as holding down a paid job, participating in community affairs, paying taxes, and being a consumer (Feinberg & Whitlatch, 1998).

In addition, such an orientation would force us to recognize that quality control cannot be assured when care is assumed to be provided by family members, so we would have to figure out how to ensure that neither party is forced into provider or receiver roles against their wishes (for an exemplar of what this might look like, see the Charlottetown Declaration [Armstrong, 2002]). At least such a stance would be reassuring to that 25% of the population with no spouse or children, for whom kin-based care is a myth. I am not saying this would be easy. What I am saying is that we would be preoccupied with a different set of issues. Such a discussion is important because it will affect the hard choices all of us have to make regarding what to support, what to steer away from, and what coalitions we participate in.

Although feminist debates about how to conceptualize as well as promote citizenship have consistently highlighted the deleterious effects of the private/public spheres split, in the 1990s the issue took on a certain edge as neo-liberalism began to equate citizenship rights with ideas of choice, in particular choice in the market place (for a synopsis of some of the arguments, see Lister, 1997). The new citizen became the consumer of goods and services in one domain and the taxpayer in another. Such a rendition permeates professional as well as market and government programs, and restricts our thinking about alternatives. Totally absent from this discourse is an awareness of how exclusionary such talk is. One needs time and money to be both consumer and taxpayer. If this is what it takes to be a citizen, then those who are carrying out caring responsibilities lack the coinage to be citizen-like. The exclusionary circle is now complete. Policies that emphasize the centrality of choice are a bad joke if your only option is sole responsibility (Gill, Hinrichsen, & DiGuiseppeet, 1998, p. 50).

The analysis I have presented is premised on the assumption that citizenship debates are critical to the well-being of carers. However, it is not caring that is the problem; rather, it is that caring takes place in a society where inequities of gender, class, race, and ability—to name but those highlighted in this paper—play themselves out to the advantage of some and the oppression of others. Through the caring labour that they do, women make major contributions to their communities as surely as they do in the labour market and within their families. Any discourse can be picked up in ways that reinforce oppression rather than promote equity. Discussions of connecting caring labour to citizenship claims are as susceptible to this as any other policy discussion. This threat notwithstanding, avoidance would be costly. Not conceptualizing caring work in terms of contributions to the community, and ultimately to the nation, reinforces its invisibility while leaving intact gendered definitions of who are "contributing" members to their society, what qualifies as work and, ultimately, who is entitled to make claims as citizens. The result will be the reinforcement of social exclusion (Craig, 2004).

In this chapter, I have attempted to articulate another way of thinking about "the caring problem." Yes, this is visionary; but having a vision is essential to protesting the discriminatory effects of policies. Responses that resources are scarce are not responses. Resources are always scarce; decisions around priorities need to be debated. If we are silent, the process of marginalizing those who provide informal care—those who do 80% of the work—will increase even more. It will not cease because we stop naming it. The work to be done is daunting. It entails ongoing contestation of definitions as well as coalition building with groups of people all of whom come with shifting alliances and unequal power. However, these are the daily ingredients of social change work. For those who wish to engage, I would argue that the caring labour done by women is as legitimate a basis for claiming social entitlements as that of individuals who currently are enshrined in images of the rights-bearing taxpayer or the sovereign consumer.

Note

1 There have been numerous attempts to create such a mechanism in Canada, but to date they have failed to garner the political support that undergirds the Canada Health Act. The most recent was the National Forum on Health in the mid-1990s (National Forum on Health, 1997). In 2002, the agenda of the Romanow Commission and similar inquiries seems to be completely highjacked by threats of a move to market-based approaches to services now covered by the CHA. In such a climate, claims of those outside this circle have little chance of being heard.

References

Armstrong, P. (2002). The evidence is in … it's time to act on home care. *Network*, 2/3. Online publication of the Canadian Women's Health Network at <www.cwhn.ca>.

Aronson, J., Denton, M., & Zeytinoglu, I. (2004). Market-modeled home care in Ontario: Deteriorating working conditions and dwindling community capacity. *Canadian Public Policy, 30*(1), 111–125.

Aronson, J., & Neysmith, S. (1997). The retreat of the state and long-term care provision: Implications for frail elderly people, unpaid family carers and paid home care workers. *Studies in Political Economy, 53*, 37–66.

Aronson, A., & Neysmith, S. (2006). Obscuring the costs of home care: Restructuring at work. *Work, Employment & Society, 20*, 27–45.

Baines, C., Evans, P., & Neysmith, S. (1998). Women's caring: Work expanding, state contracting. In C. Baines, P. Evans, & S. Neysmith (Eds.), *Women's caring: Feminist perspectives on social welfare* (pp. 3–22). Toronto: Oxford University Press.

References   Baldock, J. (1997). Social care in old age: More than a funding problem. *Social Policy and Administration, 31*(1), 73–89.

Canada. (2004). *Amendment to the Federal Provincial Fiscal Arrangements Act.* Online at <http://laws.justice.gc.ca/en/F-8/>.

Canada. (2005). *Bill C-28 amendments to the Employment Insurance Act of 1996 in relation to compassionate leave.* Online at <www.rhdcc.gc.ca/asp/gateway.asp ?hr=/en/ei/legislation/c28.shtml&hs=eyp>.

Canada. Canada Health Act R.S. 1985, c. C-6. Online at <http://laws.justice.gc.ca/ en/C-6/>.

Canada. Health Canada. *National forum on health: 1994–1997.* Online at <www. hc-sc.gc.ca/hcs-sss/com/nfh-fns/index_e.html>.

Canada. Human Resources and Skills Development Canada. (2005). *Employment Insurance* (EI) *Compassionate Care Benefits.* Online at <www.hrsdc.gc.ca/en/ei/ types/compassionate_care.shtml>.

Canadian Association of Retired Persons. (1999). *Putting a face on home care.* Kingston: Queen's Health Policy Research Unit, Queen's University.

Chappell, N.L., & Prince, M. (1997). Reasons why Canadian seniors volunteer. *Canadian Journal on Aging / La Revue canadienne du vieillissement, 16*(2), 336–353.

Cotrell, V., & Engel, R. (1998). The role of secondary supports in mediating formal services to dementia caregivers. *Journal of Gerontological Social Work, 30*(3/4), 117–132.

Craig, G. (2004). Citizenship, exclusion and older people. *Journal of Social Policy, 33*(1), 95–114.

Denton, M., Zeytinoglu, I.U., & Davies, S. (2002). Working in clients' homes: The impact on the mental health and well-being of visiting home care workers. *Home Health Care Services Quarterly, 21*(1), 1–27.

Dilworth-Anderson, P., Williams, I.C., & Gibson, B.E. (2002). Issues of race, ethnicity and culture in caregiving research: A 20-year review (1980–2000). *The Gerontologist, 42*(2), 237–272.

Evans, R., McGrail, K.M., Morgan, S., Barer, M., & Hertzman, C. (2001). Apocalypse no: Population aging and the future of health care systems. *Canadian Journal on Aging, 20*(Suppl. 1), 160–191.

Evers, A. (1993). The welfare mix approach: Understanding the pluralism of welfare systems. In A. Evers & I. Svetlik (Eds.), *Balancing pluralism: New welfare mixes in care for the elderly* (pp. 3–31). Aldershot: Avebury.

Feinberg, L.F., & Whitlatch, C. (1998). Family caregivers and in-home respite options: The consumer-directed versus agency-based experience. *Journal of Gerontological Social Work, 30*(3/4), 9–28.

Fischer, L., Mueller, D., & Cooper, P. (1991). Older volunteers: A discussion of the Minnesota Senior Study. *The Gerontologist, 31*(2), 183–194.

Fraser, N. (1989). *Unruly practices: Power, discourse and gender in contemporary social theory.* Minneapolis: University of Minnesota Press.

Fraser, N. (1997). *Justice interruptus: Critical reflections on the "postsocialist" condition.* New York: Routledge.

Gibson, D. (1996). Broken down by age and gender: The "problem of old women" redefined. *Gender and Society, 10*(4), 433–448.

Gill, C., Hinrichsen, G., & DiGuiseppeet, R. (1998). Factors associated with formal service use by family members of patients with dementia. *Journal of Applied Gerontology, 17*(1), 38–52.

Gilleard, C., & Higgs, P. (1998). Old people as users and consumers of healthcare: A third age rhetoric for a fourth age reality? *Ageing and Society, 18*(2), 233–248. **References**

Grenier, A.M. (2005). The contextual and social locations of older women's experiences of disability and decline. *Journal of Aging Studies, 19*, 131–146.

Goar, C. (2005, April 8). Compassion gets left behind. *Toronto Star*, p. A22.

Guberman, N. (1999). *Caregivers and caregiving: New trends and their implications for policy: Final report*. Ottawa: Health Canada.

Hooyman, N.R., & Gonyea, J. (1995). *Feminist perspectives on family care: Policies for gender justice*. Thousand Oaks, CA: Sage.

Horch, H.D. (1995). On the socio-economics of voluntary organizations. *Voluntas, 5*(2), 219–230.

Hughes, G. (Ed.). (1998). *Imagining welfare futures*. London: Routledge and Open University.

Jessop, R. (1993, Spring). Toward a Schumpeterian workfare state? Preliminary remarks on post-Fordist political economy. *Studies in Political Economy, 40*, 1–39.

Keefe, J., & Fancey, P. (1997). Financial compensation or home help services: Examining differences among program recipients. *Canadian Journal on Aging, 16*(2), 254–278.

Lewis, J., & Giullari, S. (2005). The Adult Worker Model family, gender equality and care: The search for new policy principles and the possibilities and problems of a capabilities approach. *Economy and Society, 34*(1), 76–104.

Light, D.W. (2001) Managed competition, governmentality and institutional response in the United Kingdom. *Social Science and Medicine, 52*, 1167–1181.

Lister, R. (1997). Citizenship: Towards a feminist synthesis. *Feminist Review, 57*, 28–48.

McBride, K.D. (2005). *Collective dreams: Political imagination and community*. University Park, PA: Pennsylvania State University Press.

Milne, A., & Williams, J. (2000). Meeting the mental health needs of older women: Taking social inequity into account. *Ageing and Society, 20*(6), 699–723.

Mitchell, L., Roos, N.P., & Shapiro, E. (2005). Patterns in home care use in Manitoba. *Canadian Journal on Aging, 24*(suppl. 1), 59–68.

National Advisory Council on Aging. (1999). *1999 and beyond: Challenges of an aging Canadian society*. Ottawa: Author.

Neysmith, S. (1995). Would a national information system promote the development of a Canadian home and community care policy? An examination of the Australian experience. *Canadian Public Policy, 31*(2), 159–173.

Neysmith, S. (Ed.). (2000). *Restructuring caring labour: Discourse, state practice and everyday life*. Toronto: Oxford University Press.

Neysmith, S. (2005, May 20). *Promoting equity: Funding mechanisms are important*. Keynote address to the Taiwan/Canadian Symposium on Women and Family Care. Taipei.

Neysmith, S., & Aronson, J. (1997). Working conditions in home care: Negotiating race and class boundaries in gendered work. *International Journal of Health Services, 27*(3), 479–499.

Neysmith, S., & McAdam, M. (1999). Controversial concepts. In S. Neysmith (Ed.), *Critical issues for future social work practice with aging persons* (pp. 1–26). New York: Columbia University Press.

References Ontario Association of Community Care Access Centres. (2005). *Contributing to the transformation of health care in Ontario: Pre-budget submission to the Standing Committee on Finance and Economic Affairs.* Toronto: Author.

Ontario Health Coalition. (2005). *Market competition in Ontario's home care system: Lessons and consequences.* Toronto: Author.

Pearce, J.L. (1993). *Volunteers: The organizational behavior of unpaid workers.* New York: Routledge.

Reitsma-Street, M., & Neysmith, S. (2000). Restructuring and community work: The case of community resource centres for families in poor urban neighbour-hoods. In S. Neysmith (Ed.), *Restructuring caring labour: Discourse, state practice, and everyday life* (pp. 142–163). Toronto: Oxford University Press.

Robertson, A. (1997). Beyond apocalyptic demography: Toward a moral economy of independence. *Ageing and Society, 17*(4), 425–446.

Shildrick, M. (1997). *Leaky bodies and boundaries: Feminism, postmoderism and (bio)ethics.* New York: Routledge.

Statistics Canada. (2005). *Population projections of visible minority groups, Canada, provinces and regions 2001–2017* (Catalogue no. 91-541-X1E). Ottawa: Supply and Services Canada.

Ungerson, C. (2004). Whose empowerment and independence? A cross-national perspective on "cash for care" schemes. *Ageing and Society 24,* 189–212.

Williams, P., Barnsley, J., Leggat, S., Deber, R., & Baranek, P. (1999). Long-term care goes to market: Managed competition and Ontario's reform of community-based services. *Canadian Journal on Aging, 18*(2), 125–153.

Peter A. Dunn

The concept of disability can be considered socially constructed. People have different views of who is disabled or what conditions constitute a disability. These ideas may change over time and location (Enns & Neufeldt, 2003; Oliver & Barnes, 1998). Policy-makers determine who is disabled and who deserves financial and other benefits as a result of disability. They often categorize people and limit services to individuals with certain types of conditions. Rather than responding to individual needs, eligibility rules are often restricted to reduce costs. This leaves many, including people with multiple disabilities, ineligible for services. Unresponsive social policies have resulted in gaps in services and regional differences in the types and number of services available in Canada. One of the challenges of social policy is to respond to the needs of Canadians with disabilities in a comprehensive, just, and effective manner (Dunn, 2003; Rioux & Prince, 2002; Torjman, 2000).

Many Canadians confront multiple oppressions in the form of environmental, economic, social, and attitudinal barriers (Baker, 2005; Beachell, 2000; Enns & Neufeldt, 2003; Hanes, 2002; Walters & Ternette, 1994). A survey of seniors with disabilities in Canada found that approximately 32% required ramps so they could get in and out of their homes, 43% had problems obtaining accessible transportation, and 53% required more help with personal supports (Dunn, 1997). Barriers to entering the labour force and extremely low public assistance payments have left Canadians with disabilities economically marginalized. Oliver and Barnes (1998) explain that capitalism has forced many to the bottom of the labour market. Roughly 31% live under Statistics Canada's poverty line (Ross, Scott, & Smith, 2000). Statistics Canada (1995) found that approximately 14% were unemployed and another 44% had given up looking for jobs and, as a result, were classified by the federal government as "not in the labour force." Approximately 65% of working-age adults with disabilities did not complete any post-secondary education. Many individuals confront multiple problems being integrated into the educational system.

Many people face discrimination and attitudes that stress charity rather than equal rights and citizenship. The many forms of oppression they experience often overlap and reinforce each other. Visible minorities who are disabled, for example, confront a double disadvantage, experiencing both racism and demeaning stereotypes related to their abilities. Women with disabilities have extremely low incomes (Dunn, 1997), and many experience physical and sexual abuse (Driedger, Feika, & Giron Batres, 1996).

Stienstra (2002) emphasizes the importance of understanding the intersections of race/ethnicity and disability as well as the social construction of these identities. Barile (2000) stresses the multiple levels of discrimination that impact individuals who are in a multiple minority status. For example, Canada's immigration policies are especially dehumanizing for immigrants with disabilities. In addition, service providers often do not consider the unique needs of individuals with disabilities from different racial or ethnic groups. Often services are not culturally appropriate; rather there is one service for everyone (Ethno-Racial People with Disabilities' Coalition of Ontario, 2000).

The incidence of disability is about twice as high for Aboriginal peoples as for the population as a whole in Canada (Stienstra, 2002). Although Aboriginal peoples often have positive attitudes towards disability, government policy responses have been very inadequate. The issues have been exacerbated as a result of jurisdictional conflicts between different levels of government. Elias and Demas (2001) found in their research that individuals with disabilities living on reserves have very limited resources. Many live in substandard housing with physical barriers in their homes. Many cannot obtain personal care attendants, accessible transportation, health care, employment training, or jobs. Durst and Bluechardt (2001) found that individuals who moved from reserves to urban areas to obtain disability supports confronted a hostile and marginalized existence.

Statistics Canada has undertaken several studies related to the number of people with disabilities in Canada and the barriers they confront. The Health Activities and Limitation Surveys (HALS) were conducted in 1983/84, 1986, and 1991. In 2001, this survey was expanded and updated into the Participation and Activity Limitation Survey (PALS). These surveys included people with physical, developmental, and mental disabilities. They illustrate the subjective nature of categorizing people. Statistics Canada (2002) defined people as disabled if they were limited in activities of daily living because of long-term physical conditions, mental conditions, or health problems, or if they were told by health professionals that they had learning or mental health disabilities. People who use technical aids such as eyeglasses or hearing aids to eliminate their limitations were not considered disabled.

The results of the Statistics Canada surveys indicate that approximately 3.6 million people in Canada—or 12.4% of the population—have some form of disability. This rate increases with age. Roughly 3.3% of the population under fifteen is disabled, 10% of those fifteen to sixty-four years old, and 40.5% of people aged sixty-five or older (Statistics Canada, 2002). As the general population in Canada has aged, the percentage of Canadians with disabilities has grown. Social policies are essential in order to respond to these overall needs and trends.

The Nature and Cause of the Problems

How social problems are defined has an impact on the types of policy responses formed by government organizations (Wharf & McKenzie, 2004). As a result of the grassroots efforts of the disability movement, there has been a transformation in our understanding of issues related to disability and their solutions. The paradigm has shifted from a medical and rehabilitation model to one based on consumer control, empowerment, and self-help (Hanes, 2001; Lord, Snow & Dingwall, 2005; Nagler, 1999).

The medical paradigm emphasizes that medical and rehabilitation practitioners are in charge. It views disability as a sickness and focuses on limitations of individuals, their inadequate performance of daily tasks, and their lack of compliance. People are considered patients or clients and often socialized to the role of a sick person. The paradigm focuses on policy principles of medicalization, categorizing people, and functional limitations. Social policies associated with the medical model emphasize institutional care, separate programs, isolation, dependency, and stigma (Dunn, 2003).

The disability movement has offered an alternative analysis of the issues related to disability and their solutions based upon a social construction of disability. This paradigm suggests that pathology can be found in the environment, in unprotected rights, in overdependency on relatives and professionals, and in a lack of responsive supports (Hanes, 2002). It focuses on how consumers are oppressed and emphasizes that people must live in the community and lead productive lives through risk taking, self-help, peer support, advocacy, and the removal of environmental, social, economic, and attitudinal barriers (Walters & Ternette, 1994). The disability movement has proposed social policies that emphasize consumer control and self-direction, choices and options, flexibility and freedom (Woodill & Willi, 1992; Lord, Snow, & Dingwall, 2005).

Government policies appear to be in transition between these paradigms. As people with disabilities were deinstitutionalized, they found some of the same attitudes and approaches to service provision in the community as they had experienced in institutional settings. These included categorization, separation, isolation, dependency, and stigma. Often community programs are unresponsive, complex, and fragmented (Dunn, 2003; Torjman, 2000). Nevertheless, there is a growing emphasis on transforming how we think of the issues related to disability and creating more consumer-driven models of service delivery. Part of this transformation is taking place because of the consumer movement in Canada. Consumers have established their own initiatives and have developed partnerships with government organizations to create new approaches to service delivery (Dunn, 2003; Lord, Snow, & Dingwall, 2005).

Historical Context

Throughout history there have been a number of trends in the way we have responded to the needs of people with disabilities. First Nations provided supports within their tribes or bands in a collective fashion. Early European settlers in Canada provided services in the community for people with disabilities who were considered deserving, although many ended up in poorhouses or jails. By the mid-nineteenth century, people were moved to newly built permanent institutions. Over time, these institutions grew in size and specialization. This period of government intervention evolved in the 1960s and 1970s with the beginning of deinstitutionalization. People were moved into the community, but often with very limited supports. Although with time more services—including preventative programs—were developed, many programs retained a medical model with an emphasis on professional control (Armitage, 2003).

During the period of deinstitutionalization, the disability movement gained strength and had an impact on government policies. The broader disability movement was made up of several submovements. Although these initiatives had somewhat different roots, they had many commonalities and joined together to lobby for change. Many of these efforts arose from the increased consciousness of social injustices and violations of human rights brought about by the human rights movement in the 1950s and 1960s (Pedlar, Haworth, Hutchison, Taylor, & Dunn, 1999).

The Independent Living movement has had a major impact on social policies and programs in Canada. This movement began in the United States in the early 1970s with the development of three Independent Living Centres. Although many of the initial consumers had physical disabilities, the centres increasingly emphasized a cross-disability approach that served people with a wide range of disabilities. They grew rapidly and, by the early 1990s, included several hundred centres in the United States. These centres lobbied for improved human rights, deinstitutionalization, and the full participation of consumers in all aspects of society (Pfeiffer, 1995). The Independent Living movement began later in Canada, but grew quickly from a few centres in the early 1980s. These Independent Living Resource Centres follow four principles: consumer control, a cross-disability approach, community-based services, and the promotion of integration and full participation. Although each centre responds to the unique needs of its particular community, they have four common core programs: information and referral, peer support, independent living/empowerment skills and development, and research and demonstration. The centres are run by and for consumers (Hanes, 2002; Walters & Ternette, 1994). In 1986, the Canadian Association of Independent Living Centres (CAILC) was formed to act as a national coordinating body for the Independent Living movement and to provide training, support, networking with government and non-governmental organizations, and information dissemination. The centres have promoted a new service delivery system in which citizens with disabilities have the responsibility for the development and management of personal and community resources (Hutchison et al., 1997).

Historical Context

The community living movement in Canada had its roots in the 1960s as parents of children with developmental disabilities began to fight for their children's right to be included in publicly funded education and recreation, to have adequate residential and vocational programs, and to live outside institutions in small residences and group homes. During this time, the normalization principle was introduced from Scandinavia. It emphasized physical and social integration. Some advocated for a continuum of services ranging from segregated services, such as group homes and sheltered workshops, to more integrated programs. The segregated services were increasingly criticized as institutionalizing people in the community. Alternatives were developed, including supported independent living (housing) arrangements, integrated education, supported employment, and participation in mainstream recreation. The focus turned in the 1990s to quality-of-life issues, people's strengths and friendships, strong social networks, consumer empowerment, and individualized planning and funding. Rights, choices, and individual preferences were emphasized. People First, an advocacy organization of people with developmental disabilities, played a critical role in lobbying for social change. They called for an end to institutional care, group homes, and sheltered workshops (Pedlar et al., 1999).

Denton (2000) has reviewed the significant developments of mental health reforms in the last century. Humanitarian reform helped change the focus of services in institutions from custody to treatment. The psychodynamic / holistic approach began to emphasize the need to understand and treat the social causes of mental health problems. It was followed by the community mental health movement, which focused on community-based services; the prevention of long-term hospitalization; and local, accessible, integrated, and coordinated services. Primary and secondary prevention programs were developed to provide early detection and intervention and the alleviation of adverse conditions, such as poverty, that contributed to mental health problems.

Lord (2000) discusses the recent growth of the psychiatric consumer/survivor movement in Canada since the 1980s. This movement developed as a reaction to people's experiences of alienation and oppression within the mental health system. The psychiatric consumer/survivor movement uses an empowerment–community integration paradigm that stresses self-help, mutual aid, peer support, and advocacy. The movement challenges approaches such as case management and clubhouses as expert-driven, segregated, and failing to respond to the social conditions they face. Psychiatric consumer/survivors propose a model that emphasizes stakeholder participation and empowerment, community support and integration, and social justice and access to valued resources. Organizations such as the National Network for Mental Health have played an active role in promoting policies based on these approaches (Everett, 2000; Nelson, Lord, & Ochocka, 2001).

Other consumer initiatives in Canada have dealt with issues related to women, Aboriginal peoples, students, and people with hearing and visual disabilities. Provincial and national organizations have helped to coordinate the efforts of some of these organizations. For example, the Council of Canadians with Disabilities (CCD) has advocated for the full and equal participation of its members. This cross-disability organization argues that institutionalization, inaccessible public places, and negative attitudes have excluded people with disabilities from the mainstream of Canadian life. The CCD advocates for citizen rights, self-determination, consumer control, and equality. Along with the Canadian Disability Rights Council, the CCD has had a major impact on disability rights and service delivery systems across Canada (Beachell, 2000).

Peters (2004) points out that the Disability Rights Movement in Canada has had some major successes, but there is a long way to go. For example, disability was included in the equality provisions of the Charter of Rights and Freedoms. However, it is difficult for individuals with disabilities to litigate the removal of every barrier under this general law, especially given the high costs of court challenges and slow progress. Disability advocates in Ontario have lobbied for the adoption of the Ontarians with Disability Act. The new, improved version of this legislation, which was adopted in 2005, will have specific enforceable standards related to goods, services, accommodation, facilities, buildings and employment in the public and private sector (ODA Committee, 2005).

Consumer groups have not worked in isolation. They have worked with disability-specific service agencies, government organizations, and other non-profit groups (Lord, 2000). Despite the disability movement's relatively recent beginnings in Canada, it has increasingly transformed notions of disability issues, developed an alternative vision of services, and created innovative interventions operated by consumers.

Evolving Roles

The 1867 British North America Act delegated to the provinces responsibility for policy development related to housing, transportation, social supports, education, and other human services. Nevertheless, the federal government plays a significant role in cost-sharing services, setting standards for programs, controlling some forms of accessible transportation, and providing direct services such as some income maintenance and employment programs. The provinces and territories have the major role in developing many areas of disability policy. They develop social policies related to personal supports, barrier-free housing, accessible transportation, education, social assistance, employment training, and other community resources such as recreation. Government agencies, non-profits, and, increasingly, for-profit organizations actually implement the programs.

Many of these services are being eroded by government funding reductions as a result of free trade agreements and globalization. Another influence on the service system has been the devolution of responsibilities from the federal government to the provinces and then to the municipalities (Dunn, 2003). The federal government established the Canada Assistance Plan (CAP) in 1966 to cost-share 50% of eligible provincial and municipal expenditures on community services and social assistance. Post-secondary education and health, including some personal support services, were covered by Established Program Financing (EPF), which included a cash payment and tax transfer from the federal to provincial governments. The federal government placed limits on CAP funding in 1990, then froze it in 1995–1996. It also froze the per capita EPF entitlements from 1991 to 1996. It eliminated both the CAP and EPF in 1996–1997 and introduced the Canada Health and Social Transfer (CHST).

CHST block funding, which consists of both cash and tax transfers, is intended to offer the provinces more flexibility and, at the same time, provide greater predictability and financial sustainability for the federal government. Many claim that the real purpose of CHST funding is to reduce transfer payments with the least political fallout by giving more discretion to the provinces. The movement to block funding and the reduction of national standards have resulted in increased disparities among the provinces (Dunn, 2003). As federal standards have diminished and provinces further fragment the service delivery system by downloading responsibilities and reducing supports, private for-profit disability agencies have emerged. Many of these agencies are concerned with profits rather than with the empowerment of consumers (Pedlar & Hutchison, 2000).

Disability Policies and Programs

This section will discuss developments in some of the major policy areas that enable Canadians with disabilities to live independently. Disability policies have moved from helping people just to function in the community to enabling consumers to participate fully in all aspects of community life and to take increased control over service delivery. To keep this section manageable, only those policies related to housing, transportation, personal supports, income, education, employment, and community supports will be discussed. A brief history of recent developments at the federal level will provide an overall context for policy development in Canada.

The International Year of the Disabled Person in 1981 was a catalyst for the federal government to work with Canada's disability community to identify and take action on outstanding issues. The Special Parliamentary Committee on the Disabled and Handicapped (1981) documented, in a report entitled *Obstacles*, the major barriers confronting people with disabilities in Canada. *Obstacles* listed 130 recommendations for actions on the part of specific federal government departments. A special follow-up report released in December 1981 listed twelve further recommendations for action on issues related to Aboriginal peoples.

In 1982, physical and mental disabilities were included under Section 15 of the Canadian Charter of Rights and Freedoms, marking the first time any national constitution referred specifically to individuals with disabilities. The United Nations declared 1983–1992 the Decade of Disabled Persons. It was not until 1985 that Prime Minister Brian Mulroney signed an agreement to recognize the Decade in Canada. That same year, a Sub-Committee on Equality of Rights produced a report entitled *Equality for All*, which highlighted the delays in implementing *Obstacles* and recommended the establishment of a federal coordinating agency as a permanent parliamentary committee to deal with disability issues. The federal government designated the Secretary of State as the Minister Responsible for the Status of Disabled Persons and established a Status of Disabled Persons Secretariat to plan and coordinate federal initiatives. It also expanded its Court Challenges program to provide funding for litigation dealing with equality rights under the new Charter. In 1987, the work of the Special Parliamentary Committee culminated in the establishment of the Standing Committee on Human Rights and the Status of Disabled Persons (Secretary of State, 1991).

The Standing Committee produced a report in 1990 entitled *A Consensus for Action: The Economic Integration of Disabled Persons*. It urged the federal government to make economic integration of Canadians with disabilities a national priority; to ensure more responsible policy, legislation, and regulations; to pursue employment equity provisions; and to develop a federal-provincial-municipal plan for consultation with consumers and follow-up actions. It documented some of the major limitations of the federal government's efforts and the frustration of consumers at having to repeat well-known and well-worn arguments for actions that they felt had been promised ten years ago. In 1991, the federal government announced a $158 million National Strategy for the Integration of Persons with Disabilities over a five-year period (Secretary of State, 1991).

In 1992, the federal, provincial, and territorial governments produced *Pathways to Integration*, better known as *Mainstream 92*, as a final report on their collaborative review of services. The Standing Committee on Human Rights and the Status of Disabled Persons continued to focus on employment issues; produced *Completing the Circle*, a report (1993a) that outlined ongoing issues related to Aboriginal peoples with disabilities; and wrote *The Grand Design*, a document (1993b) arguing for better programs and services; but when concrete actions failed to occur, consumers became increasingly bitter. They demanded that the federal government treat their concerns more seriously (Council of Canadians with Disabilities, 1996). These demands led to the creation of a Task Force on Disability Issues in 1996. Its report, *Equal Citizenship for Canadians with Disabilities: The Will to Act* incorporated many of the recommendations made by the consumer movement over the past several years (Federal Task Force on Disability Issues, 1996). It proposed an approach to disability issues that would build disability considerations into mainstream policies and programs. In 1998, the federal, provincial, and territorial ministers responsible for social services produced a report, *In Unison: A Canadian Approach to Disability Issues*, that emphasized developing a collective approach to disability issues, and they signed the Unison Accord. The Unison Accord proposed services that are accessible and portable with an individual focus. Despite all these reports and efforts, Canadians with disabilities continue to confront discrimination and multiple barriers.

Disability Policies and Programs

Disability rights' organizations have advocated for action on the Unison Accord including adequate funding for programs promoting disability inclusion. Out of frustration with the slow pace of change, they issued *A Call for Action* in 2005. This proposal urged a new investment in disability-related supports by the federal, provincial and territorial governments to break a cycle of exclusion and poverty confronting Canadians with disabilities (Council of Canadians with Disabilities, 2005).

Housing

Federal, provincial, and territorial government policies and programs have had a major impact on barrier-free housing and affordable housing arrangements. Barrier-free housing can help people with disabilities get in and out of their homes and enables independent use of facilities such as bathrooms, kitchens, and bedrooms. It also includes provisions for individuals with visual, hearing, and developmental disabilities, such as audio signals in elevators, tactile and colour-contrasting cues, visual alarms for fires, and concise, easy-to-read signs. Although housing is a provincial and territorial responsibility, the federal government's National Research Council develops national building codes approximately every five years. Since 1965, they have included some barrier-free standards. These standards act as advisory standards for provincial and territorial governments. A separate section for barrier-free standards (s. 3.7) was added to the Code in 1985, but does not include universal design standards that would ensure that all units could be unobtrusively and easily changed to accommodate individual needs. Such standards would require modifications such as adjustable counters and bathrooms large enough to accommodate wheelchair access.

The provinces and territories usually revise their building codes every five years and incorporate many of the federal provisions. Eight of the twelve provinces and territories have building codes with accessible regulations. These regulations apply primarily to new apartment buildings or those undergoing substantial renovations and do not include single-family homes or existing apartments. Although the provincial and territorial codes have become more progressive, most do not go as far as the United States' Fair Housing Act Amendment to include universal features in all apartments units. Instead, a specific percentage of units—often 5%—is usually required to be accessible (Dunn, 2003).

Disability
Policies and
Programs

The federal, provincial, and territorial governments have established housing adaptation programs to make existing housing more accessible. The federal government's role in housing is designated in the National Housing Act and is primarily carried out by the Canada Mortgage and Housing Corporation (CMHC). Its national Residential Rehabilitation Assistance Program (RRAP), which was started in 1973 as a home improvement program, was expanded in 1981 to include grants and loans to adapt existing housing. In 1986, the program was modified to become the Residential Rehabilitation Assistance Program for Persons with Disabilities [RRAP-D]. In 1992, the CMHC introduced Housing Assistance for Seniors' Independence to pay for minor modifications of seniors' homes.

Seven of the provinces and territories developed their own housing adaptation programs, and ten had home improvement programs, most of which included funding for home modifications. The most extensive programs were in Ontario and Quebec, but Ontario ended its program in 1993. Funding for many of the programs in other provinces was reduced in the 1990s. Of the programs still available, many provide limited funding and cover only a small number of home modifications. Since qualifying for these programs is often difficult, many people continue to face many barriers in their own homes (Dunn, 2003).

Canadians with disabilities confront other issues related to housing. CMHC has reduced or eliminated programs intended to increase the affordability of housing. Funds for the Rent Supplement and Non-Profit Housing Programs were reduced in the early 1990s. In 1996, CMHC indicated it would phase out its role in social housing. Many of the provinces and territories took over the administration of existing federal co-op and non-profit housing at that time. In 1997, the Ontario government decided to devolve social housing to municipal control. Not surprisingly, as governments are cutting social housing programs and budgets, many more people with disabilities are becoming homeless. Even recent federal government initiatives have not substantially changed the overall supply of affordable housing. In the meantime, many of the emergency hostels are inaccessible and unsafe. Individuals with disabilities face housing discrimination and a lack of adequate legal protection. Many who live in boarding homes or group homes are not covered by most landlord and tenant legislation, and existing legislation was weakened in many jurisdictions (Carpenter, 2001).

Transportation

Jurisdictional issues related to accessible transportation are complex. Generally, if a public carrier crosses borders between provinces or territories, it falls under the responsibility of the federal government. The federal government has jurisdiction over air travel, shipping, and interprovincial rail and buses. The provinces and territories have jurisdiction over ferries, local trains (including commuter trains and northern transport), commuter buses, buses crossing municipal boundaries, and traffic rules. The municipalities generally have responsibility for taxis, municipal buses, subways or light-rail transit, and specialized parallel transportation. Many of the municipal services receive provincial funding.

Nine of the provinces established funding for specialized parallel transportation in the late 1970s and early 1980s. The exception, Prince Edward Island, offered non-profit accessible bus services in its major communities. The northern territories have not provided specialized transportation because many northern communities are remote and not serviced by roads. Provincial government expenditures substantially increased for specialized transportation during the Decade of Disabled Persons, but by the 1990s and 2000s, eligibility was restricted and funding reduced.

During the Decade, most provinces and territories initiated programs to help municipalities or taxi companies purchase and operate accessible taxis. The advantage of these programs for consumers is increased control over the timing of rides and the reduced stigma associated with taxis as compared to segregated transit. Surprisingly few of the provinces offer funding to modify consumers' automobiles unless they qualify for specific vocational rehabilitation or workers' compensation. As a result of pressure from consumer groups, many provinces have introduced policies emphasizing a family of transportation services that give consumers more flexibility of choice. Accessible municipal and commuter buses, subways, light-rail trains, and commuter trains began to receive funding by the end of the Decade. Some municipalities introduced low-floor community buses that are operated in specific neighbourhoods for seniors and for those who have difficulty getting on and off conventional buses.

Still, many municipal, commuter, and intercity trains and buses continue to be inaccessible. The older Toronto and Montreal subways offer poor accessibility, and many trains have limited accessibility. Bus and train stations are often inaccessible too, both to people with mobility problems and to those with visual or hearing disabilities. As a result, many people cannot travel freely in Canada. Baker (2005) found in his research that mandatory, rather than voluntary, government action was critical in making transportation more accessible. In fact, since the federal government changed in the mid-1990s towards more voluntary requirements, the state of accessible federal transportation has moved backwards. For example, VIA Rail began purchasing inaccessible passenger cars and withdrew fare reductions for personal attendants.

The Americans with Disabilities Act, passed by the US Congress in 1990, offered a different approach to regulating accessible transportation (Dunn, 2003). It required all new private and public buses, train and bus stations, and rapid and light-rail trains to be accessible. All communities with conventional transportation were required to provide a specialized parallel system to serve eligible people, and bus and rail companies were required to install telephone devices for individuals with hearing limitations.

Personal Supports

Social policies related to personal supports are very complex and confusing in Canada: there are multiple levels of jurisdiction, people with different disabilities or ages may fall under different government departments or multiple ones, and these arrangements change constantly. There are no common, agreed-upon definitions of personal supports. They may include home health care, homemaker services, attendant services, respite for caregivers, technical aids, or equipment. Individuals with developmental or mental health disabilities often make use of skills training, home support workers, and community living skills coaches. Torjman (2000) raises some fundamental concerns about the overall system of personal supports, including disparities in the availability of supports, high costs for some users, and complicated eligibility rules. Personal support services are rarely portable, making it difficult for consumers to travel or to move to another location. Many services are based on a medical model. They fail to respond to individual needs, and they foster dependency.

While the provinces and territories have responsibility for personal supports, the federal government has had an indirect role through cost-sharing arrangements and as part of its responsibility for Status Indians. Today it funds many personal support services through the Canada Health and Social Transfer. Provincial and territorial departments of health and community services provide support services either directly or through purchased services, direct cash assistance or vouchers, and/or by offsetting expenses through tax provisions. Municipalities often assist in delivering and paying for these supports. Commercial agencies such as insurance organizations may also play a role in funding personal supports. Generally, non-profit agencies actually provide the services (Torjman, 2000).

Many of the provinces developed home support policies and programs in the early 1970s, primarily for seniors. During the Decade of Disabled Persons these programs were adapted and expanded to other groups. New programs were developed, including attendant services to assist individuals with long-term disabilities, children's benefits to provide funding for parents to purchase services for their children with complex needs, and independent living services for people with developmental and mental health disabilities. By the end of the Decade, all provinces and territories offered some form of personal supports and, increasingly, they coordinated services through a single entry point, provided cross-disability supports, and decentralized community services. However, funding was reduced in the 1990s and did not keep pace with the increasing demand as the population aged and more people were living independently in the community (Dunn, 2003; Krogh & Ennis, 2005). Prince (2005) points out that there is still not a national strategy of disabilities supports in Canada.

Some of the provinces and territories have developed innovative programs. One of the major innovations has been individualized funding. These programs provide money directly to consumers to obtain the supports they require. They enable consumers to hire, fire, and direct their support workers. Often less expensive than alternative models, individualized funding has been adopted in most provinces and territories, but on a limited scale. Consumer organizations, such as the Independent Living and Resource Centres in Winnipeg and Toronto, have worked with government departments to establish and administer individualized funding programs. They have also been involved in teaching consumers how to obtain and control their own services. Micro-boards are a unique innovation initially developed in British Columbia for individuals with developmental disabilities. Micro-boards are non-profit organizations of five to eight unpaid members. They are contracted by the government to provide circles of support and to oversee individualized funding to purchase supports for one or two people. Despite all of these innovations, many consumers have overwhelming problems simply obtaining basic personal supports in Canada (Dunn, 2003; Lord, Snow & Dingwall, 2005).

Income

Not only are many Canadians with disabilities poor, but they often face extraordinary costs associated with having a disability. Many cannot find paid employment because of a variety of work-related barriers, leaving them dependent on Canada's disability income security system. This system is not based on need. Rather, the amount of money a person receives depends on how she or he became disabled. There is a hierarchy of programs—from private pensions down to welfare assistance—available to different groups of people. This system has evolved in a haphazard, piecemeal fashion. It is not integrated, coordinated, comprehensive, or fair (Council of Canadians with Disabilities, 1998).

Torjman (1997) describes the different kinds of income programs for people with disabilities including personal injury awards through the courts, insurance programs, and non-insurance supports. The two key public insurance programs are the provincially administered Workers' Compensation and the Canada/Quebec Pension Plan. Workers' Compensation is designed to protect workers and their families from wage loss due to occupational injury or disease. The Canada/Quebec Pension Plan was established in 1966 as a social insurance plan for people who are retired and for previously employed people who experience severe and permanent disabilities. This program provides sickness benefits for those whose benefits have expired under Employment Insurance. These two public insurance programs are available only to those with an earnings record. People who have not worked cannot qualify and must rely on non-insurance forms of support such as welfare. Welfare provides assistance significantly below Statistics Canada's poverty line. It is stigmatizing and often has built-in disincentives to work. Other non-insurance supports include tax deductions and benefits in-kind.

A number of proposals have been made to reform the social insurance system. They focus on the need for a more comprehensive system that covers all people regardless of earning status or extent of disability. Such a system must provide adequate financial supports, recognize individual needs, and ensure labour market participation through effective rehabilitation. Many consumers have argued against a separate disability income program, instead favouring a comprehensive program for all Canadians in need (Council of Canadians with Disabilities, 1998).

Education

From the creation of special segregated classes for a few people grew the concept of inclusive, integrated education for many. Initial steps toward deinstitutionalization in the 1950s and 1960s, along with parental pressure, led to the development of segregated special education for children with disabilities at the primary and secondary school levels. These parallel segregated services proliferated in the 1970s and 1980s. In the 1980s, parents began to advocate for a shift toward integrated education for their children. They found their children were often labelled and isolated in segregated school systems, which acted as ghettos. In contrast, children in integrated schools developed new communication abilities, skills, and friendships. Non-disabled students learned how to accommodate and relate to their new peers. These changes in education occurred as the concepts of normalization and human rights gained momentum in Canada.

Although education is a provincial and territorial responsibility, a dramatic shift occurred when the Charter of Rights and Freedoms was entrenched in the Canadian constitution in 1982. When the equality rights section came into force in 1985, it provided an effective tool for parents' lobbying and litigation against segregated education (Learning Disability Association of Canada, 2002). Nevertheless, the needs of many children with disabilities have not been accommodated, especially with recent cuts to education. There is considerable variation across Canada in terms of inclusive education at the primary and secondary levels.

Porter (2001) points out that successful inclusive education depends on a number of factors. Schools must have effective mechanisms to include parents in decision-making and problem solving related to the education of their children. Children need to be accepted as having a rightful place in the school. Supports, such as staff development and flexible planning time, must be offered to teachers. Students may need concrete supports such as accessible school facilities, computer-aided technologies and other assistive devices, tutorial and interpreter support, therapeutic services, and peer support. Classroom instruction needs to take into account different learning styles. Plus, teachers, families, and students must be committed to inclusion for it to be effective. Unfortunately, many students continue to face multiple barriers within the educational system.

Inclusive post-secondary education is becoming an increasing priority in Canada, but there is little policy to support it. Funding for post-secondary education comes from both federal and provincial sources. Unfortunately, federal funding through the Canada Health and Social Transfer was reduced in the 1990s, and many provinces have decreased funding to colleges and universities. As a result, many supports for students with disabilities have decreased while tuition has increased substantially. Post-secondary students who are disabled face multiple barriers. Many cannot obtain adequate funding for their education. Often they take longer to complete their education and have to cover these costs. Some who are funded by vocational rehabilitation services may be restricted in terms of their courses or career paths. Many colleges and universities are not physically accessible or may not have technology for individuals with hearing or visual disabilities. Frequently, there is inadequate funding for sign language interpreters in classrooms. Often faculty are not trained or sensitized. Without these supports, many students will not be able to complete their studies successfully or find meaningful employment upon graduation (Canadian Centre on Disability Studies, 2004).

Disability
Policies and
Programs

Employment

Approximately one million working-age Canadians with disabilities are unemployed or remain out of the labour force in Canada. Women, Aboriginals, and other minorities who are disabled are more likely to be unemployed. It has been estimated that the resulting cost of lost productivity ranges from $35 to $38 billion annually (Crawford & Martin, 2000). Consumers have argued for inclusion in meaningful, decent-paying jobs in the regular labour force, rather than being unemployed or segregated in demeaning, sheltered workshops (Council of Canadians with Disabilities, 1998).

Canadians with disabilities are excluded from the labour market because of discrimination, inadequate public policies, and other barriers (Canadian Centre on Disability Studies, 2004). Human rights legislation has not been very effective in addressing discrimination in employment. Public policies have often segregated people into sheltered workshops and failed to achieve any meaningful employment equity. Consumers have difficulty obtaining a variety of necessary employment-related supports such as aids and devices, home supports, rehabilitation services, transportation, and adaptations to the workplace. They often do not have equal access to training and education. The current system of funding and service delivery is not well coordinated; rather, it is highly complex, fragmented, and piecemeal. Those people who become employed have problems obtaining additional income to meet their disability-related costs.

A series of policy initiatives have been developed to address some of these issues. The Canadian Human Rights Act and all provincial/territorial human rights acts prohibit discrimination in employment on the basis of disability. Some human rights legislation includes "duty to accommodate," which

Disability Policies and Programs

requires employers to make a range of modifications to a given job or workplace to promote the employment of Canadians with disabilities. The federal government and some of the provinces have employment equity legislation that requires them to report the numbers of people with disabilities and to remove workplace barriers. In 1997, the federal government replaced a program called Vocational Rehabilitation of Disabled Persons, which was over thirty-five years old, with Employability Assistance for People with Disabilities (EAPD). The name reflects a stronger emphasis on employability. The EAPD is a partnership between the federal and provincial/territorial governments. The federal government contributes 50% of the costs of eligible provincial/territorial programs and services up to a maximum total cost. The provinces and territories administer the services and have greater flexibility to tailor programs to local needs. Services include employment counselling and assessment, employment planning, pre-employment training, post-secondary education, skills training, assistive devices, wage subsidies or earning supplements, and workplace supports. There are a variety of other initiatives, including the federal government's Opportunity Fund, which supports a broad array of employment activities for Canadians with disabilities who are not eligible for employment benefits under the Employment Insurance Act.

Despite these policy initiatives, the unemployment and underemployment rate of Canadians with disabilities is extremely high. A number of policies are required to support people to obtain and retain meaningful employment. Social security programs must eliminate disincentives. People require adequate income supports, education, training, accessible housing and transportation, personal supports, and aids and devices. As part of this effort, some people require supported employment in the form of job coaches and special supports and training (Neufeldt, Sandys, Fuchs, & Logan, 1999). However, many people continue to confront barriers that do not permit them to be part of the economic mainstream of Canadian society.

Other Community Resources

Other community resources enable Canadians with disabilities to live independently. Social policies related to health care are central to this aim. Fortunately, Canada has a universal health care policy. However, in the 1990s the federal and provincial governments began to reduce funding for health care, including preventative services and drug and prescription programs. This led to the erosion of the system of personal supports, which was partially funded by health care dollars. Although funding from the health system has been used to establish many innovative services, it often perpetuates a traditional medical model that disempowers consumers. Many consumers feel oppressed by government institutions, hospitals, and rehabilitation services. The plight of psychiatric consumer/survivors in these institutions has been well documented. People are often stripped of their identity and lose control over their lives. Self-help services have provided an alternative to this model (Capponi, 2003; Lord, 2000; Nelson, Lord & Ochocka, 2001; Torjman, 2000).

Consumers continue to confront many barriers getting to and from school, work, or pursuing daily activities. Building codes are required to ensure that community facilities and housing are accessible. Other aspects of community life, such as leisure activities, have tended to be segregated. There is a movement toward more integrated recreational activities (Hutchison & McGill, 1998). Policies are evolving related to arts and culture. For example, libraries are becoming more accessible to people with visual disabilities through large-text formats and Braille. Movies and theatres are becoming more responsive through new technology for those with hearing disabilities. Nevertheless, consumers continue to confront extensive barriers in the community.

Conclusions and Future Directions

Many social policies and programs were developed for Canadians with disabilities during the Decade of Disabled Persons. The budgets of some of these programs benefitted from substantial increases in the 1980s, but by the 1990s many of these gains were eroded by funding reductions. A major recession in North America, coupled with free trade deals between Canada and the United States and then Mexico, led to pressures in Canada to cut corporate taxes, reduce government expenditures, and harmonize human services with those of trading partners. The federal government diluted national standards and downloaded more of its services to the provinces and territories—and in turn to the municipalities—creating a patchwork of services across Canada. Even as the economy improved and government surpluses increased in the 2000s, many programs continued to be cut or were not reinstated. As a result, some regions in Canada have few services and others have none.

Many programs are based on a medical model that categorizes and stigmatizes program users and leaves them with little control over services. Despite these barriers, a new concept of services is emerging in Canada—one based on consumer control, flexibility, and choice of services. Consumers have lobbied for a fundamental paradigm shift in policy development. They have advocated for universal adaptable housing features that are flexible to meet everyone's needs. Transportation policies are slowly moving from an emphasis on specialized separate transit systems to a family of accessible transportation in that consumers have more choice and flexibility. Direct individualized funding programs have been established that give consumers more control, choice, and flexibility over personal supports. There is increasing emphasis on integrated education and community resources. One challenge is to move these programs from small-scale initiatives to large-scale options.

As part of its British tradition, Canada has inherited a model of social policy that provides for a comprehensive social welfare safety net. However, this approach is crumbling under the influence of government funding reductions. In contrast, the United States has focused on developing civil rights legislation such as the Fair Housing Act Amendment and the Americans with Disability Act. This represents a promising approach for Canada, despite government jurisdictional dilemmas.

The federal government's reports *The Will to Act* and *In Unison* combine these two approaches. The Council of Canadians with Disabilities (2005) endorsed many of their proposals. These reports propose a comprehensive pan-Canadian approach that builds provisions for individuals with disabilities into mainstream policies and programs. The consumer movement has advocated for a joint federal-provincial-territorial effort to create comprehensive disability standards across Canada. *The Will to Act* and *In Unison* recommend that a Canadians with Disability Act be established and that the federal government use a disability policy lens to develop future laws, policies, programs, and human rights regulations. They highlight the need for the federal government to fulfill its commitment to Aboriginal peoples with disabilities by ensuring access to the supports and services they require. The report argues for labour market integration, in which mainstream employment programs explicitly include employment strategies for Canadians with disabilities. They suggest consumer organizations be funded to provide some of these supports. These reports recommend a renewal of vocational rehabilitation services, with a focus on broader needs. They advocate for the replacement of the patchwork of existing income programs with a coherent, comprehensive, and sustainable approach to providing income to all Canadians. The Council of Canadians with Disabilities (2005) proposes a comprehensive disability personal support program throughout the country. They emphasize the need to implement these new policy directions with concrete enabling legislation and adequate funding.

Consumer groups have also advocated for more comprehensive disability policies at the provincial and territorial level. One proposal is to develop a Canadians with Disabilities Act within the provinces and territories. Such legislation would deal with issues such as public transportation, education, provincial and municipal services and facilities, and other goods and services. It would require government bodies to identify existing barriers, design plans to deal with them within set time frames, and prevent new barriers from being created. The provisions of the Ontarians with Disabilities Act could be modified and adopted in other parts of Canada.

Future policies must be directed at all levels of government and guarantee national standards and citizenship rights. These policies must be comprehensive and respond to individual needs. Essential to this approach is consistent enforcement of legislation. Policies should stress integrated programs that ensure consumer control, choice, and flexibility. It is only though this multi-pronged approach that Canada can create an environment in which all citizens can live independently in the community.

References

Armitage, A. (2003). *Social welfare in Canada revisited.* Toronto: Oxford University Press.

Baker, D. (2005). *Moving backwards: Canada's state of transportation accessibility in an integrated approach.* Winnipeg: Council of Canadians with Disabilities.

Barile, M. (2000). Understanding the personal and political role of multiple minority status. *Disability Studies Quarterly, 20*(2), 123–128.

Beachell, L. (2000). *CCD annual report 1999–2000.* Winnipeg: Council of Canadians with Disabilities.

Canadian Centre on Disability Studies. (2004). *Students with disabilities: Transitions from post-secondary education to work.* Winnipeg: Author.

Capponi, P. (2003). *Beyond the crazy house.* Toronto: Penguin.

Carpenter, S. (2001). Housing blues from institutions to community. *CAILC New Bulletin, 6*(1), 10–13.

Council of Canadians with Disabilities. (1996). *CCD's final presentation to the Task Force on Disability.* Winnipeg: Author.

Council of Canadians with Disabilities. (1998). *Disability income supports and service project: Consultation report.* Winnipeg: Author.

Council of Canadians with Disabilities. (2005). *A call for action.* Winnipeg: Author.

Crawford, C., & Martin, T. (2000). *Job accommodation and other employment measures in Canada.* Toronto: Roeher Institute.

Denton, L. (2000). From human care to prevention. *Canadian Journal of Community Mental Health, 19*(2), 127–134.

Driedger, D., Feika, I., & Giron Batres, E. (Eds.). (1996). *Across borders: Women with disabilities working together.* Charlottetown: Gynergy Books.

Dunn, P. (1997). A comparative analysis of barrier-free housing policies for elderly people in the United States and Canada. *Canadian Journal of Rehabilitation, 12*(1), 37–53.

Dunn, P. (2003). The evolution of disability policies in Canada. *International Journal of Rehabilitation Research, 25*(3), 215–224.

Durst, D., & Bluechardt, M. (2001). *Urban Aboriginal persons with disabilities: Triple jeopardy.* Regina: Social Policy Research Unit, University of Regina.

Elias, B., & Demas, D. (2001). *A profile of Manitoba First Nations people with a disability.* Winnipeg, MB: Assembly of Manitoba Chiefs.

Enns, H., & Neufeldt, A. (2003). *In pursuit of equal participation: Canada and disability at home and abroad.* Concord, ON: Captus Press.

Ethno-Racial People with Disabilities Coalition of Ontario. (2000). *Three lives: A journey out of darkness.* Toronto: Fireweed Media Productions.

Everett, B. (2000). *A fragile revolution: Consumers and psychiatric survivors confronting the power of the mental health system.* Waterloo, ON: Wilfrid Laurier University Press.

Federal Task Force on Disability Issues. (1996). *Equal citizenship of Canadians with disabilities: The will to act.* Ottawa: Minister of Public Works and Government Services Canada.

Hanes, R. (2002). Social work with persons with disabilities. In S. Hick (Ed.), *Social work in Canada: An introduction* (pp. 217–234). Toronto: Thompson Educational.

Human Resources Development Canada. (1998). *In unison: A Canadian approach to disability issues.* Ottawa: Author.

References   Hutchison, P., & McGill, J. (1998). *Leisure, integration, and community* (2nd ed.). Toronto: Leisurability Publications.

Hutchison, P., Pedlar, A., Lord, J., Dunn, P., McGeown, M., Taylor, A., & Vanditelli, C. (1997). The impact of Independent Living Resource Centres in Canada on people with disabilities. *Canadian Journal of Rehabilitation, 10*(2), 99–112.

Krogh, K., & Ennis, M. (2005). *A national snapshot of home support from the consumer perspective.* Winnipeg: Council of Canadians with Disabilities.

Learning Disability Association of Canada. (2002). *Learning disabilities and the law.* Ottawa: Author.

Lord, J. (2000). Is that all there is? Searching for citizenship in the midst of services. *Canadian Journal of Community Mental Health, 19*(2), 165–169.

Lord, J., Snow, J. & Dingwall, C. (2005). *Building a new story: Transforming disability supports and policies.* Toronto: Individualized Funding Coalition of Ontario.

Nagler, M. (1999). *What's stopping you? Living successfully with a disability.* Toronto: Stoddart.

Nelson, G., Lord, J., & Ochocka, J. (2001). *Shifting the paradigm in community mental health: Towards empowerment and community.* Toronto: University of Toronto Press.

Neufeldt, A., Sandys, J., Fuchs, D., & Logan, M. (1999). Supported and self-directed employment support initiatives in Canada: An overview of issues. *International Journal of Practical Approaches to Disability, 23*(3), 24–36.

ODA Committee. (2005). *Ontarians with Disability Act.* Toronto: Author.

Oliver, M., & Barnes, C. (1998). *Disabled people and social policy from exclusion to inclusion.* New York: Addison Wesley Longman.

Pedlar, A., Haworth, L., Hutchison, P., Taylor, A., & Dunn, P. (1999). *A textured life: Empowerment and adults with developmental disabilities.* Waterloo, ON: Wilfrid Laurier University Press.

Pedlar, A., & Hutchison, P. (2000). Restructuring human services in Canada: Commodification of disability. *Disability and Society, 15*(4), 637–651.

Peters, Y. (2004). *Twenty years of litigating for disability equality rights: Has it made a difference?* Winnipeg: Council of Canadians with Disabilities.

Pfeiffer, D. (1995). *The disability movement and its history.* Stockholm: Independent Living Institute.

Porter, G. (2001). *Disability and education: Towards an inclusive approach.* Washington, DC: Inter-American Development Bank.

Prince, M. (2005). *A national strategy for disability supports.* Kingston, ON: Faculty of Health Sciences, Queen's University.

Rioux, M., & Prince, M. (2002). The Canadian political landscape of disability: Policy perspectives, social statuses, interest groups and rights movement. In A. Puttee (Ed.), *Federalism, democracy and disability policy in Canada* (pp. 11–28). Montreal: McGill-Queen's University Press.

Ross, D., Scott, K., & Smith, P. (2000). *The Canadian fact book on poverty.* Ottawa: Canadian Council on Social Development.

Secretary of State. (1991). *The national strategy for the integration of persons with disabilities.* Ottawa: Supply and Services Canada.

Special Parliamentary Committee on the Disabled and the Handicapped. (1981). *Obstacles.* Ottawa: Minister of Supply and Services Canada.

Standing Committee on Human Rights and the Status of Disabled Persons. (1990). *A consensus for action: The economic integration of disabled persons.* Ottawa: Minister of Supply and Services Canada.

Standing Committee on Human Rights and the Status of Disabled Persons. (1993a). **References**
    Completing the circle. Ottawa: Minister of Supply and Services Canada.
Standing Committee on Human Rights and the Status of Disabled Persons. (1993b).
    The grand design. Ottawa: Minister of Supply and Services Canada.
Statistics Canada (1995). *A portrait of persons with disabilities.* Ottawa: Ministry of
    Industry, Science and Technology.
Statistics Canada. (2002). *A profile of disability in Canada, 2001.* Ottawa: Ministry of
    Industry, Science and Technology.
Stienstra, D. (2002). *Intersections: Disability and race/ethnicity/heritage language/
    religion.* Winnipeg: Canadian Centre on Disability Studies.
Torjman, S. (1997). *The disability income system in Canada: Options for reform.*
    Ottawa: Caledon Institute.
Torjman, S. (2000). *Proposal for a national personal supports fund.* Ottawa: Cale-
    don Institute.
Walters, T., & Ternette, E. (1994, Spring). Discover independent living. *Abilities Mag-
    azine,* 1–3.
Wharf, B., & McKenzie, B. (2004). *Connecting policy to practice in human services.*
    Toronto: Oxford University Press.
Woodill, G., & Willi, V. (1992). *Independent living and participation in research:
    A critical analysis.* Toronto: Centre for Independent Living Toronto.

Additional Resources

Canadian Association of Community Living (CACL). Online at <www.cacl.ca>.
Canadian Association of the Deaf (CAD). Online at <www.cad.ca>.
Canadian Association of Independent Living Centres (CAILC). Online at <www.cailc
    .ca>.
Canadian Centre on Disability Studies (CCDS). Online at <www.disabilitystudies.ca>.
Canadian Council of the Blind (CCB). Online at <www.ccbnational.net>.
Canadian Hard of Hearing Association (CHHA). Online at <www.chha.ca>.
Canadian Mental Health Association (CMHA). Online at <www.cmha.ca>.
Canadian National Institute for the Blind (CNIB). Online at <www.cnib.ca>.
Council of Canadians with Disabilities (CCD). Online at <www.pcs.mb.ca/~ccd>.
DisAbled Women's Network of Canada (DAWN). Online at <www.dawncanada. net>.
Learning Disabilities Association of Canada (LDAC). Online at <www.ldac-taac.ca>.
National Aboriginal Network on Disability (NAND). Online at <www.schoolnet.ca/
    aboriginal/health-e.html>.
National Education Association of Disabled Students (NEADS). Online at <www
    .neads.ca>.
National Federation of the Blind Advocates for Equality (NFBAE). Online at <www
    .nfbae.ca>.
National Network for Mental Health (NNMH). Online at <www.nnmh.ca>.
Office for Disability Issues (ODI) in Service Canada. Online at <www.hrdc.gc.ca>.
Roeher Institute. Online at <www.roeher.ca>.

Looking to the Future · Part IV

Anne Westhues

The biggest challenge for policy makers and policy advocates committed to producing social policy that promotes a more just world is, as Wharf and McKenzie (2004) tell us, explicating the value issues. At least as great a challenge is getting voters to give power to a government that is committed to greater social justice. At no time is this more evident than during an election campaign. In January 2006, Canadians elected another minority government—this one led by Stephen Harper of the Conservative Party. A second minority government within two years suggests that no political party has gained sufficient confidence of Canadians to earn a clear mandate to govern, and governing means being given a mandate to shape public policy.

Political parties build the set of policies on which they run for election— their party platform—on the ideology, or values, that their party represents. We generally understand the Conservative Party to support smaller government, to believe in the devolution of service provision to the private sector, to be more socially conservative than the Liberal or New Democratic Parties, and to be more comfortable with social inequality than the other two major parties. Jost, Glaser, Kruglaski, and Sullowat (2003) conclude that the core tenets of conservatism are resistance to change, justification of inequality, and a need to manage uncertainty and threat. The ideological position most often associated with the Conservative Party has been described as "conservative" (Guest, 1997), anti-collectivist (George & Wilding, 1985), or, more recently, neo-liberal or neo-conservative (Teeple, 1995).

The New Democratic Party has demonstrated that it has the greatest commitment to public provision of health, education and social services—which leads to more public sector or non-profit sector employment and bigger government—and to be the party most committed to reducing the social exclusion of the most disadvantaged groups. Ideologically, they are usually described as social democrats (Guest, 1997). The Bloc Québécois can also be characterized as social democratic but are understood to be a "single interest" party because of their defining commitment to the creation of a sovereign Quebec. The Green Party's social policy can be defined as social democratic as well, but, because of their focus on protection of the environment, they too are characterized as a "single interest" party.

The Liberal Party tends to represent the "pragmatic" centre, balancing a commitment to reduce the effects of socio-economic disadvantage with a belief that a strong economy (and hence policies that favour the business community) is a necessary precursor to having the resources to meet the needs of the most marginalized Canadians. It is this straddling of the more extreme left and right ideological positions that has allowed the Liberal Party to form the government in Canada about eight out of ten years over the past century (Clarkson, 2005). Their ideological position is described as "reluctant collectivist" (George & Wilding, 1985) or liberal (Guest, 1997).

What do these ideological positions look like in practice, when parties convert their ideological beliefs into proposed policy? The party platforms in the 2006 federal election helped us understand the differences these value positions make to everyday Canadians and why it matters which party forms the government. Child care is an area of social policy where the ideological differences among the three major parties were particularly evident. Child care advocates (Child Care Advocacy Association of Canada, 2005) called for the passage of an Early Learning and Child Care Act that would provide quality, universal, accessible programs to address the developmental needs of all children. They also called for sufficient expansion of subsidized child care spaces to ensure access to quality programs for every child in Canada by 2010 and for a commitment to child care as a public service.

The Conservative Party did not support the legislation called for and did not support the expansion of publicly provided child care spaces. Instead, they promised a $1200-a-year taxable allowance per child that is not tied to child care spending. This meant that families where one parent (usually the mother) is an at-home caregiver would benefit as well as families where the child receives care from somebody other than their parents; more affluent families would benefit less, because the allowance would be taxable. In addition, they promised $25 million to support a program that would provide an incentive to employers to locate child care centres in the workplace (Conservative Party of Canada, 2005). They argued that this would be a benefit that might attract and retain employees. Finally, the Conservatives supported delivery of child care in the for-profit sector as well as the not-for-profit sector. These policy options reflect values that we associate with a conservative perspective: family choice about whether to care for children in the home or outside the home, support for employers to help them attract and retain employees, and support for delivery of child care services by the for-profit sector as well as the not-for-profit sector.

By contrast, the New Democratic Party supported the proposed Early Learning and Child Care Act and committed to creating 275,000 new non-profit, licensed child care spaces, with funding of $9,000 per space over a four-year period. Further, they committed to child care that is accountable to parents and communities through community boards—that is, through the non-profit sector. They did not support the growth of corporate child care (child care provided by employers) or for-profit child care (New Democratic Party of Canada, 2005). The values underlying these policy positions are quality, universal, accessible child care, through parent and community empowerment and non-profit delivery of service.

The Liberal Party also supported an Early Learning and Child Care Act but failed to pass such legislation any time during the previous twelve years they were in power. Their 2006 election platform promised to begin expanding the number of subsidized child care spaces in 2010, growing the system by 625,000 spaces by 2015, funding them at $1600 per space. Like the Conservatives, they would allow federal funding to be transferred to the commercial and corporate sectors (Liberal Party of Canada, 2006). The Liberal platform is based on the principles and values of universal accessible child care but is driven by no great sense of urgency. The party proposed to begin increasing the number of spaces beginning in 2010. While their platform claimed a commitment to quality, they proposed per-space funding of $1600, less than 20% of the proposed NDP rate. Finally, the Liberal platform showed a valuing of both the profit and the non-profit sectors for the delivery of child care services. This suggests they believed that best practices would emerge from having a variety of child care models and that parents should have choice in how they care for their children.

This analysis shows how the choices for parents looking for child care depended on which party gained power. The Conservatives promoted workplace child care, an option that may be reassuring to some parents but may tie others to a workplace they prefer to leave. The NDP supported immediate investment in well-funded group day care, which means more quality day care spaces sooner but no benefits for families who decide to care for their children at home. The Liberals supported additional funding, beginning in four years, for group care, which meant that families who decide to care for their children at home would receive no benefits and those wanting group care would be more likely to receive it, albeit after a longer wait than if the NDP were in power. In addition, the Liberals would develop some of the spaces in the profit sector and some in the non-profit sector. This meant that there would be new opportunities for small and large business as well as non-profit providers.

Other social policy issues addressed in the election platforms showed clear differences among the three major parties as well. A few examples: support for same-sex marriage; the degree of privatization in the health care sector; the degree of emphasis in our immigration policy on the economic contribution of prospective applicants versus its generosity to refugees; and the generosity of a compassionate leave program funded through Employment Insurance.

But all of this debate is occurring within the context of an overarching ideology that can best be described as global and neo-liberal (McQuaig, 1998; Teeple, 1995). This means that the policy environment—whether local,

national, or international—is now dominated by values that are less friendly
to the promotion of equality in the distribution of economic, social, and political rights than in the sixties and seventies. This environment is more concerned with punishment than care, more focused on the individual than the
community. However reluctantly, most Canadians in the post–World War II
era acknowledged that an unfettered market system did not distribute sufficient income to the poorest Canadians to meet their basic needs for food,
shelter, and clothing. There was a tolerance for—not an embrace of—the
need for government to intervene to ensure that these basic needs were met.
The previous chapters show us that the neo-liberal shift of the 1980s means
that a majority of Canadians now believe that everybody—without regard to
income level, gender, age, ability, or immigration status—will be better off if
we compete in a world market, with a minimum of government regulation.
While there is a role for government programs, it is to focus on helping people—men and women alike—to be more employable, so they can compete for
the opportunities in this "new economy." Families are expected to take on
more responsibility for dependant members—through reduction of services
like home care, or through inducement with programs like Compassionate
Leave that protect employment when care is provided for dying family members. Single mothers are expected to join the labour force, even when their
skills are limited, and they are more likely to live in poverty while employed
than they were when in receipt of social assistance, as Hunter showed us in
chapter 9. In sum, support for government intervention in meeting social
needs is contingent on there being a link with employment whenever possible.

Cameron and Stein (2000) argue that, within the context of neo-liberalism, there is still room to influence social policy. The state can be defined as
a "handmaiden to the economy" or as a "social investment" state. If it is
understood to be a handmaiden, the government of the day will secure the
competitiveness of its people by cutting taxes and shrinking the size of government by privatizing services like health care, prisons, and child care. In
addition, crime, social disorder, disease, and poverty, which reduce competitiveness, will be understood to result from dependence on the state. Dependence will be reduced by cutting benefit levels and tightening eligibility for
benefits so that individuals and their families take up their responsibilities to
support themselves. By contrast, the "social investment" model understands
crime, social disorder, disease, and poverty to be the result of social inequalities. These inequalities can be reduced through investment in education
and health, and by removing barriers to employment. A healthy, literate, well-
educated population is understood to be a draw for investors. In addition,
having a social safety net in place means that when there is a downturn in the
economy the state is positioned to respond to the social needs of its citizens
in a way that it is not if the handmaiden model has been adopted. Times of
high unemployment can be seen as opportunities for people to retrain or
upgrade their skills so that the labour force is able to meet the needs of

employers when the economy becomes stronger once again. A review of the 2005 federal budget suggests that it is the latter vision that was then shaping social policy at that level of government.

Moving Beyond a "Liberal" Ethic

So party politics still matter, but the range of social policy options considered, at least by the three major federal political parties in English Canada, is still firmly grounded in an ethic of social justice that has been described as "liberal" (Hankivsky, 2004). A "liberal" perspective assumes that universal policy solutions that emphasize rights and redistribution are needed rather than solutions that recognize the increasing diversity in Canada, or what Fraser and Honneth (2003) call our increasingly complicated "identity politics."

Hankivsky (2004) argues that a "liberal" perspective, with its emphasis on treating all citizens the same, has dominated social policy thinking in Canada during most of the post World War II years. A promising alternative to this liberal, justice-oriented ethic is the "ethic of care" offered by feminists (Baines, Evans & Neysmith, 1998; Fraser & Honneth, 2003; Hankivsky, 2004; Tronto, 1993). This relational theory, first conceptualized by Gilligan (1982), values "recognition of our interdependence with each other," understands that "these interdependencies cut across the public and private spheres," and posits that "care has a central role in sustaining us within these connective relationships" (quoted in Hankivsky, 2004, p. 8). Care theorists argue that an emphasis on "justice" or rights is necessary, but not sufficient to address the needs of those who are most likely to be excluded from society: for instance, people with serious mental illnesses or addictions, newcomers to Canada, people with physical disabilities, or older adults. These theorists argue that it is necessary to meet the financial needs of people who we are not expected to care for themselves and to protect the human rights of citizens, but that the state also has a responsibility to relieve hurt or suffering, both physical and psychological. By meeting these needs, Hankivsky (2004, p. 29) argues, we would see the rebuilding of family, community, and social relations that promote social integration and the social cohesion that we have become so fearful of losing.

Not inconsistent with the ethic of care, but in a more empirical vein, is the social determinants of health framework championed by the World Health Organization (WHO) (Raphael, 2004; Wilkinson & Marmot, 1998). Assuming a preventive health promotion perspective, the framework is grounded in research evidence about the conditions that support good health—conditions that are systemic as well as individual. The broad goals to be addressed in this framework include stress reduction; fostering a good start in the early years; reducing indicators of social exclusion like homelessness and poverty; reducing stress in the workplace; job creation and support for people who are unemployed; promotion of strong social support networks; reduction of alcohol, drug, and tobacco use; provision of an adequate food supply; and promotion of transportation alternatives to driving, such as walking, cycling, and public transport. This vision is being implemented through the Healthy Communities initiative, which now has projects in over 3,000 urban and rural communities worldwide (Directory of Pan American Healthy Cities Network, 2006). Conceived in Canada in 1984 and adopted by the WHO in 1986, this approach emphasizes participatory planning practices in trying to realize the vision chosen by each community. This is a promising partner to the ethic of care, giving more specific focus to the programming initiatives that would be consistent with an ethic of care and identifying indicators that would help us assess whether our caring activities have made positive changes in the lives of people who look to the health and social services communities for support.

Defining Your Role in Policy Advocacy

In addition to identifying a framework grounded in clearly articulated values that can be used to shape and sustain a direction in policy development, policy advocates need to reflect on how they will choose to engage in the policy development process. At what level are you most comfortable working— within your organization, in your community, provincially, nationally, or internationally? Figure 1.1 shows that policy is made at a number of levels in any country. This question is intended to help you think through which level or levels you want to target. You may seek the opportunity to work at the United Nations, or with an international NGO as described by Wichert in chapter 2. Or you may decide, as advocated by Ife (2000), to work at the personal or local level and attempt to influence policy at the agency/organizational, municipal, or community level, always cognizant of the global issues. Often, we address policy issues on more than one level at a given time, the organizational and the provincial or federal level, for instance. The challenge that Ife identifies is being able to continue to combine a focus on the public, which is increasingly defined in global terms, with one on the personal, local, or service delivery issues when the gap between the two worlds is so great.

Second, as a policy advocate you must discern whether you are most comfortable promoting system transformation or system change (Friedmann, 1987). System transformation assumes that you will work outside the policy-making or service delivery system through the mobilization of a political community. This community may be defined in relation to a specific social movement like the anti-globalization movement, through a political party as described by Wharf Higgins, Cossom, and Wharf in chapter 7, or through the activities of NGOs as described by Wichert in chapter 2. A systems change perspective, by contrast, means that you have chosen to work within a policy-making system, perhaps like the government policy analyst described by Kenny-Scherber in chapter 5, or even as a program administrator. Friedmann (1987, p. 32) describes this stand as one in which "radical proposals become integrated with the structure of the guidance system of society." He notes Policy Priorities that this process is riddled with conflict and compromise, and thus requires policy-makers who have well-developed process and political skills. Some people will be most effective working only within the system, others only outside the system, and others will be successful influencing policy, at different times and on different issues, as both insiders and outsiders.

Third, following Kenny-Scherber's suggestion, as an advocate you must ask what issues energize you, affront your sense of justice, and mobilize you to action. These may be broadly defined as concerns about children, women, people who are seriously mentally ill, people who are homeless, or the promotion of human rights. They may be more specifically focused, with a concern about the injustice of the barrier to the right to marry for people who are gay or lesbian, the lack of accommodations in the workplace for people with physical or emotional disabilities, the high levels of poverty among Aboriginal children, or the inadequacy of home care services for the frail elderly.

Finally, the advocate must answer the question that Linda McQuaig posed to the audience during a keynote address at the annual conference of the Canadian Association of Schools of Social Work in June 2002. Are you comfortable being on the losing side of a policy debate? Because if you do not share the values associated with a neo-liberal perspective, the policy positions you support are unlikely to be acted on by the governments elected today. There may be occasional dramatic wins like the Council of Canadians' ability to stall the signing of the Multilateral Agreement on International Trade that would have given private corporations the legal status of nation-states, and tools to enforce these newly acquired rights that would have compelled nation-states to safeguard corporate interests over those of their own citizens (Council of Canadians, 1999). Or like the success in preventing the movement toward privatization, as when the Harris government in Ontario attempted to sell Hydro One to private sector investors (Mackie, 2002). More left-leaning governments may be elected, but as we saw with the New Democrat Rae government in Ontario, a social democratic government may actually carry out what was recently described to me as "the mother of all cuts" in social services if the economic conditions don't support social investment. Much of the work to be done will be educational, however—planting the idea of what could be, but not seeing it germinate at this time.

Policy Priorities

Having said all of this, what are the priority issues that face us as Canadians living in a global context over the next ten years? The primary issue at the international level can be framed many ways, but I like the framing Senator Doug Roche chose in a speech to the Church Press Convention in May 2002. In the wake of the September 11, 2001, attack on the twin towers of the World Trade Center, he called for resistance to the "culture of war" ("Getting the Word Out," 2002). The culture of war calls for increased spending on guns, an incursion into long-accepted human rights, and the fostering of a belief that all people are either "friends" or "enemies." It promotes a world view supporting the belief that our friends are unconditionally right and that our enemies are unconditionally wrong.

Instead, he argues, we should participate in the UN Right to Peace initiative, which means educating people in all parts of the world to a set of values that rejects violence and fosters understanding of others. He reports that UNESCO is currently involved in hundreds of projects with this goal—some focused on human rights, some on gender, others on democratic participation, and still others on cross-cultural understanding. In keeping with Midgely's recommendation that we adopt a social development perspective, he might also have added that the most certain way to maintain peace in war-torn countries like Afghanistan or Iraq, or between Israelis and Palestinians, is to invest in economic development. This was Marshall's great inspiration after World War II, which led to the development of the Economic Recovery Program, better known as the Marshall Plan (*For European recovery*, 1997). This investment led to prosperity and peace in an area that might have erupted into yet another world war.

It is difficult to choose among many critical priorities at the national and provincial levels. The chapters that have been selected for this book are what I felt were of greatest significance at this time—the need to reduce child poverty; how we best protect children at risk of abuse or neglect; resolving long-standing issues between Aboriginal and non-Aboriginal peoples that are a consequence of colonialism; how we best support people with serious mental health issues; how we reduce homelessness; the roles we define for single mothers; whether a work requirement should be a condition for receipt of social assistance; how we include people who are gay or lesbian; how we best support recent immigrants; how we ensure universal access to health care in a timely way; and how best to provide supports to people in their old age and to people with disabilities.

The debates will continue between provincial and federal governments about how much of the responsibility each has in these areas, as they have since Confederation. We have seen historically that a provincial government may decide an issue is important enough to go ahead and pass legislation to deal with it, even without federal funding. Quebec has done this most recently in passing the Act to Combat Poverty and Social Exclusion, legislation intended to reduce child poverty in Quebec to the lowest level among industrialized societies over the next decade (Séguin, 2002). We can hope that other provinces will follow, adding some of their own revenues to the federal spending on the Canada Child Tax Benefit, or at the least allowing social assistance recipients to keep all of their CCTB payments rather than having them deducted as income from their assistance payments.

More than at any time in history, the social policy issues facing us are enormously complex. It is easy to feel that there is no way to make progress on them; but, as Linda McQuaig said in the address mentioned earlier, "It's always been hopeless." Advocates for social justice have always pressed for References change against great odds of actually achieving what they called for. And look what we have achieved anyway—a society where much remains to be done but much has been accomplished in promoting social justice.

References

Baines, C., Evans, P., & Neysmith, S. (Eds.). (1998). *Women's caring: Feminist perspectives on social welfare.* Toronto: Oxford University Press.

Cameron, D., & Stein, J.G. (2000). Globalization, culture and society: The state as place amidst shifting spaces. *Canadian Public Policy, 28*(Suppl. 2), S15–S34.

Child Care Advocacy Association of Canada. (2005). Federal election 2006: Campaign Child Care. Online at <www.childcareadvocacy.ca/action/election2006/index.html>.

Clarkson, S. (2005). *The big red machine: How the Liberal Party dominates Canadian politics.* University of British Columbia Press.

Conservative Party of Canada. (2005). Stand up for Canada. Online at <www.conservative.ca/media/20060113-Platform.pdf>.

Council of Canadians. (1999). MAI Inquiry: Confronting globalization and reclaiming democracy. Online at <www.canadians.org>.

Directory of Pan American Health Cities Networks. Online at <www.healthycommunities.org>.

For European recovery: The fiftieth anniversary of the Marshall Plan. (1997). Library of Congress. Online at <www.lcweb.loc.gov/exhibits/marshall/>.

Fraser, N., & Honneth, A. (2003). *Redistribution or recognition? A political-philosophical exchange.* New York: Verso.

Friedmann, J. (1987). *Planning in the public domain: From knowledge to action.* Princeton: Princeton University Press.

George, V., & Wilding, P. (1985). *Ideology and social welfare.* Boston: Routledge and Kegan Paul.

Getting the word out in perilous times. (2002, June 16). *Catholic New Times,* 10–11.

Gilligan, C. (1982). *In a different voice: Psychological theory and women's development.* Cambridge, MA: Harvard University Press.

Guest, D. (1997). The emergence of social security in Canada. (3rd ed.) Vancouver: University of British Columbia Press.

Hankivsky, O. (2004). *Social policy and the ethic of care.* Vancouver: University of British Columbia Press.

Ife, J. (2000). Localized needs and globalized economy: Bridging the gap with social work practice. In W. Rowe (Ed.), *Social work and globalization* (pp. 50–64). Ottawa: Canadian Association of Social Workers.

Jost, J.T., Glaser, J., Kuglanski, A.W., & Sulloway, F.J. (2003). Political conservatism as motivated social cognition. *Psychological Bulletin, 129*(3), 339–375.

Liberal Party of Canada. (2005). Securing Canada's Success. Online at <www.liberal.ca/images/dir/PDFS/platform_e.pdf>.

Mackie, R. (2002, June 13). Stopping Hydro sale gratifying. *Globe and Mail,* p. A10.

McQuaig, L. (1998). *The cult of impotence: Selling the myth of powerlessness in the global economy.* Toronto: Viking.

Midgley, J. (2000). Globalization, capitalism and social welfare: A social development perspective. In W. Rowe (Ed.), *Social work and globalization* (pp. 13–28). Ottawa: Canadian Association of Social Workers.

References   New Democratic Party of Canada. *Getting results for people: Platform 2006.* Online at <www.ndp.ca/ndp-drupal/files/platform-en-final-web.pdf>.

Raphael, D. (2004). *Social determinants of health: Canadian perspectives.* Toronto: Canadian Scholars' Press.

Séguin, R. (2002, June 13). Quebec bills sets target to reduce poverty. *Globe and Mail,* p. A12.

Teeple, G. (1995). *Globalization and the decline of social reform.* Toronto: Garamond Press.

Tronto, J. (1993). *Moral boundaries: A political argument for an ethic of care.* New York: Routledge Press.

Wharf, B., & McKenzie, B. (2004). *Connecting policy to practice in the human services.* Toronto: Oxford University Press.

Wilkinson, R., & Marmot, M. (1998). *Social determinants of health: The solid facts.* World Health Organization.

Contributors

Mike Burke is an associate professor in the Department of Politics and Public Administration at Ryerson University. He has published articles on community modes of health care delivery in Canada, the political attitudes of women physicians, the limitations of health promotion research, the policy implications of the social-environmental paradigm in health, and the obstacles academic unions face in promoting collective and progressive identities among their members. He co-edited a book with Colin Mooers and John Shields, entitled *Restructuring and resistance: Canadian public policy in an age of global capitalism* (2000), in which he examined recent transformations in Canadian health care policy and new trends in labour market inequality in Canada.

Marilyn Callahan is professor emeritus in the School of Social Work at the University of Victoria. She is currently involved in several research projects including one on risk assessment (with Karen Swift) and another examining how fathering is constructed in child welfare (with Lena Dominelli, Susan Strega, Leslie Brown, and Christopher Walmsley). She has an abiding interest in how child welfare discourses and services affect the lives of children, their mothers, and families and has published widely in this area.

Lea Caragata is an associate professor in the Faculty of Social Work at Wilfrid Laurier University. She teaches social policy, planning, and community development, following extensive experience working with marginal communities, developing social housing, and developing and analyzing public policy. Current research includes work in the areas of the social construction of knowledge, civil society, and international social work practice.

John Cossom is professor emeritus in the School of Social Work at the University of Victoria. His practice was in child welfare, family services, and corrections. He also taught at Wilfrid Laurier University and the Universities of Waterloo and Regina.

Peter A. Dunn is an associate professor in the Faculty of Social Work at Wilfrid Laurier University. His research interests include disability policies, poverty concerns, gender issues, and alternative interventions. He has

447

been involved in disability research dealing with barrier-free housing, issues confronting seniors with disabilities, the development of government independent living policies, the impact of independent living and resource centres, and the empowerment of adults with developmental disabilities.

John English holds a doctorate from Harvard University and is a senior professor of history and political science at the University of Waterloo. He served as member of Parliament for Kitchener between 1993 and 1997. Afterward, he served as a Special Ambassador for Landmines and as a Special Envoy for the election of Canada to the Security Council. He has also served as president of the Canadian Institute of International Affairs, and is currently the executive director of the Centre for International Governance Innovation, a think tank devoted to the study of international affairs.

Usha George is a professor and dean of the Faculty of Community Services at Ryerson University. Her scholarship focuses on social work with diverse communities, and her research interests are in the areas of newcomer settlement and adaptation, organization and delivery of settlement services, and community work with marginalized communities. She has completed research projects on the settlement and adaptation issues of various immigrant communities in Ontario. Her interests also include international social work, and she is currently involved in research projects in India.

Garson Hunter is an associate professor of social work at the University of Regina. He has taught courses in direct social work practice, social policy, research methods, and field education, and has published on welfare and child poverty. Currently he is researching with intravenous drug users around issues of poverty and harm reduction strategies.

Carol Kenny-Scherber is a senior policy adviser with the Ontario government who has worked in five different ministries during the twenty-seven years of her social work career. The focus of most of her work has been on education, training, and employment policy.

Iara Lessa is an associate professor at the Ryerson University School of Social Work. Her research interests are broadly focused on social policy, gender, and methodology. In the past, her research activities have explored the effects of contemporary Canadian policy on the lives and situations of certain groups such as immigrants and single mothers. She is currently participating in the development of various activities and tools to increase gender equity in Brazil's programs addressing Occupational Health and Safety and Food Security.

Geoffrey Nelson, a community psychologist, is professor of psychology at Wilfrid Laurier University. He served as the senior editor of the *Canadian*

Journal of Community Mental Health, and together with the Canadian Mental Health Association—Waterloo Region Branch, he received the Harry V. McNeill Award for Innovation in Community Mental Health from the American Psychological Foundation in 1999.

Sheila Neysmith is a professor in the Faculty of Social Work, University of Toronto. She is known nationally and internationally for her research and writing on social policy issues important to women, in particular how home care services, unpaid work, and caring labour affect the quality of women's lives as they age. She is co-editor of *Women's caring: Feminist perspectives on social welfare,* 2nd ed. (Oxford, 1998); and editor of *Critical issues for future social work practice with aging persons* (Columbia, 1999) and *Restructuring caring labour: Discourse, state practice and everyday life* (Oxford, 2000). Her most recent book is *Telling tales: Living the effects of public policy* (Fernwood, 2005).

Brian O'Neill obtained his MSW from Carleton University in 1971, and subsequently worked in child welfare management in Toronto until 1988. He received his PhD from Wilfrid Laurier University in 1994, after conducting a study of Canadian social work education from the standpoint of gay men. He is currently a faculty member at the University of British Columbia School of Social Work and Family Studies in Vancouver, where he teaches interprofessional practice in relation to HIV/AIDS, research design, and social service management. His current research focuses primarily on issues in social service policy and management for gay men and lesbians.

Malcolm A. Saulis was born on the Tobique Indian reserve. He is a Malicite Indian of the Negoot-gook tribe. He was educated at St. Thomas University in Fredericton, New Brunswick, where he received a BA Honours degree in psychology. He went on to get an MSW at Wilfrid Laurier University. He sought guidance from his elders to determine where he should put his efforts to better the reality of First Nations peoples, and was told to work in making communities better places to live. He subsequently dedicated his life to making the reality of First Nations better, primarily through community-based university educational processes. He has helped communities develop programs, services, and institutions in health, child welfare, restorative justice, education, and social policy. He has consulted with government departments on various social development areas. He is a trained Traditional Circle keeper and works extensively in holistic healing processes.

Susan Silver is an associate professor in the School of Social Work at Ryerson University. She has a PhD in social work from Bryn Mawr College, Philadelphia and an MSW from the University of Toronto. She teaches research, social work practice, and social policy. She has conducted a number of research studies exploring issues of access and inclusion in relation to health care, labour markets, and income security policy. She has just completed a national participatory action research project examining the experiences of participants attending community-based family support programs.

Linda Snyder is an associate professor in the School of Social Work at Renison College, University of Waterloo. Her research focuses on means of addressing poverty and her particular interests include women's employment initiatives and comparison of Canadian and Latin American endeavours. Prior to her doctoral studies, Linda held policy and program administration positions in Waterloo Region's Social Services Department.

Karen Swift is an associate professor in the School of Social Work at York University. She is the author of *Manufacturing "bad mothers": A critical perspective on child neglect*, as well as numerous articles and book chapters on child welfare issues, especially as they relate to women. She also publishes on issues of social policy especially related to the effects of globalizing economies on the work of women. Her current research project, which is funded by the Social Sciences and Humanities Research Council, focuses on risk and risk assessment in child welfare.

Barbara Waterfall (White Buffalo Woman, Crane Clan) is an Anishnabe-Kwe Métis. She has twenty-one years of experience working in the human services field. She became a faculty member in the Native Human Services Program at Laurentian University in 1995 and accepted a position in the Faculty of Social Work at Wilfrid Laurier University in 2002. She presently is a faculty member in the First Nations and Aboriginal Counselling Degree Program at Brandon University. Barbara has a BA degree from St. Thomas University, an MSW from Carleton University, and is a doctoral candidate in the Sociology and Equity Studies Department at the Ontario Institute for Studies in Education at the University of Toronto. Her doctoral dissertation addresses the topic of "Decolonizing Native Social Work Education." Her other research interests are in the areas of anti-colonial practice, Anishnabec-centred therapy (including Anishnabec music therapy), and the inclusion of spirituality in practice.

Ailsa Watkinson is an associate professor with the Faculty of Social Work at the University of Regina in Saskatoon. Her research interests, education, and work experience are in the area of human rights. Ailsa recently co-edited a book entitled *Contesting fundamentalisms*. She is the author of *Education, student rights and the charter*, and she co-edited two other books on systemic violence. She has published a number of articles on such topics as sexual harassment, women's and children's equality rights, employment equity, globalization, the Charter as policy advocate, religion in public spaces, and the administration of equality rights.

Anne Westhues is a professor in the Faculty of Social Work at Wilfrid Laurier University where she teaches research, social policy, and community practice. Her research interests include evaluation of policy and practice, social and strategic planning, and evidence-based practice. Her publications include articles on adoption (international adoption, disclosure, disruption, and reunions), family violence (elder abuse and prevention of wife assault), and planning (conceptualizations of social planning, human resources study of the profession of social work). Her current research is on mental health and culture and immigrant youth.

Brian Wharf is professor emeritus at the University of Victoria. During his career at this university, he was director of the School of Social Work, dean of the Faculty of Human and Social Development, professor in the graduate multidisciplinary program focused on connecting policy and practice, and acting director of the School of Public Administration. His research interests continue to focus on connecting policy and practice and on community and child welfare. The focus is reflected in two recent books: *Community work approaches to child welfare* (Broadview Press, 2002) and *Connecting policy to practice*, 2nd ed. (Oxford University Press, 2004), with Brad McKenzie.

Joan Wharf Higgins is an associate professor in the School of Physical Education and a Canada Research Chair in Health and Society at the University of Victoria. She has degrees in Leisure Studies (BA), Adult Health and Fitness (MA), and Health Promotion (PhD). Joan's research and teaching interests include planning and evaluation, social marketing, community and population health, and participatory action research methodologies.

Tim Wichert is currently a lawyer with the firm of Jackman and Associates in Toronto, focusing on refugees, immigration, and human rights. He spent seven years with the Mennonite Central Committee (MCC) in Nairobi, Geneva, and New York, and another six years as refugee programme coordinator for MCC Canada. While in Geneva, he was seconded by MCC to the Quaker United Nations Office, focusing on refugees and human rights within the UN system. He obtained his law degree from Queen's University in Kingston, Ontario, in 1984.

William R. Young received his PhD in history from the University of British Columbia. Since then he has taught at several universities (Simon Fraser, York, McGill), worked on the memoirs of Paul Martin, and since 1987 has worked in the Parliamentary Research Branch. He is currently a senior analyst with general responsibilities in the area of social policy and has served as acting director of the Political and Social Affairs Division. He has provided research assistance to many committees of Parliament (currently the Standing Committee on Human Resources Development and its subcommittees on people with disabilities and children).

Author Index

453

Subject Index